Oracle8i™ DBA Bible

Oracle8i™ DBA Bible

Jonathan Gennick
Carol McCullough-Dieter
Gerrit-Jan Linker

IDG Books Worldwide, Inc.
An International Data Group Company

Foster City, CA ✦ Chicago, IL ✦ Indianapolis, IN ✦ New York, NY

Oracle8i™ DBA Bible

Published by
IDG Books Worldwide, Inc.
An International Data Group Company
919 E. Hillsdale Blvd., Suite 400
Foster City, CA 94404
www.idgbooks.com (IDG Books Worldwide Web site)

ISBN: 0-7645-4623-6

Printed in the United States of America

10 9 8 7 6 5 4 3 2 1

1B/QZ/QT/QQ/FC

Distributed in the United States by IDG Books Worldwide, Inc.

Distributed by CDG Books Canada, Inc. for Canada; by Transworld Publishers Limited in the United Kingdom; by IDG Norge Books for Norway; by IDG Sweden Books for Sweden; by IDG Books Australia Publishing Corporation Pty. Ltd. for Australia and New Zealand; by TransQuest Publishers Pte Ltd. for Singapore, Malaysia, Thailand, Indonesia, and Hong Kong; by Gotop Information Inc. for Taiwan; by ICG Muse, Inc. for Japan; by Intersoft for South Africa; by Eyrolles for France; by International Thomson Publishing for Germany, Austria, and Switzerland; by Distribuidora Cuspide for Argentina; by LR International for Brazil; by Galileo Libros for Chile; by Ediciones ZETA S.C.R. Ltda. for Peru; by WS Computer Publishing Corporation, Inc. for the Philippines; by Contemporanea de Ediciones for Venezuela; by Express Computer Distributors for the Caribbean and West Indies; by Micronesia Media Distributor, Inc. for Micronesia; by Chips Computadoras S.A. de C.V. for Mexico; by Editorial Norma de Panama S.A. for Panama; by American Bookshops for Finland.

For general information on IDG Books Worldwide's books in the U.S., please call our Consumer Customer Service department at 800-762-2974. For reseller information, including discounts and premium sales, please call our Reseller Customer Service department at 800-434-3422.

For information on where to purchase IDG Books Worldwide's books outside the U.S., please contact our International Sales department at 317-596-5530 or fax 317-596-5692.

For consumer information on foreign language translations, please contact our Customer Service department at 800-434-3422, fax 317-596-5692, or e-mail rights@idgbooks.com.

For information on licensing foreign or domestic rights, please phone +1-650-655-3109.

For sales inquiries and special prices for bulk quantities, please contact our Sales department at 650-655-3200 or write to the address above.

For information on using IDG Books Worldwide's books in the classroom or for ordering examination copies, please contact our Educational Sales department at 800-434-2086 or fax 317-596-5499.

For press review copies, author interviews, or other publicity information, please contact our Public Relations department at 650-655-3000 or fax 650-655-3299.

For authorization to photocopy items for corporate, personal, or educational use, please contact Copyright Clearance Center, 222 Rosewood Drive, Danvers, MA 01923, or fax 978-750-4470.

Library of Congress Cataloging-in-Publication Data

Gennick, Jonathan.
    Oracle 8i DBA's bible / Jonathan Gennick, Carol McCullough-Dieter, Gerrit-Jan Linker.
       p. cm.
    ISBN 0-7645-4623-6 (alk. paper)
    1. Oracle (Computer file) 2. Operating systems (Computers) 3. Database management I. McCullough-Dieter, Carol. II. Linker, Gerrit-Jan. III. Title.
QA76.76.O63 G46 2000
005.75'85—dc21   00-022761

 is a registered trademark or trademark under exclusive license to IDG Books Worldwide, Inc. from International Data Group, Inc. in the United States and/or other countries.

IDG BOOKS WORLDWIDE

ABOUT IDG BOOKS WORLDWIDE

Welcome to the world of IDG Books Worldwide.

IDG Books Worldwide, Inc., is a subsidiary of International Data Group, the world's largest publisher of computer-related information and the leading global provider of information services on information technology. IDG was founded more than 30 years ago by Patrick J. McGovern and now employs more than 9,000 people worldwide. IDG publishes more than 290 computer publications in over 75 countries. More than 90 million people read one or more IDG publications each month.

Launched in 1990, IDG Books Worldwide is today the #1 publisher of best-selling computer books in the United States. We are proud to have received eight awards from the Computer Press Association in recognition of editorial excellence and three from Computer Currents' First Annual Readers' Choice Awards. Our best-selling ...For Dummies® series has more than 50 million copies in print with translations in 31 languages. IDG Books Worldwide, through a joint venture with IDG's Hi-Tech Beijing, became the first U.S. publisher to publish a computer book in the People's Republic of China. In record time, IDG Books Worldwide has become the first choice for millions of readers around the world who want to learn how to better manage their businesses.

Our mission is simple: Every one of our books is designed to bring extra value and skill-building instructions to the reader. Our books are written by experts who understand and care about our readers. The knowledge base of our editorial staff comes from years of experience in publishing, education, and journalism — experience we use to produce books to carry us into the new millennium. In short, we care about books, so we attract the best people. We devote special attention to details such as audience, interior design, use of icons, and illustrations. And because we use an efficient process of authoring, editing, and desktop publishing our books electronically, we can spend more time ensuring superior content and less time on the technicalities of making books.

You can count on our commitment to deliver high-quality books at competitive prices on topics you want to read about. At IDG Books Worldwide, we continue in the IDG tradition of delivering quality for more than 30 years. You'll find no better book on a subject than one from IDG Books Worldwide.

IDG
BOOKS
WORLDWIDE

John Kilcullen
Chairman and CEO
IDG Books Worldwide, Inc.

Eighth Annual Computer Press Awards ➤1992

Ninth Annual Computer Press Awards ➤1993

Tenth Annual Computer Press Awards ➤1994

Eleventh Annual Computer Press Awards ➤1995

IDG is the world's leading IT media, research and exposition company. Founded in 1964, IDG had 1997 revenues of $2.05 billion and has more than 9,000 employees worldwide. IDG offers the widest range of media options that reach IT buyers in 75 countries representing 95% of worldwide IT spending. IDG's diverse product and services portfolio spans six key areas including print publishing, online publishing, expositions and conferences, market research, education and training, and global marketing services. More than 90 million people read one or more of IDG's 290 magazines and newspapers, including IDG's leading global brands — Computerworld, PC World, Network World, Macworld and the Channel World family of publications. IDG Books Worldwide is one of the fastest-growing computer book publishers in the world, with more than 700 titles in 36 languages. The "...For Dummies®" series alone has more than 50 million copies in print. IDG offers online users the largest network of technology-specific Web sites around the world through IDG.net (http://www.idg.net), which comprises more than 225 targeted Web sites in 55 countries worldwide. International Data Corporation (IDC) is the world's largest provider of information technology data, analysis and consulting, with research centers in over 41 countries and more than 400 research analysts worldwide. IDG World Expo is a leading producer of more than 168 globally branded conferences and expositions in 35 countries including E3 (Electronic Entertainment Expo), Macworld Expo, ComNet, Windows World Expo, ICE (Internet Commerce Expo), Agenda, DEMO, and Spotlight. IDG's training subsidiary, ExecuTrain, is the world's largest computer training company, with more than 230 locations worldwide and 785 training courses. IDG Marketing Services helps industry-leading IT companies build international brand recognition by developing global integrated marketing programs via IDG's print, online and exposition products worldwide. Further information about the company can be found at www.idg.com. 1/26/00

Credits

Acquisitions Editors
Judy Brief
John Osborn

Project Editors
Terry O'Donnell
Terri Varveris

Contributing Author
Rick Greenwald

Technical Editor
Brian Laskey

Copy Editors
Chrisa Hotchkiss
Mildred Sanchez

Project Coordinators
Linda Marousek
Louigene A. Santos

Graphics and Production Specialists
Jude Levinson
Michael Lewis
Ramses Ramirez
Victor Pérez-Varela
Dina F Quan

Quality Control Specialists
Laura Taflinger
Chris Weisbart

Book Designer
Drew R. Moore

Illustrator
Mary Jo Richards

Proofreading and Indexing
York Graphic Services

Cover Design
Peter Kowaleszyn

About the Authors

Jonathan Gennick an independent consultant specializing in Oracle technologies. He got his start with relational database systems in 1990, first working with Ingres, and then later with Digital's Rdb software. In 1994, he made the leap to Oracle and hasn't looked back since. He spends much of his time providing database administration services, as well as server-side PL/SQL support, to clients.

When he isn't working with Oracle, Jonathan can often be found writing about it. Since 1997, he has been involved with a number of writing projects. He coauthored the first edition of the book *Teach Yourself PL/SQL in 21 Days*. He was the technical editor for *Oracle8™ Server Unleashed* (SAMS, 1998) and the development editor for *Teach Yourself Access 2000 in 24 Hours* (SAMS, 1999). His second book, *Oracle SQL*Plus, The Definitive Guide,* was published in 1999. In addition to coauthoring the second edition of this book, Jonathan continues to be involved in various other writing and editing projects.

Writing has given Jonathan the opportunity to pursue several interests outside of his normal day-to-day work. He is a member of the technology committee for the Greater Lansing Adventist School, where he is currently helping to set up both a LAN and an Internet connection. This satisfies his gnawing need to gain new knowledge and also his desire to help others learn.

Jonathan is a member of Mensa, and he holds a Bachelor's degree in Information and Computer Science from Andrews University in Berrien Springs, Michigan. Jonathan currently resides in Lansing, Michigan, with his wife Donna and their two children, Jenny and Jeff. You can contact Jonathan by e-mail at jonathan@gennick.com.

Carol McCullough-Dieter has specialized in Oracle databases for the past 13 years. During that time, she worked as a full-time programmer, systems analyst, project leader, database administrator, and independent consultant. She also created and taught in-house courses on PL/SQL, SQL, and SQL*Forms, and she presented two papers at Oracle OpenWorld 98.

Carol began writing books in 1995, and it quickly became her primary passion. During the past four years, she wrote four books on Oracle: *Oracle7™ for Dummies, Oracle8™ Developer's Guide, Oracle8™ for Dummies,* and her latest, *Oracle8i™ for Dummies.* From 1995 to 1999, she coauthored two other books: *Oracle8™ Bible* and *Creating Cool Web Databases.* All these books are published by IDG Books Worldwide and are available internationally.

Carol is listed in *Who's Who in America Millennium Edition,* which recognizes her for her outstanding career as an expert in Oracle database technology. She currently lives in Maui, Hawaii, with her family, conducting most of her business over the Internet.

Gerrit-Jan Linker is a self-employed systems programmer analyst and is currently working for Manchester Airport in the UK. Graduating as a computational chemist in 1995, he used Fortran77 intensively on UNIX for his computations. In his first job as a trainee at a software house in the Netherlands, he was introduced to Oracle and the developer/2000 toolset. Since then, he has fully specialized in Oracle PL/SQL programming and database interfacing. Presently, he designs and implements database systems using Oracle, VB, and C on the Windows NT platform.

As a hobby, Gerrit-Jan started to write Windows programs in Visual Basic after he graduated. Now, four years later, half a dozen commercial programs are available from his Web site. It's not surprising that his most successful program is Oracle related — Oraxcel — his add-on that gives full Oracle access to Microsoft Excel.

Together with his wife, Maartje, Gerrit-Jan enjoys life in Manchester, UK. You can access his Web site at AOL at `http://members.aol.com/gjlinker`, and you can contact him at `gjlinker@litconsulting.freeserve.co.uk`.

I dedicate this book to my son Jeff, because he's so much fun to be with.
—Jonathan Gennick

World peace one day at a time. —Carol McCullough-Dieter

Preface

Welcome to *Oracle8i™ DBA Bible*. I've been privileged to work with Carol McCullough-Dieter to revise her original work, *Oracle8™ Bible,* and bring it up-to-date with coverage of some of the important new features introduced with the 8i release of Oracle.

This book covers two major types of information:

+ It discusses the features of Oracle8i that are most important and that every database administrator (DBA) should know.

+ It provides you with a complete syntax reference to all of Oracle's SQL statements, SQL*Plus commands, and built-in SQL functions.

My coauthors and I hope that you find this book a useful and handy reference in your daily work as a database administrator.

What You Need to Know and Have

This book is targeted at beginning to intermediate DBAs. Most concepts are explained in terms that someone new to Oracle can understand. I do assume that you know what a relational database is and how to use one. If you have experience programming for Oracle or using or managing other brands of databases, that will help you absorb the information in this book.

To make the best use of this book and to use its examples, you need to have access to an Oracle8i database. You probably have that access and are responsible for managing a database. Otherwise, you most likely wouldn't have purchased this book! When using Oracle8i, you even have your choice of platforms, since Oracle8i runs on Windows NT, UNIX, and even Linux.

If you're not currently an active DBA but are trying to learn about Oracle, it's relatively easy to get your hands on some trial software. A good resource is the Oracle Technology Network's Web site, which is found at the following Web address:

```
http://technet.oracle.com.
```

Joining the Oracle Technology Network is easy, and it's free. After you've joined, you can download single-user versions of the database software and Oracle's numerous other products.

When using the CD-ROM that accompanies this book, you should have at least Windows 95 or 98, Windows NT, or compatible software.

How to Use This Book

This book wasn't designed to read cover-to-cover. The chapters are relatively self-contained, so when you find yourself needing to learn about a particular area, go to the chapter or chapters covering that area and simply read them. Of course, the more you read, the more you learn, so I encourage you to cast your net widely and at least become familiar with all that the book has to offer. Sometimes you don't know that you need something until after you read about it.

Conventions Used in This Book

Throughout this book, you'll see syntax diagrams that show you how to use SQL statements, SQL*Plus commands, Oracle's built-in functions, and so forth. The following table describes and exemplifies the conventions used in these diagrams:

Convention	Example	Explanation
Capitalized words	SELECT	Capitalized words are used to indicate keywords in the syntax. Here, the SELECT keyword is shown. While these are shown in caps to set them apart, be aware that Oracle is not case-sensitive. SQL keywords, SQL*Plus keywords, and the like may be entered in either upper- or lowercase.
Lowercase italics	column_name	Lowercase italics are used to indicate values that you must supply when entering a command. Here, column_name is used to indicate that you must supply a valid column name.
Square brackets	[ALL|DISTINCT]	Square brackets denote an optional choice, with the choices delimited by a vertical line. In this example, you may choose ALL, DISTINCT, or nothing.

Continued

Convention	Example	Explanation
Curly brackets	{*	column_name }	Curly brackets denote a mandatory choice, with the choices delimited by a vertical line. In the example, you have to choose between entering * or a column name.
Repeating an item between square brackets	table[,table...]	Repetitions are indicated by repeating the item between square brackets, adding an optional delimiter and three trailing dots at the end. In the example, you would specify one or more table names separated by commas.

What the Icons Mean

Throughout the book, I use *icons* in the left margin to call your attention to points that are particularly important. I use the following icons:

 New Feature This icon indicates that the material discussed is new to Oracle8i.

 Note This icon tells you that something is important—perhaps a concept that may help you master the task at hand or something fundamental for understanding subsequent material.

 Tip This icon indicates a more efficient way of doing something or a technique that may not be obvious.

 Caution This icon tells you when the operation described can cause problems if you're not careful.

 Cross-Reference This icon refers you to other chapters that have more to say on a subject.

How This Book Is Organized

The material in this book is divided into six parts and four appendixes. Each part focuses on a major topic area and consists of several chapters related to that topic. Three of the appendixes consist of reference material; the fourth appendix describes the book's accompanying CD-ROM.

Part I: In the Beginning

Part I covers fundamental information that you need to know about Oracle to effectively manage a database. It begins with chapters that discuss the new features in Oracle8i, moves into a discussion of Oracle8i architecture, explains how you configure Net8 and the password file, and finishes by showing you how Oracle manages space.

Part II: Database Administration Tools

Part II of this book shows you how to use the more common database administration tools and utilities. Here, you will find chapters that show you how to use the import and export utilities to move data between databases. You will also find chapters on SQL*Plus and SQL*Loader.

Part III: Nuts and Bolts

Part III, as its name implies, covers the fundamentals of managing an Oracle8i database on a day-to-day basis. The emphasis here is on practicality, not theory. You'll find chapters on security; creating and managing users; and creating and managing database objects, such as tables, views, and indexes. You'll also find chapters that show you how to write common SQL statements, such as `SELECT`, `UPDATE`, `INSERT`, and `DELETE`.

Part IV: Oracle8i Tuning

Part IV discusses the critical area of database tuning. You'll learn about Oracle's two optimizer choices: the rules-based optimizer and the cost-based optimizer. You'll also learn how to gather statistics that the cost-based optimizer can use to make intelligent decisions about how best to execute your queries. In addition to this, you'll find chapters on SQL statement tuning and on database and instance tuning.

Part V: Backup and Recovery

Part V consists of only two chapters. The first chapter is on backup, and it discusses your options for backing up an Oracle8i database. The second chapter discusses different ways to recover a database or portions of a database.

Part VI: Advanced Topics

Think of Part VI as the next step up from the nuts and bolts of Part III. Part VI consists of a number of ad hoc chapters on the more interesting Oracle8i advanced features. You'll learn how to leverage the power of Oracle's built-in procedural language, PL/SQL. There is a chapter on Java, which shows you how to load and run Java code within the database. You'll learn how to audit a database, how to partition tables, and how to manage database resources. You'll also learn to work with Oracle8i's large object types and to use PL/SQL's object-oriented features. There is also a chapter on WebDB, an exciting and relatively new feature of Oracle that enables you to develop data-driven Web sites.

Appendixes

This book has four appendixes. The first three appendixes serve as a handy reference in your daily work. When you need a quick refresher on the syntax of a SQL statement or a SQL*Plus command, this is where you should go. These three appendixes cover all of Oracle8i's SQL statements, the SQL*Plus commands, and the built-in SQL functions. The fourth appendix describes the contents of the CD-ROM that accompanies this book.

About the Companion CD-ROM

The CD-ROM in the back of this book contains the following:

1. Scripts to create and populate the sample tables used throughout this book.

2. Scripts that contain some of the longer code examples shown in Chapters 10 and 12.

3. A copy of Oraxcel Lite. Oraxcel Lite is an Excel-to-Oracle gateway that allows you to easily access Oracle data from an Excel spreadsheet.

As previously mentioned, Appendix D, "What's On the CD-ROM," describes this material further.

Reach Out

My publisher and I both want your feedback. After you have had a chance to use this book, please take a moment to register this book on the http://my2cents. idgbooks.com Web site. (Details are listed on the my2cents page in the back of this book.) Please don't hesitate to let us know about any chapters that gave you trouble, or where you thought we could have made concepts clearer. Also let us know where we've done a particularly good job.

If you have specific questions about the book, please feel free to e-mail me and ask. I respond to all the reader e-mail that I get. I can't provide extensive help and consultation, but I'm always happy to answer questions when I can. My e-mail address is the following:

    jonathan@gennick.com

You may also want to visit my Web site at the following address:

    http://gennick.com

You'll find some Oracle-related material there, and you can read about my other books. I will also post answers to frequently asked questions about this book as well as any corrections for this book.

Acknowledgments

A large number of people helped in the development of this book. Foremost, I would like to thank my co-authors. Gerrit-Jan Linker was kind enough to take on the challenging job of writing the SQL statement reference in Appendix A. Carol McCullough-Dieter took on the task of revising chapters 25 and 27 on auditing and partitioning. Rick Greenwald contributed Chapter 26, *WebDB*. Rick is also the author of the *WebDB Bible,* and it was an honor to have him contribute his expertise to this work.

I'd like to express my thanks to the many editors who labored so hard to make this book a reality. John Osborn was involved at the very beginning, and he helped shape the vision for the work. Terri Varveris and Terry O'Donnell put in some serious effort developing and editing the chapters as they were written. Brian Laskey was my technical editor, and his tireless efforts greatly contributed to the accuracy and relevance of this work. I would also like to thank my copy editors, Chrisa Hotchkiss and Mildred Sanchez, for their efforts.

Several people at Oracle Support also contributed in various small ways. I say small ways, but at the time they were large problems for me. Ronald Hahn went well above the call of duty in helping me track down information about redo log buffer and latch contention, as well as in helping me identify a related documentation bug. Peter Trent was instrumental in providing me with detailed information about how histograms really work. Thomas Kyte of Oracle Service Industries was kind enough to answer several questions relating to the new record level security features in Oracle8i.

My family's contributions to this book can't be ignored. My wife Donna allowed me to hole up in my office all day every day for a long time so that I could revise this book. She also had to run interference with the kids to prevent them from interrupting me. She was not always successful! I should thank my three-year-old son Jeff for frequently barging in, grabbing onto me, and appealing to me whenever he didn't like some decision that my wife made. That's what daddies are for, right? My 11-year-old daughter Jenny let me pick her up from school each afternoon, providing me with a much-needed mid-afternoon break. She still likes to be seen with me, and for that I'm grateful.

Jonathan Gennick

Contents at a Glance

Contents

Part II: Database Administration Tools   187

Part IV: Oracle8i Tuning   469

Chapter 18: Optimizers and Statistics 471

Chapter 19: Tuning SQL Statements 497

Part VI: Advanced Topics   585

Chapter 23: Using PL/SQL 587

Chapter 24: Using Procedures, Packages, Functions, and Triggers 633

Appendixes 827

In The Beginning

◆ ◆ ◆ ◆

◆ ◆ ◆ ◆

Introducing Oracle8i

"The Internet changes everything." Although we're not sure who first said this, Oracle certainly believes it. The release of Oracle8i and related products, such as WebDB, interMedia, and Internet File System (iFS), represent a significant push by Oracle to leverage its database expertise and become a major player in the growth of Internet computing. No longer is Oracle just a database. Now it is the Database for the Internet. Even the name has been changed, with an "i" being added to "Oracle8," giving us "Oracle8i" instead.

Oracle has done much more than just change the name of its product—the company has also added significant new functionality. A Java engine now runs within the database. Oracle interMedia enables the database to store the rich variety of sound, video, and image content so often found on the World Wide Web. Oracle Application Server (OAS) allows you to deploy robust, three-tier applications accessible to millions of people around the world. Internet File System turns the database server into a universally accessible file server. Clearly, Oracle has made some exiting changes, and at the core of all these is the database itself—Oracle8i.

This chapter tells you about many of the new features that set Oracle8i apart from its predecessors. We'll then go over some of the details that you should remember during the installation process. We'll end with a look at the starter database, followed by a quick tour of the software that you will be using to administer your database.

Introducing New Oracle8i Features

Oracle8i represents a significant increase in functionality over Oracle8. If you are still using Oracle7, the differences are even more profound. However, we're talking about an *increase* in functionality, not *changed* functionality. Oracle's backward compatibility is excellant, and applications developed for

Oracle7 and Oracle8 should work under Oracle8i as well. Oracle8i's most significant new features fall into these categories:

✦ Java

✦ Data warehousing

✦ Resource management and performance

✦ OLTP

✦ Ease-of-use enhancements

✦ Backup and recovery

✦ Security

✦ PL/SQL

This chapter doesn't discuss every last new feature, but every effort has been made to cover the most significant ones. The next few sections describe in detail the new features for each category in the preceding list.

Java

Java is certainly the big news. Oracle8i includes an embedded Java Virtual Machine (JVM) developed by Oracle specifically for its database. It runs within the same process and memory space as the database engine itself, putting it on par with Oracle's other language, PL/SQL.

You can write stored procedures, functions, and triggers in Java. Furthermore, Oracle supports two-way interoperability between PL/SQL and Java. Your Java code can make calls to PL/SQL procedures and functions, and your PL/SQL code can make calls to Java procedures and functions.

To enable you to access relational data from Java, Oracle has embedded Java database connectivity (JDBC) and SQLJ support within the database. JDBC is an industry standard set of classes and methods that allows you to query and manipulate relational data. It's similiar in concept to open database connectivity (ODBC). SQLJ is a precompiler. It works in much the same way as Pro*C and Pro*COBOL, allowing you to embed SQL statements within a Java program. When the Java program is compiled, the SQLJ precompiler translates the SQLJ statements into JDBC method calls.

Data warehousing

Oracle continues to enhance its support for data warehouses and other large databases. Significant new features include the following:

✦ **Support for materialized views and automatic query rewrites.** A *materialized view* is one where the query is executed once when the view is created, and the results are saved for future reference. The most obvious use is to store summaries of information contained in large tables. *Automatic query rewrites* cause queries that later attempt the same summarization to use the materialized view instead, resulting in a significant performance boost.

✦ **Transportable tablespaces.** *Transportable tablespaces* allow easy movement of data from an operational database to a data warehouse. Exporting data from one database and importing it into another can be time consuming. If you set things up correctly, you can now accomplish the same task more quickly by copying one or more tablespace files.

✦ **Two new aggregate operators,** CUBE **and** ROLLUP. The ROLLUP operator allows for the automatic generation of subtotals in the results returned by a GROUP BY query. The CUBE operator generates subtotals across multiple dimensions and may be used to generate crosstab reports.

✦ SAMPLE **function**. It allows you to write data-mining queries that randomly sample a specific percentage of rows in a table.

Resource management and performance

Enhancements under the resource management and performance catagory include the following:

✦ **Support for function-based indexes.** This feature allows you to create an index on the result of a SQL function applied to one or more underlying columns in the table. An index on UPPER(employee_last_name), for example, would make case-insensitive name searches not only possible, but also efficient.

✦ **Better support for index-organized tables.** An *index-organized table* is one in which the entire table is created as an index. All the data is stored in the index, and there really is no underlying table. Oracle8i allows secondary indexes to be created on these tables, allows them to store large objects, and allows you to add or modify columns using the ALTER TABLE command.

✦ **Support for resource management.** You now have the ability to allocate CPU resources among different users, or groups of users. You could, for example, limit decision support users to 10 percent of the available CPU time during the day, but allow them to use up to 80 percent at night.

OLTP

Online transaction processing (OLTP) represents one of the more common uses for relational databases. Oracle now supports stable optimizer plans. This feature allows you to store a set of optimizer-generated execution plans for an application's SQL statements on a reference database and to export those plans to other databases. An OLTP application typically generates a predefined set of SQL statements, and once an application is tuned, you generally want the same execution plan to be used anywhere that you deploy that application.

Oracle8i supports several new trigger types. You may now create triggers for the following data definition language commands:

✦ CREATE

✦ ALTER

✦ DROP

In addition, you may create triggers that execute in response to the following database events:

✦ User logon

✦ User logoff

✦ Database startup

✦ Database shutdown

✦ Server errors

Ease-of-use enhancements

Oracle8i includes several enhancements that make tasks easier for the database administrator. These include the following:

✦ DROP COLUMN **command.** No longer do you need to go through the often-agonizing process of dropping and recreating a table when all you really want to do is drop one column from that table.

✦ **Configuration Assistant.** Configuration Assistant is a wizard-based application that automates the task of creating a new Oracle database. Just answer the questions, and Configuration Assistant will write the create script for you. It will even run it for you if you like.

✦ **An enhanced Enterprise Manager.** Oracle Enterprise Manager Administrator may now be deployed in either a two-tier or a three-tier environment. Deployment in a three-tier environment allows you to perform DBA functions via your Web browser.

✦ **Support for online index rebuilds.** Previous releases of Oracle would lock a table during an index rebuild to prevent users from making changes during the rebuild process. Oracle8i allows users to update a table during an index rebuild.

Backup and recovery

Oracle8i implements the following features related to backup and recovery:

✦ Support for multiple archive log destinations, making it easier to maintain multiple copies of archived log files

✦ Support for multiple archiver processes, reducing the likelihood of bottlenecks caused by redo log files being filled faster than they can be archived

✦ The ability to set an upper limit on the time that you are willing to allow for crash recovery

✦ LogMiner, which gives you the ability to extract and analyze information from redo log files

Security

Security-related enhancements include the following:

✦ **Fine-grained access control.** This allows you to implement row-level security at the database level.

✦ **Application contexts.** This allows you to expand on fine-grained access control by making it application-specific.

✦ **Support for the invoker's rights model.** This allows you to write PL/SQL procedures and functions that execute using the privileges granted to the invoking user, as opposed to the privileges granted to the definer.

PL/SQL

Oracle8i brings a number of PL/SQL enhancements to the table. The following are the most significant:

✦ **Support for autonomous transactions.** This allows you to code completely independent transactions that you can commit regardless of whether the calling transaction commits.

✦ **Embedded dynamic SQL.** This provides a simpler and more efficient way to execute dynamic SQL than was previously available using the DBMS_SQL package.

✦ **Parameter passing by reference.** This improves the performance of applications that pass large structures as arguments to PL/SQL procedures and functions.

✦ **PL/SQL bulk binds.** This allows you to send a SQL statement to the server, together with an array of values. The SQL statement is executed once for each element in the array. The result is the same as if you had sent each element of the array one at a time, but it's much faster to send it all in one shot.

Installing Oracle8i

The process of installing Oracle software can be divided into three phases: the preinstallation phase, the installation phase, and the postinstallation phase. Most of the work should happen in the preinstallation phase. This is where you plan out the products that you want to install, decide on the hardware that you want to use, make sure that the hardware is configured properly, and read over the installation instructions. If you do your planning right, the installation phase consists of little more than watching the installer copy files.

Preinstallation preparation

The most important part of the installation process is the preperation phase. Resist the temptation to skip this phase. People often rush to put the CD in the machine and start the installation process without really thinking through just what they want to do, and without taking the time to prepare the environment. Such a rushed approach often results in a failed installation, which can lead to a lot of frustrating cleanup work, not to mention having to start over again. At best, you will end up doing a lot of rework in the postinstallation phase that you could have avoided by doing some preplanning.

Reading the Installation Guide

The process for installing Oracle varies from one operating system to the next, from one hardware platform to the next, and from one release of Oracle to the next. For each combination of operating system, hardware platform, and software release, Oracle produces an installation guide. Often, you will receive a printed version of the installation guide along with the media (usually a CD) containing the Oracle software. If you paid for the software, this is most likely the case. If you have a demo CD that you picked up free at a trade show, you should be able to find the installation guide on the CD in HTML format.

The installation guide explains the entire installation process, tells you about any prerequisites that need to be in place, and explains any configuration options for the product. The Oracle8i installation guide, for example, explains the difference between a minimal installation and a typical installation. You have to read the installation guide to find out what each configuration has to offer, as well as what each configuration requires.

If you're installing Oracle software in a UNIX environment as opposed to Windows NT, it's even more critical to read the installation guide carefully. You will likely find that you must set a number of UNIX system parameters in certain ways, and you will need to work closely with your system administrator to make the installation succeed.

A False Sense of Security

If you work with Oracle in a Windows NT environment, you may find yourself lulled into a false sense of security. The Windows NT installation is very easy to do and requires a minimum of preparation. Indeed, you are often able to just slam the CD into the machine, run setup, and install Oracle without any advance preparation. This is not a good habit to get into; when you move into other environments, such as UNIX, the installation process won't be nearly so forgiving.

Deciding What to Install

As you read through the installation guide, part of what you should be doing is deciding exactly which product options you want to install. The Oracle8i server software has many optional components to choose from. When you run the installer, you will be given a choice between a typical installation and a custom installation. A custom installation allows you to pick and choose the exact components that you want. The trick is to *know* what you want — there are a lot of components. Unless you are extremely familiar with all the components that make up an Oracle database installation, it's usually best to start with a typical installation. Chances are good that it will be sufficient, and you can add components later if it isn't. A typical installation will provide you with the following major items:

✦ The Oracle8i Server software

✦ Net8 Listener

✦ The Oracle8i utilities

✦ SQL*Plus

✦ A starter database

Reading the Release Notes

Be sure to read the release notes for any Oracle product that you install. They typically come as a stapled-together sheaf of papers. It's easy to shove them aside and lose them because they don't sit on a shelf as well as a manual. The release notes document issues and potential problems that weren't known when the manuals were printed. The issues described in the release notes may not apply to your situation, but it's possible that you could spend hours trying to make something work only to finally find the solution in the release notes.

Preparing the Server(s)

The last step before installing the software is to prepare the server. The installation guide tells you how to do this, which is another reason why you should read it. Windows NT environments are the easiest to prepare. Under Windows NT, you generally need to do the following:

✦ Check that you have enough system memory.

✦ Check that you have enough disk space.

✦ Make sure that the correct service pack is installed.

Configuring a UNIX environment is usually more complicated, and you will find yourself faced with a list of tasks that looks like this:

✦ Verify that you have enough system memory.

✦ Verify that you have enough swap space.

✦ Make sure that you have enough disk space.

✦ Verify that the correct operating system version is installed.

✦ Verify that the necessary operating system patches have been installed.

✦ Create mount points for the Oracle software and for database files.

✦ Create a dba group.

✦ Create a user to own the Oracle software.

✦ Modify various kernel parameters.

Preparing a UNIX environment involves more time and effort than preparing an NT environment. It's important to take the time to work through all the preparation steps identified in your installation guide and to work with your system administrator to ensure that your system is properly prepared for Oracle.

Installing the software

If you've done the neccessary preperation ahead of time, installing the software is a non-event. You will know what you want installed. You will know how to answer the installer prompts, and you will spend most of your time waiting and watching as the files are copied from the distribution CD to your server's disk.

Postinstallation tasks

Your installation guide contains a list of postinstallation tasks that you may need to perform. These tasks include reserving a port for the Net8 listener, starting the Net8 listener, editing configuration files for the precompilers, and so forth. Make sure that you perform the appropriate tasks for the specific product mix that you installed.

In addition to the postinstallation tasks identified in the installation guide, take the time to change the passwords for the SYS and SYSTEM users in your new database to something other than the default. You might also consider whether you really want the SCOTT user, with its set of example tables, to exist in your database. You should also change the internal password if you accepted the default during the installation.

Examining the Starter Database Contents

When you install Oracle from scratch and you accept the default installation options, the installer will create a starter database as part of the installation process. This starter database will include the following:

✦ Data dictionary tables and views

✦ A number of PL/SQL built-in packages

✦ Several default users

✦ A number of predefined roles

The *data dictionary* is a set of tables that Oracle uses to keep track of everything else in the database. Oracle creates a number of views on these data dictionary tables to make the information more accessible to database users. Throughout this book, you will find information about how you can use these data dictionary views to learn about the various objects contained in a database.

To support developers and DBAs who use PL/SQL, Oracle supplies a rich library of predefined functions and procedures. These are organized into packages, where each package focuses on a particular type of functionality. The DBMS_OUTPUT package, for example, contains procedures used to display information in SQL*Plus.

In addition to the data dictionary and the built-in packages, which are critical items that you don't want to alter, the Oracle8i starter database contains a number of predefined users and roles, some of which you may not want to keep. These users and roles are described in the next two sections, followed by a discussion of the sample tables that you can add especially for use with this book.

Users

Table 1-1 contains a list of the different users that you will find in an Oracle8i starter database. You can remove some of these users if you don't want them, but some users you should *not* remove. Users that you should never attempt to drop are marked with a "YES" in the Critical column.

Table 1-1 Preinstalled Users in Oracle8i			
User	*Password*	*Critical*	*Usage*
INTERNAL	ORACLE	YES	Alias for SYS. Not a true user.
SYS	CHANGE_ON_ INSTALL	YES	The SYS user owns the data dictionary tables and views, as well as the built-in PL/SQL packages.

Continued

Table 1-1 *(continued)*

User	Password	Critical	Usage
SYSTEM	MANAGER	YES	The SYSTEM user is created for the DBA to use. The SYSTEM user also owns a few tables and views, such as those used for advanced queuing, that are critical to the operation of the database.
SCOTT	TIGER	NO	Owns a small test schema that Oracle documentation references frequently.
DEMO	DEMO	NO	Owns a small test schema that Oracle documentation references frequently.
DBSNMP	DBSNMP	NO	Oracle Enterprise Manager Administrator.
OUTLN	OUTLN	YES	Owns stored outlines such as those created using the CREATE OUTLINE command.
MTSSYS	MTSSYS	NO	Used by Oracle Services for Microsoft Transaction Server.
AURORAORBUNAUTHENTICATED	N/A	YES	Used to allow Common Object Request Broker Architecture (CORBA) connections to log on to Oracle.

User	Password	Critical	Usage
ORDPLUGINS	ORDPLUGINS	NO	Used by Oracle interMedia
CTXSYS	CTXSYS	NO	Used by Oracle interMedia.
ORDSYS	ORDSYS	NO	Used by Oracle interMedia.
MDSYS	MDSYS	NO	Used by Oracle interMedia.

Except for SCOTT and DEMO, you should change the passwords for all these users soon after installation to protect the security of your database. Consider dropping the SCOTT and DEMO users. Their passwords are widely known, and even though they are nonprivileged users, they still pose a threat to security. Anyone logging on as SCOTT, for example, will be able to see information in any tables and views on which SELECT access has been granted to PUBLIC.

Roles

Roles help define database security. They give you a convenient way of grouping related privileges together so that you can easily assign them to a user. The starter database contains a number of predefined roles to help you get started. These are shown in Table 1-2.

Table 1-2
Preinstalled Roles in Oracle8i

Role	Usage
AQ_ADMINISTRATOR_ROLE	Allows a user to function as an advanced queuing administrator
AQ_USER_ROLE	Allows a user to make use of Oracle8i's advanced queuing features
CONNECT	Gives a user enough privileges to log on to the database and to create objects such as tables, views, synonyms, sequences, and database links

Continued

	Table 1-2 *(continued)*
Role	**Usage**
RESOURCE	Gives a user enough additional privileges to create stored procedures, triggers, object types, operators, and index types and does not confer the privileges necessary to actually connect to the database
DBA	Confers all system privileges, allowing the user to do pretty much anything
EXECUTE_CATALOG_ROLE	Allows you to execute most of the built-in PL/SQL packages
HS_ADMIN_ROLE	Allows a user to use the DBMS_HS package to administer heterogeneous services
JAVADEBUGPRIV	Allows a user to invoke the Java debug agent
JAVAIDPRIV	Allows a user to change his or her dynamic identity. Only the SYS user should ever be granted this role
JAVASYSPRIV	Allows a user access to privileged Java functionality
JAVAUSERPRIV	Allows a user who is using Java to access files and sockets
CTXAPP	Identifies a user as a Context Cartridge application user
DELETE_CATALOG_ROLE	Allows a user to delete audit trail records
EXP_FULL_DATABASE	Allows a user to export an entire database
IMP_FULL_DATABASE	Allows a user to import an entire database
RECOVERY_CATALOG_OWNER	Allows a user to run a recovery
SELECT_CATALOG_ROLE	Provides access to the data dictionary views
SNMPAGENT	Provides necessary access to Oracle Enterprise Manager's Intelligent Agent
TIMESERIES_DEVELOPER	Allows a user to make use of the time series cartridge
TIMESERIES_DBA	Allows a user to function as a time series administrator

Tables

The user named SCOTT owns several sample tables that Oracle refers to throughout its manual set. Regardless of whether you decide to keep these tables in *your* database, you should familiarize yourself with them so that you will understand the references to them. Figure 1-1 shows an entity-relationship diagram depicting these tables and their relationships.

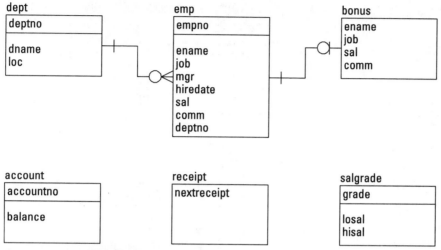

Figure 1-1: Tables in the SCOTT schema

In addition to being used for examples in the manual, the SCOTT tables provide a convenient set of data to use when you want to experiment with SQL.

Oracle8i Bible's sample tables

This book is filled with examples of code that provide step-by-step instructions on how to perform many tasks in the Oracle8i database. After installing your Oracle8i database, you can install all of the sample tables used here into your database.

For your convenience, the SQL scripts to create the Oracle8i Bible's sample tables are included (plus instructions for installing the tables into your database) on the CD-ROM that accompanies the book. Once you create these tables in your database, you can run most of the example code exactly as you see it in the book. Figure 1-2 shows a detailed relational database diagram of all of the sample tables on the CD-ROM.

Cross-Reference   Appendix D contains both the installation instructions and a detailed listing of the tables' contents.

Control menu button   Object window   Object contents window

Main menu bar   Title bar   Toolbar   Window controls

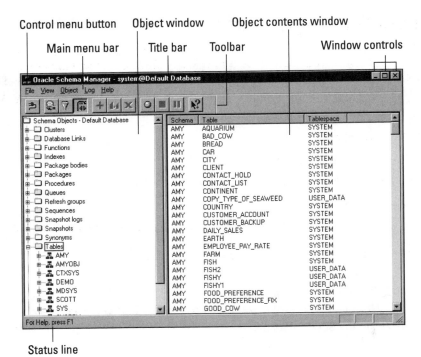

Status line

Figure 1-2: The Oracle8i Bible sample table contains many sets of relationships.

Installing WebDB

WebDB is an Oracle add-on product that allows you to develop Web sites that serve up content based on the data within your database. For example, you can easily design reports using WebDB, and then anyone using a standard Web browser can run them. WebDB is very easy to use. Besides developing reports, you can also use WebDB to design data entry forms and query forms, and you can create menus to tie together a set of forms and reports into an application. All work with WebDB is done via a standard Web browser, and any reasonably savvy user will be able to use WebDB to develop forms and reports.

Oracle includes WebDB software with an Oracle database license. It comes on a separate CD, and the WebDB installation is separate from the Oracle database installation. You don't have to install WebDB, but you should at least consider doing so. To help motivate you, WebDB includes some nifty DBA utilities that you can access through a Web browser. You'll get a glimpse of these later in this chapter, in the section titled "Taking a Quick Tour of Oracle8i."

Cross-Reference   WebDB is covered again in Chapter 26.

Preinstallation preparation

As with the database, the most important preinstallation preparation task is to read the manual. In this case, you want to read the *Getting Started — Installation and Tutorial* manual. You don't need to read the entire manual prior to installing WebDB, just be sure to read through Part 1, which talks about installing and configuring the software. The preinstallation tasks for WebDB include the following:

- ✦ Checking prerequisites
- ✦ Deciding which listener to use
- ✦ Deciding where to install the listener
- ✦ Deciding on a listener port
- ✦ Deciding between an automated installation and a manual installation

The next few sections briefly discuss each of these items.

Checking Prerequisites

WebDB requires that you run Oracle Server 7.3 or higher. This is actually fairly generous. We know of no sites running releases older than 7.3 and very few that haven't begun to migrate to either 8.0 or 8.1.

The WebDB installation process uses the SQL*Plus and SQL*Loader utilities. Make sure that these are installed on your server. Chances are that they will be, but occasionally you might run across a site where, for whatever reason, the DBA has chosen not to install these utilities on the server.

WebDB also requires that you set the MAX_ENABLED_ROLES parameter to a minimum value of 25. You set this parameter in your database initialization file. Remember that you need to stop and restart your database after changing a setting in the initialization file.

Note   You will likely need to change the MAX_ENABLED_ROLES parameter. The default value has never been so high, and even when we installed Oracle8i, we found that the value for MAX_ENABLED_ROLES was less than 25.

Deciding Which Listener to Use

WebDB requires an HTTP listener to monitor the network for incoming requests to WebDB and to serve up Web pages in response. You have three choices here:

- ✦ Use the listener that ships with WebDB.
- ✦ Use the listener that comes with Oracle Application Server.
- ✦ Use some other listener.

The easiest solution is to use the listener that ships with WebDB. WebDB Listener is a lightweight listener that provides only the necessary functionality to serve up HTML pages for WebDB applications.

Deciding Where to Install WebDB Listener

You don't need to install WebDB Listener on the same physical machine as the database server. Certainly it would be easier to put everything on one machine, but for performance reasons, you may not want to do that. Another reason to put WebDB Listener on a separate machine is that it currently runs only under Windows NT and Solaris. If your database server is on an HP-UX server, for example, then you will need to install WebDB Listener on some other machine.

Deciding on a WebDB Listener Port

By default, WebDB Listener listens on port 80. Port 80 has become the standard port that Web servers use, and all browsers connect to that port by default. If you happen to have any other Web server software running on the same machine on which you are installing WebDB Listener, you will likely have a port conflict. In that case, you must either use some other port for WebDB or remove the conflicting software.

Deciding between an Automated Installation and a Manual Installation

WebDB is such a new product that Oracle hasn't yet worked all of the bugs out of the installer. Therefore, Oracle includes instructions for doing a manual installation on the WebDB distribution CD. You can view the manual installation instructions with any Web browser, and you'll find the file at the following location on the CD:

```
\support\maninst.htm
```

Avoid performing a manual installation if possible. It's a lot of work that requires a lot of experience. You should perform a manual installation only if you haven't been able to get the automated installation to work, and even then you should consult Oracle support first.

Note   When recently trying to install WebDB on a Windows NT server that was running both Oracle 7.3.4 and 8.1.5, the WebDB installer didn't handle this well at all. The rules for placing the WebDB Oracle home are different for those two releases of the server software, and the installer tried to follow both sets of conflicting rules at the same time. This resulted in a catch-22 situation, which forced a manual installation.

If you do decide to perform a manual installation, you should review each of the SQL scripts prior to executing them. The scripts assume that you have created certain users and tablespaces. They also assume that the target database is your default database. If you're not an experienced DBA, you probably shouldn't attempt a manual installation without someone's help.

Installing the software

When you begin the actual installation process, keep two points in mind. First, WebDB expects the target database to be your default database. If you examine the SQL scripts that the installer runs, you will find that they all connect like this:

```
CONNECT sys/password
```

Notice that no service name has been specified on this CONNECT command. If you can't connect to your target database using SQL*Plus without specifying a Net8 service name, then the WebDB installer won't be able to either.

The second point to keep in mind is that if you are installing WebDB Listener, you should run the installation from the machine on which you want it to reside. The installer can run the necessary SQL scripts against a remote database, but it can't install WebDB Listener on a remote server.

The WebDB installation should be very easy as long as you've done the necessary preparation. Simply run the installer, answer the questions, and then sit back and watch while the installer does all the work.

Postinstallation tasks

The major postinstallation task for WebDB is to set up the connectivity between WebDB Listener and your database. This involves adding an entry to the tnsnames.or a file for the WebDB Oracle home. By default, WebDB expects this entry to be named WEBDB. If you use a different service name, you will have to tell that to WebDB Listener. The *Oracle WebDB Getting Started—Installation and Tutorial* manual explains how to do that.

Installing Oracle Enterprise Manager

Enterprise Manager is a set of GUI-based tools used to manage Oracle databases. Not surprisingly, Oracle has designed Enterprise Manager to fill the needs of large companies that have a lot of distributed Oracle databases. Enterprise Manager is more than just a set of GUI tools. A full-blown Enterprise Manager installation provides you with the following benefits:

✦ A set of GUI tools for managing the database

✦ A central console, from which you can monitor and manage any number of remote databases

✦ An Enterprise Manager server that allows you to schedule jobs to execute on remote servers

✦ A robust event-handling model that can alert you to impending database problems

Enterprise Manager, in a full-blown configuration, is a three-tier application. It consists of client software that sits on your PC. That client software talks to an Enterprise Manager server sitting somewhere on the network, and that server talks to the various database servers being managed. In addition, the special database known as the *repository database* contains information about database administrators, databases being monitored, jobs that are scheduled to run, and events that should be monitored. Figure 1-3 shows how all these pieces relate.

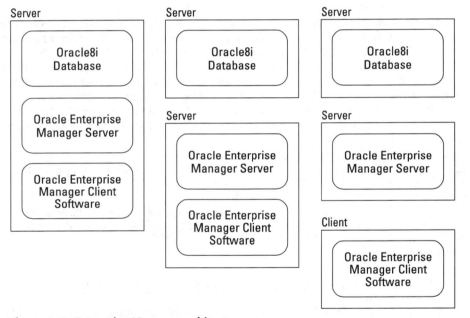

Figure 1-3: Enterprise Manager architecture

Managing Enterprise Manager in a configuration like the one shown in Figure 1-3 is almost as complex a task as managing an Oracle database. In fact, it gives you one extra database to manage — the repository. Fortunately, for small sites with only a few databases, Oracle lets you run the Enterprise Manager applications in a two-tier mode. Everything in Figure 1-3 disappears, except for the Enterprise Manager applications on the client and the databases being managed. This gives you the benefit of an easy-to-use GUI interface, without the complexity of creating a repository and configuring an Enterprise Manager server.

Preinstallation preparation

As with the other products, the fundamental piece of preinstallation advice is to read the manual. For Enterprise Manager, you should read through the *Oracle Enterprise Manager Configuration Guide*. This guide explains your options for installing the product and explains the hardware and software requirements for each option.

The major decision you have to make is whether to go with a two-tier or a three-tier installation. A two-tier installation involves installing the Enterprise Manager client software only on your PC, while a three-tier installation involves configuring an Enterprise Manager server and creating a repository database.

If you are going to perform a three-tier installation, your next task is to decide how many machines to use. It is possible to have all three tiers — the database being managed, the Enterprise Manager server, and the Enterprise Manager client software — on the same machine. A more distributed approach, and one that would probably perform better, is to have all three tiers on separate hardware platforms. Each DBA would get his or her own copy of the client software, the Enterprise Manager server and the repository database would reside on a server by themselves, and all the managed databases would reside on various other servers on the network.

Finally, it's best if you create the repository database prior to installing and configuring the Enterprise Manager server.

Note   The repository database requires that you set the *processes* initialization parameter to a minimum of 200. You will get a warning during the repository creation process if you don't do this.

Installing the Enterprise Manager software

Installing the Enterprise Manager software is no harder than installing any other Oracle software. If you've done your planning up front, you need only respond to the installer prompts, sit back, and have a cup of coffee while the files are copied from the CD.

The two-tier installation is the simpler of the two possibilities. You simply run the setup program on the Enterprise Manager CD, select the option to install only the client software, and wait while the files are copied. It's that simple.

The three-tier installation is only a bit more complex. You have to install the Enterprise Manager server software on a server machine, and you need to install the client software on one or more clients. You end up performing at least two installations. Towards the end of the server installation, the installer will fire up the Enterprise Manager Configuration Assistant. This program will query you for the name of your repository database. It will also query you for the username and password of a user with DBA privileges so that it can create the repository user, tables, views, and so forth. After you've provided the correct information, the configuration assistant connects to the repository database and creates the repository.

Postinstallation tasks

The two major postinstallation tasks are to configure Net8 for Enterprise Manager and to start the Enterprise Manager server. You need to start the server only if you installed the server, so if you just installed the client software, you have only one consideration—Net8.

Like WebDB, Enterprise Manager has it's own Oracle home directory. The setup program will have asked you to specify this directory, so you should know the correct path. This Oracle home directory has its own listener.ora file. To enable the Enterprise Manager software to connect to the databases that you want to manage, you must add entries for those databases to this file.

Finally, if you installed the Enterprise Manager server, start the server process. If the server is running on a UNIX machine, the `oemctrl` command is used to start it. If the server is running Windows NT, you will probably find it easier to start the Enterprise Manager server using the Services control panel, although the `oemctrl` command also works on NT.

Taking a Quick Tour of Oracle8i

Let's take a quick tour of Oracle8i and try out some of the tools that you'll be using to manage your Oracle database. First, you'll start by trying out two command-line utilities: SQL*Plus and Listener Control. You'll do enough to verify that your database is up and running, and you'll briefly glimpse how these tools work. Next, you'll move through several Enterprise Manager modules. Finally, the tour will end with a quick stop at the WebDB administration utility.

You may not have all of these tools installed. Oracle Enterprise Manager and WebDB are optional. If you didn't install them, you won't be able to follow along at the keyboard while reading through those sections of the tour. Read the tour anyway, though, just to see how all these tools work together.

SQL*Plus

SQL*Plus is the most venerable of the Oracle utilities. It's been around practically forever. Before Enterprise Manager came on the scene, SQL*Plus was the primary tool used to manage Oracle databases. In a nutshell, SQL*Plus is a utility that lets you enter and execute SQL statements and PL/SQL blocks. You can enter a SELECT statement, for example, and have the results displayed on the screen for you to see.

Oracle supports both a GUI and a command-line version of SQL*Plus. This tour will focus on the command-line version. Follow these steps to look at SQL*Plus:

1. Get to a command prompt.

If you're running Windows NT, you'll need to open a Command Prompt window. If you're running under UNIX, log on to the operating system to get a command prompt.

Note
If you're running Windows NT, also make sure that the correct Oracle home is in place. Installing WebDB or OEM might change your default Oracle home tree, which may make it impossible to run SQL*PLUS from the command prompt window.

2. Issue the `sqlplus` command to start SQL*Plus.

You should see results similar to those shown in Figure 1-4.

Note
Prior to the release of Oracle8i, the command to start SQL*Plus on Windows-based systems was `plusxxw`, where "xx" was the release number and the presence or absence of the "w" controlled whether you got the GUI version or the command-line version. The command `plus73` would start the command-line version of SQL*Plus for Oracle 7.3 under Windows NT (or 95), while `plus80w` would start the Windows version of SQL*Plus for Oracle 8.0 under Windows NT (or 95).

3. Connect to your Oracle database.

Enter a username and password when prompted. For this example, you could log on as the SCOTT user, with a password of TIGER. Your screen should now look like the one shown in Figure 1-4.

```
Command Prompt - sqlplus                                    _ □ ×

D:\oracle\ora81\BIN>sqlplus

SQL*Plus: Release 8.1.5.0.0 - Production on Sun Jun 13 15:38:19 1999

(c) Copyright 1999 Oracle Corporation.  All rights reserved.

Enter user-name: scott
Enter password:

Connected to:
Oracle8i Enterprise Edition Release 8.1.5.0.0 - Production
With the Partitioning and Java options
PL/SQL Release 8.1.5.0.0 - Production

SQL> _
```

Figure 1-4: Connecting to an Oracle database

If you can connect to SQL*Plus, that's a good indication that the database is up and running.

4. Execute a SQL SELECT statement by typing the following SQL statement at the SQL> prompt:

```
SELECT * FROM dual;
```

You should get results like those shown in Figure 1-5. Don't forget to type the semicolon at the end of the statement. The semicolon is important because it marks the end of the statement as far as SQL*Plus is concerned. Omit the semicolon, and you'll be prompted for another line of SQL.

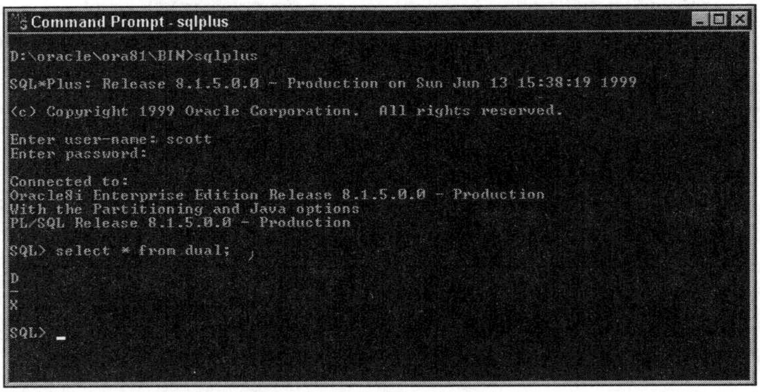

Figure 1-5: Selecting from the dual table

The dual table should be present in every Oracle database. It's a special table that has only one row and one column. It serves a variety of useful purposes. In this case, it's a known table that you can select from to prove that the database is working.

5. Exit SQL*Plus.

We're done with SQL*Plus for now, so go ahead and exit the program and return to the command prompt. Figure 1-6 illustrates this.

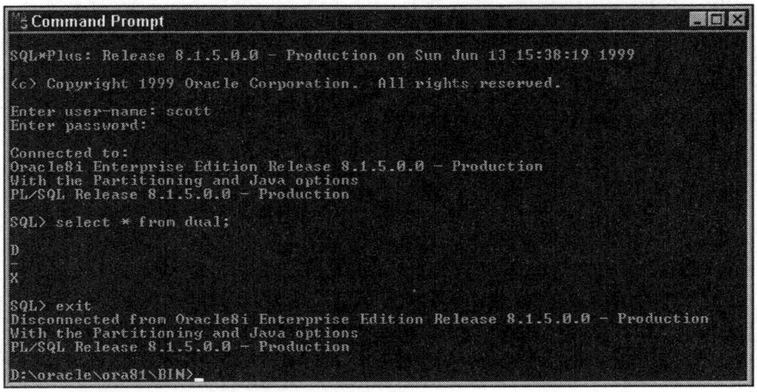

Figure 1-6: Exiting from SQL*Plus

SQL*Plus can execute any valid SQL statement or PL/SQL block, and thus allows you to perform practically any database administration task. In the past, you had to use a separate program called Server Manager to start and stop an Oracle database and to run certain administrative scripts. Beginning with the release of Oracle8i, all the Server Manager functions have been merged into SQL*Plus. Server Manager is still around, but Oracle plans to desupport it someday, leaving SQL*Plus as the only command-line interface to an Oracle database.

Listener Control

Oracle's networking product is known as Net8. Net8 allows communications between two database instances over a network. Net8 also allows for communication between a database instance and a client PC on a network. On the server, Net8 implements a process known as a *listener*. It's the listener's job to monitor the network for incomming database connections. To control the listener, you use a utility known as Listener Control. Follow these steps to have a look at the Listener Control program:

1. Get to a command prompt.

   If you're running Windows NT, you'll need to open a Command Prompt window. If you're running under UNIX, log on to the operating system to get a command prompt.

2. Start the Listener Control program.

   The command to start the Listener Control utility is `lsnrctl`. Remember, if you are running Windows NT, you'll need to open a Command Prompt window first. Listing 1-1 provides an example of what you will see after entering the command.

3. Check the status of the listener by entering the `status` command. The results will appear as shown in Listing 1-2.

4. Type `exit` at the command prompt to exit the Listener Control utility.

Listing 1-1: **Entering the lsnrctl command**

```
c:\> lsnrctl

LSNRCTL for 32-bit Windows: Version 8.1.5.0.0 - Production on 13-JUN-99 15:41:28

(c) Copyright 1998 Oracle Corporation.  All rights reserved.

Welcome to LSNRCTL, type "help" for information.

LSNRCTL>
```

Listing 1-2: **Checking the status of the listener**

```
LSNRCTL> status
Connecting to (DESCRIPTION=(ADDRESS=(PROTOCOL=IPC)(KEY=EXTPROC0)))
STATUS of the LISTENER
------------------------
Alias                     LISTENER
Version                   TNSLSNR for 32-bit Windows: Version 8.1.5.0.0
Start Date                13-JUN-99 15:43:58
Uptime                    0 days 0 hr. 0 min. 7 sec
Trace Level               off
Security                  OFF
SNMP                      OFF
Listener Parameter File   d:\oracle\ora81\network\admin\listener.ora
Listener Log File         d:\oracle\ora81\network\log\listener.log
Services Summary...
   PLSExtProc             has 1 service handler(s)
   JONATHAN               has 1 service handler(s)
The command completed successfully
LSNRCTL>
```

Instance Manager

Instance Manager is an Oracle Enterprise Manager application that shows you a high-level view of your database's current activity. Instance Manager also allows you to start and stop your database instance. This section assumes you have access to a DBA user account and password. You can use the standard Oracle8i user, SYSTEM, if you wish. The default password for SYSTEM is MANAGER.

Follow these steps to look at Instance Manager:

1. Click Start, point to Programs, point to Oracle – oem_home, point to DBA Management Pack, and select Instance Manager.

   An Oracle Enterprise Manager Login window appears and asks for your input.

2. To log on as the SYSTEM user, type SYSTEM in the Username box, MANAGER (or whatever your current system password is) in the Password box, and your Net8 service name into the Service box.

   This sequence brings you to Instance Manager's main window. It will be similar to what you see in Figure 1-7, but instead of a traffic light, you will see a splash screen on the righthand side of the window.

3. Click the Database icon that is on the left side of the screen to see the current status of the database.

   You should now see a traffic light in the righthand window, as shown in Figure 1-7.

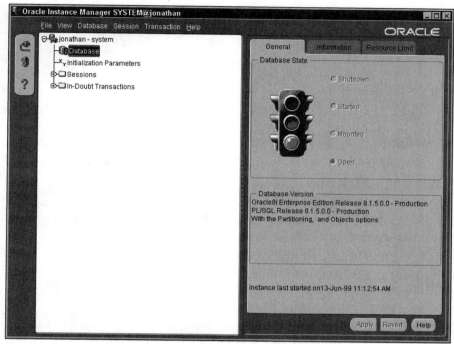

Figure 1-7: Instance Manager shows the status and current activity of the database.

4. Observe the traffic light.

If the light is green, as it likely will be, your database is open and running.

5. Double-click the Sessions folder in the left frame.

You should see a list of sessions currently active in your database. The first several sessions, the ones without usernames next to them, are the background processes for the instance. The remaining sessions are for users who are logged on to the database.

6. Click any session.

Figure 1-8 shows the details you see for each session using the database. You see the user, terminal, and the program running for the session.

7. Select the Exit command on the File menu to exit Instance Manager.

8. Close the associated Command Prompt window (Windows 95 only).

> **Note**
>
> All Enterprise Manager applications are Java applications. When you run one on a Windows 95 system, in addition to the GUI window that you just saw, an associated Command Prompt window sits in the background. Figure 1-9 shows what that window looks like. In Enterprise Manager 2.0, closing one of the applications doesn't close the associated Command Prompt window. You need to do that manually by double-clicking the window's Close button. This behavior is specific to Windows 95 and 98.

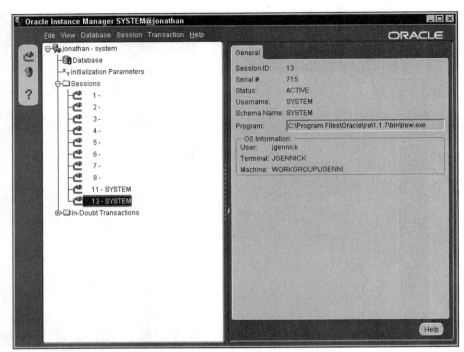

Figure 1-8: Observe your users with a click of a button.

Schema Manager

You use Schema Manager to create and modify schema objects such as tables, views, and stored procedures. Follow these steps to start Schema Manager:

1. Select Start, point to Programs, point to Oracle – oem_home, point to DBA Management Pack, and select Schema Manager to start Schema Manager.

    An Oracle Enterprise Manager Login window appears and asks for your input.

2. Log on as the SYSTEM user.

    You log on as the SYSTEM user the same way as you did previously when you ran Instance Manager. Once you log on, you will see the initial Schema Manager screen. Depending on the speed of your system, you may experience a short delay before a list of folders appears on the left side of the window.

3. Double-click the Tables folder in the left pane of the window.

    A list of tables appears in the detail pane. A list of schemas (table owners) appears under the Tables folder in the left pane of the window. Your screen should look similar to the one shown in Figure 1-9.

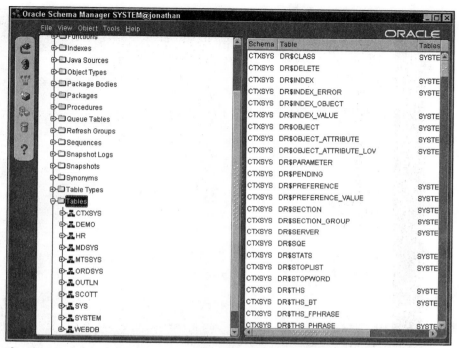

Figure 1-9: Schema Manager manages database objects such as tables.

Schema Manager arranges objects such as tables and indexes in an orderly format, similar to the way Windows NT Explorer arranges folders and files. Navigate within Schema Manager as you would in these utilities. Pull-down menus display your options. Clicking selects an item, while right-clicking displays a context-sensitive pop-up menu.

4. Double-click one of the schemas in the left pane.

A list of tables owned by that user will appear in the right pane and will also appear underneath the schema's entry in the left pane.

5. In the left pane, click the first table in the list.

The right pane changes to display a tabbed listing that describes the highlighted table (see Figure 1-10). The basic structure you see in the figure is common to most of the Enterprise Manager tools.

6. Select the Exit command on the File menu to exit Schema Manager.

7. Close the associated Command Prompt window (Windows 95 only).

Schema Manager has the same type of Command Prompt window associated with it as Instance Manager does. Switch to this window — you can press Alt+Tab to do this — and double-click the Close button to close it.

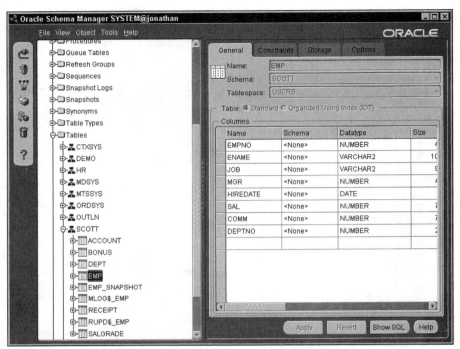

Figure 1-10: Schema Manager, showing the structure of a table

Storage Manager

Storage Manager monitors disk space and file size and also displays the mapping between tablespaces and actual files. Use Storage Manager to add new tablespaces and files to your database. Follow these steps to view Storage Manager:

1. Select Start, point to Programs, point to Oracle – oem_home, point to DBA Management Pack, and select Storage Manager to start Storage Manager.

   An Oracle Enterprise Manager Login window appears and asks for your input.

2. Log on as the SYSTEM user.

   Once you log on, you see the initial Storage Manager window.

3. Click the Tablespace folder in the left pane of the window.

   A list of tablespaces appears in the right pane. The list shows the status and size of each of your tablespaces. You may need to grab the vertical bar in the center of the window and slide it to the left before you can see all the information in the right pane. Your screen should now look similar to the one shown in Figure 1-11.

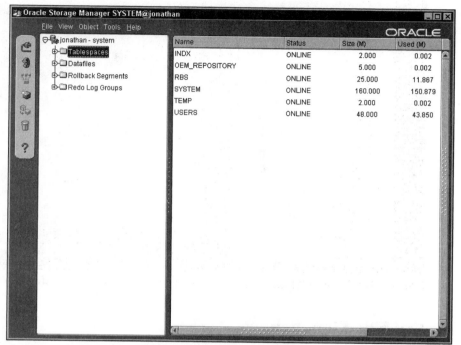

Figure 1-11: The Storage Manager window shows the status and size of each tablespace.

4. Click the plus sign next to the Datafiles folder in the left pane.

A list of files appears below the Datafiles folder in the left pane.

5. In the left pane, click the first datafile in the list.

The right pane changes to display a tabbed list describing the highlighted datafile, as shown in Figure 1-12.

6. Exit Storage Manager.

7. Close the associated Command Prompt window.

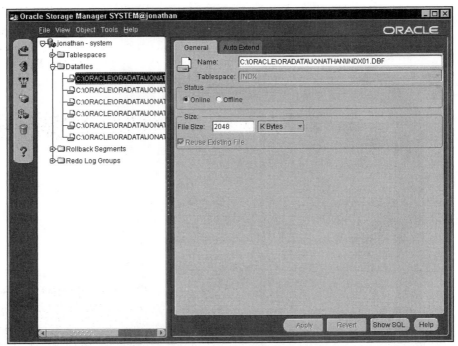

Figure 1-12: The Storage Manager window allows you to add to a datafile.

SQL*Plus Worksheet

SQL*Plus Worksheet is an Oracle Enterprise Manager tool that provides the same functionality as SQL*Plus, but it is wrapped in a GUI interface. In fact, SQL*Plus Worksheet actually calls SQL*Plus to execute whatever commands you enter. This is done to ensure absolute, 100-percent compatibility between the two products. To start SQL Worksheet, follow these steps:

1. From the Windows NT Start menu, point to Programs, point to Oracle – oem_home, point to DBA Management Pack, and select SQLP Worksheet to start the program.

2. Fill in a valid username, password, and service in the security screen that pops up.

    If you like, you can use Oracle8i's sample user account (SCOTT) and password (TIGER). The password shows up as asterisks (*) when you type it. Leave the Service box blank to connect to your local database. Otherwise, enter the Net8 service name for the Oracle database to which you will connect.

3. Accept the Connect As box as Normal. The SQL*Plus Worksheet will appear.

Figure 1-13 shows the SQLPlus Worksheet window that you can use to type your commands. The window divides horizontally into two panes. The top pane is the area in which you type SQL commands. The bottom pane displays the command and the results of the command.

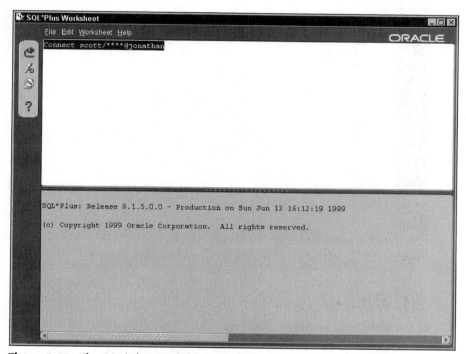

Figure 1-13: The SQL*Plus Worksheet window

4. Type the following SQL command in the top pane:

```
SELECT * FROM dual
```

5. Click the Execute button (this button has a lightning bolt on it).

You will see the results of the query appear in the bottom pane, as shown in Figure 1-14.

6. Close SQLPlus Worksheet.

7. Close the associated Command Prompt window.

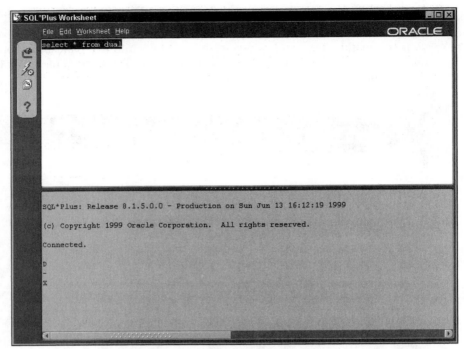

Figure 1-14: The SQLPlus Worksheet window showing the results of a query

WebDB

Do the following to start WebDB:

1. Start your Web browser.

2. In the URL box, type the name of the server where WebDB Listener is running. In the example shown in Figure 1-15, WebDB Listener is running on a node named dsat4, so "dsat4" was typed as the URL.

3. Enter your WebDB username and password, and click OK.

   A dialog box will prompt you for a username and a password. See Figure 1-15. The default WebDB username is webdb, and the default password is webdb as well.

4. Observe the WebDB opening page. It will appear similar to the one shown in Figure 1-16. From this page, you can browse the database, create new Web sites, monitor the database, and manage WebDB users.

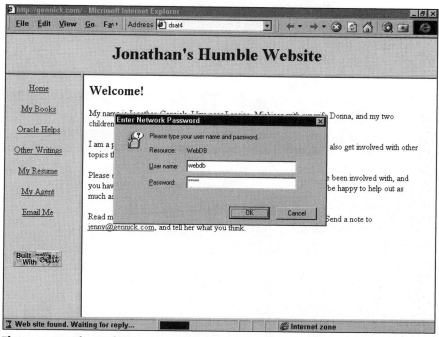

Figure 1-15: The WebDB password prompt

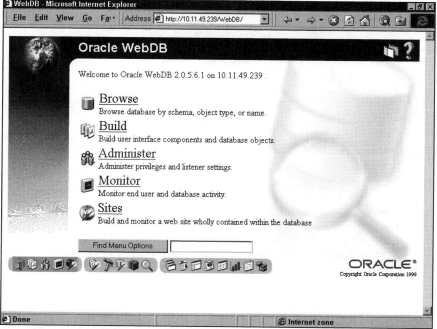

Figure 1-16: The WebDB opening page

5. Check on your database's memory usage by clicking on the following links: Monitor, Database Objects, Sessions and Memory Structures, and Chart of SGA Consumption. You should see a chart showing how much memory is being used for various purposes. See Figure 1-17.

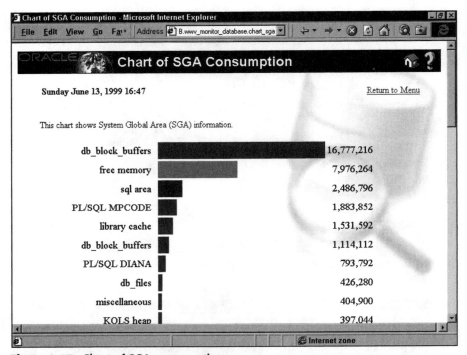

Figure 1-17: Chart of SGA consumption

6. Exit your Web browser.

Summary

In this chapter, you learned the following:

✦ Oracle8i includes a number of exiting new features, many of which are oriented to position Oracle8i as an Internet database. Leading the pack is the Java engine that allows you to run Java code within the database itself. WebDB is another Internet-related feature that takes an innovative approach to making Oracle data more accessible to end users.

✦ Oracle also added a number of features to the 8i release to make your job easier. One long-asked-for feature is the `DROP COLUMN` command that allows you to delete a column from a table without dropping and recreating that table. Oracle Enterprise Manager has been completely rewritten in Java, and you can implement it in a three-tier configuration with a Web-based interface.

✦ Before installing Oracle8i, you must be sure to spend the neccessary preliminary time in planning and preparation. Don't rush into it. UNIX systems, in particular, may require a number of steps to prepare the operating system and the environment for an Oracle installation.

✦   ✦   ✦

Oracle8i Overview

This chapter describes Oracle8i's client/server architecture. It also lists the major components that you get when you install Oracle8i's server software, and it contrasts that with the components you get as a result of installing Oracle8i's client software. Next, you will learn, step by step, how to start and stop the database. Finally, you'll see how to access and use Oracle's online documentation.

Introducing Oracle8i's Client/Server Architecture

Oracle8i is a client/server database. This means that the database server runs independently from the applications that access it. The server listens for, and accepts, requests from clients, processes those requests, and sends the results back to clients. Traditionally, most Oracle applications have been two-tier applications, but that is changing. The advent of the Web and the emphasis on Internet access to information are driving more and more applications to be implemented using a three-tier model.

Since Oracle8i is often used in a client/server architecture, you won't be surprised that it ships software both for the server and for the client. The server portion of the package includes the database software, as well as network software to enable communication to and from clients. The client portion of the package includes utilities and assistant programs, as well as a networking piece that enables communication with Oracle servers. On Windows platforms, the client portion usually includes a number of easy-to-use GUI-based programs.

Implementing a two-tier client/server architecture

Oracle applications are often implemented in a two-tier environment. This means that you have one server running the database, and one or more clients running software programs that interact with that database. Oracle's Net8 software is used to enable communications between the clients and the server. Figure 2-1 shows how this might look.

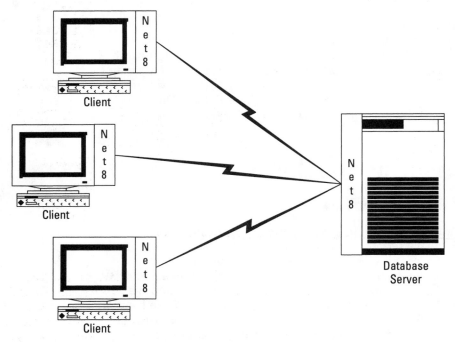

Figure 2-1: Oracle in a two-tier client/server environment

To enable easy connectivity between clients and a server, Oracle has defined a high-level networking protocol named Net8. All clients in a client/server environment have Net8 client software installed. The server will have Net8 server software installed. Net8 provides a common interface that programmers can code to, regardless of what the underlying networking protocol actually is. Oracle provides *network adapters* to transmit Net8 calls across different types of networks. TCP/IP is the most commonly used protocol, although Oracle supports a number of others as well.

Implementing a three-tier client/server architecture

Three-tier client/server configurations have gained popularity over the last few years. This is largely because of the growing importance of the Internet in the business world. The ability to interact with customers and potential clients via the Web is fast becoming a de facto requirement for being in business. Figure 2-2 shows how a typical three-tier application looks.

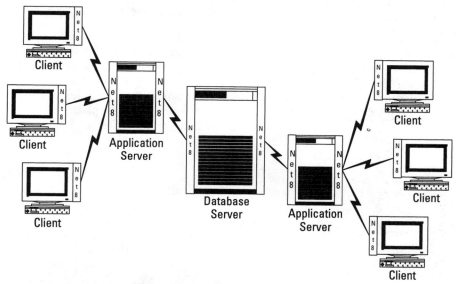

Figure 2-2: Oracle in a three-tier client/server environment

As you can see in Figure 2-2, a three-tier Oracle application still has an Oracle server and client PCs. However, an *application server* sits between the PCs and the database. Ideally, the application server contains all the application logic, the database server contains all the data, and the PCs simply manage the display and the user interaction. Three-tier configurations provide the following advantages over two-tier configurations:

✦ **Scalability.** A server can handle only a limited number of clients. Instead of having each client connect directly to the database server, the three-tier model allows you to spread clients over a number of application servers. As you add more clients, you can add more application servers to support them.

✦ **Ease of distribution.** This applies primarily to Web-based applications. Rather than distributing your software to every client using the system, you need to distribute it only to a small number of application servers, where anyone using a standard Web browser can access it.

Oracle provides a middle-tier solution called, not surprisingly, the Oracle Application Server (OAS). OAS allows you to serve up Web pages to clients and to write PL/SQL and Java code to control what goes on those pages.

In a two-tier, or even a three-tier, environment, each tier has different software installed. The next two sections describe the software that you get when you install Oracle on a server and on a client.

Taking inventory of Oracle8i's server software

When you install Oracle8i on a server, you will typically end up installing the database server software, the Net8 server software, and a core set of standard utilities. These are shown in Figure 2-3. This group of core utilities and the database behave identically — at least as far as the external world is concerned — on all platforms, whether UNIX, Windows NT, or otherwise. The differences are on the inside, where Oracle8i takes advantage of the native platform's capabilities to make the database run as efficiently as possible.

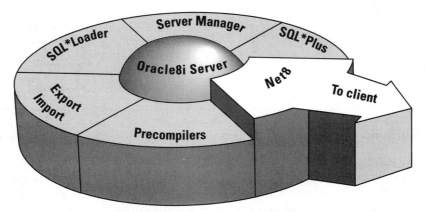

Figure 2-3: The Oracle8i database, with its core utilities, is supported on many operating system and hardware platforms.

The following are the core pieces of an Oracle server installation, as shown in Figure 2-3:

✦ **Oracle8i Server.** This is the database server. The server software contains all the logic necessary to store data, process queries, run PL/SQL code, and run Java code.

✦ **Net8.** This is Oracle's own network communication protocol. It enables rapid and efficient transmission of data between the server and the clients accessing that server.

✓ ✦ **SQL*Plus.** This is a tool that lets you execute any SQL statement, and in the case of SELECT statements, to view the results. SQL*Plus provides some limited scripting capabilities and is frequently used to run scripts that automate database administration tasks. Beginning with Oracle8i, SQL*Plus can also be used to start up, shut down, and recover a database.

✦ **Export and Import.** These utilities enable you to export data from or import data to any Oracle8i database. For example, you can use the export utility on a PC to copy data and table definitions into a file. Then, you can move the file to a UNIX computer, an IBM Mainframe, or any other platform that has an Oracle8i database, and use the import utility to place the information in that database.

✓ ✦ **SQL*Loader.** This is a utility that allows you to load data into a table from a flat file. It is most commonly used to load data from text files, such as a comma-delimited file, but it can process some types of binary files as well. While it can be difficult to learn and use, SQL*Loader is a robust utility and can quickly load large amounts of data.

✦ **Precompilers.** A number of these tools are available. Oracle8i contains one precompiler for each supported programming language, including Java, COBOL, Ada, C, C++, Pascal, and FORTRAN. The mix varies depending on the platform.

✦ **Server Manager.** Often abbreviated to SVRMGR, this utility lets you execute commands to start or stop your database. You can also run SQL commands within Server Manager. While still widely used, Oracle is beginning to phase this tool out in favor of SQL*Plus. The version of SQL*Plus shipped with Oracle8i implements all the commands that were formerly unique to Server Manager.

The previous list shows the primary tools that come with Oracle8i, regardless of the platform on which you are installing. You'll get these tools on UNIX, and you'll get them on Windows NT. However, the Windows NT version of Oracle8i has several GUI-based tools that you don't usually get on a UNIX platform:

✦ **Web Publishing Assistant.** This allows you to take the results of an Oracle SELECT statement and place them into an HTML file. Any Web browser can access the HTML file. You can do this on an ad hoc basis, or you can schedule this to occur on a regular and recurring basis.

✦ **Database Configuration Assistant.** This is a GUI-based wizard that you can use to create a new Oracle database. The SQL commands necessary to create a database can be a bit intimidating, especially to people brought up in a Windows environment where everything is point and click, so Oracle developed this wizard to generate and execute the commands for you.

✦ **Oracle Administration Assistant for Windows NT.** This is a utility that lets you perform some common DBA tasks using a GUI interface instead of commands.

✦ **Oracle for Windows NT Performance Monitor.** You will see an icon for this utility in the Database Administration program group, but it's really Microsoft's performance monitor running with some extensions (provided by Oracle) that allow it to monitor database activity.

✦ **Net8 Assistant.** Net8 is normally configured by editing several text files. Net8 Assistant provides a nice-looking GUI interface for doing the same task. The nice part about Net8 Assistant is that you don't need to remember all the keywords and syntax to use in the configuration files. If you're like most DBAs, you probably can't remember half of them anyway. Instead, you only need to fill out some forms on the screen.

✦ **Net8 Configuration Assistant**. This is a GUI-based wizard that walks you through the steps of initially configuring Net8 Listener.

✦ **Net8 Easy Config.** This is a wizard that helps you add entries to your tnsnames file.

The next two sections discuss Oracle's client software. First, we'll look at the basic elements that you might install on a user's or developer's PC. Then we'll discuss Oracle's Enterprise Manager software.

Taking inventory of Oracle8i's client software

The Oracle8i client software is installed on those users' PCs who need to interact with an Oracle database. It consists of Net8 client software used to connect the client to the server and a collection of utilities, many of which match those that get installed on the server. The client package includes the following:

✦ **Net8 Client.** This is part of both client and server components in an Oracle environment. The Net8 software on the client talks to the Net8 software on the server. Net8 enables Oracle applications to use a common networking interface regardless of the underlying network protocol.

✦ **Net8 Easy Config.** If you are installing Oracle8i client software on a Windows machine, you will get the Net8 Easy Config utility.

✦ **SQL*Plus.** This is installed on client PCs as well as on servers. If you're using a Windows machine, you'll notice that Oracle has wrapped a GUI interface around this command-line utility.

✦ **SQL*Loader.** SQL*Loader is often installed on client PCs, but it doesn't have to be. It can be omitted if the user doesn't require it.

✦ **Export and Import.** Like SQL*Plus and SQL*Loader, these utilities are often installed on the client as well as the server.

Figure 2-4 shows the configuration of client-side tools, including the main components of Enterprise Manager.

Figure 2-4 shows only the major components of the Oracle8i client package. The complete list is rather long, and it consists of a number of drivers and similar items that, unlike utilities, aren't invoked directly by an end user. The installation guide for your platform will have a complete, detailed list of client components.

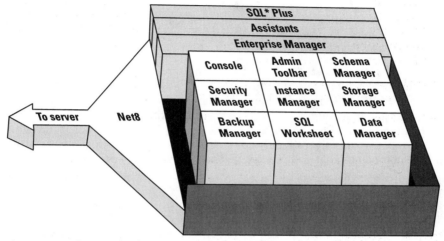

Figure 2-4: The Oracle client environment

Taking inventory of Oracle Enterprise Manager

Oracle Enterprise Manager is Oracle's GUI-based solution for managing Oracle databases. You likely already have the Oracle Enterprise Manager client software installed on your PC. The Enterprise Manager client consists of the following applications:

✦ **Enterprise Manager Console.** This is an application that enables you to monitor activity on multiple databases concurrently. The console allows you to submit database jobs to run on remote nodes, and it provides you with a unified interface that ties all the other Enterprise Manager applications together.

✦ **Schema Manager.** This tool enables you to create, alter, and drop objects such as tables, views, stored procedures, and so forth. You can navigate through lists of database objects using a tree-like interface similar to Windows NT Explorer.

✦ **Security Manager.** This tool makes creating users, setting and changing passwords, and assigning roles easy. You can also expire passwords, restrict reuse of old passwords, and more.

✦ **Instance Manager.** This tool enables you to see an overview of the activity on an Oracle database instance. You can view a list of users who are logged on, resolve in-doubt transactions, and change initialization parameters. You can also use Instance Manager to start and stop a database instance.

✦ **Storage Manager.** This tool allows you to manage database storage using a GUI interface. You use Storage Manager to add tablespaces and to add datafiles to existing tablespaces, increasing the amount of storage available for your data. You can also use Storage Manager to temporarily take a tablespace or datafile offline.

✦ **SQLPlus Worksheet.** This is a GUI tool that you can use as an alternative to running SQL*Plus. The SQLPlus Worksheet interface consists of two panes: an upper pane and a lower pane. The upper pane enables you to type and edit SQL commands. The lower pane displays the results from executing those commands. SQLPlus Worksheet makes editing SQL much easier than SQL*Plus does. It also has a very handy command-recall feature that allows you to review the commands that you've executed and select one to execute again.

Starting and Stopping an Oracle8i Instance

Before you can use an Oracle database, you have to start an Oracle instance and tell that instance to open the database. You can start an instance in several different ways, as described in this section. The startup process has several distinct phases, and it's important for you to understand these phases.

If you start a database instance, you'd probably assume that sooner or later, you would have to stop it. As with starting an instance, there are several ways to stop one. It's important that you understand your options here.

You might want your Oracle database instances to start automatically whenever you start (or reboot) your server. On UNIX machines, you accomplish this by having the dbstart script executed as part of the computer's startup process.

On a Windows NT machine, each Oracle instance is implemented as a Windows NT service. If you want an instance to start automatically, you can set the startup flag to automatic for the corresponding service, as described later in this chapter. If you'd rather start your database instances manually, you can use Instance Manager or SQL*Plus. You can also use the Services control panel to start the service. Instance Manager provides you with a GUI interface, while SQL*Plus allows you to issue commands.

Starting up in phases

If you listen to other DBAs talk, sooner or later, you will hear someone talk about "starting a database." What does it mean to "start" a database? First of all, you need to know that you really don't *start* a database. You *start* an instance, mount a database, and then you *open* a database. It's quite a mouthful, though, to say that you need to "start an instance, mount and then open a database," so most people tend to be a bit imprecise with their use of the terms.

To understand how Oracle startup works, you need to understand that a running Oracle database instance involves the following items:

✦ A collection of database files, including datafiles and control files

✦ Several processes, or programs, that operate on those files

✦ A shared memory area used by all of the processes to exchange data and coordinate activity

When you start an instance, you are really just starting the processes and allocating the shared memory area. Then, when you open a database, the instance opens all the files that make up the database. Figure 2-5 illustrates the phases in the startup process.

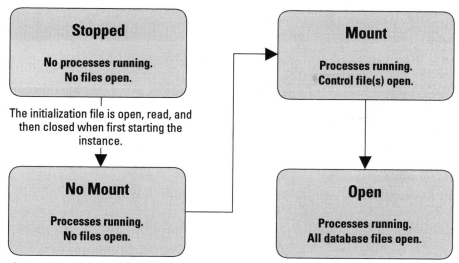

Figure 2-5: Oracle startup phases

A useful analogy is to compare Oracle to Microsoft Word. When you start up Word without opening a file, a blank screen greets you. The Word program is running, and certainly memory has been allocated to it, but that's about it. This state is comparable to the *nomount* state shown in Figure 2-5. After you've started Word, you can use the Open command on the File menu to open a file. Once you've opened a file, you are ready to get to work editing that file. This state is analogous to the *open* state shown in Figure 2-5.

Unlike Microsoft Word, however, Oracle has a state that falls between *nomount* and *open* called the *mount* state. A database is mounted when the instance has opened the control files but not any of the other database files. Figure 2-5 shows this in the frame labeled *mount*. The mount state is useful when you need to recover a database or when you need to move one or more of the datafiles. You can't move a datafile when it is open, but you must be able to record the new location of the datafile in the control file. The mount state works perfectly for that because the datafiles are closed, and the control file is open.

Shutting down an instance

When you shut down an Oracle instance, your options revolve around the questions of how quickly you want it down and how much or how little you want to inconvenience your users. You can choose from four modes when shutting down an instance:

Normal	Wait for all users to disconnect
Immediate	Wait for users to finish their current statement
Transactional	Wait for users to finish their current transaction
Abort	Don't wait for anything

The following subsections discuss each mode in detail.

Performing a Normal Shutdown

A normal shutdown generally represents the least inconvenience to your users. When you begin a normal shutdown, Oracle immediately bars any new user connections to the database. Any users currently logged on are allowed to continue whatever it is that they are doing. Eventually (hopefully), all users will log off of the database. Only when all the users have voluntarily disconnected will Oracle close the database and shut down the instance.

A normal shutdown is usually considered to be the safest choice. It can also be a frustrating choice because you effectively lose control over when the shutdown occurs. If your users tend to log on at 8:00 AM and stay logged on until 5:00 PM, you may not be able to complete a normal shutdown during business hours. Couple that with batch processing that kicks off in the evening, and you may find yourself waiting all night.

Performing an Immediate Shutdown

Doing an immediate shutdown is a good choice when you must have the database down quickly, even at the expense of inconveniencing any users who happen to be logged on at the time. When you begin an immediate shutdown, Oracle bars any new user connections to the database. So far, this is the same as a normal shutdown, but that's where the similarity ends. Any users not executing a SQL statement will have their connections terminated immediately. Users who are executing SQL statements will have their connections terminated as soon as their statements complete.

You can use immediate shutdowns before making cold database backups at night. A *cold backup* is one that occurs while the database is closed. If you're writing a script to make a cold backup of your database at 3:00 am, you don't want that script to be held up all night because one user left his or her application logged on to your database. An immediate shutdown avoids that possibility.

One other useful time for an immediate shutdown is when you need to *bounce* your instance during business hours. Hopefully, this doesn't happen to you much, because if it did, you might be out of a job. Bouncing an instance refers to the practice of quickly stopping, and then restarting, the instance. This is sometimes done when a critical initialization parameter needs to be changed. If you need to bounce an instance during the day, an immediate shutdown is often the quickest way to do it, and sometimes it's best to just get the painful process over with quickly.

Performing a Transactional Shutdown

Transactional shutdowns are a new Oracle8i feature. A transactional shutdown is just like an immediate shutdown, except that users are allowed to finish their current *transactions* rather than their current *statements*. Depending on the type and length of your transactions, this may take a bit longer, but at least you won't terminate anyone's connection in the middle of a logical unit of work.

Aborting

An abort is a good type of shutdown to avoid. When you shut down a database in the abort mode, everything just stops. All the users are disconnected immediately. All the processes are stopped. All the memory is released. Unfortunately, the database files are not left in a consistent state. It's as if you kicked the computer's plug out of the wall. Most likely, some data will exist in memory that should have been written to the datafiles, which didn't occur because of the abort. You won't lose any committed transactions because next time you start the instance, Oracle will recover those transactions from the redo log files. However, that recovery process can take some time.

Caution   Backups made after a shutdown abort are not reliable. You may not be able to restore them. If you are shutting down your database to make a backup, you should not use the abort mode. If you are forced to do a shutdown abort, you should restart your database and do a normal, immediate, or transactional shutdown before making a backup.

Consider using the abort mode most often after an instance has already crashed, and when that crash has left processes and memory in an unstable state. The characteristics of this state are that when you try to start your instance, you get an error message saying that it is already started, and when you try to stop the same instance, you get an error message saying that it is not running. Obviously, both can't be true at the same time. This state of affairs happens when an instance crashes and a few of the background processes are still running. The solution is to issue a shutdown abort command.

Using SQL*Plus to start and stop an instance

If you want to start or stop an instance by issuing commands, SQL*Plus is the tool to use. Even if you don't like to use commands, you should learn how in case GUI tools such as Enterprise Manager aren't available.

Note   Prior to the Oracle8i release (8.1.5), you could not use SQL*Plus to start or stop a database. If you are running an older release of Oracle, you will need to use Server Manager instead.

You can use SQL*Plus to start and stop an instance on the machine that you are directly connected to, or you can use it to start and stop an instance on a remote server that is connected to your network. It's easiest to use SQL*Plus to operate on a database instance when you are logged on to the server. You need to be aware of a couple of points to effectively use SQL*Plus to start or stop remote instances. We'll cover them later in this chapter.

Connecting So That You Can Start or Stop an Instance

If you are going to use SQL*Plus to start or stop a database instance, you first need to start SQL*Plus properly. SQL*Plus normally prompts you for a username and password when you first start it, and then it logs you on to the database as a normal user. You need to inhibit this behavior, because starting (or stopping) an instance requires that you connect not as a normal user, but as a DBA. Use the following command to start SQL*Plus:

```
sqlplus /nolog
```

The /nolog option tells SQL*Plus to start without automatically logging you on to the database. If you are running on Windows NT, you will find it easiest to issue this command from a Command Prompt window. Next, you need to connect to the instance that you want to start. Either of the following two commands will work:

```
CONNECT INTERNAL
CONNECT / AS SYSDBA
```

Of these two commands, Oracle prefers that you use the latter. Oracle intends to eliminate the INTERNAL user someday and discourages its use. It's included in this book because regardless of what Oracle might like, lots of DBAs still connect as the INTERNAL user. You need to be aware that it's an option, because you'll see people and scripts using it.

Note   For either of the previous two commands to work, you must be logged on to the server as a member of the dba group if you are using UNIX, or as an administrator if you are using Windows NT.

The AS SYSDBA syntax in the second CONNECT command is important. It's the reason that you must use the /nolog command-line option when you start SQL*Plus. SYSDBA is a special database role that gives you the necessary privileges to perform administrative functions such as starting a database.

Starting an Instance

Once you've connected to your instance in the SYSDBA role, you can issue one of the following STARTUP commands:

STARTUP   Use STARTUP when you want to both start the instance and open the database for general use. Most of the time, this is what you will want to do.

STARTUP NOMOUNT   Use STARTUP NOMOUNT when you just want to start the instance and nothing more. You have to use STARTUP NOMOUNT when you are going to create a new database, and that's pretty much the only time you'll need to use it.

STARTUP MOUNT   Use STARTUP MOUNT when you want to recover the database or when you want to issue ALTER DATABASE RENAME DATAFILE commands. The STARTUP MOUNT command causes the instance to open the control files, but the other database files are left closed.

Most of the time, you'll find yourself using the STARTUP command with no parameters to start an instance and open it for general use. The following example shows the entire sequence of starting SQL*Plus, connecting, and starting an instance. Listing 2-1 shows screen output from a Windows NT machine, but the commands are exactly the same on UNIX.

Listing 2-1: **Starting SQL*Plus, connecting, and starting an instance**

```
C:\>sqlplus /nolog

SQL*Plus: Release 8.1.5.0.0 - Production on Fri Jun 25 19:19:58 1999

(c) Copyright 1999 Oracle Corporation.  All rights reserved.

SQL> connect / as sysdba
Connected to an idle instance.
SQL> startup
ORACLE instance started.

Total System Global Area    38322124 bytes
Fixed Size                     65484 bytes
Variable Size               21405696 bytes
Database Buffers            16777216 bytes
Redo Buffers                   73728 bytes
Database mounted.
Database opened.
SQL>
```

If you've performed a default Oracle install on your server and you are starting the default instance, you should be able to start it by following the previous example.

Stopping an Instance

To stop an instance using SQL*Plus, issue one of the following commands:

SHUTDOWN	Performs a normal shutdown, waiting for all users to voluntarily connect.
SHUTDOWN IMMEDIATE	Does an immediate shutdown, forcibly disconnecting each user after his or her current SQL statement completes.
SHUTDOWN TRANSACTIONAL	Performs a transactional shutdown, forcibly disconnecting each user after his or her current transaction completes.
SHUTDOWN ABORT	Aborts the instance. Everything stops. Crash recovery is necessary, and the database files are not consistent with one another.

The following example shows how you would use SQL*Plus to shut down a database in the immediate mode:

```
C:\>sqlplus /nolog

SQL*Plus: Release 8.1.5.0.0 - Production on Sun Jun 27 22:19:35 1999

(c) Copyright 1999 Oracle Corporation.  All rights reserved.

SQL> connect / as sysdba
Connected.
SQL> shutdown immediate
Database closed.
Database dismounted.
ORACLE instance shut down.
SQL>
```

The only difference that you'll notice with the other modes is that normal might take longer because you have to wait until all users disconnect, and with an abort, the database is not closed and dismounted first.

Dealing with Multiple Instances on One Server

It's common to have more than one Oracle database running on the same server. In a UNIX environment, this is the norm. When you're managing several databases on one server and you want to start or stop one of them, you need a way to designate which one it is that you want to stop.

On a Windows NT machine, you can set the ORACLE_SID environment variable to indicate which database you want to start or stop. To set ORACLE_SID, you have to use the SET command. Here's an example showing the ORACLE_SID environment variable being set to PROD:

```
C:\>SET ORACLE_SID=PROD

C:\>
```

You have to issue the SET command from a Command Prompt window. Once you've done that, any Oracle utilities that you run from that window will operate on the database instance that you've specified. The ORACLE_SID setting stays in effect until you issue another SET command that changes it or until you close the window.

Note   The ORACLE_SID setting applies only to commands issued from the same Command Prompt window. Under Windows NT, it is entirely feasible to have multiple Command Prompt windows open, each with a different ORACLE_SID value.

You can view the current ORACLE_SID setting at any time by issuing the SET command with just the variable name as an argument, as shown in this example:

```
C:\>SET ORACLE_SID
ORACLE_SID=PROD
```

On UNIX systems, you also have to set the value of ORACLE_SID. However, UNIX systems usually provide an Oracle script named oraenv that you should run to do this. Here's an example showing oraenv being used to change the Oracle SID being changed on a UNIX box:

```
$ . oraenv
ORACLE_SID = [TEST] ? PROD
```

Note   Notice the space between the dot and the oraenv command. If you're using the UNIX Korn shell, that space is significant. Omit it, and your new setting won't stick.

If you look carefully at your environment variable settings, you will see that oraenv changes more than just the ORACLE_SID. It also changes ORACLE_HOME and your path setting as well.

Once you've used either the SET command or the oraenv command to change your ORACLE_SID setting, you can run SQL*Plus as shown previously, and issue the STARTUP command to start that database.

Specifying a Nondefault Parameter File

When you use SQL*Plus to start a database, SQL*Plus looks for a text file known as the *database parameter file,* reads a number of parameter settings from that file, and uses those to control various aspects of the database instance being started. Sometimes this file is referred to as the init.ora file, or even just the init file. Chapter 3, "Oracle8i Architecture," has more information about the parameter file, what it contains, and how it relates to the other database files.

SQL*Plus expects parameter files to be in a specific location and to be named according to a specific naming convention. The default location and name are different for UNIX and Windows NT. One of the following will apply:

>   **Unix**: $ORACLE_HOME/dbs/initSID.ora
>
>   **Windows NT**:   c:\oracle\ora81\database\initSID.ora

Note   The c:\oracle\ora81 portion of the path under Windows NT may be different if you installed Oracle on a drive other than c:, or if you overrode the default directory names during the installation.

As long as you place your parameter files where SQL*Plus expects them, SQL*Plus will find them, and your STARTUP commands will remain very simple. If, for some reason, you decide to place your initialization files somewhere else or to name them differently, then you must tell SQL*Plus where to look. Use the PFILE parameter of the STARTUP command to do this. The following example shows you how:

```
STARTUP PFILE=$ORACLE_BASE/admin/PROD/pfile/initPRODnight.ora
```

In this example, the PFILE parameter points SQL*Plus to a special parameter file used only for nightly processing.

The PFILE parameter is handy if you have more than one parameter file that you use to start a database. The PFILE parameter is also handy if you are starting a database remotely.

Starting and Stopping an Instance on a Remote Server

You can use SQL*Plus to start or stop a database on another computer. You won't do this often, but it is possible. Generally, if the other computer is running UNIX, you'll find it easier to Telnet in and run SQL*Plus on the server. If the other machine is Windows NT, however, Telnet won't be available, so you either have to know how to start or stop the database remotely, or you have to go to the machine.

To start or stop an instance remotely, the following prerequisites apply:

1. You need to have Net8 configured so that you can connect to the remote machine. Chapter 5, "Configuring Net8," can help you with this.

2. You need to have created a password file for the instance that you want to start, and you need to have been granted either the SYSDBA or SYSOPER role. Chapter 4, "Managing the Database Password File," can help you with this.

3. You need access to the database's parameter file. This applies only to starting. The parameter file isn't used when stopping an instance. You either need a copy of the parameter file on your local PC, or it needs to be accessible over the network.

With these prerequisites out of the way, the process for starting a remote instance is much the same as for starting an instance on your local machine. The only differences will be that you have to specify the Net8 service name in your connect statement, and you will likely need to use the startup command's PFILE parameter to specify the location of the database parameter file. Listing 2-2 shows the bible_db database being started from a remote PC:

Listing 2-2: **Starting the bible_db database from a remote PC**

```
C:\>sqlplus /nolog

SQL*Plus: Release 8.1.5.0.0 - Production on Sun Jun 27 17:09:24 1999

(c) Copyright 1999 Oracle Corporation.  All rights reserved.
SQL> connect system/manager@bible_db as sysdba
Connected to an idle instance.
SQL> startup pfile=o:\admin\jonathan\pfile\init.ora
ORACLE instance started.

Total System Global Area    38322124 bytes
Fixed Size                     65484 bytes
Variable Size               21405696 bytes
Database Buffers            16777216 bytes
Redo Buffers                   73728 bytes
Database mounted.
Database opened.
SQL>
```

Stopping an instance remotely is even more similar to stopping an instance on your local machine. The SHUTDOWN command is the same. This next example shows how you would shut down the instance that was started in the previous example:

```
C:\>sqlplus /nolog

SQL*Plus: Release 8.1.5.0.0 - Production on Sun Jun 27 22:36:05 1999
```

```
(c) Copyright 1999 Oracle Corporation.  All rights reserved.

SQL> connect system/manager@bible_db as sysdba
Connected.
SQL> shutdown
Database closed.
Database dismounted.
ORACLE instance shut down.
SQL>
```

If you intend to start and stop your database remotely like this, you need to decide how you want to handle the parameter file. Do you want to have just one parameter file, placed on a shared drive so that a remote machine can access it, or do you want to make local copies of the parameter file on each PC that you might use to start the database? If you are going to maintain multiple copies of the parameter file, how will you keep them in sync with each other? You also have to think about include files. Parameter files may contain ifile commands that link to other parameter files. Those references are resolved by SQL*Plus.

If you place your parameter file on the network and access it from a remote PC, you have to be sure that the ifile file references can be resolved from that PC, as well as from the server. For example, your parameter file might include a file named e:\admin\jonathan\pfile\configjonathan.ora. If your PC maps the server's E drive to your O drive, then the ifile directive will fail. One way to deal with this would be to map the server's E drive to your local E drive. That way the drive letters remain the same, regardless of whether you are starting the database from the server or your PC.

Using Server Manager to start and stop an instance

If you've been using Oracle for any length of time, you know that historically, Server Manager, not SQL*Plus, was the tool used to start and stop an Oracle instance. If you are using any release of Oracle prior to 8.1.5 (the 8i release), you won't be able to use SQL*Plus to start and stop a database instance. You'll have to use Server Manager instead.

Note   If you go back far enough, you'll find that SQL*DBA was the tool to use, but hopefully you aren't using any release of Oracle old enough for that to be the case.

The commands you use with Server Manager are the exact same as those that you use with SQL*Plus. Everything that you've read previously in this book about SQL*Plus, with one exception, is applicable to Server Manager as well. The one exception is the /nolog command-line option. You don't need it with Server Manager because Server Manager doesn't automatically attempt to log you on to a database.

Listing 2-3 shows Server Manager being used to start the bible_db database:

Listing 2-3: Using Server Manager to start the bible_db database

```
C:\>svrmgrl

Oracle Server Manager Release 3.1.5.0.0 - Production

(c) Copyright 1997, Oracle Corporation.  All Rights Reserved.
```

```
ORA-12560: TNS:protocol adapter error
SVRMGR> connect system/manager@bible_db.gennick as sysdba
Connected.
SVRMGR> startup pfile=o:\admin\jonathan\pfile\init.ora
ORACLE instance started.
Total System Global Area            38322124 bytes
Fixed Size                             65484 bytes
Variable Size                       21405696 bytes
Database Buffers                    16777216 bytes
Redo Buffers                           73728 bytes
Database mounted.
Database opened.
SVRMGR>
```

Note The ORA-12560 error that you see in this example occurs because NT was used, and because the ORACLE_SID environment variable was not set. It's safe to ignore the error in this case because the `connect` command includes a Net8 service name.

In this example, the `svrmgrl` command was used to start Server Manager. That command works with any UNIX release of Oracle, as well as with the 8.1.5 release on Windows NT. Previous releases of Oracle for Windows NT had the release number attached to the executable name, so the command would be `svrmgr30` for the 8.0.*x* release, `svrmgr23` for the 7.3.*x* release, and so forth.

Oracle is still shipping Server Manager with Oracle8i and will continue to do so in the future (probably for all the 8.1.*x* releases). However, Server Manager is now considered a deprecated feature, and Oracle intends to remove it someday, leaving SQL*Plus as the only command-line interface into Oracle. Therefore, avoid using Server Manager and instead get used to using SQL*Plus.

Using Instance Manager to start and stop an instance

You can also use Oracle's Instance Manager, part of Enterprise Manager's DBA Management Pack, to start or stop an Oracle instance. You can run Instance Manager as a stand-alone application, or you can run it in conjunction with an

Oracle Management server. If you run it as a stand-alone application, and if you run it from a machine other than the database server, all the prerequisites for starting a remote database need to be in place. Your database needs to have a password file, Net8 needs to be configured, and you need access to a database user who has been granted the SYSDBA or SYSOPER role.

Starting an Instance

First start the Instance Manager application. Click Start, point to Programs, point to Oracle-OraOEM, point to DBA Management Pack, and select Instance Manager. You will see a login screen similar to the one shown in Figure 2-6.

Figure 2-6: The Oracle Enterprise Manager Log in dialog box

Be sure to click the option labeled Connect Directly to a Database, and then enter your username and password in the appropriate text boxes. To start a database instance, you need to connect as either SYSOPER or SYSDBA, so select one of those options in the Connect as drop-down list box. Figure 2-6 shows everything filled out correctly for the system user to log on to a database. When you have everything correct, click OK.

Note If you are running on Windows NT, you must have a password file for your database in order to log on as SYSDBA or SYSOPER. Alternatively, you must be logged on as a Windows NT administrator.

After connecting to your instance, you'll see a screen similar to the one shown in Figure 2-7 but without the traffic light on the right-hand side. The traffic light shows the current status of your instance. To see it, click the database icon in the left-hand pane. That's the icon shown highlighted in Figure 2-7.

The traffic light not only shows you the status of your instance, but it lets you start and stop it as well. If your instance is stopped, the red light will be lit and the Shutdown option will be selected.

Note Just like when you use SQL*Plus to start a remote instance, you need to be able to pass a parameter file name to Instance Manager. You can keep a copy of the parameter file on your local PC for this purpose, or you can access one on the network.

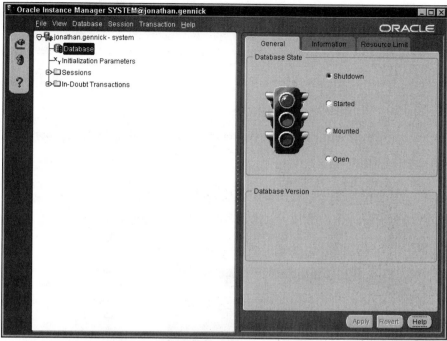

Figure 2-7: Instance Manager's traffic light

To start your instance, select the Open option and click the Apply button at the bottom of the window. Instance Manager will open a dialog box prompting you for the name of the parameter file for the instance that you are starting. Type the name and location of your parameter file, click OK, and Instance Manager will start the instance.

Tip You don't have a copy of your parameter file handy? You can use Instance Manager to create one, but you need to do it while the database is open. Click the icon labeled Initialization Parameters, and then click the Save button.

Stopping an Instance

Using Instance Manager to stop an instance is pretty much the reverse of using it to start one. It's actually a bit easier because you don't have to worry about the parameter file. To start it, click the database icon in the left pane to get the traffic light in the right pane. Next, select the Shutdown option and click Apply. Instance Manager will present you with the shutdown options shown in Figure 2-8.

These are the same options — normal, immediate, abort, and transactional — that you have when you use SQL*Plus to shut down an instance. Select the option for the shutdown mode that you want and click OK. Instance Manager will close the database and shut down the instance.

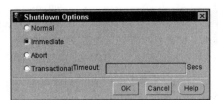

Figure 2-8: Instance Manager's Shutdown Options dialog box

Using the services control panel to start and stop an instance

Under Windows NT, the processes that make up an Oracle instance are implemented as a standard Windows NT service. You can see this service, as well as other Oracle-related services, listed in the Services control panel. Figure 2-9 shows the Oracle services on an NT server.

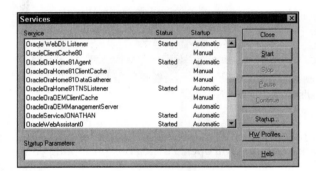

Figure 2-9: The Oracle services shown in the Services control panel applet

Like any other Windows NT service, you can start and stop the Oracle services via the Services control panel. In addition, you can also use the Oracle-supplied program named oradim to start and stop the services. Starting or stopping the service for a database instance implies starting or stopping the instance itself.

Note   Although stopping a service implies stopping an instance, the converse is not true. Stopping an instance does not stop the associated service.

Starting or stopping an Oracle service using the Services control panel is an almost trivial exercise. Figure 2-10 shows you what you will see from the control panel if the service for the instance named jonathan is not running.

To start the service, all you need to do is click the service once to highlight it, and then click the Start button. You'll see a spinning dial while Windows NT attempts to start the service, and then the status will change to read "started." To stop the service, simply click the Stop button.

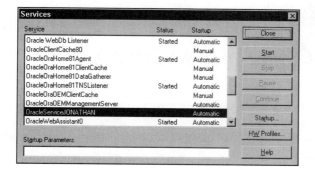

Figure 2-10: The Oracle service for jonathan is not running.

Setting the Startup Mode for an Instance

One other task you can perform from the Services control panel is to set the startup type for an Oracle database instance's service. This controls whether the database starts automatically whenever the server starts. Select the service you are interested in and click the Startup button. This opens the Service dialog box shown in Figure 2-11.

Figure 2-11: Setting the startup type for a service

As you can see in Figure 2-11, you have three choices for Startup Type: Automatic, Manual, and Disabled. Automatic means that Windows NT will automatically start the service. The manual setting means that you will have to manually start the service. When a service is disabled, Windows NT won't allow you to start it at all.

Using oradim to Start and Stop a Service

With Windows NT distribution, Oracle includes a utility named `oradim` that you can use to start and stop the service for a database instance. The `oradim` utility is useful if you are writing a batch file and you need to include a command to stop or start a database. The syntax for the `oradim` commands used to start and stop a database instance's service appears as follows:

```
ORADIM -STARTUP -SID sidname [-USRPWD password]
       [-STARTTYPE srvc|inst|srvc,inst] [-PFIFLE filename]
ORADIM -SHUTDOWN -SID sidname [-USRPWD password]
       [-SHUTTYPE srvc|inst|srvc,inst] [-SHUTMODE a|i|n]
```

The following list describes the elements in this syntax:

✦ `oradim`: The command for starting and stopping a database.

✦ `STARTUP`: Indicates that you want to start a service or an instance.

✦ `SID sidname`: Specifies the instance whose service you want to start.

✦ `USRPWD password`: Specifies the password for the internal user. You won't need this parameter if you are logged on to NT as an administrator.

✦ `STARTTYPE srvc|inst|srvc,inst`: Indicates what to start. Your choices are as follows:

 • `srvc` — Starts just the service.

 • `inst` — Starts the instance. The service must already be running for this to work.

 • `srvc,inst` — Starts both the service and the instance.

✦ `SHUTTYPE srvc|inst|srvc,inst`: Indicates what to stop. Your choices are the same as for `STARTTYPE`.

✦ `PFILE filename`: Points to the parameter file for the instance. You don't need this if the parameter file is in the default location where Oracle expects it to be.

✦ `SHUTMODE a|i|n`: Indicates the shutdown mode to use when stopping the instance. Your choices are as follows:

 • `a` — An abort

 • `i` — An immediate shutdown

 • `n` — A normal shutdown

✦ The `oradim` utility doesn't support the transaction shutdown option.

To use `oradim` to start the NT service named OracleServiceJONATHAN shown in Figure 2-11, you would issue a command like this:

```
oradim -startup -sid jonathan
```

To stop the same instance, you would issue this command:

```
oradim -shutdown -sid jonathan
```

According to the documentation, it is possible to use `STARTTYPE srvc` to start only the service, or `STARTTYPE inst` to start only the instance. However, reality doesn't seem to match the documentation. In release 8.1.5, at least, you can't use this command to start and stop an instance independent of the service.

Starting and Stopping WebDB Listener

You have two options for starting and stopping WebDB Listener. One is to use the Services control panel to start and stop the service named Oracle WebDb Listener. The other way is to use the Windows NT `net start` and `net stop` commands.

Using the services control panel to start and stop WebDB Listener

The easiest way to control WebDB Listener is to use the Services control panel. Figure 2-12 shows the control panel with the WebDB Listener service at the top of the Services control panel.

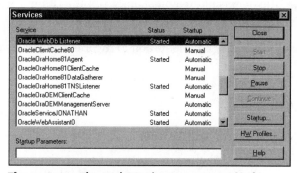

Figure 2-12: The WebDB Listener process in the Services control panel

The process for starting and stopping the WebDB Listener service is the same as for any other service. First highlight the service, and then click the Start button to start it or click the Stop button to stop it. You can also click the Startup button to open up a window that lets you set the startup type to either automatic or manual. When the startup type is automatic, Windows NT will start the service whenever the system starts; otherwise, you will have to start the service manually.

Using the wdblsnr utility to start and stop WebDB Listener

To control WebDB Listener from the command line, or from a batch file, use the `net start` and `net stop` commands. The command to start the listener is the following:

```
net start "Oracle WebDb Listener"
```

The command to stop the listener is similar, and looks like this:

```
net stop "Oracle WebDb Listener"
```

Because the WebDB Listener name contains spaces, you must enclose it in quotes. The name needs to match what is shown in the Services control panel.

Note   While the name used with the `net start` and `net stop` commands must match a service name as shown in the Services control panel, Windows NT is not case sensitive. A value of "oracle webdb listener" or "ORACLE WEBDB LISTENER" will work just as well as "Oracle WebDb Listener."

Using Oracle8i's Online Documentation

Most of the utilities that come with Oracle8i have some sort of built-in online help. For the command-line utilities, the help is often a bit skimpy, but the GUI utilities, particularly Enterprise Manager, have fairly extensive online documentation.

You can access Oracle's online-help style documentation in the following two ways:

✦ Click the Help button you find in almost every Oracle8i window.

✦ Click one of the help icons in the Oracle8i program groups.

Most of the time, you access online help by clicking the Help button from an application screen. Sometimes, however, Oracle includes an icon on the Start menu that takes you directly to the online help for a particular topic. For example, there are icons in the Network Administration program group that take you to online help for Oracle's ODBC drivers.

If you're used to standard Windows-based online help, you're in for a pleasant surprise when you start using help from any of Oracle's new Java-based utilities. You view the online help in Java-based programs, such as the Enterprise Manager applications, by using two windows. One window is a Help Navigator window. The other is a Help Topic window. These windows are shown in Figure 2-13.

The Help Navigator window allows you to browse help topics using a tree-style menu, and it also contains a searchable index. When you click on a topic in the Help Navigator, you'll see the help text for that topic in the topic window.

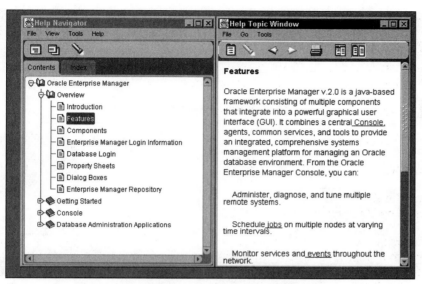

Figure 2-13: The Help Navigator and Help Topic windows

In addition to the online help, you can access Oracle's full manual set using a Web browser. Like the online help, you navigate the online manual set using a tree-style menu. Here's how you bring up the online manual set and navigate to the *Oracle8i SQL Reference* manual:

1. Place the Oracle8i distribution CD in your CD-ROM drive. You don't need to do this if you installed the online help to your local hard drive, but the default installation option leaves the help files on the CD.

2. From the Start menu, select Programs, OraHome81, and Documentation. Your Web browser will open, and after a few more seconds, the Oracle Information Manager window will open. Your screen will now look similar to Figure 2-14.

Note   Oracle also makes available a PDF version of the documentation that you can read using Adobe Acrobat. To use the PDF version, start by opening the file named index.pdf in the doc\server.815 directory on the Oracle8i distribution CD.

Note   If you don't have a Java-enabled browser, or if you have a very old browser, you won't see the Oracle Information Navigator window. In addition, you might frequently experience problems with the Oracle Information Navigator window starting improperly. You might need to try two or three times, terminating and restarting your browser each time, before it comes up properly.

At this point, you can browse the manual set either by using the tree-style navigator or by clicking the HTML links in the browser window.

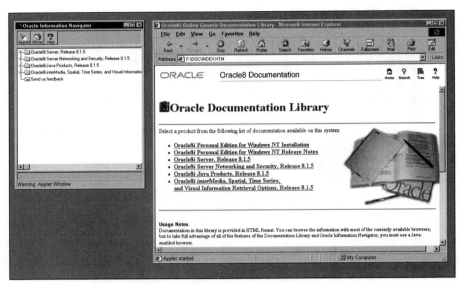

Figure 2-14: Oracle's online documentation

3. To find the *Oracle8i SQL Reference* manual, click the plus (+) sign next to the folder labeled Oracle8i Server, Release 8.1.5.

4. Open the Reference folder. You should see a list of manuals, each with an associated blue book icon.

5. Expand the SQL Reference Manual icon by either clicking the plus sign next to the manual name or by double-clicking the manual name. You will see a list of manual sections.

6. Double-click any of the manual sections, and you will see the text for that section appear in your browser window.

7. To shut down the documentation, close your browser as you normally would. The Oracle Information Navigator window will automatically close as well.

Tip

Install the HTML documentation on your local workstation. Even though it takes upwards of 140MB of space, you'll find it well worthwhile for the convenience of having the documentation always available, regardless of whether you have the CD handy.

Many people don't like to read the documentation from the CD. If you find yourself referring to a particular manual frequently, consider purchasing a printed copy from Oracle. Given the number of companies that don't like to spend money on manuals for their employees, having the documentation available electronically is a real blessing. Do everything you can to make it available to your developers and fellow database administrators.

Summary

In this chapter, you have learned:

✦ Oracle applications are implemented as client/server applications. The database server runs independent of the clients, accepts requests from clients, processes those requests, and sends results back to clients.

✦ An Oracle server software installation consists of the database software, Net8 software, and a collection of utilities.

✦ An Oracle client software installation consists of Net8 software, utilities, and possibly the Enterprise Manager applications.

✦ SQL*Plus, `oradim`, and Instance Manager are all tools that you can use to start and stop an Oracle database instance.

✦ You can stop and start WebDB Listener from the Services control panel. If you prefer to use commands, you may also stop and start it using the `net stop` and `net start` commands.

✦ The entire Oracle8i manual set is available in HTML format. Consider installing it on your workstation so that you can easily access it when needed. Make it available to developers and other database users.

✦　　✦　　✦

Oracle8i Architecture

◆ ◆ ◆ ◆

In This Chapter

Understanding the differences between an instance and a database

Examining database file architecture

Understanding memory architecture

Looking at process architecture

◆ ◆ ◆ ◆

Architecture refers to the way in which all the pieces of an Oracle8i database instance were designed to work together. It encompasses the way in which Oracle8i uses memory, the way in which Oracle8i uses disk files, and the way in which various Oracle8i processes interact with each other.

It's important for you to understand Oracle8i's architecture, particularly from a tuning standpoint, because you can't hope to properly tune an Oracle8i database if you don't know something about how Oracle operates. Understanding the architecture also gives you a lot of insight into some of the terminology that you'll encounter, and it also helps you to appreciate why things work the way that they do. For example, you'll understand why you have to mount a database before you can rename a database file. This chapter opens with a discussion of the fundamental differences between an instance and a database, and then it covers database files, memory, and process architectures.

Understanding the Differences Between Instance and Database

Instance? Database? You'll run into these two words often as a DBA. They are simple but important words because the entire Oracle8i architecture is derived from them. Chapter 2, "Oracle8i Overview," describes the difference between an instance and a database. Let's recap that discussion here.

A *database*, in the Oracle world, refers to a collection of files used to store and manage related data. The term database refers only to the files, nothing else. Of course, if you have a database full of information, you probably want to do something with that information. That's where the Oracle instance comes into play.

An *instance* is a set of processes that work together to operate on your database. For performance reasons, because these processes work so closely together, they share access to an area of memory known as the *system global area (SGA)*. The SGA is also considered to be part of the instance.

The processes that make up an Oracle instance allow you to change and retrieve your data. Some of the processes also work to protect the integrity of your data and ensure the recoverability of your data in the event of a system crash, loss of a disk, or other unforeseen event. Most Oracle processes are referred to as *background processes* because they are always running and they aren't associated with any particular user.

When an Oracle instance is running and a database is being used, the interaction between the various processes, database files, and shared memory will look something like the diagram in Figure 3-1.

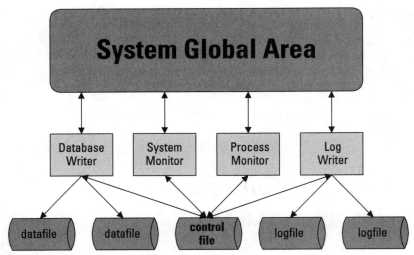

Figure 3-1: A typical Oracle instance

The configuration shown in Figure 3-1 is known as a *stand-alone instance* configuration. One instance is operating on one database. Sites that must service a lot of users and that require a high degree of availability may end up using Oracle Parallel Server. Oracle Parallel Server allows you to have many instances, all on different machines, operating on one Oracle database. Figure 3-2 shows a Parallel Server configuration.

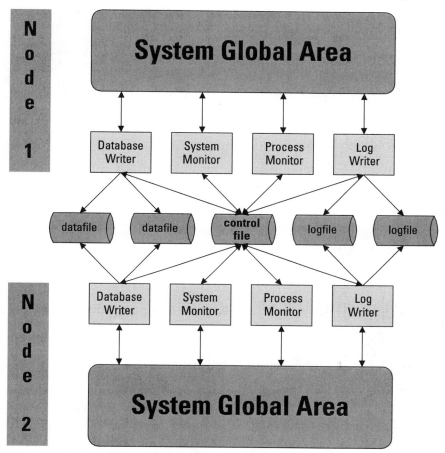

Figure 3-2: An Oracle Parallel Server configuration

Note Oracle Parallel Server is available only with the Enterprise Edition of Oracle.

Because Oracle Parallel Server allows many instances to open a database, you are somewhat insulated from problems that might occur if an instance crashes. In the event of a crash, the other instances will continue to run. Users will still be able to connect and get work done. In a stand-alone configuration, if an instance crashes, everyone is dead in the water until you can restart it.

You can also use Oracle Parallel Server to increase your database's throughput because the load can be spread over several computers instead of just one. This works best if you can partition your database tables and indexes in a way that minimizes the number of times that two instances will require access to the same data.

Examining Database File Architecture

Several different types of files combine to make up an Oracle8i database. This section describes each type. You'll learn the purpose of each type of file, see what type of information files contain, and learn how to locate the files that make up your database. Refer to Figure 3-3, which shows the files that you will see in an Oracle8i database.

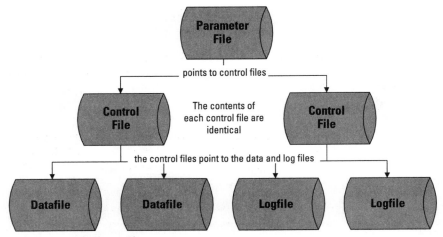

Figure 3-3: Database file types

Figure 3-3 shows the parameter file as a database file. Strictly speaking, that's not correct. However, understanding some points about the parameter file will help you better understand how Oracle keeps track of control files and archived log files. The next few sections discuss in detail each of the file types shown in Figure 3-3.

Using parameter files

The parameter file is read by either SQL*Plus, Server Manager, or Instance Manager when you use one of those programs to start an instance. It's not opened by the instance; consequently, it isn't considered to be a database file.

Even though the parameter file isn't a database file, it is important. Without the correct parameter file, you may not be able to open your database. Even if you did manage to open a database using the wrong parameter file, it might not work the way you expect because the parameter file settings greatly influence how an Oracle instance functions. You will want to treat your parameter files with the same care as you do your database files.

Parameter File Contents

Parameter files are text files. You can use any text editor to open them, If you are running UNIX, you can use the vi editor. On Windows NT, you can use Notepad. Parameter files serve much the same purpose as Windows .ini files. They contain a number of settings that influence how an Oracle database instance functions. Some of the more important aspects that you can control via settings in the parameter file are the following:

✦ The location of the database control files

✦ The amount of memory Oracle uses to buffer data that has been read from disk

✦ The amount of memory Oracle uses to buffer SQL statement execution plans, PL/SQL procedures, and data dictionary information so that they don't have to be continuously read from disk

✦ The default optimizer choice

Relative to database files, the parameter file performs two important functions. One is to point to the control files for a database. The other is to point to the archive log destination for a database. If you were to open the parameter file for an Oracle database, you would see lines like this:

```
control_files = ("E:\Oracle\oradata\jonathan\control01.ctl",
                 "F:\Oracle\oradata\jonathan\control02.ctl")
log_archive_dest_1 =
                 "location=G:\Oracle\oradata\jonathan\archive"
```

The control_files entry shown here tells Oracle where to find the control files for a database. Once an instance has found the control files, it can open those files and read the locations of all the other database files. The second entry, for log_archive_dest_1, tells Oracle where it should copy redo log files as they are filled.

Location of Parameter Files

You can place parameter files anywhere you like. However, it's usually easiest to follow some well-established conventions about where Oracle expects these files to be and how Oracle expects them to be named.

Parameter file locations on UNIX systems

On most UNIX systems, Oracle expects database parameter files to be in the following directory:

```
$ORACLE_HOME/dbs
```

The naming convention used for parameter files on UNIX systems is initXXXX.ora, where "XXXX" represents the instance name. So if you have a database instance named ORCL, which is the default name of Oracle's starter database, your parameter file would be named initORCL.ora.

Parameter file locations on Windows NT systems

On Windows NT systems, for whatever reason, Oracle expects parameter files to be in the database directory instead of the dbs directory. If you've performed a default install of Oracle on Windows NT, the full path to the database directory will look like this:

```
C:\Oracle\Ora8i\Database
```

The directory path for parameter files is different under Windows NT, but the naming convention is the same. For a database instance named ORCL, the Windows NT version of Oracle expects the parameter file to be named initORCL.ora.

Using control files

Oracle uses control files to store information about the state of your database. In a way, you could look at a control file as sort of a scratchpad. Whenever Oracle needs to save an important tidbit of information about the database, it writes it on the scratchpad. That's not to say that the information in a control file is unimportant. In fact, it's so important, and so critical, that Oracle recommends that you always mirror your control files — maintaining two or three copies so that if one is lost, you have the others to fall back on.

Control File Contents

Database control files contain the following major types of information:

✦ The database name

✦ Information about tablespaces

✦ The names and locations of all the datafiles

✦ The names and locations of all the redo log files

✦ The current log sequence number

✦ Checkpoint information

✦ Information about redo logs and the current state of archiving

The control file leads Oracle to the rest of the database files. When you start an instance, Oracle reads the control file names and locations from the parameter file. When you mount a database, Oracle opens the control file. When you finally open a database, Oracle reads the list of database files from the control file and opens each of them.

Will the Real Parameter File Please Stand Up?

Chances are, if you've installed a recent release of Oracle, your parameter files aren't where they appear to be. At least, the real parameter files won't be in either the dbs or the database directory. Instead, you will find them underneath the $ORACLE_BASE/admin/XXXX/pfile directory (UNIX) or C:\Oracle\Admin\XXXX\pfile (Windows NT), where XXXX represents the instance name.

Why is this? It has to do with a set of file-naming and placement guidelines that Oracle developed known as the optimal flexible architecture (OFA). The OFA guidelines state that the Oracle home directory should be used only for Oracle software distribution and not for any administrative or database files. This means that parameter files should not be in either the dbs or the database directories.

Rather than change the expected locations of the parameter files in its software, Oracle implemented the guidelines by taking advantage of an operating system feature known as a *file system link*. Links allow you to create directory entries that make it look like a file is in one place, when in fact it is really somewhere else.

On UNIX systems, the parameter files in the dbs directory are often nothing more than links to the real parameter files somewhere else. Windows NT doesn't support file system links, so Windows NT parameter files in the database directory often contain just one line — an include directive that points to the real parameter file somewhere else.

Finding Your Control Files

You can find the names and locations of the control files for a database in two ways. One is to look in the parameter file and find the `control_files` entry. That entry looks like this:

```
control_files = ("E:\Oracle\oradata\jonathan\control01.ctl",
                 "F:\Oracle\oradata\jonathan\control02.ctl")
```

The `control_file` entry will list all the control files that were opened when the database was started. Each control file contains identical information. If one is lost, Oracle can continue by using the other.

A second way to find the control files for a database is to log on as the SYSTEM user, or some other privileged user, and issue the following SELECT statement:

```
SELECT * FROM v$controlfile
```

You can issue this query from SQL*Plus, as shown in this screen output example:

```
SQL> SELECT * FROM v$controlfile;

STATUS  NAME
-------  ---------------------------------------------
        E:\ORACLE\ORADATA\JONATHAN\CONTROL01.CTL
        F:\ORACLE\ORADATA\JONATHAN\CONTROL02.CTL
```

Of course, for this second method to work, the instance must be running.

Using datafiles

Not surprisingly, Oracle stores your data in datafiles. Datafiles also typically represent the bulk of an Oracle database in terms of the disk space that they use. In terms of quantity also, you will probably have more datafiles than any other type of file.

Datafile Contents

Datafiles contain the following types of data:

+ Table data

+ Index data

+ Data dictionary definitions

+ Information necessary to undo transactions (rollback data)

+ Code for stored procedures, functions, and packages

+ Temporary data, often used for sorting

For performance reasons, it's usually best to separate data by type, each into its own file or set of files, and place those files on separate disks. This is especially true for data dictionary information, rollback data, and temporary data. You will almost universally store these types of data separately from the others.

Finding Your Datafiles

To generate a list of the datafiles that constitute your database, you can query a dynamic performance view named V$DATAFILE. The following query will give you the status, the size, and the name for each datafile in your database:

```
SELECT status, bytes, name
FROM v$datafile;
```

The following example shows the results you will get if you execute this query from SQL*Plus. The two COLUMN commands format the output of the bytes and name the columns to make the output more readable.

```
SQL> COLUMN name FORMAT A40
SQL> COLUMN bytes FORMAT 999,999,999
SQL> SELECT status, bytes, name
  2  FROM v$datafile;

STATUS        BYTES NAME
-------  ----------- ----------------------------------------
SYSTEM   167,772,160 E:\ORACLE\ORADATA\JONATHAN\SYSTEM01.DBF
ONLINE     3,145,728 E:\ORACLE\ORADATA\JONATHAN\USERS01.DBF
ONLINE    26,214,400 E:\ORACLE\ORADATA\JONATHAN\RBS01.DBF
ONLINE     2,097,152 E:\ORACLE\ORADATA\JONATHAN\TEMP01.DBF
ONLINE     5,242,880 E:\ORACLE\ORADATA\JONATHAN\OEMREP01.DBF
ONLINE     2,097,152 E:\ORACLE\ORADATA\JONATHAN\INDX01.DBF
ONLINE    31,457,280 E:\ORACLE\ORADATA\JONATHAN\USERS02.DBF

7 rows selected.
```

The status column tells you whether Oracle has the file open. A status of ONLINE or SYSTEM means that Oracle has the file open and that the data within that file is accessible. A status of OFFLINE means that the file is closed. Files may be offline because they were taken offline purposely by the DBA or because of a problem, such as a drive failure, that makes the file inaccessible to Oracle. You cannot access the data in an offline datafile.

The SYSTEM status indicates that a file is part of the system tablespace. The system tablespace is the one that contains the data dictionary. You'll learn more about tablespaces in Chapter 6, "Database Space Management." Oracle needs the data dictionary to access the data in the other datafiles, so the system tablespace always has to be open whenever the database is open.

Using log files

Log files, sometimes called redo log files, are an important component of any database. They exist to ensure the recoverability of a database in the event of a system crash, a drive failure, or any other unforeseen interruption to normal operations.

There are two types of redo log files: online redo log files and archived redo log files. Archived redo log files are sometimes referred to as offline redo log files. All Oracle databases use online redo log files. Archived redo log files are only generated when a database is run in archivelog mode, and allow for up-to-the-minute recovery in the event that a datafile is lost.

Log File Contents

Log files contain a sequential record of changes to a database. Any time you execute a SQL statement that changes the data in your database, Oracle generates one or more redo log entries to record that change. If you just change one row in a table, one redo log entry might be enough to document that change. If you create an index on a large table, Oracle generates a prodigious number of redo log entries to describe the changes being made.

To protect the redo log from being lost, Oracle writes it as fast as possible to a set of disk files known as redo log files. When you commit a transaction, Oracle waits until all redo log entries for that transaction have been written to the log files before telling you that the commit was successful. That way, you can't possibly lose any committed changes. Each Oracle database contains at least two redo log files, and often more. Oracle writes to these files in a circular fashion, as shown in Figure 3-4.

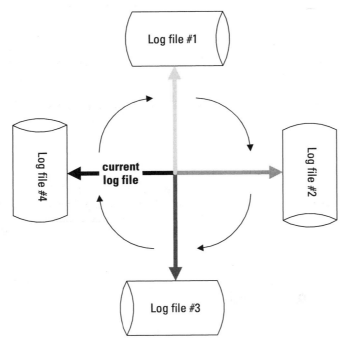

Figure 3-4: Oracle writes to the redo log files in a circular fashion.

 Note   As with control files, redo log files should always be mirrored. You can use hardware mirroring if your system is capable of it, or you can have the Oracle software mirror the files for you.

In a production setting, you should keep all redo log files that have been created since the most recent full backup of the database. Do this by having Oracle copy each redo log file as it is filled to a secure, long-term storage location. This process is known as *archiving* a redo log file. This gets to the heart of what the redo log buys you. Beginning with the most recent full backup of your database, the redo log files (both archived and online) provide you with a history of all changes made up to the current moment.

When you lose a disk drive, and someday you will, you'll lose all the datafiles on that drive. The redo log allows you to recover from what would otherwise be a disastrous event by simply performing the following three steps:

1. Replace the disk with a new one that works.

2. Restore the lost files from the most recent backup.

3. Use the redo log to reapply the changes to the restored files, bringing them up to date.

Note There are alternatives to replacing the disk. You could just as easily restore the files to a different disk and use the ALTER DATABASE RENAME FILE command to tell Oracle about the new location.

Oracle automates the third step. If you've configured your system correctly, the process of reapplying changes from the redo log is painless. All you have to do is issue one short command, sit back, and watch.

Finding Your Log Files

To generate a list of the online log files in your database, query the V$LOGFILE view. You need to be logged in as SYSTEM, or some other privileged user, to do this. The following query returns the status and name of all your online redo log files:

```
SELECT member
FROM v$logfile;
```

You can execute this query from SQL*Plus, as shown in this example:

```
SQL> COLUMN member FORMAT A40
SQL> SELECT member FROM v$logfile;

MEMBER
----------------------------------------
E:\ORACLE\ORADATA\JONATHAN\REDO04.LOG
E:\ORACLE\ORADATA\JONATHAN\REDO03.LOG
E:\ORACLE\ORADATA\JONATHAN\REDO02.LOG
E:\ORACLE\ORADATA\JONATHAN\REDO01.LOG
```

Finding your offline, or archived, log files is a different matter. Technically, they aren't considered part of the database. However, Oracle does keep track of them. You can query the v$archived_log view to get a list. You can find out the name of the directory, or device, to which Oracle is copying the archived log files by issuing an ARCHIVE LOG LIST command. Consider this example showing how to query the v$archived_log view:

```
SQL> SELECT name
  2  FROM v$archived_log
  3  ORDER BY recid;

NAME
---------------------------------
D:\ORADATA\JONATHAN\ARCH_299.1
D:\ORADATA\JONATHAN\ARCH_300.1
D:\ORADATA\JONATHAN\ARCH_301.1
D:\ORADATA\JONATHAN\ARCH_302.1
D:\ORADATA\JONATHAN\ARCH_303.1
```

To use the ARCHIVE LOG LIST command, you have to connect as either SYSDBA or SYSOPER, and issue the ARCHIVE LOG LIST command. Consider this example:

```
SQL> CONNECT system/manager@jonathan.gennick as SYSDBA;
Connected.
SQL> ARCHIVE LOG LIST
Database log mode              Archive Mode
Automatic archival             Enabled
Archive destination            G:\Oracle\Ora81\RDBMS
Oldest online log sequence     138
Current log sequence           141
```

Here, the archive destination is G:\Oracle\Ora81\RDBMS. As each redo log file is archived, it is copied to that directory. Knowing that, you can easily go to that directory, issue the dir command, and see a list of all your archived log files.

Note   The archive destination that you see with the ARCHIVE LOG LIST command is only the current destination. You can change this destination dynamically, but Oracle won't keep track of your changes. It only knows about the current destination.

Understanding Memory Architecture

When an Oracle instance starts up, it allocates a large block of memory known as the SGA. The SGA for an instance is shared by all of the background processes for that instance. In addition, each process associated with an instance will have its own private area of memory known as a program global area (PGA). Figure 3-5 illustrates this.

Sharing memory this way allows the background processes to communicate with each other quickly and minimizes the overhead of interprocess communication. This contributes greatly to Oracle's efficiency as a database.

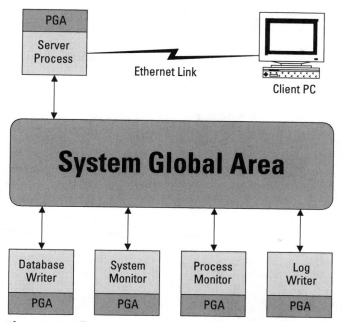

Figure 3-5: All processes share the SGA, and each process has its own PGA.

Understanding the System Global Area

The SGA is the most significant memory structure in an Oracle instance. It is composed of several major components: the database buffer cache, the shared pool, the redo log buffer, the large pool, and the fixed SGA. These are shown in Figure 3-6.

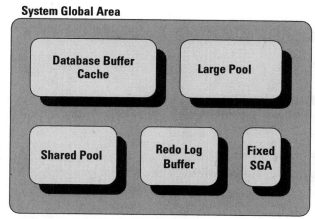

Figure 3-6: Oracle's system global area

Properly sizing the structures in the SGA is absolutely critical to proper database performance. You control their size. To properly size the structures in the SGA, you need to understand how they are used. The next few sections explain the use of each SGA structure. For suggestions on sizing these structures, see Chapter 20, "Database and Instance Tuning."

Understanding the database buffer cache

If Oracle had to read every block of data from disk each time you executed a query and had to write each block back to disk after you changed it, then Oracle would be a slow database indeed. Instead, Oracle caches frequently used data blocks in memory where they can be accessed quickly. The area in memory used to store frequently accessed data is known as the *database buffer cache.*

The database buffer cache consists of a number of buffers in memory. The size of each buffer matches the database block size. As blocks are read from disk, they are placed into the buffers. The number of buffers in the buffer cache is controlled by the db_block_buffers parameter. Thus, if your parameter file specifies db_block_buffers = 8192, then Oracle will reserve enough memory to hold 8,192 database blocks.

Note The size of a database block is controlled by the db_block_size parameter. To get the size of the buffer cache in bytes, multiply the db_block_size value by the db_block_buffers value. If your block size is 4,096, and you have 8,192 buffers in the cache, then the total size of the cache is 33,554,432 bytes.

Buffer Pools

The database buffer cache is frequently the largest part of the SGA. It consists of three smaller structures known as *buffer pools,* each of which is used to cache data with different access characteristics. Figure 3-7 shows these three buffer pools.

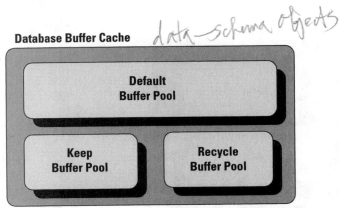

Figure 3-7: The buffer pools in the database buffer cache

Two of the buffer pools, the *keep buffer pool* and the *recycle buffer pool,* are optional. Every instance has at least one buffer pool — the *default buffer pool.* The (= *data* buffer pools serve the following purposes:

keep buffer pool	Use the keep buffer pool for frequently accessed schema objects, such as code tables, that you want to keep in memory all the time. Data read into the keep buffer pool is retained until you shut down the database. It is never aged out of memory to make room for new data.
recycle buffer pool	Use the recycle buffer pool for schema objects that you want flushed out of memory as quickly as possible. A large table that you frequently scan in its entirety would be a good candidate for the recycle buffer pool.
default buffer pool	Use the default buffer pool for all objects that don't fall into the keep or recycle category.

Note Prior to the release of Oracle8, Oracle supported only one buffer pool. It was the equivalent of the default buffer pool, but it wasn't named because there was no need to distinguish it from other buffer pools.

Sizing buffer pools

The `buffer_pool_keep` and the `buffer_pool_recycle` parameters control the size of the keep and recycle buffer pools. The size of the default buffer pool is what's left over after subtracting the size of the keep and recycle pools from the total size of the buffer cache. Let's take a look at a sample configuration:

```
db_block_buffers        8192
buffer_pool_keep        2000
buffer_pool_recycle     1000
                        ----
size of DEFAULT pool    5192
```

In this example, the total size of the database buffer cache is 8,192 buffers. You set this by using the `db_block_buffers` parameter. Of those 8,192 buffers, 2,000 were allocated to the keep buffer pool. Another 1,000 were allocated to the recycle buffer pool. This leaves 5,192 for the default buffer pool.

Assigning objects to a buffer pool

Database objects, such as tables and indexes, are assigned to a buffer pool when you create them. You must decide which buffer pool is most appropriate. You make the buffer pool assignment using the `STORAGE` clause of the `CREATE` statement, as shown in this example:

```
CREATE TABLE state_codes (
    state_abbr          varchar2(2),
    state_name          varchar2(30)
) TABLESPACE users
STORAGE (BUFFER_POOL KEEP);
```

Here, the `state_codes` table was assigned to the keep buffer pool. This makes sense because the `state_codes` table won't be very big, and in all likelihood, it will be a frequently referenced table.

Dirty Lists and the LRU Lists

Oracle uses two lists to manage each buffer pool: a dirty list and a least recently used (LRU) list. The *dirty list* keeps track of which buffers in the pool have been modified and are in need of being written back to disk. The LRU list keeps track of how recently each buffer has been accessed. Figure 3-8 shows how these lists might look in relation to the DEFAULT buffer pool.

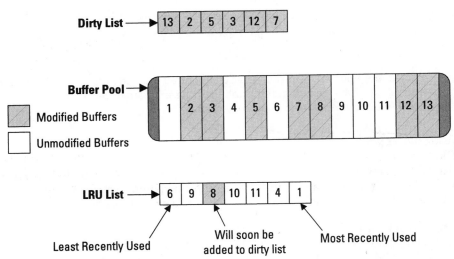

Figure 3-8: The dirty list and the LRU list keep track of buffers in a buffer pool.

Oracle uses the LRU list to decide which buffers to overwrite when new data needs to be read in from disk. The LRU list has two ends: a least recently used (LRU) end and a most recently used (MRU) end. Every time a buffer is accessed to satisfy a SQL statement, Oracle moves the pointer to that buffer to the most recently used end of the LRU list. This results in the LRU list always containing a list of buffers in the order in which they have recently been accessed.

When Oracle needs to read new data from disk, it starts at the least recently used end of the LRU list and looks for a buffer that hasn't been modified. When it finds one, the newly read data is placed in that buffer. Pointers to frequently accessed data blocks will tend to migrate to the most recently used end of the LRU list, and consequently, they will be the last to be overwritten. Keeping the most frequently used data in memory is a great asset in terms of performance. Memory is much faster than disk.

The dirty list is used to keep track of which buffers have been changed and need to be written back to disk. Whenever a buffer is modified, usually as a result of a SQL statement, Oracle will mark the buffer as *dirty*. Dirty buffers are quickly added to the dirty list. The database writer background processes, which you will read more about later in this chapter, check the dirty list regularly, and write those modified blocks back to disk.

> **Note**   Buffers aren't always added to the dirty list immediately when they are modified. Oracle tends to perform processes asynchronously, and it is possible for dirty buffers to remain in the LRU list for a short period of time. Ultimately, though, they'll be moved to the dirty list and then written to disk.

Caching in the shared pool

The *shared pool* is an area in memory where Oracle caches PL/SQL program units, parsed versions of SQL statements, execution plans for those parsed SQL statements, and data dictionary information. Like the database buffer cache, the shared pool is a major piece of the SGA, and its size has a significant impact on database performance.

Components of the Shared Pool

The two major components of the shared pool are the library cache and the data dictionary cache. The library cache is further subdivided into the shared SQL area and the PL/SQL area. Figure 3-9 shows these structures in the shared pool.

program units
pl/sql program, pased version of SQL stm / stm
execution plan for the sql stm
dictinary info.

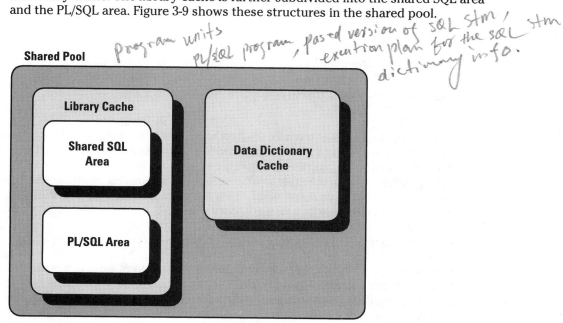

Figure 3-9: Memory structures in the shared pool

In addition to what is shown in Figure 3-9, the shared pool contains several relatively minor items such as locks, library cache handles, and memory-for-character-set conversion.

Sizing the Shared Pool

The `shared_pool_size` parameter controls the size of the shared pool. You can set the size at 50 million bytes, for example, by placing the following line in your database's parameter file:

```
shared_pool_size = 50000000
```

You can also use M and K prefixes to specify the size in megabytes or kilobytes.

Oracle determines the size of all the structures within the shared pool automatically based on the total size that you specify. You have no control over how much shared pool space gets allocated to the library cache vs. the data dictionary cache. Oracle determines that.

The Library Cache

The Library Cache contains the shared SQL area and the PL/SQL area, which work similarly. The shared SQL area holds parsed versions of SQL statements so that they don't have to be reparsed if they are used again. The PL/SQL area holds the compiled versions of PL/SQL procedures, functions, packages, and other program units so that all the database users can share them.

The shared SQL area

The shared SQL area holds parsed versions of SQL statements that database users have executed. The shared SQL area also holds the execution plans for those statements. The purpose is to speed the process along if and when those statements are reused.

Think for a minute about what Oracle has to do when you execute a SQL statement. First it has to parse the statement. *Parsing* refers to the process of taking the syntax of the statement apart, verifying that it is correct, and validating that the table and column names used in the statement are correct. Parsing can be an expensive operation in terms of time and disk I/O because Oracle needs to read information from the data dictionary to parse a SQL statement. To get that information, Oracle actually issues SQL statements internally. These are referred to as *recursive SQL* statements, and they too must be parsed.

After a statement has been parsed and Oracle understands what you want to do, Oracle must then figure out *how* to do it. It must build an *execution plan* for the statement. Figure 3-10 provides an example of one. Given the SELECT statement on the left, Oracle might come up with the execution plan shown on the right. Building the execution plan might involve even more recursive SQL statements, and Oracle often needs to consider several possible plans before it can determine which is most efficient.

Query	Execution Plan
| ```
SELECT id_no, animal_name
FROM aquatic_animal a
WHERE NOT EXISTS (
    SELECT *
    FROM checkup_history ch
    WHERE ch.id_no = a.id_no
    AND ch.checkup_date >
add_months(trunc(sysdate),-12));
``` | ```
0 SELECT STATEMENT    Cost = 1
1   FILTER
2     TABLE ACCESS FULL AQUATIC_ANIMAL
3     TABLE ACCESS FULL CHECKUP_HISTORY
``` |

Figure 3-10: A SQL statement and its execution plan

Although all this parsing and execution-plan building is expensive, you can short-circuit much of it. Typically, the programmers define the SQL statements used by any given application when they write that application. You may have a lot of people using an application, but they will all be executing the same SQL statements over and over again. The people developing the Oracle software recognized that they could gain efficiency by simply saving the parsed SQL statements together with their execution plans. When the statement is next executed, Oracle simply needs to retrieve the preexisting plan. What a savings! No parsing. No rebuilding of the execution plan. No recursive SQL.

The shared SQL area is the part of the SGA that stores parsed SQL statements and their execution plans. Being able to reuse execution plans is critical to good database performance. Consequently, it's important to size the shared pool so that the shared SQL area is large enough to hold all the SQL statements that you use regularly. Chapter 20, "Database and Instance Tuning," provides some techniques that you can use to determine whether your shared SQL area is large enough.

The PL/SQL area

The PL/SQL area serves much the same purpose for PL/SQL code as the shared SQL area does for SQL statements. It allows multiple users to share the compiled version of one PL/SQL program unit.

When you execute a PL/SQL program unit, such as a trigger or a stored procedure, Oracle must load the compiled version of that program unit into memory. Sometimes, especially with PL/SQL packages, a program unit can be quite large. If a second user comes along and needs to execute the same trigger, stored procedure, or function, you don't want to have to load that same code into memory twice. Doing so costs both disk I/O and memory usage. To avoid this, Oracle loads compiled PL/SQL code into an area of the Library Cache set aside for that purpose. If two people execute the same code, they will both share the same copy.

Note
While users share copies of PL/SQL code, they don't share copies of the variables. Each user actually gets his or her own private PL/SQL area where any variables are stored. This is what enables many users to execute the same code without conflicting with one another.

The Dictionary Cache

The dictionary cache is an area in the shared pool that Oracle uses to cache data dictionary information. Oracle frequently refers to the data dictionary when parsing SQL statements to verify table names, column names, datatypes, and so forth. By caching the most frequently used data dictionary information in memory, Oracle reduces the performance hit caused by recursive SQL statements.

Note
The dictionary cache is sometimes referred to as the row cache.

Writing to the redo log buffer

The *redo log buffer* is an area in memory where Oracle places redo log entries that need to be written to disk. Every Oracle database has a background process called the log writer that constantly checks for new redo log entries and writes those entries to disk as quickly as possible. However, disk I/O is a lot slower than memory, and the log writer process can't keep up during heavy bursts of activity. The buffer evens things out. When changes are coming thick and fast, redo log entries are added to the buffer faster than they can be written, and the buffer starts to fill up. When the rate of redo generation subsides, the log writer process will catch up, and the buffer will empty out. For good database performance, the redo log buffer needs to be large enough to accommodate any sudden burst of activity, and the overall rate of redo log generation needs to be in a range that the log writer can handle.

Organization of the Redo Log Buffer

The redo log buffer is a first-in, first-out buffer that Oracle uses in a circular fashion. Oracle maintains two pointers, one pointing to the head of the log and the other pointing to the tail of the log. See Figure 3-11.

As changes are made to the database, Oracle always adds redo entries onto the head of the log, advancing the head pointer each time. The log writer process, which writes these entries to disk, always writes from the tail of the log. Thus, the tail chases the head in a circular fashion. In Figure 3-11, the buffer contains 11 entries. As each pointer advances past entry 11, it will be reset to point at entry 1, and the process of advancing through the buffer will begin all over again. This continues for as long as the database is running.

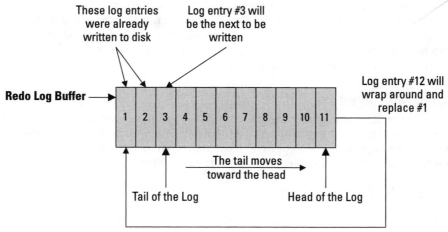

Figure 3-11: The redo log buffer

Sizing the Redo Log Buffer

You use the `log_buffer` parameter to size the redo log buffer. To allocate a 1MB redo log buffer, you would place the following entry in your database's parameter file:

```
log_buffer = 1024000
```

You want the redo log buffer to be large enough to accommodate normal bursts of activity that occur during daily operations. Chapter 20, "Database and Instance Tuning," tells you how to monitor for problems related to the redo log buffer size.

Using the large pool

The large pool is an optional feature introduced with the release of Oracle8 that provides a separate memory area where large blocks of memory can be allocated. You don't have to have one, but it's a good idea if you use either the multithreaded server option or Oracle's RMAN utility for backup and restore operations.

Large Pool Uses

Oracle's multithreaded server option uses the large pool as a place to allocate session memory. Session memory tends to be quite large when a multithreaded server is being used, and it works better to allocate that memory in the large pool. The large pool is also used by Oracle's RMAN utility to allocate I/O buffers used for backup and restore operations.

If you don't allocate a large pool, memory for user sessions and backup and restore operations end up being allocated from the shared pool. Oracle may sometimes be forced to reduce the amount of memory available for caching SQL statements to allocate enough memory for a multithreaded server session or for a backup operation. This can have a negative impact on performance.

Sizing the Large Pool

You size the large pool using the `large_pool_size` initialization parameter. The default size is zero. The minimum size is 600KB. The maximum size is operating-system specific but will always be at least 2GB. To allocate a 600KB large pool, you would place the following line in your database's parameter file:

```
large_pool_size = 600K
```

If you don't explicitly set the large pool's size using the `large_pool_size` parameter, Oracle will default to not using a large pool at all.

Understanding the fixed SGA

The fixed SGA is an area in the SGA that Oracle uses to store the myriad number of values that it needs to keep track of internally for the instance to operate. You can't size the fixed SGA. You don't need to tune the fixed SGA; just be aware that it exists.

Understanding program global areas

In addition to the shared memory available in the SGA, each process connected to an Oracle database needs a private memory area of its own. Oracle refers to this area as a program global area (PGA). Processes use PGAs to store variables, arrays, and other information that do not need to be shared with other processes.

Contents of the PGA

The exact contents of the PGA depend on whether you are using Oracle's multithreaded server option. Figure 3-12 shows the contents of the PGA in both the standard and the multithreaded server configurations.

The session information box is sometimes referred to as the user global area (UGA) because it contains information specific to a particular database user connection. When a multithreaded server is being used, the UGA is stored in either the shared pool or the large pool because it must be accessible to more than one server process.

Note   Under the multithreaded server configuration, the server process handling a user's SQL statements may change from one statement to the next; hence, the need for the UGA to be accessible to more than one process.

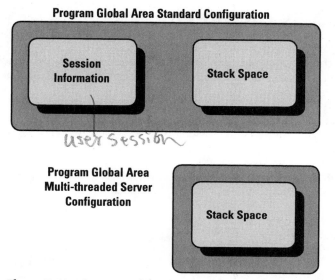

user Session

Figure 3-12: Contents of the PGA

Sizing the PGA

The sort_area_size and sort_area_retained_size parameters have the greatest effect on the size of the PGA. Together, these parameters control the amount of memory available to a process for sorting. Under the standard configuration, the entire sort area is contained in the PGA, so the PGA's size can potentially range up to the size specified by the sort_area_size initialization parameter. Actually, it can exceed that, because there are other structures in the PGA as well.

Note The maximum sort area space is not allocated unless required. If the sort area size is 10MB, and the largest sort you do requires only 2MB, then only 2MB will be allocated.

When you are using the multithreaded server option, the retained portion of the sort area is allocated in the SGA, and the amount allocated in the PGA will be equivalent to sort_area_size – sort_area_retained_size.

The sort area isn't the only structure in the PGA, and the sort area parameters aren't the only ones that affect the size of the PGA. The open_links and db_files parameters also affect the size of the PGA. However, as far as tuning goes, you need to worry about the sort area parameters.

Looking at Process Architecture

An Oracle instance is composed of processes and memory structures. You've already learned about the memory part; now it's time for the processes. An Oracle instance is composed of a number of processes called *background processes*. They're called background processes because they are always running, whether or not any users are connected to the database. Figure 3-13 shows a typical collection of background processes for an instance.

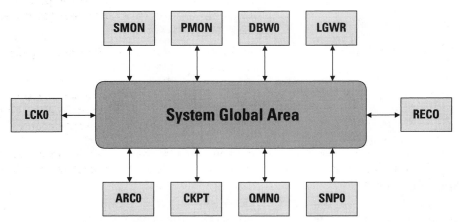

Figure 3-13: A typical Oracle instance

Each of the processes shown in Figure 3-13 has a specific job to do. You'll read more about each process later. For now, here's a brief synopsis of each process's function:

Database Writer (DBW0)	Database Writer processes write-modified data blocks back to the datafiles.
Log Writer (LGWR)	Log Writer processes write-redo log entries to the redo log files.
System Monitor (SMON)	System Monitor processes perform crash recovery and coalesces free space.
Process Monitor (PMON)	Process Monitor processes watch for processes that are prematurely disconnected, release any locks that they hold, and take care of any other necessary cleanup tasks.
Recoverer (RECO)	Recoverer processes resolve distributed transactions.

Snapshot (SNP0)	Snapshot processes run jobs from the database job queue.
Queue Monitor (QMN0)	Queue Monitor processes are used by the Advanced Queueing option to manage message queues.
Lock (LCK0)	Lock processes are used by the Parallel Server option to manage interinstance locking.
Checkpoint (CKPT)	Checkpoint processes periodically checkpoint the database. Checkpointing is the process of recording the current system change number in all of the database files.
Archiver (ARC0)	Archiver processes copy filled redo log files to the archive log destination.

Not all processes will be present for every Oracle instance. Some of them are optional, such as the SNP0 processes. You will see them only if you have set the job_queue_processes initialization parameter to a value greater than zero.

Using the appropriate operating system commands, you can list the processes that are running for any given Oracle instance. This is sometimes useful as a quick check to be sure that the instance is up and running.

Oracle processes under UNIX

On most UNIX systems, you can use the ps command to list processes. To see the Oracle background processes, you'll want to use ps -ef to get an extended process listing. Unless you want to wade through a list of all the processes running on your computer, you'll also want to use grep to search for the instance name. The following example shows how you would generate a list of all the background processes running for the PROD instance:

```
$ ps -ef | grep PROD
  oracle  3592    1  0 17:00:05 ?          0:00 ora_smon_PROD
  oracle  3590    1  0 17:00:05 ?          0:03 ora_lgwr_PROD
  oracle  3588    1  0 17:00:05 ?          0:05 ora_dbw0_PROD
  oracle  3586    1  0 17:00:05 ?          0:03 ora_pmon_PROD
  oracle  3594    1  0 17:00:05 ?          0:00 ora_reco_PROD
  oracle  3597    1  0 17:00:05 ?          0:03 ora_arc0_PROD
```

You can use a variation of this technique to quickly see which databases are running. For instance, instead of using grep to search for an instance name, use grep to search for one of the mandatory processes instead. You'll get a line of output for each instance that is currently running. Here's an example:

```
$ ps -ef | grep smon
    oracle  2564     1  2 07:00:01 ?            0:05 ora_smon_TEST
    oracle  2588     1  2 07:00:05 ?            0:05 ora_smon_DEVL
    oracle  2576     1  1 07:00:03 ?            0:06 ora_smon_PROD
    oracle  3351  3336  1 17:19:02 ttyp2        0:00 grep dbw0
```

This example searched for the SMON process. You could just as easily use grep for LGWR or DBW0. Be careful with the numbered processes, though. If you use grep for DBW9 and not all instances are configured to run nine database writers, you'll miss some.

Oracle processes under Windows NT

Under Windows NT, the Oracle processes are implemented as threads that run within a service. Oracle provides a utility, the Database Administration Assistant for Windows NT, that allows you to view a list of these threads. You can find this utility on the Database Administration menu, which you get to by selecting Start and pointing to Programs and Oracle – OraHome1. When you run it, you can navigate to the instance you want, right-click it, choose Process Information from the pop-up menu, and you'll see a screen like the one shown in Figure 3-14.

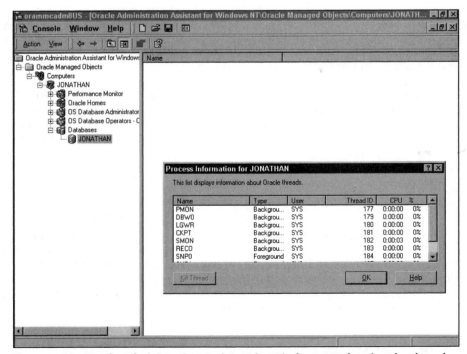

Figure 3-14: Oracle Administration Assistant for Windows NT showing the threads in an Oracle instance

Note In order to use the Oracle Administration Assistant for Windows NT, you need to install the Microsoft Management Console version 1.1. You can download it from Microsoft's website.

If you need to know which instances are running, your best bet is to look at the Services control panel. It will tell you which Oracle database services are running, although it's still possible for an instance to be shut down even though its service is running.

Database Writer processes

An Oracle instance can have up to ten Database Writer processes (DBW0). These will be numbered DBW0 through DBW9. The Database Writer's job is to write modified data blocks back to disk.

Every instance gets one Database Writer by default. You can change the number of Database Writer processes by using the db_writer_processes initialization parameter. To configure an instance for the full complement of ten Database Writer processes, add the following line to the parameter file:

```
db_writer_processes = 10
```

Multiple Database Writers make sense only in a system with multiple CPUs because they allow you to spread the task of writing data evenly over those CPUs. If you are running on a single-CPU system, you should use just one Database Writer process.

The Log Writer process

The Log Writer's job is to write redo log entries to the database's online redo log files. Recall that as changes are made to a database, Oracle places redo log entries into the redo log buffer. For the Log Writer process (LGWR), these entries are always added to the head of the log. The Log Writer pulls these entries off the tail of the log and writes them to disk.

Archiver processes

Archiver processes (ARC0) have the task of copying filled redo log files to the archive log destination. An Oracle database has a finite number of redo log files, and Oracle writes to these in a circular fashion. It fills up each online redo log file in sequence, and when it gets to the end, it circles around and starts filling up the first redo log file again. If you want to save the log files for possible use in recovering the database, you need to make a copy of each log file before it is reused. You can do this manually, or you can start one or more archiver processes to automate the process.

As with database writers, Oracle allows you to have up to ten Archiver processes. The `log_archive_max_processes` parameter is used to set the maximum number that you want to allow. For example, the following entry in your database parameter file will set a maximum of five Archiver processes:

```
log_archive_max_processes = 5
```

Unlike the case with database writers, Oracle won't necessarily start five archiver processes just because you tell it to. Instead, it automatically starts and stops archiver processes as necessary to keep up with the amount of redo being generated. As the name indicates, the `log_archive_max_processes` parameter sets an upper limit on the number of archiver processes that Oracle can start.

The Checkpoint process

The Checkpoint process (CKPT) is responsible for recording Checkpoint information in all database file headers. Periodically, when an instance is running, Oracle records a Checkpoint in all database file headers indicating the most recent redo log entry for which all changes have been written to the database files. Oracle uses this information during a recovery operation to determine which log files must be read and which log entries must be reapplied.

The System Monitor process

The System Monitor process (SMON) has three functions in life:

✦ Crash recovery

✦ Cleanup of temporary segments

✦ Coalescing free space

Crash recovery happens when you restart the database after a system crash or an instance crash. When a crash occurs, you will very likely lose changes that were buffered in memory, but not written to disk, before the crash occurred. Some of these changes might represent committed transactions. When the instance is restarted, SMON recovers these transactions by reapplying the lost changes based on the information in the online redo log files. This works because Oracle always ensures that all changes for a committed transaction have been recorded in the redo log and that those log entries have been physically written to disk.

Another of SMON's tasks, and a more mundane one, is to deallocate temporary segments used for sorting. When you issue a `SELECT` statement, or any other SQL statement that requires a lot of data to be sorted, the sort may not be done entirely in memory. When too much data exists to be sorted in memory, Oracle sorts a piece at a time and uses disk space to temporarily hold the results. When the sort is over, it is SMON's task to deallocate this space.

Coalescing free space is the last of SMON's major functions. For tablespaces with a default PCTINCREASE setting that is greater than 0, SMON continuously checks data files, looking for two or more adjacent areas of free space. Whenever it finds adjacent areas of free space, SMON combines them into one larger area. This helps avoid fragmentation and also lets you allocate larger extents that might not be possible otherwise.

The Process Monitor process

The Process Monitor (PMON) performs the same kind of tasks for processes that the System Monitor does for an instance. The difference is that instead of cleaning up after an instance crash, the PMON cleans up after processes that abnormally terminate. When a process aborts, PMON does the following:

✦ Releases any locks held by the process

✦ Rolls back any transactions that the process had started but had not yet committed

✦ Removes the process ID from the list of active processes

The Recoverer process

The Recoverer process (RECO) resolves distributed transactions that have failed. This process will be present only if the `distributed_transactions` initialization parameter is greater than 0, indicating that the database supports distributed transactions. If a distributed transaction fails, Recoverer will communicate with the other nodes involved with the transaction to either commit or roll back the transaction.

Job queue processes

Job queue processes (SNP0) are used to run scheduled PL/SQL jobs. If you are using Oracle's replication features and you have created snapshots that refresh automatically at predefined intervals, a job queue process makes that happen. Job queue processes also run jobs that have been scheduled using the built-in DBMS_JOBS package.

The `job_queue_processes` initialization parameter controls how many of these processes are started, and you can have up to 36. The following entry, placed in a parameter file, would cause the maximum of 36 job queue processes to be started:

```
job_queue_processes = 36
```

The 36 job queue processes are named `SNP0` through `SNP9`, and then `SNPA` through `SNPZ`.

Queue Monitor processes

Queue Monitor processes (QMNO) are used with Oracle's Advanced Queuing option. You can have up to ten Queue Monitor processes, and they are configured using the `aq_tm_processes` initialization parameter. The following parameter file entry would configure an instance to have three Queue Monitor processes:

```
aq_tm_processes = 3
```

Queue Monitor processes are named QMN0 through QMN9, depending on how many you create.

Summary

In this chapter, you learned:

✦ An Oracle instance consists of a set of processes and an area of shared memory. A database consists of files that contain related data.

✦ Three types of files make up an Oracle database: datafiles, log files, and control files.

✦ The system global area (SGA) is a large memory structure that Oracle background processes use.

✦ The major components of the SGA are the database buffer cache, the shared pool, the redo log buffer, and the large pool.

✦ Several processes combine to make an Oracle instance. Each has a specific function to perform.

✦   ✦   ✦

Managing the Database Password File

CHAPTER

4

✦ ✦ ✦ ✦

In This Chapter

Connecting as an administrative user

Creating a password file

Managing administrative users

Deleting a password file

Rebuilding a password file

✦ ✦ ✦ ✦

The database *password file* is an operating system file, separate from the database, in which Oracle stores the passwords of database administrators. The password file is key to authenticating DBAs who must connect remotely to a database over a network and who must perform administrative tasks such as starting and stopping that database. As a DBA, you need to be able to connect and perform these tasks even when the database isn't open. If a database isn't open, then the passwords stored within that database are not accessible. By storing the administrative passwords in a separate file that isn't part of the database, Oracle enables remote authentication even when the database is not running. This chapter covers creating and managing password files.

Connecting as an Administrative User

What does it mean to connect as a database administrator? Depending on your point of view, it may not mean a whole lot. You'll find that you can perform almost all administrative tasks, such as creating users, tables, tablespaces, and so forth, while logged on normally as a user with DBA privileges. However, the following commands may be issued only by someone connected as an administrator:

✦ STARTUP

✦ SHUTDOWN

✦ ALTER DATABASE OPEN

✦ ALTER DATABASE MOUNT

✦ ALTER DATABASE BACKUP

✦ ARCHIVE LOG

✦ RECOVER

✦ CREATE DATABASE

The brevity of this list may make it seem insignificant, but these are really some very significant commands. When you need to restore a damaged database file, the RECOVER command becomes quite significant indeed. Generally, connecting as an administrator allows you to perform tasks that involve the database being in some state other than fully open.

The internal connection

Years ago, the only way to connect as an administrator to an instance was to run Server Manager and connect internally by using the keyword INTERNAL. That method still works today, although it's not the method that Oracle recommends. The following example shows how it is done:

```
C:\>svrmgrl

Oracle Server Manager Release 3.1.5.0.0 - Production

(c) Copyright 1997, Oracle Corporation.  All Rights Reserved.

Oracle8i Release 8.1.5.0.0 - Production
With the Partitioning and Java options
PL/SQL Release 8.1.5.0.0 - Production

SVRMGR> connect internal
Connected.
SVRMGR>
```

Beginning with the release of Oracle8i, SQL*Plus can connect internally. Oracle added this ability in preparation for the eventual phase-out of Server Manager, so if you have Oracle8i installed, you should probably get used to using SQL*Plus instead. The only difference between using SQL*Plus and using Server Manager to connect internally is that you will want to start SQL*Plus using the /nolog option on the command line. Normally, SQL*Plus forces you to connect to the database as a normal user before it gives you a command prompt. The /NOLOG option gets you a command prompt right away. You can then issue a CONNECT INTERNAL command to connect internally. Here's an example:

```
$sqlplus /nolog

SQL*Plus: Release 8.1.5.0.0 - Production on Wed May 19 22:24:15 1999
```

```
(c) Copyright 1999 Oracle Corporation.  All rights reserved.

SQL> connect internal
Connected.
SQL>
```

Even though Oracle no longer promotes the use of the INTERNAL keyword, you will likely see this method used quite often. It's easy, and it's simple. In a UNIX environment, DBAs are given UNIX accounts that are part of the dba group. Being part of the dba group allows DBAs to connect internally. Other UNIX users that are not part of the dba group won't be able to connect as internally.

For added security, or to enable internal connections to be made over the network, you can create a password file with just one password—for use when connecting internally. Once that's done, you can log on remotely.

Note   If you connect internally over the network to start a database, remember that the path to the initialization file is relative to your machine and not the database server.

The following example shows how you would connect to the PROD database as the internal user from a remote PC somewhere on the network:

```
SQL> connect internal@prod
Password:
Connected.
SQL>
```

Notice that the password characters were not echoed to the screen. That prevents any passersby from seeing them. If you prefer not to be prompted for the password, you can supply it with the CONNECT command. For example:

```
SVRMGR> connect internal/oracle@prod
Connected.
SVRMGR>
```

Remember, before you can connect as an internal user from a remote system, you need to create a password file. Otherwise, Oracle won't be able to authenticate you, and you won't be allowed to connect. You'll see how to do this later in the chapter.

The SYSOPER and SYSDBA connection

Another method for making an administrative connection to an Oracle database is to connect in one of two special roles known as SYSDBA and SYSOPER. This is the method that Oracle Enterprise Manager uses. To connect this way, you need to have an Oracle username and you need to have been granted either the SYSDBA or SYSOPER privilege.

The SYSDBA privilege gives you full control over the database. The SYSOPER privilege allows you to grant someone, perhaps a system operator, the ability to perform straightforward and routine tasks such as starting and stopping a database. Table 4-1 shows the capabilities that these two privileges provide and compares them to what you can do through an internal connection.

Table 4-1
Capabilities Provided by SYSDBA, SYSOPER, and INTERNAL

Command/Privilege/Feature	SYSDBA	SYSOPER	INTERNAL
Start the database	*	*	*
Close the database and shutdown the instance	*	*	*
Open the database	*	*	*
Mount the database	*	*	*
Place tablespaces into backup mode	*	*	*
Issue ARCHIVE LOG commands to view the status of archiving	*	*	*
Perform database recovery	*	*	*
Recover the database to a specific point in time	*		*
Create a new database	*		*
Connect when only DBAs are permitted to connect	*	*	*
Receive all system privileges, with the ADMIN option	*		*

A user connecting as SYSOPER will be limited and will be able to perform only the specific tasks shown in Table 4-1. Users connecting as SYSDBA have full control over the database and are not limited only to the tasks shown in Table 4-1. Since they have all possible system privileges, they can create tables, modify data, drop objects, and pretty much execute any valid SQL statement.

To connect in one of these administrative roles, you issue a special form of the CONNECT command that looks like this:

```
CONNECT username/password AS {SYSDBA|SYSOPER}
```

If you are connecting remotely, you need to include a Net8 service name:

```
CONNECT username/password@service AS {SYSDBA|SYSOPER}
```

If you are connecting through Oracle Enterprise Manager, you need to select either SYSDBA or SYSOPER from the drop-down list on the Oracle Enterprise Manager

Login screen. Figure 4-1 shows how this looks for Oracle Enterprise Manager 2.0. Note the Connect as drop-down list, and note that SYSDBA is being selected.

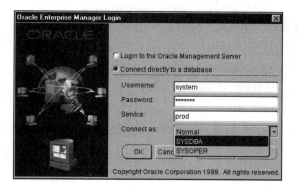

Figure 4-1: Select either SYSDBA or SYSOPER in the Oracle Enterprise Manager to be connected to your Oracle database.

A user can actually be granted both of these roles. In that case, the user has the choice of whether to connect as SYSOPER or as SYSDBA.

Note Strange as it may seem, when you connect remotely to a database as the user SYS, and you connect as SYSDBA or SYSOPER, you must use the INTERNAL password and not the SYS user's password. When you connect as SYS without specifying SYSOPER or SYSDBA, you use the SYS user's password.

Oracle's official position is that you should connect as SYSOPER or SYSDBA when performing administrative tasks. The internal connection is a deprecated feature that Oracle keeps around for backwards compatibility. A lot of Server Manager scripts still exist out there that make use of it. Someday, though, Oracle will probably remove the ability to connect internally.

The default schema

Each database user in an Oracle database is associated with a schema. Normally, the user's name and the schema's name are the same, and people often use the terms user and schema interchangeably. One of the few times that they are not the same is when you log on as an administrator. Any time that you log on as INTERNAL, SYSDBA, or as SYSOPER, your session is associated with the SYS schema.

What is the effect of this? What does it mean to be associated with the SYS schema? Take a look at the following example, where a user named Jaimie connects in the normal fashion and issues a SELECT statement to confirm her username:

```
SQL> connect jaimie/upton
Connected.
SQL> select user from dual;
USER
------------------------------
```

```
JAIMIE
1 row selected.
SQL>
```

As expected, the SELECT statement confirms that Jaimie is indeed connected as the user named "jaimie." Now, take a look at a second example. This time, Jaimie connects as an administrator using the SYSDBA keyword:

```
SQL> connect jaimie/upton as sysdba
Connected.
SQL> select user from dual;
USER
------------------------------
SYS
1 row selected.
SQL>
```

Even though Jaimie logged on using her username and password, she is connected as the user SYS. If Jaimie were to create a table, a view, or any other schema object, it would end up being owned by SYS, not Jaimie. Because of this, and to reduce the possibility of mistakenly creating objects in the wrong schema, you should avoid creating any database objects while logged on as INTERNAL, SYSDBA, or SYSOPER.

The OSOPER and OSDBA roles

As an alternative to using a password file for authentication, on many platforms, Oracle uses two operating system roles named OSOPER and OSDBA to provide DBA operating system authentication. These correspond to SYSOPER and SYSDBA, respectively.

To use operating system authentication, your system administrator must grant you and the other DBAs either the OSOPER or the OSDBA role. Alternatively, all the DBAs can be made part of the dba group. Remember, OSOPER and OSDBA are operating system roles. The grants are done from the operating system and not from within Oracle. Your system administrator should be able to help you with that. Once granted the proper privilege, you can run SQL*Plus (or Server Manager) and connect to Oracle with a command like this:

```
CONNECT / AS SYSDBA
```

The forward slash is used instead of a username because you don't even need a database username at this point. You are connected to the SYS schema, just as if you had logged on internally. When you connect this way, Oracle checks to see if you have been granted the proper operating system role. If you try to connect as SYSDBA, Oracle checks to see if you have the OSDBA role. If you try to connect as SYSOPER, Oracle checks to see if you have the OSOPER role. If you have the correct role, you are allowed to connect. If not, you aren't.

Creating a Password File

You will need a password file when you connect remotely. It's easy enough to rely on operating system authentication when you're running in a UNIX environment, where all the DBAs log on to the UNIX server to perform administrative tasks. It's a different matter when you are a DBA running Enterprise Manager on a PC and you are connecting to that same database over the LAN. Operating system authentication won't work because you aren't even logging on to the server operating system. You can't depend on the normal user passwords that are stored in the database either, because the database may not be up when you try to connect. The solution is to create a password file, allowing the DBA passwords to be stored outside of the database. To create a password file for a database, you need to perform these five steps:

1. Determine the proper location and name for the password file.

2. Shut down the database.

3. Use the ORAPWD utility to create the password file.

4. Set the value of the REMOTE_LOGIN_PASSWORDFILE initialization parameter.

5. Restart the database.

Properly setting the REMOTE_LOGIN_PASSWORDFILE initialization parameter is a key part of this procedure. First of all, it determines whether your password file even gets used. Secondly, it determines whether you can set administrative passwords for any user, or for just the INTERNAL user. This parameter is discussed further later in this section.

Password file name and location

The location in which Oracle expects to find password files is specific to each operating system. The same is true for the naming convention used to name these files. UNIX systems use one convention, and Windows NT systems use another. Table 4-2 shows the location and naming conventions used in these two environments.

| Table 4-2 |
| **Location and Naming Conventions for Oracle Password Files** |

Operating System	*Password File Location*	*Naming Convention*
UNIX (and Linux too)	$ORACLE_HOME/dbs	orapwXXXX
Windows NT	c:\oracle\ora81\Database	PWDXXXX.ora

The letters XXXX in Table 4-2 represent the Oracle SID, or instance name. For example, if you had an instance named `PROD`, then your password file should be named `orapwPROD` in UNIX, and `PWDPROD.ora` in Windows NT. The password file location in the Windows NT environment is in the Database folder underneath your Oracle home folder. The first part of the path may vary depending on choices that you made when you installed Oracle.

If you don't get the file name right, Oracle will tell you about it when you try to start the database. You will see a message like this:

```
ORA-01990: error opening password file '/ORACLE_BASE/product/733/dbs/orapwPROD'
```

Fortunately, this message includes the full path and file name that Oracle is looking for. That's everything you need to solve the problem. Just re-create the password file where Oracle expects to find it.

The orapwd utility

Once you've figured out where to place the password file, and what to name it, it's time to create it. To create a password file, you need to run the Oracle command-line utility named `orapwd`. You run it from a command prompt and pass several pieces of information as parameters to the command. The syntax for running `orapwd` looks like this:

```
orapwd file=filename password=password
[entries=max_administrators]
```

The `filename` is the name to use for the password file that you are creating. You may include a path as part of the name. The `password` sets the password for use when connecting internally, and `max_administrators` is an optional parameter that specifies the maximum number of DBA users you can ever expect to support. This value is used to size the password file. It includes room for the internal password and for passwords of all users to which you ever expect to grant `SYSDBA` or `SYSOPER` privileges.

Note   The `orapwd` utility does not allow for spaces on either side of the equal sign. You must type `file=filename`, **not** `file = filename`.

The following example shows how to use the `orapwd` utility. It creates a password file for a database named `PROD`. The password file is created large enough to hold six database administrator passwords in addition to the internal password. The password for `INTERNAL` is set to *gorf*.

```
$ orapwd file=$ORACLE_HOME/dbs/orapwPROD password=gorf entries=7
```

The password file has seven entries and not six because the internal password always gets one slot. That leaves six remaining slots for the individual DBAs.

Tip Always be generous with the number of entries that you allow for. These files aren't expandable. To add more administrators than you originally planned for, you need to re-create the file. That's a bit of a pain. Password files aren't that large, so allow plenty of room for growth.

The REMOTE_LOGIN_PASSWORDFILE parameter

The `REMOTE_LOGIN_PASSWORDFILE` initialization parameter, which, as noted earlier, is a key part of creating a password file, controls how your database instance uses the password file. You can set three possible values:

✦ **None** — No password file is used. This is the default setting.

✦ **Shared** — Multiple databases may share one password file. You are limited to one entry for the internal password.

✦ **Exclusive** — The password file is used exclusively by one database. It may contain entries for any number of users.

You set `REMOTE_LOGIN_PASSWORDFILE` by placing a line like the following in your database's parameter file:

```
REMOTE_LOGIN_PASSWORDFILE = EXCLUSIVE
```

In the above example, the exclusive value is set. The next subsections describe each of the options in more detail.

Using the None Option

The default value, none, is used for the starter database that you get when you first install Oracle. If you are using operating system authentication, or if you don't want to allow for remote administration by tools such as Oracle Enterprise Manager, you can leave the setting at none.

Using the Shared Option

Setting the `REMOTE_LOGIN_PASSWORDFILE` parameter to shared allows you to share one password file among several databases. When you share a password file, you are limited to just one entry for the internal password. You won't be allowed to grant `SYSDBA` or `SYSOPER` privileges. The practical effect of sharing a password file is that the internal password will be the same for all of the databases using that file. Once you give a DBA access to one database, you've given him or her access to all.

Sharing password files can be a bit of a trick. Remember, the SID forms part of the password file name, so if you have two databases, you will have two SIDS, and Oracle will be looking for two different file names. To get two databases to use the same password file, you need to create one of the files as a link to another. For example:

```
$ orapwd file=orapwGOLD password=justin
$ ln -f orapwGOLD orapwSEED
```

The UNIX `ln` command in this example creates a link from `orapwSEED` to `orapwGOLD`. In effect, UNIX is making one file look like two. When Oracle tries to open `orapwSEED`, it will really be opening `orapwGOLD`. By linking your files in this way, you can have several databases sharing the same password file.

Using the Exclusive Option

You use the exclusive option when you want a password file to be used by only one database. When you have an exclusive, one-to-one relationship between password file and database, Oracle allows you to grant `SYSDBA` and `SYSOPER` to users other than `INTERNAL` and `SYS`. The number of users to which you can grant those privileges is determined by the number of entries that you allocate when creating the password file. The following command, for example, creates a password file sized to hold records for ten users:

```
orapwd file=orapwGOLD password=justin entries=10
```

If you are using Oracle Enterprise Manager to manage your databases and you want to allow yourself and other database administrators to connect remotely, then you need to use the exclusive option.

Managing Administrative Users

Once you've created the password file and set the `REMOTE_LOGIN_PASSWORDFILE` parameter to *exclusive*, you can enroll database users as administrators. You do this by connecting as an administrator yourself and granting the appropriate privileges (either `SYSDBA` or `SYSOPER`) to the users who need them. Once you've granted a user the `SYSDBA` privilege or the `SYSOPER` privilege, that user gets an entry in the password file. The entry remains until you revoke the privilege.

Granting administrator privileges

To grant a user either the `SYSDBA` or `SYSOPER` privilege, you need to be connected to Oracle as `SYSDBA` or using the internal connection. You might think that you could log on as a user with full DBA privileges, such as the user SYSTEM, and grant `SYSDBA` privileges, but you can't. Here's what happens if you try:

```
SQL> connect system/manager
Connected.
SQL> grant sysdba to jaimie;
grant sysdba to jaimie
*
ORA-01031: insufficient privileges
```

The reason the grant failed is because you logged on normally and not as `SYSDBA`. In this next example, the user correctly logs on as an administrator before attempting the grant:

```
SQL> connect system/manager as sysdba;
Connected.
SQL> grant sysdba to jaimie;
Statement processed.
```

This time the statement worked. The user Jaimie now has the SYSDBA role. She has something else, too — a record in the password file. From this point forward, Jaimie's database password will be stored both within the database and inside the password file. When Jaimie issues an ALTER USER command to change her password, that password is changed in the password file as well.

Using Oracle Security Manager

SYSDBA and SYSOPER privileges may also be granted from Oracle Security Manager, which is part of the Oracle Enterprise Manager toolset. Security Manager treats SYSDBA and SYSOPER as if they were just another system privilege. Figure 4-2 shows SYSDBA being granted to a user named JONATHAN:

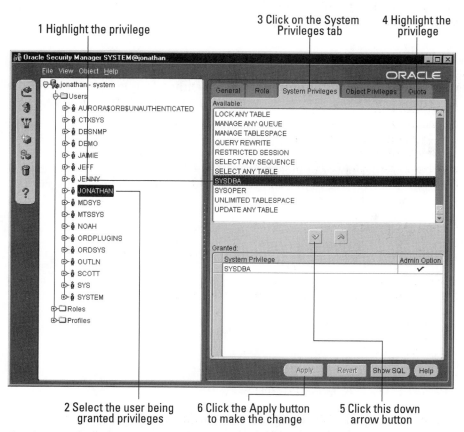

Figure 4-2: The SYSDBA role has been granted to JONATHAN.

Just as with SQL*Plus and Server Manager, you need to be connected as SYSDBA when using Security Manager to grant either the SYSOPER or SYSDBA privileges.

Making the First Privilege Grant

One problem that you might encounter when you first create a password file is that none of your users will have the SYSDBA privilege to start with. If no one has it, how can you grant it? You can usually get around this by connecting internally. When you connect using the keyword INTERNAL, you have full control over the database, and you will be able to grant the SYSDBA privilege. Here's an example:

```
SQL> connect internal
Connected.
SQL> grant sysdba to system;
Statement processed.
```

Another solution, and probably the one that Oracle would recommend, would be to log on to the server as the Oracle software owner and connect as SYSDBA using operating system authentication. For example:

```
SQL> connect / as sysdba
Connected.
SQL>
```

Connecting this way using operating system authentication should work if you have logged on as the Oracle software owner or as a member of the dba group.

Listing administrators

The dynamic performance view named V$PWFILE_USERS reflects the current contents of the password file, and you can query it to see which users currently have administrator privileges. To see a list of administrators, issue a SELECT query such as the following:

```
SQL> SELECT * FROM v$pwfile_users;
USERNAME                        SYSDBA SYSOPER
------------------------------- ------ -------
INTERNAL                        TRUE   TRUE
SYS                             TRUE   TRUE
JAIMIE                          TRUE   FALSE
SYSTEM                          TRUE   FALSE
JENNY                           FALSE  TRUE
JEFF                            FALSE  TRUE
6 rows selected.
```

The results are easy to interpret. Users with a value of TRUE in the SYSDBA column have the SYSDBA privilege. Users with a value of TRUE in the SYSOPER column have the SYSOPER privilege. Users not in the list have neither privilege.

Revoking administrator privileges

To revoke SYSOPER and SYSDBA privileges, you need to log on either as SYSDBA or connect internally. Once you've done that, you'll be able to revoke the privileges from users who no longer need them. The following example shows the SYSDBA privilege being revoked from the user named JEFF:

```
SQL> $sqlplus /nolog

SQL*Plus: Release 8.1.5.0.0 - Production on Wed May 19 22:24:15 1999

(c) Copyright 1999 Oracle Corporation.  All rights reserved.

SQL> CONNECT system/manager AS SYSDBA;
Connected.
SQL> REVOKE SYSDBA FROM jeff;
Statement processed.
SQL>
```

Once you've revoked a user's administrator privileges, his or her entry in the password file is no longer necessary. The entry will be deleted, and the space will be made available for use next time you grant a user SYSDBA or SYSOPER privileges.

You can never revoke SYSDBA or SYSOPER privileges from the internal connection. Oracle simply won't let you do that. If you try, you will get an error. Anyone connecting as internal always has full control over the database.

Deleting a Password File

If you currently have a password file for your database, you can remove it if you decide that you no longer want to support remote connections. To delete a password file, you should follow these steps:

1. Shut down the instance to close the database.

2. Change the value of the REMOTE_LOGIN_PASSWORDFILE parameter to none.

3. Delete the password file.

4. Restart the instance and open the database.

With the password file deleted, remote users will no longer be able to connect as SYSDBA, SYSOPER, or using the INTERNAL keyword.

Rebuilding a Password File

Someday, you may find that you need to add more users to a password file than you had originally planned for. You'll know when this happens because you'll get the error shown in the following example:

```
SVRMGR> grant sysdba to noah;
grant sysdba to oem
*
ORA-01996: GRANT failed: password file 'C:\Oracle\Ora81\DATABASE\PWDcoin.ORA' is
 full
SVRMGR>
```

When your password file is full and you still want to add another user, your only recourse is to delete the existing password file and create a new one with more entries. Here is the procedure that you should follow to do this:

1. Connect to the database and grab a list of current password file entries. You can use SELECT * FROM v$pwfile_users to do that.

2. Revoke each user's SYSDBA and SYSOPER privileges. Remember that you must be connected as SYSDBA to do this.

3. Make a note of the current internal password if you want to keep it.

4. Shut down the database.

5. Create a new password file with a sufficient number of entries. You can supply your current internal password to the orapwd command if you would like to keep it the same.

6. Restart the database.

7. Grant SYSDBA and SYSOPER to the users who need those privileges.

The key to this procedure is the first step, where you make a list of current password file entries. This won't give you the passwords for those users, but you don't need their passwords anyway. After you've re-created the password file, you need to regrant the same privileges to the same users. As you do that, Oracle creates a password file entry for each user. When you are done, everyone's privileges will be back to the way they were before you started.

Summary

In this chapter, you learned:

✦ Oracle supports three ways to connect to an instance when you want to perform administrative tasks such as starting or stopping the instance. You can connect internally, which uses a deprecated feature of Oracle, or you can connect in either the SYSDBA or SYSOPER role.

✦ Oracle uses password files to authenticate database administrators who must connect remotely from another computer on the network. These password files are external to the database so that they can be accessed even when the database is closed. This is necessary, for example, when a DBA connects in order to start a database.

✦ To grant `SYSDBA` and `SYSOPER` privileges to your DBAs, enabling them to connect remotely, you must have a password file with more than just one entry. You must also set the value of the `REMOTE_LOGIN_PASSWORDFILE` initialization parameter to *exclusive*.

✦ On Windows NT, password files are located in the Database folder underneath the Oracle home directory (`c:\oracle\ora81\database`, for example), and password files are named `PWDXXXX.ora`, where `XXXX` represents the instance name.

✦ On most UNIX systems, the password file location is `$ORACLE_HOME/dbs`, and the naming convention is `orapwXXXX`, with no file extension being used.

✦   ✦   ✦

Configuring Net8

It's a networked world out there, and Oracle is smack dab in the middle of it. Not only do client-server applications hit Oracle databases, but databases also communicate with each other, and application servers execute database queries on behalf of Internet and intranet clients.

In this chapter, you'll learn about Net8, which is Oracle's networking software. You'll learn about the various Net8 components, both on the server and on the client. You'll also learn some of the more common ways to configure Net8 server and client software. Finally, you'll read about some useful troubleshooting techniques that you can use to resolve Net8 connectivity problems.

Describing the Net8 Oracle Networking Software

Net8 is Oracle's networking software. Its purpose is to provide a common communication protocol for all Oracle software to use. Oracle clients can use Net8 to communicate with database servers; servers use Net8 to communicate with other servers. From an application development standpoint, Net8 provides a common interface that works the same regardless of the underlying networking technology or hardware platforms being used.

Note　　Oracle's networking software used to be called SQL*Net. With the release of Oracle8, the name was changed to Net8.

Figure 5-1 shows a simplified representation of how Net8 fits into the client/server picture. As you can see, requests from a client software application are passed to Net8. Net8 then transmits those requests to the database server using a low-level networking protocol such as TCP/IP or SPX.

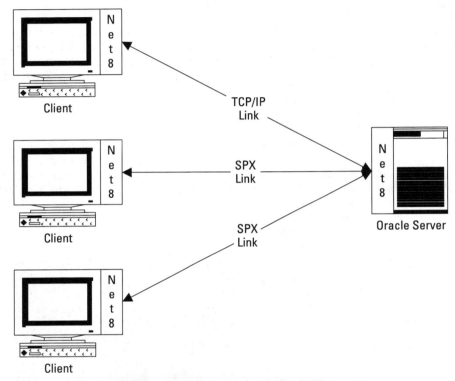

Figure 5-1: Net8 enables client applications to communicate with an Oracle database.

Because Net8 works the same from an application point of view, regardless of the underlying networking protocol being used, it is said to be *network transparent*. To move an application from one network environment to another, all you have to do is use the appropriate Net8 protocol adapter for that environment.

Net8 is also location transparent and operating-system transparent. It is *location transparent* because application programs do not need to know the name of the server to which they are connecting. Net8 is *operating-system transparent* because it works the same regardless of whether it is running on Windows NT, UNIX, Novell, or any other operating system that Oracle supports.

Net8 server components

The Net8 server component that you will be most concerned with is Net8 listener. The listener is a process that runs on a database server to monitor the network for incoming database connection requests. You interact with the listener by using a program called the Listener Control program.

In addition to the listener is the Net8 Assistant, a Java program that gives you an easy-to-use GUI interface for setting and modifying a variety of Net8 parameters. Oracle servers usually have the Net8 Client components, such as Net8 Easy Config and `tnsping`, installed as well. You'll read more about these client components later in this chapter.

The Net8 listener

The Net8 listener's job is to monitor the network, or *listen,* for requests to connect to one of the databases on a database server. When an incoming request is detected, the listener validates that request, logs the client on to the database, and hands the client off to a server process, or possibly a dispatcher process. Figure 5-2 illustrates this sequence of events.

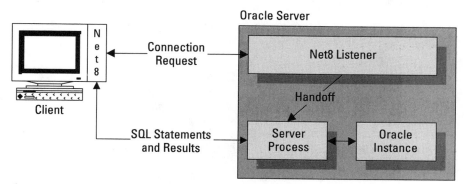

Figure 5-2: Net8 Listener accepts incoming connection requests.

Once the connection has been made and the remote user has been logged on to the database, the listener has no further role to play. All further communication takes place between the client and either a server process or a dispatcher process. However, the listener does listen for other connection requests.

Listener Control

The Listener Control program is your primary means of interacting with the Net8 listener. You can use the Listener Control program to stop and start the listener, check the status of the listener, turn on tracing, or set one of several options. The screen output shown in Listing 5.1 demonstrates Listener Control being used to *bounce*, that is, to stop and start, a listener:

Listing 5-1: **Using the Listener Control program**

```
C:\>lsnrctl

LSNRCTL for 32-bit Windows: Version 8.1.5.0.0 - Production on 25-JUL-99 18:11:50


(c) Copyright 1998 Oracle Corporation.  All rights reserved.

Welcome to LSNRCTL, type "help" for information.

LSNRCTL> set password bonk
The command completed successfully
LSNRCTL> stop
Connecting to (DESCRIPTION=(ADDRESS=(PROTOCOL=IPC)(KEY=EXTPROC0)))
The command completed successfully
LSNRCTL> start
Starting tnslsnr: please wait...

Service OracleOraHome81TNSListener start pending.
Service OracleOraHome81TNSListener started.
TNSLSNR for 32-bit Windows: Version 8.1.5.0.0 - Production
System parameter file is E:\ORACLE\ORA81\NETWORK\ADMIN\listener.ora
Log messages written to E:\Oracle\Ora81\network\log\listener.log
Listening on: (DESCRIPTION=(ADDRESS=(PROTOCOL=IPC)(KEY=EXTPROC0)))
Listening on: (DESCRIPTION=(ADDRESS=(PROTOCOL=TCP)(HOST=jonathan)(PORT=1521)))
Listening on: (DESCRIPTION=(PROTOCOL_STACK=(PRESENTATION=GIOP)(SESSION=RAW))(ADD
RESS=(PROTOCOL=TCP)(HOST=jonathan)(PORT=2481)))

Connecting to (DESCRIPTION=(ADDRESS=(PROTOCOL=IPC)(KEY=EXTPROC0)))
STATUS of the LISTENER
------------------------
Alias                    LISTENER
Version                  TNSLSNR for 32-bit Windows: Version 8.1.5.0.0 - Produc
tion
Start Date               25-JUL-99 18:12:00
Uptime                   0 days 0 hr. 0 min. 2 sec
Trace Level              off
Security                 ON
SNMP                     OFF
Listener Parameter File  E:\ORACLE\ORA81\NETWORK\ADMIN\listener.ora
Listener Log File        E:\Oracle\Ora81\network\log\listener.log
```

```
Services Summary...
  PLSExtProc           has 1 service handler(s)
  JONATHAN             has 1 service handler(s)
The command completed successfully
LSNRCTL>
```

 Cross-Reference The most common Listener Control commands are described later in this chapter in the section "Configuring Net8 on the Server."

Multiple Listeners

In Figure 5-2 and in the previous example, the server was assumed to have only one Net8 listener process running; however, you can have multiple listener processes running at once. You might do this to ensure the complete separation of production and test databases. Having separate listeners means that you can take the listener for one database down without affecting the other database. There's an example later in this chapter showing you how to configure multiple listeners.

Net8 Assistants

In addition to the listener and the Listener Control program, a server may have two assistants: Net8 Assistant and Net8 Configuration Assistant. Oracle uses the term assistant to describe what Microsoft calls a wizard. An *assistant* is a program that helps you perform a complex task by gathering information from you in a user-friendly manner, and then it carries out the task for you.

Net8 Assistant is a nice GUI interface that you can use to configure the Net8 software on your server. You perform most Net8 configuration by editing various text files, some of which use some rather arcane syntax. Net8 Assistant lets you fill in forms and dialog boxes and then uses that information to edit the text files for you. Net8 Configuration Assistant walks you through some of the common Net8 configuration tasks that you need to perform after first installing Oracle8i software on a server.

Net8 Client components

A PC running Oracle client software will typically have the following Net8 components installed:

✦ Net8 Client

✦ Net8 Easy Config

Releases of Oracle prior to 8.1 also included protocol adapters as part of the Net8 Client software. You would pick which protocol adapters to install based on the network protocols in use at your site. With Oracle8i, the protocol adapters have been bundled into the basic Net8 Client software. You can no longer install them separately.

Net8 Client

For the most part, Net8 Client software consists of dynamic link libraries (DLLs on Windows NT) that are used by programs written to interact with an Oracle database. There's no process, like the listener, always running in the background. There's no stand-alone *program* that you can run from the Start menu.

From a configuration standpoint, the most significant part of the Net8 Client software installation is the two configuration files named sqlnet.ora and tnsnames.ora. Correctly configuring these files is the key to being able to connect to an Oracle database running on a server.

Net8 Easy Config

Net8 Easy Config is an assistant that puts a user-friendly face on the task of editing your local tnsnames.ora file. The tnsnames.ora file is a critical Net8 configuration file. You use it to define the remote databases to which you will be able to connect. The syntax used in the tnsnames.ora file is tough to follow and involves multiple levels of nested parentheses. If you edit this file by hand, it's easy to make a mistake, perhaps by leaving out a parenthesis. Oracle created Net8 Easy Config to simplify the process of editing the tnsnames.ora file and to reduce the risk of error.

Note   The version of Net8 Easy Config that shipped with Oracle 8.1.5 is the first one that truly merits "easy" as part of its name. Previous versions didn't deal well with tnsnames.ora files that had been edited by hand. In release 8.1.5, Net8 Easy Config can not only handle manually edited tnsnames.ora files, but it also reformats them in a standard way so that they are easy to read.

Configuring Net8 on the Server

Configuring Net8 on a database server generally involves editing a text file named listener.ora. After editing listener.ora, you will need to use the Listener Control program to stop and restart the listener so that your changes can take effect.

As an alternative to editing the listener.ora file, you may be able to use Net8 Assistant. It provides a GUI interface that you can use to edit the listener.ora file. In your listener.ora file, you need to specify the following:

✦ The number of listeners that you want to run

✦ The protocols that you want to support

✦ The databases for which you will accept connections

In addition, you may want to configure the tnsnames.ora file on a server just as you would on a client so that you can access databases on other servers.

Using the Listener Control program

You use the Listener Control program to control and monitor the operation of the Net8 listeners on a server. Use Listener Control to perform the following functions:

✦ Start a listener

✦ Stop a listener

✦ Check the status of a listener

The next few sections show you how to start the Listener Control program and how to use it to perform each of the above tasks.

Starting Listener Control

Listener Control is not a GUI utility. It's a command-line-based utility, and it must be started from the command prompt. The command used to start the Listener Control program is `lsnrctl`. Here is an example:

```
C:\>lsnrctl

LSNRCTL for 32-bit Windows: Version 8.1.5.0.0 - Production on 25-JUL-99 18:11:50


(c) Copyright 1998 Oracle Corporation.  All rights reserved.

Welcome to LSNRCTL, type "help" for information.

LSNRCTL>
```

Tip
Remember that "control" is abbreviated in the command as "ctl" and not as "ctrl." You may find yourself occasionally typing "lsnrctrl" instead.

Starting a Listener

For remote clients to connect to a database on a server, a listener process must be running on that server. You use the `start` command to start a listener, and the syntax looks like this:

```
start [listener_name]
```

The syntax is described as follows:

✦ `start` — The command to start a listener.

✦ `listener_name` — The name of the listener that you want to start. This defaults to "listener."

Listing 5-2 shows a listener being started.

Listing 5-2: **Starting a listener**

```
LSNRCTL> start listener
Starting tnslsnr: please wait...

Service OracleOraHome81TNSListener start pending.
Service OracleOraHome81TNSListener started.
TNSLSNR for 32-bit Windows: Version 8.1.5.0.0 - Production
System parameter file is E:\ORACLE\ORA81\NETWORK\ADMIN\listener.ora
Log messages written to E:\Oracle\Ora81\network\log\listener.log
Listening on: (DESCRIPTION=(ADDRESS=(PROTOCOL=IPC)(KEY=EXTPROC0)))
Listening on: (DESCRIPTION=(ADDRESS=(PROTOCOL=TCP)(HOST=jonathan)(PORT=1521)))
Listening on: (DESCRIPTION=(PROTOCOL_STACK=(PRESENTATION=GIOP)(SESSION=RAW))(ADD
RESS=(PROTOCOL=TCP)(HOST=jonathan)(PORT=2481)))

Connecting to (DESCRIPTION=(ADDRESS=(PROTOCOL=IPC)(KEY=EXTPROC0)))
STATUS of the LISTENER
------------------------
Alias                      LISTENER
Version                    TNSLSNR for 32-bit Windows: Version 8.1.5.0.0 - Produc
tion
Start Date                 25-JUL-99 18:12:00
Uptime                     0 days 0 hr. 0 min. 2 sec
Trace Level                off
Security                   ON
SNMP                       OFF
Listener Parameter File    E:\ORACLE\ORA81\NETWORK\ADMIN\listener.ora
Listener Log File          E:\Oracle\Ora81\network\log\listener.log
Services Summary...
  PLSExtProc               has 1 service handler(s)
  JONATHAN                 has 1 service handler(s)
The command completed successfully
LSNRCTL>
```

Once you've started a listener, remote clients will be able to connect to any databases served by that listener.

Stopping a Listener

You use the stop command to stop a listener. The syntax looks like this:

```
stop [listener_name]
```

The syntax is described as follows:

✦ stop — The command to stop a listener.

✦ *listener_name* — The name of the listener that you want to stop. This defaults to "listener."

The following example shows a listener being stopped:

```
LSNRCTL> stop listener
Connecting to (DESCRIPTION=(ADDRESS=(PROTOCOL=IPC)(KEY=EXTPROC0)))
The command completed successfully
LSNRCTL>
```

Stopping a listener prevents remote clients from connecting to databases served by that listener.

Checking a Listener's Status

You use the `status` command to check the status of a listener. It is often used when troubleshooting connectivity problems to verify that the listener is running. The syntax looks like this:

```
status [listener_name]
```

The syntax is described as follows:

- ✦ `status` — The command used to get a listener's status.

- ✦ `listener_name` — The name of the listener that you are interested in. This defaults to "listener."

Listing 5-3 shows how you would check the status of the default listener.

Listing 5-3: **Checking a listener's status**

```
LSNRCTL> status listener
Connecting to (DESCRIPTION=(ADDRESS=(PROTOCOL=IPC)(KEY=EXTPROC0)))
STATUS of the LISTENER
------------------------
Alias                     LISTENER
Version                   TNSLSNR for 32-bit Windows: Version 8.1.5.0.0 - Produc
tion
Start Date                25-JUL-99 20:23:22
Uptime                    0 days 0 hr. 1 min. 46 sec
Trace Level               off
Security                  ON
SNMP                      OFF
Listener Parameter File   E:\ORACLE\ORA81\NETWORK\ADMIN\listener.ora
Listener Log File         E:\Oracle\Ora81\network\log\listener.log
Services Summary...
Service "PLSExtProc"            has 1 instances.
    Instance "PLSExtProc"            has 0 handlers.
Service "jonathan.gennick"          has 1 instances.
    Instance "JONATHAN"        has 0 handlers.
The command completed successfully
LSNRCTL>
```

The status command gives you several pieces of useful information. It tells you where the listener parameter file, listener.ora, is located. It tells you when the listener was started and how long it has been running. It also gives you a list of services, usually databases, for which the listener is listening. Take a look at the services summary section of the previous status output:

```
Services Summary...
Service "PLSExtProc"          has 1 instances.
    Instance "PLSExtProc"          has 0 handlers.
Service "jonathan.gennick"          has 1 instances.
    Instance "JONATHAN"       has 0 handlers.
The command completed successfully
```

The first service is PLSExtProc. This isn't a database service; PLSExtProc is a service that allows PL/SQL code running on Windows NT servers to make calls to external DLL routines. The second service is named jonathan.gennick, and it is a database service. This tells you that this listener will handle incoming connection requests for the database named jonathan in the gennick domain.

Setting a Password

You have the option of password-protecting your listeners to prevent unauthorized people from starting them, stopping them, or otherwise affecting their operation. If you have password-protected a listener, you will need to use the set password command to enter the appropriate password before you can operate that listener. The syntax for the set password command looks like this:

```
set password [password]
```

✦ set password — The command for setting the listener password.

✦ password — The password that you want to set. If you omit this argument, you will be prompted for the password.

The following example shows the set password command being used:

```
LSNRCTL> set password
Password:
The command completed successfully
LSNRCTL>
```

Note that the password was not passed as an argument. It could be, but in this case the argument was omitted so that Listener Control would prompt for the password. This is because Listener Control doesn't echo the characters typed in response to the prompt. This prevents people from looking over your shoulder and spotting the password as you type it.

Note You password-protect a listener by placing a PASSWORDS_LISTENER entry into your listener.ora file.

Locating the listener.ora file

The listener.ora file is a text file containing a number of settings that control the operation of the listener and that tell the listener which databases to listen for. Finding this file can sometimes be a challenge. The default location depends on the operating system that you are using. On Windows NT running Oracle8i, you'll find the listener.ora file in the following subdirectory underneath the Oracle software directory:

```
network\admin
```

 Note　The 8.0.*x* releases of Oracle on Windows NT used net8\admin for the directory. The 7.*x.x* releases used network\admin.

On UNIX systems, the default location for `listener.ora` will be one of the following directories:

```
/var/opt/oracle
/etc
$ORACLE_HOME/network/admin
```

The directory used as the default location on UNIX systems can vary from one vendor's version of UNIX to another. If you have any doubts about the location on your system, consult the operating-system-specific documentation that came with your Oracle8i software distribution.

If you don't want to use the default listener.ora location, you can specify some other directory as the location. The `TNS_ADMIN` environment variable is used for that purpose.

Using the TNS_ADMIN environment variable

If you don't like Oracle's default location for your Net8 files, you can use the `TNS_ADMIN` environment variable to point to whatever directory you want. Just make sure that you copy or move your Net8 configuration files (listener.ora, tnsnames.ora, sqlnet.ora, and so on) to the location that you have specified.

If you're running Windows NT, you have a choice between specifying `TNS_ADMIN` as an environment variable or as a registry entry. To set it as an environment variable, open the System control panel, click the Environment tab, and create a new variable named `TNS_ADMIN`. Figure 5-3 shows the `TNS_ADMIN` variable in the Windows NT System Properties dialog box. In this case, Oracle will look in the e:\oracle\ora81\ network\admin directory for any Net8 configuration files.

If you prefer to specify `TNS_ADMIN` as a registry setting, then be aware that it is Oracle home-specific. For example, the registry entries controlling the operation of Oracle Enterprise Manager can be in the following key on a Windows NT system:

```
HKEY_LOCAL_MACHINE\SOFTWARE\ORACLE\HOME2
```

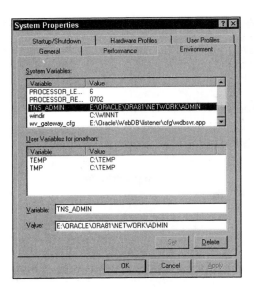

Figure 5-3: The TNS_ADMIN environment variable pointing to the directory containing the Net8 configuration files

Underneath that key in our example, a TNS_ADMIN variable is pointing to the network\admin directory for the database software. That way, both Enterprise Manager and the database share the same Net8 configuration files. (See Figure 5-4.)

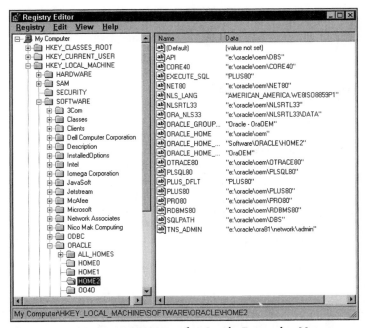

Figure 5-4: A TNS_ADMIN entry for Oracle Enterprise Manager

With the release of Oracle8i, Oracle has moved toward a model of installing each product in its own Oracle home. So if you have installed Oracle8i, WebDB, and Enterprise Manager, you will have three Oracle homes on your server. In a case like that, TNS_ADMIN provides a handy mechanism to point all those products to the same set of Net8 configuration files.

Looking at the listener.ora syntax

The listener.ora file defines one or more Net8 listeners that monitor the network for incoming database connection requests. For each listener, the file contains the following:

✦ Listener address information

✦ A list of Oracle instances for which the listener is listening

✦ Optional control parameters

The default installation of Oracle results in one listener being defined. The name of that listener is LISTENER, which tends to confuse some people more then help them because of the way the listener name is worked into the listener.ora syntax.

Listener Names and listener.ora Parameters

If you look in the listener.ora file created by a fresh install of the Oracle server software, you'll see two entries that look like this:

```
LISTENER =
  (
  ...
  )

SID_LIST_LISTENER =
  (
  ...
  )
```

The first entry defines the protocols that the listener recognizes, as well as the addresses on which the listener listens. The second entry contains a list of instances for which the listener will accept connections. In each case, the listener's name forms part of the keyword that begins each entry. The listener name in this example is LISTENER.

If you wanted to, you could define a second listener. To do that, just pick a name and place two corresponding entries in the listener.ora file. For example, suppose that you want a second listener named PRODUCTION_LISTENER. The entries for that listener would look like this:

```
PRODUCTION_LISTENER =
  (
  . . .
  )

SID_LIST_PRODUCTION_LISTENER =
  (
  . . .
  )
```

This naming convention—that is, using the listener name as part of the keyword—is used for all entries in the listener.ora file. You can see some examples later, in the section "Studying Listener.ora Examples."

The Listener Address Section

The listener address entry defines the protocols that your listener will recognize and the addresses (ports for TCP/IP) that the listener monitors. The syntax for this section is shown in Listing 5-4.

Listing 5-4: Syntax for the listener address

```
LISTENER =
  (DESCRIPTION_LIST =
    (DESCRIPTION =
      (ADDRESS =
        (PROTOCOL = TCP)(HOST = oak.gennick.com)(PORT = 1521))
      (PROTOCOL_STACK =
        (PRESENTATION = TTC)
        (SESSION = NS)
      )
    )
    (DESCRIPTION =
      (ADDRESS =
        (PROTOCOL = TCP)(HOST = oak.gennick.com)(PORT = 2481))
      (PROTOCOL_STACK =
        (PRESENTATION = GIOP)
        (SESSION = RAW)
      )
    )
  )
```

Whoever dreamed up this syntax must have had a fetish for parentheses! It's easy to get a bit cross-eyed trying to make the parentheses match up when editing one of these files by hand. Here are descriptions of each of the syntax elements shown in the example:

`DESCRIPTION_LIST`	Identifies list protocol addresses, together with their respective protocol stack specifications.
`DESCRIPTION`	Identifies a specific protocol address and protocol stack specification.
`ADDRESS`	Defines the address used by a listener for a specific protocol. The format for this parameter varies with the protocol being used. See Table 5-1.
`PROTOCOL_STACK`	Specifies the presentation layer and session layers to use. There are only two choices: `(PRESENTATION = TTC) (SESSION = NS)`, which is the default, is used for Net8 connections to the database; `(PRESENTATION = GIOP)` `(SESSION = RAW)` allows connections to Java code using the General Inter-orb Protocol (GIOP).

Consider the following points about the syntax used in listener.ora, as well as in the other Net8 configuration files that you will read about later in this chapter:

✦ The `listener.ora` file keywords are not case sensitive. The values used with those keywords usually aren't either, but they may be, depending on the specific operating system and network protocol being used.

Note   Although SQL*Net is not case sensitive, it turns out that the Intelligent Agent used by OEM requires that the keywords all be in uppercase. You will not be able to use some of the OEM options (tuning, change management) if these are not included correctly.

✦ The spacing and line breaks don't have to be exactly as shown. The format you see here is that produced by Oracle's Net8 Assistant.

✦ The specific order of elements within an enclosing element isn't important. If you are specifying a TCP/IP address, for example, it would be just as acceptable to use `(PROTOCOL = TCP)(HOST = oak.gennick.com)` `(PORT = 1521))` as it would be to use `(HOST = oak.gennick.com)` `(PROTOCOL = TCP) (PORT = 1521))`.

This TCP/IP address tells the listener that the database server is named `oak` and that the listener should monitor TCP/IP port 1521 for incoming database connection requests. Table 5-1 shows the address entry format for TCP/IP and all the other protocols supported by Net8.

Table 5-1
Listener.ora Address Entry Formats

Protocol	ADDRESS Entry Syntax	Notes

TCP/IP	```(ADDRESS =```
	 ``` (PROTOCOL = TCP)```
	 ``` (HOST = host_name)```
	 ``` (PORT = port_number)```
	 ```)```
		The port number 1521 is generally used for the listener. Port 2481 is used for connections to Java routines in the database. The server's IP address may be used in place of the host name. The port number in the listener.ora file must match that used in the tnsnames.ora file on client machines.

IPC	```(ADDRESS =```
	 ``` (PROTOCOL = IPC)```
	 ``` (KEY = service_name)```
	 ```)```
		IPC is used to connect to remote procedures, such as those in a Windows DLL file.

Named Pipes	```(ADDRESS =```
	 ``` (PROTOCOL = NMP)```
	 ``` (SERVER = server_name)```
	 ``` (PIPE = pipe_name)```
	 ```)```
		The pipe name may be any arbitrary value, but it must match an entry in a client's tnsnames.ora file for a connection to be made.

LU6.2	```(ADDRESS =```
	 ``` (PROTOCOL = LU62)```
	 ``` (LU_NAME = server_name)```
	 ``` (LOCAL_LU =```
	 ``` local_lu_alias)```
	 ``` (LOCAL_LU_NAME =```
	 ``` local_lu_name)```
	 ``` (MODE = log_mode_entry)```
	 ``` (PARTNER_LU_NAME =```
	 ``` server_name)```
	 ``` (PARTNER_LU_```
	 ``` LOCAL_ALIAS =```
	 ``` partner_lu_alias)```
	 ``` (TP_NAME = transaction_```
	 ``` program_name)```
	 ```)```
		You can use LLU, LLU_NAME, MDN, PLU, and PLU_LA in place of LU_NAME, LOCAL_LU_NAME, MODE, z PARTNER_LU_NAME, and PARTNER_LU_LOCAL_ ALIAS, respectively. You either have to use an alias or a name, but not both. For example, you have to choose between LU_NAME and LOCAL_LU. Local names cannot be used with local aliases.

SPX	```(ADDRESS =```
	 ``` (PROTOCOL = SPX)```
	 ``` (SERVICE = service_name)```
	 ```)```
		SPX service names are arbitrary, but the name used in the tnsnames.ora file on client PCs must match the name used on the server.

The SID_List Entry

The SID_LIST entry for a listener contains a list of Oracle database instances for which the listener will accept connections. The SID_LIST entry also controls the number of dedicated server processes that the listener will prestart to have one ready and waiting when a user connects. The syntax for the SID_LIST entry is shown in Listing 5-5.

Listing 5-5: The syntax for the SID_LIST entry

```
SID_LIST_LISTENER =
  (SID_LIST =
    (SID_DESC =
      (GLOBAL_DBNAME = bible_db.oak.gennick.com)
      (SID_NAME = BIBDB)
      (PROGRAM_NAME = extproc)
      (ORACLE_HOME = /oracle/ora81)
      (PRESPAWN_MAX = 99)
      (PRESPAWN_LIST =
        (PRESPAWN_DESC =
          (PROTOCOL = TCP)
          (POOL_SIZE = 10)
          (TIMEOUT = 5)
        )
      )
    )
  )
)
```

The following list provides descriptions for each of the elements in the SID_LIST:

SID_LIST_LISTENER	Introduces the SID list entry for the listener named LISTENER. If your listener is named PRODUCTION_LISTENER, then you can use SID_LIST_PRODUCTION_LISTENER.
SID_LIST	Identifies a list of database instances associated with the listener in question. You need only one of these entries.
SID_DESC	Defines one database instance to the listener. You can have as many SID_DESC entries as you have databases. A number of entries falling underneath SID_DESC further define how the listener services a particular database.

GLOBAL_DBNAME — Specifies the global database name, including the domain, identifying a database. This must match the value of the SERVICE_NAMES parameter in the database's initialization file. This entry is optional. Use it if you want to reference the database by its global name when connecting to it.

SID_NAME — Specifies the instance name. This value should match the value of the INSTANCE_NAME parameter in the database's initialization file. This entry is optional, but you need to specify at least one SID_NAME or GLOBAL_DBNAME.

PROGRAM_NAME — Associates the SID_DESC entry with an executable program name.

ORACLE_HOME — Specifies the path of the Oracle home directory for the database in question.

PRESPAWN_MAX — Specifies the maximum number of prespawned dedicated server processes that the listener is allowed to create. A *prespawned server process* is one that is created in anticipation of a future user connection. This parameter must not be less than the sum of the POOL_SIZE parameters for the SID_LIST. This parameter is ignored in Windows NT because prespawned dedicated server processes can't be created on that operating system.

PRESPAWN_LIST — Introduces a list of prespawned dedicated server processes for a SID_DESC entry.

PRESPAWN_DESC — Defines a number of dedicated server processes to be prespawned for a particular Net8 protocol. You may have as many PRESPAWN_DESC entries as you desire.

PROTOCOL — Specifies the Net8 protocol for which you want to prespawn the dedicated server processes. The processes are protocol-specific, so if you are supporting multiple protocols, you will need to use multiple PRESPAWN_DESC entries to configure prespawned processes for those protocols. Note, however, that you don't need to create prespawned processes for each protocol that you support.

POOL_SIZE — Specifies the number of *unused* dedicated server processes that you want to keep on hand for possible user connections. Set this value to match what you expect the average number of connection attempts to be at any given time.

TIMEOUT   Applies to dedicated server processes that have been used, and from which a user has disconnected. The timeout controls the number of minutes that the process will remain in the pool waiting for a new connection before being terminated.

Control Parameters

In addition to the listener address information and the SID list, the listener.ora file may optionally contain any of several miscellaneous entries. These are referred to as control parameters, and they are described in Table 5-2.

Table 5-2
Listener.ora Control Parameters

Parameter Name and Example	Description
CONNECT_TIMEOUT CONNECT_TIMEOUT_ LISTENER = 10	Default: 10 seconds Specifies that the listener will wait up to 10 seconds for a valid connection request after a connection has been initiated.
LOG_DIRECTORY LOG_DIRECTORY_ LISTENER = $ORACLE_HOME/ network/log	Default: $ORACLE_HOME/network/log Tells the listener to write the listener log file to the $ORACLE_HOME/network/log directory.
LOG_FILE LOG_FILE_LISTENER = LISTENER.LOG	Default: LISTENER.LOG Tells the listener that the listener log file should be named LISTENER.LOG.
PASSWORDS PASSWORDS_LISTENER = (oracle) PASSWORDS_LISTENER = (oracle,big_secret, little_secret)	Default: none Specifies one or more unencrypted passwords that must be supplied by the DBA (using Listener Control's SET PASSWORD command) before Listener Control can be used to control the listener. The first example specifies a password of "oracle." The second example specifies several passwords, any one of which may be used.

Continued

Table 5-2 *(continued)*

Parameter Name and Example	Description
STARTUP_WAITTIME STARTUP_WAITTIME_ LISTENER = 5	Default: 0 seconds Tells the listener to sleep five seconds before responding to the first status command from the Listener Control program.
TRACE_DIRECTORY TRACE_DIRECTORY_ LISTENER = $ORACLE_HOME/ network/trace	Default: $ORACLE_HOME/network/trace Default: $ORACLE_HOME/network/trace Tells the listener to write trace files into the $ORACLE_HOME/network/trace directory.
TRACE_FILE TRACE_FILE_LISTENER = LISTENER.TRC	Default: LISTENER.TRC Controls the name to be used for a listener trace file.
TRACE_LEVEL TRACE_LEVEL_ LISTENER = SUPPORT	Default: OFF Controls the type of information written to a listener trace file. The OFF value means that no trace information will be generated. Values of USER, ADMIN, and SUPPORT result in trace files containing increasing levels of detail.
USE_PLUG_AND_PLAY USE_PLUG_AND_PLAY_ LISTENER = ON	Default: OFF Tells the listener whether it should automatically register itself with an Oracle Names server. Valid values are OFF and ON.

Pay attention to the fact that each control parameter has the listener name attached to it. The examples in Table 5-2 all used the default listener name LISTENER. If you had two listeners defined, named LISTENER and PRODUCTION_ LISTENER, you could specify parameters for each by qualifying the parameter name with the listener name. Here is an example that sets a password for each of those listeners:

```
PASSWORDS_LISTENER = (oracle)
PASSWORDS_PRODUCTION_LISTENER = (big_secret)
```

In this example, oracle is the password for the default listener, while big_secret is the password to the production listener named PRODUCTION_LISTENER.

Studying listener.ora examples

Sometimes it's easier to learn by example, and where Net8 is concerned, that's often the case. This section contains three sample listener.ora files that demonstrate some common configurations. To start with, you will see a basic, single-database configuration. Next, you will see how to modify that configuration to handle multiple databases. Finally, you will see how to configure multiple listeners and split several databases between them. These examples also use some of the control parameters.

One Listener, One Database

The following example in Listing 5-6 shows a listener.ora file that is pretty close to the default that you get when you first install Oracle. It defines one listener and gives it the default name of LISTENER. Only one protocol is supported, TCP/IP, and one database is in the SID list.

Listing 5-6: **A listener.ora file supporting one protocol and one listener**

```
LISTENER =
  (DESCRIPTION_LIST =
    (DESCRIPTION =
      (ADDRESS = (PROTOCOL = IPC)(KEY = EXTPROC0))
      (PROTOCOL_STACK =
        (PRESENTATION = TTC)
        (SESSION = NS)
      )
    )
    (DESCRIPTION =
      (ADDRESS =
        (PROTOCOL = TCP)
        (HOST = OAK.GENNICK.COM)
        (PORT = 1521))
      (PROTOCOL_STACK =
        (PRESENTATION = TTC)
        (SESSION = NS)
      )
    )
    (DESCRIPTION =
      (ADDRESS =
        (PROTOCOL = TCP)
        (HOST = OAK.GENNICK.COM)
        (PORT = 2481))
      (PROTOCOL_STACK =
        (PRESENTATION = GIOP)
        (SESSION = RAW)
      )
    )
```

Continued

Listing 5-6: *(continued)*

```
    )

SID_LIST_LISTENER =
  (SID_LIST =
    (SID_DESC =
      (SID_NAME = PLSExtProc)
      (ORACLE_HOME = E:\Oracle\Ora81)
      (PROGRAM = extproc)
    )
    (SID_DESC =
      (GLOBAL_DBNAME = BIBLE_DB.OAK.GENNICK.COM)
      (ORACLE_HOME = E:\Oracle\Ora81)
      (SID_NAME = BIBDB)
    )
  )
```

In this example, the `DESCRIPTION` entry referencing port 2481 supports connections to Oracle8i's internal Java engine. If you weren't using any Java features, you could omit that entry. The entry referring to `EXTPROC0` exists to allow PL/SQL to call external DLL routines. It too could be omitted.

One Listener, Two Databases

This example, shown in Listing 5-7, is similar to the previous example, but it eliminates support for Java and external DLLs, and it listens for two databases instead of just one. It also specifies a password `MUNISING` for the listener.

Listing 5-7: A listener.ora file supporting two databases

```
LISTENER =
  (DESCRIPTION_LIST =
    (DESCRIPTION =
      (ADDRESS =
        (PROTOCOL = TCP)
        (HOST = OAK.GENNICK.COM)
        (PORT = 1521))
      )
    )
  )

SID_LIST_LISTENER =
  (SID_LIST =
    (SID_DESC =
      (GLOBAL_DBNAME = BIBLE_DB.OAK.GENNICK.COM)
      (ORACLE_HOME = E:\Oracle\Ora81)
      (SID_NAME = BIBDB)
```

```
        )
(SID_DESC =
        (GLOBAL_DBNAME = PROD)
        (ORACLE_HOME = E:\Oracle\Ora81)
        (SID_NAME = PROD)
    )
)

PASSWORDS_LISTENER = (MUNISING)
```

In this example, the PASSWORDS_LISTENER entry defines a password for the listener. There are also two instances shown in the SID_LIST entry. One instance is named PROD, while the other is named BIBDB.

Two Listeners, Two Databases, and Two Protocols

The example shown in Listing 5-8 configures two listeners. One is listening for two databases, the other for one. The production listener supports only the TCP/IP protocol, while the development listener supports both TCP/IP and SPX. The listeners each have a password. The production listener is running in trace mode, generating a trace file for Oracle support to use in debugging a connectivity problem. The development listener isn't running in trace mode.

Listing 5-8: A listener.ora file supporting two listeners, two protocols, and two databases

```
DEVELOPMENT_LISTENER =
  (DESCRIPTION_LIST =
    (DESCRIPTION =
      (ADDRESS =
        (PROTOCOL = TCP)
        (HOST = OAK.GENNICK.COM)
        (PORT = 1521))
      )
      (ADDRESS =
        (PROTOCOL = SPX)
        (SERVICE = OAK)
        )
    )
  )

PRODUCTION_LISTENER =
  (DESCRIPTION_LIST =
    (DESCRIPTION =
      (ADDRESS =
        (PROTOCOL = TCP)
        (HOST = OAK.GENNICK.COM)
```

Continued

Listing 5-8: *(continued)*

```
        (PORT = 1522))
      )
    )
  )

SID_LIST_DEVELOPMENT_LISTENER =
  (SID_LIST =
    (SID_DESC =
      (GLOBAL_DBNAME = BIBLE_DB_TEST.OAK.GENNICK.COM)
      (ORACLE_HOME = E:\Oracle\Ora81)
      (SID_NAME = TEST)
    )
    (SID_DESC =
      (GLOBAL_DBNAME = BIBLE_DB_DEV.OAK.GENNICK.COM)
      (ORACLE_HOME = E:\Oracle\Ora81)
      (SID_NAME = DEV)
    )
  )

SID_LIST_PRODUCTION_LISTENER =
  (SID_LIST =
    (SID_DESC =
      (GLOBAL_DBNAME = BIBLE_DB_PROD.OAK.GENNICK.COM)
      (ORACLE_HOME = E:\Oracle\Ora81)
      (SID_NAME = PROD)
    )
  )

TRACE_DIRECTORY_DEVELOPMENT_LISTENER = c:\trace
TRACE_DIRECTORY_PRODUCTION_LISTENER = c:\trace
TRACE_FILE_DEVELOPMENT_LISTENER = DEV_LISTENER.TRC
TRACE_FILE_PRODUCTION_LISTENER = PROD_LISTENER.TRC
TRACE_LEVEL_DEVELOPMENT_LISTENER = OFF
TRACE_LEVEL_PRODUCTION_LISTENER = SUPPORT
PASSWORDS_DEVELOPMENT_LISTENER = (MUNISING)
PASSWORDS_PRODUCTION_LISTENER = (MARQUETTE)
```

Notice that this listing defines two listeners. One is named DEVELOPMENT_
LISTENER, and the other is named PRODUCTION_LISTENER. The entries defining
these two listeners are the first two in the file. Notice how the listener names
are made part of all the other parameter names in the file. The password for the
listener named PRODUCTION_LISTENER is defined by the PASSWORDS_PRODUCTION_
LISTENER entry. The password for the listener named DEVELOPMENT_LISTENER
is defined by the PASSWORDS_DEVELOPMENT_LISTENER entry. This naming
convention is used for all the other entries as well.

Using Oracle's Net8 Assistant

Having looked at the listener.ora syntax, you can see how easily you might make a mistake when editing this file by hand. It's particularly easy to end up with mismatched parentheses; in fact, Oracle support has historically been deluged with calls related to missing parentheses or other syntax errors in the Net8 configuration files.

Partly to combat the listener.ora syntax problems, and partly just to simplify life for DBAs in a world where everything is point and click, Oracle created a GUI-based program named Net8 Assistant for editing the Net8 configuration files. In Oracle8i, Net8 Assistant is a Java utility that allows you to configure general Net8 parameters in the sqlnet.ora file, Net8 service names in the tnsnames file, and listener parameters in the listener.ora file. Listener parameters are divided into these four categories:

✦ General parameters

✦ Listening locations

✦ Database services

✦ Other services

Figure 5-5 shows the General Parameters window for the default listener. The general parameters correspond to the control parameters that you read about earlier, and they are divided into three tabs named General, Logging & Tracing, and Authentication.

Editing these parameters is fairly intuitive — Net8 Assistant works like any other Windows application and comes complete with drop-down list boxes, radio button fields, check boxes, and text boxes. The Listening Locations window, shown in Figure 5-6, corresponds to the listener address section of the listener.ora file, and it allows you to specify the protocols that the listener will recognize. Figure 5-6 shows the address entry for the TCP/IP protocol.

The Database Services window, shown in Figure 5-7, corresponds to the SID list section of the listener.ora file. It allows you to define the databases for which the listener in question will accept connection requests.

You use the Other Services window, shown in Figure 5-8, to define nondatabase services, such as the PLSExtProc service, that are used when you make calls from PL/SQL to external DLL routines.

To run Net8 Assistant on a Windows NT system, go to the Start menu, point to Oracle, point to OraHome81, point to Network Administration program group, and select the Net8 Assistant icon. Make whatever changes you want and then use the File Save menu option to write out a new listener.ora file. You may have to bounce the listener, that is, stop and restart the listener, for some changes to take effect.

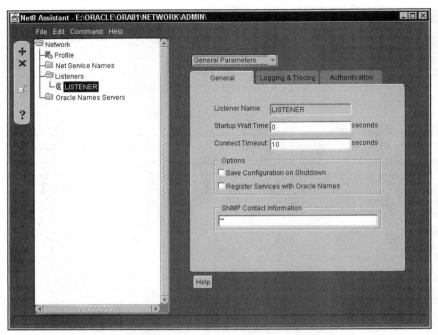

Figure 5-5: General parameters for the default listener

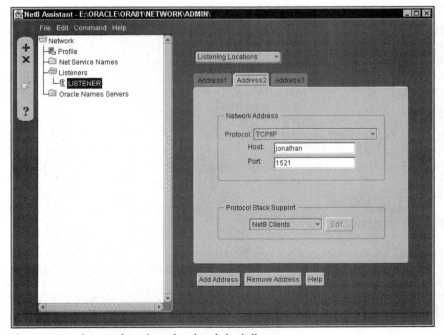

Figure 5-6: Listener locations for the default listener

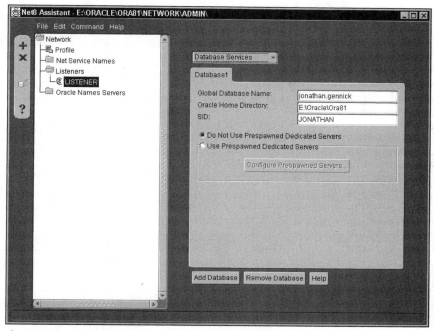

Figure 5-7: Database services for the default listener

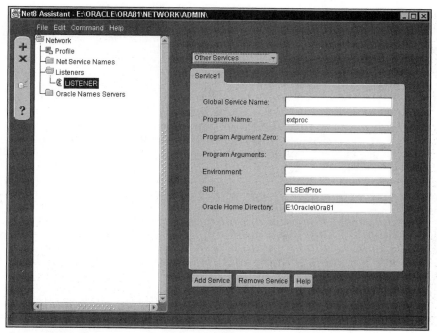

Figure 5-8: Other services for the default listener

Tip   Take a little time to become familiar with Net8 Assistant. Compare what you see on its screens with the information in your listener.ora file. Add database services or listeners using Net8 Assistant, and observe how it changes your listener.ora file.

Configuring Net8 on the Client

Configuring Net8 on a client involves editing two text files named sqlnet.ora and tnsnames.ora. As with the listener.ora file, these files—especially the tnsnames.ora file—tend to be burdened with multiple sets of nested parentheses. On a client, you place entries in the sqlnet.ora file to configure some general items such as the following:

✦ The name and location of the Net8 log file

✦ The order in which naming methods are used to try and resolve Net8 service names

✦ Preferred names servers

✦ The name and location of trace files

✦ The level of tracing, if any, that you want

If you are using the local naming method, you also place entries in a file named `tnsnames.ora` that define the following:

✦ Net8 service names

✦ The databases that those service names refer to

✦ The servers on which those databases reside

✦ The protocol (TCP/IP, SPX, and so on) used to communicate with those databases

The next few sections discuss how to locate the client configuration files, show you the syntax to use in these files, and provide some examples of typical configurations.

The client configuration files

The same considerations apply to finding the client configuration files as apply to finding the listener.ora file on the server. On Windows NT machines, you will find these files in:

```
c:\Oracle\Ora81\network\admin
```

Note that the `c:\Oracle\Ora81` directory represents the Oracle home directory that you created when you installed the software. If you choose a different Oracle home location, look in the `network\admin` directory underneath that Oracle home instead.

On UNIX platforms, the exact location of the Net8 configuration files depends on the operating system being used. Look in the following locations:

```
/var/opt/oracle (e.g. Unix System V)
/etc
$ORACLE_HOME/network/admin (e.g. HP-UX)
```

As on the server, you can set the `TNS_ADMIN` environment variable on the client to specify any directory you like as the location for the Net8 configuration files.

The sqlnet.ora syntax

The sqlnet.ora file contains parameters that control how Net8 operates. Far more parameters exist (many of which are related to the use of Oracle Names or to the different authentication methods that Oracle supports) than can be described in one chapter. Table 5-3 summarizes the most common among these parameters.

Table 5-3 Common sqlnet.ora Parameters	
Parameter Name and Example	**Description**
`NAMES.DEFAULT_DOMAIN` `NAMES.DEFAULT_DOMAIN = idg.com`	Default: `null` Specifies the default domain to append to unqualified Net8 service names. In this example, if a client attempts to connect to a service named `prod`, Net8 will automatically translate that to `prod.idg.com`.
`NAMES.DIRECTORY_PATH` `NAMES.DIRECTORY_PATH = (TNSNAMES, ONAMES)`	Default: (`TNSNAMES, ONAMES, HOSTNAME`) Specifies the naming methods that Oracle uses and the order in which Oracle uses them when trying to resolve a Net8 service name. In this example, Oracle will first look in the `tnsnames.ora` file, then look for an Oracle Names server, and finally attempt to use host naming to match the service name with a database.

Continued

Table 5-3 *(continued)*

Parameter Name and Example	Description
NAMES.INITIAL_ RETRY_TIMEOUT NAMES.INITIAL_ RETRY_TIMEOUT = 15	Default: 15 seconds Specifies the time, in seconds, that a client will wait for a request from one Oracle Names server before trying the next server in the preferred servers list. The valid range for this value is from 1 to 600 seconds.

NAMES.PREFERRED_SERVERS
 	
NAMES.PREFERRED_SERVERS]
  (ADDRESS_LIST =
    (ADDRESS =
      (PROTOCOL = TCP)
      (HOST = jonathan)
      (KEY = 1575))
    (ADDRESS =
      (PROTOCOL = IPC)
      (KEY = n01))
  ...
)
	Default: none
	Defines a list of Oracle Names servers in the order in which they will be used, in an attempt to resolve a Net8 service name.

SQLNET.EXPIRE_TIME SQLNET.EXPIRE_TIME = 10	Default: 0 minutes Sets the time interval between probes to see if a session is still alive. Sessions that don't respond to the probe are assumed to represent dropped user sessions and are terminated.
TRACE_DIRECTORY_CLIENT TRACE_DIRECTORY_CLIENT = c:\trace	Default: $ORACLE_HOME/network/trace Specifies the directory to which Net8 client trace files are to be written.
TRACE_FILE_CLIENT TRACE_FILE_CLIENT = sqlnet.trc	Default: SQLNET.TRC Specifies the name to use for client trace files.
TRACE_UNIQUE_CLIENT TRACE_UNIQUE_CLIENT = ON	Default: ON Controls whether each client Net8 trace file is uniquely identified. Valid values are ON and OFF. If ON is used, then any Net8 trace files will have the process ID number appended to the file name.

The tnsnames.ora syntax

The tnsnames.ora file resides on a client and contains entries that resolve Net8 service names to specific databases on specific servers. Take a look at Figure 5-9, which shows the Oracle Enterprise Manager Login window for SQLPlus Worksheet, where a user logs on to a database named bible_db.

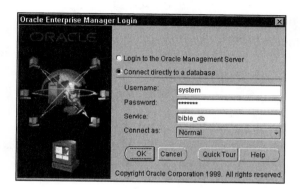

Figure 5-9: Using SQLPlus Worksheet to log on to the bible_db **database**

Just what database does the service name bible_db refer to, and where is it? Oracle needs a way to determine this, and there are several methods to choose from. One method is referred to as *local naming* and consists of looking up the service name in a text file that contains the details of where the database for that service is. The name of this text file is tnsnames.ora.

The syntax for a basic entry in the tnsnames.ora file looks like this:

```
BIBLE_DB =
  (DESCRIPTION =
    (ADDRESS_LIST =
      (ADDRESS =
        (PROTOCOL = TCP)
        (HOST = OAK.GENNICK.COM)
        (PORT = 1521))
    )
    (CONNECT_DATA =
      (SERVICE_NAME = BIBLE_DB.OAK.GENNICK.COM)
      (SID = BIBDB)
    )
  )
```

The following list describes each of the syntax elements shown in this example:

BIBLE_DB   Represents the Net8 service name. You can use simple names like this, or you can specify a name and a domain using Internet-style notation—for example, BIBLE_DB.OAK.GENNICK.COM. If you don't specify a domain, Net8 will use the value from the NAMES.DEFAULT_DOMAIN parameter in your sqlnet.ora file.

DESCRIPTION   Defines both a listener address and a database to which you want to connect via that listener.

ADDRESS_LIST   Defines a list of listener addresses for the Net8 service.

ADDRESS   Specifies the host address used to contact the listener. The format matches that used for the ADDRESS entry in the listener.ora file, and it varies depending on the network protocol being used. See Table 5-1 for details.

CONNECT_DATA   Specifies the database to which you want to connect when using the Net8 service name.

SERVICE_NAME   Defines the service name of an Oracle8i database. This is valid only for Oracle releases 8.1.x and above. The service name must match a name in the SERVICE_NAMES parameter in the database's parameter file. Typically, the service name will match the global name and domain of the database.

SID   Specifies the name of the specific Oracle instance that you want to connect to when using this Net8 service name. The SID is used when connecting to a database running under Oracle release 8.0.x or prior.

You may see other parameters in a tnsnames.ora file that involve load balancing and failover, but those are outside the scope of this book. The parameters described in this section are those used most commonly.

Net8 Easy Config

Net8 Easy Config is a network administration utility that ships with Oracle8i that allows you to easily add new entries to your tnsnames.ora file. It also allows you to modify or delete existing entries. Net8 Easy Config is a wizard-like tool that prompts you for the information required for the network protocol you are using and that tests the new or modified connection before making the change permanent.

If you are running Windows NT, you can find Net8 Easy Config in the Network Administration folder under the Oracle software program group. Click Start, point to Programs, point to Oracle – OraHome81, point to Network Administration, and select Net8 Easy Config. Figure 5-10 shows the opening page.

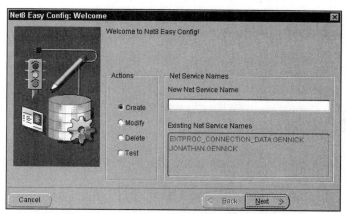

Figure 5-10: Net8 Easy Config's opening wizard page

The radio buttons on the left allow you to choose whether you want to create a new entry, modify or delete an existing entry, or simply test an existing entry. The text box at the bottom shows you a list of the existing entries in your tnsnames.ora file. Let's assume that you are going to add a new entry.

Your first job would be to think up a new service name. It can be anything you like that fits your naming conventions and that makes sense to your users. Next, click the Create radio button. After that, type the new Net8 service name into the text box, as shown in Figure 5-11.

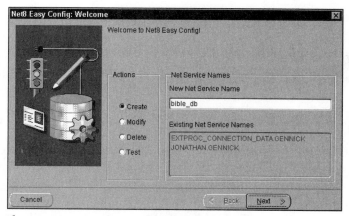

Figure 5-11: Creating a new Net8 service name

After entering the new name, as shown in Figure 5-11, click the Next button. You will see the page shown in Figure 5-12. Your task now is to select the network protocol to use for this new entry.

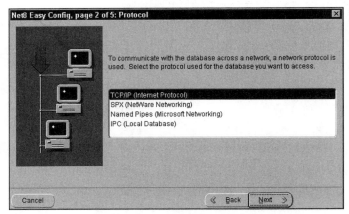

Figure 5-12: Selecting the network protocol for a service name

By far, the most commonly used protocol is TCP/IP, so let's assume that you've selected that and clicked Next. You should now see the page shown in Figure 5-13. Your job here is to specify the host name of the database server and the port number that the listener is monitoring.

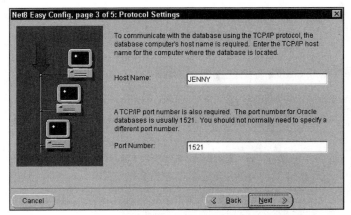

Figure 5-13: Entering the host name and port number for a service name

In this example, the host name JENNY is used. The port number has been left at the default of 1521. The port number here must match the port number specified in the listener.ora file on the server in question. If you are uncertain, 1521 is a good bet to start with because it's the default, and most people don't change it. Click Next, and you will see the page shown in Figure 5-14.

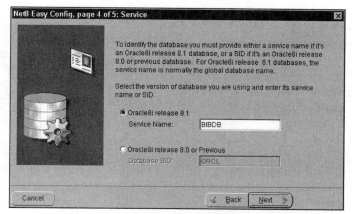

Figure 5-14: Choosing the Oracle database for a service name

Now you need to choose the database instance or database service on the remote host to which you want to connect. If you are running a release of Oracle that precedes the 8i release, then your only choice here is to specify the SID name of an instance on the server. If you are running release 8.1.*x* or greater, you should specify a database service name. The database service name here should match up with a GLOBAL_DBNAME entry in your server's listener.ora file.

The next step is to test the new connection. Click the Next button, and you will see the page shown in Figure 5-15.

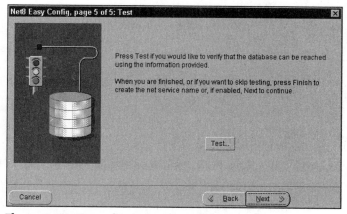

Figure 5-15: Preparing to test a new Net8 service name

Click the Test button, and Net8 Easy Config will attempt to connect to the remote database using the SCOTT/TIGER login. The SCOTT user is a demo user, and the test will fail if you have deleted that user from your database, as many DBAs do. Figure 5-16 shows you the page that you will see if an error occurs.

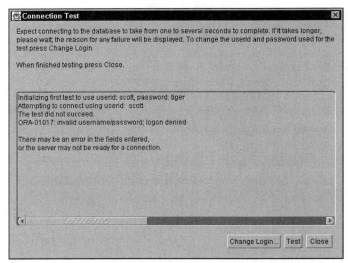

Figure 5-16: A new Net8 service name that fails the connection test

If the test failed because SCOTT/TIGER wasn't a valid login, click the Change Login button to enter a different username and password.

Note After entering a new username and password, you must remember to click the Test button to retry the test. Otherwise, Net8 Easy Config won't respond.

When you're done testing, click the Close button to close the test page, and click the Next button to continue with Net8 Easy Config. The last page that you will see is shown in Figure 5-17.

This is where you finalize your changes. You have one last chance to click the Back button and review or change your new entry. If you're satisfied with it, click the Finish button to have Net8 Easy Config write your changes out to your tnsnames.ora file.

Note If you need to add two or more databases, you have to invoke the program for each database. You have to *finish* the program to save the data for the first database before going back.

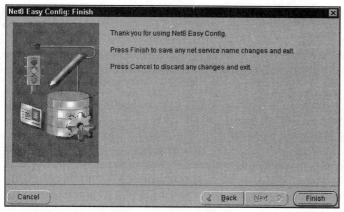

Figure 5-17: Net8 Easy Config's final page

Troubleshooting Net8

When Net8 works, it works very well. When it doesn't work, troubleshooting the problem can be a frustrating experience. A few techniques and utilities can be helpful, though, and they are discussed in the last part of this chapter.

Examining types of problems

The most common Net8-related problems you may encounter have the following causes:

✦ Net8 Listener isn't running.

✦ The address information in the tnsnames.ora file is incorrect.

✦ The service name being used isn't correct.

✦ The default domain specified in the sqlnet.ora file doesn't match the domain in the tnsnames.ora file for the service that you are trying to use.

The trick to solving most connectivity problems is to start from the physical connection and work your way up through each layer of networking until you find exactly where the problem occurs. When you troubleshoot a connectivity problem, you should generally check the following items in the order they are listed:

1. The physical LAN connection

2. Connectivity to the server using the underlying network protocol: TCP/IP, for example

3. Connectivity to the listener

4. Connectivity to the database

Checking the physical connection is as simple as making sure that the network cable is plugged into the PC and that the other end of the cable is plugged into the wall. Only occasionally is this the problem, but still it's worth a try. You'll feel pretty silly after you spend an hour searching for the problem only to finally find that someone accidentally kicked the network cable loose.

Using ping and tnsping

Testing the connectivity between client and server often involves the use of two utilities known as ping and tnsping. With TCP/IP networks, which are the most common, you can use the ping utility to verify connectivity between a client and a server. For testing the Net8 connectivity, Oracle supplies a utility analogous to ping named tnsping. The tnsping utility tells you whether the remote Net8 listener process can be contacted.

Pinging a Server

The TCP/IP ping utility verifies that a given host can be contacted via the network. The ping command is simple. It takes the host name as an argument and reports back on whether the host could be contacted. Here is an example:

```
ping jonathan.gennick
```

The output from this example is as follows:

```
Pinging jonathan.gennick [10.11.49.241] with 32 bytes of data:

Reply from 10.11.49.241: bytes=32 time<10ms TTL=128
Reply from 10.11.49.241: bytes=32 time<10ms TTL=128
Reply from 10.11.49.241: bytes=32 time<10ms TTL=128
Reply from 10.11.49.241: bytes=32 time<10ms TTL=128
```

If ping replies like this, then all is good. The target host is reachable, and you should move on up to the next level. If ping fails to contact the remote host, then you need to find out why. The following are some areas to look at:

✦ Is the remote server up and running?

✦ Did you supply ping with the correct host name?

✦ Is the IP address that the ping command reported correct?

✦ Is ping able to resolve the server name to an IP address?

✦ Can you ping using the IP address but not the server name?

IP address problems almost always require that you work together with your system or network administrators to resolve them. Many networks will use Dynamic Host Configuration Protocol (DHCP) or something similar to translate a host name into an IP address. If you can `ping` using an IP address but not using the host name, then your DHCP server might be down, or it might not be configured properly.

Note   Some networks still use hosts files on individual PCs to equate IP addresses with host names. If your network is one of these, you should verify that your hosts file contains the correct address for the server you are trying to reach.

The `ping` command will usually report back the IP address of the server that you are pinging. If that IP address isn't correct, or if `ping` is unable to translate the server name to an IP address, then you should contact your network administrator and work with him or her to resolve the problem.

Tnspinging a Listener

The `tnsping` utility is similar to `ping` and is provided by Oracle to help resolve Net8 connectivity problems. It verifies that the listener on the remote server can be contacted from the client. The `tnsping` utility has one advantage over `ping`: It is not network-specific. Even if you aren't using TCP/IP as your network protocol, you can still use `tnsping` to test connectivity to the server.

To run `tnsping`, you issue the `tnsping` command and supply a Net8 service name as an argument to that command. For example:

```
tnsping jonathan.gennick
```

generates the following output:

```
TNS Ping Utility for 32-bit Windows: Version 8.1.5.0.0 - Production on 25-JUL-99
 21:09:53

(c) Copyright 1997 Oracle Corporation.  All rights reserved.

Attempting to contact (ADDRESS=(PROTOCOL=TCP)(HOST=jonathan)(PORT=1521))
OK (60 msec)

C:\>
```

The `tnsping` utility will report back the address entry for the server that it is trying to contact, and it will tell you whether the listener could be contacted. If the listener couldn't be contacted, you should check the following:

◆ Is the listener up and running?

◆ Can you `ping` the server (TCP/IP), or otherwise verify connectivity to the server?

◆ Is the port number in your `tnsnames.ora` file correct? The `tnsping` utility will report the port number to you. Make sure it matches the port number in the `listener.ora` file on the server.

If `tnsping` is successful and the listener could be contacted, then you should be able to log on to your database.

Tip   The SQL*Plus utility is convenient to use to test your ability to log on to a database.

If, even after `tnsping`ing the listener, you still can't log on to the database, check the following:

✦ Is the database instance running?

✦ Is the database open?

✦ Are you using the correct username and password?

✦ Does the user that you are logging on have `CREATE SESSION` privileges?

If you've performed all the tests up to this point and still haven't isolated a connectivity problem, you have reached the point where no pat answers exist. You have reached a point in the troubleshooting process that calls for a good understanding of Net8, the underlying network protocols, the Oracle database software, and networking in general. You will need a healthy amount of intuition and experience to guide your next steps. Now is the time for you to consult with other professionals and consider calling Oracle support for help as well.

Summary

In this chapter, you learned:

✦ Net8 enables connectivity between an Oracle database and a client, or between two Oracle databases. Net8 supports multiple physical protocols, and provides location and protocol transparency to clients.

✦ The task of configuring Net8 on the server consists largely of editing the listener.ora file and adding entries that define the databases available on that server, that specify the number of listeners to start, and that associate each database with a listener.

✦ The task of configuring Net8 on a client consists mainly of adding entries to the sqlnet.ora and tnsnames.ora files. Oracle provides two utilities to make this task easier. Net8 Easy Config is a wizard-like assistant that automates the task of adding a new Net8 service name to the listener.ora file. Net8 Assistant is a GUI-based utility allowing you to change sqlnet.ora settings, as well as edit entries in listener.ora.

✦ The Listener Control program is used on the server to start and stop the Net8 listeners. Listener Control is also used to report the current status of the various listeners.

✦ The best way to troubleshoot Net8 connection problems is to work your way up through each layer of networking, beginning with the physical layer. If your physical connection is good, check the connectivity via the network protocol that you are using. Lastly, check the Net8 connectivity, to be sure that you can reach the listener on the server to which you are trying to connect.

✦ The `ping` utility is a widely available operating system utility that allows you to check TCP/IP connectivity between a client and a server. The `tnsping` utility is an Oracle-supplied utility that allows you to check the connectivity between a Net8 client and a Net8 listener running on a server.

✦   ✦   ✦

Database Space Management

In a popular TV series, space is the final frontier, and it's full
of surprises for the adventurous explorer. For the Oracle
DBAs, space—in the form of disk storage space—is more often
a big worry, one that hopefully won't lead to any surprises. As
an Oracle DBA, you have to concern yourself with storage
space at a variety of levels. You need to know how much the
database as a whole uses. You also need to know, or be able to
find out, how much storage space is used by any given table,
index, or other object. Not only do you need to know how much
storage space is being used now, but you also need to forecast
your needs for the future. Storage space, and how Oracle
manages it, is the subject of this chapter.

Managing Storage Space

Oracle8i uses logical structures to manage a database's
storage space. This section discusses how storage space for
a table is managed logically by way of segments, extents, and
blocks. Of course, the logical structures must eventually be
mapped onto physical structures, and we'll look at this as
well. As you learn these structures, you'll gain an appreciation
for all the work that Oracle does behind the scenes to manage
the storage of your data.

Understanding storage related terms

Logical database structures provide a conceptual framework for
managing data that is somewhat independent of the underlying
physical hardware. One of the major benefits to using a database
is that it frees you from having to remember the physical details
of how your data is stored. The database software handles that
for you. There are five types of logical structures:

✦ **Database objects**—A database object is a logical object
containing the data that you want to store in a database.
A table is such an object, as is an index.

✦ **Segments**—A segment represents a set of extents that contain data for a database object. Segments are stored in tablespaces.

✦ **Tablespaces**—A tablespace is the logical equivalent of a file.

✦ **Blocks**—A block is the smallest logical unit of storage managed by Oracle.

✦ **Extents**—An extent is a contiguous allocation of data blocks within a tablespace.

These logical structures allow you to manage your storage for your database in a platform-independent manner. No matter whether you are running Oracle8i on NT, VMS, or UNIX, you always manage disk storage in terms of objects, segments, tablespaces, extents, and blocks—the five items listed previously.

Aside from platform independence, logical structures provide you with flexibility. You can change the underlying physical structure of a database (by moving files around, for example) without changing its logical structure. Thus, your applications, which only see the logical structure, are completely unaffected by the changes.

Database objects

Tables and indexes are the two primary examples of *database objects*. They are the reason you have the database in the first place. You have tables of information that you want to store and retrieve, and you create indexes on those tables to facilitate retrieving that information.

Tables and indexes store data; thus, they are the database object types you are most concerned about relative to understanding how Oracle logically manages your data using tablespaces, extents, and data blocks. The one other database object that you should be aware of here is the cluster. A *cluster* is a database object that combines related tables together in such a way that related rows from one table are stored next to the related rows from the other table.

Segments

Tables, indexes, and clusters are stored in *segments*. For a nonpartitioned object, you always have exactly one segment. Partitioned objects get one segment per partition. Figure 6-1 shows the relationship between objects and segments for both a partitioned and a nonpartitioned object.

The nonpartitioned table in Figure 6-1 is stored in one segment. The other table is stored in two segments, one for each partition. Segments stand between an object and the tablespace or tablespaces used to store that object. Tablespaces, in turn, get you to files.

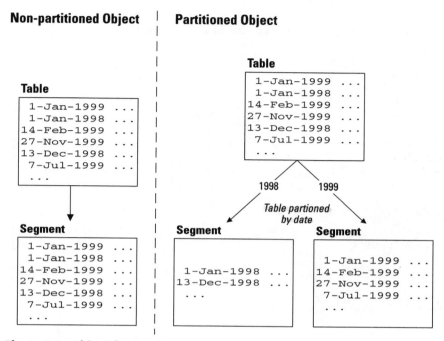

Figure 6-1: Objects have segments.

Tablespaces

You could consider a *tablespace* to be the logical equivalent of a data file. Rather than link each table and index directly to the file where the table or index data is stored, Oracle instead has you link each table and index segment to a tablespace. Data for a tablespace is then stored in one or more files. Figure 6-2 diagrams how the whole scheme looks.

Having a tablespace standing between a segment and the file used to store data for that segment provides you with some flexibility that you wouldn't otherwise have. For one thing, it allows you to transparently add files to a tablespace whenever you need more space. You don't have to do anything special to have Oracle use those files to store data for segments assigned to that tablespace. Another option is to move the files for a tablespace without having to change the definitions of objects stored within that tablespace.

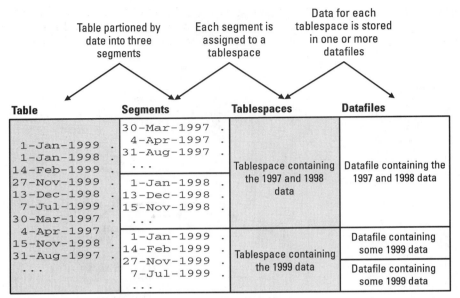

Figure 6-2: A table's segments are stored in a tablespace.

Data blocks

Data blocks are the smallest, most fundamental units of storage within a database. They are the smallest units of storage that Oracle can allocate to an object. Don't confuse Oracle data blocks with operating system blocks. An *operating system block* is the smallest unit that the operating system can read from or write to disk. Oracle data blocks are the smallest units that Oracle will read from or write to disk. Figure 6-3 diagrams how a tablespace is subdivided into Oracle data blocks and how those blocks relate to operating system blocks.

When Oracle reads data from disk, the amount of data it reads is always a multiple of the data block size. The data block size should always be an integer multiple of the operating system block size. Otherwise, you waste I/O and space because Oracle can't split an operating system block in half.

Extents

An *extent* is a contiguous allocation of data blocks. When Oracle needs to allocate space to an object, it doesn't just add one block. Instead, it allocates a whole group of blocks, and that group is referred to as an extent. Oracle does this to avoid having to constantly assign blocks one at a time to rapidly growing tables. You control the size of the extents that Oracle allocates to an object, and you should set the size large enough so that the object doesn't need to be extended often.

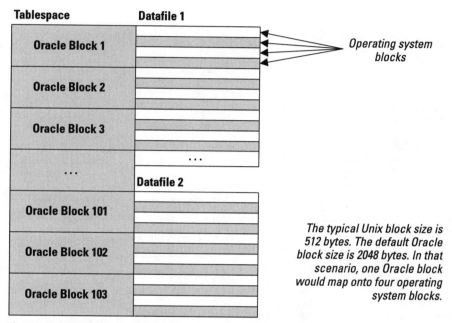

Figure 6-3: A tablespace contains many Oracle data blocks.

Figure 6-4 diagrams how extents figure into the space-allocation picture. Starting on the left, you have a table that is partitioned into two segments, each of which is assigned to a tablespace. Within each tablespace, the segments each have two extents. Extents are made up of Oracle data blocks. The tablespaces are each mapped onto two physical datafiles, and you can see how the Oracle datablocks are related to the operating system blocks.

You can see in Figure 6-4 that none of the extents crosses a datafile boundary. This is a rule that Oracle enforces. The blocks in an extent must be adjacent to each other, and they must also be in the same datafile.

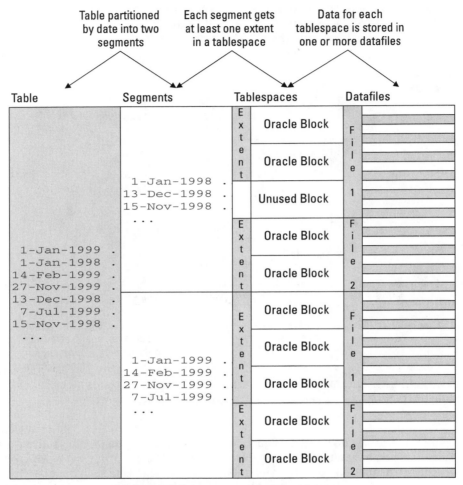

Figure 6-4: Extents in the overall space-management picture

Allocating and Managing Storage Space

To manage storage in an Oracle database, you need to be able to specify storage options for the tablespaces that you create. You also need to be able to specify storage options for the objects that you create in those tablespaces. In general, you need to know how to do the following:

✦ Create a tablespace

✦ Set tablespace options, such as the minimum extent, whether to autoextend, and so forth.

✦ Set default storage parameters for a tablespace

✦ Set the storage parameters for an object

✦ Add space when needed

✦ Coalesce extents

Each of these topics is covered in one the following sections.

Creating a tablespace

You use the CREATE TABLESPACE command to create a tablespace. At a minimum, when creating a tablespace, you need to tell Oracle how large to make the tablespace and where to put it. For example:

```
CREATE TABLESPACE CHECKUP_HISTORY
    DATAFILE '/m01/oradata/BIBDB/checkup_history.dbf'
    SIZE 1000M;
```

This statement creates a file named checkup_history.dbf that is 1,000MB in size. That file will be used to hold all data stored within the CHECKUP_HISTORY tablespace.

Tablespace Storage Parameters

When you create a tablespace, Oracle allows you to specify default storage parameters to be used for objects that you later create and assign to that tablespace. The five parameters that you can set at the tablespace level are the following:

INITIAL	The INITIAL parameter sets the size of the initial extent that is allocated to each new object when you create it.
NEXT	The NEXT parameter sets the size to use for subsequent extents. Often, the INITIAL and NEXT settings are identical.
MINEXTENTS	The MINEXTENTS parameter defines the minimum number of extents to allocate when a new object is created. Most of the time, it makes sense to set MINEXTENTS to 1.
MAXEXTENTS	The MAXEXTENTS parameter defines the maximum number of extents that Oracle will allow an object to have. You can supply a specific number, or you can use the keyword UNLIMITED.
PCTINCREASE	The PCTINCREASE parameter establishes a percentage by which to increase the NEXT value each time a new extent is added for an object. It's usually best to set this to 0.

For example, to specify that objects created and assigned to a tablespace have extent sizes of 50MB, and that no limit is placed on the number of extents for an object, you could issue the following command:

```
CREATE TABLESPACE checkup_history
    DATAFILE '/m01/oradata/BIBDB/checkup_history.dbf'
    SIZE 1000M
DEFAULT STORAGE (    INITIAL 50M
                     NEXT 50M
                     MINEXTENTS 1
                     MAXEXTENTS UNLIMITED
                     PCTINCREASE 0);
```

Storage parameter values specified at the tablespace level represent defaults. They are used only when you create a new object in the tablespace without specifying storage parameters specifically for the object. The table created by the following command, for example, will inherit the default storage parameters shown previously:

```
CREATE TABLE checkup_history (
        CHECKUP_NO            NUMBER(10,0) NOT NULL,
        ID_NO                 NUMBER(10,0),
        CHECKUP_TYPE          VARCHAR2(30),
        CHECKUP_DATE          DATE,
        DOCTOR_NAME           VARCHAR2(50)
        ) TABLESPACE checkup_history;
```

Since no STORAGE clause was given in the CREATE TABLE statement, the checkup_history table will inherit its storage parameter settings from the tablespace. An initial extent of 50MB will be allocated immediately, and future extents of 50MB will be allocated as needed. Figure 6-5 illustrates this allocation of space.

CHECKUP_HISTORY Tablespace

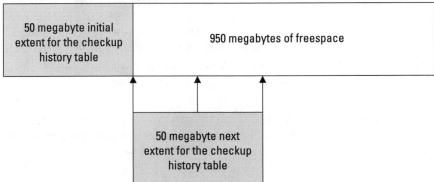

Figure 6-5: The initial extent for the checkup_history table

The tablespace default storage parameters are referenced when you create a new object in the tablespace. Subsequently changing the parameters at the tablespace level won't affect objects that have already been created.

The Minimum Extent Size

When many objects with different extent sizes are stored in a tablespace, it can become fragmented. The upcoming section, "Coalescing Extents," talks more about fragmentation. For now, though, realize that fragmentation may create extents of free space that aren't big enough to be very useful. Figure 6-6 illustrates how this might happen.

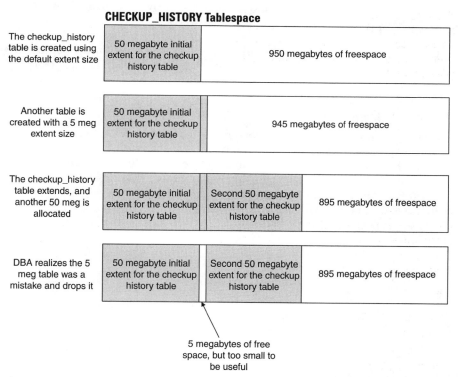

Figure 6-6: Events leading up to fragmentation and a uselessly small extent

To help you prevent a tablespace from being fragmented into extents that are too small to be useful, Oracle allows you to specify a minimum extent size for a tablespace. The following statement creates a tablespace and specifies a minimum extent size of 25MB:

```
CREATE TABLESPACE checkup_history
    DATAFILE '/m01/oradata/BIBDB/checkup_history.dbf'
    SIZE 1000M
    MINIMUM EXTENT 25M
DEFAULT STORAGE (    INITIAL 50M
                     NEXT 50M
                     MINEXTENTS 1
                     MAXEXTENTS UNLIMITED
                     PCTINCREASE 0);
```

Oracle will not allow any extents less than 25MB to be allocated in the `checkup_history` tablespace created with this statement. With respect to the sequence of events shown in Figure 6-6, the command to create a table with an initial size of 5MB will succeed, but Oracle will silently allocate a 25MB initial extent, because that is the minimum size allowed.

By preventing extents of such a small size from ever being created, you ensure that even if fragmentation occurs, the fragmented extents will at least be of a usable size.

The Autoextend Option

Normally, when you create the initial datafile for a tablespace, the size of that datafile is fixed. Adding more space to the tablespace requires that you create more datafiles. Historically, that was the way it worked—period. However, in one of the Oracle7 releases, Oracle began allowing you to create datafiles that can extend in size automatically. You do this by specifying AUTOEXTEND ON when you create a tablespace, or when you add a datafile to a tablespace. Following is an example showing a tablespace being created with a 100MB datafile that will grow in 100MB chunks:

```
CREATE TABLESPACE checkup_history
    DATAFILE 'e:\Oracle\Oradata\jonathan\checkup_history.dbf'
    SIZE 100M
    AUTOEXTEND ON NEXT 100M MAXSIZE UNLIMITED
    MINIMUM EXTENT 25M
DEFAULT STORAGE (    INITIAL 50M
NEXT 50M
MINEXTENTS 1
MAXEXTENTS UNLIMITED
PCTINCREASE 0);
```

Turning the autoextend option on for your datafiles truly puts your database's storage space management on automatic. The tablespace created with the command just shown can grow in 100MB chunks until you run out of disk space, and objects created within the tablespace can grow in 50MB chunks, also until you run out of disk space.

Locally Managed Tablespaces

New with Oracle8i is the ability to create locally managed tablespaces. With regular tablespaces, referred to now as *dictionary-managed tablespaces,* the data dictionary keeps track of how space has been allocated. A *locally managed tablespace* is one where the space management is done using bitmaps that are stored within the tablespace itself, hence, the term *local*. The result is faster extent allocation as objects grow.

The LOCAL keyword is used to create a locally managed tablespace, and two options exist for managing extents: AUTOALLOCATE and UNIFORM. The following two statements illustrate these options:

```
CREATE TABLESPACE checkup_history
    DATAFILE '/m01/oradata/BIBDB/checkup_history.dbf'
    SIZE 1000M
    EXTENT MANAGEMENT LOCAL AUTOALLOCATE;

CREATE TABLESPACE checkup_history
    DATAFILE '/m01/oradata/BIBDB/checkup_history.dbf'
    SIZE 1000M
    EXTENT MANAGEMENT LOCAL UNIFORM SIZE 50M;
```

The AUTOALLOCATE option causes the tablespace to be created with a bitmap containing one bit for each data block. Oracle controls extent size. When you create an object in the tablespace, Oracle will start out by allocating a 64KB extent to that object. As the object grows in size, more 64KB extents will be added. Oracle will eventually increase the size of extents allocated to that object.

The UNIFORM clause allows you to manage storage space in extents that are larger than one block. All extents must be the same size, hence, the term *uniform*. In this example, the uniform extent size is 50MB, and the bitmap will contain one bit for each 50MB of storage space in the tablespace.

Note   The uniform extent size will be rounded up to the nearest integer multiple of the database block size.

Setting storage parameters for an object

You've seen how to use the DEFAULT STORAGE clause to specify the default storage characteristics for objects created within a tablespace. You can use a similar clause when you create an object that allows you to override those default characteristics.

Dictionary-Managed Tablespaces

You can use the STORAGE clause when you create an object to specify the storage parameters to use for that object. For example, the following statement creates a table with a 15MB initial extent. Subsequent extents will be 5MB each.

```
CREATE TABLE checkup_history (
        CHECKUP_NO          NUMBER(10,0) NOT NULL,
        ID_NO               NUMBER(10,0),
        CHECKUP_TYPE        VARCHAR2(30),
        CHECKUP_DATE        DATE,
        DOCTOR_NAME         VARCHAR2(50)
        ) TABLESPACE checkup_history_local
          STORAGE (INITIAL 15M NEXT 5M);
```

Anything that you specify in the STORAGE clause for an object overrides the corresponding DEFAULT STORAGE value that you specify at the tablespace level. The same values, INITIAL, NEXT, PCTINCREASE, MINEXTENTS, and MAXEXTENTS, which you can specify in the DEFAULT STORAGE clause, may also be used in the STORAGE clause.

Locally Managed Tablespaces

When you are creating objects in a locally managed tablespace, the rules for extent allocation change. If you are using the AUTOALLOCATE option, Oracle will control the size and number of extents based on an internal algorithm. While the details of this algorithm haven't been published, the following statements are true:

✦ Oracle will allocate an initial extent of 64KB by default.

✦ Oracle will allocate an initial extent of 64KB, even if you ask for less.

✦ If you ask for an initial extent greater than 64KB, Oracle will allocate enough 64KB extents to give you at least the amount of space that you asked for.

✦ Oracle will ignore any value that you supply for PCTINCREASE.

✦ Oracle will ignore any value that you supply for NEXT.

✦ Beginning with the 16th extent, Oracle will increase the extent size from 64KB to 1MB.

✦ Oracle will ignore any MAXEXTENTS value.

If you configure a locally managed tablespace to use uniform extents, then Oracle ensures that all extents in the tablespace are the same size. As with the AUTOALLOCATE option, enough uniform extents will be allocated to at least match the amount of space requested for the initial extent.

Just remember that when you use a uniform extent size, all extents will be that size. When you use the AUTOALLOCATE option, Oracle uses an internal algorithm to control the extent size.

Coalescing extents

Figure 6-6 illustrated how you can end up with a small orphan extent of free space in a tablespace. In cases where you have a large amount of extent creation and deletion, it's possible to end up with several contiguous extents of free space. Figure 6-7 diagrams how this might look.

CHECKUP_HISTORY Tablespace

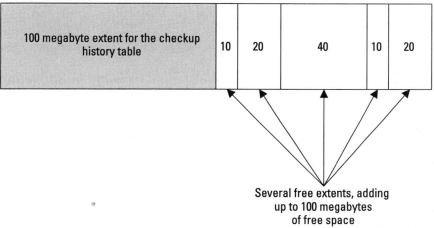

Several free extents, adding
up to 100 megabytes
of free space

Figure 6-7: Several contiguous extents of free space

The tablespace shown in Figure 6-7 contains 100MB of free space organized into several extents ranging in size from 10–40MB each. Sometimes this can present a problem. Even though there are 100MB of contiguous free space, it doesn't appear that way because that space has been fragmented into several smaller pieces.

The solution to this problem of fragmented free space is to *coalesce* all the adjacent free extents into one large extent. There are two ways you can do this. One is to just wait. One of the functions of the SMON background process is to continuously scan for this type of situation and to coalesce adjacent free extents whenever it finds them. However, SMON only does this for tablespaces with a nonzero default PCTFREE setting. Oracle's extent allocation algorithm is also supposed to do this for you. However, if you run into problems allocating storage space and you need the space right away, you can manually coalesce the extents. The following ALTER TABLESPACE command will do that:

```
ALTER TABLESPACE tablespace_name COALESCE;
```

Figure 6-8 shows the same tablespace as the one shown in Figure 6-7, but after the free space has been coalesced. Notice that there is now one large 50MB extent of free space.

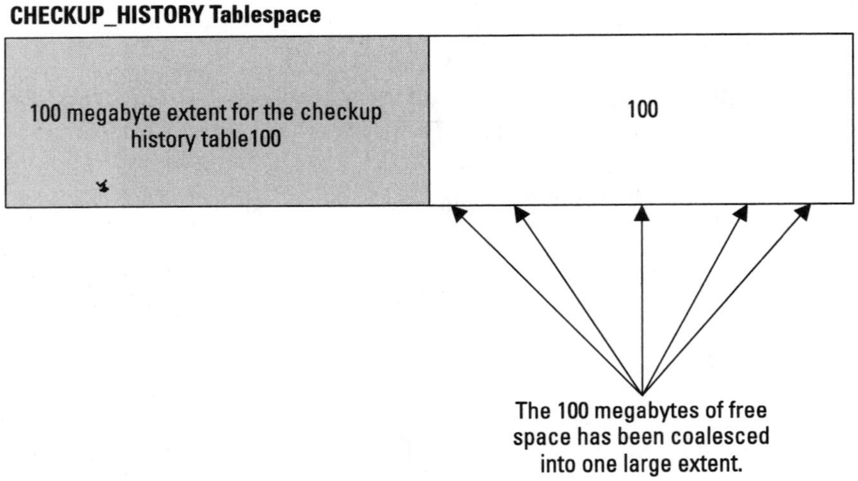

CHECKUP_HISTORY Tablespace

100 megabyte extent for the checkup history table100	100

The 100 megabytes of free space has been coalesced into one large extent.

Figure 6-8: The free space has been coalesced into one large extent.

Adding storage space when needed

Over time, the objects in your database will grow in size, and sooner or later, you will need to add more space to your database. As long as you have enough disk space, adding storage space is actually quite easy. The trick is in knowing when, and how much.

Knowing When You Need More Space

You know that you need more storage space when one of your users calls you about an error message like this:

```
ORA-01653: unable to extend table HR.EMPLOYEE by 2560 in tablespace HR_DATA
```

Of course, this isn't the way that you want to find out! You won't last long as a DBA if your space-management methodology is to wait until you run out. When you drive a car on a trip, you have some general idea of how far you can go on one tank of gas, and you monitor the gas gauge periodically so that you know ahead of time when you need to fill up. You need to do the same with your database. You need to monitor and to plan for the future. To do this, you need to be able to answer the following questions:

✦ How large are your objects (tables, indexes, and so on) now?

✦ How fast are your objects growing?

✦ How much free space do you have left now?

The next few sections will help you answer the first and last questions in this list. They are easy questions because they refer to the current state of the database. Predicting the future is a bit tougher, though.

The most reliable way to see how fast your database objects are growing is to check their size regularly. Once you've determined how much space is added to an object every day, every week, or during whatever interval you choose to measure, you can use that value to extrapolate into the future. For example, if a table is growing by 1MB per day, you can extrapolate that out to 30MB a month.

 Tip
It can be cumbersome to regularly monitor the size of every object in a database. Often, only a few tables and indexes grow significantly on a daily basis, with the remaining tables being relatively static. Focus your efforts on the fast-growing objects, and monitor them often, perhaps daily. Choose a longer interval for the more static objects.

In addition to watching how fast your objects are growing, keep a close eye on the amount of free space remaining in each of your tablespaces. You should have some idea of an acceptable minimum for each tablespace. Think in terms of extents here. If the objects in a tablespace all have 50MB extent sizes, then you need some multiple of that amount free. When the amount of free space drops below this minimum, allocate more space.

Adding Storage Space to a Tablespace

You can take two approaches to add storage space to a tablespace. You can add a datafile to the tablespace, or you can attempt to extend one of the existing datafiles.

You use the ALTER TABLESPACE command to add a datafile to a tablespace. The following example adds a 1000MB datafile to the checkup_history tablespace:

```
ALTER TABLESPACE checkup_history
    ADD     DATAFILE '/m02/oradata/BIBDB/checkup_history_2.dbf'
            SIZE 1000M;
```

You can add as many datafiles to a tablespace as you like, subject to the overall limit on the number of database files set by the DB_FILES initialization parameter.

Adding Space to a Datafile

Another way to add space to a tablespace is to resize one or more datafiles associated with the tablespace. You use the ALTER DATABASE command to do this. The following example resizes the checkup_history_2.dbf datafile to 1,500MB:

```
ALTER DATABASE
    DATAFILE '/m02/oradata/BIBDB/checkup_history_2.dbf'
    RESIZE 1500m;
```

Resizing a datafile works both ways: You can make a file larger, or you can attempt to shrink it smaller. You can resize a file downward as long as you are not throwing away blocks that are being used.

Manually Adding an Extent to a Table

You can arbitrarily allocate space to a table by using the ALTER TABLE command. The command in the following example causes Oracle to allocate a 5MB extent for the checkup_history table:

```
ALTER TABLE checkup_history
    ALLOCATE EXTENT (SIZE 5M);
```

Allocating space for a table involves some overhead. One advantage to manually allocating space like this is that you control when that overhead is incurred. The alternative is that some random user is going to absorb the overhead of extending the table.

Note   The SIZE parameter shown in the previous example is optional. You can issue the command ALTER TABLE checkup_history ALLOCATE EXTENT, and the size will default to the value for NEXT.

Another advantage to manually allocating storage space like this is that you can assure yourself that the table has enough space for some well-defined time period. For example, if you know the checkup_history table is growing by 5MB per month, you could manually allocate a 5MB extent at the beginning of each month. Then you can be pretty sure, barring some sudden spurt of growth, that you won't run out of space during the next month.

If you have a tablespace with several datafiles, you can force the extent to be allocated in a file of your choosing. For example:

```
ALTER TABLE checkup_history
    ALLOCATE EXTENT (
        SIZE 5M
        DATAFILE '/m02/oradata/BIBDB/checkup_history_2.dbf'
        );
```

This gives you the ability to manually strip your data across disks. If you have 20MB of data and four disks, you can create a datafile on each disk and manually allocate a 5MB extent in each of those datafiles. The result is that your 20MB of data is spread over four disks, which may reduce disk contention somewhat.

Note While you can specify the datafile to use when manually extending an existing object, you cannot specify the datafile to use for the initial extent when you first create the object.

Reporting an object's storage space usage

Two data dictionary views are key to finding out how a database is using storage space. These views are:

✦ DBA_EXTENTS

✦ DBA_FREE_SPACE

The DBA_EXTENTS view tells you about extents that have been allocated to objects such as tables, indexes, and so forth. The DBA_FREE_SPACE view returns information about chunks of free space within a tablespace.

While the DBA_EXTENTS view returns information about space that has been allocated to an object, it doesn't tell you how much of that space has been used. The ANALYZE command can help in this area. To find out how many blocks are actually being used to store information for a table, you can issue an ANALYZE TABLE command, followed by a query to DBA_TABLES.

The next few subsections show you how to determine the amount of space allocated to an object such as a table or a view; how to determine the free and used space within a tablespace; and how to use the ANALYZE command to find out how much data a table (or index) really contains.

Storage Space Allocated to an Object

To find out how much storage space has been allocated to an object, you need to query the DBA_EXTENTS view. The following query will tell you how much space the CHECKUP_HISTORY table has used:

```
SELECT COUNT(*) extents,
       SUM(bytes) bytes_used,
       SUM(blocks) blocks_used
FROM dba_extents
WHERE owner='SEAPARK'
  AND segment_name='CHECKUP_HISTORY'
  AND segment_type='TABLE';
```

The blocks column in DBA_EXTENTS tells you how many Oracle blocks make up the extent. The bytes column tells you how many bytes those blocks represent. It is the number of blocks multiplied by the database block size (from the DB_BLOCK_SIZE initialization parameter).

In this example, we are querying for the space allocated to a table, so we used a segment type of TABLE. If you were interested in the size of an index, you would use the index name and a segment type of INDEX. The valid segment types are CACHE, CLUSTER, DEFERRED ROLLBACK, INDEX, INDEX PARTITION, LOBINDEX, LOBSEGMENT, NESTED TABLE, ROLLBACK, TEMPORARY TABLE, and TABLE PARTITION.

You can get a report showing the space allocated to all objects in a tablespace by using the following query. Just replace *tablespace_name* with the name of the tablespace that you are interested in.

```
SELECT owner,
       segment_name,
       segment_type,
       count(*) extents,
       SUM(bytes) bytes_used,
       SUM(blocks) blocks_used
FROM dba_extents
WHERE tablespace_name='SYSTEM'
GROUP BY owner, segment_name, segment_type
ORDER BY owner, segment_name, segment_type;
```

The queries shown previously will work for partitioned and nonpartitioned objects that don't contain large objects or nested tables stored in their own segments. For example, say that you created a table with a large object, and you stored that large object in its own tablespace. Your CREATE TABLE command might look like this:

```
CREATE TABLE items (
item_no         NUMBER,
item_photo      BLOB
) TABLESPACE item_data
  LOB (item_photo)
      STORE AS items_item_photo (TABLESPACE item_photos);
```

In this case, except for the item_photo column, the table data is stored in a segment named ITEMS, in the tablespace named item_data. The item_photo column, however, has been relegated to a separate tablespace named item_photos, where it will be stored in a segment named items_item_photo. To find the total space used by this table, you would need to issue the two queries shown in Listing 6-1.

The first query returns the amount of space allocated to the main table, while the second query returns the amount of space allocated to the item_photo column.

Listing 6-1: **Finding total space in a table**

```
SELECT COUNT(*) extents,
       SUM(bytes) bytes_used,
       SUM(blocks) blocks_used
FROM dba_extents
WHERE owner='SEAPARK'
  AND segment_name='ITEMS'
  AND segment_type='TABLE';

SELECT COUNT(*) extents,
       SUM(bytes) bytes_used,
       SUM(blocks) blocks_used
FROM dba_extents
WHERE owner='SEAPARK'
  AND segment_name='ITEMS_ITEM_PHOTO'
  AND segment_type='LOBSEGMENT';
```

Space Used in a Tablespace

The queries are quite simple to determine how much storage space has been used within a tablespace, versus how much is still free. The following query will tell you how much space each of your tablespaces has used:

```
SELECT ts.tablespace_name,
       NVL(COUNT(extent_id),0) extents,
       SUM(NVL(bytes,0)) bytes_used,
       SUM(NVL(blocks,0)) blocks_used
FROM dba_tablespaces ts, dba_extents ex
WHERE ts.tablespace_name = ex.tablespace_name(+)
GROUP BY ts.tablespace_name;
```

This query is written to return zeros for tablespaces where no extents have been allocated. If you didn't care to see that, you could eliminate the outer join, making the query a bit simpler.

Free Space in a Tablespace

The DBA_FREE_SPACE view returns information about the *unused* space within a tablespace. The following query returns the amount of unused space within each tablespace, as well as the size of the largest free extent in each tablespace:

```
SELECT ts.tablespace_name,
       NVL(COUNT(fs.block_id),0) free_extents,
       SUM(NVL(bytes,0)) bytes_free,
       SUM(NVL(blocks,0)) blocks_free,
       MAX(NVL(bytes,0)) largest_free_extent
FROM dba_tablespaces ts, dba_free_space fs
WHERE ts.tablespace_name = fs.tablespace_name(+)
GROUP BY ts.tablespace_name;
```

Knowing the largest free extent is helpful because when an object extends, it not only needs enough free space to extend, but it needs that space in one contiguous chunk.

Blocks Actually Used by an Object

The DBA_EXTENTS view tells you how much space has been allocated to an object, such as a table, but that's not always a good indicator of how large that object really is or how much space it is really using. Extents of any size can be allocated to empty tables, and it's common to allocate large extents in anticipation of future growth. How, then, do you find out how much space a table is really using versus what has been allocated to it?

One way to find out exactly how much storage space a table or an index is really using is to use the ANALYZE command. When you analyze a table, Oracle counts up the number of rows in the table, computes the average row size, and tallies the number of blocks actually being used to store data. Oracle does much the same thing when you analyze an index, except that it counts keys instead of rows, and it computes some other information that is specific to indexing.

The example in Listing 6-2 shows the ANALYZE command being used on the SEAPARK user's CHECKUP table:

Listing 6-2: Using the ANALYZE command

```
SQL> ANALYZE TABLE SEAPARK.CHECKUP COMPUTE STATISTICS;

Table analyzed.

SQL> SELECT blocks,
  2         num_rows,
  3         empty_blocks,
  4         avg_space,
  5         avg_row_len
  6  FROM dba_tables
  7  WHERE owner='SEAPARK'
  8    AND table_name='CHECKUP';

  BLOCKS  NUM_ROWS EMPTY_BLOCKS AVG_SPACE AVG_ROW_LEN
--------- --------- ------------ --------- -----------
        1         3            3      1904          16
```

As you can see, after the ANALYZE command has completed, the following columns were selected from DBA_TABLES:

> BLOCKS   The BLOCKS column lists the number of blocks that have actually been used to store data.

NUM_ROWS | The NUM_ROWS column lists the number of rows in the table.

EMPTY_BLOCKS | The EMPTY_BLOCKS column lists the number of blocks allocated to the table that have never been used.

AVG_SPACE | The AVG_SPACE column lists the average amount of free space per block.

AVG_ROW_LEN | The AVG_ROW_LEN column lists the average row length.

Note The value for EMPTY_BLOCKS doesn't include blocks that were once used but are now empty. It only includes those blocks that have never been used.

The CHECKUP table in the previous example has three rows with an average row length of 16 bytes. Multiplying those two numbers gives a total of 48 bytes of data. Only one block is being used to store that data. To properly interpret the AVG_SPACE figure, you need to know the block size. In this case, the block size is 2,048 bytes, so 2,048 − 1,904 = 144 bytes used per block, on average. Note that the bytes used per block includes overhead, so that figure won't necessarily match the result of multiplying NUM_ROWS by AVG_ROW_SIZE.

Estimating Space Requirements

When you create a new table or a new index, you need to estimate how much storage space will be required for the amount of data that you expect to have. There are three ways of going about this task:

✦ You can make an educated guess.

✦ You can extrapolate from a subset of data.

✦ You can calculate an estimate based on row size, block size, estimated free space within a block, and so forth.

Making an educated guess is by far the simplest approach, and in some cases it may be the most appropriate to use. Consider the SALAD_TYPE table owned by the user named AMY in the sample database for this book, and which is made up of the following columns:

```
SALAD_TYPE         VARCHAR2(10)
DESCRIPTION_TEXT   VARCHAR2(40)
ORGANIC_FLAG       VARCHAR2(3)
PRICE_PER_POUND    NUMBER(10,2)
LAST_CHANGE_DATE   DATE
```

How many types of salads could there possibly be? For a table this small, unless you just can't afford to make any mistake at all, you probably don't need to be too rigorous. If you allocated a 100KB extent and ended up wasting 80KB of space, so what? If you allocated a 10KB extent and ended up needing another 10KB extent, that also would be no big deal.

Perhaps the most reliable method of estimating the space required for a table or an index is to extrapolate based on a small amount of sample data. Let's go back to the SALAD_TYPE example. Assume for a moment, absurd as it may seem, that you are expecting 10,000 rows to be in that table. Maybe there really are 10,000 types of salad in the world. One way of estimating the amount of space required for those rows would be to populate the table with 100 representative rows, find out how much space is required for those rows, and multiply that value by 100. You can use the ANALYZE command to determine the space actually used in a table. The following example shows ANALYZE being used on a SALAD_TYPE table that contains 100 rows:

```
SQL> ANALYZE TABLE salad_type COMPUTE STATISTICS;

Table analyzed.

SQL> SELECT blocks, avg_row_len
  2  FROM user_tables
  3  WHERE table_name='SALAD_TYPE';

  BLOCKS AVG_ROW_LEN
--------- -----------
       4          54

1 row selected.
```

In this example, the average length of a row in the SALAD_TYPE table is 54 bytes, and it took four blocks to hold 100 records. Extrapolating from this, you can be pretty safe in assuming that 400 blocks would hold 10,000 records.

Note With such a small initial sample, you may end up allocating more space than is absolutely necessary for a table. Ninety-nine rows may fit in three blocks, and the 100th row might have been barely enough to spill over into the fourth.

Remember, unused space is also being multiplied by 100. You can refine the estimate by increasing the sample size. This example predicts 40 blocks for 1,000 rows, but when you increase the sample to 1,000 rows, you'll find that only 34 blocks are used. Extrapolating from that, you would expect 340 blocks for 10,000 rows. In fact, only 325 blocks were necessary. In this case, the estimate based on 1,000 rows was closer to the final result than the estimate based on 100 rows.

Estimating future storage space requirements based on existing data works only when you have some representative data to look at. If you are developing or implementing a new system, you may be forced, because of the schedule, to create a database well before you have any data to put in it. If that's the case, and you still need a rigorous size estimate, you can still use some calculations to get that. The next few sections describe the information that you need and show you the formulas to use.

Sizing Small Code Tables

How would you really size a small table like SALAD_TYPE? First of all, look at other code tables in the system. If the INITIAL and NEXT extent sizes are consistent for the other small tables, you would probably follow that pattern for SALAD_TYPE. Often, a database will have a tablespace set aside specifically for small code tables, with reasonable default storage parameters already set. If no pattern exists to follow, you might choose to make a rough estimate of the space required.

The sum of the VARCHAR2 column lengths in the table is 53. The DATE columns are 7 bytes each, and the NUMBER column in this case will use about 5 bytes. That works out to 65 bytes per row. Allowing for 25 salad types, you would have 25 rows × 65 bytes = 1,625 bytes total. If you were doing this calculation in your head, you might round up the row size to 100, to make the math easier. Whatever value you came up with for a total size, you would then round up to the nearest block size increment and use that value for your initial and next extent sizes.

You'll recognize that this calculation yields only a crude estimate. Often, though, that's enough to get you in the ballpark. See the section, "Estimating the Space for a Table," for a more rigorous set of calculations.

Collecting prerequisite information

The formulas described in this chapter come from the *Oracle8 Administrator's Guide*. To use them, you need to query your database to find out your database block size. You also need to retrieve the sizes for the following types: KCBH, UB1, UB2, UB4, KTBBH, KTBIT, KDBH, and KDBT. You can retrieve the database block size from the V$PARAMETER view. The type sizes come from the V$TYPE_SIZE view. Listing 6-3 provides an example that shows how you can query for these values.

Listing 6-3: **Retrieving the database block size value**

```
SQL> SELECT value
  2  FROM v$parameter
  3  WHERE name='db_block_size';

VALUE
-----------------------------------------------------------
2048

1 row selected.

SQL>
SQL> SELECT component, type, description, type_size
```

Continued

Listing 6-3: *(continued)*

```
2   FROM v$type_size
3   WHERE type IN ('KCBH','UB1','UB2','UB4',
4                  'KTBBH','KTBIT','KDBH','KDBT',
5                  'SB2');

COMPONENT TYPE    DESCRIPTION                        TYPE_SIZE
--------- ------- ---------------------------------- ---------
S         UB1     UNSIGNED BYTE 1                            1
S         UB2     UNSIGNED BYTE 2                            2
S         UB4     UNSIGNED BYTE 4                            4
S         SB2     SIGNED BYTE 2                              2
KCB       KCBH    BLOCK COMMON HEADER                       20
KTB       KTBIT   TRANSACTION VARIABLE HEADER               24
KTB       KTBBH   TRANSACTION FIXED HEADER                  48
KDB       KDBH    DATA HEADER                               14
KDB       KDBT    TABLE DIRECTORY ENTRY                      4

9 rows selected.
```

In addition to the type sizes and the database block size, you need to know the values that you are going to use for the INITRANS and PCTFREE parameters when you create the table. If you aren't going to specify those parameters, then use the defaults for the calculations. The default value for INITRANS is 1, and the default for PCTFREE is 20.

Estimating the space for a table

To estimate the size of a table, you need to do the following:

1. Figure out how much space in each database block is available for data.

2. Determine an average row size on which to base your estimate.

3. Compute the number of blocks required based on the previous two values.

The following sections show you some formulas that you can use for each of these steps. After that, there is an example based on the SALAD_TYPE table scenario discussed earlier.

Estimating the Amount of Available Space per Block

The amount of storage space available in a block depends primarily on the block size, the amount of overhead, and the PCTFREE value. Oracle provides the following formula:

```
SPACE_FOR_DATA = CEIL((DB_BLOCK_SIZE - KCBH - UB4 -KTBBH
- ((INITTRANS - 1) * KTBIT) - KDBH)
* (1-PCTFREE/100)) - KDBT
```

The CEIL function is an Oracle function that rounds fractional values up to the nearest integer. For example, CEIL (5.3) results in a value of 6.

Estimating the Row Size

Estimating the row size is perhaps the trickiest part of this entire process. It's fairly easy to come up with a maximum row size. It's tougher to settle on a good average to use for estimation purposes.

The first step in calculating the row size is to sum up the lengths of the individual columns. Table 6-1 will help you do this. As you work with each column, give some thought about your expectations in terms of the average amount of data the column will hold. A description field, for example, may be defined as a VARCHAR(40), but how often are you likely to save a description that uses all 40 characters? You may want to compute column sizes based on what you expect a reasonable average to be.

Table 6-1 Column Sizes	
Datatype	**Size**
CHAR(x)	The column size will be x bytes.
NUMBER(x,y)	Number columns have a maximum size of 21 bytes. The amount used depends on the value being stored. Figure two digits per byte: one digit for the exponent, and one more for the negative sign (only when the number is negative). A value of 123.45 would take 3 + 1 + 0, or 4 bytes. A value of −123.45 would take 3 + 1 + 1, or 5 bytes.
VARCHAR2(x) VARCHAR(x)	If the length is 250 or less, the column size will be x+1; otherwise, it will be x+3.
DATE	Date columns always consume 7 bytes.
LONG LONGRAW RAW	Same as for the VARCHAR2 datatype.
NVARCHAR2(x)	If x is in bytes, the calculation is the same as for the VARCHAR2 datatype. If x represents some number of multibyte characters, then you have to multiply by the number of bytes per character.
NCHAR(x)	If x is in bytes, the calculation is the same as for the CHAR datatype. If x represents some number of multibyte characters, then you have to multiply by the number of bytes per character.

Once you have the sum of the column sizes, you can estimate the space required for each row using this formula:

```
ROWSIZE = MAX(UB1 * 3 + UB4 + SB2, (3 * UB1)
              + SUM_OF_COLUMN_SIZES)
```

The MAX function is an Oracle function that returns the larger of two values. For example, MAX(4, 5) returns a value of 5.

Estimating the Number of Blocks Required

The last step, once you've computed the available space per block and the row size, is to compute the number of blocks required for the number of rows that you expect to store. The calculation for this is:

```
BLOCKS_REQUIRED = CEIL(ROWS_TO_STORE
                  / FLOOR(SPACE_FOR_DATA / ROWSIZE)
```

The FLOOR function is similar to CEIL, but it rounds any fractional value down to an integer value. For example, FLOOR(9.9) returns a value of 9.

Estimating the SALAD_TYPE Table's Row Space Requirement

Returning to the SALAD_TYPE table scenario described earlier, let's work through the process of estimating the space required by 10,000 rows. We'll use the type sizes listed earlier, in the section "Collecting prerequisite information." The columns in the SALAD_TYPE table are defined like this:

```
SALAD_TYPE         VARCHAR2(10)
DESCRIPTION_TEXT   VARCHAR2(40)
ORGANIC_FLAG       VARCHAR2(3)
PRICE_PER_POUND    NUMBER(10,2)
LAST_CHANGE_DATE   DATE
```

Assuming a 2KB block size, and assuming that default values are used for PCTFREE and INITRANS, the calculation to find the space in each block that is available for data is as follows:

```
SPACE_FOR_DATA = CEIL((2048 - 20 - 4 -48
- ((1 - 1) * 24) - 14)
* (1-20/100)) - 4
```

This works out to 1,566 bytes per block. The next step is to compute an average row size. Let's assume that the SALAD_TYPE and DESCRIPTION_TEXT fields will, on average, be 50 percent full. For the remaining fields, we will use the maximum size as the basis for our estimate. The following calculations demonstrate how the column lengths are computed:

SALAD_TYPE   Average of 5 bytes used, plus one more for the length, yields a total of 6 bytes.

DESCRIPTION_TEXT	Average of 20 bytes used, plus one more for the length, yields a total of 21 bytes.
ORGANIC_FLAG	Three bytes, plus one for the length, yields a total of 4 bytes.
PRICE_PER_POUND	Ten digits ÷ 2 per byte = 5 bytes. Add one for the exponent to get a total of 6 bytes.
LAST_CHANGE_DATE	Dates are always 7 bytes.

The sum of the column sizes is 44 bytes. Plug that into the `rowsize` formula, and we get:

```
ROWSIZE = MAX(UB1 * 3 + UB4 + SB2, (3 * UB1)
          + 44)
```

The average rowsize works out to 47 bytes. The calculation to compute the space required for 10,000 rows then becomes:

```
BLOCKS_REQUIRED = CEIL(10000
                  / FLOOR(1566 / 47)
```

Work out the math, and you'll find that the estimated number of blocks required to hold 10,000 rows of data is 304. That's fairly close to, but a bit lower than, the 325 blocks that were actually used for 10,000 rows earlier in the chapter when the extrapolation method was used. If you look back, though, you'll find that those rows had an average length of 54 bytes. Plug that value into the previous formula, instead of 47, and the estimate works out to be 345 blocks. That almost exactly matches the earlier extrapolation estimate based on 1,000 representative rows.

Remember that an estimate is just that, an estimate. Don't expect reality to exactly match your estimates. The best that you can hope for is that your estimated space requirements will be just a bit higher than what is actually required. That way, you don't waste too much space, and you don't have to create more extents than originally planned.

Estimating the storage space for an index

The process for estimating the space requirements for an index is similar to that for a table. The calculations are different because the structure of an index differs from that of a table, but you still follow the same basic steps:

1. Figure out how much space in each database block is available for index data.

2. Determine an average index entry size on which to base your estimate.

3. Compute the number of blocks required based on the previous two values.

You can use the calculations shown in the following sections to estimate the space required for the traditional B*Tree index that is most often used in an Oracle database.

Estimating the Amount of Available Space per Block

Oracle provides the following formula for use in estimating the available space in an index block:

```
AVAILABLE_SPACE = ((DB_BLOCK_SIZE - (113 + 24 * INITRANS))
- ((DB_BLOCK_SIZE - (113 + 24 * INITRANS))
* (PCTFREE / 100))
```

The default values for PCTFREE and INITRANS are the same for indexes as for tables. Use 20 for PCTFREE and 1 for INITRANS, if you don't plan to specify different values when creating the index.

Estimating the Entry Size

With a table, you need to calculate an average row size. For an index, you need to calculate the average size of an index entry. The first step in this process is to compute the sum of the column lengths for all columns involved in the index. Table 6-1 can help with this.

Once you have summed the column lengths, you can use the following formula to estimate the size of an index entry:

```
ENTRY_SIZE = 2 + 10 + SUM_OF_COLUMN_SIZES
```

When you are computing the column sizes for columns in the index, take into account the average amount of space that you expect to be used. If you are indexing a VARCHAR(40) field, but you expect the average entry to be only 20 characters long, you will get a more accurate estimate using 20 for the size.

Estimating the Number of Blocks Required

After you've estimated the available space and the average entry size, compute the number of blocks required using the following formula:

```
BLOCKS_REQUIRED = CEIL(1.05 * (NUM_ROWS
                    / FLOOR (AVAILABLE_SPACE / ENTRY_SIZE)))
```

In this formula, NUM_ROWS is the number of rows that you expect to be indexed. If you are indexing columns that are allowed to be null, allow for that when estimating the number of rows. For example, if your table will contain 10,000 rows, but you expect 2,000 rows to have null values for the indexed fields, then use a value of 8,000 for NUM_ROWS.

Estimating the SALAD_TYPE_PK Index's Block Size Requirement

Return one more time to the SALAD_TYPE scenario used earlier. This time, we'll estimate the number of blocks required for an index on the SALAD_TYPE column. The SALAD_TYPE column is defined as follows:

```
SALAD_TYPE          VARCHAR2(10)
```

Assuming a 2KB block size, and assuming the default values of 20 for PCTFREE and 1 for INITRANS, the following calculation returns the available space in each index block:

```
AVAILABLE_SPACE = ((2048 - (113 + 24 * 1))
- ((2048 - (113 + 24 * 1))
* (20 / 100))
```

In this case, the available space works out to 1,529 bytes per block. In computing the average entry size, assume that the SALAD_TYPE FIELD will be 75 percent full—say seven characters on average. Add one byte for the length, and you have 8 bytes for the column length. Plug that value into the entry size formula, and you get the following:

```
ENTRY_SIZE = 2 + 10 + 8
```

This works out to an average entry size of 20 bytes. You can now obtain an estimate of the number of blocks required by using this formula:

```
BLOCKS_REQUIRED = CEIL(1.05 * (10000
                 / FLOOR (1528 / 20)))
```

This finally produces an estimate of 139 blocks for an index on the SALAD_TYPE field.

Summary

In this chapter, you learned:

✦ Oracle manages space in terms of blocks, extents, segments, and tablespaces.

✦ An Oracle block is the smallest unit of space managed by Oracle.

✦ When Oracle allocates space to an object, it allocates a group of contiguous blocks. Such a group is referred to as an extent.

✦ Tablespaces are the logical containers for database objects. Each tablespace uses one or more physical files to store its data.

✦ You can use the DEFAULT STORAGE clause when creating a tablespace to specify default storage attributes for objects stored within that tablespace. When creating an object, you can use the STORAGE clause to override the default storage attributes.

✦ The DBA_EXTENTS and DBA_FREE_SPACE views are the keys to understanding how the space within a database has been allocated.

✦ There are three basic methods for estimating the size of a database object: You can make an educated guess; you can extrapolate from a small sample; or you can calculate an estimate using a set of formulas.

✦   ✦   ✦

Database Administration Tools

SQL*Plus and Server Manager

SQL*Plus and Server Manager are two popular Oracle utilities that DBAs use. Both tools have similar interfaces, and both tools can be used to perform pretty much the same function. This chapter focuses on the use of SQL*Plus because of its superior functionality, and also because Server Manager is on its way out. Server Manager used to have a few capabilities that SQL*Plus didn't have, notably the ability to start and stop a database. With the release of Oracle8i, Oracle has folded these functions into SQL*Plus and has further indicated that support for Server Manager will be dropped in a future release of Oracle.

What Is SQL*Plus?

SQL*Plus is an interactive tool that allows you to type and execute ad-hoc SQL statements and PL/SQL blocks. SQL*Plus also allows you to run scripts and generate simple reports. Beginning with the Oracle8i release, you can use SQL*Plus to start and stop a database or to recover a database. SQL*Plus is frequently used to query the data dictionary, to execute DDL commands, and sometimes just to query a table and see what's out there.

SQL*Plus has been a part of Oracle's software distribution almost from the beginning. Originally a command-line utility, SQL*Plus has been dressed up a bit for Windows platforms, where it is also available in a command-line–oriented GUI interface. SQL*Plus is also used by Oracle Enterprise Manager's SQLPlus Worksheet tool as the underlying engine for executing the commands that you enter. You would never know it to look at it, but underneath that slick-looking, Java-based GUI interface lies good old command-line SQL*Plus.

What Is Server Manager?

Server Manager is a command-line tool that allows you to perform administrative tasks on an Oracle database. These tasks include starting an instance, stopping an instance, and recovering a database. Oracle releases 7.3 and 8.0 used Server Manager to run a large number of administrative scripts that shipped with the Oracle software.

The Server Manager interface is similar to the SQL*Plus interface. At first glance, they both appear to work the same. However, Server Manager doesn't have the built-in line-editing capabilities of SQL*Plus, and Server Manager supports only a small subset of SQL*Plus's formatting functionality.

Since the list of Server Manager-specific functions is so small, and since the interface is already so similar to SQL*Plus, Oracle decided that it simply wasn't worth the trouble to maintain two sets of code. The Oracle8i release of SQL*Plus (release 8.1.5.0.0) now allows you to perform functions such as starting and stopping an instance that previously could only be accomplished using Server Manager. Server Manager is still around because many sites depend on it, but its days are numbered.

Comparing SQL*Plus and Server Manager

SQL*Plus and Server Manager differ in several ways. Table 7-1 lists these differences and highlights how the functionality of SQL*Plus has been enhanced to absorb Server Manager.

<table>
<tr><th colspan="4">Table 7-1
SQL*Plus vs. Server Manager</th></tr>
<tr><th>Function</th><th>SQL*Plus 8.1.x</th><th>SQL*Plus Prior to 8.1</th><th>Server Manager</th></tr>
<tr><td>Start and stop a database</td><td>Yes</td><td>No</td><td>Yes</td></tr>
<tr><td>Recover a database, tablespace, or datafile</td><td>Yes</td><td>No</td><td>Yes</td></tr>
<tr><td>Issue ARCHIVE LOG commands</td><td>Yes</td><td>No</td><td>Yes</td></tr>
<tr><td>Run Oracle-supplied scripts such as CATPROC and CATALOG</td><td>Yes</td><td>No</td><td>Yes</td></tr>
</table>

Function	SQL*Plus 8.1.x	SQL*Plus Prior to 8.1	Server Manager
Execute ad-hoc queries	Yes	Yes	Yes
Format output (placing commas in numbers and so forth)	Yes	Yes	No
Format reports (column headings, page titles, and so forth)	Yes	Yes	No
Execute SQL* Plus scripts	Yes	Yes	No
Connect as SYSDBA or SYSOPER	Yes	No	Yes
Support SET commands	Yes	Yes	Very limited
Prompt a user for input	Yes	Yes	No
Use line-editing commands to edit SQL statements and PL/SQL blocks	Yes	Yes	No

You can see in Table 7-1 that SQL*Plus has the edge when it comes to formatting data and creating reports. SQL*Plus also has the edge in terms of user interaction. It can display messages, prompt a user for input, and implement a rudimentary set of line-editing commands that are useful for correcting mistakes. The only reason to use Server Manager, really, is to start, stop, and recover the database.

Converting Server Manager scripts to SQL*Plus

Many DBAs have written scripts for Server Manager. Since Server Manager is fading away, sooner or later, every Server Manager script will need to be converted to run under SQL*Plus. At first glance, this seems like a simple task, and it almost is. However, when converting from one to the other, you have to take into account the following differences in how the two products work:

✦ Server Manager allows comment lines to begin with the pound-sign (#) character; SQL*Plus does not.

✦ Server Manager allows blank lines within SQL statements; SQL*Plus does not.

✦ SQL*Plus uses the ampersand (&) character to mark substitution variables; Server Manager does not support substitution variables.

✦ SQL*Plus supports the use of the hyphen (-) character as a line continuation character; Server Manager does not.

✦ SQL*Plus requires that the CREATE TYPE and CREATE LIBRARY commands be terminated by a forward-slash (/) on a line by itself. Server Manager does not require this.

When you convert a Server Manager script to SQL*Plus, you have to work through each one of these issues.

Comment Lines

Server Manager allows you to mark a line as a comment by preceding it with a pound-sign (#) character. Here's an example:

```
# This is a comment in Server Manager
```

Nothing will happen when you type this comment line into Server Manager. Type the same line into SQL*Plus, however, and you will receive an Unknown Command error. To mark a line as a comment in SQL*Plus, precede it with either the REM command or by a double-hyphen (--). Consider this example:

```
REM This is a comment in SQL*Plus
-- This is also a comment in SQL*Plus
```

When converting a script from Server Manager to SQL*Plus, check your comments and change any that start with the pound sign (#) so that they start with REM or -- instead.

Blank Lines

Both Server Manager and SQL*Plus allow you to enter SQL statements that span multiple lines. Server Manager, however, allows you to include blank lines in a SQL statement, while SQL*Plus does not. Here's an example:

```
SVRMGR> SELECT *
    2>
    3> FROM dual;
D
-
X
1 row selected.
```

Try to enter that same statement, including the blank line, into SQL*Plus, and here's what will happen:

```
SQL> SELECT *
  2
SQL> FROM dual;
SP2-0042: unknown command "FROM DUAL" - rest of line ignored.
```

What's happening here? SQL*Plus recognizes a blank line as the end of a statement, so the blank line after `SELECT *` causes SQL*Plus to terminate entry of the statement, leaving it in the buffer where you can edit it using line-editing commands. As far as SQL*Plus is concerned, the line `FROM dual;` is a new command. Because it terminates with a semicolon, SQL*Plus attempts to execute it. The `FROM dual;` command, of course, is not a valid statement, so the result is an error message.

Oracle does provide some relief from this problem through the use of the `SQLBLANKLINES` setting. This setting is a new feature added to SQL*Plus in the 8.1.5 release, specifically to make it easier to convert Server Manager scripts. The following command causes SQL*Plus to allow blank lines in SQL statements:

```
SET SQLBLANKLINES ON
```

Here's an example showing how the `SET SQLBLANKLINES ON` command allows the same command that failed earlier to run successfully:

```
SQL> SET SQLBLANKLINES ON
SQL> SELECT *
  2
  3  FROM dual;

D
-
X

1 row selected.
```

If you have a Server Manager script to convert, and you don't want to go through and remove blank lines from SQL statements, place a `SET SQLBLANKLINES ON` command at the beginning of the script.

Tip   If you use `SET SQLBLANKLINES ON` at the beginning of a script, you may want to add `SET SQLBLANKLINES OFF` to the end. That way, if you run several scripts interactively in one SQL*Plus session, you won't inadvertently cause subsequent scripts to fail.

Substitution Variables

To enable you to write generic scripts that you can run multiple times using different input values, SQL*Plus allows you to embed substitution variables in SQL statements. When SQL*Plus encounters one of these variables, it stops and prompts for a value before continuing. Consider this example:

```
SQL> SELECT animal_name
  2  FROM aquatic_animal
  3  WHERE id_no=&animal_id;
Enter value for animal_id: 100
old   3: WHERE id_no=&animal_id
new   3: WHERE id_no=100

ANIMAL_NAME
------------------------------
Flipper

1 row selected.
```

Notice how SQL*Plus prompted for an animal ID number when it encountered the
&animal_id variable. Server Manager doesn't support this feature at all. At first
that may not seem like a problem when converting away from Server Manager, but
it actually is. Because Server Manager doesn't support substitution, you can place
ampersands (&) in Server Manager scripts with impunity. The following statement
will run just fine in Server Manager:

```
SELECT tank_no
FROM tank
WHERE tank_name = 'Blue & Red';
```

Try this same statement in SQL*Plus, however, and you suddenly find yourself
being prompted for the value of red:

```
SQL> SELECT tank_no
  2  FROM tank
  3  WHERE tank_name = 'Blue & Red';
Enter value for red:
```

A relatively easy fix for this, if you don't want to hunt through your Server Manager
script looking for ampersands, is to place the following commands at the beginning
and end of your script:

```
SET DEFINE OFF
...
SET DEFINE ON
```

The command SET DEFINE OFF turns off the SQL*Plus substitution feature.

Continuation Characters

The use of the hyphen as a continuation character in SQL*Plus presents a subtle
problem. Since Server Manager doesn't support continuation characters at all, you
might think you don't need to worry about this. In fact, you do. The following SQL
statement illustrates the problem:

```
SELECT 10 -
       3 FROM dual;
```

Server Manager will interpret this as a subtraction and will return a value of 7. SQL*Plus will interpret the hyphen as a continuation character, will combine the two lines into one, and will return an error, as shown here:

```
SQL> SELECT 10 -
>       3 FROM dual;
SELECT 10        3 FROM dual
                    *
ERROR at line 1:
ORA-00923: FROM keyword not found where expected
```

Unfortunately, no easy fix exists. It's a very subtle problem. You won't encounter it often, because it's rare for anyone to break up a subtraction by leaving the minus sign at the end of a line. Your only recourse here is to manually scan your Server Manager scripts, look for this problem, and fix it when you find it.

The CREATE TYPE and CREATE LIBRARY Commands

The last issue that you need to worry about is the one involving the CREATE TYPE and CREATE LIBRARY commands. Server Manager will allow these commands to be terminated by a semicolon, as in this example:

```
CREATE TYPE PERSON AS OBJECT (
    NAME VARCHAR2(30)
);
```

SQL*Plus, on the other hand, requires that these commands be terminated with a forward slash on a line by itself. For example:

```
CREATE TYPE PERSON AS OBJECT (
    NAME VARCHAR2(30)
);
/
```

The forward slash must be the first character on the line, and the semicolon at the end of the type definition is still required. There is no magic solution to this problem. If you convert a script containing CREATE TYPE or CREATE LIBRARY commands from Server Manager to SQL*Plus, you have to go in and add the forward-slash characters.

Using SQL*Plus to Enter and Execute SQL Statements

This section shows you how to start SQL*Plus and how to enter and execute SQL statements. You will see how you can edit those SQL statements, which can be quite helpful when you've mistyped something. Finally, you'll see how you can save a SQL statement to a file so that you can return to it later.

Starting SQL*Plus

How you start SQL*Plus depends on whether you are running the Windows platform, and, if you are running Windows, whether you want to run the GUI version. If you are running UNIX, or if you want to start SQL*Plus from a Windows command prompt, use the `sqlplus` command, as shown in this example:

```
C:\>sqlplus

SQL*Plus: Release 8.1.5.0.0 - Production on Wed Aug 4 18:02:53 1999

(c) Copyright 1999 Oracle Corporation.  All rights reserved.

Enter user-name:
```

If you are running Windows and you want to run the GUI version of SQL*Plus, click Start, point to Programs, point to Oracle – OraHome81, point to Application Development, and select SQL Plus. The SQL*Plus icon is shown in Figure 7-1.

Figure 7-1: The SQL*Plus icon

No matter how you start SQL*Plus, you will be prompted for a username and a password. The GUI version will also prompt you for a Net8 service name (the field title on the screen is actually Host String), so if you are connecting to a remote database, you may want to use that version.

Entering commands in SQL*Plus

How you enter a command in SQL*Plus depends partly on whether the command is a SQL statement, a PL/SQL block, or a command to SQL*Plus itself. For the most part, you just type commands. The differences are in how you terminate those commands.

Entering SQL Statements

To enter and execute a SQL statement, just type it and terminate it with a semicolon, as shown in this example:

```
SELECT * FROM dual;
```

You can also use a forward slash to terminate a SQL statement, as shown here:

```
SELECT * FROM dual
/
```

Don't mix the two methods in the same statement. Use either a semicolon or a forward slash, but not both. You can also terminate a SQL statement with a blank line. When you do that, the statement is not executed, it is simply held in the buffer of SQL*Plus, where you can edit it.

Entering PL/SQL Blocks

To enter and execute a PL/SQL block, you must terminate the block both with a semicolon and a forward slash, as shown in this example:

```
BEGIN
   NULL;
END;
/
```

Using both a semicolon and a forward slash together when PL/SQL is involved but not when SQL is involved doesn't represent an inconsistency in design. The semicolon is necessary because it is part of PL/SQL syntax. Because semicolons are used as statement terminators in PL/SQL, they can't be relied on to mark the end of a block — hence, the need for the forward slash.

You can enter a PL/SQL block without executing it, by terminating it with a period (.) instead of a forward slash. Consider this example:

```
BEGIN
   NULL;
END;
.
```

Using the period causes SQL*Plus to hold the block in the buffer for further editing.

Entering SQL*Plus Commands

In addition to accepting SQL statements and PL/SQL blocks, both of which are executed by the Oracle database software, SQL*Plus also recognizes a large number of commands. A good example is the COLUMN command, used to format output from a query:

```
COLUMN animal_name FORMAT A30
```

Commands like the COLUMN command have meaning only to SQL*Plus and are not passed on to the Oracle database. Because of that, these commands don't need any special terminator characters.

Sometimes, SQL*Plus commands can be quite long. This is especially true of the TTITLE and BTITLE commands that are used to define page headers and footers.

If you have a long command, SQL*Plus allows you to continue it across multiple lines by using the hyphen (-) as a continuation character. Consider this example:

```
TTITLE CENTER "IDG's Seapark" SKIP 1-
       LEFT "Animal Management" -
       RIGHT "Animal Feeding Report"
```

When you continue commands like this, you must have at least one space preceding the continuation character.

Editing your work in SQL*Plus

SQL*Plus contains a rudimentary set of editing commands. These commands allow you to edit SQL statements that you have entered into the buffer, and they allow you to save and restore SQL statements to and from files. The line-editing commands can be quite handy when you find that you've made a mistake typing a long SQL statement. If you don't like line editing, or if you have extensive changes to make, you can use the EDIT command to invoke an external editor such as vi (UNIX) or Notepad (Windows).

The Line-editing Commands

The line-editing commands that SQL*Plus implements are rudimentary but quite functional. They are useful for correcting small mistakes in SQL queries and PL/SQL blocks. The following list summarizes these commands:

✦ L—Lists the current SQL statement in the buffer.

✦ L n—Displays line n of the current SQL statement.

✦ L n m—Displays lines n–m of the current SQL statement.

✦ C/x/y/—Changes the first occurrence of x on a line into y. This command operates on the current line.

✦ DEL—Deletes the current line.

✦ DEL n—Deletes line n.

✦ DEL n m—Deletes lines n–m.

✦ I—Inserts a new line below the current line.

✦ A text—Appends text onto the end of the current line.

✦ /—Executes the statement in the buffer.

When you are editing a SQL statement, the concept of the current line is an important one to understand. Put simply, the *current line* is always the most recent line displayed by SQL*Plus. Unless you specify a line number, which you can do with the L and DEL commands, all line-editing commands operate on whichever line is current when you issue the commands. Read through the following example and commentary to get a feel for how the line-editing commands work:

A query is entered that has several mistakes. The result is an error message.

```
SQL> SELECT id_no, tank_num, animal_name
  2  Animal_parent
  3  FROM
  4  WHERE birth_date > SYSDATE;
WHERE birth_date > SYSDATE
      *
ERROR at line 4:
ORA-00903: invalid table name


SQL>
```

The L command is used to list the first line so that a correction can be made.

```
SQL> L 1
  1* SELECT id_no, tank_num, animal_name
SQL>
```

The C command is used to change tank_num to tank_no.

```
SQL> C /tank_num/tank_no/
  1* SELECT id_no, tank_no, animal_name
SQL>
```

Line 2 is a mistake, and the DEL command is used to delete it.

```
SQL> DEL 2
SQL>
```

The buffer is relisted so that you can reorient yourself. Note that all the lines following the deleted line have been renumbered.

```
SQL> L
  1  SELECT id_no, tank_no, animal_name
  2  FROM
  3* WHERE birth_date > SYSDATE
SQL>
```

Line 2 is listed because it has the next and last error to be fixed.

```
SQL> L 2
  2* FROM
SQL>
```

The A command is used to append the table name onto the end of line 2.

```
SQL> A  aquatic_animal
  2* FROM aquatic_animal
SQL>
```

The command is listed one last time before it is executed.

```
SQL> L 1 3
  1  SELECT id_no, tank_no, animal_name
  2  FROM aquatic_animal
  3* WHERE birth_date > SYSDATE
SQL>
```

The forward slash is used to execute the command as it stands now.

```
SQL> /

no rows selected
```

Take time to experiment with the line-editing commands and become familiar with them. They may seem crude — they are crude — but they can still save you a lot of time.

The SAVE and GET Commands

SQL*Plus includes commands that allow you to save a statement from the buffer to a file and to load a statement from a file back into the buffer. The commands are SAVE and GET.

The SAVE command writes the current SQL statement (or PL/SQL block) from the buffer into a file. You have to supply a file name as an argument to SAVE, as shown in this example:

```
SQL> SELECT * FROM AQUATIC_ANIMAL
  2
SQL> SAVE c:\a\save_example.sql
Created file c:\a\save_example.sql
```

This SAVE command works if you are creating a new file. If you intend to overwrite an existing file, then you must use the REPLACE option, as shown here:

```
  SAVE c:\a\save_example.sql REPLACE
```

The GET command does the reverse of SAVE. It loads a SQL statement from a file into the buffer where you can edit it. The following example shows an empty buffer and then demonstrates using the GET command to load a statement into that buffer:

```
SQL> L
SP2-0223: No lines in SQL buffer.
SQL> GET c:\a\save_example.sql
  1* SELECT * FROM AQUATIC_ANIMAL
```

Once you have loaded the SQL statement into the buffer, you can either execute it right away using the forward-slash command, or you can use the line-editing commands to change it first.

The EDIT Command

The SQL*Plus EDIT command allows you to invoke an external text editor to edit the statement in the buffer. On Windows platforms, the Notepad editor is used. Generally, you use these steps when using the EDIT command:

1. Type a SQL statement.

2. Invoke an editor by using the EDIT command.

3. Edit the statement in the editor.

4. Save the statement and exit the editor.

5. Use the forward slash (/) to execute the statement.

Figure 7-2 shows the results of entering a statement and then issuing the EDIT command on a Windows platform.

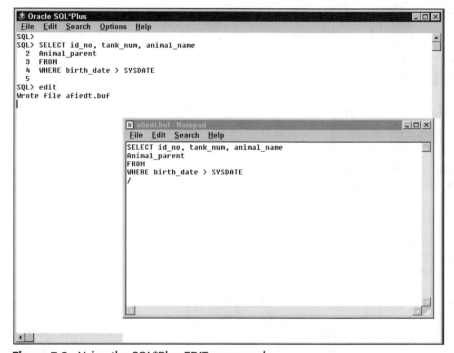

Figure 7-2: Using the SQL*Plus EDIT command

For large statements or those with major mistakes, it's often easier to edit them with an external editor than it is to use the line-editing commands. The advantage of using the internal editor is that it is always the same, and always available, regardless of the operating system being used.

Using SQL*Plus to Generate Reports

To its credit, SQL*Plus allows you to quickly create decent-looking ad-hoc reports. The SQL*Plus environment enables you to create column titles, page headers, and page footers, and even to prompt for variables. This section highlights the major steps to completing reports quickly.

Basic report commands

When writing a report with SQL*Plus, start by creating the query. Then you can add report features such as column headings, page titles, and so forth using SQL*Plus commands. This section shows you how to do the following basic reporting tasks:

✦ Modify the format and heading for a column

✦ Add a title to the report

✦ Write the formatted query results (that is, the report) to a file

The SQL*Plus COLUMN, TTITLE, BTITLE, and SPOOL commands are used for these tasks.

Note
You can run all the report examples in this chapter if you install the sample schema from the CD-ROM. Appendix A contains instructions on how to install the sample schema into an Oracle8i database.

The COLUMN Command

The COLUMN command enables you to change the heading of a column, set the width of a column, and set the display format to use for a column. A simplified version of the syntax for the COLUMN command looks like this:

```
COLUMN columnname [HEADING headingtext]
       [FORMAT formattext] [WORD_WRAPPED|TRUNCATED]
```

Replace columnname with the actual column name from your query, and replace headingtext with your desired column heading. If the heading includes spaces, enclose it in double quotes (" "). To make a heading that contains two lines, use the vertical bar (|) as a divider. For example, the following COLUMN command results in a heading with Birth and Date aligned vertically for the column named BIRTH_DATE.

```
COLUMN BIRTH_DATE HEADING "Birth|Date"
```

The resulting column heading looks like this:

```
Birth
Date
-----
```

The FORMAT clause, together with formattext, controls the display format used for the column. The FORMAT clause is most useful for numbers. For text columns, you can control only the display width. For numeric columns, you can control both the column width and the appearance of the numbers.

Table 7-2 shows examples of some format specifications. The column on the right shows a sample of some data formatted according to each specification.

Table 7-2
Formats in the SQL*Plus COLUMN Command

Datatype	Sample Format	Sample Results
Number	COLUMN x FORMAT 999,999.00	4,550.00
Number	COLUMN x FORMAT 000,000.00	004,550.00
Number	COLUMN x FORMAT $9999.99	$4550.00
Character	COLUMN y FORMAT A10	Supercalif
Character	COLUMN y FORMAT A20	Supercalifragilistic

For text columns, you can use Axx, where xx is a number to control the number of characters displayed in a column. Wrap text data within the column by adding the WORD_WRAP parameter to the COLUMN command. For example, the following COLUMN command allows the MARKINGS_DESCRIPTION column to wrap data:

```
COLUMN MARKINGS_DESCRIPTION FORMAT A10 WORD_WRAP
```

The resulting report will look like the one shown in this example:

```
SQL> COLUMN MARKINGS_DESCRIPTION FORMAT A10 WORD_WRAP
SQL> SELECT ANIMAL_NAME, MARKINGS_DESCRIPTION
  2  FROM AQUATIC_ANIMAL;

ANIMAL_NAME                     MARKINGS_D
------------------------------- ----------
Flipper                         Gray with
                                pink
                                tongue

Skipper                         Small scar
                                on right
                                fin
```

The WORD_WRAPPED setting is optional. If you don't specify it, then the lines in the column will be broken exactly at the column boundary, even if that means breaking the line in the middle of a word. If you don't want multiline columns, use the TRUNCATE option. This causes SQL*Plus to chop values that are longer than the column is wide, instead of wrapping them.

For numeric columns, you specify the format using a pattern of 9 0, . and $ characters. The 9 and 0 characters control the number of digits to be displayed. Leading "0" characters cause the number to be displayed with leading zeros; otherwise, leading zeros are suppressed. A leading $ can be used to print a dollar sign in front of dollar values. The . indicates the location of the decimal point, and the , s indicate how you want to use commas to separate groups of digits.

For date columns, you can't use SQL*Plus to define the display format for the date. Instead, you have to treat date columns as you would character columns, and you have to specify the date format in your SELECT statement by using Oracle's built-in TO_CHAR function. The TO_CHAR function has its own set of formatting characters. Table 7-3 shows the characters commonly used for dates.

Cross-Reference   See Appendix B, "SQL Built-in Function Reference," for a complete list.

Table 7-3
Date Conversion in the TO_CHAR(DATE) Function

Abbreviation	Meaning
DD	Day (01 through 31)
Day	Day of the week with initial letter capitalized (such as Saturday)
MM	Month (01 through 12)
Month	Month spelled out and initial letter capitalized
MON	First three letters of month in capital letters
YY	Year (00 through 99)
YYYY	Four-digit year (for example, 1999, 2000, and so on)
MI	Minute (00 through 59)
HH	Hour (01 through 12)
HH24	Hour (01 through 24)
SS	Second (00 through 59)

Tip   Watch out for the small but critical difference between MM (the month abbreviation) and MI (the minute abbreviation).

The following example demonstrates using the TO_CHAR function to format a date column in a report:

```
SQL> COLUMN animal_name FORMAT A11
SQL> COLUMN b_date FORMAT A11
SQL> SELECT animal_name,
  2         TO_CHAR(birth_date,'dd-Mon-yyyy') b_date
  3  FROM aquatic_animal;

ANIMAL_NAME BIRTH_DATE
----------- -----------
Flipper     01-Feb-1968
Skipper     01-Jan-1978
Bopper      11-Mar-1990
```

When you use the TO_CHAR function to format a date like this, be sure to provide a column alias in your SQL query. That's what gives the resulting column a name that you can work with. In this example, the alias is b_date. The column alias must match the name used with the COLUMN command.

The TTITLE and BTITLE Commands

SQL*Plus allows you to create page headers, or titles, for reports that you generate. You can also create page footers if you like. You use the TTITLE and BTITLE commands for these purposes. Title commands can get fairly long, and they contain a mixture of text strings and modifiers that control how and where those text strings print. Listing 7-1 demonstrates using the TTITLE command to place a multiline title at the top of a report:

Listing 7-1: **Placing a title at the top of a report**

```
SQL> SET LINESIZE 47
SQL> TTITLE CENTER "SeaPark" SKIP 1 -
>        LEFT "Animal Report" RIGHT "Page " -
>        FORMAT 999 SQL.PNO SKIP 3
SQL> COLUMN id_no FORMAT 999 HEADING "ID"
SQL> COLUMN animal_name FORMAT A30 HEADING "Name"
SQL> COLUMN birth_date FORMAT A11 HEADING "Birth Date" -
>          JUST RIGHT
SQL> SELECT id_no,
  2         animal_name,
  3         TO_CHAR(birth_date,'dd-Mon-yyyy') birth_date
  4    FROM aquatic_animal
  5   WHERE death_date IS NULL;

                    SeaPark
Animal Report                          Page    1


   ID Name                          Birth Date
 ---- ----------------------------- -----------
  100 Flipper                       01-Feb-1968
  105 Skipper                       01-Jan-1978
  112 Bopper                        11-Mar-1990
  151 Batty                         06-Jun-1996
  166 Shorty                        06-Jun-1996
  145 Squacky                       06-Jun-1996
  175 Paintuin                      14-May-1997
  199 Nosey                         05-Jan-1990
  202 Rascal                        01-Oct-1994

9 rows selected.

SQL>
```

Let's take a look at the TTITLE command used for this report. It is a rather long command that continues over three lines. The first line looks like this:

```
TTITLE CENTER "SeaPark" SKIP 1 -
```

The keyword CENTER causes subsequent text to be aligned to the center of the page. In this case, the subsequent text is "SeaPark", which did indeed print top and center. The SKIP 1 clause causes the title to advance one line. The second line of the TTITLE command is:

```
LEFT "Animal Report" RIGHT "Page " -
```

The keyword LEFT functions similarly to CENTER, except that it causes subsequent text to print aligned to the left of the page. After "Animal Report", the RIGHT keyword forces the page number to print flush right. The third line of the TTITLE command looks like this:

```
FORMAT 999 SQL.PNO SKIP 3
```

The FORMAT clause specifies a numeric format used for any numbers in the title that might follow this clause. In this case, the number being formatted is the page number. The SQL.PNO parameter is a special construct that SQL*Plus recognizes and replaces with the current page number. A final SKIP clause is used to advance three lines to allow some vertical space between the page title and the column headings.

Note   The SKIP 3 clause results in only two blank lines. The report advances three lines, but the first advance simply gets it past the title line.

There are a couple of points worth examining about this report. First, the SET LINESIZE command sets the line width at 47. Why such an odd number? Because that's what it took to get the page number to print flush right with the right edge of the Birth Date column. The TTITLE command's CENTER and RIGHT clauses reference the linesize setting to determine exactly where the center and the right edge of a page are.

Also notice the use of the JUST RIGHT clause in the COLUMN command for the birth date data. This clause causes the column heading to print flush with the right edge of a character column, rather than the left, which looks better where dates are concerned.

The BTITLE command functions exactly like TTITLE. All the same clauses may be used. The only difference is that BTITLE defines a page footer that prints at the *bottom* of each page.

Titles and Dates

SQL*Plus makes it easy to get the page number into a report title; you just place SQL.PNO in the title where you want the page number to appear. Since it's so easy to get the page number, you might think that SQL*Plus would make it just as easy to get the date in the title. It doesn't.

Getting the current date into a report title requires that you use an arcane incantation of SQL*Plus commands and SQL statements. Essentially, you need to do the following:

1. Think up a name for a substitution variable that will hold the current date.

2. Place this substitution variable name in the TTITLE command where you want the date to appear. Do not use an ampersand here. SQL*Plus will replace the variable with its contents when it prints the page title.

3. Add a date column to your query. Use TO_CHAR to format the date the way you want it to appear.

4. Use the COLUMN command's NEW_VALUE clause to have SQL*Plus place the value of the date column into the substitution variable. Also use the NOPRINT clause so the date doesn't print as a column on the report.

5. Execute the query to produce the report. The date will appear in the report header.

The following code snippet provides an example of the technique just described:

```
TTITLE LEFT TODAYS_DATE CENTER 'The Animal Report' SKIP 2
COLUMN TODAYS_DATE NEW_VALUE TODAYS_DATE NOPRINT
SELECT TO_CHAR (SYSDATE, 'dd-Mon-yyyy') TODAYS_DATE,
       ID_NO,
       ANIMAL_NAME
FROM AQUATIC_ANIMAL
WHERE TANK_NO = 1;
```

When you execute this code, the results will look like this:

```
05-Aug-1999                          The Animal Report

    ID_NO ANIMAL_NAME
--------- ------------------------------
      100 Flipper
      105 Skipper
      112 Bopper

3 rows selected.
```

As you can see, the date shows up in the report header in the position indicated by the TODAYS_DATE substitution variable in the TTITLE command.

Note   You can use this same technique to place other information into a title. Anything that you can query from your database, you can place into a substitution variable, which can then be used in a TTITLE or BTITLE command.

The SPOOL Command

The SQL*Plus SPOOL command is a useful command that writes the results of your query to a file. In fact, if you want to print a report generated with SQL*Plus, the only way you can do it is to first spool it to a file. Later, you can copy the file to the printer to print the report. The syntax for the SPOOL command looks like this:

```
SPOOL filename
```

The filename argument may optionally include a path and an extension. If you don't specify an extension, SQL*Plus automatically adds one (usually .lis or .lst).

Once you issue the SPOOL command, SQL*Plus writes everything to the spool file that it writes to the display. It does this until you issue the following command to stop the spooling:

```
SPOOL OFF
```

Listing 7-2 demonstrates using the SPOOL command to send the output of a report to a file.

Listing 7-2: **Spooling a report to a file**

```
SET LINESIZE 47
TTITLE CENTER "SeaPark" SKIP 1 -
        LEFT "Animal Report" RIGHT "Page " -
        FORMAT 999 SQL.PNO SKIP 3
COLUMN id_no FORMAT 999 HEADING "ID"
COLUMN animal_name FORMAT A30 HEADING "Name"
COLUMN birth_date FORMAT A11 HEADING "Birth Date" -
        JUST RIGHT

SPOOL animal_report
SELECT id_no,
        animal_name,
        TO_CHAR(birth_date,'dd-Mon-yyyy') birth_date
FROM aquatic_animal
WHERE death_date IS NULL;
SPOOL OFF
```

Notice that the two SPOOL commands bracket the SELECT statement. There's no sense issuing the commands earlier, unless you also want your COLUMN commands to be written to the spool file.

Having written the report to the animal_report file, you can print the report by sending the file to a printer. On UNIX systems, you can easily do this using the lp command. On Windows systems, if you have a DOS printer mapped, you can copy the file to that printer. Otherwise, you can load the file into an editor such as Notepad or Microsoft Word, and print the file from there.

The BREAK and COMPUTE Commands

SQL*Plus provides a way to summarize and group sets of rows in a report. Using the BREAK and COMPUTE commands, you can make a report with details, breaks, and summaries.

The general syntax of the BREAK command follows:

```
BRE[AK] [ON report_element [action]
ON report_element [action]...]
```

The BREAK command is actually one of the more difficult SQL*Plus commands to master. Generally, you replace the report_element parameters with column names. Each report element in a BREAK command has an action associated with it. Whenever the value of one of the report elements changes, SQL*Plus executes the action that you specified for that element. Typical actions include suppressing repeating values, skipping one or more lines, or skipping to a new page.

The following example shows one of the more common uses for the BREAK command, which is to suppress repeating values in a column. The query returns a list of animals and tank numbers that is sorted by tank number. Since all the animals for one tank are grouped together, the results will look better if the tank number is printed only once for each group. You use the BREAK command to accomplish this. Take a look at the example shown in Listing 7-3.

Listing 7-3: Suppressing repeating values in a column

```
SQL> BREAK ON tank_no NODUPLICATES SKIP 1
SQL> SELECT tank_no, id_no, animal_name
  2  FROM aquatic_animal
  3  ORDER BY tank_no, id_no;

TANK_NO    ID_NO ANIMAL_NAME
--------- -------- ------------------------------
        1      100 Flipper
               105 Skipper
               112 Bopper

        2      145 Squacky
               151 Batty
               166 Shorty
               175 Paintuin

        3      199 Nosey
               202 Rascal
               240 Snoops

10 rows selected.
```

Notice that two break actions are listed for the tank_no column. The first action is NODUPLICATES, which causes the value of the tank_no column to print only when it changes. The result is that the tank number is printed only once per group.

The second action is SKIP 1, which tells SQL*Plus to skip a line. Whenever the value of the tank_no column changes, SQL*Plus executes both these actions. The result of SKIP 1 is that a blank line separates each group of animals, making it easy to quickly ascertain which animals are in which tank.

Note   When you break on a column, you must also sort the report on the same column. In the previous example, the break column is also the first column listed in the SQL statement's ORDER BY clause. If your break columns and your ORDER BY columns don't correspond, your data won't be grouped in any rational fashion, and your report will look bad.

SQL*Plus can print summary information about the rows in the group. You use the COMPUTE command to do this. The COMPUTE command works in conjunction with the BREAK command, allowing you to print summary information on breaks. The general syntax of the COMPUTE command follows:

```
COMP[UTE] [function [LABEL] text OF
expression|column|alias  ON
expression | column | alias | REPORT | ROW]
```

The COMPUTE command is another difficult SQL*Plus command to master. Like the BREAK command, the COMPUTE command is most easily explained by using an example. Using the SEAPARK tables, you can create a report showing the number of animals each caretaker handles, listed by the caretaker name and then by the tank number. You can report a count of animals for each tank, each caretaker, and the entire report. To create this report, you will need three COMPUTE commands. The first causes SQL*Plus to report a count of records for the entire report, and it looks like this:

```
COMPUTE COUNT OF ID_NO ON REPORT
```

This command tells SQL*Plus to generate a count based on the ID_NO column. The ON REPORT clause generates that count for all the records in the report. You could actually count any non-null column. The ID_NO column is just a convenient choice because it is the table's primary key.

The next COMPUTE command looks like this:

```
COMPUTE COUNT OF ID_NO ON C_NAME
```

This COMPUTE command is similar to the previous one, except that it computes a count of records for each distinct value of C_NAME, or for each caretaker. For the results of this command to make sense, you must sort the report on the same value.

The last of the three COMPUTE commands is this:

```
COMPUTE COUNT OF ID_NO ON TANK_NO
```

This final command tells SQL*Plus to generate a count of records (animals) in each tank. When you are counting records for specific columns, as in this report, you must have the report sorted correctly. It's also important that you break on the same columns that you name in your COMPUTE commands. This report is computing totals for each caretaker and tank combination, and for each caretaker. The BREAK command used looks like this:

```
BREAK ON REPORT ON C_NAME SKIP 2 ON TANK_NO SKIP 1
```

The COMPUTE command tells SQL*Plus to generate summary information for a column, but it's the BREAK command that allows SQL*Plus to print that information. Notice that this BREAK command lists all the columns — REPORT, C_NAME, and TANK_NO — that were mentioned in the three COMPUTE statements.

The final requirement is to sort the query results to match the break order. The ORDER BY clause used in the query is:

```
ORDER BY T.CHIEF_CARETAKER_NAME, T.TANK_NO, A.ID_NO;
```

This ORDER BY clause sorts the report first on the caretaker's name, then within that on the tank number, and within that on the animal ID number. The leading columns in the ORDER BY clause match the column order in the BREAK command. That's important. If that order doesn't match, you'll get a mixed-up report. It's okay to have other columns in the ORDER BY clause, beyond those listed in the BREAK command, but they must come at the end.

The complete SQL*Plus script to generate this report looks like this:

```
COLUMN C_NAME FORMAT A15
BREAK ON REPORT ON C_NAME SKIP 2 ON TANK_NO SKIP 1
COMPUTE COUNT OF ID_NO ON REPORT
COMPUTE COUNT OF ID_NO ON C_NAME
COMPUTE COUNT OF ID_NO ON TANK_NO
SELECT T.CHIEF_CARETAKER_NAME C_NAME,
       T.TANK_NO,
       A.ID_NO,
       A.ANIMAL_NAME
FROM TANK T, AQUATIC_ANIMAL A
WHERE T.TANK_NO = A.TANK_NO
ORDER BY T.CHIEF_CARETAKER_NAME, T.TANK_NO, A.ID_NO;
```

Listing 7-4 presents the results from executing this script.

Listing 7-4: **Animal counts by tank and caretaker**

```
C_NAME                TANK_NO      ID_NO ANIMAL_NAME
-----------------   ----------   -------------------
Harold Kamalii           1         100 Flipper
                                   105 Skipper
                                   112 Bopper
                    *********      -----
                    count             3


***************                    -----
count                                 3


Jan Neeleson             3         199 Nosey
                                   202 Rascal
                                   240 Snoops
                    *********      -----
                    count             3


***************                    -----
count                                 3


Joseph Kalama            2         145 Squacky
                                   151 Batty
                                   166 Shorty
                                   175 Paintuin
                    *********      -----
                    count             4

***************                    -----
count                                 4


                                   -----
count                                10
10 rows selected.
```

The results of the query give you a count for each tank, as well as for each caretaker. You can tell which count is which by the position of the label count, which SQL*Plus automatically places in the column corresponding to the ON clause of the COMPUTE command. Thus, the count label for the animals per caretaker is under the C_NAME column. Together, the COMPUTE and BREAK commands allow you to produce some sophisticated reports using SQL*Plus.

Substitution variables

Substitution variables help you write flexible queries that you can easily reuse. For example, you can write a script to produce a report and have that script prompt you for selection criteria each time that you run it.

Defining and Using a Substitution Variable

The DEFINE command allows you to define a SQL*Plus substitution variable. You can then use that variable anywhere in a SQL query. Typically, you would use it to supply a value in the query's WHERE clause.

The syntax for defining a variable looks like this:

```
DEF[INE] [variable = text]
```

Note

> You actually don't need to define a variable before using it. The only real reasons to use the DEFINE command are to define a constant or to define a variable with an initial value.

You can place a substitution variable in a query by preceding it with an ampersand (&). When you place a substitution variable in a SQL statement, SQL*Plus prompts you to supply a value for that variable when it executes the statement. Take a look at the following statement, which uses a substitution variable named STARTS_WITH:

```
SELECT ID_NO, ANIMAL_NAME
FROM AQUATIC_ANIMAL
WHERE ANIMAL_NAME LIKE '&STARTS_WITH%';
```

The ampersand is a sign to SQL*Plus that the word that follows is the name of a substitution variable — in this case, STARTS_WITH. When you execute the query, SQL*Plus asks you to supply a value for this variable. SQL*Plus then displays the before and after versions of the line involved. Finally, it executes the query and returns the results. The following example illustrates how this process works:

```
SQL> SELECT ID_NO, ANIMAL_NAME
  2  FROM AQUATIC_ANIMAL
  3  WHERE ANIMAL_NAME LIKE '&STARTS_WITH%';
Enter value for starts_with: B
old   3: WHERE ANIMAL_NAME LIKE '&STARTS_WITH%'
new   3: WHERE ANIMAL_NAME LIKE 'B%'

    ID_NO ANIMAL_NAME
--------- ------------------------------
      112 Bopper
      151 Batty

2 rows selected.
```

In this case, the user supplies a value of B for the variable. This causes the query to become a query for the names of all animals whose names begin with B. There are two of those, named Bopper and Batty.

Using substitution variables like this doesn't make much sense when you are executing queries interactively. They make a lot of sense when you encapsulate a query into a script file that you can execute repeatedly, because they allow you to supply different inputs each time. It's a lot faster and easier to answer a prompt than it is to load a query, edit it to change the selection criteria, execute it, edit it again, and so forth.

Using Double-Ampersand Variables

When you preface a substitution variable with a single ampersand, as shown in the previous example, SQL*Plus will prompt for a value each time it encounters the variable. This can be a bit of a nuisance if you use a variable in two different places in the same SQL statement. Not only will you get prompted twice, but you must also be sure to supply the same value each time, or risk having your query return the wrong results.

There's a solution to this problem, and that is to use a double ampersand (&&) when you are referencing the same variable twice. The double ampersand tells SQL*Plus not to prompt twice for the same variable. If the variable has already been defined, then SQL*Plus reuses the previous value. Here's an example showing the STARTS_WITH variable being used twice in the same query:

```
SQL> SELECT ANIMAL_NAME, ' Begins with a '||'&&STARTS_WITH'
  2  FROM AQUATIC_ANIMAL
  3  WHERE ANIMAL_NAME LIKE '&&STARTS_WITH%';
Enter value for starts_with:
old   1: SELECT ANIMAL_NAME, ' Begins with a '||'&&STARTS_WITH'
new   1: SELECT ANIMAL_NAME, ' Begins with a '||'B'
old   3: WHERE ANIMAL_NAME LIKE '&&STARTS_WITH%'
new   3: WHERE ANIMAL_NAME LIKE 'B%'

ANIMAL_NAME                      'BEGINSWITHA'||'
-------------------------------- ----------------
Bopper                           Begins with a B
Batty                            Begins with a B

2 rows selected.
```

As you can see from the example, SQL*Plus prompts for the STARTS_WITH variable once but uses it twice.

Using SQL*Plus to Write Scripts

When you start to use SQL*Plus to generate reports, you'll quickly find that it often takes several commands executed in succession to get the results that you want, as you've already seen in some of the examples in this chapter. Naturally, if you have a complex report that you want to run occasionally, you don't want to have to type all the commands each time. The good news is that you don't need to. You can place all the commands for a report into a text file and tell SQL*Plus to execute the commands in that file. Such a file is referred to as a script file. *Script files* allow you to store complex reports, or other series of commands, so that you can easily execute them later. Script files also allow you to submit SQL*Plus commands as background jobs.

Using the @ command

The SQL*Plus @ command invokes a script file. Suppose you have a text file named list_tables.sql with the following commands in it:

```
COLUMN index_name FORMAT A15 WORD_WRAPPED HEADING "Index"
COLUMN column_name FORMAT A30 HEADING "Column"
SELECT index_name, column_name
FROM user_ind_columns
WHERE table_name=UPPER('&table_name')
ORDER BY index_name, column_position;
```

This script prompts you for a table name and then displays a list of indexes for that table. You can execute this script file from SQL*Plus using the @ command, as shown in this example:

```
SQL> @list_indexes
Enter value for table_name: aquatic_animal
old   3: WHERE table_name=UPPER('&table_name')
new   3: WHERE table_name=UPPER('aquatic_animal')

Index           Column
--------------- ------------------------------
AQ_ANIMAL_PK    ID_NO

1 row selected.
```

Using substitution variables in scripts like this is a powerful technique. You can automate any number of repetitive tasks by writings scripts such as the one shown here.

Note   SQL*Plus also supports an @@ command. Use @@ in a script when you want to execute another script that is stored in the same directory as the first.

Executing a script from the command line

If you're writing batch jobs or shell scripts, you can invoke SQL*Plus and run a SQL*Plus script all with one command. You can do this by passing your database username and password and the script file name as arguments to the *sqlplus* command. The general format to use looks like this:

```
sqlplus username/password[@service] @script_file
```

Replace *username* and *password* with your database username and password. If you are connecting to a remote database, replace *service* with the Net8 service name of that database. Be sure to separate the service name from the password with an ampersand, and don't leave any spaces. After the username and password, you can place the @ command to run the script file. This time, you do need a space before the @ character. This is how SQL*Plus tells the difference between a service name and a script file name.

When you invoke a script from the operating system prompt like this, you probably don't want to be prompted for any values. That's especially true if you are planning to run the script as a background job. You can still use substitution variables in the script, but you may want to use the special variables &1, &2, and so forth. These correspond to arguments that you can pass on the command line. Here is a different version of the list_indexes script, which accepts the table name as a command-line argument:

```
COLUMN index_name FORMAT A15 WORD_WRAPPED HEADING "Index"
COLUMN column_name FORMAT A30 HEADING "Column"
SELECT index_name, column_name
FROM user_ind_columns
WHERE table_name=UPPER('&1')
ORDER BY index_name, column_position;
EXIT
```

Notice the use of &1 to hold the place of the table name. In just a moment, you will see how that value is passed into the script. First, though, take a look at the last line. An EXIT command is added so that SQL*Plus exits immediately after the script finishes. Listing 7-5 demonstrates invoking this version of the list_indexes script from the operating system command line.

Listing 7-5: **Passing parameters to a script**

```
E:\bible_scripts>sqlplus seapark/seapark@bible_db @list_indexes aquatic_animal

SQL*Plus: Release 8.1.5.0.0 - Production on Thu Aug 5 14:51:26 1999

(c) Copyright 1999 Oracle Corporation.  All rights reserved.
```

```
Connected to:
Oracle8i Personal Edition Release 8.1.5.0.0 - Production
With the Partitioning and Java options
PL/SQL Release 8.1.5.0.0 - Production

old   3: WHERE table_name=UPPER('&1')
new   3: WHERE table_name=UPPER('aquatic_animal')

Index           Column
--------------- ------------------------------
AQ_ANIMAL_PK    ID_NO

Disconnected from Oracle8i Personal Edition Release 8.1.5.0.0 - Production
With the Partitioning and Java options
PL/SQL Release 8.1.5.0.0 - Production

E:\Jonathan\Oracle_Bible\ch7>
```

You can see that SQL*Plus picks up the word following @list_indexes and places it in the &1 substitution variable. This is then substituted into the query, which returns the list of indexes defined on the table. No user interaction is required, other than the initial command to invoke the script.

Summary

In this chapter, you learned:

✦ SQL*Plus allows you to enter and execute ad-hoc SQL statements and PL/SQL blocks.

✦ Server Manager is phasing out, so you should convert your Server Manager scripts to run under SQL*Plus.

✦ SQL*Plus has a number of line-editing commands, and you can use the EDIT command to invoke an external text editor.

✦ Use the COLUMN command to format column data and to provide column headings.

✦ Use the TTITLE and BTITLE commands to define page headers and footers.

✦ Use BREAK and COMPUTE to generate summary data.

✦ Use the @ command to execute commands from a file.

✦   ✦   ✦

Using Oracle8i's Export Utility

Oracle's Export utility allows you to extract data from a database and write that data to an operating system file. Together with the Import utility, which you will read about in the next chapter, this provides you with a convenient way to move data between databases. You can export an entire database, or you can choose to limit the export to objects owned by a specific user or to a specific list of tables. This chapter discusses how you can use the Export utility and all of its options to export data to operating system files.

Using Oracle8i's Export Utility

The file to which you extract data when you use Oracle8i's Export utility is referred to as a *dump file*. Export's dump files contain both metadata and data. *Metadata* refers to the data definition language (DDL) statements necessary to re-create the objects that have been exported. If you export your entire database, for example, the dump file will contain CREATE TABLE statements, GRANT statements, and everything else necessary to re-create your database. Some of the more important uses for the Export utility include the following:

✦ Copying tables, or entire schemas, from one database to another.

✦ Reorganizing a table by exporting the data, re-creating the table with different storage parameters, and reloading the data — all in the same database.

✦ Storing data as a secondary backup, in case the primary backup fails. This works well only for small databases.

✦ Creating a logical backup that you can use to restore specific tables rather than the entire database.

✦ Creating a temporary backup of objects that you are going to delete, just in case you later find that you really do need them.

You almost always use the Export utility in conjunction with the Import utility. About the only time that you ever export data without importing it again is when you are using the Export utility as a backup. Even then, you have to be *prepared* to import it again. The Import utility is described in Chapter 9, "Using Oracle8i's Import Utility." To effectively use the Export utility, you need to know how to do several operations, including:

✦ Starting the Export utility

✦ Passing parameters to it

✦ Running it interactively

✦ Getting help when you need it

✦ Using its prerequisites

Starting the Export utility

The proper command to start the Export utility depends on the release of and the platform on which you are running Oracle. On UNIX systems, and on Windows systems beginning with the Oracle8i release, you use the exp command to start the Export utility. On Windows releases prior to Oracle8i, the command contains the release number, so the command you use — exp80, exp73, or so on — depends on the specific release of Oracle that you are using.

Export is a command-line utility, so you have to run it from the command prompt. On Windows systems, this means that you need to open a Command Prompt window. The following example shows Export being invoked from a Windows NT command prompt to export all the tables, indexes, and other objects owned by the user named AMY:

```
C:\> exp system/manager@bible_db file=amy log=amy owner=amy

Export: Release 8.1.5.0.0 - Production on Fri Aug 6 11:45:53 1999

(c) Copyright 1999 Oracle Corporation.  All rights reserved.


Connected to: Oracle8i Release 8.1.5.0.0 - Production
With the Partitioning and Java options
PL/SQL Release 8.1.5.0.0 - Production
Export done in WE8ISO8859P1 character set and WE8ISO8859P1 NCHAR character set
About to export specified users ...
```

There are two basic modes in which to invoke and use Export. You can invoke it either interactively or from the command line. When you run Export interactively, you enter your username and password, respond to some prompts for information about what you want to export, and then let the utility export the data. While this mode is easy to use, the interactive interface is limited. It doesn't support all the functionality that Export provides. The second way to invoke Export, the one shown in the previous Windows NT platform example, and the one you should focus your efforts on learning, is to pass information to Export using command-line parameters.

Getting help

Export supports a large number of parameters, and it's difficult to remember the ones that you don't use frequently. To help jog your memory, you can run Export with the HELP=Y parameter, causing it to display a brief help screen. An example help screen is shown in Listing 8-1.

Listing 8-1: **Export's online help**

```
C:\>exp help=y

Export: Release 8.1.5.0.0 - Production on Fri Aug 6 11:23:00 1999

(c) Copyright 1999 Oracle Corporation.  All rights reserved.



You can let Export prompt you for parameters by entering the EXP
command followed by your username/password:

    Example: EXP SCOTT/TIGER

Or, you can control how Export runs by entering the EXP command followed
by various arguments. To specify parameters, you use keywords:

    Format:  EXP KEYWORD=value or KEYWORD=(value1,value2,...,valueN)
    Example: EXP SCOTT/TIGER GRANTS=Y TABLES=(EMP,DEPT,MGR)
             or TABLES=(T1:P1,T1:P2), if T1 is partitioned table

USERID must be the first parameter on the command line.

Keyword  Description (Default)         Keyword      Description (Default)
--------------------------------------------------------------------------
USERID    username/password           FULL         export entire file (N)
BUFFER    size of data buffer         OWNER        list of owner usernames
FILE      output files (EXPDAT.DMP)   TABLES       list of table names
COMPRESS  import into one extent (Y)  RECORDLENGTH length of IO record
GRANTS    export grants (Y)           INCTYPE      incremental export type
INDEXES   export indexes (Y)          RECORD       track incr. export (Y)
ROWS      export data rows (Y)        PARFILE      parameter filename
CONSTRAINTS export constraints (Y)    CONSISTENT   cross-table consistency
```

```
LOG      log file of screen output    STATISTICS  analyze objects (ESTIMATE)
DIRECT   direct path (N)              TRIGGERS    export triggers (Y)
FEEDBACK display progress every x rows (0)
FILESIZE maximum size of each dump file
QUERY    select clause used to export a subset of a table

The following keywords only apply to transportable tablespaces
TRANSPORT_TABLESPACE export transportable tablespace metadata (N)
TABLESPACES list of tablespaces to transport

Export terminated successfully without warnings.
```

You may find that HELP=Y is one of the parameters you will use most frequently.

Using Export parameters

The general form for invoking the Export utility looks like this:

```
exp [username[/password[@service]]] [param=value
[param=value]...]
```

Replace *username* and *password* with your username and password. If you omit either of these, Export will prompt you for them. If you are exporting data from a remote database, you can include a Net8 service name after the password. The parameters, shown as *param* in the syntax, are those listed on the help screen. Table 8-1 provides a brief description of each. You can place as many parameters as you need to use on the command line.

Table 8-1	
Export Parameters	
Parameter	*Description*
BUFFER	Specifies the size of the buffer used to fetch rows from the database. This value is in bytes, and it is ignored for direct-path exports. (Direct-path exports will be discussed later in the chapter.) Larger values lead to better performance. The default value for this parameter is operating-system–specific.

Parameter	Description
COMPRESS	Specifies whether you want the data for each table to be loaded into one extent, in the event that you import the data back into the database. The default is Y, causing the data to be compressed. Use N if you don't want to do this.
CONSISTENT	Specifies whether you want *all* the data exported to be consistent with respect to a single point in time. The default is N, meaning that each table is exported as a separate transaction. Use Y to have the entire export done as one transaction. You might do this if you expect users to be changing data while you are exporting it.
CONSTRAINTS	Controls whether table constraints are exported. The default is Y. Use N if you want tables to be exported without constraint definitions.
DIRECT	Controls whether a direct-path export is done. (Direct-path exports will be discussed later in the chapter.) The direct method is much faster than the conventional export path. The default is N, which provides a conventional export. Use DIRECT=Y to do a direct-path export.
FEEDBACK	Specifies for Export to indicate progress by displaying periods on the screen. The default is FEEDBACK=0, resulting in no progress display. The FEEDBACK=10 parameter causes a period to be written for every ten rows written to the export file, FEEDBACK=20 causes a period to be written for every 20 rows, and so forth. Be careful with this parameter. If you have a billion-row table, you could be watching a lot of periods pass by.
FILE	Specifies the name of the export file. The default is FILE=expdat.dmp. The default file extension is .dmp.
FILESIZE	Allows you to spread exported data over multiple files. The value used with FILESIZE places an upper limit on the number of bytes written to a file. The default is FILESIZE=0, causing all data to be written to one file. Here are some other possibilities: FILESIZE = 1024 (Generate 1k files) FILESIZE = 1K (Generate 1k files) FILESIZE = 1M (Generate 1 megabyte files) FILESIZE = 1G (Generate 1 gigabyte files)

Continued

Table 8-1 *(continued)*

Parameter	Description
	If an export requires multiple files, you will be prompted for more file names. If you don't want to be prompted, you can include a list of file names with the FILE parameter. For example: `FILE=(bibdb_1,bibdb_2,bibdb_3)` If you don't specify enough names, Export will prompt you for more.
FULL	Specifies that the entire database is to be exported when the FULL=Y parameter is used. The default is FULL=N.
GRANTS	Specifies that grants are to be exported with tables. Grants allow other users to use the tables. The GRANTS=Y parameter is the default. The GRANTS=N parameter causes tables to be exported without their associated grants.
HELP	Controls the display of the help screen shown earlier in this chapter. The parameter is HELP=Y; there is no HELP=N option.
INCTYPE	Specifies the incremental Export options. You can use the following option values:
INCREMENTAL	Exports all database objects that have changed since the last incremental, cumulative, or complete export
CUMULATIVE	Exports all database objects that have changed since the last cumulative or complete export
COMPLETE	Exports all objects Oracle plans to remove support for these options in a future release, in favor of using Recovery Manager. Recovery Manager is a utility that helps you manage the backup and recovery of your database.
INDEXES	Specifies whether indexes should be exported. The default is INDEXES=Y. Use INDEXES=N if you don't want index definitions to be exported.
LOG	Specifies the name of a log file that will accumulate information about the export, including any error messages. The default file extension is .log.
OWNER	Allows you to export data and objects for a specific user or a list of users.

Parameter	Description
PARFILE	Allows you to read export parameters from a file. (This option is discussed later in the chapter.)
QUERY	Specifies exporting only a subset of rows from one or more tables. The value for this parameter must be a WHERE clause, and it is applied to the SELECT statement that Export executes against each table.
RECORD	Indicates whether to record an incremental or cumulative export in the export system tables. The default is RECORD=Y. Use RECORD=N if you want to take an incremental or cumulative export without recording that fact.
RECORDLENGTH	Specifies the length, in bytes, of the records in the export file. This option is useful if you are planning to transfer the export file to an operating system that supports smaller record sizes than the one on which you are doing the export. The default is operating-system-specific.
ROWS	Controls whether or not table data is exported. The default is ROWS=Y, which causes data to be exported. Use ROWS=N if you want to export table definitions, but not the data.
STATISTICS	Specifies the type of database optimizer statistics to generate when you import the data that you are now exporting. The valid options are ESTIMATE, COMPUTE, and NONE. If your are importing tables for which statistics existed prior to the export, then the Import utility will automatically regenerate statistics unless you specify STATISTICS=NONE.
TABLES	Allows you to export a specific table or a list of tables.
TABLESPACES	Allows you to export a specific tablespace or a list of tablespaces. The tablespaces must be locally managed, and you must use this parameter in conjunction with TRANSPORT_TABLESPACE=Y.
TRANSPORT_TABLESPACE	Allows you to export the metadata for transportable tablespaces. The default is TRANSPORT_TABLESPACE=N.
TRIGGERS	Controls whether trigger definitions are exported with tables. The default is TRIGGERS=Y, which causes triggers to be exported. Use TRIGGERS=N to export tables, but not their triggers.
USERID	Specifies the username and password of the user invoking the export.

The examples in this chapter show the more common uses of the Export utility. Many of these examples demonstrate the use of the parameters shown in Table 8-1. The PARFILE parameter is significant because it allows you to read parameters from a file. Placing parameters in a file allows you to save complex exports for use again in the future. You'll see how to do this later in this chapter.

Using interactive mode vs. command-line mode

Although you get full access to Export's functionality only when you invoke the utility using command-line parameters, Export does support a limited interactive mode. To invoke Export interactively, simply start it without passing any parameters. The format to use is:

```
exp [username[/password[@service]]]
```

Although you can't pass any parameters, you can pass in the username and password on the command line. It's best not to place the password on the command line, though, lest other people see it. The example shown in Listing 8-2 shows you how to invoke Export with only the Net8 service name and your username on the command line, so that you will be prompted for the password. The benefit of this is that the password is not displayed when you type it. This example goes on to further export the AQUATIC_ANIMAL table owned by the user named SEAPARK.

Listing 8-2: Invoking the Export utility with a Net8 service name

```
E:\Jonathan\Oracle_Bible\ch8> exp seapark@bible_db

Export: Release 8.1.5.0.0 - Production on Fri Aug 6 13:01:05 1999

(c) Copyright 1999 Oracle Corporation.  All rights reserved.

Password:

Connected to: Oracle8i Release 8.1.5.0.0 - Production
With the Partitioning and Java options
PL/SQL Release 8.1.5.0.0 - Production
Enter array fetch buffer size: 4096 >

Export file: EXPDAT.DMP > aquatic_animal

(2)U(sers), or (3)T(ables): (2)U > t

Export table data (yes/no): yes >
```

```
Compress extents (yes/no): yes >

Export done in WE8ISO8859P1 character set and WE8ISO8859P1 NCHAR character set

About to export specified tables via Conventional Path ...
Table(T) or Partition(T:P) to be exported: (RETURN to quit) > aquatic_animal

. . exporting table              AQUATIC_ANIMAL         10 rows exported
Table(T) or Partition(T:P) to be exported: (RETURN to quit) >

Export terminated successfully without warnings.
```

In this example, defaults were taken for pretty much everything except the file name and the table name. As you can see, the AQUATIC_ANIMAL table was exported, and it would have been written to a file named aquatic_animal.dmp. The Enter key (or Return key on some systems) was pressed at the end to exit the utility.

Normal users can use Export interactively like this to export specific tables or to export their entire schema. As a DBA, you will have the additional options of exporting the entire database and exporting other schemas.

Using Export prerequisites

To use the Export utility, a user must have the CREATE SESSION privilege on the target database. That's all you need as long as you are executing objects that you own. To export tables owned by another user or to export the entire database, you must have the EXP_FULL_DATABASE role, and you must have it enabled. Typically, you will have the DBA role, which includes the EXP_FULL_DATABASE role, so you can export pretty much anything that you want to export.

Some schemas are special, and you can't export them even if you are the DBA. The list of restricted schemas includes SYS, ORDSYS, CTXSYS, MDSYS, and ORDPLUGINS. These schemas are special in that they own software and other objects that are very specific to a database, and to a database release. You could damage another database by importing objects into the SYS schema, for example, so Export simply doesn't allow you to export those objects in the first place.

Before using Export against a database, you must run the CATEXP.SQL script once to create views and tables that the Export utility requires. The EXP_FULL_DATABASE role is one of the items that CATEXP.SQL creates. The CATEXP.SQL script is run by CATALOG.SQL, so if you ran CATALOG.SQL when you first created the database, you're all set. If you find that you do need to run either of these scripts, you'll find them in the $ORACLE_HOME/RDBMS/ADMIN directory.

Exporting Databases

You can export the entire database by using the FULL=Y option. This has the effect of exporting all tables, indexes, and other objects for all users. The example shown in Listing 8-3 demonstrates a full export being done:

Listing 8-3: **Exporting an entire database**

```
E:\ch8> exp system/manager file=bible_db log=bible_db full=y

Export: Release 8.1.5.0.0 - Production on Fri Aug 6 14:23:33 1999

(c) Copyright 1999 Oracle Corporation.  All rights reserved.


Connected to: Oracle8i Release 8.1.5.0.0 - Production
With the Partitioning and Java options
PL/SQL Release 8.1.5.0.0 - Production
Export done in WE8ISO8859P1 character set and WE8ISO8859P1 NCHAR character set

About to export the entire database ...
. exporting tablespace definitions
. exporting profiles
. exporting user definitions
. exporting roles
. exporting resource costs

...

. exporting job queues
. exporting refresh groups and children
. exporting dimensions
. exporting post-schema procedural objects and actions
. exporting user history table
. exporting default and system auditing options
Export terminated successfully without warnings.

E:\Jonathan\Oracle_Bible\ch8>
```

Sometimes, you may want to export just the definitions from a database and not the data. One reason you might do this is when you want to make a copy of a database — perhaps for use in testing or development — where you want the same structure but not the same data. Use ROWS=N, as shown in the following example, to prevent any data from being exported, leaving only the object definitions in the export file:

```
exp system/manager file=bible_db log=bible_db full=y rows=n
```

One use for the ROWS=N option, and this is one that Oracle doesn't officially support, is to generate the DDL statements necessary to re-create your objects. Export files are binary files, but you can usually load them into a text editor and clean them up a bit. If you do, you'll find that they contain all the CREATE TABLE, CREATE INDEX, and other statements necessary to re-create your schema objects.

Exporting by User

You can export tables for one specific user or a group of users with the OWNER parameter. The following command, for example, exports all objects owned by the user named SEAPARK:

```
exp system/manager file=seapark log=seapark owner=seapark
```

If you want to export several users at once, place a comma-separated list of usernames within parentheses, as shown in the following example, which exports tables for all the users in the sample database used for this book:

```
exp system/manager file=seapark log=seapark
    owner=(seapark, amy, amyc, harold)
```

One issue to be aware of when exporting a user is that although you get all objects owned by the user you are exporting, you don't get any public synonyms that reference those objects. This can be troublesome if you are attempting to copy a schema from a production database into a test database, and the software that you are testing expects synonyms to be in place.

If you run into this situation, you can use SQL*Plus to generate the needed CREATE PUBLIC SYNONYM commands. The following SQL*Plus commands, for example, will create a script file with commands to re-create all public synonyms that point to objects owned by SEAPARK:

```
SET LINESIZE 132
SET PAGESIZE 0
SET TRIMSPOOL ON
SPOOL C:\A\SEAPARK.SYN
SELECT 'create public synonym '
       || synonym_name
       || ' for '
       || table_owner || '.' || table_name
       || ';'
  FROM dba_synonyms
 WHERE table_owner = 'SEAPARK'
   AND owner = 'PUBLIC';
SPOOL OFF
```

Once you've executed these commands and generated the script, you can connect to the target database and run the script there (using the @*filename* command) to re-create the synonyms.

Exporting by Table

You can export a database, you can export a user, and you can also export a table. Use the TABLES parameter to do this. The following command will export just the TANK table:

```
exp seapark/seapark file=tank log=tank tables=tank
```

In this case, because it is the SEAPARK user running the export, it will be SEAPARK's TANK table that is exported. If you are a privileged user (EXP_FULL_DATABASE), you can export a table owned by another user simply by prefacing the table name with the username, using the standard dot notation. In this example, the SYSTEM user is exporting SEAPARK's TANK table:

```
exp system/manager file=tank log=tank tables=seapark.tank
```

Note   Don't try to use the OWNER parameter to specify the owner when you want to export someone else's table. The OWNER and TABLES parameters are not compatible, and they can't be used in the same command. Use the dot notation as shown in the example.

To export multiple tables, enclose a comma-separated list of table names within parentheses. Consider this example:

```
exp system/manager file=tank log=tank
    tables=(seapark.tank, amy.artist)
```

Exporting and importing a single table gives you a way to reorganize how a table is stored. For example, suppose that you want to move a table from one tablespace to another. Perhaps you accidentally created the table in the SYSTEM tablespace, which is not a good place for user tables. One way to move the table is to export it, drop it, re-create it in the correct tablespace, and then import it back again. Chapter 9, "Using Oracle8i's Import Utility," contains information about the Import utility that you need to know to do this.

Estimating the Size of Export Files

If you're exporting a large table or a large database, you need to give some thought to the size of the export file. Based on size, you can choose to export the file to the appropriate disk. One way to estimate size is to query the DBA_SEGMENTS view. The following query returns the total bytes allocated to all tables in the database:

```
SELECT SUM(bytes)
FROM dba_segments
WHERE segment_type = 'TABLE';
```

Since tables may not use all the space that was allocated to them, the results returned by this query can represent only an approximation. Chances are good that it will be on the high side.

If you are exporting by user or by table, you can further qualify the query so that it returns information only related to the tables that you are exporting. The following two queries return the total bytes used by all tables for the SEAPARK user, and for just the AQUATIC_ANIMAL table, respectively:

```
SELECT SUM(bytes)
FROM dba_segments
WHERE segment_type = 'TABLE'
AND owner='SEAPARK';

SELECT SUM(bytes)
FROM dba_segments
WHERE owner='SEAPARK'
AND segment_type='TABLE'
AND segment_name='AQUATIC_ANIMAL';
```

These queries return information only about table data. Large object data, such as BLOB columns, CLOB columns, and so forth, are often stored in segments of type LOBSEGMENT. If you are exporting tables with large object columns, be sure to query that segment type as well.

Using Export Options

You should be aware of at least five significant export options. Each of these options is associated with a parameter that you can specify on the Export utility's command line. The following five options are discussed in this section:

✦ Using export paths

✦ Compressing extents

✦ Exporting a subset of table data

✦ Splitting exports across multiple files

✦ Using parameter files

Using export paths

Direct-path exports have been around at least since the Oracle 7.3 days. But while they are nothing new, they do provide a significant performance boost over conventional-path exports. The ability to export a subset of a table's data and the ability to split exports across multiple files are new with Oracle8i. Oracle's Export utility provides the following two paths for exporting table data:

✦ Conventional

✦ Direct

The conventional-path export represents the way exports have been done from day one. The direct-path export option is a performance enhancement that was added a few years ago.

Conventional-Path Exports

The conventional-path export retrieves data in exactly the same way that a user program would. You use a SQL SELECT statement to retrieve the data for each table being exported. As with any other executed query, the data is read from disk and placed into the database buffer cache. From there, the data is moved to a work area where the rows are pulled out, examined to see if they match the query's WHERE clause, and then sent on to the Export utility. Conventional-path exports are the default, although you can use the DIRECT=N parameter to explicitly ask for one.

Direct-Path Exports

A direct-path export bypasses the evaluation of the individual rows and extracts data much faster than the conventional path. A SQL query is still issued, and blocks from the table are still read into the database buffer cache, but from there they are passed back directly to the Export utility. Figure 8-1 shows the difference between the two methods.

Direct-path exports do have some limitations. Using the QUERY parameter is incompatible with direct-path exports because you have to evaluate each row to export a subset of a table. Direct-path exports also cannot be used when the tables that you are exporting contain LOB columns. However, when you can use the direct-path, the performance impact is significant. Add the DIRECT=Y parameter to your export commands to ask for direct-path exports.

Compressing extents

If you have a table with data stored in several small extents, you can use the Export and Import utilities together to reorganize the table's data into one large extent. This reduces fragmentation in the tablespace and can have a positive impact on performance. The process of reorganizing a table looks like this:

1. Export the table using the COMPRESS=Y parameter

2. Drop the existing table

3. Import the table back

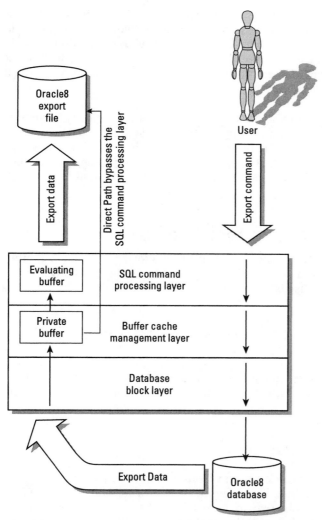

Figure 8-1: Direct-path exports vs. conventional-path exports

The COMPRESS=Y parameter, which happens to be the default anyway, causes the Export utility to modify the INITIAL storage parameter for the table, and to make it large enough so that when the table is imported back, the initial extent will hold all the data.

If you have a large table, and the size of that table is greater than the largest block of freespace in your database, then you won't be able to import it as one large extent. In such cases, export the table using COMPRESS=N, so that Import won't try to create one large extent when you import the table back.

Note If you're curious about how extent compression works, pick a table and export it both ways, once with COMPRESS=Y and once with COMPRESS=N. Be sure to pick a table that is using multiple extents. Use an editor to view both export dump files. The files will contain a lot of binary data, but you should be able to find the CRE-ATE TABLE commands in each file. Look at the STORAGE clauses. You'll see that the value for INITIAL is different.

When many people first learn about COMPRESS=Y, it seems strange to them to have to specify this parameter when exporting the data, while the change is really taking place on the import operation. The reason for this is simple. The Export utility generates the DDL to re-create the table, so the Export utility generates the modified STORAGE clause. The Import utility simply reads and executes what the Export utility wrote.

Exporting a subset of a table's data

Oracle8i implements an interesting new option that allows you to export only a subset of a table's data. You do this by including a WHERE clause as an export parameter. This WHERE clause is then appended to the SQL select statement that Export uses to retrieve data from the table.

Note You cannot use a direct-path export to extract a subset of data.

You use the QUERY parameter to pass a WHERE clause to the Export utility. The following example shows an export of the SALAD_TYPE table that includes only 'FRUIT':

```
exp system/manager query='where salad_type=''FRUIT'''
    tables=amy.salad_type file=fruit log=fruit
```

Using the QUERY parameter can get messy because of the way operating systems treat quotes in a command line. This example works for NT. The entire WHERE clause is inside a quoted string (single quotes), and the single quotes around FRUIT have been doubled so that the operating system will treat them as one quote inside the string and not as the terminating quote. On a UNIX system, you would have to use backslashes to escape the special characters, and you would need to enclose the WHERE clause in double quotes. For example:

```
exp system/manager query=\"where salad_type=\'FRUIT\'\"
    tables=amy.salad_type file=fruit log=fruit
```

If you are exporting multiple related tables, you can subset all of them in one export operation. The only requirement is that the WHERE clause must apply equally to all tables involved in the export. The command in the following example exports the two related tables, SALAD_TYPE and SALAD_TRAY:

```
exp system/manager query='where salad_type=''FRUIT'''
    tables=(amy.salad_type,amy.salad_tray) file=fruit log=fruit
```

Since both of these tables contain a SALAD_TYPE column, the WHERE clause applies equally well to each one. By exporting both together like this and using the same WHERE clause, you get a consistent set of related data in the export file. In this case, you have all the fruit salad records.

Splitting an export across multiple files

The ability to split an export across multiple files is a new enhancement that became available with the release of Oracle8i. Databases today can be quite large, and as the size of a database increases, so does the size of its export file. In many environments, full exports of production databases are difficult because the resulting files are too large. Many UNIX systems limit file sizes to 2GB or less. If you are exporting a 4GB table, that presents a problem.

Using the new FILESIZE parameter, you can export a large table into several smaller files. For example, if you have a 4GB table named PAYCHECK, and you want to export it into four 1GB files, you can now do that with this command:

```
exp system/manager
    file=(paycheck_1, paycheck_2, paycheck_3, paycheck_4)
    log=paycheck, filesize=1g tables=hr.paycheck
```

The result of this export will be four files named paycheck_1.dmp, paycheck_2.dmp, paycheck_3.dmp, and paycheck_4.dmp. In this example, those four file names were placed in a comma-separated list after the FILE parameter. Export will work through the files one at a time, in the order that you list them. As each file fills to the size you specified, Export will close that file and open the next. If you don't provide enough files in the list for the amount of data being exported, Export will prompt you for more.

Note If you are running an export like this as a background job, be certain to provide more than enough file names. Otherwise, the export might hang, waiting for you to provide another file name, which you won't be able to do.

Using parameter files

Some of the example export commands in this chapter have been quite long. In real life, the commands can get much larger yet. It's normal to run exports where you list dozens of tables after the TABLES parameter. That's a lot to type on the command line, and if you make a mistake, you have to type it all in again. If you are working with long export lists, or if you want to define export jobs that you can execute repeatedly, you can use the PARFILE parameter to have the Export utility read parameters from a text file.

Suppose that you want to export all the sample tables used for this book, and that you want to be able to do this from time to time without having to rethink how to do it. One solution would be to create a text file with the contents shown in Listing 8-4.

Listing 8-4: **An export parameter file**

```
# Export the sample tables used for
# the Oracle8i Database Administrator's Bible.

file=bible_tables
log=bible_tables
tables = (
amy.ARTIST
amy.BOOKS
amy.BOOKS_LOANED
amy.BOOKS_RESERVED
amy.BREAD
amy.CLIENT
amy.DAILY_SALES
amy.FISH
amy.MILLIES_MAILING_LIST
amy.MONTHLY_SALES
amy.SALAD_TRAY
amy.SALAD_TYPE
amy.STUDENTS
amy.STUDENTS_FINES
amy.TICKET
seapark.AQUATIC_ANIMAL
seapark.CARETAKER
seapark.CHECKUP
seapark.CHECKUP_HISTORY
seapark.ITEMS
seapark.PARK_REVENUE
seapark.PLAN_TABLE
seapark.TANK
amyc.student
)
```

If the name of this text file was bible_tables.par, you could then issue the following export command whenever you wanted to export the tables:

```
exp system/manager parfile=bible_tables.par
```

The PARFILE parameter in this example would tell the Export utility to read parameters from the file bible_tables.par. This is a great way to eliminate a lot of typing and retyping of parameters, as well as to ensure that each subsequent export is consistent with the first.

Note   In a parameter file, pound signs (#) indicate comment lines. Items in a list may either be separated by commas, or they may each be placed on separate lines.

Summary

In this chapter, you learned:

✦ The Export utility allows you to export a database, a schema, or a table to an operating system file. You can then import the data into other databases, import it back into the same database, or simply hold it as a backup.

✦ The HELP=Y parameter gets you a concise help screen that lists the other export parameters.

✦ You must have the EXP_FULL_DATABASE role to export data owned by other users. The DBA role typically includes EXP_FULL_DATABASE.

✦ Parameter files can be used when you have long parameter lists or when you have export jobs that must be run repeatedly. You use the PARFILE parameter to point the Export utility to a parameter file.

✦ You can use the QUERY parameter to supply a WHERE clause, which is used to export a subset of data from one or more tables. The WHERE clause that you supply must be applicable to all the tables being exported.

✦ You use the FILESIZE parameter to limit the size of export files and to spread large exports over multiple files. This makes it possible to export large tables where the export file's size would otherwise be larger than the operating system allows.

✦ You can reorganize the storage for a table, and you can reduce the number of extents, by exporting the table with COMPRESS=Y, dropping the table, and importing it back again.

✦ ✦ ✦

Using Oracle8i's Import Utility

Oracle's Import utility reads data and object definitions from a file and loads them into an Oracle database. Import is the complement to Oracle's Export utility and can read files produced only by the Export utility. Import allows you to do the following:

- ✦ Load data that was exported from another database.
- ✦ Load object definitions that were exported from another database.
- ✦ Restore objects that you accidentally deleted. If you drop a table, for example, you can import it from the most recent export file.
- ✦ Import tables that you have exported as part of a reorganization process.

Much of the Import utility's functionality parallels that of the Export utility. Export is described in Chapter 8, "Using Oracle8i's Export Utility." It is recommended that you read Chapter 8 first, or at least be familiar with the Export utility, before you attempt to use the Import utility.

Using Oracle8i's Import Utility

To use the Import utility to import data into a database, you need to know how to do several operations, including:

- ✦ Starting the Import utility
- ✦ Getting help when you need it
- ✦ Passing parameters to it
- ✦ Running it interactively
- ✦ Using its prerequisites

Starting the Import utility

You start the Import utility the same way that you start the Export utility, except that the command is imp instead of exp. Prior to the release of Oracle8i, the Windows versions of Oracle embedded the first two digits of the release number as part of the executable name. If you are running one of those versions, the command will be imp80, imp73, or so on, depending on the specific release of Oracle that you are using.

Like Export, Import is also a command-driven utility. On Windows NT, this means opening a Command Prompt window. The following example shows how you might import just one specific table from an export file:

```
E:\Jonathan\Oracle_Bible\ch9> imp system/manager file=bibdb log=bibdb_import
fromuser=seapark tables=caretaker

Import: Release 8.1.5.0.0 - Production on Mon Aug 9 10:52:12 1999

(c) Copyright 1999 Oracle Corporation.  All rights reserved.


Connected to: Oracle8i Release 8.1.5.0.0 - Production
With the Partitioning and Java options
PL/SQL Release 8.1.5.0.0 - Production

Export file created by EXPORT:V08.01.05 via direct path
import done in WE8ISO8859P1 character set and WE8ISO8859P1 NCHAR character set
. importing SEAPARK's objects into SEAPARK
. . importing table                    "CARETAKER"          3 rows imported
About to enable constraints...
Import terminated successfully without warnings.
```

You might import one table like this after accidentally dropping the table. Restoring only one table from a file-system backup of the Oracle datafiles is a difficult and cumbersome process. If you can afford the time to make a database export regularly, that provides you with a convenient method for restoring just one database object.

Note When using the Import utility to restore an object, you do have to think about the volatility of the object. After the restore, the data will be only as current as the most recent export. You can't roll forward like you can when you do a file-based recovery. The result is that you may lose data. You may also run into referential integrity problems if the data that you are importing is dependent on rows in other tables that no longer exist.

You can invoke the Import utility both in an interactive mode and a command-line mode. The interactive mode exists only for purposes of backwards compatibility with earlier releases. When you run the Import utility interactively, you respond to a number of prompts to tell the Import utility what to do. Only a small subset of Import's functionality is available this way. The command-line interface, where you pass all information as parameters on the command line, gives you full access to all the import options. The earlier example used the command-line interface.

Getting help

The Import utility has an online help facility similar to that provided by Export. Just run Import using the HELP=Y parameter, and you will get a brief display showing all possible parameters. Listing 9-1 provides an example.

Listing 9-1: **Import's online help**

```
E:\Jonathan\Oracle_Bible\ch9>imp help=y

Import: Release 8.1.5.0.0 - Production on Mon Aug 9 09:30:59 1999

(c) Copyright 1999 Oracle Corporation.  All rights reserved.


You can let Import prompt you for parameters by entering the IMP
command followed by your username/password:

    Example: IMP SCOTT/TIGER

Or, you can control how Import runs by entering the IMP command followed
by various arguments. To specify parameters, you use keywords:

    Format:  IMP KEYWORD=value or KEYWORD=(value1,value2,...,valueN)
    Example: IMP SCOTT/TIGER IGNORE=Y TABLES=(EMP,DEPT) FULL=N
             or TABLES=(T1:P1,T1:P2), if T1 is partitioned table

USERID must be the first parameter on the command line.

Keyword  Description (Default)        Keyword      Description (Default)
--------------------------------------------------------------------------
USERID   username/password           FULL         import entire file (N)
BUFFER   size of data buffer         FROMUSER     list of owner usernames
FILE     input files (EXPDAT.DMP)    TOUSER       list of usernames
SHOW     just list file contents (N) TABLES       list of table names
IGNORE   ignore create errors (N)    RECORDLENGTH length of IO record
GRANTS   import grants (Y)           INCTYPE      incremental import type
INDEXES  import indexes (Y)          COMMIT       commit array insert (N)
ROWS     import data rows (Y)        PARFILE      parameter filename
LOG      log file of screen output   CONSTRAINTS  import constraints (Y)
DESTROY  overwrite tablespace data file (N)
INDEXFILE write table/index info to specified file
```

Continued

Listing 9-1 *(continued)*

```
SKIP_UNUSABLE_INDEXES  skip maintenance of unusable indexes (N)
ANALYZE  execute ANALYZE statements in dump file (Y)
FEEDBACK display progress every x rows(0)
TOID_NOVALIDATE  skip validation of specified type ids
FILESIZE maximum size of each dump file
RECALCULATE_STATISTICS recalculate statistics (N)

The following keywords only apply to transportable tablespaces
TRANSPORT_TABLESPACE import transportable tablespace metadata (N)
TABLESPACES tablespaces to be transported into database
DATAFILES datafiles to be transported into database
TTS_OWNERS users that own data in the transportable tablespace set

Import terminated successfully without warnings.
```

The parameter explanations that you get using HELP=Y are very concise, but they are helpful if you know their functionality but need a brief reminder of syntax.

Using Import parameters

The general form for invoking the Import utility looks like this:

```
imp [username[/password[@service]]] [param=value
[param=value]...]
```

Replace *username* and *password* with your username and password. If you omit either of these, Import will prompt you for them. You can use a Net8 service name to allow you to import data into a remote database. The parameters, shown as *param* in the syntax, are the ones listed in Table 9-1. You may place as many parameters on the command line as you need.

Table 9-1
Import Parameters

Parameter	Description
ANALYZE	Controls whether any ANALYZE commands that may be in the export file are executed. Also controls whether any statistics that were exported are loaded.

Parameter	Description
BUFFER	Specifies the size of the buffer used to send rows to the database. This value is in bytes. The buffer must be large enough to hold the largest row in the table.
COMMIT	Specifies whether a commit should occur after each array insert. The default setting is COMMIT=N, causing a commit to occur after loading each table. The COMMIT=Y parameter causes commits to occur more frequently, thus lessening the pressure on rollback segments. However, using COMMIT=Y slows the import down quite a bit. Another problem with COMMIT=Y is that if an import fails while a table is being loaded, the changes already made to that table cannot be rolled back. This could lead to duplicate rows after you retry the import. Use of COMMIT=Y is safest when you have a primary key or a unique key defined for the table.
CONSTRAINTS	Controls whether you want table constraints to be imported. The default is CONSTRAINTS=Y.
DATAFILES	Supplies a list of the datafile names for that tablespace if you are importing a transportable tablespace.
DESTROY	Specifies having the REUSE option automatically added to all CREATE TABLESPACE commands. The default is DESTROY=N, causing the import to fail if an attempt is made to overwrite any existing datafiles.
FEEDBACK	Specifies that Import indicate progress by displaying periods on the screen. The default is FEEDBACK=0, resulting in no progress display. The FEEDBACK=10 parameter causes a period to be written for every ten rows that are inserted, FEEDBACK=20 causes a period to be written for every 20 rows, and so forth.
FILE	Specifies the name of the export file. The default is FILE=expdat.dmp. The default file extension is .dmp.
FILESIZE	Specifies the file size that was used for a multifile export. This should match the FILESIZE setting used when you exported the data.
FROMUSER	Allows you to import specific schemas, ignoring anything else in the export file. You can list one schema or several, as shown in these two examples: FROMUSER=AMY FROMUSER=(AMY,SEAPARK) These two clauses limit an import to objects owned by AMY, or by AMY and SEAPARK, respectively. Objects in the export file owned by users that you do not list will be ignored.

Continued

Table 9-1 *(continued)*	
Parameter	**Description**
FULL	Specifies that everything in the export file is to be imported when the FULL=Y parameter is used. The default is FULL=N.
GRANTS	Specifies that GRANT statements are to be imported with their tables. The GRANTS=Y parameter is the default. The GRANTS=N parameter causes tables to be imported without their associated grants.
HELP	Controls the display of the help screen shown earlier in the chapter. The parameter is HELP=Y; there is no HELP=N option.
IGNORE	Controls Import's behavior when it fails to create a table that is being imported. When you use the IGNORE=N parameter, which is the default, a table creation error will cause Import to skip to the next table. When you use the IGNORE=Y parameter, even though a table could not be created, Import will attempt to import that table's data. Use IGNORE=Y if you have manually created the tables that you are trying to import. The IGNORE=Y parameter is frequently used when reorganizing storage.
INCTYPE	Specifies the incremental import options. You can use the following option values: SYSTEM. Imports system objects RESTORE. Imports all user objects There is no default value for INCTYPE.
INDEXES	Specifies whether indexes should be imported with their tables. The default is INDEXES=Y. Use INDEXES=N if you don't want index definitions to be imported, or if you want to create the indexes manually after the import is finished.
INDEXFILE	Specifies having Import generate a text file of CREATE INDEX commands for all indexes found in the export file. The following example results in a file named BIBDB_INDEXES.SQL: INDEXFILE=BIBDB_INDEXES.SQL When the INDEXFILE parameter is used, no objects are imported. Import will create only the requested text file. There is no default value for this parameter.
LOG	Specifies the name of a log file that will accumulate information about the import, including any error messages. The default file extension is .log.
PARFILE	Allows you to read export parameters from a file. Read more on this option later in the chapter.

Parameter	Description
RECALCULATE_STATISTICS	Specifies that Import may execute ANALYZE commands for all tables and indexes that are imported, or it may import precalculated statistics that were written by the Export utility, when ANALYZE=Y is used. The Import utility makes the choice. Setting RECALCULATE_STATISTICS=Y forces Import to ignore any precalculated statistics and to execute ANALYZE commands instead. The default is RECALCULATE_STATISTICS=N.
RECORDLENGTH	Specifies the record length used in the export file. You may not need it, but the RECORDLENGTH parameter can be useful when transferring export files between operating systems. The value specified for RECORDLENGTH when importing should match that used when exporting.
ROWS	Controls whether table data is imported. The default is ROWS=Y, which causes data to be imported. Use ROWS=N if you just want to import table definitions. This results in empty tables.
SHOW	Specifies Import to display all the SQL statements that would be executed if it were to actually import the file being read. This is a good way to find out what's in an export file. When using SHOW=Y, no data or objects are imported—you get only the display. The default is SHOW=N.
SKIP_UNUSABLE_INDEXES	Specifies that Import not update or build indexes where the state has been set to *index unusable,* when using SKIP_UNUSABLE_INDEXES=Y. The default is SKIP_UNUSABLE_INDEXES=N.
TABLES	Allows you to import a specific table or a list of tables.
TABLESPACES	Allows you to export a specific tablespace or a list of tablespaces. The tablespaces must be locally managed, and you must use this parameter in conjunction with TRANSPORT_TABLESPACE=Y.
TOID_NOVALIDATE	Allows you to import a table based on object types without validating that the unique identifier for those types in the export file matches the unique identifier for the same types in the target database.
	This parameter expects a list of type names, and it should be formatted like this:
	`TOID_NOVALIDATE = ([schema.]type [,[schema.]type...])`
	There is no default value for this parameter.
TOUSER	Specifies a target list of schemas when used in conjunction with FROMUSER. This option allows you to copy objects from one schema to another. Objects owned by the users listed with the FROMUSER parameter are loaded into schemas for the users listed with the TOUSER parameter.

Continued

Table 9-1 *(continued)*	
Parameter	*Description*
TRANSPORT_ TABLESPACE	Allows you to import the metadata for transportable tablespaces. The default is TRANSPORT_TABLESPACE=N.
TTS_OWNERS	Lists the owners of the data in the transportable tablespaces being imported and can be used with TRANSPORT_TABLESPACE=Y. If this list of owners doesn't match the export file, Import will return an error.
USERID	Specifies the username and password of the user invoking the import.
VOLSIZE	Specifies the maximum number of bytes in export files when those files are stored on tape volumes.

The examples in this chapter show the more common uses of the Import utility. Many of these examples demonstrate the use of the parameters shown in Table 9-1.

Using interactive mode vs. command-line mode

The Import utility supports a limited interactive mode. To invoke Import interactively, simply start it without passing any parameters. The format to use is:

```
imp [username[/password[@service]]]
```

You can leave out the password, and Import will prompt you for it. If you aren't connecting to a remote database, you can leave out both the username and the password, and Import will prompt you for both. Listing 9-2 shows Import being used interactively to import the CARETAKER table owned by the user SEAPARK.

Listing 9-2: **Performing an interactive import**

```
E:\Jonathan\Oracle_Bible\ch9> imp system@bibdb

Import: Release 8.1.5.0.0 - Production on Mon Aug 9 10:55:54 1999

(c) Copyright 1999 Oracle Corporation.  All rights reserved.

Password:

Connected to: Oracle8i Release 8.1.5.0.0 - Production
With the Partitioning and Java options
PL/SQL Release 8.1.5.0.0 - Production

Import file: EXPDAT.DMP > bibdb
```

```
Enter insert buffer size (minimum is 8192) 30720>

Export file created by EXPORT:V08.01.05 via direct path
import done in WE8ISO8859P1 character set and WE8ISO8859P1 NCHAR character set
List contents of import file only (yes/no): no >

Ignore create error due to object existence (yes/no): no >

Import grants (yes/no): yes >

Import table data (yes/no): yes >

Import entire export file (yes/no): no >
Username: seapark

Enter table(T) or partition(T:P) names. Null list means all tables for user
Enter table(T) or partition(T:P) name or . if done: caretaker

Enter table(T) or partition(T:P) name or . if done:

. importing SEAPARK's objects into SEAPARK
. . importing table                    "CARETAKER"            3 rows imported
About to enable constraints...
Import terminated successfully without warnings.
```

When you use Import interactively like this, you don't have access to the utility's full functionality like you do when you pass parameters on the command line.

Using Import prerequisites

To use the Import utility, you must have the following:

✦ The CREATE SESSION privilege, allowing you to log on to the target database.

✦ The CREATE privileges for any objects that you are importing. For example, to import new tables, you need the CREATE TABLE privilege.

✦ The IMP_FULL_DATABASE role if you are importing from an export file that you did not create, or if you are importing objects owned by another user.

✦ Execute privileges on the DBMS_RLS package if you are importing tables with fine-grained access policies attached.

Before using Import against a database, you must run the CATEXP.SQL script once to create views and tables that the Import utility requires. The IMP_FULL_DATABASE role is one of the items that CATEXP.SQL creates. The CATEXP.SQL script is run by CATALOG.SQL, so if you ran CATALOG.SQL when you first created the database, you are all set. If you need them, you will find these scripts in the $ORACLE_HOME/RDBMS/ADMIN directory.

Importing an Entire Database

You can use the FULL=Y option to import the entire contents of an export file. If the export was a full database export, then importing that file results in a full database import. Listing 9-3 shows the results of a full database import:

```
E:\Jonathan\Oracle_Bible\ch9> imp system@bibdb full=y ignore=y file=bibdb
log=bib
db_import

Import: Release 8.1.5.0.0 - Production on Mon Aug 9 11:17:15 1999

(c) Copyright 1999 Oracle Corporation.  All rights reserved.

Password:

Connected to: Oracle8i Release 8.1.5.0.0 - Production
With the Partitioning and Java options
PL/SQL Release 8.1.5.0.0 - Production

Export file created by EXPORT:V08.01.05 via direct path
import done in WE8ISO8859P1 character set and WE8ISO8859P1 NCHAR character set
. importing SEAPARK's objects into SEAPARK
. importing AMY's objects into AMY
. importing SYS's objects into SYS
. importing SYSTEM's objects into SYSTEM
. importing SYS's objects into SYS
. importing SYSTEM's objects into SYSTEM
. . importing table                "DEF$_AQCALL"          0 rows imported
. . importing table                "DEF$_AQERROR"         0 rows imported

...


About to enable constraints...
. importing SCOTT's objects into SCOTT
. importing SEAPARK's objects into SEAPARK
. importing SYSTEM's objects into SYSTEM
. importing SCOTT's objects into SCOTT
. importing ORDSYS's objects into ORDSYS
. importing MDSYS's objects into MDSYS
. importing SEAPARK's objects into SEAPARK
Import terminated successfully with warnings.
```

When you do a full import like this, you may want to set the IGNORE=Y parameter. Otherwise, you will see a veritable plethora of error messages regarding system objects that couldn't be created because they already exist. Remember, though, that the IGNORE=Y parameter can cause duplicate rows in your tables if you aren't importing into an empty database.

Note   The issue of attempting to create system objects that already exist, and having to deal with the resulting error messages, is one reason why you might try to avoid doing full database imports if you can. Instead, consider importing at either the user or the table level, where you'll have a way to know for sure whether an error message is something to be concerned about. Importing an entire database can be too broad a stroke to paint.

While Import gives you the capability to import specific tables, or to import specific users, the only way to import other database objects, such as profiles, public synonyms, and tablespace definitions, is to do a full export and import using the FULL=Y option.

Importing Users

You can use the FROMUSER and TOUSER options to import specific schemas from an export file. The FROMUSER option specifies a list of schemas to import. The TOUSER option allows you to specify a list of target schemas that differ from the original, effectively giving you a way to rename users.

Importing a specific list of users

You can import one user or a specific list of users, using the FROMUSER parameter. The format to use for FROMUSER is:

```
FROMUSER=username
FROMUSER=(username, username,...)
```

When you use the FROMUSER option, you must create the specified users in the target database before you attempt to import them. You don't have to create any of their objects before you import, but Import will expect the users to exist. Be sure, too, that you have granted the necessary CREATE privileges to the users based on the objects that you are importing.

Listing 9-4 shows FROMUSER being used to import only objects owned by AMY and SEAPARK.

> ### Listing 9-4: **Importing objects owned by a specific set of users**
>
> ```
> E:\Jonathan\Oracle_Bible\ch9> imp system@bibdb fromuser=(amy,seapark) file=bibdb
> log=bibdb_log
>
> Import: Release 8.1.5.0.0 - Production on Mon Aug 9 12:12:15 1999
>
> (c) Copyright 1999 Oracle Corporation.  All rights reserved.
>
> Password:
>
> Connected to: Oracle8i Release 8.1.5.0.0 - Production
> With the Partitioning and Java options
> PL/SQL Release 8.1.5.0.0 - Production
>
> Export file created by EXPORT:V08.01.05 via direct path
> import done in WE8ISO8859P1 character set and WE8ISO8859P1 NCHAR character set
> . importing SEAPARK's objects into SEAPARK
> . importing AMY's objects into AMY
> . importing SEAPARK's objects into SEAPARK
> . . importing table              "AQUATIC_ANIMAL"       10 rows imported
> . . importing table                    "CARETAKER"       3 rows imported
> . . importing table                      "CHECKUP"       3 rows imported
>
> ...
>
> . importing AMY's objects into AMY
> . . importing table                        "ARTIST"      10 rows imported
> . . importing table                         "BOOKS"       3 rows imported
> . . importing table                  "BOOKS_LOANED"       1 rows imported
>
> ...
>
> About to enable constraints...
> Import terminated successfully without warnings.
> ```

If the users in question own no objects before the import starts, the import should run to completion without generating any error message.

Importing one user into another

You can use the TOUSER parameter to import data owned by one user into another user's schema. If you need to make a copy of a user for testing purposes, the TOUSER parameter allows you to do that.

The syntax for TOUSER is the same as for FROMUSER. You supply either one schema name or a list of schema names separated by commas. The schema names listed in TOUSER correspond to the schema names listed with FROMUSER on a positional basis. Take a look at this example:

```
FROMUSER=(AMY,SEAPARK,HAROLD)
TOUSER=(SEAPARK, AMY)
```

In this rather extreme example, AMY's objects would be imported into the SEAPARK schema, SEAPARK's objects would be imported into AMY's schema, and you would have one mixed-up database. HAROLD's objects, since no corresponding TOUSER entry existed for HAROLD, would be imported into the HAROLD schema.

Note   Schemas in the FROMUSER list without corresponding entries in TOUSER are imported unchanged.

TOUSER is commonly used to make a duplicate copy of a schema for testing purposes. Say that you want to make a copy of the SEAPARK schema and call it SEAPARK_COPY. You could do that by following these steps:

1. Export the current SEAPARK user. You could use a command like this:

   ```
   exp system@bibdb file=seapark log=seapark owner=seapark
   ```

2. Create a new user named SEAPARK_COPY. For example:

   ```
   CREATE USER seapark_copy identified by seapark
   DEFAULT TABLESPACE users
   TEMPORARY TABLESPACE temp
   QUOTA UNLIMITED ON users
   QUOTA UNLIMITED ON temp;
   GRANT CONNECT, RESOURCE TO seapark_copy;
   ```

3. Import the SEAPARK data into SEAPARK_COPY's schema. The following import command will do this:

   ```
   imp system@bibdb fromuser=seapark touser=seapark_copy
       file=seapark log=seapark_import
   ```

When copying a schema, you can use any export file containing that schema's objects. One approach, the one shown in Step 1, is to create a brand new export for just the one schema. Another approach is to simply use a recent full database export, if you have one. Whichever method you choose, the FROMUSER parameter in Step 3 controls which schema's data gets imported. The TOUSER parameter then determines the destination schema.

Importing a Table

You can use the TABLES parameter to limit an import to just one table or to a specific list of tables. The syntax for TABLES takes either of these forms:

```
TABLES=table_name
TABLES=(table_name, table_name...)
```

Be aware that while the Export utility allows table names listed after the TABLES parameter to be qualified with schema names, the Import utility does not. If you are trying to restore the SEAPARK user's CARETAKER table, you can't use the following parameter to do that:

```
TABLES=seapark.caretaker
```

Instead, to restore a table for a user other than yourself, you need to use both FROMUSER and TABLES together. For example:

```
FROMUSER=seapark TABLES=caretaker
```

The FROMUSER parameter gets you to the specific schema, in this case, the SEAPARK schema, while TABLES gets you to a specific list of tables within that schema, in this case, the CARETAKER table.

Note   If an export was done by a user who was not a DBA, then another user may import that data into his or her own schema without using FROMUSER/TOUSER. If an export was done by a DBA, then it must be imported by a DBA.

Using Import Options

A lot of parameters affect how the Import utility operates. Some of the more significant parameters allow you to do the following:

✦ Ignore create errors

✦ Generate CREATE INDEX statements

✦ Import from multiple-file exports

✦ Use parameter files

This section shows you how and why to use these features.

Ignoring create errors

You will often import data into tables that you have already created. Maybe you are just using Export and Import to copy data from one database to another. Or maybe you want to export a nonpartitioned table and import it back as a partitioned table. Whatever the reason, this conflicts with Import's standard practice of attempting to create objects that it imports. When Import loads a table, it goes through the following steps:

1. It creates the table.

2. It inserts the data.

3. It creates indexes on the table.

4. It creates integrity constraints on the table.

Step 1 presents a problem if the table already exists. Import's normal behavior is to skip an object if any type of error occurs. If a table exists, Import will try to create it, the create will fail, and Import will move to the next table. The result is that no data gets loaded.

You can use IGNORE=Y to change Import's behavior in response to creation errors. When the IGNORE=Y setting is used, Import will still try to create each table that it imports. The difference is that if the table already exists, Import will ignore the creation error and proceed to insert the table's data into the preexisting table. Listing 9-5 shows a simple example that demonstrates Imports normal response to a creation error. The AQUATIC_ANIMAL table has already been created, but it contains no data. The import attempt doesn't specify IGNORE=Y, so look what happens.

Listing 9-5: **Import skips a table because of a creation error**

```
E:\Jonathan\Oracle_Bible\ch9> imp system/manager@bibdb fromuser=seapark
tables=aquatic_animal file=bibdb log=bibdb_import

Import: Release 8.1.5.0.0 - Production on Mon Aug 9 14:36:31 1999

(c) Copyright 1999 Oracle Corporation.  All rights reserved.


Connected to: Oracle8i Release 8.1.5.0.0 - Production
With the Partitioning and Java options
PL/SQL Release 8.1.5.0.0 - Production

Export file created by EXPORT:V08.01.05 via direct path
import done in WE8ISO8859P1 character set and WE8ISO8859P1 NCHAR character set
```

Continued

Listing 9-5 *(continued)*

```
importing SEAPARK's objects into SEAPARK
IMP-00015: following statement failed because the object already exists:
 "CREATE TABLE "AQUATIC_ANIMAL" ("ID_NO" NUMBER(10, 0), "TANK_NO" NUMBER(10, "
 "0), "ANIMAL_NAME" VARCHAR2(30), "MARKINGS_DESCRIPTION" VARCHAR2(30), "BIRTH"
 "_DATE" DATE, "DEATH_DATE" DATE)  PCTFREE 10 PCTUSED 40 INITRANS 1 MAXTRANS "
 "255 LOGGING STORAGE(INITIAL 10240 NEXT 10240 MINEXTENTS 1 MAXEXTENTS 121 PC"
 "TINCREASE 50 FREELISTS 1 FREELIST GROUPS 1 BUFFER_POOL DEFAULT) TABLESPACE "
 ""USERS""
Import terminated successfully with warnings.
```

What happened was that no data was loaded. Import detected an error when it tried to create the AQUATIC_ANIMAL table and did not do anything more. Listing 9-6 shows the same import again, but this time with the IGNORE=Y parameter setting.

Listing 9-6: **Using IGNORE=Y to ignore creation errors**

```
E:\Jonathan\Oracle_Bible\ch9> imp system/manager@bibdb fromuser=seapark
tables=aquatic_animal file=bibdb log=bibdb_import ignore=y

Import: Release 8.1.5.0.0 - Production on Mon Aug 9 14:38:56 1999

(c) Copyright 1999 Oracle Corporation.  All rights reserved.


Connected to: Oracle8i Release 8.1.5.0.0 - Production
With the Partitioning and Java options
PL/SQL Release 8.1.5.0.0 - Production

Export file created by EXPORT:V08.01.05 via direct path
import done in WE8ISO8859P1 character set and WE8ISO8859P1 NCHAR character set
. importing SEAPARK's objects into SEAPARK
. . importing table              "AQUATIC_ANIMAL"          10 rows imported
About to enable constraints...
Import terminated successfully without warnings.
```

This time, because of the IGNORE=Y setting, the creation error was ignored. In fact, you don't even see the error message. Import goes on to load the data into the existing table.

When you create a table before importing it, you can make almost any change that you want involving the way that the table is stored. You can change the tablespace, partition the table, change the storage parameters, and even add new columns to the table. You do, however, need to keep the following points in mind:

✦ Column names in the table must match those in the export file.

✦ Column types must be compatible. You can import a NUMBER(10) into a FLOAT, but you cannot import a NUMBER into a VARCHAR2.

✦ Column lengths must not shrink. Don't try to import a VARCHAR2(30) into a VARCHAR2(10).

✦ You can't add NOT NULL columns. Since the old rows will not contain values for these columns, the NOT NULL constraint will always fail.

Another issue to consider, unrelated to compatibility between column types, is the effect of referential integrity constraints, especially if you are loading multiple tables. Referential integrity constraints define dependencies between tables. Normally, Import doesn't apply any referential integrity constraints until after all data has been imported. If you have first created tables with referential integrity constraints and you are importing data into these tables, you may find rows being rejected because the required parent rows don't exist. You can work around this problem by disabling all involved referential integrity constraints before you load your data. After all data in all related tables have been loaded, you can enable the constraints again.

Generating CREATE INDEX statements

If you are doing an export followed by an import to reorganize your database, you may not want the Import utility to create your indexes for you. The reason for this is that by default, Import will create the indexes in the same tablespace that they were in when they were exported, and with the same storage parameters. You may want the opportunity to change things around. You can get that opportunity by following this process:

1. Run Import with the INDEXFILE parameter, which generates a SQL file containing CREATE INDEX commands.

2. Edit the index creation commands so that they contain the desired storage and tablespace options.

3. Create the tables that you are going to import before importing.

4. Run Import using IGNORE=Y and INDEXES=N to load the data into your created tables without creating the indexes.

5. Run the index creation script.

The following example in Listing 9-7 shows how you can use the `INDEXFILE` parameter to generate a file containing `CREATE INDEX` commands.

Listing 9-7: **Placing CREATE INDEX statements into a file**

```
E:\Jonathan\Oracle_Bible\ch9> imp system/manager@bibdb
indexfile=seapark_indexes.sql fromuser=seapark file=bibdb log=bibdb_indexes

Import: Release 8.1.5.0.0 - Production on Mon Aug 9 15:20:05 1999

(c) Copyright 1999 Oracle Corporation.  All rights reserved.


Connected to: Oracle8i Release 8.1.5.0.0 - Production
With the Partitioning and Java options
PL/SQL Release 8.1.5.0.0 - Production

Export file created by EXPORT:V08.01.05 via conventional path
import done in WE8ISO8859P1 character set and WE8ISO8859P1 NCHAR character set
. . skipping table "AQUATIC_ANIMAL"

. . skipping table "CARETAKER"

. . skipping table "CHECKUP"

. . skipping table "CHECKUP_HISTORY"

. . skipping table "ITEMS"

. . skipping table "PARK_REVENUE"

. . skipping table "TANK"

Import terminated successfully without warnings.
```

The resulting file, in this instance named seapark_indexes.sql, will look like the one shown in Listing 9-8.

Listing 9-8: **The resulting seapark_indexes.sql file**

```
REM   CREATE TABLE "SEAPARK"."AQUATIC_ANIMAL" ("ID_NO" NUMBER(10, 0),
REM   "TANK_NO" FLOAT(126), "ANIMAL_NAME" VARCHAR2(30),
REM   "MARKINGS_DESCRIPTION" VARCHAR2(30), "BIRTH_DATE" DATE, "DEATH_DATE"
REM   DATE) PCTFREE 10 PCTUSED 40 INITRANS 1 MAXTRANS 255 LOGGING
REM   STORAGE(INITIAL 10240 NEXT 10240 MINEXTENTS 1 MAXEXTENTS 121
REM   PCTINCREASE 50 FREELISTS 1 FREELIST GROUPS 1 BUFFER_POOL DEFAULT)
REM   TABLESPACE "USERS" ;
```

```
REM  ... 10 rows
CONNECT SEAPARK;
CREATE INDEX "SEAPARK"."AA_NAME" ON "AQUATIC_ANIMAL" ("ANIMAL_NAME" )
PCTFREE 10 INITRANS 2 MAXTRANS 255 STORAGE(INITIAL 10240 NEXT 10240
MINEXTENTS 1 MAXEXTENTS 121 PCTINCREASE 50 FREELISTS 1 FREELIST GROUPS 1
BUFFER_POOL DEFAULT) TABLESPACE "USERS" LOGGING ;
REM  ALTER TABLE "SEAPARK"."AQUATIC_ANIMAL" ADD CONSTRAINT "AQ_ANIMAL_PK"
REM  PRIMARY KEY ("ID_NO") USING INDEX PCTFREE 10 INITRANS 2 MAXTRANS 255
REM  STORAGE(INITIAL 10240 NEXT 10240 MINEXTENTS 1 MAXEXTENTS 121
REM  PCTINCREASE 50 FREELISTS 1 FREELIST GROUPS 1 BUFFER_POOL DEFAULT)
REM  TABLESPACE "USERS" ENABLE NOVALIDATE ;
```

While the format is a bit messy, the file contains a remarked-out version of the CREATE TABLE statement, followed by CREATE INDEX statements for all indexes on the table, followed by an ALTER TABLE statement creating the table's primary key.

Note   By uncommenting the CREATE TABLE and ALTER TABLE statements, you can even use this SQL script as a basis for recreating the table prior to importing the data.

Importing from multiple-file exports

In Chapter 8, "Using Oracle8i's Export Utility," you saw how to use the FILE and FILESIZE parameters to create exports that spanned multiple files. When you import from such an export, you can use the same FILE and FILESIZE parameters for the import command as you originally used when exporting the data. Doing this enables Import to perform two functions:

✦ Check the FILESIZE that you specify against that recorded in the export files

✦ Automatically advance through the export files

If the file size specified in the import command doesn't match the size recorded in the export file, the import terminates with an error. For example, the import command shown in Listing 9-9 specifies a file size of 20KB when, in fact, a 10KB size was used when creating the export.

Listing 9-9: **An import specifying a 20KB file size**

```
E:\Jonathan\OR98C7~1\ch9> imp system/manager@jonathan.gennick
file=(seapark_1,seapark_2,seapark_3) full=y filesize=20k

Import: Release 8.1.5.0.0 - Production on Mon Aug 9 17:12:38 1999

(c) Copyright 1999 Oracle Corporation.  All rights reserved.
Connected to: Oracle8i Release 8.1.5.0.0 - Production
```

Continued

Listing 9-9 *(continued)*

```
With the Partitioning and Java options
PL/SQL Release 8.1.5.0.0 - Production

Export file created by EXPORT:V08.01.05 via conventional path
import done in WE8ISO8859P1 character set and WE8ISO8859P1 NCHAR character set
IMP-00040: FILESIZE does not match the value used for export: 10240
IMP-00000: Import terminated unsuccessfully
```

In most cases, it's probably easiest just to leave off the FILESIZE parameter altogether. Oracle records the file size in the export files and will automatically advance from one file to the next as long as you list all the file names using the FILE parameter. See Listing 9-10.

Listing 9-10: A multifile import

```
E:\Jonathan\OR98C7~1\ch9> imp system/manager@jonathan.gennick
file=(seapark_1,seapark_2,seapark_3) full=y

Import: Release 8.1.5.0.0 - Production on Mon Aug 9 17:18:29 1999

(c) Copyright 1999 Oracle Corporation.  All rights reserved.


Connected to: Oracle8i Release 8.1.5.0.0 - Production
With the Partitioning and Java options
PL/SQL Release 8.1.5.0.0 - Production

Export file created by EXPORT:V08.01.05 via conventional path
import done in WE8ISO8859P1 character set and WE8ISO8859P1 NCHAR character set
IMP-00046: using FILESIZE value from export file of 10240
. importing SYSTEM's objects into SYSTEM
. importing SEAPARK's objects into SEAPARK
. . importing table                 "AQUATIC_ANIMAL"         10 rows imported
. . importing table                     "CARETAKER"          3 rows imported
. . importing table                       "CHECKUP"          3 rows imported
. . importing table               "CHECKUP_HISTORY"          0 rows imported
. . importing table                         "ITEMS"          0 rows imported
. . importing table                  "PARK_REVENUE"          4 rows imported
. . importing table                    "PLAN_TABLE"          4 rows imported
. . importing table                          "TANK"          3 rows imported
Import terminated successfully with warnings.
```

In this case, the warning occurs only if you did not explicitly use the FILESIZE parameter. This is nothing to worry about. Import used the size recorded in the export file.

If you've done a multifile export, but you forget to specify all the file names when doing the import, the Import utility will prompt you for the missing files, as shown in Listing 9-11.

Listing 9-11: **The Import utility prompting for missing files**

```
E:\Jonathan\OR98C7~1\ch9> imp system/manager@jonathan.gennick file=seapark_1
full-y

Import: Release 8.1.5.0.0 - Production on Mon Aug 9 17:22:36 1999

(c) Copyright 1999 Oracle Corporation.  All rights reserved.


Connected to: Oracle8i Release 8.1.5.0.0 - Production
With the Partitioning and Java options
PL/SQL Release 8.1.5.0.0 - Production

Export file created by EXPORT:V08.01.05 via conventional path
import done in WE8ISO8859P1 character set and WE8ISO8859P1 NCHAR character set
IMP-00046: using FILESIZE value from export file of 10240
. importing SYSTEM's objects into SYSTEM
. importing SEAPARK's objects into SEAPARK
. . importing table            "AQUATIC_ANIMAL"      10 rows imported
. . importing table                 "CARETAKER"       3 rows imported
. . importing table                   "CHECKUP"       3 rows imported
. . importing table         "CHECKUP_HISTORY"         0 rows imported
. . importing table                     "ITEMS"       0 rows imported
. . importing table             "PARK_REVENUE"        4 rows imported
. . importing table                "PLAN_TABLE"
Import file: EXPDAT.DMP > seapark_2
```

When Import prompts for a file name, it won't know what the next file name should be. The default, shown in the prompt, will be EXPDAT.DMP. You'll have to type the name of the next export file to open. However, if you get the files out of sequence, Import will detect that and return an error message.

Using parameter files

You use parameter files with the Import utility for the same reason that you use them with the Export utility. Parameter files allow you to define import jobs that you can run repeatedly. For example, if you were regularly importing the SEAPARK user's objects into the SEAPARK_COPY schema, you could build a text file with the following contents:

```
FROMUSER=seapark
TOUSER=seapark_copy
FILE=seapark
LOG=seapark_import
```

If the text file containing these parameters were named copy_seapark.par, you could invoke the import using this short command:

```
imp system@bibdb PARFILE=copy_seapark.par
```

Using parameter files like this allows you to maintain consistency from one import to the next and also allows you to deal with extremely long parameter lists. If you need to list 1,000 tables after the TABLES parameter, for example, it's unlikely that your operating system will support a command that long. Parameter files provide you with a way to handle those situations.

Summary

In this chapter, you learned:

✦ The Import utility is the complement of the Export utility and is used to load data from an export file back into a database.

✦ You use the HELP=Y command-line parameter to get a brief help screen describing all the import parameters.

✦ The FULL=Y parameter tells Import to import everything in the file. To limit the import to a specific user, use the FROMUSER parameter. To further limit the export to a specific table, use the TABLES parameter.

✦ If you are reorganizing storage and you have first created the tables that you are importing, specify IGNORE=Y as a parameter so that Import will ignore any errors it receives while trying to create those tables again.

✦ If you don't want Import to create your indexes for you, specify INDEXES=N. Then, run the import again using the INDEXFILE parameter to get a SQL file containing CREATE INDEX statements. You can then edit those statements before executing the file.

✦　✦　✦

Using SQL*Loader

SQL*Loader is an Oracle utility that enables you to efficiently load large amounts of data into a database. If you have data in a flat file, such as a comma-delimited text file, and you need to get that data into an Oracle database, SQL*Loader is the tool to use. This chapter introduces you to the SQL*Loader utility, discusses its control file, provides the syntax for using the SQL*Loader command, and provides examples of using SQL*Loader to load data into databases.

Introducing SQL*Loader

SQL*Loader's sole purpose in life is to read data from a flat file and to place that data into an Oracle database. In spite of having such a singular purpose, SQL*Loader is one of Oracle's most versatile utilities. Using SQL*Loader, you can do the following:

+ Load data from a delimited text file, such as a comma-delimited file

+ Load data from a fixed-width text file

+ Load data from a binary file

+ Combine multiple input records into one logical record

+ Store data from one logical record into one table or into several tables

+ Write SQL expressions to validate and transform data as it is being read from a file

+ Combine data from multiple data files into one

+ Filter the data in the input file, loading only selected records

✦ Collect *bad* records — that is, those records that won't load — into a separate file where you can fix them

✦ And more!

The alternative to using SQL*Loader would be to write a custom program each time you needed to load data into your database. SQL*Loader frees you from that, because it is a generic utility that can be used to load almost any type of data. Not only is SQL*Loader versatile, it is also fast. Over the years, Oracle has added support for direct-path loads, and for parallel loads, all in an effort to maximize the amount of data that you can load in a given time period.

Understanding the SQL*Loader Control File

To use SQL*Loader, you need to have a database, a flat file to load, and a control file to describe the contents of the flat file. Figure 10-1 illustrates the relationship between these.

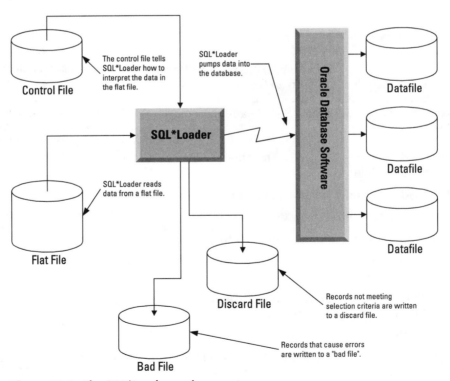

Figure 10-1: The SQL*Loader environment

Control files, such as the one illustrated in Figure 10-1, contain a number of commands and clauses describing the data that SQL*Loader is reading. Control files also tell SQL*Loader where to store that data, and they can define validation expressions for the data. Understanding control file syntax is crucial to using SQL*Loader effectively.

The control file is aptly named, because it controls almost every aspect of how SQL*Loader operates. The control file describes the format of the data in the input file and tells SQL*Loader which tables and columns to populate with that data. When you write a control file, you need to be concerned with these questions:

✦ What file, or files, contain the data that you want to load?

✦ What table, or tables, are you loading?

✦ What is the format of the data that you are loading?

✦ What do you want to do with records that won't load?

All of these items represent things that you specify when you write a SQL*Loader control file. Generally, control files consist of one long command that starts out like this:

```
LOAD DATA
```

The keyword DATA is optional. Everything else in the control file is a clause of some sort that is added onto this command.

SQL*Loader is a broad subject that's difficult to condense into one chapter. The control file clauses shown in this chapter are the ones most commonly used when loading data from text files. The corresponding examples will help you understand SQL*Loader and how it's used, and should provide enough background for you to easily use the other features of SQL*Loader as explained in the *Oracle8i Server Utilities* manual.

Many of the control file clauses you'll encounter in this chapter are explained by example. The task of loading data into the following table forms the basis for those examples:

```
CREATE TABLE animal_feeding (
animal_id          NUMBER,
    feeding_date   DATE,
    pounds_eaten   NUMBER (5,2),
    note           VARCHAR2(80)    );
```

Some examples are based on loading data from a fixed-width text file into the animal_feeding table, while others are based on loading the same data from a comma-delimited file.

Specifying the input file

You use the INFILE clause to identify the file containing the data that you want to load. The data can be in a file separate from the control file, which is usually the case, or you can place the data within the control file itself. Use multiple INFILE clauses if your data is spread across several files.

Control File Data

If you are loading data from a text file, you have the option of placing the LOAD command at the beginning of that file, which then becomes the control file. To specify that SQL*Loader looks in the control file for the data, supply an asterisk (*) for the file name in the INFILE clause. For example:

```
LOAD DATA
  INFILE *
 . . .
 . . .
 . . .
BEGINDATA
data
data
data
```

If you do include your data in the control file, the last clause of your LOAD command must be the BEGINDATA clause. This tells SQL*Loader where the command ends and where your data begins. SQL*Loader will begin reading data from the line immediately following BEGINDATA.

Data in a Separate File

Although you can have data in the control file, it's more common to have it in a separate file. In that case, you place the file name after the keyword INFILE, as shown in this example:

```
LOAD DATA
  INFILE 'animal_feeding.csv'
 . . .
 . . .
 . . .
```

Placing quotes around the file name often isn't necessary, but it's a good habit to get into. If the file name happens to match a SQL*Loader keyword, contains some strange punctuation, or is case sensitive (UNIX), you could run into problems unless it's quoted. You can use either single or double quotes. If necessary, you may include a path as part of the file name. The default extension is .dat.

Data in Multiple Files

You can use multiple INFILE clauses to load data from several files at once. The clauses must follow each other, as shown here:

```
LOAD DATA
  INFILE 'animal_feeding_fixed_1.dat'
  INFILE 'animal_feeding_fixed_2.dat'
...
...
...
```

When you specify multiple files like this, SQL*Loader will read them in the order in which they are listed.

Loading data into nonempty tables

After listing the input file, or files, in SQL*Loader, you need to specify whether you expect the table that you are loading to be empty. By default, SQL*Loader expects that you are loading data into a completely empty table. If, when the load starts, SQL*Loader finds even one row in the table, the load will be aborted. This is sometimes frustrating to people who haven't used SQL*Loader before, because it's not the behavior that you would intuitively expect.

Four keywords control SQL*Loader's behavior when it comes to dealing with empty vs. nonempty tables:

INSERT	Specifies that you are loading an empty table. SQL*Loader will abort the load if the table contains data to start with.
APPEND	Specifies that you are *adding* data to a table. SQL*Loader will proceed with the load even if preexisting data is in the table.
REPLACE	Specifies that you want to *replace* the data in a table. Before loading, SQL*Loader will *delete* any existing data.
TRUNCATE	Specifies the same as REPLACE, but SQL*Loader uses the TRUNCATE statement instead of a DELETE statement to delete existing data.

Place the keyword for whichever option you choose after the INFILE clause, as shown in this example:

```
LOAD DATA
  INFILE 'animal_feeding.csv'
  APPEND
...
...
...
```

If you don't specify an option, then INSERT is assumed by default.

Specifying the table to load

In SQL*Loader, you use the `INTO TABLE` clause to specify which table or tables you want to load. It also specifies the format of the data contained in the input file. The `INTO TABLE` clause is the most complex of all the clauses, and what you see here represents only a fraction of what it can include.

Loading One Table

To load one table, just place the `INTO TABLE` clause in your `LOAD` statement, as shown in the following example:

```
LOAD DATA
   INFILE 'animal_feeding.dat'
   APPEND
INTO TABLE animal_feeding
   (
      animal_id        POSITION (1:3) INTEGER EXTERNAL,
      feeding_date     POSITION (4:14) DATE "dd-mon-yyyy",
      pounds_eaten     POSITION (15:19) ZONED (5,2),
      note             POSITION (20:99) CHAR
   )
```

The table name shown in this example is the `animal_feeding` table. The same issues apply to table names as to file names. If the table name matches a reserved word or is case sensitive, enclose it within quotes.

A big part of the `INTO TABLE` clause is the list of field definitions. These describe the input file format for SQL*Loader and map the data in the input file onto the appropriate columns within the table being loaded. The sections "Describing delimited columns" and "Describing fixed-width columns," later in this chapter, explain more about writing field definitions.

Loading More than One Table

You can use multiple `INTO TABLE` clauses to load more than one table. Each `INTO TABLE` clause gets its own set of field definitions. Listing 10-1 shows an example of how you can split data among two tables.

Listing 10-1: **Loading data into two tables**

```
LOAD DATA
   INFILE 'animal_feeding_fixed.dat'
   APPEND
INTO TABLE animal_feeding
   (
```

```
           animal_id       POSITION (1:3) INTEGER EXTERNAL,
           feeding_date    POSITION (4:14) DATE "dd-mon-yyyy",
           pounds_eaten    POSITION (15:19) ZONED (5,2)
       )
INTO TABLE animal_feeding_note
   (
       animal_id       POSITION (1:3) INTEGER EXTERNAL,
       feeding_date    POSITION (4:14) DATE "dd-mon-yyyy",
       note            POSITION (20:99) CHAR
       )
```

In this example, `animal_id` and `feeding_date` are loaded into both tables. After that, however, the `animal_feeding` table gets the `pounds_eaten` value, while the `animal_feeding_note` table gets the `note` value.

Loading Multiple Tables from Delimited Data

When you load data into multiple tables like this, you can run into complications if the data that you are loading is delimited. Consider the LOAD command shown in Listing 10-2.

Listing 10-2: **Problems loading delimited data into multiple tables**

```
LOAD DATA
  INFILE 'animal_feeding.csv'
  APPEND
INTO TABLE animal_feeding
   (
       animal_id       INTEGER EXTERNAL TERMINATED BY ',',
       feeding_date    DATE "dd-mon-yyyy" TERMINATED BY ',',
       pounds_eaten    DECIMAL EXTERNAL TERMINATED BY ','
       )
INTO TABLE animal_feeding_note
   (
       animal_id       INTEGER EXTERNAL TERMINATED BY ',',
       feeding_date    DATE "dd-mon-yyyy" TERMINATED BY ',',
       note            CHAR TERMINATED BY ','
                       OPTIONALLY ENCLOSED BY '"'
       )
```

The problem that you experience here is that SQL*Loader works through delimited fields in the order in which they are listed, and this order cuts across all the INTO

TABLE clauses. Thus, SQL*Loader would expect `animal_id` for the `animal_feeding_note` table to follow the `pounds_eaten` value in the input file. The second `feeding_date` would have to follow that, and so forth. To reset SQL*Loader to the beginning of the line where the second `INTO TABLE` clause is applied to a record, you need to add a `POSITION` clause to the first field listed for that table. The `LOAD` statement in Listing 10-3 would work here.

Listing 10-3: Repositioning SQL*Loader's pointer into the record

```
LOAD DATA
  INFILE 'animal_feeding.csv'
  APPEND
INTO TABLE animal_feeding
   (
      animal_id        INTEGER EXTERNAL TERMINATED BY ',',
      feeding_date     DATE "dd-mon-yyyy" TERMINATED BY ',',
      pounds_eaten     DECIMAL EXTERNAL TERMINATED BY ','
   )
INTO TABLE animal_feeding_note TRAILING NULLCOLS
   (
      animal_id        POSITION (1) INTEGER EXTERNAL
                       TERMINATED BY ',',
      feeding_date     DATE "dd-mon-yyyy" TERMINATED BY ',',
      pounds_eaten     FILLER DECIMAL EXTERNAL
                       TERMINATED BY ',',
      note             CHAR TERMINATED BY ','
                       OPTIONALLY ENCLOSED BY '"'
   )
```

Notice the following in the example shown in Listing 10-3:

✦ The second definition of `animal_id` contains the clause `POSITION (1)`. This causes SQL*Loader to start scanning from the first character of the record. This is the behavior you want because you are loading the same field into two tables. Otherwise, SQL*Loader would look for another `animal_id` following the `pounds_eaten` column.

✦ The `TRAILING NULLCOLS` clause has been added to the second `INTO TABLE` clause because not all records in the input file contain notes.

✦ Even though you aren't storing it in the `animal_feeding_note` table, the `pounds_eaten` column doesn't go away. The `FILLER` keyword has been used to specify that SQL*Loader not load this field.

You can see that life does get a bit complex when loading a delimited file into multiple tables.

Describing fixed-width columns

The INTO TABLE clause contains a field list within parentheses. This list defines the fields being loaded from the flat file into the table. Each entry in the field list has this general format:

```
column_name    POSITION (start:end) datatype
```

✦ **column_name.** The name of a column in the table that you are loading.

✦ **POSITION (start:end).** The position of the column within the record. The values for *start* and *end* represent the character positions for the first and last characters of the column. The first character of a record is always position 1.

✦ **datatype.** A SQL*Loader datatype (not the same as an Oracle datatype) that identifies the type of data being loaded. Table 10-1 lists some of these.

You will need to write one field list entry for each column that you are loading. As an example, consider the following record:

```
10010-jan-200002350Flipper seemed unusually hungry today.
```

This record contains a three-digit ID number, followed by a date, followed by a five-digit number, followed by a text field. The ID number occupies character positions 1 through 3 and is an integer, so its definition would look like this:

```
animal_id      POSITION (1:3) INTEGER EXTERNAL,
```

The date field is next, occupying character positions 4 through 14, and its definition looks like this:

```
feeding_date   POSITION (4:14) DATE "dd-mon-yyyy",
```

Notice the "dd-mon-yyyy" string following the datatype. This tells SQL*Loader the specific format used for the date field. SQL*Loader uses this in a call to Oracle's built-in TO_DATE function, so any format that works for TO_DATE may be specified for SQL*Loader DATE fields.

You could continue to use the same method to define the rest of the fields that you want to load. The complete field list would look like this:

```
(
animal_id      POSITION (1:3) INTEGER EXTERNAL,
feeding_date   POSITION (4:14) DATE "dd-mon-yyyy",
pounds_eaten   POSITION (15:19) ZONED (5,2),
note           POSITION (20:99) CHAR
)
```

Using SQL*Loader Datatypes

SQL*Loader supports a wide variety of datatypes. Table 10-1 lists those that are most useful when loading data from text files.

Table 10-1 SQL*Loader Text-based Datatypes	
Datatype Name	**Description**
CHAR	Identifies character data. Don't confuse this with the CHAR datatype used within the database. No relationship exists between the two. If you are loading data into any type of text field, such as VARCHAR2, CHAR, or CLOB, use the SQL*Loader CHAR datatype.
DATE ["*format*"]	Identifies a date. Even though it's optional, specify a format. That way, you avoid problems if the default date format in the database is different from what you expect.
INTEGER EXTERNAL	Identifies an integer value that is stored in character form. For example, the character string "123" is a valid INTEGER EXTERNAL value.
DECIMAL EXTERNAL	Identifies a numeric value that is stored in character form and that may include a decimal point. The string "-123.45" is a good example of a DECIMAL EXTERNAL value.
ZONED (*precision, scale*)	Identifies a zoned decimal field, such as you might find in a file generated by a COBOL program. *Zoned decimal fields* are numeric values represented as character strings and that contain an assumed decimal point. For example, a definition of ZONED (5,2) would cause "12345" to be interpreted as 123.45. See the note following this table regarding zoned decimal and negative values.

Note   Be careful with the ZONED datatype. It can be handy for loading numeric values with assumed decimal places, but you have to be aware of how it expects the sign to be represented. This datatype harks back to the old card-punch days when data was stored on 80-character-wide punch cards. The sign for zoned decimal numbers was stored as an *overpunch* on one of the digits. The practical effect of that is that the ZONED data type will not recognize a hyphen (-) as a negative sign. It will, however, recognize some letters of the alphabet as valid digits. If you're not loading true zoned decimal data, such as a COBOL program might create, then use ZONED only for non-negative numbers.

SQL*Loader supports a number of other datatypes, most of which are well beyond the scope of this chapter. One other that you will read about later is the LOBFILE type. An example near the end of this chapter shows you how to load files into CLOB columns.

Converting Blanks to Nulls

When you're dealing with data in fixed-width columns, you'll find that missing values appear as blanks in the data file. Take a look at the following two lines of data:

```
   10-jan-200002350Flipper seemed unusually hungry today.
10510-jan-200009945Spread over three meals.
```

The first record is missing the three-digit animal ID number. Should that be interpreted as a null value? Or should it be left alone, causing the record to be rejected because spaces do not constitute a valid number? The latter behavior is the default.

If you prefer to treat a blank field as a null, you can use the NULLIF clause to tell SQL*Loader to do that. The NULLIF clause comes after the datatype and takes the following form:

```
NULLIF field_name=BLANKS
```

To define animal_id so that blank values are stored as nulls, you would use this definition:

```
animal_id          POSITION (1:3) INTEGER EXTERNAL
                   NULLIF animal_id=BLANKS,
```

You can actually have any valid SQL*Loader expression following the NULLIF clause, but comparing the column to BLANKS is the most common approach taken.

Describing delimited columns

The format for describing delimited data, such as comma-delimited data, is similar to that used for fixed-width data. The difference is that you need to specify the delimiter being used. The general format of a delimited column definition looks like this:

```
column_name    datatype TERMINATED BY 'delim'
               [OPTIONALLY ENCLOSED BY 'delim']
```

The elements of this column definition are described as follows:

column_name	The name of a column in the table that you are loading.
datatype	A SQL*Loader datatype. (See Table 10-1.)
TERMINATED BY *'delim'*	Identifies the delimiter that marks the end of the column.
OPTIONALLY ENCLOSED BY *'delim'*	Specifies an optional enclosing character. Many text values, for example, are enclosed by quotation marks.

When describing delimited fields, you must be careful to describe them in the order in which they occur. Take a look at this record, which contains some delimited data:

```
100,1-jan-2000,23.5,"Flipper seemed unusually hungry today."
```

The first field in the record is a three-digit number, an ID number in this case, and can be defined as follows:

```
animal_id     INTEGER EXTERNAL TERMINATED BY ',',
```

The remaining fields can be defined similarly to the first. However, the note field represents a special case because it is enclosed within quotation marks. To account for that, you must add an ENCLOSED BY clause to that field's definition. For example:

```
note          CHAR TERMINATED BY ','
              OPTIONALLY ENCLOSED BY '"'
```

The keyword OPTIONALLY tells SQL*Loader that the quotes are optional. If they are there, SQL*Loader will remove them. Otherwise, SQL*Loader will load whatever text it finds.

Working with short records

When dealing with delimited data, you occasionally run into cases where not all fields are present in each record in a data file. Take, for example, these two records:

```
100,1-jan-2000,23.5,"Flipper seemed unusually hungry today."
151,1-jan-2000,55
```

The first record contains a note, while the second does not. SQL*Loader's default behavior is to consider the second record as an error because not all fields are present. You can change this behavior, and cause SQL*Loader to treat missing values at the end of a record as nulls, by using the TRAILING NULLCOLS clause. This clause is part of the INTO TABLE clause, and appears as follows:

```
...
INTO TABLE animal_feeding
    TRAILING NULLCOLS
    (
        animal_id       INTEGER EXTERNAL TERMINATED BY ',',
        feeding_date    DATE "dd-mon-yyyy" TERMINATED BY ',',
        pounds_eaten    DECIMAL EXTERNAL TERMINATED BY ',',
        note            CHAR TERMINATED BY ','
                        OPTIONALLY ENCLOSED BY '"'
    )
```

When you use TRAILING NULLCOLS, any missing fields in the record will be saved in the database as nulls. *what abbut the missing value of middle col ?*

Error-causing records

When SQL*Loader reads a record from the input file, and for one reason or another is unable to load that record into the database, two things happen:

✦ An error message is written to the log file.

✦ The record that caused the error is written to another file called the *bad file*.

Bad files have the same format as the input file from which they were created. The reason that SQL*Loader writes bad records to a bad file is to make it easy for you to find and correct the errors. Once the load is done, you can edit the bad file (assuming that it is text), correct the errors, and resubmit the load using the same control file as was originally used.

The default name for the bad file is the input file name, but with the extension . bad. You can specify an alternate bad file name as part of the INFILE clause. For example:

```
INFILE 'animal_feeding.csv'
    BADFILE 'animal_feeding_bad.bad'
```

Each input file gets its own bad file. If you are using multiple INFILE clauses, each of those can specify a different bad file name.

Concatenating records

SQL*Loader has the ability to combine multiple physical records into one logical record. You can do this in one of two ways. You can choose to combine a fixed number of logical records into one physical record, or you can base that determination on the value of some field in the record.

The CONCATENATE Clause

If you have a case where a logical record is always made up of a fixed number of physical records, you can use the CONCATENATE clause to tell SQL*Loader to combine the records. The CONCATENATE clause appears in the LOAD statement, as shown in this example:

```
LOAD DATA
   INFILE 'animal_feeding_concat.csv'
     BADFILE 'animal_feeding_concat'
   APPEND
   CONCATENATE 2
...
```

In this example, every two physical records in the input file will be combined into one longer, logical record. The effect will be as if you took the second record and added it to the end of the first record. The following two records, for example:

```
100,1-jan-2000,23.5,
"Flipper seemed unusually hungry today."
```

will be combined into this one:

```
100,1-jan-2000,23.5,"Flipper seemed unusually hungry today."
```

The CONCATENATE clause is the appropriate choice if the number of records to be combined is always the same. Sometimes, however, you have to deal with cases where a particular field in a record determines whether the record is continued. For those cases, you must use CONTINUEIF.

The CONTINUEIF Clause

The CONTINUEIF clause allows you to identify continuation characters in the input record that identify whether a record should be continued. There are three possible variations on the CONTINUEIF clause. Which one you use depends on how the continuation characters are specified in your input file:

CONTINUEIF THIS	Use this option if each record in your input file contains a flag indicating whether the next record should be considered a continuation of the current record.

CONTINUEIF NEXT   Use this option if the continuation flag is not in the first record to be continued, but rather in each subsequent record.

CONTINUEIF LAST   Use this option if the continuation flag is always the last nonblank character or string of characters in the record.

One you've made this choice, your next two tasks are to specify the string that marks a continued record and to tell SQL*Loader the character positions where that string can be found. Let's say you have an input file that uses a dash as a continuation character and that looks like this:

```
-17510-jan-200003550
 Paintuin skipped his first meal.
-19910-jan-200000050
 Nosey wasn't very hungry today.
 20210-jan-200002200
```

The hyphen (-) character in the first column of a line indicates that the record is continued to the next line in the file. Records need to be concatenated until one is encountered that doesn't have a hyphen. Because the hyphen is in the record being continued, and because it is not the last nonblank character in the record, the CONTINUEIF THIS option is the appropriate one to use. The proper CONTINUEIF clause then becomes:

```
CONTINUEIF THIS (1:1) = '-'
```

The (1:1) tells SQL*Loader that the continuation string starts in column 1 and ends in column 1. The equal sign (=) tells SQL*Loader to keep combining records as long as the continuation field contains the specified string.

When concatenating records, be aware that SQL*Loader removes the continuation string when it does the concatenation. Thus, the following two records:

```
-17510-jan-200003550
 Paintuin skipped his first meal.
```

will be combined into one like this:

```
17510-jan-200003550Paintuin skipped his first meal.
```

Notice that the leading character from each record, the one indicating whether the record is continued, has been removed. With one exception, SQL*Loader always does this. The exception is when you use CONTINUEIF LAST. When you use CONTINUEIF LAST, SQL*Loader leaves the continuation character or characters in the record.

The CONTINUEIF NEXT parameter works similarly to CONTINUEIF THIS, except that SQL*Loader looks for the continuation flag in the record subsequent to the one being processed. The CONTINUEIF LAST parameter always looks for the continuation string at the end of the record, so you don't need to specify an exact position. The CONTINUEIF LAST parameter is ideal for delimited records, and there's an example later in this chapter showing how it's used.

Understanding the SQL*Loader Command

You must invoke the SQL*Loader utility from the command line. The command is usually sqlldr, but it can vary depending on the operating system you're using.

Note Older releases of Oracle on Windows NT embedded part of the release number into the file name. So this command would be sqlldr80, sqlldr73, and so forth.

As with other Oracle command-line utilities, SQL*Loader can accept a number of command-line arguments. SQL*Loader can also read command-line arguments from a separate parameter file (not to be confused with the control file). The syntax for the SQL*Loader command looks like this:

```
sqlldr [param=value[, param=value...]]
```

If you invoke SQL*Loader without any parameters, a short help screen will appear. This is similar to the behavior of the Export and Import utilities. Table 10-2 documents the SQL*Loader parameters.

	Table 10-2 SQL*Loader Parameters
Parameter	**Description**
userid	Passes in your username, password, and Net8 service name. The syntax to use is the same as for any other command-line utility, and looks like this: userid=username[/password][@service]
control	Passes in the control file name. Here's an example: control=[path]filename[.ext] The default extension for control files is .ctl.
log	Passes in the log file name. Here's an example: log=[path]filename[.ext] The default extension used for log files is .log. If you don't supply a file name, the log file will be named to match the control file.

Parameter	Description
bad	Passes in the bad file name. Here's an example: `bad=[path]filename[.ext]` The default extension for bad files is .bad. If you don't supply a file name, the bad file will be named to match the control file. Using this parameter overrides any file name that may be specified in the control file.
data	Passes in the data file name. Here's an example: `data=[path]filename[.ext]` The default extension used for data files is .dat. Specifying a data file name on the command line overrides the name specified in the control file. If no data file name is specified anywhere, it defaults to the same name as the control file, but with the .dat extension.
discard	Passes in the discard file name. Here's an example: `discard=[path]filename[.ext]` The default extension used for discard files is .dis. If you don't supply a file name, the discard file will be named to match the control file. Using this parameter overrides any discard file name that may be specified in the control file.
discardmax	Optionally places a limit on the number of discarded records that will be allowed. The syntax looks like this: `discardmax=number_of_records` If the number of discarded records exceeds this limit, the load is aborted.
skip	Allows you to skip a specified number of logical records. The syntax looks like this: `skip=number_of_records` Use the `skip` parameter when you want to continue a load that has been aborted and when you know how far into the file you want to go before you restart.
load	Optionally places a limit on the number of logical records to load into the database. The syntax looks like this: `load=number_of_records` Once the specified limit has been reached, SQL*Loader will stop.

Continued

Table 10-2 *(continued)*

Parameter	Description
errors	Specifies the number of errors to allow before SQL*Loader aborts the load. The syntax looks like this: `errors=number_of_records` SQL*Loader will stop the load if more than the specified number of errors has been received. The default limit is 50. There is no way to allow an unlimited number. The best you can do is to specify a very high value, such as 999999999.
rows	Indirectly controls how often commits occur during the load process. The rows parameter specifies the size of the bind array used for conventional-path loads in terms of rows. SQL*Loader will round that value off to be some multiple of the I/O block size. The syntax for the rows parameter looks like this: `rows=number_of_rows` The default value is 64 for conventional-path loads. Direct-path loads, by default, are saved only when the entire load is done. However, when a direct-path load is done, this parameter can be used to control the commit frequency directly.
bindsize	Specifies the maximum size of the bind array. The syntax looks like this: `bindsize=number_of_bytes` The default is 65,536 bytes (64KB). If you use `bindsize`, any value that you specify overrides the size specified by the `rows` parameter.
silent	Allows you to suppress messages displayed by SQL*Loader. You can pass one or more arguments to the silent parameter, as shown in this syntax: `silent=(keyword[, keyword...]])` Valid keywords are the following: `header` Suppresses introductory messages `feedback` Suppresses the "commit point reached" messages `errors` Suppresses data-related error messages `discards` Suppresses messages related to discarded records
partitions	Disables writing of partition statistics when loading a partitioned table

Parameter	***Description***
`all`	Disables all the messages described above
`direct`	Controls whether SQL*Loader performs a direct-path load. The syntax looks like this: `direct={true|false}` The default is `false`, causing a conventional-path load to be performed.
`parfile`	Specifies the name of a parameter file containing command-line parameters. The syntax looks like this: `parfile=[path]filename[.ext]` When the `parfile` parameter is encountered, SQL*Loader opens the file and reads command-line parameters from that file.
`parallel`	Controls whether direct loads are performed using parallel processing. The syntax looks like this: `parallel={true|false}` The default value is `false`.
`readsize`	Controls the size of the buffer used to hold data read from the input file. The syntax looks like this: readsize=size_in_bytes The default value is 65,536 bytes. SQL*Loader will ensure that the `readsize` and `bindsize` values match. If you specify different values for each, SQL*Loader will use the larger value for both settings.
`file`	Specifies the database datafile in which the data is to be stored and may be used when doing a parallel load. The syntax looks like this: `file=`*`datafile_name`* The file must be one of the files in the tablespace for the table or partition being loaded.

Using keywords by position

SQL*Loader allows you to pass command-line parameters using two different methods. You can name each parameter (recommended), or you can pass them positionally. The naming method is the easiest to understand, and looks like this:

```
sqlldr userid=system/manager control=animal_feeding.ctl
```

sqlldr txn/txnachange autoad_d.ctl external_table=generate-only

The positional method allows you to pass parameters without explicitly naming them. You must pass the parameters in the exact order in which Table 10-2 lists them, and you must not skip any. Converting the previous command to use positional notation yields the following:

```
sqlldr system/manager animal_feeding.ctl
```

You can even mix the two methods, passing one or more parameters by position and the remaining parameters by name. For example:

```
sqlldr system/manager control=animal_feeding.ctl
```

Since it's conventional for Oracle utilities to accept a username and password as the first parameter to a command, this last example represents a good compromise between the two methods. With the one exception of the username and password, it is recommended that you name all your parameters. You're much less likely to make a mistake that way.

Using parameter files

As with the Export and Import utilities, SQL*Loader also allows you to place command-line parameters in a text file. You can then use the `parfile` parameter to point to that file. For example, suppose you have a text file named `animal_feeding.par` that contains these lines:

```
userid=system/manager
control=animal_feeding.ctl
```

You could invoke SQL*Loader, and use the parameters from the text file, by issuing this command:

```
sqlldr parfile=animal_feeding.par
```

Parameter files provide a stable place in which to record the parameters used for a load and can serve as a means of documenting loads that you perform regularly.

Studying SQL*Loader Examples

SQL*Loader is best explained through the use of examples, and that is what you are going to see in the remainder of this chapter. The five examples in this section illustrate how to do to the following:

✦ Loading comma-delimited data

✦ Concatenating multiple physical records into one logical record

✦ Loading fixed-width, columnar data, and loading from multiple files

✦ Using expressions to modify data before loading it

✦ Loading large amounts of text into a large object column

With one exception, all the examples in this section will load data into the following table:

```
CREATE TABLE animal_feeding (
animal_id        NUMBER,
    feeding_date    DATE,
    pounds_eaten    NUMBER (5,2),
    note            VARCHAR2(80)
    );
```

The one exception involves the last example, which shows you how to load large objects. For that example, the note column is assumed to be a CLOB rather than a VARCHAR2 column. If you want to try these examples yourself, you can find the scripts on the CD in the directory sql_loader_examples.

Loading comma-delimited data

Let's assume that you have the following data in a file named animal_feedings.csv:

```
100,1-jan-2000,23.5,"Flipper seemed unusually hungry today."
105,1-jan-2000,99.45,"Spread over three meals."
112,1-jan-2000,10,"No comment."
151,1-jan-2000,55
166,1-jan-2000,17.5,"Shorty ate Squacky."
145,1-jan-2000,0,"Squacky is no more."
175,1-jan-2000,35.5,"Paintuin skipped his first meal."
199,1-jan-2000,0.5,"Nosey wasn't very hungry today."
202,1-jan-2000,22.0
240,1-jan-2000,28,"Snoops was lethargic and feverish."
...
```

This format is the typical comma-separated values (CSV) format that you might get if you had entered the data in Excel and saved it as a comma-delimited file. The fields are all delimited by commas, and the text fields are also enclosed within quotes. The following control file, named animal_feedings.ctl, would load this data:

```
LOAD DATA
  INFILE 'animal_feeding.csv'
    BADFILE 'animal_feeding'
  APPEND
  INTO TABLE animal_feeding
    TRAILING NULLCOLS
    (
```

```
animal_id          INTEGER EXTERNAL TERMINATED BY ",",
feeding_date       DATE "dd-mon-yyyy" TERMINATED BY ",",
pounds_eaten       DECIMAL EXTERNAL TERMINATED BY ",",
note               CHAR TERMINATED BY ","
                   OPTIONALLY ENCLOSED BY '"'
)
```

Here are some points worth noting about this control file:

✦ Any records that won't load because of an error will be written to a file named animal_feeding.bad. The BADFILE clause specifies the file name, and the extension .bad is used by default.

✦ The APPEND keyword causes SQL*Loader to insert the new data regardless of whether the table has any existing data. While not the default, the APPEND option is one you'll often want to use.

✦ The TRAILING NULLCOLS option is used because not all records in the input file contain a value for all fields. The note field is frequently omitted. Without TRAILING NULLCOLS, omitting a field would result in an error, and those records would be written to the bad file.

✦ The definition of the date field includes a format mask. This is the same format mask that you would use with Oracle's built-in TO_DATE function.

The following example shows SQL*Loader being invoked to load this data:

```
E:\> sqlldr seapark/seapark@bible_db control=animal_feeding

SQL*Loader: Release 8.1.5.0.0 - Production on Wed Aug 18 11:02:24 1999

(c) Copyright 1999 Oracle Corporation.  All rights reserved.

Commit point reached - logical record count 28
```

The command-line parameter control is used to pass in the control file name. The extension defaults to .ctl. The same command, but with different control file names, can be used for all the examples in this section.

Concatenating physical records into one logical record

Some of the lines in the animal_feeding.csv file shown in the previous example are quite long. That's because the note field can be up to 80 characters long. If you took that same file, named it animal_feeding_concat.csv, and placed each note on a line by itself, you would have a file containing records like those shown in Listing 10-4.

Listing 10-4: **Placing each note on its own line**

```
100,4-jan-2000,23.5,
"Flipper seemed unusually hungry today."
105,4-jan-2000,99.45,
"Spread over three meals."
112,4-jan-2000,10,
"No comment."
151,4-jan-2000,55
166,4-jan-2000,17.5,
"Shorty ate Squacky."
145,4-jan-2000,0,
"Squacky is no more."
175,4-jan-2000,35.5,
"Paintuin skipped his first meal."
199,4-jan-2000,0.5,
"Nosey wasn't very hungry today."
202,4-jan-2000,22.0
240,4-jan-2000,28,
"Snoops was lethargic and feverish."
...
```

This presents an interesting problem, because sometimes you want to concatenate two records into one, and sometimes you don't. In this case, the key lies in the fact that for each logical record that contains a comment, a trailing comma (,) has been left at the end of the physical record containing the numeric and date data. You can use the control file shown in Listing 10-5, which is named animal_feeding_concat.ctl, to key off of that comma, combine records appropriately, and load the data.

Listing 10-5: **A control file that combines two records into one**

```
LOAD DATA
  INFILE 'animal_feeding_concat.csv'
    BADFILE 'animal_feeding_concat'
  APPEND
  CONTINUEIF LAST = ","
  INTO TABLE animal_feeding
    TRAILING NULLCOLS
    (
      animal_id        INTEGER EXTERNAL TERMINATED BY ",",
      feeding_date     DATE "dd-mon-yyyy" TERMINATED BY ",",
      pounds_eaten     DECIMAL EXTERNAL TERMINATED BY ",",
      note             CHAR TERMINATED BY ","
                       OPTIONALLY ENCLOSED BY '"'
    )
```

There are two keys to making this approach work:

✦ If a line is to be continued, the last nonblank character must be a comma. Since all fields are delimited by commas, this is pretty easy to arrange.

✦ The `CONTINUEIF LAST = ","` clause tells SQL*Loader to look for a comma at the end of each line read from the file. Whenever it finds a comma, the next line is read and appended onto the first.

You aren't limited to concatenating two lines together. You can actually concatenate as many lines as you like, as long as they each contain a trailing comma. For example, you could enter the 5-Jan-2000 feeding for animal #100 as follows:

```
100,
5-jan-2000,
19.5,
"Flipper's appetite has returned to normal."
```

All four lines can be concatenated because the first three end with a comma. The fourth line doesn't end with a comma, and that signals the end of the logical record.

Loading fixed-width data

The following example shows you how to load fixed-width data and how to combine data from two files into one load. When you load fixed-width data, you need to use the `POSITION` keyword to specify the starting and ending positions of each field. Say you had two files, named animal_feeding_fixed_1.dat and animal_feeding_fixed_2.dat, containing records that looked like these:

```
10001-jan-200002350Flipper seemed unusually hungry today.
10501-jan-200009945Spread over three meals.
11201-jan-200001000No comment.
15101-jan-200005500
16601-jan-200001750Shorty ate Squacky.
14501-jan-200000000Squacky is no more.
17501-jan-200003550Paintuin skipped his first meal.
19901-jan-200000050Nosey wasn't very hungry today.
20201-jan-200002200
24001-jan-200002800Snoops was lethargic and feverish.
. . .
```

You could load this data, reading from both files, using the control file shown in Listing 10-6.

Listing 10-6: **Loading fixed-width data from two files**

```
LOAD DATA
  INFILE 'animal_feeding_fixed_1.dat'
    BADFILE 'animal_feeding_fixed_1'
  INFILE 'animal_feeding_fixed_2.dat'
    BADFILE 'animal_feeding_fixed_2'
  APPEND
  INTO TABLE animal_feeding
    TRAILING NULLCOLS
    (
      animal_id        POSITION (1:3) INTEGER EXTERNAL,
      feeding_date     POSITION (4:14) DATE "dd-mon-yyyy",
      pounds_eaten     POSITION (15:19) ZONED (5,2),
      note             POSITION (20:99) CHAR
    )
```

Notice the following about this control file:

✦ Two `INFILE` clauses are used, one for each file. Each clause contains its own `BADFILE` name.

✦ The `POSITION` clause, instead of the `TERMINATED BY` clause, is used for each field to specify the starting and ending column for that field.

✦ The datatype for the `pounds_eaten` field has been changed from `DECIMAL EXTERNAL` to `ZONED` because the decimal point is assumed to be after the third digit and doesn't really appear in the number. For example, 123.45 is recorded in the input file as 12345. COBOL programs commonly create files containing zoned decimal data.

✦ The `POSITION` clause appears before the datatype, whereas the `TERMINATED BY` clause appears after the datatype. That's just the way the syntax is.

Other than the use of the `POSITION` clause, there really is no difference between loading fixed-width data and delimited data.

Writing expressions to modify loaded data

SQL*Loader provides you with the ability to write expressions to modify data read from the input file. Look at this comma-delimited data, which is similar to what you loaded earlier:

```
100,13-jan-2000,23.5,"Flipper seemed unusually hungry today."
105,13-jan-2000,99.45,"Spread over three meals."
112,13-jan-2000,10,"No comment."
```

```
151,13-jan-2000,55
166,13-jan-2000,17.5,"Shorty ate Squacky."
145,13-jan-2000,0,"Squacky is no more."
175,13-jan-2000,35.5,"Paintuin skipped his first meal."
199,13-jan-2000,0.5,"Nosey wasn't very hungry today."
202,13-jan-2000,22.0
240,13-jan-2000,28,"Snoops was lethargic and feverish."
```

Imagine for a moment that you want to uppercase the contents of the note field. Imagine also that the weights in this file are in kilograms, and that you must convert those values to pounds as you load the data. You can do that by writing expressions to modify the note field and the pounds_eaten field. The following example shows you how to multiply the weight by 2.2 to convert from kilograms to pounds:

```
pounds_eaten    DECIMAL EXTERNAL TERMINATED BY ","
                ":pounds_eaten * 2.2",
```

As you can see, the expression has been placed within quotes, and it has been added to the end of the field definition. You can use a field name within an expression, but when you do, you must precede it with a colon (:). You can use any valid SQL expression that you like, but it must be one that will work within the VALUES clause of an INSERT statement. Indeed, SQL*Loader uses the expression that you supply as part of the actual INSERT statement that it builds to load your data. With respect to the pounds_eaten example, SQL*Loader will build an INSERT statement like this:

```
INSERT INTO animal_feeding
   (animal_id, feeding_date, pounds_eaten, note)
   VALUES (:animal_id, :feeding_date,
           :pounds_eaten * 2.2, :note)
```

Listing 10-7 shows a control file that will both convert from kilograms to pounds and uppercase the note field.

Listing 10-7: **Using expressions to transform data**

```
LOAD DATA
  INFILE 'animal_feeding_expr.csv'
    BADFILE 'animal_feeding_expr'
  APPEND
  INTO TABLE animal_feeding
    TRAILING NULLCOLS
    (
      animal_id      INTEGER EXTERNAL TERMINATED BY ",",
      feeding_date   DATE "dd-mon-yyyy" TERMINATED BY ",",
      pounds_eaten   DECIMAL EXTERNAL TERMINATED BY ","
```

```
                               ":pounds_eaten * 2.2",
        note                   CHAR TERMINATED BY ",",
                               OPTIONALLY ENCLOSED BY '"'
                               "UPPER(:note)"

    )
```

Oracle has a rich library of such functions that you can draw from. These are documented in Appendix B, "SQL Built-in Function Reference."

Loading large amounts of text

So far, all of the examples in this section have shown you how to load *scaler data*. This is the type of data that is normally associated with business applications, and it consists of character strings, dates, and numbers. In addition to loading simple, scaler data, you can also use SQL*Loader to load large object types. Consider this variation of the `animal_feeding` table:

```
CREATE TABLE animal_feeding (
        animal_id               NUMBER,
    feeding_date     DATE,
    pounds_eaten     NUMBER (5,2),
    note             CLOB
    );
```

Instead of an 80-character-wide note column, this version of the table defines the note column as a character-based large object, or CLOB. CLOBs may contain up to 2GB of data, effectively removing any practical limit on the length of a note. Can you load such a column using SQL*Loader? Yes.

For purposes of our example, let's assume that you have created note files for each animal, and that each file contains information similar to what you see here:

```
NAME: Shorty
DATE: 16-Jan-2000
TEMPERATURE: 115.2
ACTIVITY LEVEL: High
HUMOR: Predatory, Shorty caught Squacky and literally ate
       him for supper. Shorty should be isolated from the
       other animals until he can be checked out by
       Seapark's resident marine psychologist.
```

Let's also assume that you have modified the comma-delimited file so that instead of containing the note text, each line in that file contains the name of the note file to load. For example:

```
100,13-jan-2000,23.5,note_100.txt
105,13-jan-2000,99.45,note_105.txt
112,13-jan-2000,10,note_112.txt
151,13-jan-2000,55
166,13-jan-2000,17.5,note_166.txt
145,13-jan-2000,0,note_145.txt
175,13-jan-2000,35.5,note_175.txt
199,13-jan-2000,0.5,note_199.txt
202,13-jan-2000,22.0
240,13-jan-2000,28,note_240.txt
```

To load this data using SQL*Loader, do the following:

✦ Define a `FILLER` field to contain the file name. This field will not be loaded into the database.

✦ Define a `LOBFILE` field that loads the contents of the file identified by the `FILLER` field into the `CLOB` column.

The resulting control file is shown in Listing 10-8.

Listing 10-8: Loading files into a large object column

```
LOAD DATA
  INFILE 'animal_feeding_clob.csv'
    BADFILE 'animal_feeding_clob'
  APPEND
  INTO TABLE animal_feeding
    TRAILING NULLCOLS
    (
      animal_id        INTEGER EXTERNAL TERMINATED BY ",",
      feeding_date     DATE "dd-mon-yyyy" TERMINATED BY ",",
      pounds_eaten     DECIMAL EXTERNAL TERMINATED BY ",",
      note_file_name   FILLER CHAR TERMINATED BY ",",
      note             LOBFILE (note_file_name)
                       TERMINATED BY EOF
    )
```

Each time SQL*Loader inserts a record into the `animal_feeding` table, it will also store the entire contents of the associated note file in the note field.

Summary

In this chapter, you learned:

✦ SQL*Loader is a versatile utility for loading large amounts of data into an Oracle database.

✦ SQL*Loader control files are used to describe the data being loaded and to specify the table(s) into which that data is stored.

✦ You can use the INFILE clause to identify the file, or files, that you want SQL*Loader to read.

✦ You can use the INTO TABLE clause to identify the table, and the columns within that table, that you wish to populate using the data read from the input file.

✦ You can use the APPEND option after the INFILE clause to tell SQL*Loader to insert data into a table that already contains data to begin with.

✦ You can use SQL*Loader to load delimited data, such as comma-delimited data, or you can use it to load data stored in fixed-width columns.

✦ SQL*Loader fully supports all of Oracle8i's datatypes, even to the point of allowing you to populate LOB columns.

✦   ✦   ✦

Nuts and Bolts

◆ ◆ ◆ ◆

◆ ◆ ◆ ◆

Managing Users and Security

For many systems, the DBA is in charge of security. Security often becomes a time-consuming task that needs regular attention. Oracle's Security Manager, part of Enterprise Manager's DBA Management Pack, makes your tasks more intuitive and helps you manage users, passwords, and database privileges more efficiently and accurately.

This chapter explores how you can use Security Manager to create users and roles, assign privileges, and control passwords. It also shows you how to perform these tasks manually, executing SQL statements from the SQL*Plus tool. While Security Manager provides a GUI interface that substitutes for handwritten SQL code, underneath that interface, SQL statements are still being generated and executed. Security Manager will let you view those statements. Viewing the SQL statements generated by Security Manager is one way to reinforce your knowledge of SQL.

Creating and Managing Users

Often, one of your first tasks involves defining new users. Later, when a definitive security plan evolves, you can establish roles with specialized sets of privileges to enforce security. Typically, each end user becomes a member of at least one role that you create.

Creating a new user

The SQL command for creating a user is, aptly enough, CREATE USER. Before using this command to create a new user, keep the following in mind:

✦ A value for the user's initial password

✦ A default tablespace in which you want to store objects owned by the user

✦ The temporary tablespace to be used when the user executes queries requiring sorts

✦ The amount of disk space that you wish to allow the user to use in the default tablespace

Once you have these items in mind, you can create a new user by issuing a SQL statement like this one:

```
CREATE USER joseph IDENTIFIED BY big_cave
    DEFAULT TABLESPACE users
    TEMPORARY TABLESPACE temp
    QUOTA UNLIMITED ON users;
```

Note   It is not necessary to give quota on the temporary tablespace.

This statement creates a new user named JOSEPH and assigns him an initial password of BIG_CAVE. Joseph's default tablespace will be the USERS tablespace, and his temporary tablespace will be TEMP. Joseph has been given unlimited quota on the USERS tablespace, so he can use any amount of disk space in that tablespace.

Default Tablespaces

When a user creates an object such as a table or an index, that object must be stored somewhere. In Oracle, you control an object's storage by assigning it to a tablespace. If you don't specify a tablespace when you create an object, Oracle will pick one for you. The tablespace that Oracle picks will be the one specified as your default tablespace when your user ID was created.

The benefit of being able to specify a default tablespace for a user is that it allows users who aren't very sophisticated or knowledgeable about Oracle to create tables, indexes, and so forth, without having to worry about where they are stored. As the DBA, you can still exert some control over where objects are placed because you control the default tablespace assignments.

You should assign every user a default tablespace. If you don't specify a default tablespace when creating a user, then the SYSTEM tablespace is used as the default, which isn't good. The SYSTEM tablespace contains the data dictionary and is heavily used by Oracle. Placing user objects in the same tablespace can lead to performance degradation because of disk contention. Even if you don't ever expect a user to create any objects, specify a default tablespace anyway. That way, you won't be surprised later.

Temporary Tablespaces

Several types of SQL queries require data to be sorted. The obvious examples are those queries containing ORDER BY clauses, but Oracle can also perform sorts for GROUP BY queries, DISTINCT queries, and for certain types of joins. Some sorts can be done in memory, but if the amount of data to be sorted is large enough, the sorting process requires that some of it be temporarily written to disk.

When Oracle needs temporary storage, it will look to see if the user has been assigned a temporary tablespace and will perform the sort there. If that tablespace has been created specifically as a temporary tablespace, the result will be better performance, because Oracle's sorting routines have been optimized to take advantage of temporary tablespace features.

Quotas

A *quota* is a limit on the amount of disk space that one user is allowed to use. When you create a user, you have the option of granting the user permission to use some disk space in your database. You do this by placing one or more QUOTA clauses in the CREATE USER command. The earlier example used the keyword UNLIMITED to allow the user JOSEPH to use any amount of disk space in the USERS and TEMP tablespaces.

You aren't limited to specifying quota for just the default and temporary tablespaces. You can assign quota on any tablespace in the database. If you were to later decide that JOSEPH needed to create objects in the SEAPARK_DATA and SEAPARK_INDEXES tablespaces, you could issue this command:

```
ALTER USER joseph
    QUOTA 10M ON SEAPARK_DATA
    QUOTA 5M ON SEAPARK_INDEXES;
```

Here, Joseph has been granted the authority to use up to 10MB of space in the SEAPARK_DATA tablespace, and up to 5MB of space in the SEAPARK_INDEXES tablespace. The M following the numbers in the command stands for MB. You can also use a suffix of K (for KB). If you give a user quota on a tablespace, and later decide that you don't want the user to have any quota on that tablespace, you can set the user's quota for that tablespace to zero.

Choosing Names for Users and Passwords

As a DBA, you have the responsibility of creating every new username for your Oracle8i database. When setting up a name for a new user, you must follow the same rules that apply for naming any Oracle object:

✦ Names may be up to 30 characters long.

✦ Names must begin with a letter.

✦ After the first letter, names may consist of any combination of letters (A-Z), digits (0-9), underscores (_), pound signs (#), and dollar signs ($).

✦ Names are not case sensitive unless they are enclosed within double quotes.

✦ Names within double quotes may contain any combination of characters, in any order, but may not contain embedded quotes.

Using Security Manager to create a user

Security Manager makes quick work of creating a user. Its GUI interface is easy to follow and does not require you to remember any SQL syntax. To use Security Manager to create a user, follow these steps:

1. Start up Security Manager and log on to the database.

   Figure 11-1 shows the opening window of Security Manager.

2. Right-click the Users folder, and select Create to create a new user.

   This will open the Create User dialog box, which is shown in Figure 11-2.

Note You can also click the Create button on the toolbar or select Create from the Object menu to begin creating a user. With either of these two methods, you will need to proceed through another dialog box where you choose the type of object (user, role, or profile) that you are creating.

3. Type a new username.

4. Select a profile set from the pull-down list.

   Refer to the section "Creating and Assigning User Profiles" later in this chapter to learn how to create new profiles.

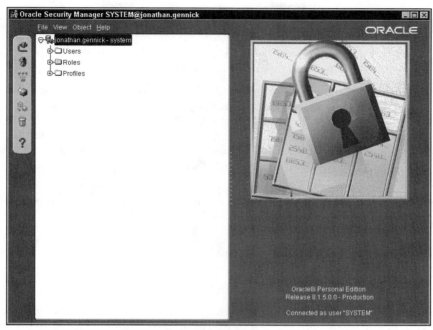

Figure 11-1: Security Manager's opening window

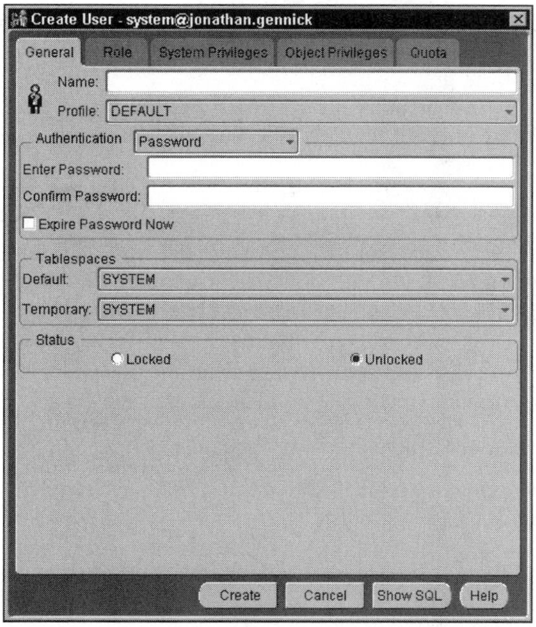

Figure 11-2: The Create User dialog box

5. Select the authentication type.

Three types of authentication exist:

- **Global.** A username can be defined as unique across multiple databases by selecting global authentication.

- **External.** Oracle validates the user through the operating system. In these cases, you append a common prefix to the user's operating system name to create the Oracle username. The default prefix is OPS$. If a user logs on to the operating system as JOSEPH, then the user's Oracle username is OPS$JOSEPH. The user doesn't enter a password when logging on to Oracle with external authentication.

- **Password.** The user must enter a password when logging on to the database. This is the traditional method. Use it if you are uncertain which choice to make.

6. If the user type is Password, type the password in both the Enter Password box and the Confirm Password box.

To prevent other people from seeing it, the password will appear on the screen as a string of asterisks (*).

Oracle enables you to require the user to enter a new password the first time the user logs on. Select the Expire Password Now check box to use this feature.

7. Select a default tablespace.

This is the tablespace in which Oracle puts the new user's tables if the user creates tables without explicitly assigning them to a different tablespace.

8. Click the Temporary drop-down list arrow to select a temporary tablespace.

Temporary tablespaces are normally named with TEMP as part of the name. The default database that you get with Oracle8i uses TEMP for the name of the temporary tablespace.

9. Click the Quota tab (optional).

Figure 11-3 shows the Quota tab. Here you can assign limits to the amount of space a user is allowed to use in each of the tablespaces in the database. To assign a limit, select the tablespace, click the Value option, type a number, and then select either K Bytes or M Bytes from the drop-down list. Do this for each tablespace that you want the user to use, except for the temporary tablespace. You do not need to assign quota for temporary tablespaces.

10. Click the Create button to finish.

Oracle creates the new username and displays a message telling you that the creation was successful.

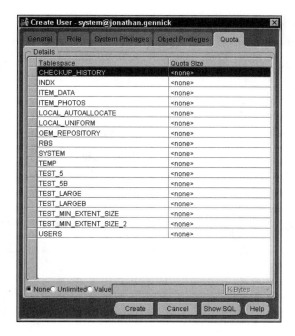

Figure 11-3: The Quota tab in the Create User dialog box

Tip   There's an easy way to use an existing user as a template when creating a new user. Right-click the template user in the user list, and then select Create Like from the pop-up menu. Fill in a new username and password. Make any other changes that you would like, and then click the Create button to create the new user.

Changing a user's password

Oracle does not contain a utility to display a user's password — it always appears as asterisks or in an encrypted form. If a user forgets his or her password, you must assign a new one. You can either use the ALTER USER command to change a password, or you can do it from Security Manager.

Changing a Password Using the ALTER USER Command

The following example shows you how to use the ALTER USER command to change a user's password. It changes Joseph's password to BROWN_BAG.

```
ALTER USER joseph IDENTIFIED BY brown_bag;
```

As you can see, this command is simple. You can issue it from either SQL*Plus or SQLPlus Worksheet.

Using Security Manager to Change a Password

To change a user's password from Security Manager, follow these steps:

1. Start Security Manager, and log on to the database.

2. Double-click the User folder in the left pane.

   This brings up a list of users on the left side of the screen.

3. Click the user whose password you are changing.

   The General tab of the user's Profile appears in the right pane, as shown in Figure 11-4.

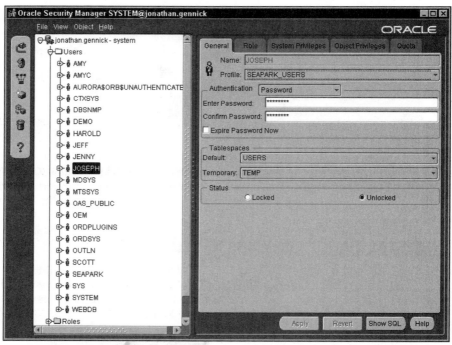

Figure 11-4: Editing a user's profile

4. Type the new password in the Enter Password box and again in the Confirm Password box.

5. Click the Apply button to complete the job.

   Security Manager executes the SQL statements necessary to apply the change and returns you to the main window.

Changing user settings

You can change the default tablespaces, account lock, profile, or quotas assigned to any user. Use the `ALTER USER` command to perform these tasks, or if you prefer, you can do them from Security Manager.

Note The account lock/unlock feature enables you to lock out users from accessing a database.

To make any of these changes from Security Manager, follow the procedure described earlier for making a password change. Once you have a user record selected for editing, you can make any changes you like to that record. The following sections show you how to make these changes from SQL*Plus.

Changing Tablespaces

You can change the default tablespace for a user by issuing a command like this:

```
ALTER USER username
    DEFAULT TABLESPACE tablespace_name;
```

You can change a user's temporary tablespace using the same method; just use the keyword `TEMPORARY` in place of `DEFAULT`.

Note If you change a user's default tablespace, don't forget to assign quota on that tablespace.

Locking Out a User

You can temporarily lock a user's account and prevent him or her from accessing the database by using this command:

```
ALTER USER username ACCOUNT LOCK;
```

You can re-enable the user's access by unlocking the account, using this command:

```
ALTER USER username ACCOUNT UNLOCK;
```

This account lock feature was introduced in Oracle release 8.0, and it provides a convenient method for temporarily disabling a user without having to drop the user.

Changing a User's Profile

To change a user's profile, use the `ALTER USER` command as follows:

```
ALTER USER username PROFILE profile_name;
```

Replace *profile_name* with the name of any valid profile defined for the database.

Changing a User's Quota

To change a user's disk quota on a tablespace, issue an ALTER USER command like this:

```
ALTER USER username
    QUOTA {UNLIMITED|VALUE[M|K]} ON tablespace_name;
```

For example, to reduce Joseph's quota on the USERS tablespace from 10MB to 5MB, issue the following command:

```
ALTER USER username
    QUOTA 5M ON users;
```

You can use as many QUOTA clauses in the command as necessary. Reducing a user's quota doesn't affect data that the user already has stored. Had Joseph already been using 8MB of data, for example, in the USERS tablespace, reducing his quota to 5MB would not result in any data being deleted.

Dropping a user

There are two ways to delete a user from the database. One way is to issue the DROP USER command from SQL*Plus or SQLPlus Worksheet. The other way is through Server Manager. If a user owns tables, indexes, or other objects, you normally need to delete those objects before you can drop the user. Using the CASCADE option allows you to drop a user and his or her data in one shot.

Using the DROP USER Command

Use the DROP USER command to delete a user from the database. The syntax is simple. To drop the user named JOSEPH, you issue the following command:

```
DROP USER joseph;
```

This form of the command requires that there are no tables, indexes, or other objects owned by the user.

Dropping a User and the User's Data

To drop a user, together with all tables and other objects owned by that user, add the CASCADE option to the DROP USER command. For example:

```
DROP USER joseph CASCADE;
```

Be careful with this command. You can easily delete a lot of data by mistake.

Using Security Manager to Drop a User

In addition to creating users, Security Manger allows you to delete them. To use Security Manager to delete (or drop) a user, follow these steps:

1. Run Security Manager, and log on to the database.

2. Expand the Users folder. You can do this by double-clicking the folder or by clicking the plus (+) sign to the left of the folder.

3. Find the user that you want to delete. Right-click that user, and select the Remove option from the pop-up menu.

4. You will be asked to confirm your intention to drop the user, as shown in Figure 11-5.

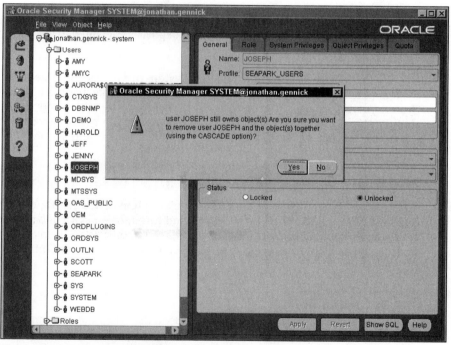

Figure 11-5: Using Security Manager to delete a user

Unlike issuing the DROP USER command, you don't need to decide ahead of time whether you need to use the CASCADE option. If you are deleting some objects that the user owns, Security Manager will warn you and then apply the CASCADE option automatically.

Granting Roles and Privileges to Users

For a user to do anything to a database, you need to grant that user one or more system privileges. A *system privilege* is a privilege defined by Oracle that allows a user to perform a certain task, such as creating a table. Oracle has defined a rich set of privileges that you can grant or not grant to closely control what a user is allowed to do. Even just logging on to a database requires a privilege—the CREATE SESSION privilege.

Privileges are frequently bundled together into roles. You'll learn more about roles, including how to create them, later in this chapter. One of the most commonly granted roles is the CONNECT role, a default role that you get when you create a database. It conveys the privileges required to log on to the database and to create common objects such as views, tables, indexes, and so forth.

 Tip   To see a list of privileges conveyed by a role such as CONNECT, navigate to that role in Security Manager and click it. The list of privileges granted to the role will appear in the right pane.

Oracle provides two types of privileges: system privileges and object privileges. System privileges give you the ability to do various tasks in an Oracle database. System privileges are not used to provide access to the tables and views within that database. Object privileges are used to specify the type of access to the data a user can have in various objects such as tables, views, and sequences.

Granting system privileges and roles

You can use the GRANT command to assign a system privilege or a role to a user. Similarly, you can use the REVOKE command to remove a system privilege or a role from a user. You can issue the GRANT and REVOKE commands from a command-line utility such as SQL*Plus, or you can use Security Manager's GUI interface to manage privileges.

The GRANT Command

To grant a system privilege or a role to a user, use the GRANT command as follows:

```
GRANT {privilege|role}[,{privilege|role}...]
TO {username|rolename};
```

You can list as many privileges and roles in the command as you need. The CREATE SESSION privilege allows a user to log on to a database. The CREATE TABLE command allows a user to create tables and indexes. You can grant both to the user named JOSEPH using this command:

```
GRANT CREATE SESSION, CREATE TABLE TO joseph;
```

You grant a role in the same way that you grant a privilege. To grant Joseph the CONNECT role, you can issue this command:

```
GRANT CONNECT TO joseph;
```

You can grant a privilege or a role to all users in the database by using the keyword PUBLIC in place of a username. For example, the following GRANT allows any user to use any amount of disk space within the database:

```
GRANT UNLIMITED TABLESPACE TO PUBLIC;
```

Granting UNLIMITED TABLESPACE to a user has the same effect as if you had given that user an unlimited quota on each tablespace within the database.

Commonly Granted Privileges

The list of privileges that Oracle supports is quite long. Some are used more frequently than others. Table 11-1 contains a list of some of the more commonly used privileges.

Table 11-1
Commonly Granted Privileges and Roles

Privilege/Role	Description
CREATE SESSION	Allows a user to log on to the database.
CONNECT	Allows you to log on and create the most-used objects. The CONNECT privilege is a predefined role that conveys a bundle of useful system privileges.
RESOURCE	Conveys UNLIMITED TABLESPACE and is similar to CONNECT. The list of objects that you can create is longer, but RESOURCE does not convey the CREATE SESSION privilege. When you grant RESOURCE to a user, the UNLIMITED TABLESPACE privilege is automatically granted as well.
CREATE TABLE	Allows the user to create tables.
CREATE VIEW	Allows the user to create views.
CREATE SEQUENCE	Allows the user to create sequences.
CREATE PROCEDURE	Allows the user to create procedures, functions, and packages.
CREATE TRIGGER	Allows the user to create triggers on tables owned by that user.
CREATE SYNONYM	Allows the user to create private synonyms.

For a complete list of Oracle database privileges, see the entry for the GRANT command in Appendix A, "SQL Statement Reference."

The ADMIN Option

By default, only database administrators can grant roles or privileges to other users. If you happen to have a specific role or privilege that you want someone else to manage for you, you can grant it to him or her using the ADMIN option. For example:

```
GRANT CREATE TABLE TO joseph WITH ADMIN OPTION;
```

The ADMIN option allows Joseph to further grant CREATE TABLE to other users besides himself. The ADMIN option can be very useful if you have created a set of roles in support of a specific application. You can grant those roles, with the ADMIN option, to an application administrator, who can then shoulder the burden of properly granting those roles to application users.

Revoking System Privileges and Roles

You can use the REVOKE command to remove a role or a privilege from a user. The syntax looks like this:

```
REVOKE {privilege|role}[,{privilege|role}...]
FROM {username|rolename}
```

For example, the following command revokes CREATE TABLE from the user named JOSEPH:

```
REVOKE CREATE TABLE FROM joseph;
```

If you have granted a privilege to PUBLIC, you can revoke it by using PUBLIC in place of the username. For example:

```
REVOKE UNLIMITED TABLESPACE FROM PUBLIC;
```

As with the GRANT statement, you may revoke any number of roles and privileges using one command.

Granting object privileges

Object privileges allow a user access to the data within a table, view, sequence, procedure, or other object. The five commonly used object privileges are the following:

SELECT	Allows a user to retrieve data from a table, sequence, or view
UPDATE	Allows a user to change data in a table or view

DELETE	Allows a user to delete data from a table or view
INSERT	Allows a user to add new rows to a table or view
EXECUTE	Allows a user to execute a stored procedure, function, or package

You use the GRANT and REVOKE commands to manage object privileges, but the syntax is slightly different than that used when dealing with system privileges and roles.

Note   Object privileges must be granted and revoked by the owner of the object in question. Even database administrators cannot grant object privileges for objects owned by another user.

Granting an Object Privilege

The format of the GRANT command you can use when granting object privileges looks like this:

```
GRANT {privilege_list|ALL} [(column_list)]
ON object TO {user|role|PUBLIC}
[WITH GRANT OPTION];
```

The following list describes the parameters of this command:

privilege_list	This is a comma-delimited list of object privileges.
ALL	This grants all privileges relevant to the object in question.
column_list	This is a comma-delimited list of columns, and is only applicable when granting INSERT, UPDATE, or REFERENCES on a table or a view.
object	This is an object name. This may optionally be qualified with a schema name, using the standard dot notation.
user	This is the user to whom you want to grant the privilege(s).
role	This is the role to which you want to grant the privilege(s).
PUBLIC	This is used to grant one or more privileges to all users.
WITH GRANT OPTION	This allows the user to further grant the privilege to another user.

Only an object owner can grant access to its objects. Even database administrators, who may be able to read that data because of system privileges that they hold, are not allowed to grant access to objects owned by another user.

> **Note** By using WITH GRANT OPTION, an object owner can grant a specific object privilege to another user and allow that user to further grant it to others.

As an example, suppose that you want to grant the user named HAROLD the ability to query the checkup history of animals in Seapark, and that you also want HAROLD to be able to insert new checkup records. To do all this, you need to log on as the SEAPARK user and issue the following commands:

```
GRANT SELECT ON AQUATIC_ANIMAL TO harold;
GRANT SELECT ON CHECKUP TO harold;
GRANT SELECT, INSERT ON CHECKUP_HISTORY TO harold;
```

The SELECT privileges are needed on the first two tables, because HAROLD will need to query for the animal names and for the checkup types. The INSERT privilege is needed on CHECKUP_HISTORY, because each checkup is recorded by adding a record to that table.

Revoking an Object Privilege

The format of the REVOKE command to remove object privileges from a user looks like this:

```
REVOKE {privilege_list|ALL} ON object
FROM {user|role|PUBLIC} [CASCADE CONSTRAINTS] [FORCE];
```

With two exceptions, the syntax elements in the REVOKE command have the same meanings as in the GRANT command. The two exceptions are CASCADE CONSTRAINTS and FORCE; the GRANT command doesn't have these two options.

✦ **CASCADE CONSTRAINTS.** This option causes any referential integrity constraints that have been defined using the REFERENCES privilege to be dropped as well.

✦ **FORCE.** This option forces the revocation of EXECUTE privileges on user-defined object types, where the revokee has tables that depend on those types.

The following REVOKE command revokes the object privileges granted in the previous section:

```
REVOKE SELECT ON AQUATIC_ANIMAL FROM harold;
REVOKE SELECT ON CHECKUP FROM harold;
REVOKE ALL ON CHECKUP_HISTORY FROM harold;
```

Note Take note of the use of the REVOKE ALL command in the previous example. You can use the REVOKE ALL command if you want to save typing or if you can't remember exactly what was granted and you want to revoke everything anyway.

Using Security Manager to manage privileges and roles

Security Manager provides you with an easy-to-use interface for managing privileges and roles. You can use Security Manager to manage both system privileges and roles. You can also use Security Manager to view a list of object privileges that have been granted to various users and roles. However, using Security Manager to grant and revoke object privileges depends on the ability of the object owner to run the application.

Using Security Manager to Grant System Privileges

To grant privileges to or revoke privileges from a user, perform the following steps:

1. Start Security Manager, and log on to the database.

2. Double-click the Users folder to expand the list of users in the database.

3. Click the user of interest. You'll see the definition for that user appear in the right pane.

4. Click the System Privileges tab. Your screen will now look similar to the one shown in Figure 11-6.

The list at the top of the right pane contains all possible system privileges. The list at the bottom shows the privileges assigned to the user in question. The arrows in between the lists allow you to move privileges back and forth. To grant a privilege to a user, click that privilege in the top list, and then click the Down Arrow button. The privilege will be moved to the bottom list. Reverse the process to revoke a privilege.

When you have finished editing a user's privileges, click the Apply button to make your changes permanent. If you make a mistake during the editing process, you can press the Revert button to cancel all the edits that you've made.

You can manage roles by using Security Manager in the same manner as system privileges. Just click the Role tab.

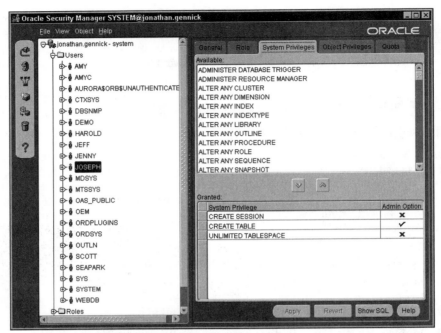

Figure 11-6: Editing a user's system privileges

Using Security Manager to Grant Object Privileges

Although it's possible to grant object privileges using Security Manager, when you try to do so, you'll find yourself in this catch-22 situation: Only an object's owner can grant privileges on an object, but only privileged users, such as DBAs, can run Security Manager.

You probably don't want to grant the DBA role to all your users just so they can use Security Manager to grant object privileges, so what are you to do? One solution to this problem is to grant your users the role named SELECT_CATALOG_ROLE. Another is to grant them the SELECT ANY TABLE system privilege. Either solution allows them to select from the data dictionary views, which allows them to run Security Manager.

Note   Granting SELECT_CATALOG_ROLE is preferable to granting SELECT ANY TABLE, but there have been problems with the SELECT_CATALOG_ROLE not working for some releases of Oracle Enterprise Manager. The SELECT ANY TABLE privilege gives a user access to *all* tables in the database, including those owned by other users. Consequently, you must consider security implications before granting this privilege to a user.

Once a user has access to the data dictionary views, he or she can use Security Manager to grant other users access to his or her tables, views, and so forth. Just follow these steps:

1. Run Security Manager, and log on to the database.

2. Navigate to the user to whom you want to grant privileges, and highlight that user. The right pane will change to allow you to edit information for that user.

3. Click the Object Privileges tab. Your screen should look similar to the one shown in Figure 11-7.

4. Grant whatever object privileges are necessary, and then click the Apply button.

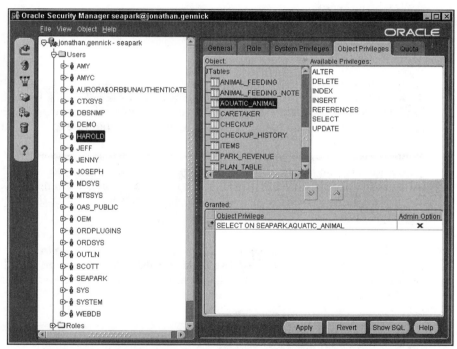

Figure 11-7: Granting the SELECT privilege on the AQUATIC_ANIMAL table to user HAROLD

Other than the need to log on as the object owner, the process you use for managing object privileges is identical to the process you use for managing system privileges.

Creating Roles

You use roles to pull together sets of privileges, such as access to tables, for easier management. Consider the task of creating 1,000 users and granting the following privileges to each:

```
CREATE TABLE
CREATE SEQUENCE
CREATE VIEW
CREATE SYNONYM
CREATE SESSION
ALTER SESSION
CREATE CLUSTER
CREATE DATABASE LINK
```

Granting these privileges individually would be a daunting task. It would be more so if someone asked you to go back later and grant CREATE TRIGGER to each of those same users. Your task would be easier if you created a role, say the CONNECT role, granted those privileges to the role, and then granted that one role to your users.

When you grant a role to a user, that user inherits all privileges granted to the role. A user can be assigned any number of roles. A role can be assigned any number of privileges. Roles simplify the tasks of managing the privileges granted to users. They allow changes to be made at one central point—the role—rather than having to be made to each user individually.

> **Note** The initialization parameter max_enabled_roles limits the number of enabled roles that may be held by a user at any given time. Make sure that this is set high enough to accommodate the number of roles that you will be granting to your users.

Creating a role

You use the CREATE ROLE command to create a role. The syntax looks like this:

```
CREATE ROLE role_name [IDENTIFIED BY password];
```

If you wish to require a password, use the IDENTIFIED BY clause. This requires a user to enter a password before using the privileges conveyed by the role. Besides using passwords, there are some other role authentication options that aren't described here. See Appendix A, "SQL Statement Reference," for details.

You must log on as a user with DBA authority or the CREATE ROLE privilege to create roles. To modify roles, you must have the ALTER ANY ROLE privilege. To remove a role, you must have the DROP ANY ROLE privilege. Role names are subject to the naming rules for Oracle objects. Refer to the sidebar "Choosing Names for Users and Passwords" for a quick summary of object-naming guidelines.

As an example, to create a role for the SEAPARK application administrator, you might issue this command:

```
CREATE ROLE seapark_administrator;
```

Of course, a role isn't very useful until you've had a chance to grant some privileges to that role. You'll see how to do that in the next section.

Adding privileges to a role

The task of granting privileges to a role is no different than the task of granting privileges to a user. Use the GRANT command; the syntax is the same. For example, the following commands grant some system privileges to the SEAPARK_ADMINISTRATOR role:

```
GRANT CREATE USER, GRANT ANY ROLE TO seapark_administrator;
GRANT CREATE SESSION TO seapark_administrator WITH ADMIN OPTION;
```

You can grant two types of privileges to a role. The example just shown grants system privileges. It's also common to grant object privileges to roles. Object privileges allow access to objects such as tables and views, and must be granted by the owner of the objects in question. For example, the application administrator might log on as the SEAPARK user and make the following grants:

```
GRANT SELECT ON caretaker TO seapark_administrator;
GRANT SELECT ON aquatic_animal TO seapark_administrator;
```

After you've created a role and granted privileges to that role, you are ready to grant that role to the users who need it. You've already seen how to use the GRANT command to do that earlier in this chapter.

Removing (revoking) privileges from roles

Use the REVOKE command to revoke a privilege from a role. To revoke system privileges or roles from a role, the syntax looks like this:

```
REVOKE {system privilege|role} FROM role;
```

Object privileges, such as SELECT, INSERT, and so forth, must be removed by the object's owner. The syntax is different because you have to supply the name of the object involved. It looks like this:

```
REVOKE object privilege ON object name FROM role;
```

As an example, the following statements revoke the privileges granted by the examples in the previous section:

```
REVOKE CREATE USER, GRANT ANY USER,
    CREATE SESSION
FROM seapark_administrator;
REVOKE SELECT ON caretaker FROM seapark_administrator;
REVOKE SELECT ON caretaker FROM seapark_administrator;
```

Using Security Manager to create roles

You can create roles and delete them by using Security Manager in much the same manner as you create and delete users. You can create a role in Security Manager by right-clicking the Roles folder and selecting Create from the pop-up menu. This will display the Create Role dialog box shown in Figure 11-8.

Figure 11-8: Using Security Manager to create a role

You can use the Role, System Privileges, and Object Privileges tabs to grant roles, system privileges, and object privileges, respectively, to the new role. When you're done, click the Create button, and Security Manager will execute the necessary SQL statements to create the role as you have defined it.

Creating and Assigning User Profiles

Profiles, like roles, can simplify and streamline your work. A profile is a collection of parameters given a name and assigned to one or more Oracle users. For the most part, profiles place limits on what a user can do. Profiles allow you to limit the system resources used by a particular group of users. For example, you can cause the database to end a query that is executing for more than one hour.

Profiles, once created, can be assigned to users. Oracle has one profile preloaded with its default database. This profile is named DEFAULT. Unless you specify otherwise, all new users are assigned the DEFAULT profile.

Creating and assigning a new profile

The syntax shown in Listing 11-1 creates a new profile.

Listing 11-1: **Syntax for creating a new profile**

```
CREATE PROFILE profile_name
[SESSIONS_PER_USER { n | UNLIMITED | DEFAULT } ]
[CPU_PER_SESSION { n | UNLIMITED | DEFAULT } ]
[CPU_PER_CALL { n | UNLIMITED | DEFAULT } ]
[CONNECT_TIME { n | UNLIMITED | DEFAULT } ]
[IDLE_TIME { n | UNLIMITED | DEFAULT } ]
[LOGICAL_READS_PER_SESSION { n | UNLIMITED | DEFAULT } ]
[LOGICAL_READS_PER_CALL { n | UNLIMITED | DEFAULT } ]
[PRIVATE_SGA { n [ K | M ] | UNLIMITED | DEFAULT } ]
[FAILED_LOGIN_ATTEMPTS { n | UNLIMITED | DEFAULT } ]
[PASSWORD_LIFE_TIME { n | UNLIMITED | DEFAULT } ]
[PASSWORD_REUSE_TIME { n | UNLIMITED | DEFAULT } ]
[PASSWORD_REUSE_MAX { n | UNLIMITED | DEFAULT } ]
[PASSWORD_LOCK_TIME { n | UNLIMITED | DEFAULT } ]
[PASSWORD_GRACE_TIME { n | UNLIMITED | DEFAULT } ]
[PASSWORD_VERIFY_FUNCTION [ function_name | NULL | DEFAULT ] ]
[COMPOSITE_LIMIT [n | UNLIMITED | DEFAULT ] ];
```

When you select DEFAULT for any of the parameters, that profile parameter receives the value of the same parameter in the default profile. Notice that you can control password parameters in the syntax for creating a new profile. The upcoming subsection "Using a profile to manage password features" provides more information.

You specify time for the password limits in days. Use fractions to represent periods of less than one day. For example, one hour is expressed as $\frac{1}{24}$. CPU times are expressed in hundredths of a second. So a CPU_PER_SESSION limit of 100 allows the use of one second of CPU time.

After creating a profile, you can assign it to a user. Use the following syntax to do that:

```
ALTER USER username PROFILE profile_name;
```

Replace *username* in this syntax with the name of a database user. Replace *profile_name* with the name of a profile.

Using a profile to manage password features

Oracle implements several features that give you control over how users manage their passwords. These features include the ability to do the following:

✦ Expire a password

✦ Prevent reuse of passwords

✦ Enforce password complexity

Expiring a User's Password

You need to use profiles to take advantage of these features, with one exception: expiring a user's password. The command to do that is user-specific and looks like this:

```
ALTER USER username PASSWORD EXPIRE;
```

When you expire a user's password, the user will still be able to log on, but upon logon, he or she will be forced to immediately choose a new password.

Preventing Password Reuse

You can prevent users from reusing old passwords by assigning them to a profile that keeps a password history. You can choose to base the history list on either the number of days before reuse is allowed or the number of passwords before reuse is allowed.

To retain a user's password history for a specific number of days, you must set the PASSWORD_REUSE_TIME parameter in the user's profile. Note that if you set PASSWORD_REUSE_TIME to a specific number of days, you must also set PASSWORD_REUSE_MAX to UNLIMITED. In addition to altering a profile, you can set these values when you create the profile. The following example creates a profile named SEAPARK_USERS that retains a 180-day password history:

```
CREATE PROFILE seapark_users
    LIMIT PASSWORD_REUSE_TIME 180
        PASSWORD_REUSE_MAX UNLIMITED;
```

Rather than have the retention period based on a period of time, you can choose to base it on a fixed number of passwords. The following example changes the SEAPARK_USERS profile so that the history for a user always includes the ten most recently used passwords:

```
ALTER PROFILE seapark_users
    LIMIT PASSWORD_REUSE_MAX 10
        PASSWORD_REUSE_TIME UNLIMITED;
```

These two methods for determining password retention time are mutually exclusive. You may limit reuse based on elapsed days, or on the number of passwords, but you can't use both methods at once in the same profile.

Enforcing Password Complexity

You can enforce password complexity by specifying the name of a function that Oracle calls whenever a user changes a password. The function can check to be sure that the password is really two words, that it contains one or more nonalpha characters, and so forth. You can use a third-party function, or you can write your own.

To specify a password complexity verification function, you need to modify a profile and supply the function name as the value for the PASSWORD_VERIFY_FUNCTION setting. For example, the following command makes the SEAPARK_PW function the complexity verification function for the SEAPARK_USERS profile:

```
ALTER PROFILE seapark_users LIMIT
        PASSWORD_VERIFY_FUNCTION seapark_pw;
```

Password verification functions must be owned by the user named SYS, and the function header must match this format:

```
function_name (
    username IN VARCHAR(30),
    password IN VARCHAR (30),
    old_password IN VARCHAR (30)
)RETURN BOOLEAN
```

The function returns a value of TRUE if the user's new password is acceptable. Otherwise, it should return FALSE. The syntax for the CREATE PROFILE and ALTER PROFILE commands is almost identical. Any clause that you've seen used with ALTER PROFILE may also be used with CREATE PROFILE, and vice-versa.

Tip

Oracle does provide a working password template function that can be modified to meet your specific requirements. Using this is a whole lot easier than writing one from scratch, especially if you're not familiar with PL/SQL. The file containing the template function is $ORACLE_HOME/rdbms/admin/utlpwdmg.sql.

Using Security Manager to manage profiles

Instead of using commands, you can use Security Manager to manage profiles. The process to create, edit, and delete profiles is the same as the process used to create, edit, and delete users and roles.

To edit an existing profile using Security Manager, just navigate to that profile, highlight it, and edit its properties in the dialog box that appears in the right pane of the Security Manager window. Figure 11-9 shows Security Manager being used to edit the SEAPARK_USERS role:

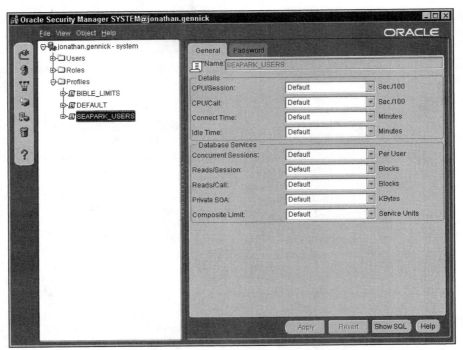

Figure 11-9: Editing the SEAPARK_USERS profile

To create a new profile, right-click the Profiles folder and select Create. The tabs in the Create Profile dialog box are the same as those used to edit a profile. Profiles are assigned to users when you create them. Just choose the appropriate profile from the drop-down list on the General tab of the Create User dialog box.

Becoming a User

When troubleshooting a security problem for a user, it's sometimes helpful to log on as the user involved. However, you may not know the user's password. Asking users for their password is a bad practice because it gets them used to giving it out on request. Before you know it, they'll be giving it out to someone who is not authorized to have it.

Temporarily changing a user's password

So how do you log on as another user when you need to? While Oracle won't let you query the data dictionary to find a user's password in clear text form, you can retrieve the encrypted version of a password. You can then temporarily change the user's password. Later, using the undocumented IDENTIFIED BY VALUES clause of the ALTER USER command, you can change the password back to its original value, by following these steps:

1. Retrieve the user's encrypted password from the DBA_USERS view. The password will be in the form of a string of hexadecimal digits. Write this down or otherwise save it so that you can restore it later.

2. Change the user's password to something you do know. Use the ALTER USER command to do this.

3. Log on as the user in question, using the temporary password that you set.

4. Using the hexadecimal password that you saved, issue an ALTER USER command to change the password back to its original value. Use the IDENTIFIED BY VALUES clause, as shown in this example:

```
ALTER USER joseph IDENTIFIED BY VALUES 'AD923596D59E92AA'
```

When you alter a user's password in this manner, the password history is not checked, the expiration date is not reset, and the complexity function is not called. However, Step 2, where you change the user's password to a temporary value, will cause all these to be done. Your temporary password will be added to the user's password history list, and the password expiration date will be set based on when you set the temporary password.

A become_user script

The code in Listing 11-2 represents one possible approach to the task of writing a SQL*Plus script that allows you to become another user.

Listing 11-2: **A SQL*Plus script to become another user**

```
ACCEPT username CHAR PROMPT 'Become User >'
ACCEPT temp_pass CHAR PROMPT 'Temporary Password >'

SET TERMOUT OFF
COLUMN password NOPRINT NEW_VALUE current_password
SELECT password
FROM dba_users
WHERE username=UPPER('&&username');
SET TERMOUT ON

ALTER USER &&username IDENTIFIED BY &&temp_pass;
CONNECT &&username/&&temp_pass

PAUSE Press ENTER to reset the password back to what it was.
ALTER USER &&username
IDENTIFIED BY VALUES '&&current_password';
```

This script uses the COLUMN command's NEW_VALUE clause to store the user's current password in a SQL*Plus user variable named current_password. Only the encrypted hex representation of the password will be stored. The script then changes the user's password, in the normal fashion, to the temporary value that you specified, and logs you on to the database as that user. Listing 11-3 shows this script being used to temporarily log on as the SEAPARK user:

Listing 11-3: **Temporarily logging on as SEAPARK**

```
SQL> connect system/manager
Connected.
SQL> @become_user
Become User >seapark
Temporary Password >temp
old   1: ALTER USER &&username IDENTIFIED BY &&temp_pass
new   1: ALTER USER seapark IDENTIFIED BY temp

User altered.

Connected.
Press ENTER to reset the user's password back to what it was.

old   1: ALTER USER &&username IDENTIFIED BY VALUES '&&current_password'
new   1: ALTER USER seapark IDENTIFIED BY VALUES 'E42711E67FF7A82E'

User altered.
```

The PAUSE command in the script allows you to control exactly when the password is reset to its original value. This gives you the ability to also run any third-party software that the user may be using and to connect to the database using the temporary password. Then, after you connect, you press Enter on your SQL*Plus session, and the user's password is reset.

Viewing Users, Security, and the Data Dictionary

If you need to find out information about users, roles, and profiles in your database, you can query Oracle's data dictionary. Several data dictionary views return information about profiles, users, and the privileges that you have granted to those users. These views include:

DBA_USERS	Returns one row for each database user. Use this view to retrieve information about account status, password expiration, default and temporary tablespace settings, and profile name.
DBA_ROLES	Returns one row for each role defined in the database.
DBA_PROFILES	Returns one row for each user profile setting. Use this view when you want to list profiles that have been defined, or when you want to list the settings defined for a particular profile.
DBA_SYS_PRIVS	Returns one row for each system privilege that has been granted to a user or to a role.
DBA_TAB_PRIVS	Returns one row for each object privilege held by a user. Use this parameter when you want to see a list of objects to which a user has access.
DBA_ROLE_PRIVS	Returns one row for each role granted to a user or for each role granted to another role.

Listing users in the database

The DBA_USERS view provides information about the users that exist in your database. You can use this view to generate a list of users by executing a query such as this:

```
SELECT username, account_status, profile
FROM dba_users
ORDER BY username;
```

You can also use this view to find out the default and temporary tablespace settings for a user.

Listing privileges granted to a user

When it comes to discovering the privileges held by a user, there are four areas that you need to look at:

✦ System privileges granted directly to the user

✦ Roles granted directly to the user

✦ System privileges and roles granted to roles held directly by the user

✦ Object privileges granted to the user

The third item in the list can be the most difficult to track down. When you discover that a user has been granted a role, to get a complete picture of the user's privileges, you need to in turn find out what has been granted to that role. In the process of doing that, you might discover yet another role to look at, and so forth.

Listing System Privileges Held by a User

To list the system privileges held directly by a user, query the DBA_SYS_PRIVS view. For example, the query in the following example returns all of the privileges granted directly to the user named SYSTEM:

```
SQL> SELECT privilege, admin_option
  2  FROM dba_sys_privs
  3  WHERE grantee='SYSTEM';

PRIVILEGE                                ADM
---------------------------------------- ---
UNLIMITED TABLESPACE                     YES
```

In this case, the SYSTEM user holds the UNLIMITED TABLESPACE privilege with the ADMIN option. The ADMIN option allows the SYSTEM user to grant this privilege to other users. This may not seem like much considering that the user in question is SYSTEM, and it's not. The SYSTEM user gets most of its privileges via the DBA role. To find out what privileges the DBA role conveys, you would also query the DBA_SYS_PRIVS view, as shown in Listing 11-4.

Listing 11-4: **Querying for DBA privileges**

```
SQL> SELECT privilege, admin_option
  2  FROM dba_sys_privs
  3* WHERE grantee='DBA';

PRIVILEGE                                ADM
---------------------------------------- ---
ADMINISTER DATABASE TRIGGER              YES
ADMINISTER RESOURCE MANAGER              YES
```

```
ALTER ANY CLUSTER                    YES
ALTER ANY DIMENSION                  YES
ALTER ANY INDEX                      YES
ALTER ANY INDEXTYPE                  YES
...
...
...
```

This is a much longer list. It still doesn't give you the complete picture, though, because the DBA role also conveys some roles that have been granted to it.

Listing Roles Held by a User

Roles may be held by a user or by another role. You can list these roles by querying the DBA_ROLE_PRIVS view. The following example shows how to query for roles held by the DBA role:

```
SQL> SELECT granted_role, admin_option
  2  FROM dba_role_privs
  3  WHERE grantee='DBA';

GRANTED_ROLE                         ADM
------------------------------------ ---
DELETE_CATALOG_ROLE                  YES
EXECUTE_CATALOG_ROLE                 YES
EXP_FULL_DATABASE                    NO
IMP_FULL_DATABASE                    NO
SELECT_CATALOG_ROLE                  YES
```

The ADMIN option, represented here by the column titled ADM, indicates whether the role can be further granted to other users. Use the same approach for listing the roles held directly by a user: Simply compare the grantee column to a username instead of a role name.

Listing Object Privileges Held by a User

The DBA_TAB_PRIVS view returns information about object privileges held by a user. Listing 11-5 demonstrates how you can query this view to find the objects to which a user has been granted direct access.

Listing 11-5: **Querying the DBA_TAB_PRIVS view**

```
SQL> COLUMN object_name FORMAT A30
SQL> COLUMN privilege FORMAT A11
SQL> COLUMN grantable FORMAT A10
```

Continued

Listing 11-5 *(continued)*

```
SQL> SELECT owner || '.' || table_name object_name,
  2          privilege, grantable
  3  FROM dba_tab_privs
  4  WHERE grantee = 'SYSTEM'
  5  ORDER BY owner, table_name, privilege;

OBJECT_NAME    PRIVILEGE          GRANTABLE
------------------------------ ----------- ----------
SYS.DBMS_AQ                     EXECUTE     YES
SYS.DBMS_AQADM                  EXECUTE     YES
SYS.DBMS_AQ_IMPORT_INTERNAL     EXECUTE     YES
SYS.DBMS_DEFER_IMPORT_INTERNAL  EXECUTE     NO
SYS.DBMS_RULE_EXIMP             EXECUTE     YES
```

The COLUMN commands in this example are not strictly necessary, but the nature of this particular query makes for some very long lines of output. The COLUMN commands limit the display width of the columns so that the output isn't wrapped around on the screen. It's a lot easier to read this way.

Object privileges may be granted to roles as well as to users. In this example, the user of interest was SYSTEM, but you can substitute any other username or role name in its place.

Listing information about roles

You can generate a list of roles defined in the database by querying the DBA_ROLES view. For example:

```
SQL> SELECT role
  2  FROM dba_roles;

ROLE
------------------------------
CONNECT
RESOURCE
DBA
SELECT_CATALOG_ROLE
```

To find out which privileges have been granted to a role, follow the same process described earlier for listing privileges granted to a user.

Listing the definition for a profile

To see the definition of a user profile, you can query the DBA_PROFILES view. The DBA_PROFILES view contains the following columns:

```
PROFILE          NOT NULL VARCHAR2(30)
RESOURCE_NAME    NOT NULL VARCHAR2(32)
RESOURCE_TYPE             VARCHAR2(8)
LIMIT                     VARCHAR2(40)
```

The columns contain the following data:

PROFILE	Contains the name of the profile
RESOURCE_NAME	Contains the name of a resource limit that you can specify as part of the CREATE PROFILE command
RESOURCE_TYPE	Will be either KERNEL or PASSWORD, depending on whether the resource has to do with password management
LIMIT	Contains the resource limit as specified in the CREATE PROFILE command

For each profile that you define, the DBA_PROFILES view will return several rows, one for each resource limit in the profile. Listing 11-6 demonstrates how you can return the definition of the profile named DEFAULT.

Listing 11-6: **Retrieving the definition for a profile**

```
SQL> SELECT resource_name, limit
  2  FROM dba_profiles
  3  WHERE profile='DEFAULT';

RESOURCE_NAME                        LIMIT
------------------------------------ ----------------
COMPOSITE_LIMIT                      UNLIMITED
SESSIONS_PER_USER                    UNLIMITED
CPU_PER_SESSION                      UNLIMITED
CPU_PER_CALL                         UNLIMITED
LOGICAL_READS_PER_SESSION            UNLIMITED
LOGICAL_READS_PER_CALL               UNLIMITED
IDLE_TIME                            UNLIMITED
CONNECT_TIME                         UNLIMITED
PRIVATE_SGA                          UNLIMITED
FAILED_LOGIN_ATTEMPTS                UNLIMITED
PASSWORD_LIFE_TIME                   UNLIMITED
PASSWORD_REUSE_TIME                  UNLIMITED
```

Continued

Listing 11-6 *(continued)*

```
PASSWORD_REUSE_MAX                UNLIMITED
PASSWORD_VERIFY_FUNCTION          UNLIMITED
PASSWORD_LOCK_TIME                UNLIMITED
PASSWORD_GRACE_TIME               UNLIMITED

16 rows selected.
```

The DBA_PROFILES view will return a row for each possible resource limit, regardless of whether you specified all of them when you created the profile.

Summary

In this chapter, you learned:

✦ You use system privileges to control what a user can and can't do to the database. Object privileges control what a user can and can't do to individual objects such as a table or a view.

✦ Roles enable the DBA and the application developer to simplify privilege management by lumping related privileges together under a single role. Subsequently, a new user can be assigned (granted) to a single role rather than assigned numerous privileges individually.

✦ You can use profiles to limit a user's consumption of CPU resources and to enforce rules regarding password complexity. Profiles also define how often passwords need to be changed.

✦ When you create a user, always define both a default and a temporary tablespace. Don't forget to provide quota on the default tablespace.

✦   ✦   ✦

Using Fine-Grained Access Control

◆ ◆ ◆ ◆

In This Chapter

Using application
security

Understanding
application security
contexts

Writing security
policies

Using pre-8i
alternatives

◆ ◆ ◆ ◆

## CHAPTER 12

An exciting new Oracle8i feature is the ability to implement
row-level security within the database. Oracle refers to
this as *fine-grained access control*. It addresses a problem that
has plagued application developers and security administrators
ever since client/server computing came into vogue. The
problem is that an impedance mismatch has existed between
the typical relational database's implementation of security
at the object level, and the application developer's need for
security to be implemented at the row level. For a long time
now, we have been able to define access rights to objects
such as tables or views at the database level, but row-level
security has almost always been forced down into the
application. Oracle8i changes all this by implementing features
that support fine-grained access control at the database level.

Using Application Security

Application security is loosely defined as the enforcement of
limits on what a particular user can do using a given application.
Take a payroll application, for example. Any payroll application
is capable of adding new employees to the payroll, changing pay
rates, and so forth. Even though all these features are available,
you certainly don't want all users to avail themselves of them.
Instead, you have a limited number of users who are allowed to
see and change sensitive data such as an employee's pay rate.
You might have a larger pool of users with "look only" access.
You may have further restrictions; for instance, a manager
is allowed to see only his or her own employees. All of these
restrictions are typically enforced through some type of
row-level security.

Implementing security in the application

Historically, implementing detailed security policies at the database level has been difficult. Sometimes you can do it using a combination of views and stored procedures, but the amount of human overhead needed to manage all that is high. Third-party development tools, such as Visual Basic and Powerbuilder, are designed around using tables and views, making it cumbersome to funnel all access through stored procedures. Because of these difficulties, row-level security is often implemented at the application level, as illustrated in Figure 12-1.

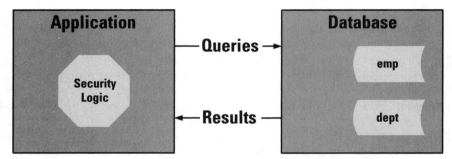

Figure 12-1: Row-level security is often implemented within the application.

When row-level security is implemented as shown in Figure 12-1, you typically run into these problems:

- ✦ The programmers don't always get it right.
- ✦ Implementation is inconsistent from one application to another.
- ✦ The application maintenance burden is greatly increased.
- ✦ There is no security when ad-hoc query tools are used.

Oracle8i now offers an alternative approach. Read on to learn about it.

Using application contexts and policies

With the release of Oracle8i, you now have two new database features that enable you to define row-level security within the database consistently, and in a way that is transparent to users and applications accessing the database: security policies and application contexts. Together, you can use these two features to move row-level security from the application into the database, as shown in figure 12-2.

You can use application contexts and security policies separately. Application contexts have uses other than for security. Security policies can be implemented without using an application context. However, any reasonably robust security scheme is likely to leverage both features.

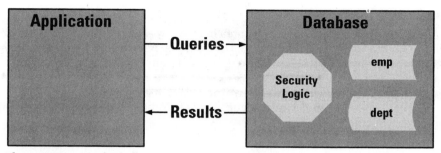

Figure 12-2: Oracle8i allows you to move application security into the database.

Using Security Policies

A *security policy* is a set of rules, attached to an object such as a table or a view, that defines who is allowed to see data from the object, what rows they are allowed to see, and whether those rows can be updated or deleted. You implement security policies by writing PL/SQL code to dynamically modify the WHERE clauses of queries against the object being secured.

Figure 12-3 illustrates how a security policy actually works. A query has been issued against the EMP table in an attempt to select all rows from that table. When the query is issued, Oracle automatically invokes the security policy for the EMP table. The security policy is nothing more than a PL/SQL package that looks up some information about the user, and uses that information to modify the query's WHERE clause. All this is done transparently. The user never sees the modified query. In this case, the end result is that a manager will be allowed to see only his or her own employees.

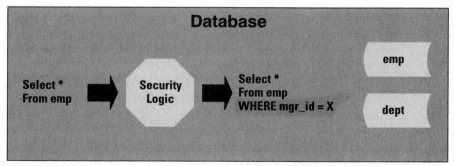

Figure 12-3: Security policies dynamically rewrite the WHERE clause of a query.

For performance reasons, if nothing else, you will want to use application contexts in a row-level security scheme. If a security policy needs to retrieve information from the database and needs to retrieve that information each time it is invoked, performance will suffer.

Using Application Contexts

An *application context* is a scratchpad area in memory that you can use to store bits of information that security policies need. For example, when a user logs on, you might store his or her username, ID number, department number, and other information in an application context. That information can then be referenced by the code that enforces the security policies on objects that the user accesses. Figure 12-4 shows the complete relationship between security policies, application contexts, and the object being secured.

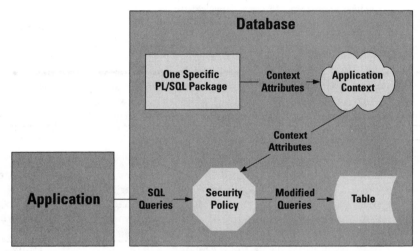

Figure 12-4: Security policies and application contexts work together to secure an object.

Application contexts are restricted to prevent users from arbitrarily updating their context data. When you create an application context, you also need to create a PL/SQL package that you can use to define attributes in that context. The command to create the context links the context to the package. After a context is created, Oracle ensures that only the specified package can be used to define attributes (save values) in that context.

Examining a Seapark Example

The rest of this chapter implements a row-level security model for the Seapark database. The basic rule of that model is this:

> The records of animals and tanks may be modified only by the caretaker responsible for the animal or tank in question.

The examples throughout this chapter illustrate how to build the context and the policies to support this model. This won't be a comprehensive implementation. The example is limited to just the AQUATIC_ANIMAL and TANK tables, but that should be enough to provide you with a good understanding of how all this works.

Understanding Application Security Contexts

An *application security context* functions as a glorified scratchpad. It is an area in memory where you can store information that you may need occasionally during a session. You define the information that you need to store in terms of attributes. Each attribute in a context has a name and a value. Both the name and the value are text strings that you supply when you create the attribute.

Creating and dropping a context

You manage contexts using the CREATE CONTEXT and DROP CONTEXT commands. The CREATE command creates; the DROP command deletes. There is no ALTER CONTEXT command.

Creating a Context

Before creating a context, you m̶   anything you like, as long as it ⌐   y to give the context a name t̶   h. The syntax for the CREATE

```
CREATE [OR REPLA
    USING [schema
```

The package name that y̶   PL/SQL package that is allowed t̶   ackage doesn't need to exist wher   's.

> **Note** Creating a context does   ̶le
> does. When you create a   ̶ry
> in the data dictionary. C̶   ̶y
> when attributes are set.

You must have the CREATE AN   ̶e a context. Because contexts aren't created   ̶y are global to the entire database, you may want to do a̶   ̶reating yourself, rather than grant this role to a user.

Dropping a Context

You use the DROP CONTEXT command to remove a context. The syntax is simple, and it looks like this:

```
DROP CONTEXT context_name;
```

When you drop a context, its entry is removed from the data dictionary, and you can no longer define attributes for that context. However, users who currently have attributes set for the context will retain those attributes until they disconnect.

Defining and retrieving context attributes

Once you have created a context, you can define attributes in that context using the DBMS_SESSION package. Later, you can retrieve the values of those attributes using the new SYS_CONTEXT function.

Defining Attributes

You define an attribute in a context by making a call to DBMS_SESSION.SET_CONTEXT. The syntax of that call looks like this:

```
DBMS_SESSION.SET_CONTEXT (
'context_name','attribute_name','attribute_value');
```

For example, if you had a Seapark application user responsible for tank #4, and you wanted to store that information in the SEAPARK context, you could call SET_CONTEXT like this:

```
DBMS_SESSION.SET_CONTEXT('SEAPARK','TANK','4');
```

You can't execute a SET_CONTEXT call interactively using SQL*Plus or any similar tool. Context attributes can be changed only by the package named when the context was created. You must code calls to SET_CONTEXT within that package.

Retrieving Attributes

You can retrieve attribute values from a context using Oracle's new built-in SYS_CONTEXT function. The syntax for calling that function is as follows:

```
attribute_value:=SYS_CONTEXT('context_name','attribute_name');
```

Unlike the case when setting an attribute value, SYS_CONTEXT doesn't need to be invoked from any particular PL/SQL package. You can use SYS_CONTEXT from within any PL/SQL code. You can also use it as part of a SELECT statement. This example shows SYS_CONTEXT being used from within a SELECT statement to retrieve the value of the USERNAME attribute from the SEAPARK context:

```
SQL> select sys_context('seapark','username') from dual;

SYS_CONTEXT('SEAPARK','USERNAME')
--------------------------------------------------------
HAROLD

1 row selected.
```

As you can see from this example, context names and attribute names are not case-sensitive.

Using Oracle's Predefined Context — USERENV

Oracle implements a predefined context containing some attributes that are useful when implementing fine-grained security. The context name is USERENV, and the predefined attributes are the following:

SESSION_USER	The username that was used to log into the database.
CURRENT_USER	If a PL/SQL procedure, function, or package is being executed, this will be the name of the user who created it. Otherwise, this will be the same as SESSION_USER.
CURRENT_SCHEMA	The name of the current schema. Most often, this will be identical to the CURRENT_USER value.
SESSION_USERID	The numeric user ID corresponding to the session user. This is the same value as found in the USER_ID column of the DBA_USERS view.
CURRENT_USERID	The numeric user ID corresponding to the current user.
CURRENT_SCHEMAID	The numeric user ID corresponding to the current schema.
NLS_CALENDAR	The name of the NLS calendar currently being used for dates, for example, "GREGORIAN".
NLS_CURRENCY	The currency indicator, for example, "$".
NLS_DATE_FORMAT	The current default date format, for example, "DD-MON-YY".
NLS_DATE_LANGUAGE	The current date language, for example, "AMERICAN".
NLS_SORT	The current linguistic sorting method being used, for example, "BINARY".
NLS_TERRITORY	The current territory setting, for example, "AMERICA".

For security purposes, SESSION_USER is by far the most useful of all these attributes. In the past, detecting the logon username from within a stored PL/SQL procedure was difficult. Now, it's easy. Just code the following:

```
username := SYS_CONTEXT('USERENV','SESSION_USER');
```

matchs 1 on P332

Later in the chapter, you'll see how the USERENV context's SESSION_USER attribute forms the cornerstone of the row-level security model for the Seapark database.

Examining the Seapark context

Getting back to our Seapark scenario, remember that our security goal was this:

> The records of animals and tanks may be modified only by the caretaker responsible for the animal or tank in question.

To help implement that goal, we will create a context for the Seapark application. Within that context, we will define attributes that contain the current user's username and the tanks for which he or she is responsible.

You can find scripts to create the SEAPARK context and the package used to define attributes within that context on the companion CD in the directory named fine_grained_security_examples.

Creating the Seapark Context

Creating the context is the simple part. Log on as the SYSTEM user and execute a CREATE CONTEXT command, as shown in this example:

```
SQL> CREATE OR REPLACE CONTEXT seapark
  2       USING seapark.seapark_context;
```

This creates the context. The file named seapark_context.sql on the CD contains this command. The next task is to create the SEAPARK_CONTEXT package referenced in the command.

Creating the SEAPARK_CONTEXT Package

The SEAPARK_CONTEXT package is the only package that is allowed to define attributes in the SEAPARK context's namespace. Application users should not have access to this package because if they were able to change it, they would have an opening to bypass security. For this example, we will store the package in the SEAPARK schema. The assumption is that application users all have their own user IDs, and that only the DBA or other trusted users are allowed to log on as SEAPARK. If you want to secure the data from even the schema owner, you can do this by creating a different schema just for this one package.

To create the package, log on to the database as the SEAPARK user, and execute the two files on the CD named seapark_context_package.sql and seapark_context_body.sql. For an example, see Listing 12-1.

Listing 12-1: **Creating the SEAPARK_CONTEXT package**

```
SQL> @seapark_context_package
SQL> SET ECHO ON
SQL>
SQL> CREATE OR REPLACE PACKAGE seapark_context IS
  2       PROCEDURE set_attributes;
```

```
  3  END seapark_context;
  4  /
Package created.

SQL>
SQL> @seapark_context_body
SQL> SET ECHO ON
SQL>
SQL> CREATE OR REPLACE PACKAGE BODY seapark_context IS
  2      PROCEDURE set_attributes IS
  3          username caretaker.caretaker_name%type;
  4          tank_list VARCHAR2(100);
  5      BEGIN
  6          --Set a flag to temporarily disable policies on
  7          --the tank table.
  8          DBMS_SESSION.SET_CONTEXT
  9              ('seapark','logon','true');
 10
 11          --Use the new SYS_CONTEXT function to grab
 12          --the username of the currently logged on
 13          --user.
 14          username := SYS_CONTEXT('userenv','session_user');
 15
 16          --Now, query the tank table to see which tanks,
 17          --if any, this user is responsible for.
 18          tank_list := '';
 19
 20          FOR tank IN (
 21          SELECT tank_no
 22          FROM tank
 23          WHERE chief_caretaker_name = username)
 24          LOOP
 25              IF tank.tank_no IS NOT NULL THEN
 26                  IF (LENGTH(tank_list) > 0)  THEN
 27                      tank_list := tank_list || ',';
 28                  END IF;
 29
 30                  tank_list :=tank_list
 31                          || to_char(tank.tank_no);
 32              END IF;
 33          END LOOP;
 34
 35          --Store the username and the tank list in
 36          --the Seapark application context.
 37          DBMS_SESSION.SET_CONTEXT
 38              ('seapark','username',username);
 39          DBMS_SESSION.SET_CONTEXT
 40              ('seapark','tank_list',tank_list);
 41
 42          --Reset the logon flag, and enable security.
 43          DBMS_SESSION.SET_CONTEXT
```

Continued

Listing 12-1 *(continued)*

```
44               ('seapark','logon','false');
45      END;
46  END seapark_context;
47  /

Package body created.
```

The purpose of the SET_ATTRIBUTES procedure in this package is to determine the tank(s) for which a user is responsible, and to store that information in the SEAPARK context. Notice that the previous code does the following:

1. Makes a call to SET_CONTEXT to set a logon flag to TRUE

2. Makes a call to SYS_CONTEXT to get the logon username

3. Uses the logon username to query the TANK table

4. Builds a list of tanks for which the caretaker is chiefly responsible

5. Uses the SET_CONTEXT function to store the username and the tank list in the SEAPARK context for the user

6. Makes a call to SET_CONTEXT to set the logon flag to FALSE

This procedure is designed to be called from a database logon trigger. The logon flag is set to TRUE at the beginning and FALSE at the end to avoid the catch-22 of having security enforced on the tank table before the tank list has been retrieved for the user. The reason for this will become more apparent when you read the section on policies.

The last issue to deal with, now that the context and the context's package have been created, is to find some way to run the SET_ATTRIBUTES procedure for each user. One possibility is to have the application call the procedure. Another possibility is to write a logon trigger to call SET_ATTRIBUTES automatically whenever a user connects.

Note   Even if users were to manually invoke SET_ATTRIBUTES, they wouldn't be able to control the attributes that it defined in the context. The keys here are to ensure that users can't log on as SEAPARK (give them their own usernames to use), and that you don't grant CREATE ANY PROCEDURE to users you do not trust.

Creating a Logon Trigger

Logon triggers are a new Oracle8i feature that provides an excellent method for ensuring that a user's application context attributes are properly set no matter how that user connects to the database.

To create a logon trigger to call the SET_ATTRIBUTES procedure, log on as SYSTEM and execute a CREATE TRIGGER statement like that shown in the following example:

Note

Before attempting to create this trigger, you must grant execute privileges on the SEAPARK_CONTEXT package to the SYSTEM user.

```
SQL> CREATE OR REPLACE TRIGGER seapark_logon
  2      AFTER LOGON ON DATABASE
  3      CALL seapark.seapark_context.set_attributes
  4  /
```

Note

If you change the SEAPARK_CONTEXT package after creating the logon trigger, you will need to recompile the trigger. Do that by logging on as SYSDBA and issuing an ALTER TRIGGER SYSTEM.SEAPARK_CONTEXT command.

Once you have created the trigger, you can log on as any user, and the attributes for the Seapark application will automatically be set. You can see these attributes through the SESSION_CONTEXT view, as the following example shows:

```
SQL> CONNECT harold/harold
Connected.
SQL> SELECT * FROM session_context;

NAMESPACE   ATTRIBUTE   VALUE
----------  ----------  ----------
SEAPARK     USERNAME    HAROLD
SEAPARK     TANK_LIST   1,4
```

Note

If you run the schema creation scripts from the CD included with this book, HAROLD will be the only database user created who also manages a tank.

Once the logon trigger sets these attributes, the user can't do anything to change them. They stay set until the user logs off. The logon trigger ensures that no matter how the user connects to the database, these attributes get defined.

Caution

Be careful when creating logon triggers. If you create a trigger with errors, those errors will prevent all database users from logging on to the database. If a bad logon trigger prevents you from connecting, you can bypass it by connecting as either SYSDBA or as INTERNAL. Then you can drop the offending trigger. For more information, see Chapter 24, "Using Procedures, Packages, Functions, and Triggers."

Getting the context set up and the attributes properly defined is the first big step towards implementing row-level security for an application. The next step is to write some security policies to enforce security based on those attributes.

Writing Security Policies

A *policy* is a set of rules that governs the data that a user is allowed to see and modify within a table. In Oracle8i, you implement policies by writing functions that return query predicates. These predicates are then appended to queries issued by a user. Thus, while a user might issue a query like this:

```
DELETE
FROM aquatic_animal
WHERE id_no = 151
```

the security policy on the AQUATIC_ANIMAL table would transparently add a predicate to the query so that the end result would look like this:

```
DELETE
FROM aquatic_animal
WHERE id_no = 151
AND tank_no IN (1,4)
```

In this example, the list of tank numbers represents the tanks for which the currently logged-on user is responsible. The additional predicate prevents the user from deleting animals from other caretaker's tanks.

Implementing a policy

To implement a policy, you generally follow these steps:

1. Write a stored function or package that conforms to the policy specifications.

2. Use the DBMS_RLS.ADD_POLICY procedure to associate the policy function with the table(s) that you are protecting.

One policy function can protect more than one table, and a table can have different policies for selecting, inserting, updating, and deleting. Examples of both scenarios are provided throughout this section.

Creating a Policy Function

Policies are written as PL/SQL functions. Oracle calls these functions automatically and expects them to conform to this specification:

```
FUNCTION function_name (
        object_schema IN VARCHAR2,
        object_name IN VARCHAR2) RETURN VARCHAR2;
```

Oracle uses the two input arguments to pass in the owner name and object name of the object being queried. In return, Oracle expects a character string that can be appended onto the end of a SQL statement's WHERE clause. This return value is referred to as a *predicate*.

Your function may do whatever it needs to do to determine the proper predicate to return. It can query other database tables, check the username of the currently logged on user, and reference values stored in an application context. For example, the function shown in Listing 12-2 retrieves the user's tank list from the SEAPARK context and uses it to build a predicate that limits the results of a query to records with tank numbers that are found in the user's list.

Listing 12-2: **Returning a predicate**

```
FUNCTION update_limits (
      object_schema IN VARCHAR2,
      object_name IN VARCHAR2) RETURN VARCHAR2
   IS
      tank_list VARCHAR2(100);
      predicate VARCHAR2(113);
   BEGIN
      --Retrieve the tank list for this user
      tank_list := SYS_CONTEXT('seapark','tank_list');

    --Limit the user to his or her own tanks
      predicate := 'tank_no IN (' || tank_list || ')';

      --Return the predicate so it can be appended
      --to the query's WHERE clause.
      RETURN predicate;
   END;
```

The predicate returned by this function looks like this:

```
tank_no IN (1,4)
```

Note that there is no trailing semicolon, and the word WHERE isn't included as part of the predicate. Policy functions may return any valid predicate. Predicates may contain subqueries or any other valid SQL construct.

Implementing the Seapark Policies

If you have several related policies, consider implementing those policies as part of a package. The SEAPARK_POLICY package shown in this section implements the row-level security requirements discussed earlier for the Seapark database, and it contains these two functions:

✦ UPDATE_LIMITS

✦ SELECT_LIMITS

The UPDATE_LIMITS function is intended to be called whenever the user issues a query that changes the data in either the TANK table or the AQUATIC_ANIMALS table. It returns the predicate necessary to limit changes to the tanks for which the user is responsible. It also disallows changes to dead animals. In addition, users who aren't caretakers — in other words, who don't have a tank list — aren't allowed to make any changes.

The SELECT_LIMITS function is intended to be called whenever a SELECT statement is issued against one of the two tables. The rules are different for SELECTS. Caretakers are allowed to see each other's records, and they may see information about dead animals.

The code to create the SEAPARK_POLICY package is contained on the CD in the two files named seapark_policy_package.sql and seapark_policy_body.sql. You can create the package by logging on as the user SEAPARK and executing those scripts from SQL*Plus, as shown in Listing 12-3.

Listing 12-3: **Creating the SEAPARK_POLICY package**

```
SQL> @seapark_policy_package
SQL> SET ECHO ON
SQL>
SQL> CREATE OR REPLACE PACKAGE seapark_policy IS
  2      FUNCTION update_limits (
  3          object_schema IN VARCHAR2,
  4          object_name IN VARCHAR2) RETURN VARCHAR2;
  5
  6      FUNCTION select_limits (
  7          object_schema IN VARCHAR2,
  8          object_name IN VARCHAR2) RETURN VARCHAR2;
  9  END seapark_policy;
 10  /

Package created.
SQL>
SQL> @seapark_policy_body
SQL> SET ECHO ON
SQL>
SQL> CREATE OR REPLACE PACKAGE BODY seapark_policy IS
  2      FUNCTION update_limits (
  3          object_schema IN VARCHAR2,
  4          object_name IN VARCHAR2) RETURN VARCHAR2
  5      IS
  6          tank_list VARCHAR2(100);
  7          predicate VARCHAR2(113);
  8      BEGIN
  9          --Retrieve the tank list for this user
```

```
10          tank_list := SYS_CONTEXT('seapark','tank_list');
11
12          --If the tank list is null, the user has
13          --NO access. Otherwise, the user can change
14          --data related to his or her tank.
15          IF tank_list IS NULL THEN
16              --No data will match this condition.
17              predicate := '1=2';
18          ELSE
19              --Limit the user to his or her own tanks
20              predicate := 'tank_no IN ('
21                          || tank_list || ')';
22          END IF;
23
24          --Prevent changes to dead animals
25          IF object_schema = 'SEAPARK'
26          AND object_name = 'AQUATIC_ANIMAL' THEN
27              predicate := predicate
28                          || ' AND death_date IS NULL';
29          END IF;
30
31          --Return the predicate so it can be appended
32          --to the query's WHERE clause.
33          RETURN predicate;
34      END;
35
36      FUNCTION select_limits (
37          object_schema IN VARCHAR2,
38          object_name IN VARCHAR2) RETURN VARCHAR2
39      IS
40          tank_list VARCHAR2(100);
41          predicate VARCHAR2(113);
42      BEGIN
43          --If logging in, then return null so
44          --the logon trigger can see values in
45          --the tank table.
46          IF SYS_CONTEXT('seapark','logon') = 'true' THEN
47              RETURN '';
48          END IF;
49
50          --Retrieve the tank list for this user
51          tank_list := SYS_CONTEXT('seapark','tank_list');
52
53          --If the tank list is null, the user has
54          --NO access. Otherwise, the user can see
55          --anything.
56          IF tank_list IS NULL THEN
57              --No data will match this condition.
58              predicate := '1=2';
59          ELSE
60              --The user is a caretaker. Let him or her
```

Continued

Listing 12-3 *(continued)*

```
61              --see data for the other caretakers.
62              predicate := '';
63          END IF;
64
65          --Return the predicate so it can be appended
66          --to the query's WHERE clause.
67          RETURN predicate;
68      END;
69  END seapark_policy;
70  /

Package body created.
```

You can see that the two functions are pretty much the same, except that the SELECT_LIMITS function allows caretakers to see any data. One other difference is that SELECT_LIMITS issues a call to SYS_CONTEXT to see if the logon attribute is defined as 'true'; if true, it returns a null value as the predicate. The function does this because the logon trigger needs to query the tank table to retrieve the list of tanks for which a user is responsible. Because that list can't be known until after the query has been made, the logon trigger needs a way to bypass the security policy for that one query, hence the use of the logon flag.

Note   Users will not be able to bypass security by setting the logon flag themselves. Only the SEAPARK_CONTEXT package can change the value of an attribute in the SEAPARK context.

Three other points are worth noting about these functions, and about policy functions in general:

✦ When you want to allow a user unrestricted access to a table, have your policy function return a null string. The SELECT_LIMITS function does that when the logon flag is true.

✦ When you want to prevent a user from seeing any data in a table, return a predicate that will always be false. These functions use 1=2 for that purpose.

✦ The OBJECT_SCHEMA and OBJECT_NAME arguments may be used to code rules that are specific to a particular table. The UPDATE_LIMITS function uses these to apply the dead animal rule only to the AQUATIC_ANIMAL table.

With the policy functions created, the next step is to associate them with the tables that you want to secure.

Adding a Policy to an Object

Once you have created a policy, you associate that policy with a table using the DBMS_RLS package.

Note

You must have execute access on DBMS_RLS to use it. Because the package is owned by SYS, you will need to log on as SYS to grant that access.

You use the DBMS_RLS.ADD_POLICY procedure to link a policy function with a table. The syntax looks like this:

```
DBMS_RLS.ADD_POLICY (
'object_schema','object_name','policy_name',
'function_schema','function_name'
'statement_types',update_check)
```

The following list describes the syntax in detail:

✦ *object_schema* — The name of the schema containing the object that you are protecting. In this chapter, we are dealing with the SEAPARK schema.

✦ *object_name* — The name of the object, table, or view that you are protecting.

✦ *policy_name* — A name for the policy. This can be any name that you like. It's used with other DBMS_RLS calls to identify the policy that you are working with.

✦ *function_schema* — The owner of the policy function. For the examples in this book, the object owner (SEAPARK) also owns the function. It is possible, though, to have someone else own the function.

✦ *function_name* — The name of the policy function. If the function is part of a package, you must qualify the function name with the policy name.

✦ *statement_types* — A comma-separated list of data manipulation language (DML) statements for which you want this function to be invoked. The valid DML statements are SELECT, INSERT, UPDATE, and DELETE.

✦ *update_check* — A Boolean argument (not a string), which can be either TRUE or FALSE. A value of TRUE prevents a user from updating a row in such a way that the result violates the policy. A value of FALSE prevents that check from being made.

To associate the Seapark policies with the TANK and AQUATIC_ANIMALS tables, you can log on as SEAPARK using SQL*Plus and execute the calls to DBMS_RLS.ADD_POLICY as found in the file named seapark_add_policy.sql. See Listing 12-4.

Listing 12-4: **Associating policies with tables**

```
SQL> @seapark_add_policy
SQL> SET ECHO ON
SQL>
SQL> EXECUTE DBMS_RLS.ADD_POLICY ( -
>      'SEAPARK','TANK','TANK_UPDATE', -
>      'SEAPARK','SEAPARK_POLICY.UPDATE_LIMITS', -
>      'INSERT, UPDATE, DELETE', TRUE);

PL/SQL procedure successfully completed.

SQL>
SQL> EXECUTE DBMS_RLS.ADD_POLICY ( -
>      'SEAPARK','TANK','TANK_SELECT', -
>      'SEAPARK','SEAPARK_POLICY.SELECT_LIMITS', -
>      'SELECT', TRUE);

PL/SQL procedure successfully completed.

SQL>
SQL> EXECUTE DBMS_RLS.ADD_POLICY ( -
>      'SEAPARK','AQUATIC_ANIMAL','AQUATIC_ANIMAL_UPDATE', -
>      'SEAPARK','SEAPARK_POLICY.UPDATE_LIMITS', -
>      'INSERT, UPDATE, DELETE', TRUE);

PL/SQL procedure successfully completed.

SQL>
SQL> EXECUTE DBMS_RLS.ADD_POLICY ( -
>      'SEAPARK','AQUATIC_ANIMAL','AQUATIC_ANIMAL_SELECT', -
>      'SEAPARK','SEAPARK_POLICY.SELECT_LIMITS', -
>      'SELECT', TRUE);

PL/SQL procedure successfully completed.
```

Two policies have been linked with each table: one for selecting and one for everything else. You now have the situation shown in Table 12-1.

Each table has two policies. Each policy function is used for two objects. Having the tank number field named the same in both tables makes that easy to do. The exception — where AQUATIC_ANIMAL is the only table with a death date — is handled by having the UPDATE_LIMITS function check the object name.

Table 12-1
Seapark Security Policies

Table	Policy	DML	Function
TANK	TANK_UPDATE	INSERT UPDATE DELETE	SEAPARK_POLICY.UPDATE_LIMITS
	TANK_SELECT	SELECT	SEAPARK_POLICY.SELECT_LIMITS
AQUATIC _ANIMAL	AQUATIC_ ANIMAL_ UPDATE	INSERT UPDATE DELETE	SEAPARK_POLICY.UPDATE_LIMITS
	AQUATIC_ ANIMAL_ SELECT	SELECT	SEAPARK_POLICY.SELECT_LIMITS

Verifying Policy Enforcement

If you've been following along with all the examples in this chapter, you can see the effects of policy enforcement by logging on as the user named HAROLD. If you log on as HAROLD and select data from the AQUATIC_ANIMAL table, you'll see all the records, as shown in Listing 12-5.

Listing 12-5: **HAROLD can see all animal records.**

```
SQL> SELECT id_no, tank_no, animal_name
  2  FROM seapark.aquatic_animal;

   ID_NO    TANK_NO ANIMAL_NAME
--------- --------- ------------------------------
     100         1 Flipper
     105         1 Skipper
     112         1 Bopper
     151         2 Batty
     166         2 Shorty
     145         2 Squacky
     175         2 Paintuin
     199         3 Nosey
     202         3 Rascal
     240         3 Snoops

10 rows selected.
```

This ability to see all the records is consistent with the policy of allowing caretakers to view data about each other's animals. However, if you try to delete or update those same records, the results are different:

```
SQL> DELETE FROM seapark.aquatic_animal;

3 rows deleted.
```

Even though the table contains ten rows, Harold was able to delete only three. Harold is the caretaker for tank 1, so he is allowed to delete records only for animals in that tank.

Note   You may want to roll back this deletion.

Here is another example showing the update check option at work:

```
SQL> UPDATE seapark.aquatic_animal
  2  SET death_date = SYSDATE;
UPDATE seapark.aquatic_animal
              *
ERROR at line 1:
ORA-01402: view WITH CHECK OPTION where-clause violation
```

Harold has attempted to define a death date for all his animals. The UPDATE_LIMITS policy doesn't allow records for dead animals to be altered. By setting the update check option to true, we have prevented Harold from changing a record from a state in which it can be altered to a state in which it cannot.

Note   You might want to disable the update check on the AQUATIC_ANIMAL_UPDATE policy because you probably do want Harold to be able to record the death of one of his animals.

To see the effect of the policies on a user who is not a caretaker, log on as SEAPARK and try selecting from either the TANK or AQUATIC_ANIMAL tables. You won't get any rows back because SEAPARK isn't listed in the TANK table as a caretaker.

Listing policies on an object

You can get a list of policies on an object by querying one of these views:

DBA_POLICIES	Returns information about all policies defined in the database
ALL_POLICIES	Returns information about policies defined on all objects to which you have access
USER_POLICIES	Returns information about policies on objects that you own

These views are fairly self-explanatory. The column names make obvious the type of data they contain. The following example shows how you can generate a list of all policies on all objects that you own:

```
SQL> SELECT object_name, policy_name, sel, ins, upd, del
  2  FROM user_policies
  3  ORDER BY object_name, policy_name;

OBJECT_NAME       POLICY_NAME               SEL INS UPD DEL
----------------  ------------------------  --- --- --- ---
AQUATIC_ANIMAL    AQUATIC_ANIMAL_SELECT     YES NO  NO  NO
AQUATIC_ANIMAL    AQUATIC_ANIMAL_UPDATE     NO  YES YES YES
TANK              TANK_SELECT               YES NO  NO  NO
TANK              TANK_UPDATE               NO  YES YES YES
```

The yes/no flags indicate the type of DML statements to which the policy applies. The USER_OBJECTS view also contains columns to return the name of the package and function used to enforce the policy, if you need that information. The ALL_POLICIES and DBA_POLICIES views differ from USER_POLICIES by one additional field that identifies the owner of an object.

Enabling and disabling a policy

The DBMS_RLS package allows you to temporarily disable a policy without having to drop it. This comes in handy if you have some maintenance work to do on a table and you don't want to be thwarted by your own security. The DBMS_RLS.ENABLE procedure is used both to disable and to enable a policy. The syntax looks like this:

```
DBMS_RLS.ENABLE_POLICY (
object_schema,
object_name,
policy_name,
enable_flag);
```

The *enable_flag* argument is a Boolean, and you set it to either TRUE or FALSE, depending on whether you want the policy enforced.

Dropping a policy

You can drop (remove) a policy by making a call to the DBMS_RLS package's DROP_POLICY procedure. The syntax for this looks like the following:

```
DBMS_RLS.DROP_POLICY (
    object_schema,
    object_name,
     policy_name);
```

If you've been following along through the examples in this chapter, you may want to drop any policies that you have created. The SQL*Plus script on the CD named drop_policy_examples.sql will do this for you.

Using Pre-8i Alternatives

People have used a few approaches in the past to implement row-level security within the database. These approaches generally include some combination of the following:

✦ Views to restrict the data that a user can see

✦ Triggers to prevent unauthorized updates to tables

✦ Stored procedures as a vehicle for managing updates and deletes

Enforcing security using these features can work, but it takes careful application design because use of these features isn't always transparent to the application.

Enforcing security with views

You can use views as a mechanism to enforce row-level security. They work best when you're only selecting data, not changing or deleting it. The following view on the TANK table limits users to viewing information only about their tanks:

```
CREATE OR REPLACE VIEW user_tank AS
    SELECT *
    FROM tank
    WHERE CHIEF_CARETAKER_NAME = USER;
```

By granting users SELECT access on this view but not the underlying table, you limit them to seeing only tanks that they manage. Since this particular view doesn't contain any joins or subqueries, it could be used to control INSERTS, UPDATES, and DELETES as well as SELECTS.

Oracle uses the view method extensively in its data dictionary. The ALL views, for example, are defined in such a way as to allow you to see information about any objects to which you have access. That's all done through the WHERE clause. You will run into some issues, however, when using views for security:

✦ The WHERE clauses can quickly become complex. Subqueries and joins may become necessary, thus rendering the views nonupdateable.

✦ When a view is nonupdateable, you need a different mechanism for securing INSERTS, UPDATES, and DELETES.

✦ You may need different views for different classes of users. Your application programs need to be aware of which view to use for any given user.

✦ If the number of views is quite high, and especially if they change frequently, the maintenance burden can be significant.

In spite of these issues, views do have a place in a security plan. They remain the only method of limiting a user's access to specific columns within a table.

Enforcing security with triggers

Triggers provide another mechanism for enforcing security on a table. The trigger on the TANK table shown in Listing 12-6 restricts users to their own tanks.

Listing 12-6: Using a trigger to enforce security on a table

```
CREATE OR REPLACE TRIGGER user_tank
    BEFORE UPDATE OR INSERT OR DELETE ON tank
    FOR EACH ROW
BEGIN
    IF UPDATING OR DELETING THEN
        IF :old.chief_caretaker_name = USER THEN
            NULL;
        ELSE
            RAISE_APPLICATION_ERROR (
                -20000,
                'You can''t update another caretaker''s tank.');
        END IF;
    END IF;
    IF INSERTING THEN
        IF :old.chief_caretaker_name = USER THEN
            NULL;
        ELSE
            RAISE_APPLICATION_ERROR (
                -20000,
                'You can''t insert a tank for another caretaker.');
        END IF;
    END IF;
END;
/
```

One advantage of using triggers is that they are transparent to the application. A major disadvantage, however, is that they work only for inserts, updates, and deletes. You still need to depend on some other method, such as using views, to secure selects.

Note

It is possible to grant SELECT on a view, and only INSERT, UPDATE, and DELETE on the underlying table. Applications would then select from the view, but update (or delete or insert into) the table.

Enforcing security with procedures

You can sometimes use stored procedures to enforce business rules and security at the database level. The following procedure, for example, allows you to change an animal's name, but only if that animal is still alive:

```
CREATE OR REPLACE PROCEDURE change_animal_name (
    id_no IN NUMBER,
    animal_name IN VARCHAR2) AS
BEGIN
    UPDATE aquatic_animal
    SET animal_name = change_animal_name.animal_name
    WHERE id_no = change_animal_name.id_no
    AND death_date IS NULL;
END;
/
```

To make this secure, you would grant users execute access on the stored procedure, but you wouldn't grant UPDATE access to the underlying table. That would force all updates to be done through procedure calls. One problem with this approach is that it isn't transparent to the application. Instead, the application has to be coded to perform updates through procedure calls. Depending on the development tool that you are using, this may not be as easy as you would like it to be. Another problem with using stored procedures is that prior to the release of Oracle8i, with its SYS_CONTEXT function, getting the name of the currently logged-on ser from a stored procedure wasn't possible.

Summary

In this chapter, you learned:

✦ In Orace8i, you can use policies and contexts to enforce fine-grained security, giving you control over which rows a user is allowed to access.

✦ Application contexts serve as scratchpad areas in memory. Users can freely read from a context, but updates can be made only by the specific PL/SQL package named when the package was created.

✦ You can use logon triggers to ensure that context attributes for a user are set when a user first logs on. This is done by having the logon trigger call the specific package allowed to update the context.

✦ Security policies function by dynamically adding a predicate to a user's queries. This transformation is transparent to the user, and the user never sees the final version of the query.

✦ Fine-grained security offers advantages over previous methods for implementing row-level security in that it allows for a unified and consistent approach to be taken, and it doesn't require any specific coding at the application level.

✦   ✦   ✦

Managing Tables

This chapter shows you how to use SQL commands to create tables and indexes, define primary and foreign keys, and define other constraints. Some consider the command-line approach as old fashioned, preferring instead to use GUI-based tools. Don't worry, this chapter also shows you how to create tables using Enterprise Manager's Schema Manager application.

Note   All the SQL commands shown in this chapter are also listed in Appendix A, "SQL Statement Reference." Because the commands are so complex, relevant examples are given here, but the full syntax is left to Appendix A.

Understanding Tables

Tables are the cornerstone of a relational database, and they typically consist of the following major elements:

+ **Columns.** Define the data that may be stored in the table

+ **Constraints.** Restrict the data that may be stored in a table, usually for the purpose of enforcing business rules

+ **Indexes.** Allow fast access to a table's data based on values in one or more columns

    Oracle also uses indexes as a mechanism for enforcing unique and primary key constraints

Oracle is even more than a relational database. It is an object-relational database. In addition to the elements just described, Oracle tables may contain objects, arrays, and nested tables.

Cross-Reference   Chapter 29, "Using Oracle8i's Object Features," discusses these exciting features: objects, arrays, and nested tables.

In This Chapter

Understanding tables

Creating tables

Altering tables

Deleting tables

Using the data dictionary

Columns

Columns are mandatory elements of a table definition. You can define a table without indexes, and without constraints, but you can't define a table without columns. When creating columns, you'll want to consider names, datatypes, and null values.

Column Names

The rules for naming columns are the same as for any other object, including tables:

   ✦ Column names must begin with a letter.

   ✦ Column names may be up to 30 characters long.

   ✦ After the first letter, column names may consist of any combination of letters, digits, pound signs (#), dollar signs ($), and underscores (_).

   ✦ Oracle automatically converts all column names to uppercase unless they are enclosed within quotes.

Note   Column names that are enclosed within quotes may contain other special characters besides those listed here, but creating such names usually ends up causing more trouble than it's worth.

Column names are not normally case-sensitive, unless they are enclosed in quotes. You'll find that it's usually best to avoid case-sensitive column names, although the ability to use them does come in handy when converting databases to Oracle from Microsoft Access, where mixed-case column names, and spaces in column names, are the rule.

Oracle8i Datatypes

Columns are defined during the process of creating a new table in the database. After naming the column, you must specify in Oracle what kind of data goes into the column. You do this by specifying a *datatype* for the column. Table 13-1 lists the datatypes available when you define columns in Oracle8i.

Table 13-1
Oracle8i Datatypes

Datatype	Length	Description
BFILE	0–4GB	A pointer to a binary file stored outside the database. The maximum supported file size is 4GB.

Datatype	Length	Description
BLOB	0–4GB	A binary large object. The maximum supported size is 4GB.
CHAR(*length*)	1–2000	A string with a fixed length. The default length is 1. Prior to the release of Oracle8, the maximum length of a CHAR field was 255.
CHARACTER(length)	1–2000	A string with fixed length. Provided for ANSI compatibility, it is the same as CHAR.
CHAR VARYING (*length*)	1–4000	A variable-length string. It is the same as CHARACTER VARYING.
CHARACTER VARYING (length)	1–4000	A variable-length string type provided for ANSI compatibility. It is the same as VARCHAR2.
CLOB	0–4GB	A character-based large object. It has a 4GB maximum size.
DATE	N/A	A date value. Valid dates range from January 1, 4712 B.C., to December 31, A.D. 4712. In Oracle, DATE fields always include the time in hours, minutes, and seconds.
DECIMAL (*precision,scale*)	precision: 1–38 scale: -84–127	A decimal datatype provided for ANSI compatibility. It is the same as NUMBER.
DOUBLE PRECISION	126 binary digits	A numeric datatype provided for ANSI compatibility. It is the same as FLOAT.
FLOAT(bdigits)	1–126	A floating-point type provided for ANSI compatibility. It is the same as NUMBER(bdigits). The default precision is 126.
INT	38 digits	An integer type provided for ANSI compatibility. It is the same as NUMBER(38).
INTEGER	38 digits	An integer type provided for ANSI compatibility. It is the same as NUMBER(38).
LONG	0–2GB	A large text string. The LONG datatype is obsolete. Use CLOB or BLOB instead for all new designs.

Continued

Table 13-1 (continued)

Datatype	Length	Description
LONG RAW	0–2GB	Raw binary data. Use BLOB instead.
MLSLABEL	N/A	A binary format of a label used on a secure operating system. This datatype is used only with Trusted Oracle.
NATIONAL CHAR (length)	1–2000	A national language type provided for ANSI compatibility. It is the same as NCHAR.
NATIONAL CHARACTER (length)	1–2000	A national language type provided for ANSI compatibility. It is the same as NCHAR.
NATIONAL CHAR VARYING (length)	1–4000	A national language type provided for ANSI compatibility, and which is the same as NVARCHAR2.
NATIONAL CHARACTER VARYING (length)	1–4000	A national language type provided for ANSI compatibility. It is the same as NVARCHAR2.
NCHAR(length)	1–2000	A fixed-length character string using the national character set. The NCHAR type has the same attributes as CHAR, except that it stores characters that depend on a national character set. Oracle8i supports many languages this way. The length is in bytes. In some character sets, one character may be represented by more than one byte.
NCLOB	0–4GB	A character-based large object. It uses a national character set.
NUMBER (precision,scale)	precision: 1–38 scale: -84–127	A number. The precision indicates the number of digits, up to 38. The scale indicates the location of the decimal point. For example, a column of type NUMBER (9,2) would store seven digits to the left of the decimal, and two to the right, for a total of nine digits.
NUMBER(bdigits)	1–126 binary digits	A floating-point number with up to 126 binary digits of precision. The default precision is 126.

Datatype	Length	Description
NUMBER	38 digits	A floating-point number. When no precision and scale are specified, a declaration of NUMBER results in a floating-point value with 38 digits of precision.
NVARCHAR2(*length*)	1–4000	A variable-length character string using the national character set. The NVARCHAR2 datatype has the same attributes as VARCHAR2, except that it stores characters using the national language character set. The length is in bytes, not characters.
RAW(*length*)	1–2000	Raw binary data. You should consider using BLOB instead.
REAL	63 binary digits	A real number. This is provided for ANSI compatibility and is the same as FLOAT(63).
REF	N/A	A pointer. It points to a particular instance of an Oracle8i object type.
ROWID	N/A	A rowid type. It allows you to store row IDs in a table.
SMALLINT	38 digits	Provided for ANSI compatibility. It is the same as NUMBER(38).
UROWID	N/A	Allows you to store universal row IDs, such as those that are used with index-organized tables (IOTs).
VARCHAR(*length*)	1–4000	Same as VARCHAR2. Oracle recommends using VARCHAR2 instead.
VARCHAR2(*length*)	1–4000	A text string of variable length. You must specify the maximum length when defining the column. Prior to the release of Oracle8, the maximum length of a VARCHAR2 was 2000 bytes.

The most common datatypes are VARCHAR2, DATE, and variations of NUMBER. Oracle rarely uses the datatypes provided for ANSI compatibility, and if they are used, Oracle converts them to the corresponding Oracle datatype.

Constraints

Constraints are rules about your data that you define at the database level. Constraints are declarative. You don't specify the process for enforcing a rule; you simply specify what that rule is to be. Oracle supports these types of constraints:

- ✦ Primary key
- ✦ Unique key
- ✦ Foreign key
- ✦ Check

Primary key constraints identify the set of columns whose values uniquely identify a record in a table. Oracle won't allow two records to have the same primary key value. For example, the ID_NO column is the primary key of the AQUATIC_ANIMAL table. Because ID_NO has been defined as the primary key, Oracle will not allow two records to have the same value in that column. Furthermore, primary key columns become required columns — they can never be null.

Unique key constraints identify sets of columns that must be unique for each row in a table. Unique key constraints are similar to primary key constraints, and they often represent alternative primary key choices. The one difference between a unique key and a primary key is that columns in a unique key may be null.

Note   When you create a primary key or unique key constraint on a table, Oracle will create a unique index to enforce that constraint. The name of the index will match the name that you give the constraint.

Foreign key constraints are used to link two tables that contain related information. They are most often used in parent-child relationships, such as the one between the TANK table and the AQUATIC_ANIMAL table. A foreign key constraint can be placed on the AQUATIC_ANIMAL table, requiring that any TANK_NO value match a record in the TANK table. In this way, you can prevent erroneous tank numbers from being entered in the AQUATIC_ANIMAL table. Foreign keys must be linked to a corresponding primary or unique key.

Check constraints allow you to define an arbitrary condition that must be true before a row can be saved in a table. The most common check constraint is the NOT NULL constraint, which requires that a column have a value. You can supply almost any arbitrary expression for a check constraint, provided that it returns a value of TRUE or FALSE.

Indexes

Indexes on tables function much like the index in a book. They allow Oracle to quickly zero in on the data necessary to satisfy a query. Consider the TANK table, which contains the following information:

```
TANK_NO TANK_NAME
-------- ----------------
      1 Dolphin Tank
      2 Penguin Pool
      3 Sea Lion Den
      4 Beer Tank
    . . .
```

If you were to issue a SELECT statement looking for tanks named "Dolphin Tank," how would Oracle find the correct rows to return? One possible way would be to read each row in the table one by one, checking each to see if the name matched. With only four rows in the table, that's probably the fastest way, but what if there were a million rows to look through? With a million rows, it would take a long time to check each one to see if the name was "Dolphin Tank." An index on the TANK_NAME column would allow you to find the tank named "Dolphin Tank" quickly.

Chapter 14, "Managing Indexes," discusses the various index types that Oracle supports, showing you how to take advantage of them. With respect to creating and managing tables, be aware that Oracle creates indexes automatically to enforce primary and unique key constraints.

Creating Tables

When you create a relational table in an Oracle database, you need to do the following:

✦ Name the table.

✦ Name and define the columns within the table.

✦ Define constraints on the table.

✦ Specify physical properties for the table.

The last item, specifying physical properties, can be a large task in its own right, especially if you are creating a partitioned table, a clustered table, or a table containing large object types. Each of those topics is discussed in other chapters within this book.

There are two ways to create a table. One is to write a CREATE TABLE statement and execute it using a tool such as SQL*Plus. The other is to use Enterprise Manager's Schema Manager application.

Using the CREATE TABLE statement

Depending on what you are doing, the CREATE TABLE statement can be one of the most complex SQL statements to write. At a minimum, you should define the columns and specify a tablespace in which to store the table. For example:

```
CREATE TABLE aquatic_animal (
    ID_NO               NUMBER(10),
    TANK_NO             NUMBER(10),
    ANIMAL_NAME         VARCHAR2(30),
    BIRTH_DATE          DATE,
    DEATH_DATE          DATE,
    MARKINGS_DESCRIPTION VARCHAR2(30)
    ) TABLESPACE users;
```

This statement creates the AQUATIC_ANIMAL table used in the sample database and places it in the tablespace named USERS. The tablespace clause is optional. Omit it, and the table will be created as your default tablespace.

Note   In a production setting, it's rare that you can store all your tables in the default tablespace. Production databases tend to have many tablespaces, and you'll find yourself including the TABLESPACE clause in most CREATE TABLE commands that you write.

Defining columns

Columns define the data that a table can store. As you've seen by looking at the previous CREATE TABLE statement, you define a column by providing a column name and a datatype. The exact syntax looks like this:

```
column_name datatype [DEFAULT default_value]
                     [[NOT] NULL]
                     column_constraint
```

The column name may be up to 30 characters long, and it must conform to the same rules used for naming tables and other objects. The datatype, unless you've defined your own, must be one of those listed in Table 13-1. The examples in this chapter focus on using the traditional scaler datatypes such as NUMBER, DATE, and VARCHAR2. Other chapters in this book delve into the more exotic areas of nested tables, large object types, and varying arrays.

When you define a column, you may define a default value for that column. You may also define one or more column constraints.

Default Values

Default values represent values that are stored in a column when no other value is supplied. They have meaning only when new rows are inserted, and you specify them using the DEFAULT clause in the column definition. The following example defines a default value for the MARKINGS_DESCRIPTION column:

```
MARKINGS_DESCRIPTION VARCHAR2(30) DEFAULT 'No unusual markings'
```

With this default value in place, if you insert a row into the AQUATIC_ANIMAL table without supplying a value for the MARKINGS_DESCRIPTION field, the default value would be stored automatically. For example:

```
SQL> INSERT INTO aquatic_animal
  2     (id_no, animal_name)
  3     VALUES (995,'Herman');

1 row created.

SQL> select id_no, markings_description
  2     FROM aquatic_animal
  3     WHERE id_no = 995;

 ID_NO MARKINGS_DESCRIPTION
--------- ------------------------------
   995 No unusual markings
```

Because no value is supplied for the MARKINGS_DESCRIPTION column, the default value is picked up and used instead. You can use default values for columns defined as NOT NULL to prevent errors caused when application programs insert a row without supplying a value for those columns.

Nullability

By default, Oracle doesn't require you to supply a value for every column when you are inserting a row into a table. Instead, columns that you omit are simply stored as null values. If you have important columns for which you always want the user to supply a value, you can use the NOT NULL keywords to indicate that. The ANIMAL_NAME column in the AQUATIC_ANIMAL table is a good candidate for a required field. Here's how you would make required fields out of both the ANIMAL_NAME column and the MARKINGS_DESCRIPTION column:

```
animal_name           VARCHAR2(30)
   CONSTRAINT animal_name_required NOT NULL,
markings_description VARCHAR2(30)
   DEFAULT 'No unusual markings'
   CONSTRAINT markings_description_required NOT NULL
```

When you define a column as a NOT NULL column, you are actually defining a constraint on that column. A NOT NULL constraint is a specific implementation of a CHECK constraint. In this example, a NOT NULL constraint was defined for each field, and the CONSTRAINT keyword was used to give each constraint a name.

Column Constraints

You can define constraints at the column level by adding a CONSTRAINT clause to the column definition. The NOT NULL keywords just discussed actually represent one form of a constraint clause. You may also define primary keys, foreign keys, unique keys, and check constraints at the column level. The following example shows how you can define a primary key constraint for the AQUATIC_ANIMAL table:

```
ID_NO              NUMBER(10)
                   CONSTRAINT aquatic_animal_pk
                   PRIMARY KEY,
```

Defining constraints at the column level like this limits you somewhat, because you can't define a constraint over multiple columns. To do that, you need to use a table constraint. Since Oracle treats all constraints the same anyway, consider defining all your constraints at the table level.

Note   The NOT NULL constraint is the constraint that makes sense at the column level. The ANSI standard supports the NOT NULL keywords, and people are quite used to using them.

Defining constraints

You can define constraints at the table level by including one or more constraint clauses along with your column definitions. Defining constraints on your tables is beneficial for the following reasons:

✦ Constraints prevent bad data from being saved.

✦ Constraints serve as a form of documentation. Foreign key and primary key constraints, for example, serve to document the relationships between tables. Reporting tools, such as Oracle Reports, can make use of that information.

You have four types of constraints to choose from: primary key, unique key, foreign key, and check.

Primary Key Constraints

You can use primary key constraints to define and document the columns in a table that can be depended upon to uniquely identify a record. One of the hallmarks of good relational design is that every table has a primary key. Primary keys enforce the following rules:

✦ Each column making up the key becomes a required column. Null values in primary key columns are not allowed. To do otherwise would mean that a primary key could not be depended upon to identify a record.

✦ No two rows in a table may have the same set of values for the primary key columns.

When you define a primary key constraint on a table, Oracle silently creates a unique index to support that constraint. Consequently, on all but the most trivial tables, when you create a primary key constraint, you need to give some thought to where that index will be stored and what it will be named. The following example demonstrates how to define a primary key constraint on the AQUATIC_ANIMAL table, including the clauses necessary to name the constraint, and how to specify the tablespace in which the underlying index is stored:

```
CREATE TABLE aquatic_animal (
    ID_NO               NUMBER(10),
    TANK_NO             NUMBER(10),
    ANIMAL_NAME         VARCHAR2(30),
    BIRTH_DATE          DATE,
    DEATH_DATE          DATE,
    MARKINGS_DESCRIPTION VARCHAR2(30),
    CONSTRAINT aquatic_animal_pk
        PRIMARY KEY (id_no)
        USING INDEX TABLESPACE indx
) TABLESPACE users;
```

Notice that the constraint clause follows immediately after the column definitions. You can mix table constraints in with the column definitions, but common practice is to list the constraints at the end.

When Oracle creates an index in support of a constraint, the index is named to match the constraint name. In this case, both the constraint and the index will be named AQUATIC_ANIMAL_PK. Naming your constraints is optional, but it's a good idea to give each constraint a unique name. Otherwise, Oracle generates a name. The names sometimes show up in error messages, and it's much easier to understand at a glance what a constraint named AQUATIC_ANIMAL_PK is all about than it is to guess at what SYS_C001765 might be.

Having explicit names for constraints also makes it easier to write database maintenance and migration scripts. If you have four copies of a database, the system-generated constraint names will be different in each of the four. If you then need to perform maintenance related to constraints, it becomes impossible to write a generic script that works across all four databases.

The USING INDEX clause of a constraint definition allows you to specify a tablespace name and other parameters for the index that Oracle creates to enforce the constraint. The USING INDEX clause applies only to primary key and unique key constraints.

Unique Key Constraints

Unique key constraints are similar to primary key constraints. In fact, in many cases, unique keys represent alternative primary key choices. There is one major difference between unique and primary keys: Columns that form part of a unique key constraint may be null.

Listing 13-1 uses the AQUATIC_ANIMAL table and defines a unique key constraint on the animal name and tank number fields.

Listing 13-1: **Defining a unique key constraint**

```
CREATE TABLE aquatic_animal (
   ID_NO NUMBER(10),
   TANK_NO            NUMBER(10),
   ANIMAL_NAME        VARCHAR2(30),
   BIRTH_DATE         DATE,
   DEATH_DATE         DATE,
   MARKINGS_DESCRIPTION VARCHAR2(30),
   CONSTRAINT aquatic_animal_pk
         PRIMARY KEY (id_no)
         USING INDEX TABLESPACE indx,
   CONSTRAINT unique_name_tank
         UNIQUE (animal_name, tank_no)
         USING INDEX TABLESPACE indx
         STORAGE (INITIAL 50K NEXT 10K)
) TABLESPACE USERS;
```

As you can see, the definition of a unique key constraint is almost identical to that of a primary key. In this example, a storage clause has been added following the tablespace name to override the default storage parameters for the tablespace. As with a primary key constraint, Oracle will create an index to enforce the unique key constraint. The index name will match the constraint name.

When you create a unique constraint, you need to understand how Oracle treats null values when enforcing that constraint. As long as at least one column is not null, Oracle will enforce the constraint using the remaining values. If all columns are null, Oracle won't enforce the constraint. Consider the sequence of inserts into the AQUATIC_ANIMAL table that are shown in Table 13-2.

Table 13-2
The Effect of Nulls on a Unique Key Constraint

Sequence	ID_NO	TANK_NO	ANIMAL_NAME	Results
1	1	1	Flipper	Success.
2	2	1	Skippy	Success. The names are different.
3	3	1	Skippy	Failure. An existing record with the same tank number and animal name exists.
4	3	1		Success. No other record has a tank number of 1 with a null animal name.
5	4		Flipper	Success. No other record has a null tank number with an animal name of Flipper.
6	5		Flipper	Failure. An existing record already has a null tank number and an animal name of Flipper.
7	6			Success. Both tank number and animal name are null.
8	7			Success. Both tank number and animal name are null.

The key areas to focus on in Table 13-2 are sequences 5, 6, 7, and 8. Sequence numbers 5 and 6 show that when some columns are null, Oracle still enforces the constraint by looking for identical cases where the same columns are null. Sequences 7 and 8 show that any number of rows may be inserted when all columns listed in a unique constraint are null.

Foreign Key Constraints

Use foreign key constraints when you want to make certain that the values in a set of columns in one table exist in at least one row of another table. The AQUATIC_ANIMAL table provides a good example of the need for this. It contains a tank number for each animal in the table. The Seapark database also contains a TANK table, presumably with a list of valid tanks. You wouldn't want someone to enter an animal and place that animal in a tank that doesn't exist. You can prevent that from ever happening by defining a foreign key on the AQUATIC_ANIMAL table, like this:

```
CREATE TABLE aquatic_animal (
...
CONSTRAINT assigned_tank_fk
        FOREIGN KEY (tank_no)
        REFERENCES tank
...
```

This constraint tells Oracle that every tank number value in the AQUATIC_ANIMAL table must also exist in the TANK table. How does Oracle know if a tank number is listed in the TANK table? It looks at the primary key. Oracle knows that the primary key of the TANK table is TANK_NO. Listing 13-2 illustrates how the foreign key is enforced.

Listing 13-2: **Enforcing a foreign key**

```
SQL> SELECT tank_no FROM tank;

TANK_NO
---------
        1
        2
        3
        4

SQL> INSERT INTO aquatic_animal
  2      (id_no, tank_no, animal_name)
  3      VALUES (970, 1, 'Sippy');

1 row created.

SQL> INSERT INTO aquatic_animal
  2      (id_no, tank_no, animal_name)
  3      VALUES (971, 5, 'Sappy');
insert into aquatic_animal
            *
ERROR at line 1:
ORA-02291: integrity constraint (SEAPARK.ASSIGNED_TANK_FK) violated -
parent key not found
```

The tank table contains entries for tanks numbered from 1 through 4. The first insert succeeds because it assigns the animal named Sippy to tank #1, a valid tank. The second insert fails because it assigns the animal named Sappy to tank #5, which is not a valid tank. In this way, a foreign key constraint prevents erroneous data from being entered into the database.

Foreign keys don't always have to relate to primary keys. They may also relate to unique keys. In that case, you must explicitly specify the matching columns in the parent table when defining the constraint. For example:

```
CREATE TABLE aquatic_animal (
...
CONSTRAINT assigned_tank_fk
        FOREIGN KEY (tank_no)
        REFERENCES tank (tank_no)
...
```

This example explicitly states that the TANK_NO column in the AQUATIC_ANIMAL table must match a value in the TANK_NO column of the TANK table. The column names don't need to match, although it is less confusing if they do match. They do need to be of the same datatype, and the referenced column(s) must represent either a primary key or a unique key.

Oracle doesn't need to create an index to enforce a foreign key constraint because primary and unique keys are already indexed. For performance reasons, though, consider indexing the foreign key fields in the child table. The reason for this is that if you ever delete a parent record (a tank record), Oracle must check to see if there are any child records (aquatic animal records) that reference the record being deleted. If there is no index on the foreign key fields in the child table, Oracle is forced to lock the table and read each record to see if any matching records exist.

If you know that you are never going to delete a parent record, fine. But if you do expect to delete parents, then index your foreign key. With respect to this example, you can index the TANK_NO column in the AQUATIC_ANIMAL table.

One last word on foreign key constraints: If at least one column listed in a foreign key constraint is null, Oracle will not check to see if a parent record exists. You can add the NOT NULL constraint to your foreign key fields if you always want to require a value.

Check Constraints

Check constraints allow you to define an arbitrary condition that must be true for each record in a table. The NOT NULL constraint is a form of check constraint where the condition is that a column must not be null. Earlier, you saw how to use the NOT NULL keywords to make MARKINGS_DESCRIPTION a required column. You can do the same thing by defining the following constraint:

```
CONSTRAINT markings_description_ck
    CHECK (markings_description IS NOT NULL)
```

It's probably better to define NOT NULL constraints in the normal fashion, using the NOT NULL keywords in the column definition.

Check constraints do have a place, though, as they allow you to define other useful conditions. Take the relationship between birth and death dates, for example. Most animals are born *before* they die. You can require that behavior by defining the following constraint:

```
CREATE TABLE aquatic_animal (
...
CONSTRAINT death_after_birth
       CHECK (death_date > birth_date),
...
```

Whenever a row is inserted into the AQUATIC_ANIMAL table, or whenever a row is updated, Oracle will evaluate the condition specified by the constraint. If the condition evaluates to TRUE (or to UNKNOWN), Oracle will allow the insert or update to occur.

When one of the columns in a check expression is null, that will cause the expression to evaluate to UNKNOWN, and Oracle will consider the constraint to be satisfied. The exception to this is when you explicitly write the expression to check for null values using IS NULL, IS NOT NULL, NVL, or some other construct designed to evaluate nulls.

Using Schema Manager to create a table

Rather than type a long command to create a table, you can use Enterprise Manager's Schema Manager to create a table using a GUI interface. To create a table using Schema Manager, follow these steps:

1. Run Schema Manager and connect to the database.

2. Right-click the Tables folder and select Create from the pop-up menu. See Figure 13-1.

   A Create Table window opens, and its tabbed interface allows you to enter the information needed to create the table.

3. Define the table's columns on the General tab.

   Figure 13-2 shows this tab filled out for the AQUATIC_ANIMALS table.

4. Switch to the Constraints tab and define the table's constraints.

5. Enter storage options and other options using the Storage and Options Tabs.

6. Click the Create button when you are ready to actually create the table.

The Schema Manager interface is fairly intuitive and easy to use. It functions just like any of the other Enterprise Manager applications. If you like, you can click the Show SQL button and watch Schema Manager build your CREATE TABLE statement for you as you fill in the tabs.

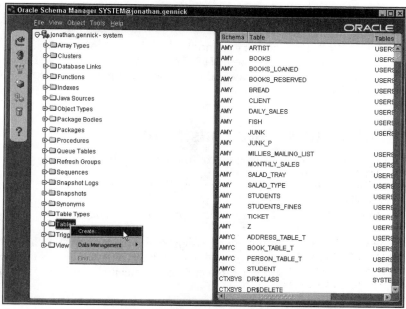

Figure 13-1: Creating a table in the Schema Manager window

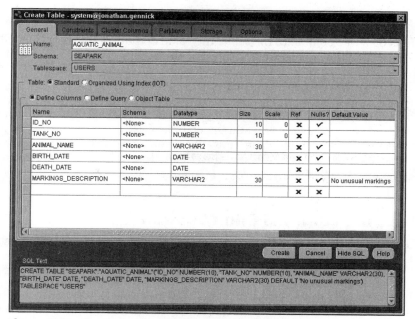

Figure 13-2: The General tab in the Create Table window

Altering Tables

From time to time, it's necessary to modify a table that you have created. In most cases, you will be able to use the ALTER TABLE command to make the changes that you need; however, you may find that some changes require you to drop and re-create the table.

Adding columns and constraints

You can easily add columns or constraints to a table by using the ALTER TABLE command as follows:

```
ALTER TABLE table_name
    ADD (column_or_constraint [,column_or_constraint...]);
```

The syntax you can use for columns or constraints that you wish to add to a table is identical to the syntax you use for creating a table. The following example adds a SEX column to the AQUATIC_ANIMAL table and constrains it to values of 'M' and 'F':

```
ALTER TABLE aquatic_animal
    ADD (animal_sex            CHAR,
        CONSTRAINT animal_sex_mf
            CHECK (animal_sex IN ('M','F'))
        );
```

When you add a column to the table, the value of that column is set to null for all rows that are currently in the table. For this reason, you can never add a new column with a NOT NULL constraint to a table that contains data. The very act of adding the column causes the constraint to be violated.

Another issue to be aware of is that if you add a column and specify a default value for the column at the time you add the column, Oracle will populate every row in the table with that default value. However, if you alter the table to add the column, and then alter the table and modify the column to add a default value, Oracle will only use the default value for rows added after that point.

Dropping columns and constraints

You can use the ALTER TABLE DROP command to drop columns and constraints. The syntax is slightly different for columns than it is for constraints.

Note   The option of dropping a column is new with Oracle8i.

Dropping a Constraint

To drop a constraint, issue a command like this:

```
ALTER TABLE aquatic_animal
    DROP CONSTRAINT animal_sex_mf;
```

If you are dropping a primary key constraint or a unique key constraint and you have foreign key constraints that refer to the constraint that you are dropping, Oracle will disallow the drop unless you specify the CASCADE option. The following example demonstrates this option:

```
ALTER TABLE tank
    DROP CONSTRAINT tank_pk CASCADE;
```

Using the CASCADE option causes Oracle to drop not only the constraint that you named, in this case TANK_PK, but also any foreign key constraints that refer to it.

Dropping a Column

With the release of Oracle8i, Oracle implemented a feature long awaited by Oracle DBAs everywhere—the ability to drop a column from a table. Previously, the only way to do that was to drop the entire table and re-create it from scratch—a process made tedious by the need to save and restore the data, as well as by the need to disable and reenable constraints that referenced the table. Now, dropping a column is as simple as issuing a command like this:

```
ALTER TABLE aquatic_animal
    DROP COLUMN animal_sex;
```

Tip Use care when dropping a column on a large table. Oracle actually reads each row in the table and removes the column from each one. On a large table, that can be a time-consuming process.

If you want to drop a column in a hurry and you don't want to take the time to remove it from all the rows in the table, you can mark the column unused and delete it later. The command to mark a column unused is as follows:

```
ALTER TABLE aquatic_animal
    SET UNUSED (animal_sex);
```

Once you've marked a column as unused, it appears for all practical purposes as if the column is really gone. The only difference between setting a column unused and actually dropping the column is that the unused column still takes up space.

Note It's not easy to see the space freed by dropping a column. That's because the number of database blocks that the table uses doesn't change. Space is freed within the individual blocks, but the table as a whole is not compacted.

When you want to actually drop columns that you have marked as unused, you can issue a command like this:

```
ALTER TABLE aquatic_animal
    DROP UNUSED COLUMNS;
```

This command causes Oracle to go through and actually drop any columns that have been set unused.

Modifying columns

You can modify existing columns by issuing an ALTER TABLE MODIFY command and writing new column definitions for the columns that you want to change. For example, the following command changes the length of the ANIMAL_NAME column in the AQUATIC_ANIMAL table from its original maximum of 30 characters to a new maximum of 60 characters:

```
ALTER TABLE aquatic_animal
    MODIFY (animal_name    VARCHAR2(60));
```

You can use the same technique to add default values and constraints, such as a NOT NULL constraint, to the column.

Working with existing data

When you make changes to a table that contains existing data, you can run into a number of problems, including the following:

✦ The inability to add NOT NULL columns

✦ Incompatible datatypes when changing a column definition

✦ Preexisting records that violate foreign key constraints that you are trying to add

✦ Duplicate records that violate primary constraints that you are trying to add

Creating NOT NULL Columns

If you need to add a NOT NULL column to a table that already contains data, you can do so by breaking the task down into three steps:

1. Add the column without a NOT NULL constraint. Oracle will do this, and all existing rows will have the value for that column set to null.

2. Issue an UPDATE statement on the table that sets the column to a non-null value.

3. Modify the table and apply the NOT NULL constraint to the column.

Step 2 in this process requires some thought. You need some way to determine what the appropriate non-null value is for each row in the table. This may be a trivial task, and it may not be. You may find that step 2 becomes a significant process in its own right.

Working with Incompatible Datatypes

Sometimes you want to modify the datatype of a column, and the target datatype isn't compatible with the original. For example, Oracle won't let you convert a NUMBER column to a VARCHAR2 column when that column contains data. Oracle will, however, let you freely change datatypes on empty columns (that is, when all values are null). This leads to the following possible approach of changing a column's datatype.

1. Create a temporary table with the column defined as you want it to be, using the new datatype. The temporary table should include all the primary key columns as well, from the table that you are changing. For example, if you need to change the AQUATIC_ANIMAL table's TANK_NO field to a character string, you can create this working table:

```
CREATE TABLE aquatic_animal_work (
    ID_NO     NUMBER(10),
    TANK_NO   VARCHAR2(10));
```

2. Execute an INSERT statement that copies data from the table being changed to the work table. Code this INSERT statement to explicitly convert the column that you are changing. Consider this example:

```
INSERT INTO aquatic_animal_work
    SELECT id_no, TRIM(TO_CHAR(tank_no))
    FROM aquatic_animal;
```

3. Set the column that you are changing to null. Do this for all rows in the table. Consider this example:

```
UPDATE aquatic_animal
SET tank_no = NULL;
```

4. Modify the column, changing the datatype to what you want it to be. Oracle should allow this because the column contains no data. Consider this example:

```
ALTER TABLE aquatic_animal
MODIFY (tank_no   VARCHAR2(10));
```

5. Move the saved column data from the work table back into the original table. Use the primary key to make sure that you get the correct value back in each row. Consider this example:

```
UPDATE aquatic_animal aa
SET tank_no = (SELECT tank_no
               FROM aquatic_animal_work aaw
               WHERE aaw.tank_no = aa.tank_no);
```

6. Drop the work table.

One critical point about using this approach is that you must do this when users are not accessing the table that you are changing.

Resolving Duplicate Primary or Unique Keys

If you are attempting to add a primary or unique key constraint to a table, and the existing data contains duplicate occurrences of the key values, you will receive an error like this one:

```
ORA-02437: cannot validate (SEAPARK.TANK_PK) - primary key violated
```

To resolve this issue, your first task is to get a list of offending rows. You can do that with a query like the following, which lists cases in the TANK table where two rows have the same tank number:

```
SELECT t1.tank_no, t1.tank_name
FROM tank t1
WHERE EXISTS (
    SELECT t2.tank_no
    FROM tank t2
    WHERE t2.tank_no = t1.tank_no
    GROUP BY t2.tank_no
    HAVING COUNT(*) > 1)
ORDER BY t1.tank_no;
```

Your next problem is deciding what to do with the duplicate rows. If they are truly duplicates, or if you are dealing with test data, you can do a mass delete by issuing a statement like the following:

```
DELETE
FROM tank t1
WHERE EXISTS (
    SELECT t2.tank_no
    FROM tank t2
    WHERE t2.tank_no = t1.tank_no
    GROUP BY t2.tank_no
    HAVING COUNT(*) > 1)
AND ROWID NOT IN (
    SELECT MIN(ROWID)
    FROM tank t3
    WHERE t3.tank_no = t1.tank_no);
```

You can depend on the ROWID psuedo-column to be unique for each record in the table, even if all the other columns are identical. This makes it useful for picking the one row to save out of each set of duplicates. The previous query arbitrarily chooses to save the row with the minimum ROWID value.

Another approach to this problem is to create an exceptions table, and use the EXCEPTIONS INTO clause with the constraint definition to cause Oracle to populate the exceptions table with the rowids of records that violate the constraint. You can then work from that table to resolve the exceptions. Consider this example that shows how to use this technique:

```
ALTER TABLE aquatic_animal
    ADD ( CONSTRAINT tank_no_uk
            UNIQUE (tank_no)
            EXCEPTIONS INTO exceptions);
```

The attempt to add this constraint to the `aquatic_animal` table will fail because there are many animals in each tank. If even one row fails to meet the condition specified by the constraint, Oracle will not add it. However, since the `EXCEPTIONS INTO` clause is used, Oracle will write the `rowids` of the offending rows into the table named exceptions. You can query the exceptions table, and join it to the `aquatic_animal` table, to see the list of rows that caused this constraint to fail. Consider this example:

```
SELECT id_no, tank_no, animal_name
FROM aquatic_animal, exceptions
WHERE exceptions.row_id = aquatic_animal.rowid
AND exceptions.table_name = 'AQUATIC_ANIMAL'
AND exceptions.constraint = 'TANK_NO_UK';
```

The exceptions table must be in a specific format. You can create it using an Oracle-supplied script named utlexcpt1.sql (utlexcpt.sql for releases prior to 8i), which you will find in the $ORACLE_HOME/rdbms/admin directory.

Resolving Nonexistent Foreign Keys

If you are trying to add a foreign key constraint to a table and parent keys don't exist for some of the records, you will get an error message like this:

```
ORA-02298: cannot validate (SEAPARK.ASSIGNED_TANK_FK) - parent keys not found
```

To find the offending rows, you can issue a query like this one:

```
SELECT id_no, tank_no
FROM aquatic_animal
WHERE NOT EXISTS (
    SELECT *
    FROM tank
    WHERE tank.tank_no = aquatic_animal.tank_no);
```

This query returns a list of all `AQUATIC_ANIMAL` records with tank numbers that don't exist in the `TANK` table.

Note

The sample data, as created, does not contain any orphan tank numbers in the `AQUATIC_ANIMAL` **table. If you want to execute this query and see results, delete one of the tank records first.**

Of course, once you find the offending records, you have to decide what to do with them. That's the tough part. If you didn't care about them, you could convert the previous SELECT statement into a DELETE statement and delete them. A more reasonable approach might be to go in and correct them.

Changing storage parameters

When it comes to changing how the data for a table is physically stored, about the only way that you can make any significant changes is to drop and re-create the table. That makes sense when you begin to think about it. If, for example, you want to move a table's data from the USERS tablespace to a new tablespace named SEAPARK_DATA, you need to read the data from one tablespace and reinsert it into the other. No matter how you cut it, changing the way data is stored involves reading it and writing it back again.

If you need to make a significant change, such as moving a table from one tablespace to another, you can do so by following these steps:

1. Export the table. For more information about the Export utility, see Chapter 8, "Using Oracle8i's Export Utility."

2. Use the DROP TABLE statement to drop the table, including any constraints that reference the table.

3. Re-create the table, and don't forget to re-create foreign key constraints on other tables that reference the one that you are reorganizing.

4. Use the Import utility, with the IGNORE=Y option, to reload the table's data from the export file you created in step 1. For more information about the Import utility, see Chapter 9, "Using Oracle8i's Import Utility." You may also want to specify INDEXES=N so that you can re-create the indexes yourself after the import. That will generally give you better performance.

5. Re-create any indexes on the table. These will have been dropped when the table was dropped.

With large tables, this process can take some time. During the time that you are reorganizing the table, it won't be available to database users. This underscores the need for careful planning when you create your tables so that you don't need to reorganize them often.

Deleting Tables

When you no longer need a table, you can delete it using the DROP TABLE command. The syntax is simple and looks like this:

```
DROP TABLE [schema.]tablename [CASCADE CONSTRAINTS];
```

The CASCADE CONSTRAINTS option is necessary only if other tables have foreign key constraints that refer to the table you are dropping. The following example shows the AQUATIC_ANIMAL table being dropped:

```
SQL> DROP TABLE aquatic_animal CASCADE CONSTRAINTS;

Table dropped.
```

Of course, once a table is dropped, the data that it contained is gone too.

Using the Data Dictionary

The easiest way to look at the definition of a table is to use Schema Manager. Schema Manager's GUI interface allows you to easily browse column definitions, constraint definitions, and other information for any table in the database.

The SQL*Plus DESCRIBE command is also useful for viewing information about a table. Unlike Schema Manager, DESCRIBE tells you only about columns, their datatypes, and whether they can be null. The DESCRIBE command doesn't provide information about constraints, default values, or storage parameters. The following example shows the output that you get from DESCRIBE:

```
SQL> DESCRIBE aquatic_animal
 Name                             Null?     Type
 ------------------------------   --------  -------------
 ID_NO                            NOT NULL  NUMBER(10)
 TANK_NO                                    NUMBER(10)
 ANIMAL_NAME                                VARCHAR2(30)
 BIRTH_DATE                                 DATE
 DEATH_DATE                                 DATE
 MARKINGS_DESCRIPTION                       VARCHAR2(30)
```

If you don't have Schema Manager and you need more information than the DESCRIBE command provides, you can query Oracle's data dictionary views. In this section, you'll see how to use the following four views:

✦ DBA_TABLES. Returns information about each table in the database

✦ DBA_CONSTRAINTS. Returns information about constraints defined on a table

✦ DBA_TAB_COLUMNS. Returns information about the columns in a table

✦ DBA_CONS_COLUMNS. Returns information about the columns in a constraint

Typically, only database administrators have access to the DBA views because these views list information about every object in the database. If you aren't the DBA, you can replace DBA in the view names with either ALL or USER. For example, ALL_TABLES returns information about all tables that you have access to, and USER_TABLES returns information about all tables that you own.

Listing tables for a user

You can get a list of tables owned by any user in the database by querying the
DBA_TABLES view. The DBA_TABLES view returns one row for each table in the
database. The following query, executed from SQL*Plus, returns a list of all tables
owned by SEAPARK:

```
SELECT table_name
FROM dba_tables
WHERE owner = 'SEAPARK'
ORDER BY table_name;
```

In addition to table names, you can also use the DBA_TABLES view to get information
about a table's storage parameters, including its tablespace assignment.

Listing constraints on a table

The DBA_CONSTRAINTS view is quite useful because it provides information on the
constraints defined for a table. There are four types of constraints, and you can use
three different queries to see them. Primary and unique keys are similar enough
that the same query works for both.

Check Constraints

Check constraints are the easiest to list because you can get everything you need
from one view. The following query displays all the check constraints defined on
the AQUATIC_ANIMAL table:

```
SELECT constraint_name,
       search_condition
FROM dba_constraints
WHERE owner = 'SEAPARK'
AND table_name = 'AQUATIC_ANIMAL'
AND constraint_type = 'C';
```

This query lists both the name of the constraint and the expression that must be
satisfied. The SEARCH_CONDITION column returns the check expression. A constraint
type of 'C' indicates that the constraint is a check constraint.

Primary and Unique Key Constraints

Returning information about primary key and unique key constraints is a bit more
difficult than for check constraints because you have to join two views to get the
list columns involved in the constraints. Primary key constraints are identified by a
type of 'P', while unique key constraints have a type of 'U'. The following query
lists primary and unique key constraints for the AQUATIC_ANIMAL table:

```
SELECT c.constraint_name,
       c.constraint_type,
       cc.column_name
```

```
FROM dba_constraints c,
     dba_cons_columns cc
WHERE c.owner='SEAPARK'
AND c.table_name = 'AQUATIC_ANIMAL'
AND c.owner = cc.owner
AND c.constraint_name = cc.constraint_name
AND c.constraint_type IN ('P','U')
ORDER BY c.constraint_type,
         c.constraint_name,
         cc.position;
```

The ORDER BY clause is necessary. This query will return one row for each column in a constraint. Sorting on the constraint name causes all columns for a constraint to be listed together. Further sorting by the POSITION field is done to get the columns to list in the proper order. The DECODE at the beginning of the ORDER BY clause is optional and causes any primary key constraint to be listed first, before any unique key constraints.

Foreign Key Constraints

Foreign key constraints are the most difficult to query for. Not only must you list the columns involved in the constraint, but you must also join DBA_CONS_COLUMNS to itself to determine the parent table and the matching list of columns in the parent table. Foreign key constraints are identified by a type code of 'R'. The query shown in Listing 13-3 lists all foreign key constraints defined on the AQUATIC_ANIMAL table.

Listing 13-3: **Listing a table's foreign key constraints**

```
SELECT c.constraint_name,
       cc.column_name,
       rcc.owner,
       rcc.table_name,
       rcc.column_name
FROM dba_constraints c,
     dba_cons_columns cc,
     dba_cons_columns rcc
 WHERE c.owner='SEAPARK'
AND c.table_name = 'AQUATIC_ANIMAL'
AND c.constraint_type = 'R'
AND c.owner = cc.owner
AND c.constraint_name = cc.constraint_name
AND c.r_owner = rcc.owner
AND c.r_constraint_name = rcc.constraint_name
AND cc.position = rcc.position
ORDER BY c.constraint_name, cc.position;
```

The results are sorted by constraint name and column position so that the columns will be listed in the proper order.

Listing the columns in a table

The DBA_CONS_COLUMNS view returns information about the columns in a table. It's the same view that SQL*Plus queries when you issue the DESCRIBE command. For the most part, you're better off using DESCRIBE than trying to query this view. The exception to that is if you need to see the default value for a column. The DESCRIBE command won't provide you with that information. The following query lists all columns in the AQUATIC_ANIMAL table that have default values defined, and it shows you what those default values are:

```
SELECT column_name, data_default
FROM dba_tab_columns
WHERE owner = 'SEAPARK'
AND table_name = 'AQUATIC_ANIMAL'
AND data_default IS NOT NULL;
```

The DATA_DEFAULT column is a LONG column, which allows for values up to 2GB in size. By default, SQL*Plus will display only the first 80 characters. If you are dealing with long strings, you can issue the SET LONG command to increase the number of displayed characters. For example, SET LONG 160 causes SQL*Plus to display the first 160 characters of each LONG value.

Summary

In this chapter, you learned:

- ✦ Tables are composed of columns and constraints. Columns define what a table can store, while constraints help prevent the introduction of invalid data.

- ✦ Oracle supports a number of datatypes. The most common scaler types are NUMBER, VARCHAR2, DATE, and CHAR.

- ✦ Use the CREATE TABLE statement to create a new table. Be sure to specify a tablespace and to define a primary key.

- ✦ Oracle uses indexes to enforce primary key and unique key constraints. Be sure to assign these indexes to a tablespace when creating these types of constraints.

- ✦ To modify a table, use the ALTER TABLE command. Changing physical storage parameters may require a full export and import of the table. If the table contains data, you may have to work around that data to make your changes.

✦ If you don't have Enterprise Manager installed, you can still get information about a table from Oracle's data dictionary views. The DBA_CONSTRAINTS and DBA_CONS_COLUMNS views provide information about table constraints. The DBA_TABLES and DBA_TAB_COLUMNS views provide information about table and column definitions.

✦ If you are not the DBA, you won't have access to the DBA views. Use ALL_TABLES, ALL_TAB_COLUMNS, ALL_CONSTRAINTS, and ALL_CONS_COLUMNS instead.

✦   ✦   ✦

Managing Indexes

Indexes are structures that allow you to quickly access rows in a table based on the value of one or more columns in that table. You use indexes for two primary purposes:

✦ **Faster queries.** Indexing columns frequently referenced in queries helps Oracle retrieve data at maximum speed.

✦ **Unique values.** Oracle automatically generates an index to enforce unique values in the primary key of a table. You can also use this feature for any other column (or set of columns) that you require to be unique.

Like anything else in life, using an index involves some tradeoffs. When you create an index, you are trading disk space and increased insert, update, and delete time in return for faster query response. Indexes require overhead during inserts and updates because the index needs to be updated in response to new rows, or to changes in indexed columns in existing rows. Even when deleting a row, you must take the time to remove that row's entry from the index.

Indexes also require disk space. The columns to be indexed must be reproduced as part of the index. If you have many indexes on a table, it's possible that the total space the indexes use will exceed the space the table itself uses.

In this chapter, you'll read about the different types of indexes that Oracle supports. You'll see how to create them, how to reorganize them, and how to drop them. You'll also learn about the data dictionary views that you can use to retrieve information about indexes.

Understanding Index Types

Oracle8i supports two fundamental types of indexes: B*Tree indexes and bitmapped indexes. B*Tree indexes have been around for years, and they are the most commonly used indexes. Bitmapped indexes are relatively new, and they were introduced as a data-warehousing feature.

Using B*Tree indexes

The most common type of index used is the B*Tree index, which uses an inverted tree structure to speed access to rows in a table. Figure 14-1 illustrates this structure.

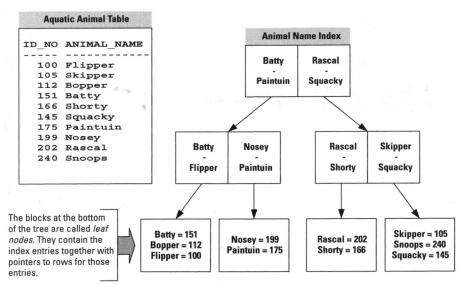

Figure 14-1: An example of the inverted tree structure used by B*Tree indexes

When you query for a particular value, Oracle navigates down through the tree to the leaf node containing the entry you are after. That entry contains a pointer to the row in the table. B*Tree indexes have several characteristics that make them a good choice for most uses:

✦ They maintain the sort order of the data, making it easy to look up a range of records. For example, you might want to find all animals whose names begin with "S."

✦ With multicolumn indexes, you can use the leading-edge columns to resolve a query, even if that query doesn't reference *all* columns in the index.

✦ They automatically stay balanced, at least they are supposed to, with all leaf nodes at the same depth, so the time you need to retrieve one entry is consistent for all entries in the index.

✦ Performance remains relatively constant, even as the size of the indexed table grows.

Within the B*Tree structure, you have some flexibility in how the index operates. When you create a B*Tree index, you can choose from among these two options:

REVERSE	Reverses the bytes in each index entry. The name Justin, for example, can be indexed as nitsuJ. If Oracle Parallel Server is being used, and primary keys are being generated from a numeric sequence, reversing the index can help prevent multiple instances from competing for the same index blocks.
UNIQUE	Requires that each index entry be unique. This also inherently prevents two rows in the underlying table from having the same value for the indexed columns. Oracle normally uses unique indexes to enforce primary key constraints.

The REVERSE option is compatible with UNIQUE. The default, if you choose neither option, is for the index to be stored unreversed, and for it to allow multiple entries for the same value.

Using bitmapped indexes

Bitmapped indexes were introduced in Oracle8. You can use them to index columns that contain a relatively small number of distinct values. Bitmapped indexes always contain one entry for each row in the table. The size of the entry depends on the number of distinct values in the column you are indexing. Figure 14-2 shows a conceptual view of two bitmapped indexes: In one, you see Yes and No columns, and in another, you see state abbreviation columns.

Bitmapped indexes are very compact because they are composed of long strings of bits. The bit-string for one value in a million-row table would take up only around 122KB. Oracle can quickly scan that bit-string for rows that match the criteria specified in a query. Bitmapped indexes really shine when you can use several together to resolve a query. Consider the following SELECT statement:

```
SELECT *
FROM employee
WHERE retired = 'Y'
AND state = 'MI';
```

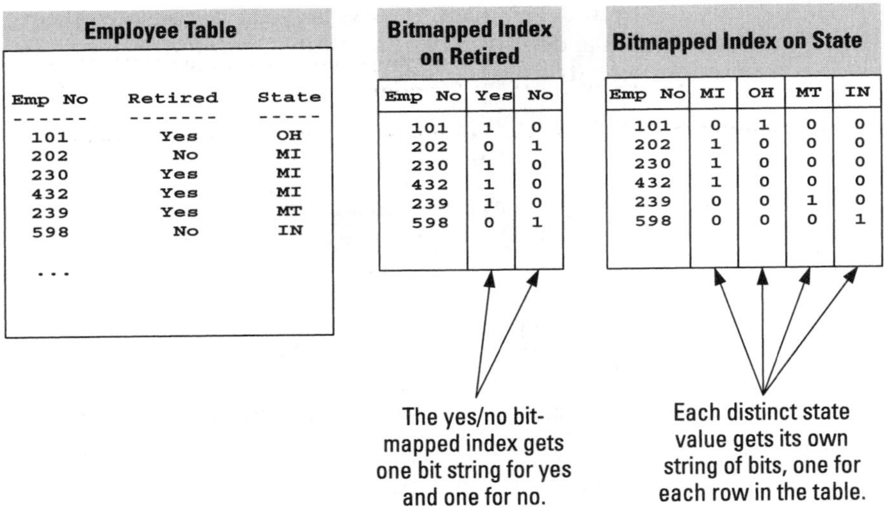

Figure 14-2: A conceptual view of a bitmapped index

With bitmapped indexes on both the RETIRED column and the STATE column, as shown in Figure 14-2, Oracle can easily retrieve the bitmaps for Y and for MI, and then *and* them together. Oracle *ands* two bitmaps by merging them into one bitmap that flags rows that meet the condition represented by both of the original bitmaps. Table 14-1 provides an example.

Table 14-1
Anding Two Bitmaps Together

RETIRED = Y	STATE = MI	Anded Result
1	0	0
0	1	0
1	1	1
1	1	1
1	0	0
0	0	0

Anding two bit streams is a logic operation that most computers can do extremely quickly. Oracle can then use the resulting bitmap to identify those rows that match all the criteria.

As great as bitmapped indexes are, they do have some disadvantages. They were designed for query-intensive databases, so you shouldn't use them in online transaction processing (OLTP) systems. They aren't good for range queries, and you shouldn't use them for columns that contain more than just a few distinct values. Creating a bitmapped index on a name column would be a poor choice. The greater the number of distinct values in a column, the less efficient bitmapped indexing becomes.

Note   Bitmapped indexes are available only in Oracle Enterprise Edition.

Creating an Index

Indexes are created using the `CREATE INDEX` statement. When you create an index, you need to specify the table on which the index is to be built. After identifying the table, you should also consider the following questions:

- ✦ Which columns should be part of the index?
- ✦ Should the index be B*Tree or bitmapped?
- ✦ Should the index be unique?
- ✦ Should the `REVERSE` option be used?
- ✦ In what tablespace should the index be stored?

Once you have answered these questions, you are ready to create the index using Schema Manager, or by executing a `CREATE INDEX` command from SQL*Plus.

Choosing the columns for an index

Most of the time, you choose the columns for an index because you are using them in the `WHERE` clause of queries that you write. However, there are times when you might want to add columns to an index that aren't used in a `WHERE` clause, or when you want to exclude some that are. Suppose that you have the following table, which contains both a first and last name column, in your database:

```
CREATE TABLE employee (
   last_name       VARCHAR2(30),
   first_name      VARCHAR2(30),
   department_no   NUMBER
);
```

Further suppose that you are running an application that frequently queries for employees based on their first and last names. Perhaps the application uses a query like this:

```
SELECT last_name, first_name, department_no
FROM employee
WHERE last_name = 'Burgers'
AND first_name = 'Jenny';
```

At first glance, you might think to create an index on both the first and last name columns. However, if you think more about it, you may have only a few employees with any given last name. By creating the index on last name only, you cut the space required by the index in half. The tradeoff is increased I/O. If three people have the same last name, Oracle will need to follow each of the three index entries to the table, retrieve the row, and then check the first name. Sometimes this tradeoff is worth making, and sometimes it isn't. You may need to experiment a bit to be sure.

Rather than cutting fields from an index, another strategy is to add more fields than are required. Let's assume that your application allows queries based only on the last name, and that it always issues SQL statements like this: *I/O ⇆ disk space*

```
SELECT last_name, first_name, department_no
FROM employee
WHERE last_name LIKE 'Nue%';
```

Further, assume that once this query is executed, the name and department number of each matching employee will be listed on a screen from which you can choose the specific employee that you want. Which index would you create to support this query? The obvious answer is to create an index on last name. However, you might gain some efficiency in terms of response time if you create the following index instead:

```
CREATE INDEX emp_name_dept ON employee (
  last_name,
  first_name,
  department_no
);
```

Why place all three columns in the index when the query bases its search on only one? Doing so allows Oracle to retrieve from the index all the data that the query requires. Instead of reading each index entry and following it back to the table to get the first name and department number, Oracle can just get all three values from the index. The tradeoff here is more disk space for the index in return for the potentially faster response time.

Tip   No hard and fast rules exist for making these types of choices. The best strategy is to develop some relevant metrics, measure the performance that you get with different types of indexes, and compare that to the disk space that they use. Base your decision on those numbers.

Note You cannot index LONG or LONG RAW columns.

Choosing the index type

You've already read about the differences between bitmapped and B*Tree indexes. You've also learned about reversed indexes and unique indexes. Follow these guidelines to make the appropriate choice from among those options:

✦ Use unique indexes only when you need to enforce a business rule requiring unique values in a column.

✦ Consider the REVERSE option when you have large numbers of index entries all starting with the same characters and when reversing those characters would eliminate that clustering. The classic example of when to use a reversed index is when you are indexing a numeric column that is sequentially incremented each time a row is added to the database.

✦ Do not use the REVERSE option if you are querying for ranges of data. The reversed index entries randomize the location of entries. To find a specific range of values requires the entire index to be scanned.

✦ Consider bitmapped indexes for columns containing a low number of distinct values — a Yes or No type of column, for example — and where the primary use of the table is for query purposes (that is, few updates).

If you are uncertain about which choice to make, stick with the plain-vanilla, nonunique, nonreversed B*Tree index.

Using SQL to create an index

The SQL statement for creating an index is CREATE INDEX. You can issue it from SQL*Plus, Server Manager, or any other suitable tool. The following example shows a standard B*Tree index being created on the CHECKUP_HISTORY table. The UNIQUE keyword is used because two checkups on the same date should really be treated as one.

```
CREATE UNIQUE INDEX animal_checkup_history
ON checkup_history (
    id_no,
    checkup_date
) TABLESPACE indx;
```

If you were creating this index, and you didn't want it to be unique, you would just leave the keyword UNIQUE out of the command. To make it a reverse index, you can add the keyword REVERSE immediately following the tablespace name.

The CHECKUP_TYPE field in the CHECKUP_HISTORY table is a good candidate for a bitmapped index. This field is a foreign key to the CHECKUP table, and contains only the three distinct values ANNUAL, MONTHLY, and DAILY. You can create a bitmapped index on that column using this command:

```
CREATE BITMAP INDEX checkup_history_type
ON checkup_history (
    checkup_type
) TABLESPACE indx;
```

Bitmapped indexes may not be unique, so you can't combine the two types.

The NOLOGGING Option

The NOLOGGING option specifies to create the index without logging the index creation work to the database redo log files. The NOLOGGING option goes into the CREATE INDEX command, as shown in this example:

```
CREATE UNIQUE INDEX animal_checkup_history
ON checkup_history (
    id_no,
    checkup_date
) TABLESPACE indx
    NOLOGGING;
```

The advantage of using the NOLOGGING option is greater speed, which results from not having to write the index data out to the redo log. The risk you are taking is that if you lose some of your database files because of a disk failure and you have to recover those files, the index won't be recovered. That's a pretty small risk, because you can always create the index again. You just have to remember to do that.

The NOSORT Option

If you've just loaded a large table, say using SQL*Loader, and you know for a fact that all the rows were presorted on the same columns that you are indexing, you can create the index using the NOSORT option. Consider this example:

```
CREATE UNIQUE INDEX animal_checkup_history
ON checkup_history (
    id_no,
    checkup_date
) TABLESPACE indx
    NOSORT;
```

The NOSORT option does exactly what its name implies. Normally, when you create an index, Oracle sorts the table based on the index columns. When you use NOSORT, Oracle skips the sort step and assumes that the data in the table is ordered correctly to start with. Needless to say, skipping the sort can save you significant time. If, while creating the index, Oracle discovers that the rows in the table are in fact not presorted, the operation will abort, and you will have to create the index in the usual manner.

The ONLINE Option

Normally, when you create an index, Oracle places a lock on the table being indexed to prevent users from changing any of the data within that table. As you might imagine, if the indexing operation takes any amount of time, the users of that table will be inconvenienced. Oracle8i implements a new feature allowing you to create indexes in a way that leaves the table available for use. To take advantage of this feature, add the ONLINE keyword to your CREATE command, as shown here:

```
CREATE UNIQUE INDEX animal_checkup_history
ON checkup_history (
    id_no,
    checkup_date
) TABLESPACE indx
    ONLINE;
```

You can't create all indexes while the table remains online. Whether you can use ONLINE depends on the exact mix of options that you are using when you create the index.

table statistics
index statistics

The COMPUTE STATISTICS Option

If you are using the cost-based query optimizer, it's important to maintain current statistics on database objects such as tables and indexes. Index statistics provide Oracle with information on the number of distinct index entries, the total number of leaf blocks, the average number of data blocks per key, and so forth. This information is critical to the optimizer, relative to determining the most efficient way to execute a query.

Cross-Reference
You'll learn more about how the optimizer works in Chapter 19, "Tuning SQL Statements."

Index statistics aren't maintained automatically. You have to periodically regenerate them using ANALYZE TABLE commands.

Cross-Reference
Chapter 18, "Optimizers and Statistics," talks more about the importance of doing this.

Generating statistics via the ANALYZE command uses a significant amount of CPU and I/O resources. You end up reading through either the entire index or at least a significant part of it. When you create a new index, however, you have a perfect opportunity to sidestep this overhead by combining the generation of the statistics with the creation of the index. To do that, use the COMPUTE STATISTICS keyword in your CREATE command, as shown here:

```
CREATE UNIQUE INDEX animal_checkup_history
ON checkup_history (
    id_no,
    checkup_date
) TABLESPACE indx
    COMPUTE STATISTICS;
```

(Nologging)
(Nosort)
✗ online

There is one disadvantage to the COMPUTE STATISTICS option, and that is that you can't mix it with the ONLINE option.

Using function-based indexes

Function-based indexes are an exciting new feature in Oracle8i. Rather than indexing based just on the column contents, you can create an index on the result of an expression applied to the column. One use for this is to create indexes to support case-insensitive queries. The following command creates a function-based index on the ANIMAL_NAME column of the AQUATIC_ANIMAL table:

```
CREATE INDEX animal_name_upper
ON aquatic_animal (
   UPPER(animal_name)
) TABLESPACE indx
   NOLOGGING;
```

Note   To create function-based indexes, you must have the QUERY REWRITE system privilege.

Once you've created an index such as the one shown previously, you can place the function call UPPER(animal_name) in the WHERE clause of a SELECT statement, and Oracle will be able to use the function-based index ANIMAL_NAME_UPPER to resolve the query. Without a function-based index, wrapping a function around a column name in the WHERE clause of a query would prevent any index on that column from ever being used.

Using Enterprise Manager to create an index

If you have Enterprise Manager installed, you can use Schema Manager to create your indexes. Schema Manager provides a convenient graphical user interface. To create an index using Schema Manager, follow these steps:

1. Start Schema Manager and log on to the database.

2. Right-click the Indexes folder and select Create from the pop-up menu. See Figure 14-3.

3. Fill in the Create Index form that appears.

   Figure 14-4 shows you a completed General tab in the Create Index dialog box to create the ANIMAL_CHECKUP_HISTORY index shown in the previous section.

4. Click the Create button.

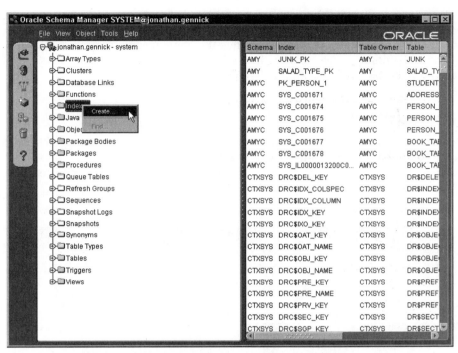

Figure 14-3: Selecting the Create option to create a new index

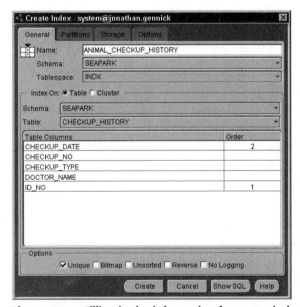

Figure 14-4: Filling in the information for a new index

When you're selecting the columns to be included in an index, click those columns in the order in which you want them to appear. If you click the wrong column, or if you click a column out of order, just click the column again to deselect it. As you click each column to be included in the index, Schema Manager displays the order on the right-hand side of the Create Index dialog box.

Browsing indexes

You can easily browse indexes using Schema Manager and quickly get a look at the definitions for any that interest you. Do this by expanding the Indexes folder and drilling down to the schema of interest. Figure 14-5 illustrates using Schema Manager to list the indexes in the SEAPARK schema.

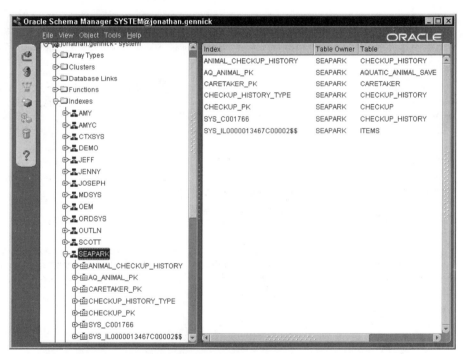

Figure 14-5: Listing the SEAPARK indexes

If a particular index interests you, click that index, and Schema Manager displays the details in the right pane of the window.

Altering an Index

You can change an index after you create it, but for the most part, you are limited to changing only its physical characteristics. You can't add columns to an index. To do that, you would have to drop the index and re-create it. However, Oracle does allow you to make the following changes:

✦ Move an index to another tablespace

✦ Rebuild an index using different storage parameters

✦ Rename an index

✦ De-allocate unused space

Many of the changes that you can make, such as relocating an index to another tablespace, actually require the complete re-creation of the index. However, Oracle automates the process and can often keep the index online and usable while the rebuild proceeds.

 Note   When Oracle rebuilds an index, it does so using only the information in the index. If the index is corrupt (missing a value or containing a pointer to a nonexistent row), the corruption will still exist in the rebuilt index.

Using SQL to alter an index

You can use the `ALTER INDEX` command to change an index. To rename an index, for example, issue a command like the following:

```
ALTER INDEX animal_checkup_history RENAME TO an_chk_hist;
```

You can make many of the physical changes by using the `REBUILD` clause. When you rebuild an index, Oracle re-creates the index from scratch by using a new set of storage parameters. The following example rebuilds the `animal_checkup_history` index by changing a number of parameters and settings:

```
ALTER INDEX animal_checkup_history REBUILD
   TABLESPACE users
   ONLINE
   NOLOGGING
   STORAGE (INITIAL 5K NEXT 5K);
```

Let's go through these clauses one by one:

✦ `ALTER INDEX animal_checkup_history REBUILD`—Specifies that you want to rebuild the index named `an_chk_hist`.

✦ `TABLESPACE users`—Creates the new version of the index in the tablespace named `USERS`.

✦ `ONLINE`—Specifies that you want users to be able to access the table while the rebuild is in progress.

Note You can't rebuild an index online if you are also using the COMPUTE STATISTICS or REVERSE clause. Bitmapped indexes cannot be rebuilt online either.

✦ NOLOGGING—Prevents Oracle from recording the rebuild in the redo log. This will speed the rebuild process (less I/O), but if you ever need to recover the database from a backup and roll forward through the changes, the index rebuild will not be included. Instead, you may need to manually rebuild the index again.

✦ STORAGE (INITIAL 5K NEXT 5K)—Specifies to allocate an initial extent of 5KB for the index. Subsequent extents will also be 5KB each. These values override the default settings for the tablespace in which the index is being created.

Certain types of changes are not allowed when the ONLINE option is requested. For example, you can't compute statistics during an online rebuild. If you try to do a rebuild online that Oracle doesn't support, you will get the following error:

```
ORA-08108: may not build or rebuild this type of index online
```

If you get an ORA-08108 error, you will have to rebuild the index offline. This means that no one will be able to insert, update, or delete from the table until the rebuild is finished.

Using Enterprise Manager to alter an index

You can use Enterprise Manager's Schema Manager to modify an index using a GUI interface. Schema Manager builds the necessary ALTER INDEX statement based on information that you provide and then executes it for you. To alter an index using Schema Manager, follow these steps:

1. Start Schema Manager and log on to the database.

2. Open the Indexes folder and navigate to the index that you want to change. Figure 14-6 shows the Indexes folder open to the ANIMAL_ CHECKUP_HISTORY index.

3. Right-click the index and select Edit from the pop-up menu.

   You will see the General tab in an Edit Indexes dialog box, which is similar to the Create Index dialog box shown in Figure 14-6.

4. Fill in the General tab's information.

   Figure 14-6 shows how you can fill in the information on this tab to create the ANIMAL_CHECKUP_HISTORY index shown in the previous section.

5. Go through the tabs and modify fields that you want to change. Dimmed fields indicate items that you can't change. Most of what you can change is on the Storage tab shown in Figure 14-7.

6. Click the Create button.

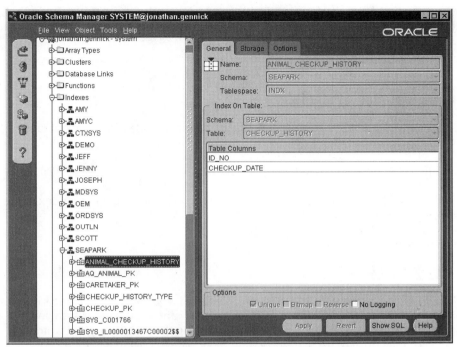

Figure 14-6: Selecting the ANIMAL_CHECKUP_HISTORY index

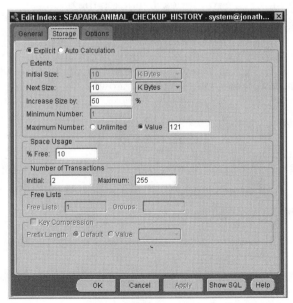

Figure 14-7: Using Schema Manager to change an Index's storage properties

One task that Schema Manager can't perform is to rebuild an index. To do that, you have to write the ALTER INDEX REBUILD statement yourself and submit it using SQL*Plus.

Deleting an Index

You can use the DROP INDEX command to delete an index from a database. Consider this example:

```
DROP INDEX animal_checkup_history;
```

In Schema Manager, you can drop an index by right-clicking on the index name and selecting Remove from the pop-up menu.

Listing Indexes

If you need to find out information about indexes, you can query Oracle's data dictionary. The data dictionary will tell you the names of the indexes in your database, the names of the columns that make up those indexes, and which options you chose to use when creating them. The following two data dictionary views are relevant to indexes:

DBA_INDEXES	Returns one row for each index in the database
DBA_IND_COLUMNS	Returns one row for each indexed column

If you don't have access to the DBA views, remember that you do have access to the ALL and USER views. The ALL_INDEXES view lists indexes on all tables to which you have access, and USER_INDEXES lists indexes that you own.

Listing indexes on a table

You can get a list of all the indexes defined for a table by querying DBA_INDEXES. The following query returns the index name and type and a flag indicating whether it is a unique index:

```
SELECT index_name, index_type, uniqueness
FROM DBA_INDEXES
WHERE table_owner = 'schema_name'
AND table_name = 'table_name';
```

If you don't have access to the DBA_INDEXES view, use ALL_INDEXES instead. The DBA_INDEXES view contains many more columns than those listed here. The contents of most columns are self-evident from the column names.

Listing the columns in an index

The DBA_IND_COLUMNS view, or ALL_IND_COLUMNS if you aren't the DBA, returns information about the columns that make up an index. The following query returns a list of columns for a given index:

```
SELECT column_name, column_position, descend
FROM dba_ind_columns
WHERE index_owner = 'schema_name'
AND index_name = 'index_name'
ORDER BY column_position;
```

You must order the results by COLUMN_POSITION to get them to list in the correct order. The DESCEND column tells you whether the index sorts a particular column in ascending order or descending order. Most indexes are sorted in ascending order.

Note

The COLUMN_NAME field in DBA_IND_COLUMNS is defined as a VARCHAR2(4000). That's rather wide. If you are executing a query from SQL*Plus that includes that column, you may want to enter a command like COLUMN COLUMN_NAME FORMAT A30 to set the display width to a more reasonable value, which in this case would be 30 characters.

Summary

In this chapter, you learned:

✦ Indexes on a database function like an index in a book: They speed your access to the data in a table.

✦ Oracle supports two types of indexes: B*Tree and bitmapped. B*Tree indexes are structured in an inverse tree and are good all-around choices. Bitmapped indexes excel when you are querying columns containing a small number of distinct values (a Yes or No column, for example).

✦ Function-based indexes, a new feature in Oracle8i, allow you to create indexes based on the result of an expression applied to a column. Queries that use the same expression in their WHERE clause can take advantage of these indexes.

✦ The DBA_INDEXES view returns information about the indexes in a database. DBA_IND_COLUMNS tells you which columns make up an index.

✦   ✦   ✦

Working with Views, Synonyms, and Sequences

Views, synonyms, and sequences are relatively minor objects in terms of the effort you must expend to create and manage them. *Views* are nothing more than stored SELECT statements. Once you create them, Oracle allows you to treat a view as if it were another table. *Synonyms* represent alternative names for a database object. The primary use of synonyms is to provide schema independence. *Sequences* are transaction-independent counters that are stored in the database and managed by Oracle. Their primary application is to generate unique keys for tables.

Views have applications for security and for convenience. In terms of security, views can limit the data that a user is allowed to see. In terms of convenience, views may encapsulate complex SQL needed for reporting, reducing the amount of complexity that goes into generating the reports. Synonyms allow users to access tables owned by an application schema without having to preface each table name with the schema name. This chapter discusses views, synonyms, and sequences, and explains why you use each type as well as how to create and manage them.

Managing Views

To create and manage views, you first need to know what a view is. It also helps to understand how and why views are used and why they are important. A view is a stored `SELECT` statement that presents data in a more convenient form than you might find in your tables. You can encapsulate complex SQL statements into a view, relieving users from having to write those statements themselves. Consider the following view on the `AQUATIC_ANIMAL` table:

```
CREATE OR REPLACE VIEW animals AS
   SELECT id_no,
          animal_name name,
          TO_CHAR(birth_date,'dd-Mon-yyyy') birth_date
FROM aquatic_animal
WHERE death_date IS NULL;
```

Consider this a convenience view. It limits the results to only those animals who are still alive. It formats the date field to use a four-digit year, and it simplifies the title of the `ANIMAL_NAME` column to just `NAME`. Here's what your output will look like when you select from this view:

```
SQL> select * FROM animals;

    ID_NO NAME                               BIRTH_DATE
--------- ------------------------------     ----------
      100 Flipper                            01-Feb-1968
      105 Skipper                            01-Jan-1978
      112 Bopper                             11-Mar-1990
```

What really happens when you select from a view like this? Let's say that you issue the following `SELECT` statement against the view:

```
SELECT *
FROM animals
WHERE name = 'Skipper';
```

From a conceptual standpoint, when you query a view, Oracle first executes the view's query and then executes your query against the results. It would be as if you had written a SQL statement like this:

```
SELECT *
FROM (
SELECT id_no,
          animal_name name,
          TO_CHAR(birth_date,'dd-Mon-yyyy') birth_date
FROM aquatic_animal
WHERE death_date IS NULL
)
WHERE name = 'Skipper';
```

Conceptually, this is what happens. In some cases, if a view is complex enough, Oracle will actually execute the view this way. In practice, though, completely executing the view's query each time the view is referenced doesn't lead to good performance. When it can, the optimizer will do one of the following for queries against a view:

✦ Merge your query into the view's query

✦ Merge the view's query into your query

Believe it or not, the optimizer does consider these as two separate approaches. The result is that the query against the ANIMALS view for the animal named Skipper would be translated into something like this:

```
SELECT id_no,
       animal_name name,
       TO_CHAR(birth_date,'dd-Mon-yyyy') birth_date
FROM aquatic_animal
WHERE animal_name = 'Skipper'
AND death_date IS NULL;
```

Merging the two queries is a much more efficient means of processing a query against a view than to execute the view's query first, and Oracle will do this whenever possible. Remember the conceptual model, though. No matter how Oracle optimizes a query against a view, the results must match the conceptual model. When writing queries against views, you'll find it helpful to always think in terms of that model.

Determining when to use views

Views have a number of uses, including the following:

✦ **Security.** You can use views to limit a user's access to the rows in a table, to limit a user's access to columns in a table, and to restrict a user's ability to insert data into a table.

✦ **Convenience.** You can use views to encapsulate complex SQL queries, making report generation easier.

✦ **Consistency.** You can encapsulate standard reports into views. Users querying these views will get consistent results. Views can also insulate you from changes to the underlying tables.

Security

Views are often used to prevent a user from seeing all the data within a table. For example, you might limit a user to a certain subset of rows, or you might block out certain columns. Chapter 12, "Using Fine-Grained Access Control," contains an example of views being used for security. When you use a view for security, you must take the following approach:

✦ Deny users access to the underlying table. You don't want the users going around the view and querying the table directly.

✦ Create a view that limits what a user can see.

✦ Grant users access to the view.

A key feature of views is that users don't need access to the underlying table to select from the views. Views were purposely designed this way so that they can be used as a way to limit a user's access to data. The following view, for example, limits a user to seeing only animal ID numbers and names:

```
CREATE VIEW animal_name AS
SELECT id_no,
       animal_name
FROM aquatic_animal;
```

In terms of the sample database, one could hardly consider an animal's birth date to be sensitive information. However, if you were dealing with an HR application, you might consider an employee's pay rate to be sensitive, and you could create a view that didn't contain that column.

Another, possibly security-related purpose of views, is to use them to limit what a user can insert into a table. You can do this by taking advantage of the WITH CHECK OPTION. Take a look at the following view, which returns a list of live animals:

```
CREATE OR REPLACE VIEW live_animals AS
SELECT *
FROM aquatic_animal
WHERE death_date IS NULL
WITH CHECK OPTION;
```

The keywords WITH CHECK OPTION prevent someone from using this view to insert any records that contain a death date. In other words, users are prevented from entering an already dead animal into the system. Users would also be prevented from entering a death date for any existing animals. The following example shows the error that you would get if you tried to insert a record that violated the view's conditions:

```
SQL> INSERT INTO live_animals
  2  (id_no, animal_name, death_date)
  3  VALUES (576, 'Scampi',
  4          TO_DATE('3-Sep-1999','dd-Mon-yyyy'));
INSERT INTO live_animals
            *
ERROR at line 1:
ORA-01402: view WITH CHECK OPTION where-clause violation
```

You might consider this to be as much a data integrity issue as a security issue. Presumably, however, you would have a few select people who were allowed access directly to the table so that they could record the death of an animal.

If you have different classes of users, you can create many different views, one for each class. As the number of views increases, so does the effort needed to manage them. If you find yourself dealing with an unmanageable number of views, you might take a look at Chapter 12 to see if you can make use of Oracle8i's new fine-grained access control features.

Convenience

You can also use views for convenience. If you have complex queries on which reports are based, you can encapsulate those queries into views. That makes the programmer's job easier, and if he or she is using the same query repeatedly, using a view instead of replicating the query over and over reduces the risk of introducing an error.

Another way you can use convenience views is to make life easy for end users who are querying the database using ad-hoc query tools. In spite of the nice GUI interfaces that these tools support, querying a database still requires knowledge of how to deal with many subtle issues. Users need to know about nulls and their impact on true or false expressions. They need to understand outer joins vs. inner joins. There may be subtleties in the data or exceptions to the rule that the average user won't know about or understand. Instead of leaving your users to deal with these issues, you can create views that pull together the data that they most often require. Here's a good example:

```
CREATE OR REPLACE VIEW animal_caretakers AS
SELECT id_no,
       t.tank_no,
       animal_name,
       full_name caretaker_name
FROM aquatic_animal a, tank t, caretaker c
WHERE a.tank_no = t.tank_no(+)
AND t.chief_caretaker_name = c.caretaker_name (+)
AND a.death_date IS NULL;
```

This view returns information about animals and their caretakers. Note that it omits dead animals, because presumably the average user doesn't need to be concerned about animals that don't exist. The view also includes an outer join, so animals without a tank assignment will still be included. Both of these issues represent complexities that an end user might not think about.

Note   The ANIMAL_CARETAKERS **view shown in this section is a relatively simple view. In production systems, the queries behind views can be several pages long. Placing those queries into a view makes a huge difference in usability because the user no longer has to type in, or even think about, such a long query.**

Consistency

If a great deal of specialized knowledge is required to properly query your tables, different users will tend to get different results even when producing ostensibly identical reports. You may have two users producing a list of animals in the Seapark facilities, but only one might remember to exclude those animals who have died. By creating a standardized set of views that take these subtleties into account, and by requiring ad-hoc reports to be written against those views, you promote consistency in results across the organization. For example, an organization can use this technique with its financial data so that reports produced by different departments will be consistent with one another.

Creating a view

If you've read this far into the chapter, you've already seen several examples showing how to create a view. To start with, you need three items:

✦ A name for the view

✦ A SQL query

✦ The CREATE VIEW system privilege

Once you have these three items, you can use the CREATE VIEW statement to create a view. Consider this example:

```
CREATE VIEW animal_checkup AS
    SELECT a.id_no,
           a.animal_name,
           c.checkup_date,
           c.checkup_type,
           c.doctor_name
    FROM aquatic_animal a, checkup_history c
    WHERE a.id_no = c.id_no;
```

You can specify some useful options when you create a view. These include the following:

✦ OR REPLACE—Allows the new view to replace an existing view of the same name. This saves you the trouble of dropping the old view first. These keywords should immediately follow CREATE: for example, CREATE OR REPLACE.

✦ FORCE—Creates the view even if the underlying tables don't exist or if you don't have access to those tables. However, the view will remain in an invalid state until the tables are created and you have been granted access to them. If you use this option, FORCE should precede the VIEW keyword: for example, CREATE FORCE VIEW.

Note The export utility generates `CREATE FORCE VIEW` statements to ensure that views get created on import, regardless of whether all objects referenced by a view have been created yet.

✦ `WITH READ ONLY`—Prevents all but query access to the view. These keywords follow the SQL query.

✦ `WITH CHECK OPTION`—Restricts users to inserting and updating rows that fit within the view. Consider using this option for views that are used for `UPDATES` and `INSERTS`.

Caution This option may not work properly if the view contains a subquery.

If you prefer to use a GUI interface, you can use Schema Manager to create a view. Just follow these steps:

1. Start Schema Manager and log on to the database.

2. Right-click the Views folder and select Create from the pop-up menu.

   The Create View dialog box, shown in Figure 15-1, will open.

3. Fill in the fields of the General tab with the information necessary to create the view.

   Figure 15-1 shows the `ANIMAL_CHECKUP` view being created.

4. Click the create button.

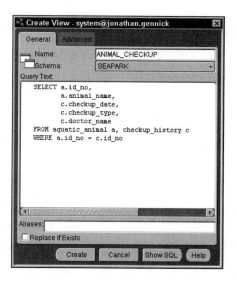

Figure 15-1: Using Schema Manager to create a view

Schema Manager doesn't really provide any advantages over the command-line option for creating views. You still need to type the SQL query. In fact, that little text box might complicate matters if your SQL query is particularly long.

You can use any valid SQL query in a view. The query can use Oracle's built-in SQL functions, column aliases, group functions, and so forth. To learn more about constructing queries, see Chapter 16, "Selecting Data with SQL."

Selecting from a view

Once you've created a view, you can select from it just as if it were a table. Consider this example:

```
SQL> SELECT * FROM animal_checkup;

  ID_NO ANIMAL_NAME  CHECKUP_D CHECKUP_TY  DOCTOR_NAME
------- ------------ --------- ----------  ------------------
    105 Skipper      03-SEP-99 ANNUAL      Justin Nue

1 row selected.
```

You can even join views and tables together. The following query joins the ANIMAL_CHECKUP view to the CHECKUP table and returns only those checkups for which a blood sample should have been obtained:

```
SELECT *
FROM animal_checkup, checkup
WHERE animal_checkup.checkup_type = checkup.checkup_type
AND blood_test_flag = 'Y';
```

While views and tables may be used interchangeably when selecting data, that isn't always the case when you are changing data.

Using views to manipulate data

Where possible, Oracle allows you to issue UPDATE, INSERT, and DELETE statements against a view. However, when it comes to views, these types of statements present a problem. All of these statements modify the data in the underlying table. To update or delete a row through a view, you need to be able to track the row in the view back to one row in a table underlying the view. This gets difficult when you are dealing with summarized data, columns based on expressions, unions, and certain types of joins.

Generally, if a view includes all columns from the underlying table and uses only a WHERE clause to restrict the rows returned, Oracle will allow you to update the view. Certain types of join views are also updateable, but the following rules apply:

✦ Only one of the tables represented in a view can be updated.

✦ The columns that you are updating must map back to a table whose primary key columns are all preserved in the view.

✦ If you are deleting from a join view, then the view must include primary key columns from only one of the tables involved in the join. The delete will apply to only that table.

✦ If you are inserting into a view, you must not reference nonupdatable columns. If the join view is created using the WITH CHECK OPTION, you won't be able to insert into it at all.

Join views that don't preserve the primary keys of at least one underlying table can never be updated. Other types of views are also never updated. These include the following:

✦ Views with set operators such as INTERSECT, UNION, and MINUS

✦ Views with GROUP BY, CONNECT BY, or START WITH clauses

✦ Views with group functions such as AVG, SUM, or MAX

✦ Views using the DISTINCT function

If you have any doubts about which views you can update or about which columns in a specific view you can update, you can query the USER_UPDATABLE_COLUMNS data dictionary view. For example, if you create a view named TANK_ANIMALS_VIEW that joins two tables, the following query will show which columns you can update:

```
SELECT column_name, updatable
FROM user_updatable_columns
WHERE table_name = 'TANK_ANIMALS_VIEW';
```

If you need to make a nonupdateable view updateable, you may be able to do that by writing some instead-of triggers. An *instead-of trigger* defines PL/SQL code to be invoked by Oracle in response to updates, inserts, and deletes issued against a view.

 Cross-Reference You can read about instead-of triggers in Chapter 24, "Using Procedures, Packages, Functions, and Triggers."

Altering a view

Oracle does implement an ALTER VIEW command, but the only operation that you can do with it is to recompile the view. To make any other changes, you must re-create the view.

Recompiling a View

Recompiling a view causes Oracle to check the underlying SQL statement to be sure that it is still valid. The syntax to use is as follows:

```
ALTER VIEW [schema.]view_name COMPILE;
```

Any time that you change an object referenced by a view's query, Oracle will mark that view as invalid. Before you can use the view again, it must be recompiled. You can either recompile it yourself, or leave Oracle to do it automatically. If you're in doubt about whether you have any views that need to be recompiled, you can get a list of invalid views by issuing this query:

```
SELECT object_name, status
FROM user_objects
WHERE object_type = 'VIEW'
AND status = 'INVALID'
```

You can even use SQL to automatically generate the needed ALTER VIEW commands to do the recompiles. Execute a query like the following using SQL*Plus, and spool the output to a file:

```
SELECT 'ALTER VIEW ' || object_name || ' COMPILE;'
FROM user_objects
WHERE object_type = 'VIEW'
AND status = 'INVALID'
```

When you leave the recompiling for Oracle to do automatically, you run the risk that the view won't compile correctly. Explicitly compiling invalid views is a safer approach because it allows you to spot any errors up front, allowing you to fix them before the users encounter them.

Re-creating a View

Aside from recompiling a view, you must make any other changes by re-creating the view. Oracle makes this fairly easy: All you have to do is use OR REPLACE with the CREATE VIEW command. For example:

```
CREATE OR REPLACE VIEW animal_checkup AS
    SELECT a.id_no,
            a.animal_name,
            c.checkup_date,
            c.checkup_type,
            c.doctor_name
    FROM aquatic_animal a, checkup_history c
    WHERE a.id_no = c.id_no;
```

If you store your CREATE VIEW statements in text files, you can quickly make changes to a view by editing the view's CREATE statement in the file and then executing that file using SQL*Plus.

Note   For convenience, the CREATE OR REPLACE syntax is valid even if the view does not already exist.

Using Schema Manager to Alter a View

You can use Schema Manager to modify a view in much the same way as you use it to modify a table. Simply follow these steps:

1. Start Schema Manager and log on to the database.

2. Open the Views folder and navigate to the view that you want to change.

3. Right-click the view name and select Edit from the pop-up menu.

    Schema Manager opens an Edit View window for you.

4. Make your changes to the view by editing the fields in the window.

5. Click the OK button.

If you click the Show SQL button while editing a view in Schema Manager, you will see that Schema Manager makes the changes by writing CREATE OR REPLACE statements to re-create the view.

Removing a view

You can use the DROP VIEW command to remove a view from the database. The following statement, for example, removes the view named ANIMAL_CHECKUP:

```
DROP VIEW animal_checkup;
```

You can use Schema Manager to drop a view by right-clicking the view and selecting Remove from the pop-up menu.

Using views with the data dictionary

Two data dictionary views are useful when it comes to managing views. The DBA_OBJECTS view allows you to query for views that are currently in an invalid state and that need to be recompiled. The DBA_OBJECTS view is similar to USER_OBJECTS, which was discussed previously in the section "Altering a View."

The DBA_VIEWS view is another useful view. You can use DBA_VIEWS to get a list of views owned by a user and to get the query behind a view. If you're not a DBA, you can use ALL_VIEWS instead of DBA_VIEWS.

Listing Views Owned by a User

You can query the DBA_VIEWS view to generate a list of all views owned by any particular user. The query in the following example returns a list of views owned by SEAPARK:

```
SQL> SELECT view_name
  2  FROM all_views
```

```
  3  WHERE owner='SEAPARK';

VIEW_NAME
-------------------------------
ANIMALS
ANIMAL_CARETAKERS
ANIMAL_CHECKUP
ANIMAL_NAME
CHECKUP_TYPE_COUNT
LIVE_ANIMALS
USER_TANK
```

If you're interested only in your own views, select from USER_VIEWS instead and omit the WHERE clause. That will save you some typing.

Displaying the Query behind a View

The query behind a view is returned by the column named TEXT in the DBA_VIEWS view. Listing 15-1 shows the query being returned for the view named ANIMAL_CHECKUP.

Listing 15-1: **Retrieving a view's query**

```
SQL> SET LONG 2000
SQL> COLUMN text WORD_WRAPPED
SQL>
SQL> SELECT text
  2  FROM DBA_VIEWS
  3  WHERE owner = 'SEAPARK'
  4  AND view_name = 'ANIMAL_CHECKUP';

TEXT
-----------------------------------------------
SELECT a.id_no,
        a.animal_name,
        c.checkup_date,
        c.checkup_type,
        c.doctor_name
   FROM aquatic_animal a, checkup_history c
   WHERE a.id_no = c.id_no


1 row selected.
```

The datatype of the TEXT column is LONG. By default, SQL*Plus displays only the first 80 characters of a LONG column. Unless you write very short queries for your views, that won't do you any good. The `SET LONG 2000` command tells SQL*Plus to display up to 2000 characters of the `LONG` value. For complex views, you may need to increase the value even more. In SQL*Plus, the `COLUMN` command specifies to wordwrap the results. If you tend to use long lines in your `CREATE VIEW` statements, you may need this to avoid having words chopped in the middle when line breaks occur.

Managing Synonyms

A synonym is an alternate name for an object. Primarily, synonyms enable multiple users to reference an object without them having to prefix the object name with the schema name. You manage synonyms by using the `CREATE SYNONYM` and `DROP SYNONYM` commands. You can also use Schema Manager to create and drop them.

Understanding synonyms

To better understand the issue that synonyms address, consider the `AQUATIC_ANIMAL` table in the `SEAPARK` schema. If you log on as the user named HAROLD and you want to select from that table, you could refer to it as `SEAPARK.AQUATIC_ANIMAL`. That's a lot to type. Further, if you were writing an application, you would need to embed the schema name throughout the application, forcing your application to depend on the tables stored in a schema named `SEAPARK`.

Synonyms provide you with a way to refer to objects in a schema-independent manner, as shown in Figure 15-2.

Once you create a synonym for an object, you can use that synonym in place of the object's name in `SELECT` statements, and in DML statements such as `INSERT`, `UPDATE`, or `DELETE`. With respect to Figure 15-2, you can use `AQUATIC_ANIMAL` any time that you want to refer to the `SEAPARK.AQUATIC_ANIMAL` table.

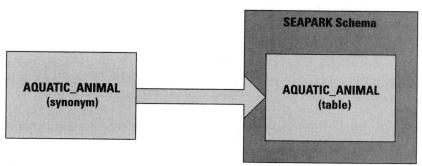

Figure 15-2: Synonyms point to schema objects.

Oracle uses synonyms extensively to refer to the data dictionary views, all of which are owned by the user named SYS. It's only because of these synonyms that you can select from DBA_TABLES without having to reference it as SYS.DBA_TABLES.

You can make a synonym for a table, a view, or even for another synonym. In addition, you can create synonyms for functions, packages, procedures, sequences, and database links to remote databases. After you create a synonym, you can use it as though it were the underlying object. Synonyms don't contain their own data; they are only a pointer to an object.

Types of Synonyms

Oracle supports two types of synonyms: private and public. *Private synonyms* are created by a user, and they apply only to statements issued by that one user. *Public synonyms* are created by the DBA and are shared by all users. Figure 15-3 illustrates the difference.

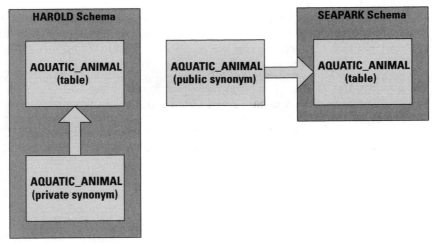

Figure 15-3: Public versus private synonyms

In Figure 15-3, you can see that a public synonym named AQUATIC_ANIMALS exists, and that it points to the SEAPARK.AQUATIC_ANIMALS table. All users but one will use this synonym. That one user is HAROLD. User HAROLD has his own private synonym pointing to his own copy of the AQUATIC_ANIMALS table.

Note Synonym names don't need to match table names, but making them match is a common practice.

Private synonyms always override public synonyms. When a SQL command contains an object name that isn't prefixed with a schema name, Oracle resolves the name by checking for objects in this order:

1. Objects and private synonyms owned by the current user

2. Public synonyms

Public synonyms are most often used when the purpose is to avoid having to code schema names within applications.

When to Use Synonyms

Application developers typically use private synonyms as shorthand for tables they need to reference often during SQL code development. This approach avoids the retyping of long table names. Public synonyms simplify the migration of applications. If the schema names are different but the tables are the same, synonyms allow an application to be migrated easily from one database to another.

Sometimes, you use public synonyms for common lookup tables that all database users need. The synonyms for the DBA views in the data dictionary provide a good example of this use.

Another use for synonyms is to enable two applications to refer to a single table with two different names. Views can also perform this task, but if the sole purpose is to give each application a business-rule appropriate name, a synonym may be a good solution. For example, an accounting department application may refer to the customer table as CUSTOMER, while a sales department application may use CLIENT instead. Although this wouldn't be an ideal situation to create, sometimes you do have to deal with legacy applications.

Note   When creating public synonyms, Oracle users often mistakenly assume they can immediately share their tables with other Oracle users. Creating a public synonym for a table doesn't automatically enable other users to view or change the data in that table. You must still assign the appropriate privileges using Security Manager or the SQL GRANT command.

Creating synonyms

You can use the CREATE SYNONYM command to create synonyms, or you can use Enterprise Manager's Schema Manager. You will need the CREATE SYNONYM privilege, and if you are creating public synonyms, you will need the CREATE PUBLIC SYNONYM privilege.

Using SQL to Create Synonyms

The CREATE SYNONYM statement allows you to create both public and private synonyms. The syntax is extremely simple. The most difficult part is getting your fingers to type *synonym* correctly. To create a private synonym referring to a table in another schema, issue the following command:

```
CREATE SYNONYM animal FOR seapark.aquatic_animal;
```

Having created this synonym, you can select from ANIMAL instead of SEAPARK.AQUATIC_ANIMAL. Consider this example:

```
SQL> SELECT id_no, animal_name
  2  FROM animal;

  ID_NO ANIMAL_NAME
--------- --------------------
    100 Flipper
    105 Skipper
    112 Bopper
    151 Batty
```

Note   Remember that creating a synonym doesn't give you access to another user's table. That user must grant you SELECT privileges for you to be able to select data from the table.

To create a public synonym on a table, add the PUBLIC keyword to the CREATE SYNONYM command. All database users may use the synonym you can create in this example:

```
CREATE PUBLIC SYNONYM animal FOR seapark.aquatic_animal;
```

Synonyms are also useful in making access to data in remote databases transparent to both users and applications. For example, if you have a remote database containing a human resource application, you might create a synonym like the following so that you could tie into it:

```
CREATE PUBLIC SYNONYM employee
FOR payroll.employee_public_data@hr;
```

With this synonym in place, your applications would be able to select from EMPLOYEE without having to worry about the fact that the table was actually in another database.

Using Schema Manager to Create Synonyms

You can use Schema Manager to create a synonym by following these steps:

1. Start Schema Manager and log on to the database.

2. Right-click the Synonyms folder and select Create from the pop-up menu.

   The General tab of the Create Synonym dialog box, shown in Figure 15-4, will display.

3. Fill in the fields of the General tab with the information needed to create the synonym.

   Figure 15-4 shows the ANIMAL synonym being created.

4. Click the Create button.

After you carry out these four easy steps, you have your synonym.

Figure 15-4: Creating the ANIMAL synonym

Removing synonyms

You can remove a synonym from the database by issuing a SQL statement or by using Schema Manager. The SQL statement to remove a synonym is as follows:

```
DROP [PUBLIC] SYNONYM synonym_name;
```

Be sure to include the keyword PUBLIC if you are dropping a public synonym. To use Schema Manager to remove a synonym, navigate to the synonym that you want to remove, right-click its name, and select Remove from the pop-up menu.

Using synonyms with the data dictionary

Only one data dictionary view is directly related to synonyms, and that's the DBA_SYNONYMS view. Like other DBA views, DBA_SYNONYMS is usually visible only to the DBA. If you aren't the DBA, use ALL_SYNONYMS instead.

Listing Synonyms Owned by a User

You can use the following query to list the synonyms owned by a particular user:

```
SELECT synonym_name, table_owner, table_name
FROM dba_synonyms
WHERE owner = 'username';
```

In spite of the columns being named TABLE_OWNER and TABLE_NAME, this view does return information about synonyms pointing to views as well as to tables.

Listing Public Synonyms

To list the public synonyms that have been created on a database, query the DBA_SYNONYMS view using PUBLIC as the owner name. Consider this example:

```
SELECT synonym_name, table_owner, table_name
FROM dba_synonyms
WHERE owner = 'PUBLIC';
```

Oracle allows all users to see all public synonyms, regardless of whether they have access to the objects pointed to by those synonyms.

Listing Synonyms That Refer to an Object

Occasionally, you might need to find out if any synonyms refer to an object. You can do that by using the following query:

```
SELECT owner, synonym_name
FROM dba_synonyms
WHERE table_owner = 'object_owner'
AND table_name = 'object_name';
```

Similarly, you can also find all synonyms referring to objects owned by a user. Just drop the last condition of the WHERE clause.

Listing Synonyms That Reference a User

If you frequently export users from one database and import them into another, you'll soon find that when you export just one user, the Export utility doesn't export public synonyms that reference objects owned by that user. This makes sense, but it can be inconvenient if you are using the Export utility to migrate a schema from a development database to a test database, because in that case, you probably do want the relevant public synonyms to go along.

If you need to re-create a user's public synonyms in another database, you can use the data dictionary to generate the necessary SQL commands automatically. Listing 15-2 shows an example of a SQL*Plus script that does this. It generates a file of CREATE PUBLIC SYNONYM commands for all public synonyms referencing objects owned by SEAPARK.

Listing 15-2: **Rebuilding public synonyms**

```
set linesize 200
set pagesize 0
set trimspool on
spool c:\a\seapark_syn.sql
select 'create public synonym '
           || synonym_name
           || ' for '
           || table_owner || '.' || table_name
           || DECODE (db_link, null, '','@' || db_link)
           || ';'
    from dba_synonyms
  where table_owner = 'SEAPARK'
    and owner = 'PUBLIC';
spool off
```

After executing these commands against your source database, the file seapark_syn.sql will contain CREATE PUBLIC SYNONYM commands for objects owned by SEAPARK. You can create those on the target database by logging on to that database with SQL*Plus and executing the file.

Managing Sequences

A sequence is an Oracle object used to deliver a series of unique numbers. Sequences are transaction-independent. Each time you access a sequence, the value of that sequence is incremented (or decremented) by a predetermined amount. Committing or rolling back a transaction doesn't affect changes to a sequence. Sequences are stored in the database. They don't occupy a lot of space like tables do, but their values persist through shutdowns and startups. Sequences are most often used to generate unique, primary keys for tables. The example shown in Listing 15-3 demonstrates how you can select a series of incrementing values from a sequence.

Listing 15-3: Sequences are used to generate a series of sequential values.

```
SQL> SELECT checkup_history_seq.NEXTVAL
  2  FROM dual;

  NEXTVAL
---------
        1

1 row selected.

SQL> SELECT checkup_history_seq.NEXTVAL
  2  FROM dual;

  NEXTVAL
---------
        2

1 row selected.

SQL> SELECT checkup_history_seq.NEXTVAL
  2  FROM dual;

  NEXTVAL
---------
        3

1 row selected.
```

By themselves, Oracle sequences aren't worth much. You have to write some code somewhere that uses the sequences that you create. Many databases, such as Microsoft SQL Server and Microsoft Access, allow you to define fields in a table that autoincrement each time a row is inserted. These autoincrement fields are most often used as primary key generators.

You can perform the same function from Oracle, but with Oracle, the incrementing function (the sequence) is separate from the field being incremented. You need to tie the two together with some code, and you'll see how to do that later in the section "Creating an Autoincrementing Field."

Determining when to use sequences

Consider using sequences whenever you are faced with one of the following situations:

✦ You want the primary key of a table to be a number, and you want that number to autoincrement each time you insert a new row into the table.

✦ You are creating an audit trail table, and you need to know the exact order in which the audit trail entries were made. Timestamps alone aren't usually enough to do this.

In general, consider using a sequence whenever you need to generate unique numbers.

Creating a sequence

You can use the CREATE SEQUENCE statement to create a sequence. Issue the statement using SQL*Plus, or you can use Schema Manager's GUI interface, and Schema Manager will write and execute the statement for you.

Before you create a sequence, consider the following questions:

✦ Do you want the sequence to start with 1, or do you want some other value used as the starting point?

✦ Do you want the values to increment by 1, or by some other value? Do you want the values to decrement?

✦ What do you want the behavior to be when the sequence reaches its maximum value?

✦ Must you have the values generated sequentially, or can you receive the values out of order?

✦ How many values can you afford to lose if the instance goes down?

When you create a sequence, Oracle allows you to choose the starting value. You may also set a maximum value, and you may set an increment value. The increment defaults to 1, but you may choose another increment if you prefer. You can create a descending sequence by making the increment a negative value. An increment of -1, for example, results in a sequence that counts down like this: 10, 9, 8, and so on.

You may specify maximum and minimum values when you create a sequence. The default minimum is 1. The default maximum is 1.0E+27 (1 with 27 zeros after it). You can also control Oracle's behavior once that maximum is hit. By default, Oracle will stop generating values when the sequence reaches its maximum. Using the CYCLE option, you can create sequences that automatically start over again at the beginning.

Note

If you are using sequences to generate unique keys for records, you should avoid the CYCLE option, unless, that is, you have some way to be sure that older records have been deleted from the table by the time the sequence cycles back to the beginning again.

Another consideration when creating a sequence is whether you want the values to be generated in numeric order. This may seem like a silly issue. After all, why call it a sequence if the values aren't in sequence, right? Ordering is an issue only when you're using Parallel Server, and it's an issue because of how Oracle caches sequence values in memory. Each instance accessing a database maintains a cache of sequence values in memory. This is to avoid the overhead of disk access each time a new sequence value is requested. You end up with the situation shown in Figure 15-5.

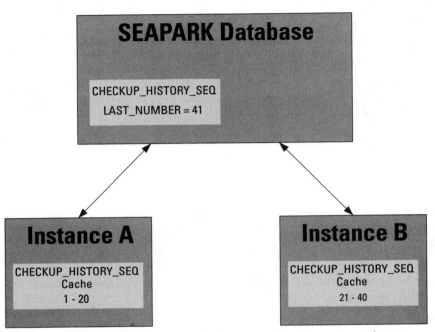

Figure 15-5: Each Oracle instance gets its own cache of sequence values.

In Figure 15-5, if two users are connected to instances A and B, respectively, and are alternately inserting new records into the database, the sequence values used will be 1, 21, 2, 22, 3, 23, and so forth. This really shouldn't present a problem if you are using the sequence only to generate unique keys. If you absolutely must have sequence values generated in order, you can use the ORDER option when creating the sequence. However, there's a slight performance cost in doing this.

Tip Challenge anyone who claims that ordering is a requirement. Sometimes, in the case of an audit trail table, it really is a requirement. More often, it's an issue of someone's sense of "neatness" being violated by out-of-order values. If all you need is a unique number to identify a record, does it really matter if that number is in sequence or not?

The last issue to think about is how many sequence values you want to cache in memory. This is a performance tradeoff. By default, Oracle caches 20 values from each sequence in memory. That means that you can access a sequence 19 times without causing disk access. On the 20th time, Oracle will need to access the disk to refresh the cache. The tradeoff that you make when you cache sequence numbers is that the values in memory are lost if an instance crashes. This results in gaps. If you are using sequences to generate primary keys, you could end up jumping from 100 to 121 and not have any records for numbers 101 to 120. You can use the NOCACHE option to prevent Oracle from caching values.

> **Note** Using the NOCACHE option will hurt performance because Oracle will be forced to access the disk each time a new sequence value is requested. Also, by itself, NOCACHE won't eliminate the problem of gaps in autoincremented fields. There is still a risk of loss due to transactions that are rolled back, including uncommitted transactions that are rolled back due to an instance failure.

Using the CREATE SEQUENCE Statement

You can use the CREAT SEQUENCE statement to create a sequence from SQL*Plus. To use the command in its simplest form, taking all the defaults, you just need to supply a sequence name after the command. Consider this example:

```
SQL> CREATE SEQUENCE aquatic_animal_seq;

Sequence created.
```

If you're using a sequence for a primary key or for an audit trail log, then you may want to specify some nondefault settings. The command in the following example creates a sequence that would be useful for an audit trail log:

```
SQL> CREATE SEQUENCE aquatic_animal_audit_trail_seq
  2   START WITH 1
  3   INCREMENT BY 1
  4   ORDER
  5   NOCYCLE;

Sequence created.
```

The ORDER and NOCYCLE options are significant here. For an audit trail, you need to know the exact order in which events occur. Hence, you use the ORDER option to guarantee that each sequence value will be greater than the previous value. You use the NOCYCLE option to prevent the sequence from automatically wrapping around to 1 again, which could cause primary key violations if the audit trail table is keyed by the sequence value.

Using Schema Manager to Create a Sequence

You can use Schema Manager to create a sequence in much the same way that you create a table or any other object. Follow these steps:

1. Start Schema Manager and log on to the database.

2. Right-click on Sequences and select Create from the pop-up menu.

3. Fill in the General tab in the Create Sequence dialog box.

   Figure 15-6 shows the CHECKUP_HISTORY_SEQ sequence being created.

4. Click the Create button, and Schema Manager will execute the CREATE SEQUENCE command for you.

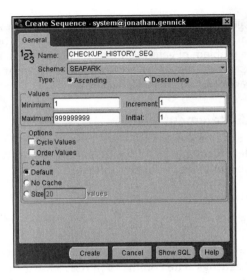

Figure 15-6: Using Schema Manager to create the CHECKUP_HISTORY_SEQ sequence

Creating an autoincrementing field

People moving to an Oracle environment after having worked with SQL Server or Microsoft Access often become frustrated with the task of defining an autoincrementing field in a table. While some database products make this easy by supporting autoincrementing fields as a distinct datatype, Oracle requires you to write code.

To create an autoincrementing field in Oracle, follow these steps:

1. Define the column that you want to increment as a number.

2. Create a sequence in support of that column.

3. Write a trigger to set the value of the column from the sequence whenever a row is inserted.

4. Optionally, write a trigger to prevent updates to the column.

As an example, let's say that you want the primary key for the CHECKUP_HISTORY table to automatically increment by 1 each time a new record is inserted. The structure of the CHECKUP_HISTORY table looks like this:

```
SQL> DESCRIBE checkup_history
```

```
Name                             Null?     Type
------------------------------   --------  -------------
CHECKUP_NO                       NOT NULL  NUMBER(10)
ID_NO                                      NUMBER(10)
CHECKUP_TYPE                               VARCHAR2(30)
CHECKUP_DATE                               DATE
DOCTOR_NAME                                VARCHAR2(50)
```

The CHECKUP_NO field is the primary key, and it is already a number. You can create a stored sequence for this field by using the following command:

```
CREATE SEQUENCE checkup_no_seq
NOCYCLE
MAXVALUE 9999999999
START WITH 2;
```

The maximum value was chosen to match the field definition. The CHECKUP_NO field is 10 digits long, so the maximum value that it can hold is 9,999,999,999. You could start the sequence at 1, but if the table already contains data, you might need to start at a higher number to avoid conflicts with the existing data. In this case, the sequence starts at 2.

Your next task is to make certain that the sequence is always used to set the CHECKUP_NO field each time a new row is inserted into the table. You could code all your application programs to do this, but a more robust approach is to create an insert trigger on the CHECKUP_HISTORY table. Listing 15-4 demonstrates a trigger that ensures that the key is always properly set, no matter how a row is inserted.

Listing 15-4: A trigger to implement an autoincrementing primary key field

```
CREATE OR REPLACE TRIGGER set_checkup_no
BEFORE INSERT ON checkup_history
FOR EACH ROW
DECLARE
  next_checkup_no NUMBER;
BEGIN
   --Get the next checkup number from the sequence.
   SELECT checkup_no_seq.NEXTVAL
   INTO next_checkup_no
   FROM dual;

   --Use the sequence number as the primary key
   --for the record being inserted.
   :new.checkup_no := next_checkup_no;
END;
/
```

With this trigger in place, the CHECKUP_NO field will always be set using the sequence that you have created. This will be true even if an INSERT statement specifies some other value for that field. The trigger will override any value supplied by the INSERT statement, ensuring that the sequence is always the source for primary keys.

In this situation, it's possible for someone to update an existing record and change the primary key value to something that might conflict with a future insertion. You may want to head off that possibility by creating an update trigger like the following:

```
CREATE OR REPLACE TRIGGER upd_checkup_no
BEFORE UPDATE OF checkup_no ON checkup_history
FOR EACH ROW
BEGIN
   RAISE_APPLICATION_ERROR (-20000,
      'UPD_CHECKUP_NO Trigger: Updates of the CHECKUP_NO field'
      || ' are not allowed.');
END;
/
```

The BEFORE UPDATE OF checkup_no clause ensures that this trigger will fire only when a user attempts to update the CHECKUP_NO column. This minimizes the overhead incurred by normal updates. If an illegal update is detected, the RAISE_APPLICATION_ERROR procedure is used to send a human readable error message back to the application.

Altering a sequence

You can alter a sequence in one of two ways. You can use the ALTER SEQUENCE command to change any of the options, such as the amount of values cached, the minimum and maximum values, and the increment. Or you can use Schema Manager by right-clicking on a sequence name and selecting Edit from the pop-up menu.

Unfortunately, you can't alter a current value for the sequence itself. The best way to change the value of a sequence is to drop it and re-create it using the START WITH clause. When you do this, you will lose any access granted on the sequence. You'll have to regrant access after you re-create it. You will also need to recompile any triggers that depend on the sequence.

If you absolutely must change the value of a sequence without dropping and recreating it, you may be able to use a workaround to temporarily change the increment value so that the next time a value is retrieved, the sequence will be advanced to where you want it to be. For this workaround to work reliably, you must be absolutely certain that no other users will access the sequence while you are making the change.

As an example, assume that you must change the CHECKUP_HISTORY_SEQ sequence so that the next value to be retrieved is 1,000. The first step is to ascertain the current value of the sequence. You can do that as shown in the following example:

```
SQL> SELECT checkup_history_seq.NEXTVAL
  2  FROM dual;

  NEXTVAL
---------
        2
```

The current value is 2. The next value to be selected is now 3. You want the next value to be 1,000. Subtract 3 from 1,000, and you have an increment of 997. Now, issue the commands shown in Listing 15-5 to temporarily set the increment to 997, select from the sequence, and then reset the increment back to 1.

Listing 15-5: **Changing the sequence value**

```
SQL> ALTER SEQUENCE checkup_history_seq
  2       INCREMENT BY 997;

Sequence altered.

SQL> SELECT checkup_history_seq.NEXTVAL
  2  FROM dual;

  NEXTVAL
---------
      999

1 row selected.

SQL> ALTER SEQUENCE checkup_history_seq
  2       INCREMENT BY 1;

Sequence altered.
```

You can see that after the increment was modified, the sequence returned a value of 2+997, or 999. Setting the increment back to 1 afterwards causes the next value retrieved to be 1,000, as shown in the following example:

```
SQL> SELECT checkup_history_seq.NEXTVAL
  2  FROM dual;

  NEXTVAL
---------
     1000
```

For this to work, you need to be certain that no other user accesses the sequence while you have the increment modified. Otherwise, you may find yourself jumping to 1997 (2 + 997 + 997 + 1) instead of 1,000.

> **Tip** Sometimes the risk of other users accessing a sequence while you are modifying it is worth taking. You do have to be sure that you can stand a big gap in the values, though. While making a change on the fly, when other users could potentially access the sequence, write out all the necessary SQL statements ahead of time and execute them from a script. This greatly reduces the period of time during which you are exposed.

Removing a sequence

You can use the `DROP SEQUENCE` command to remove a sequence. Consider this example:

```
DROP SEQUENCE checkup_history_seq;
```

You may also use Schema Manager to drop sequences. Simply right-click the sequence that you want to drop and select Remove from the pop-up menu.

Dropping a sequence causes Oracle to remove any privileges granted on the sequence. Synonyms remain but are invalid. Triggers using the dropped sequence remain but will also be invalid, and you'll get error messages each time those triggers are fired.

Using sequences with the data dictionary

The `DBA_SEQUENCES` view returns information about all the sequences defined in a database. You are typically the only person who can see this view. If you aren't the DBA, use `ALL_SEQUENCES` or `USER_SEQUENCES` instead. To get a list of all sequences owned by a particular user, issue a query like the one that follows:

```
SELECT sequence_name
FROM dba_sequences
WHERE sequence_owner = 'schema_name';
```

To find out information about one sequence in particular, issue the following query:

```
SELECT *
FROM dba_sequences
WHERE sequence_owner = 'schema_name'
AND sequence_name = 'sequence_name';
```

One of the values returned by the `DBA_SEQUENCES` view is named `LAST_NUMBER`. This isn't the last sequence number returned to a user. It is the most recent value recorded on disk. It is set when Oracle fills its cache with values for the sequence, and it will be one increment higher than the highest value that Oracle has cached so far.

Summary

In this chapter, you learned:

✦ Views help streamline access to the data by hiding complexities of the underlying tables. Views can also help to separate data for different users as a security measure. You can reference views almost anywhere you reference a table.

✦ Views are stored in the database as a SQL SELECT command and have no data of their own.

✦ Synonyms enable developers to reference tables with shorthand names. Synonyms also allow different applications to reference the same object with different names. Synonyms can help simplify migration of applications from one schema or database instance to another.

✦ Oracle supports two types of synonyms: public and private. Public synonyms affect all users in the database. Private synonyms affect only the user who owns them. Private synonyms take precedence over public synonyms of the same name.

✦ You can use sequences to generate unique numbers for primary keys. Sequences are safer than other application-based methods of key generation because they are independent of transactions.

✦ If you are creating a sequence in support of an audit trail table, you need to be sure that the sequence numbers are assigned in strict order. Be sure to specify the ORDER option.

✦   ✦   ✦

Selecting Data with SQL

The SQL SELECT statement is the key to getting data out of your database. And if the SELECT statement is the key to getting the data, the WHERE clause is the key to getting the correct data. Programmers must master both these constructs if they expect to do productive programming for a database. As a database administrator, you probably don't need quite the same level of mastery as a programmer, but you do need to be familiar with the basic concepts of selecting data, joining tables, and summarizing data.

Note   All of the examples in this chapter are based on the sample tables owned by the user named AMY.

Using the Basic SELECT Query

You use SELECT statements to retrieve data from an Oracle database. You use them to specify which tables you are interested in and which columns you want back from those tables. The general form of a SELECT statement looks like this:

```
SELECT column_list
FROM table_list
WHERE conditions
GROUP BY column_list
HAVING conditions
ORDER BY column_list;
```

Each of the clauses in this example has a specific function:

✦ SELECT column_list — Specifies which columns you want to see

✦ FROM table_list — Specifies which tables contain those columns

✦ WHERE *conditions*—Restricts the data that Oracle returns so that you see only rows that match the specified conditions

✦ GROUP BY *column_list*—Causes Oracle to summarize data over the values in the specified columns

✦ HAVING *conditions*—Restricts the summarized data so that you see only summary rows that match the specified conditions

✦ ORDER BY *column_list*—Specifies how to sort the data

You'll learn about each of these clauses as you read this chapter.

Selecting data

A simple SELECT statement might look like this:

```
SELECT last_name, first_name, specialty
FROM artist;
```

This statement returns the three named columns from the ARTIST table. If you were to execute it using SQL*Plus, your results would look like this:

```
LAST_NAME        FIRST_NAME       SPECIALTY
---------------  ---------------  --------------
Smith            Ken              DIGITAL
Palionis         Lina             OTHER
Ahrens           Lorri            WATERCOLOR
Mosston          Nikki            ACRYLIC
Perry            Robert           MIXED MEDIA
Stone            Sharron          DIGITAL
Michael          Sherry           WATERCOLOR
Roberts          Stephen          MIXED ON PAPER
Joyce            Terence          DIGITAL
Taylor           Thomas           OIL
```

Notice that these rows aren't sorted in any particular order. That's because an ORDER BY clause wasn't used.

Sorting data

You can use the ORDER BY clause to specify sorting the data returned by a query. The clause goes at the end of the query and consists of a comma-delimited list of columns. Oracle will sort the query results based on those columns. For example, to sort the artist list by last name and first name, you could write a query like this:

```
SELECT last_name, first_name, specialty
FROM artist
ORDER BY last_name, first_name;
```

Oracle will sort the results in ascending order on the columns that you specify. You can also sort in descending order by using the DESC keyword after a column name. The query in Listing 16-1 sorts in descending order by specialty and then in ascending order by name within specialty.

Listing 16-1: Using the ORDER BY clause

```
SQL> SELECT last_name, first_name, specialty
  2  FROM artist
  3  ORDER BY specialty DESC, last_name, first_name;

LAST_NAME      FIRST_NAME      SPECIALTY
-------------  --------------  ----------------
Ahrens         Lorri           WATERCOLOR
Michael        Sherry          WATERCOLOR
Palionis       Lina            OTHER
Taylor         Thomas          OIL
Roberts        Stephen         MIXED ON PAPER
Perry          Robert          MIXED MEDIA
Joyce          Terence         DIGITAL
Smith          Ken             DIGITAL
Stone          Sharron         DIGITAL
Mosston        Nikki           ACRYLIC
```

You can use an ASC keyword to indicate ascending order, but it's rarely used because an ascending sort is the default.

Caution   If you want data to be returned in a certain order, you must use an ORDER BY clause to specify the sort order that you want. Some common misconceptions are that Oracle returns records in primary key order, in index order, or in the order in which records were inserted. All of these arrangements are true sometimes, under the right circumstances, but you can't count on them being true all of the time. If the order of your query results is important, use an ORDER BY clause.

Restricting the results

Chances are good that you won't want to see all the data in a table when you issue a query. You can use the WHERE clause to restrict the data returned by Oracle to those rows that interest you. The WHERE clause, if one exists, follows immediately after the FROM clause. The following query, for example, returns only those artists whose specialty is 'DIGITAL':

```
SELECT last_name, first_name, specialty
FROM artist
WHERE specialty = 'DIGITAL'
ORDER BY specialty DESC, last_name, first_name
```

This WHERE clause is very simple and contains a test only for equality. Oracle supports a number of operators that you may use, and these are listed in Table 16-1.

	Table 16-1 Comparison Operators	
Operator	**Purpose**	**Example**
=	Equality.	Specialty = 'DIGITAL'
<>	Inequality.	Specialty <> 'DIGITAL'
<	Less than.	book_due < sysdate
>	Greater than.	book_due > sysdate
<=	Less than or equal to.	book_due <= sysdate
>=	Greater than or equal to.	book_due >= sysdate
LIKE	Limited wildcard comparisons. Use '%' to match any string. Use '_' to match any one character.	Specialty LIKE 'DIGI%' Specialty LIKE 'DIG_TAL'
BETWEEN	Tests to see if one value is between two others. The range is inclusive.	Specialty BETWEEN 'D' and 'E'
IN	Tests to see if a value is contained within a list of values.	Specialty IN ('DIGITAL', 'WATERCOLOR')
IS NULL	Tests to see if a value is null.	Specialty IS NULL
IS NOT NULL	Tests to see if a value is not null.	Specialty IS NOT NULL

Keep these points in mind while writing WHERE clauses:

✦ Quoted strings must be within single quotes, not double quotes.

✦ If you need to place an apostrophe inside a string, you should double it. For example, if you need to compare a column to the string "Won't," write it in the WHERE clause as 'Won''t'.

✦ Always think about the effects of null values. For each column in a WHERE clause, you have to ask yourself what would happen if that column was null. See the section "Beware of Nulls!" later in this chapter.

✦ Use care when applying a function to a database column because this can prevent indexes from being used. See the section "Using SQL Functions in Queries" later in this chapter.

✦ If you are summarizing data, try to eliminate all the data that you can in the WHERE clause rather than the HAVING clause. See the section "Summarizing Data" later in this chapter.

The WHERE clause may be the most important part of a SQL statement. It's usually the most difficult to write, yet it's also where you can be the most creative.

Joining Tables

When a query combines data from two tables, it is called a *join*. The ability to join tables is one of the most fundamental operations of a relational database. That's where the term *relational* comes from — joining two tables that contain related data.

There are different ways of classifying joins, and you'll often hear people bandy about terms such as "right outer join," "left outer join," "equi-join," and so forth. Most of those terms don't really matter or are useful only to academics who spend a lot of time theorizing about SQL. When it comes to Oracle, there are two keys to understanding joins:

✦ You need to understand the concept of a Cartesian product.

✦ You need to understand the difference between an inner join and an outer join.

If you get these two concepts down, you won't have any trouble joining tables together in your queries.

Deriving a Cartesian product

Whenever you join two tables in a relational database, conceptually, you begin working with the Cartesian product of those two tables. The *Cartesian product* is defined as every possible combination of two rows from the two tables. Figure 16-1 illustrates this concept using the BOOKS and BOOKS_LOANED table.

As you can see in Figure 16-1, the Cartesian product has a multiplying effect. The BOOKS table contains three rows, and the BOOKS_LOANED table contains two rows. The resulting Cartesian product consists of six rows. This has some serious performance implications when you are dealing with large tables, and companies such as Oracle expend a great deal of time, money, and effort looking for ways to optimize table joins.

Note   In practice, Cartesian products are rarely generated. Conceptually, though, all joins start with the Cartesian product and are then winnowed down by conditions in the WHERE clause. You might find visualizing this Cartesian product to be an effective aid to writing correct join conditions in your WHERE clauses.

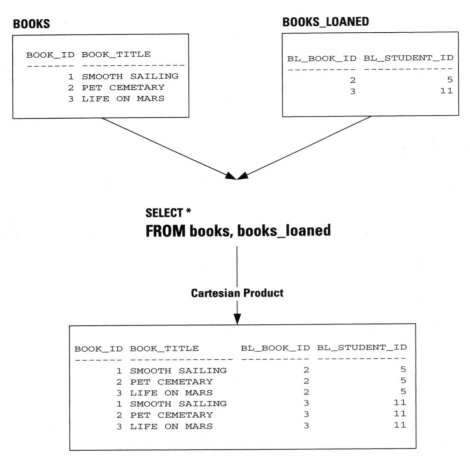

Figure 16-1: The Cartesian product of the BOOKS and BOOKS_LOANED tables

You would rarely ever really want the Cartesian product to be returned as the result when you join two tables. You will almost always end up adding conditions to your WHERE clause to eliminate combinations of rows that don't make sense.

Using equi-joins to compare columns

Equi-joins are the most common type of join, and they are most often used to join two tables that have a parent-child relationship. Equi-joins compare one or more columns in a set of tables for equality.

For example, the BOOKS table is related to the BOOKS_LOANED table by a parent-child relationship. Any one book may be loaned out several times over its lifetime, and each loan will be recorded with an entry in the BOOKS_LOANED table. If you want to report on the loan history of your books, you could start by querying the BOOKS_LOANED table, as follows:

```
SQL> SELECT bl_book_id, bl_student_id, bl_loan_date
  2  FROM books_loaned;

BL_BOOK_ID BL_STUDENT_ID BL_LOAN_D
---------- ------------- ---------
         2             5 04-MAY-98
```

This report really doesn't tell you much, because unless you have a good memory for ID numbers, you won't know the name of the book or student involved with any particular loan. However, you can get the book name from the BOOKS table. To do that, you must join the BOOKS and BOOKS_LOANED tables. The query in this next example does this. Notice that the BOOKS table has been added to the FROM clause, and the BOOK_TITLE and BOOK_ID columns have been added to the SELECT list.

```
SQL> SELECT book_id, book_title,
  2         bl_book_id, bl_student_id, bl_loan_date
  3  FROM books_loaned, books;

 BOOK_ID BOOK_TITLE      BL_BOOK_ID BL_STUDENT_ID BL_LOAN_D
-------- --------------- ---------- ------------- ---------
       1 SMOOTH SAILING           2             5 04-MAY-98
       2 PET CEMETARY             2             5 04-MAY-98
       3 LIFE ON MARS             2             5 04-MAY-98
```

Yuck! These results clearly aren't what you want. There was only one loan, yet the report now lists three loans, one for each book. What you are seeing here is the Cartesian product. The two tables were joined without the proper join condition being added to the WHERE clause. If you look at the BOOK_ID and BL_BOOK_ID columns, you'll see that the results make sense in only one case, and that's where the two columns are equal. Add a WHERE clause with that condition to the query, and it will now return the result you're after, as shown in the following example:

```
SQL> SELECT book_id, book_title,
  2         bl_book_id, bl_student_id, bl_loan_date
  3  FROM books_loaned, books
  4  WHERE book_id = bl_book_id;

 BOOK_ID BOOK_TITLE      BL_BOOK_ID BL_STUDENT_ID BL_LOAN_D
-------- --------------- ---------- ------------- ---------
       2 PET CEMETARY             2             5 04-MAY-98
```

Now that you have the query returning the loan history, including the book name, it's time to think about adding the student name into the mix. The relationship between STUDENTS and BOOKS_LOANED is the same as between BOOKS and

BOOKS_LOANED, so you can add the STUDENTS table to the query using the same technique as you used for BOOKS. The resulting query looks like this:

```
SELECT book_id, book_title,
       bl_book_id, bl_student_id,
       student_id, first_name, last_name,
       bl_loan_date
FROM books_loaned, books, students
WHERE book_id = bl_book_id
AND student_id = bl_student_id;
```

The queries in this section include the book ID number from both the BOOKS table and the BOOKS_LOANED table. It just so happens that the column names were slightly different between the two tables. However, what if the column names were identical? Would you write WHERE book_id = book_id in your query? How would Oracle tell the difference? These are good questions, and form the subject of the next section.

Using table aliases

When you join two tables, you may run into column names that are identical in each table. That begs the question of how to uniquely identify the columns when you refer to them in your query. One way is to prefix each column name with its respective table name. Consider this example:

```
SELECT books.book_id, books.book_title,
       books_loaned.bl_book_id, books_loaned.bl_student_id,
       students.student_id, students.first_name,
       students.last_name,
       books_loaned.bl_loan_date
FROM books_loaned, books, students
WHERE books.book_id = books_loaned.bl_book_id
AND students.student_id = books_loaned.bl_student_id;
```

Qualifying each column name with a table name is effective, but it often makes the query difficult to read, especially if your table names are on the long side. Because of this, in SQL, you are allowed to define aliases for the tables within a query. An *alias* is simply an alternate, and usually shorter, name for a table. You specify table aliases in the FROM clause by placing them immediately after the table names, separated by at least one space, as shown in this example:

```
FROM books_loaned bl, books b, students s
```

This FROM clause specifies aliases of BL for BOOKS_LOANED, B for BOOKS, and S for STUDENTS. Now you can use these aliases to qualify the column names within the query, as shown in this example:

```
SELECT b.book_id, b.book_title,
```

```
        bl.bl_book_id, bl.bl_student_id,
        s.student_id, s.first_name, s.last_name,
        bl.bl_loan_date
FROM books_loaned bl, books b, students s
WHERE b.book_id = bl.bl_book_id
AND s.student_id = bl.bl_student_id;
```

Short one- or two-letter aliases are typical because they make the query easier to read. They allow you to focus more on the column names than the table names.

Tip   When you define table aliases, try to make them mnemonic. Sometimes, you will see people using "a," "b," "c," and so forth. Avoid that because it becomes difficult to remember which table is "a" and which table is "b." The example in this section uses "bl" for "books loaned," making it easy to associate the two.

Using outer joins

An *outer join* allows you to join two tables and return results even when the second table doesn't have any records corresponding with the first. To really understand this, you have to know what an inner join is. An *inner join* between two tables returns rows where there are corresponding records in *both* tables. The join between BOOKS and BOOKS_LOANED is such a join. It returns a record only for the one book that had been loaned out, not for all books. Those results look like this:

```
BOOK_ID BOOK_TITLE      BL_BOOK_ID BL_STUDENT_ID BL_LOAN_D
------- --------------- ---------- ------------- ---------
      2 PET CEMETARY             2             5 04-MAY-98
```

Books that had never been loaned out weren't returned by the query. Why not? Because the join condition requires that the BOOK_ID column in the BOOKS table equal a BL_BOOK_ID value in the BOOKS_LOANED table. Since there were no loans recorded for books 1 and 3, that condition could never be true.

That's all well and good, but what if you want to produce a report listing all books, including loan history if there was any, but not excluding any books without a loan history? The solution is to write an outer join so you'll have one table that is the anchor table. You will always get at least one row back for each row in the anchor table. In this case, the BOOKS table will be the anchor. When you write the query, you indicate that you want an outer join by placing a (+) in the WHERE clause after the column names from the optional table. That's probably clear as mud, so here's an example:

```
SELECT book_id, book_title,
       bl_book_id, bl_student_id, bl_loan_date
FROM books_loaned, books
WHERE book_id = bl_book_id (+);
```

The (+) notation following the BL_BOOK_ID column specifies that you are doing an outer join. In return, whenever a book is encountered that doesn't have a loan history, Oracle will return one row for the book, but with null values for all the loan-related columns. The output will look like this:

```
BOOK_ID BOOK_TITLE      BL_BOOK_ID BL_STUDENT_ID BL_LOAN_D
--------- ---------------  ---------- ------------- ---------
      1 SMOOTH SAILING
      2 PET CEMETARY            2             5 04-MAY-98
      3 LIFE ON MARS
```

Note   Oracle is the only database vendor to use this rather strange (+) notation. Other database vendors allow you to specify outer joins in the FROM clause. This actually makes more sense because an outer join is table-specific, not column-specific.

Outer joins can become increasingly complex as you add more tables to the join, especially if these additional tables relate to the optional table. If you want to join the STUDENTS table to the query shown here, you need to also make that an outer join, because STUDENTS relates to BOOKS_LOANED. If BOOKS_LOANED is optional, then STUDENTS must be too. The following query will return all books, their loan records, if any exist, and the name of the student who goes with each loan record.

```
SELECT book_id, book_title,
       bl_book_id, bl_student_id,
       student_id, first_name, last_name,
       bl_loan_date
FROM books_loaned, books, students
WHERE book_id = bl_book_id (+)
AND student_id (+) = bl_student_id;
```

With the addition of the STUDENTS table, the (+) notation has been appended following the STUDENT_ID column in the WHERE clause. This makes the STUDENTS table optional. That way, when no BOOKS_LOANED record exists for a book, the lack of a student record won't matter, and the query will still return information for that book. Here are the results of executing this query:

```
BOOK_ID BOOK_TITLE      BL_BOOK_ID BL_STUDENT_ID STUDENT_ID...
------- ---------------  ---------- ------------- ----------...
      2 PET CEMETARY           2             5          5...
      1 SMOOTH SAILING                                   ...
      3 LIFE ON MARS                                     ...
```

Oracle places one restriction on outer joins: One table can't be the optional table in two outer joins. You could not, for example, change the last line in the previous query to read AND student_id = bl_student_id (+).

Summarizing Data

Several SQL functions exist that allow you to summarize data. These are referred to as *aggregate functions* because they return values aggregated from more than one row of data. Table 16-2 describes each of these aggregate functions.

Table 16-2 SQL Aggregate Functions	
Function	*Description*
AVG	Returns the average of all values in the column
COUNT	Returns a count of rows or a count of values in a column
MAX	Returns the maximum value of a column
MIN	Returns the minimum value of a column
STDDEV	Returns the standard deviation of all values in the column
SUM	Returns the sum of all values in a column
VARIANCE	Returns the variance (related to standard deviation) of all values in a column

The summary functions listed in Table 16-2 are almost always used in conjunction with a GROUP BY clause. The one exception is when you are summarizing all the data returned by a query.

Performing query-level summaries

The simplest form of summarization is when you use one of the aggregate functions to summarize the results of an entire query. This is often done to return a count of rows in a table. The following example shows the COUNT function being used to return the number of rows in the ARTISTS table:

```
SQL> SELECT COUNT(*)
  2  FROM artist;

COUNT(*)
---------
      10

1 row selected.
```

The asterisk used as an argument to COUNT indicates that you want the function to include every row in the table. You can pass in a column name instead, in which case, Oracle will count the number of values in that one column. The results may be different because null values in a column are not counted. Here's an example illustrating that point:

```
SQL> SELECT COUNT(city)
  2  FROM artist;

COUNT(CITY)
-----------
          9

1 row selected.
```

It seems that one artist has a null value for the CITY column. Since nulls represent the lack of a value, they aren't counted. In this case, the ARTIST table contains nine city values.

Using the GROUP BY clause

In addition to summarizing data for an entire table, you can use the GROUP BY clause to summarize data for a specific set of columns. This is almost better explained by example. Suppose you want to know how many artists of each specialty you have. You could determine this by writing a query like the one shown in Listing 16-2.

Listing 16-2: **Using the GROUP BY clause to summarize data**

```
SQL> SELECT specialty, COUNT(*)
  2  FROM artist
  3  GROUP BY specialty;

SPECIALTY        COUNT(*)
--------------- ---------
ACRYLIC                 1
DIGITAL                 3
MIXED MEDIA             1
MIXED ON PAPER          1
OIL                     1
OTHER                   1
WATERCOLOR              2

7 rows selected.
```

Notice what's going on here. The select list contains one column not used in an aggregate function. That column is also listed in the GROUP BY clause. The aggregate function COUNT(*) is also in the select list, causing Oracle to count up the number of rows for each distinct value in the specialty column.

Oracle evaluates a GROUP BY query like this by going through these steps:

1. Oracle retrieves the data for the query and saves it in temporary storage (possibly in memory, or possibly on disk).

2. Oracle sorts the data enough to group all records with like GROUP BY values together. The results might look like this:

```
WATERCOLOR
WATERCOLOR
DIGITAL
DIGITAL
DIGITAL
MIXED MEDIA
MIXED ON PAPER
ACRYLIC
OIL
OTHER
```

   Note that the sort is not a complete sort. Oracle is concerned only with grouping like values together. A strict alphabetical sort isn't necessary at this point.

3. Oracle applies the specified aggregate function to each group of records and returns one row for each group.

Because summary queries return one row for each group, you can't have columns in your select list that aren't also listed in your GROUP BY clause, unless those columns have an aggregate function applied to them. You cannot, for example, write this query:

```
SELECT specialty, last_name, first_name, COUNT(*)
FROM artist
GROUP BY specialty;
```

Why can't you do this? Because one specialty may represent many artists. Three artists have a specialty of 'DIGITAL'. Since the query is returning only one row for a specialty, how is it supposed to choose which first and last names go with that row? The answer is that there is no automatic way to do this. You either need to apply an aggregate function to the first and last name fields, or you must remove them from the select list.

You can group query results by more than one column, and COUNT is certainly not the only aggregate function at your disposal. The following example shows a GROUP BY query consisting of a join and two aggregate functions:

```
SELECT book_title, bl_student_id, COUNT(*), SUM(bl_fine)
FROM books, books_loaned
WHERE bl_fine > 0
AND books.book_id = bl_book_id
GROUP BY book_title, bl_student_id;
```

This query lists all books for which fines were paid, uses the COUNT function to tell you how many fines were paid for each book, and uses the SUM function to tell you the total dollar amount of fines for any one book. It does this for each combination of book and student.

Using the HAVING clause

The HAVING clause is a clause that you can add to a GROUP BY query to restrict the rows returned by that query. HAVING is just like WHERE, except that the conditions in the HAVING clause are applied to the data after it is summarized. You can use HAVING when you are interested only in specific groups. A good example might be if you wanted to see a list of artist specialties that were represented only by one artist. You could generate that list using the query shown in Listing 16-3.

Listing 16-3: **Restricting rows in a query**

```
SQL> SELECT specialty
  2  FROM artist
  3  GROUP BY specialty
  4  HAVING COUNT(*) = 1;

SPECIALTY
--------------
ACRYLIC
MIXED MEDIA
MIXED ON PAPER
OIL
OTHER

5 rows selected.
```

Notice that the HAVING clause in this query restricted the results based on an aggregate function. It has to do that because the HAVING clause is applied only after the data has been summarized. The HAVING clause can use only the GROUP BY columns and aggregate functions on other columns. Column values for individual rows aren't available. The aggregate functions used in the HAVING clause do not necessarily need to be the ones listed in the SELECT clause.

While it's possible to use the GROUP BY columns in the HAVING clause, it's often more efficient if you take another approach. For example, you could write the following query, which excludes the specialty named 'OTHER':

```
SELECT specialty
FROM artist
GROUP BY specialty
HAVING COUNT(*) = 1
AND specialty <> 'OTHER';
```

This query will work as expected, but think about what Oracle needs to do to resolve it. All the rows containing 'OTHER' must be read from the database, then grouped and summarized like those for any other value. Only after that data is summarized can the result be excluded. You could make this query much more efficient by avoiding the need to read those rows in the first place. You can do that by moving the specialty condition to the WHERE clause:

```
SELECT specialty
FROM artist
WHERE specialty <> 'OTHER'
GROUP BY specialty
HAVING COUNT(*) = 1;
```

This query will return the same results but will execute more efficiently because rows containing 'OTHER' never need to be read, placed in temporary storage, sorted, and summarized. Any time that you find yourself using GROUP BY columns in the HAVING clause, you should consider the possibility of moving those conditions to the WHERE clause.

Using the DISTINCT keyword vs. the ALL keyword

You can use two keywords with aggregate functions that affect how the data is summarized. These keywords are DISTINCT and ALL. The difference lies in whether the aggregate function summarizes each value in a group or each distinct value in a group. Let's use artist specialties as the basis for an example. You can count the values in the SPECIALTY column like this:

```
SQL> SELECT COUNT(specialty)
  2  FROM artist;

COUNT(SPECIALTY)
----------------
              10
```

This query returns a value of 10 because there are 10 artists in the table and each has a specialty. That isn't a very useful number, though. You might be more interested in the number of distinctly different specialties that exist. For that, you could use the DISTINCT keyword, as in this example:

```
SQL> SELECT COUNT(DISTINCT specialty)
  2  FROM artist;

COUNT(DISTINCTSPECIALTY)
-----------------------
                      7
```

Because the DISTINCT keyword is used, Oracle counts each distinct specialty value only once. In this case, there are seven different specialties. You can use the ALL keyword in place of DISTINCT, but that's rarely done since ALL represents the default behavior anyway.

 Note   Given this scenario, you'd probably be better off selecting the SPECIALTY column and grouping by that column, since your next question after finding out that there are seven specialties is going to be, "What are they?" — unless, of course, you were using this as a subquery.

When developing SQL queries, you can follow the steps outlined in the following sidebar. It discusses a methodology for query development.

Using Subqueries

Subqueries are queries that are nested within a larger query. You can use subqueries in a WHERE clause to express conditions that can't be expressed using simple comparison expressions. You should be aware of three types of subqueries:

✦ Noncorrelated subqueries, which execute independently of the parent query

✦ Correlated subqueries, which are executed once for each row returned by a parent query, and which use values from that row

✦ Inline views, which are subqueries that appear in the FROM clause

A Methodology for Query Development

I would like to share with you my personal methodology for developing SQL queries. I've often thought that standard SQL syntax encourages a backwards approach to query development. Since SELECT comes first, people tend to write that clause first. If the syntax were to match my order of query development, it would look like this:

```
FROM table_list
WHERE conditions
GROUP BY column_list
HAVING conditions
SELECT column_list
```

I generally find it helpful to follow the steps listed here when I'm developing a new SQL query. I start my work with the FROM clause. As I work through each step, I continuously test and modify the query. Usually, I do that by executing the partially completed query using SQL*Plus, and viewing the results. Here are my steps:

1. I figure out which tables contain the data that I want.

2. I work out the join conditions for these tables. At this point, I write the WHERE clause for those join conditions, and I place all the join columns in my select list. If I'm joining a number of tables, I add one at a time to the query and test the results after each addition.

3. Once I'm sure of having the joins correct, I add any other needed conditions to the WHERE clause. I never do this earlier because doing so could mask problems with the joins.

4. Having narrowed the results down to the data that I need, I look at any grouping that needs to be done.

5. If I did use a GROUP BY clause, I write the HAVING clause only after I know that I have the GROUP BY clause correct.

6. Finally, I go back and make the SELECT list look right. I remove columns that I had listed, to verify that joins were working correctly, I apply any needed SQL functions, and I add any other miscellaneous columns that I wasn't forced to add in any earlier steps.

There you have it. I've found that this process can reduce the development of some complex queries to a relatively routine task. The key here is to build up your queries a piece at a time, testing and validating each piece as you go.

Noncorrelated subqueries

A *noncorrelated subquery* doesn't depend on any values from rows returned by the parent query. You can use a noncorrelated subquery to obtain a list of values for use with the IN operator. Say you're interested in generating a list of students who don't appear to be using the school library. You might decide to use borrowing a book as a basis for that list, and you assume that if a student has never borrowed a book, then that student isn't using the library. That may not always be a correct assumption, but it's the only data that you have to work with. The following query uses the BOOKS_LOANED table to return a list of students who *have* borrowed at least one book:

```
SELECT DISTINCT bl_student_id
FROM books_loaned;
```

The DISTINCT keyword eliminates duplicate values from the result list. Even if a student borrowed a hundred books, you need only one copy of his or her ID number. Now that you have this query, you can use it as part of a larger query that answers the original question. For example:

```
SELECT student_id, first_name, last_name
FROM students
WHERE student_id NOT IN (
    SELECT DISTINCT bl_student_id
    FROM books_loaned
    );
```

The outer query here returns a list of students not represented by the inner query; in other words, it returns a list of students who have never borrowed a book. The subquery in the WHERE clause is independent of the parent query, making it noncorrelated. The acid test here is that you can pull the subquery out as it stands, execute it on its own, and get results.

Correlated subqueries

A *correlated subquery* is one in which the result depends on values returned by the parent query. Because of this dependency, Oracle must execute these queries once for each row examined by the parent query: hence, the term correlated.

We can also use the problem of identifying students who have never borrowed books to demonstrate the use of correlated subqueries. We want a list of students who have never borrowed books, so for any given student, we need to check the BOOKS_LOANED table to see if any records exist. Here, a correlated subquery is used to do that:

```
SELECT student_id, first_name, last_name
```

```
FROM students s
WHERE NOT EXISTS (
   SELECT *
   FROM books_loaned bl
   WHERE bl.bl_student_id = s.student_id
   );
```

The NOT EXISTS operator is used here, and it will return a value of TRUE if no rows are returned by the subquery that goes with it. Notice the WHERE clause of this subquery. It contains a reference to a value in the STUDENTS table, which is listed in the FROM clause of the outer query. That makes this a correlated subquery. It must be executed once for each student. You couldn't pull this subquery out and execute it as it stands because the STUDENT_ID column will not be recognized. The subquery makes sense only in the context of the outer query.

Tip

Specify table aliases when you write correlated subqueries, and use them to qualify all your column names. This is necessary if your subquery is against the same table as the parent query, but even when it's not necessary, the aliases will help you keep straight to which table a column belongs.

You've now seen the same query implemented in two ways: using NOT IN and using NOT EXISTS. Which is better? That really depends on the execution plan that the optimizer puts together for the query. You might hear debates between those who feel that NOT IN is always the best approach and those who believe that NOT EXISTS is always best. Don't waste your time with debates. If you're ever in doubt about which approach to take, just test it out. Chapter 19, "Tuning SQL Statements," shows you how to discover the optimizer's execution plan for a statement. Arm yourself with that information, and perhaps with some statistics from a few trial executions, and let the numbers speak for themselves.

Inline views

An *inline view* is a subquery used in the FROM clause in place of a table name. Such a subquery functions the same as if you had created and used a view based on the query. Here's an example:

```
SELECT student_id, books_borrowed
FROM (
   SELECT s.student_id student_id,
          COUNT(bl.bl_student_id) books_borrowed
   FROM students s, books_loaned bl
   WHERE s.student_id = bl.bl_student_id (+)
   GROUP BY s.student_id
   )
WHERE books_borrowed = 0;
```

The inline view in this example returns a complete list of students, together with the number of books that they have borrowed. You accomplish this by using an outer join from STUDENTS to BOOKS_LOANED and counting up the number of BL_STUDENT_ID values. Remember, nulls don't count. Whenever a student has no corresponding loan records, the BL_STUDENT_ID value will be null, and that student will get a value of 0. Column aliases are specified for both columns returned by the inline view, and these become the column names visible to the parent SELECT statement. The outer SELECT statement, then, selects only those records where the BOOKS_BORROWED count is equal to zero.

Note   The number of different solutions to the problem of finding students who have never borrowed books shows just how creative you can get when writing SQL queries. You haven't seen the last of this problem yet, either. There's at least one more solution shown later in this chapter.

Inline views function just as any other view, and you can join them to other tables, views, or even other inline views. You can join the inline view just discussed to the STUDENTS table to allow the parent SELECT statement to retrieve the first and last names for each student. Here's an example showing how to do that:

```
SELECT bb.student_id, bb.books_borrowed,
       s.last_name, s.first_name
FROM (
   SELECT s.student_id student_id,
          COUNT(bl.bl_student_id) books_borrowed
   FROM students s, books_loaned bl
   WHERE s.student_id = bl.bl_student_id (+)
   GROUP BY s.student_id
   ) bb, students s
WHERE books_borrowed = 0
AND bb.student_id = s.student_id;
```

In this case, because the inline view and the STUDENTS table both contain columns named STUDENT_ID, you use table aliases of BB and S to make it clear just which table is being referred to at any time.

Beware of Nulls!

Null values have a strangely unintuitive effect on the values of expressions, especially those returning Boolean values such as those that you often find in a WHERE clause. To write queries that properly handle null values, you need to understand three-valued logic. You also need to understand the built-in operators and functions that have been specifically designed to deal with null values.

The two primary problems that people encounter when using nulls are three-valued logic and the effect of nulls on expressions.

Recognizing three-valued logic

The primary problem with nulls is that SQL deals with them using a system known as *three-valued logic*. In our day-to-day lives, most of us become accustomed to two-valued logic. A statement may be either true or false. Three-valued logic introduces another option referred to as *unknown*. The following statement demonstrates this nicely:

```
SELECT first_name, last_name
FROM artist
WHERE city = 'Madison'
OR city <> 'Madison';
```

Intuitively, most people would expect this statement to return every row in the ARTIST table. After all, we are asking for the records for Madison, and also for other cities. In reality, though, if you execute this statement against the data in the sample database, you'll only get nine of the ten artists' records back because one artist has a null value for the CITY column. Is null equal to 'Madison'? The answer is unknown. Is null not equal to 'Madison'? That answer is also unknown. Is unknown the same as true? No, it's not, so the record with a null is never returned.

Understanding the impact of nulls on expressions

Another problem with nulls is that if any value in an expression happens to be a null, then the result of the expression will also be a null. Theoretically, this is reasonable behavior. Practically, it's often not what you need to get the job done.

You typically need to deal with null values in two parts of a query: the select list and the WHERE clause.

Using nulls in the SELECT list

Your primary concern with the SELECT list is whether you want NULL values to be returned to your program. Or, if you are writing a SQL*Plus report, you need to be concerned with what the report displays when a value is null. The following query returns three columns, all of which could be null:

```
SELECT bl_book_id, bl_student_id, bl_fine
FROM books_loaned;
```

Assuming for a moment that you would never have a loan record without a student and a book, how do you want to deal with the BL_FINE field? One choice is to leave it as it is and allow nulls to be returned by the query. Your other choice is to supply a reasonable alternate value to use in place of nulls. You can use Oracle's built-in NVL function to do this. The following example shows the query rewritten to return 0 whenever the fine field is null:

```
SELECT bl_book_id, bl_student_id, NVL(bl_fine,0)
FROM books_loaned;
```

The NVL function takes two arguments. One is a column name or an expression. The other is the value to be returned when the first argument evaluates to null. In this example, NVL will return 0 whenever BL_FINE is null. Otherwise, it will return the value of BL_FINE.

Using nulls in the WHERE clause

With WHERE clauses (and HAVING clauses, too), your primary concern is whether you want records with null values included in the query results. Take a look at this query, for example:

```
SELECT *
FROM books_loaned
WHERE bl_fine <= 10;
```

This query is asking for all records where the fine was less than or equal to $10. That seems straightforward enough, but what about records where the BL_FINE column is null? Should those be included? If your answer is yes, you can include them by adding a condition that uses the IS NULL operator. Consider this example:

```
SELECT *
FROM books_loaned
WHERE bl_fine <= 10
OR bl_fine IS NULL;
```

You could also use NVL in the WHERE clause and write WHERE NVL(bl_fine,0) <= 10, but as you'll find out in the next section, using functions on columns in the WHERE clause isn't always a good idea.

In addition to IS NULL, there is the IS NOT NULL operator. Use IS NULL when you want to check for a value being null; use IS NOT NULL when you want to check a value to see if it is something other than null.

Tip Always use IS NULL or IS NOT NULL when testing for nullity. Don't ever write anything like WHERE bl_fine = NULL. The equality operator can't test for nullity, and that expression will always evaluate to unknown.

Using SQL Functions in Queries

Oracle implements a number of built-in functions that you can use in your queries. You've already seen one example in the NVL function used to translate null values to something other than null. A few of the more interesting and useful functions are described here. See Appendix B, "SQL Built-in Function Reference," for a complete list.

Using functions on indexed columns

When you use functions in a query, especially in the WHERE clause of a query, be aware of the potential for those functions to preclude the use of an index. Say, for example, that you have indexed the SPECIALTY column in the ARTIST table. A query such as the following, which selects for a specific specialty, could take advantage of that index:

```
SELECT last_name, first_name
FROM artist
WHERE specialty = 'WATERCOLOR';
```

Applying a function to the specialty column, however, changes the rules. Look at this example, where the UPPER function has been applied to make the query case-insensitive:

```
SELECT last_name, first_name
FROM artist
WHERE UPPER(specialty) = 'WATERCOLOR';
```

This query no longer searches for a specific value in the SPECIALTY column; rather, it is searching for rows where the expression UPPER(specialty) returns a specific value. This distinction is important to make, because this normally precludes Oracle from using any indexes on the SPECIALTY column. Instead, in this case, Oracle will be forced to read every row in the table, evaluate the expression for each row, and test the result. On a large table, this can be a significant performance issue.

New Feature Oracle8i implements a new feature that allows you to index the results of an expression. You can use this feature to create an index on an expression such as UPPER(specialty), which Oracle will then be able to use when you make such a function call in your queries. See Chapter 14, "Managing Indexes," for information on creating function-based indexes.

If you're not using function-based indexes, you need to carefully consider your use of functions in the WHERE clause. Avoid applying them to indexed columns, if at all possible.

Using the DECODE function

You can use the DECODE function to work as an inline IF statement inside a query. A call to DECODE includes a variable number of arguments used to transfer an input argument into some other value. The first argument is the input argument. The second and third arguments form a pair. If the input argument matches the second argument, the function returns the third argument. You can have as many argument pairs as you like. The final argument, which is optional, represents the value to be returned if the input argument doesn't match any of the pairs.

The FISH table contains a death date column that can be used to illustrate the use of DECODE. Suppose that you are producing a report of fish, and that you want to know whether each fish is alive. The actual death date, if one exists, doesn't matter to you. You can use the DECODE function to translate the DEATH_DATE column from a date field to a text field containing either 'ALIVE' or 'DEAD', as shown in this example:

```
DECODE(death_date,NULL,'ALIVE','DEAD')
```

Note   The DECODE function is one of the few functions that can properly test for nulls.

The input argument is DEATH_DATE. The first value pair is NULL, 'ALIVE'. If the DEATH_DATE is null, meaning that the fish hasn't died yet, the DECODE function will return the character string 'ALIVE'. If the date doesn't match any value pair—in this case, there is only one—then the default value of 'DEAD' will be returned. The following example shows this DECODE function being used in a query to retrieve a list of fish:

```
SQL> SELECT name_of_fish,
  2         DECODE(death_date,null,'ALIVE','DEAD')
  3  FROM fish;

NAME_OF_FI DECOD
---------- -----
Fish Two   DEAD
Fish Three DEAD
Fish Four  ALIVE
Wesley     ALIVE
```

If this is the first time you've seen the DECODE function being used, you may think it's a rather strange function. It is a strange function, but it's extremely useful. As you work more with Oracle, you'll see a number of creative applications for the DECODE function.

Using the INSTR function

The INSTR (short for INSTRING) function is a function that you apply to a character-datatype column. The INSTR function hunts down a text string or letter and tells you exactly where it starts within that column. If the text string you are searching for isn't found, the INSTR function will return a value of 0.

For example, you might want to find all the fish with comments referring to the fish named Wesley. You could do this using the following query:

```
SELECT name_of_fish, comment_text
FROM fish
WHERE INSTR(comment_text,'Wesley') <> 0;
```

In this case, it doesn't matter where in the COMMENT_TEXT column the string occurs. All that matters is that it does occur. Any nonzero value indicates that. If you execute this query, the results will look like this:

```
NAME_OF_FI COMMENT_TEXT
---------- -------------------------------------------

Fish Two   Eaten by Wesley
Fish Three Eaten by Wesley
Fish Four  Died while I was on vacation, probably
           eaten by Wesley
```

Using the SUBSTR function

You can use the SUBSTR function to return a specific portion of a character column. The SUBSTR function takes three arguments. The first is the string itself. The second argument indicates the starting position. The third argument indicates the number of characters that you want to extract.

Following is an example showing how you can use the SUBSTR function. This is the same query that you saw in the previous section, but the SUBSTR function has been used to make the fish names display without "Fish" in front of each one:

```
SQL> SELECT SUBSTR(name_of_fish,6,5), comment_text
  2  FROM fish
  3  WHERE INSTR(comment_text,'Wesley') <> 0;

SUBST COMMENT_TEXT
----- -------------------------------------------
Two   Eaten by Wesley
Three Eaten by Wesley
Four  Died while I was on vacation, probably
      eaten by Wesley
```

As you can see, this query displays only the last five characters of each fish's name.

Using the concatenation operator

The concatenation operator is not really a function, but this seems as good a place as any to talk about it. You can use the concatenation operator to combine any two text strings into one. If you want to insert the words "The Honorable" in front of your fish's names, for example, you could use the concatenation operator, as shown in the following example:

```
SQL> SELECT 'The Honorable ' || name_of_fish
  2  FROM fish;

'THEHONORABLE'||NAME_OF_
------------------------
The Honorable Fish Two
The Honorable Fish Three
The Honorable Fish Four
The Honorable Wesley
```

When concatenating strings, take care to insert spaces between them so that your words don't run together. In this example, a space is appended to the word "Honorable."

Using the NVL function

The NVL function enables you to substitute a phrase, number, or date for a null value in a query. Here's an easy example:

```
SELECT name_of_fish, NVL(sex,'Unknown') sex
FROM fish;
```

In this example, when a fish has a null value for sex, the word "Unknown" will be returned in its place. The results look like this:

```
NAME_OF_FI SEX
---------- ----------
Fish Two   Female
Fish Three Male
Fish Four  Unknown
Wesley     Male
```

Notice that in this example, a column alias was used to give the SEX column back its original name. Otherwise, Oracle generates a name based on the expression that was used. If you're writing ad-hoc SQL*Plus reports, it's easier to set up column headings if you name columns that are the result of expressions.

Combining Query Results

A *union* combines the results of several queries into one result set. Unions are useful when you find it difficult to write just one query to get the results that you want. With unions, you can combine the results of two or more queries. SQL supports four types of unions. The operators for the four types are as follows:

UNION	Combines the results of two SELECT statements, and weeds out duplicate rows
UNION ALL	Combines the results of two SELECT statements, and doesn't weed out duplicate rows
MINUS	Returns rows that are from one SELECT statement that are not also returned by another
INTERSECT	Returns rows that are returned by each of two SELECT statements

Using the UNION and UNION ALL keywords

The UNION operator combines the results of two SELECT statements and weeds out duplicate rows at the same time. For example, the following UNION query returns a list of students who have either borrowed or reserved a book:

```
SELECT bl_student_id
FROM books_loaned
UNION
SELECT reserved_student_id
FROM books_reserved;
```

Because UNION is used in this example, no student will be listed twice in the results. If you don't want duplicate records to be eliminated, use UNION ALL instead.

Using the MINUS operator

The MINUS operator subtracts the results of one query from another. Remember the queries earlier in the chapter that produced a list of students who had never borrowed books? Here is yet one more approach to solving that problem, this time using the MINUS operator:

```
SQL> SELECT student_id
  2  FROM students
  3  MINUS
  4  SELECT bl_student_id
  5  FROM books_loaned;
```

```
STUDENT_ID
----------
         1
         7
        11
```

The first SELECT statement, from the STUDENTS table, provides a complete list of ID numbers. The second SELECT statement, from the BOOKS_LOANED table, provides a list of ID numbers for students who have borrowed books. The MINUS operator causes Oracle to look at the results of the first query and to delete any rows where those rows match a row returned by the second query. Oracle looks at all the columns in the row when it does this.

Using the INTERSECT operator

The INTERSECT operator causes Oracle to return rows only when they occur in both SELECT statements. The following query, for example, returns a list of students who have borrowed books:

```
SQL> SELECT student_id
  2  FROM students
  3  INTERSECT
  4  SELECT bl_student_id
  5  FROM books_loaned;

STUDENT_ID
----------
         5
```

As with the MINUS example presented earlier, the first query returns a list of all student ID numbers. The second query returns ID numbers only for students who have borrowed books. The INTERSECT operator causes Oracle to return rows represented only in both result sets.

Summary

In this chapter, you learned:

✦ Learning to write queries is a basic SQL skill. The same skills are used when writing other commands, such as INSERT and UPDATE. The SQL SELECT command is the mechanism for queries. The SELECT command has five basic components: the SELECT, FROM, WHERE, GROUP BY, and ORDER BY clauses.

✦ Oracle supports two types of joins. Inner joins return results only when both tables contain corresponding records. Outer joins can be used to make one table an optional table.

✦ You can use the GROUP BY clause to summarize data. Aggregate functions such as COUNT are used when doing this. You can also use the HAVING clause when summarizing data, to eliminate summary rows that you don't want to see in the results.

✦ Functions modify column contents within the context of the query. When used in a query, the underlying data doesn't change. You can use functions anywhere that you can use a column.

✦ You should develop your SQL queries systematically and test them each step of the way to be sure the results are what you expect.

✦ Unions allow you to combine the results of two SELECT statements. There are four types of unions: UNION, UNION ALL, MINUS, and INTERSECT. The UNION operator combines the rows from two SELECT statements and eliminates any duplicates. The UNION ALL operator performs the same functionbut without eliminating duplicates. The MINUS operator removes any rows that are returned by the second query. The INTERSECT operator returns only rows that are returned by both queries.

✦   ✦   ✦

Using DML Statements

C hapter 16, "Selecting Data with SQL," covers constructing queries, and if you've read that chapter, you understand how to choose particular rows out of a table. You call upon this ability when you modify data in the data-base as well. If you want to change the data in one or more rows of a table, you must know how to specify which rows you are after. This chapter describes how to modify data using three SQL commands: INSERT, UPDATE, and DELETE. Each command has several variations, which will be illustrated with examples.

Modifying Data in Tables and Views

The real power of SQL derives from its operation on many rows of data at one time. A single line of SQL code can change every row in a table. You can use the same techniques you use to gather many rows together for a report to modify many rows at the same time. The three basic commands for data manipulation are UPDATE, INSERT, and DELETE.

You can insert, update, or delete rows from a table or a view. You must have the corresponding privilege (INSERT to insert rows, UPDATE to modify rows, and DELETE to delete rows) on the table or view. Modifying the rows in a view actually modifies the rows in the underlying table. For more information about modifying data in a view, you can read the sidebar.

Modifying Data in a View

Some restrictions apply when using INSERT, UPDATE, and DELETE commands on a view rather than on a table. If the view was created with the WITH CHECK OPTION, you can modify data through view only if the resulting data satisfies the view's defining query. You can't insert data into a view created using this option.

You cannot modify data using a view if the view's defining query contains any of the following constructs:

✦ Certain types of joins

✦ Set operator (UNION, UNION ALL, MINUS, INTERSECT)

✦ The GROUP BY clause

✦ Group function (MAX, MIN, AVG, and so forth)

✦ The DISTINCT operator

Cross-Reference For more information about updateable views, including details on the type of joins that are updateable, see Chapter 15, "Working with Views, Synonyms, and Sequences."

Inserting New Data

The INSERT command has two forms. The first allows you to supply values for one specific row to be inserted, while the second uses a subquery to return values for new rows. This section describes each variation on using the INSERT command to modify data.

Inserting one row

The following example demonstrates the usual way to insert a row into a table:

```
INSERT INTO tablename
    (columnname1, columnname2,...)
    VALUES (value1, value2,...);
```

Replace *tablename* with the name of the table into which you are inserting the row. Replace *columnname1, columnname2,...* with the names of the columns for which you are supplying data. Replace *value1, value2,...* with the actual data that you are inserting. You must supply one value for each column in the column list. Text strings should be enclosed within single quotes. Dates should be enclosed in quotes, and the TO_DATE function should be used to explicitly convert them from text to a date value.

You can omit the entire list of columns (`columnname1, columnname2,...`) as long as your list of values matches the table's columns exactly.

Suppose that you add a new type of salad to your lunch counter. You need to add a new row to the SALAD_TYPE table for this new salad type. Here's an insert statement you can use to add this new variety:

```
INSERT INTO salad_type
   (salad_type, description_text,
    organic_flag, price_per_pound)
   VALUES ('CEASAR', 'Ceasar Salad', 'YES', 9.50);
```

This insert supplies values for all columns, except LAST_CHANGE_DATE. When you insert a row like this without supplying values for all the columns in the table, Oracle will need to do something with those remaining columns. Usually, it will set those columns to null. The exception is when a default value has been defined. If a default value was defined, and no value was supplied for the column in the INSERT statement, Oracle stores the default value in the column for the new row. See Chapter 13, "Managing Tables," for more information on defining default values for columns in a table.

You can explicitly place null values into a column by using the NULL keyword. For example, the following INSERT statement explicitly sets the ORGANIC_FLAG column to null:

```
INSERT INTO SALAD_TYPE
   (salad_type, description_text,
    organic_flag, price_per_pound, last_change_date)
 values ('GREENS','Garden Greens, Dandelions, etc',
        NULL, 2.75, TRUNC(SYSDATE));
```

When you explicitly specify a null value this way, the column will be set to null regardless of any default value that may be defined for that column.

Inserting the results of a query

If you're trying to copy data from one table to another, or if you can derive the data that you want to insert from other tables in the database, you can use a subquery as the source of values for an INSERT statement. This allows you to insert many rows at one time. The basic format for this kind of insert is the following:

```
INSERT INTO tablename (column1, column2, ... ) subquery;
```

You may omit the list of columns if the subquery returns a value for every column in the table. You'll probably want to do this often when you're duplicating the contents of a table.

As an example of this technique, suppose that you acquire a mailing list and that you import that list into your database as a table named MILLIES_MAILING_LIST. Having imported the data, you now want to insert all the rows into your CLIENT table. You can do this by writing an INSERT statement with a subquery on the imported table. For example:

```
SQL> INSERT INTO client
  2  SELECT customer_id+125, name_of_client,
  3         street_address || ' ' || city_state_zip, NULL
  4  FROM millies_mailing_list;

4 rows created.
```

Consider these interesting points about this example:

✦ No column list was given in the INSERT statement, meaning that all columns in the CLIENT table must be populated from corresponding columns in the SELECT query.

✦ The MILLIES_MAILING_LIST table has a two-column address that is concatenated and stored as one column in the CLIENT table.

✦ A value of 125 is added to each new customer ID to avoid possible conflicts with existing data.

✦ Since MILLIES_MAILING_LIST did not have a country column, the subquery returned a NULL for that value.

Another use of subqueries in INSERT statements is to generate missing parent records in preparation for creating a foreign key constraint. Say that you intend to create a foreign key from SALAD_TRAY to SALAD_TYPE and that you know you have a number of salad trays defined with invalid types. If you want to create the constraint and yet keep those trays, you can issue an INSERT statement like this:

```
INSERT INTO salad_type tp
   (salad_type, description_text, organic_flag)
   SELECT ty.salad_type, MAX(ty.sample_description), MAX('NO')
   FROM salad_tray ty
   WHERE ty.salad_type NOT IN (
         SELECT tp2.salad_type
         FROM salad_type tp2
         )
   GROUP BY ty.salad_type;
```

This is certainly a mind-bending statement. It actually contains two subqueries, one nested inside the other. The innermost subquery retrieves a list of salad types that have already been defined. These don't need to be redefined, so the parent query excludes those types from the rows that it selects. The GROUP BY clause exists to ensure that only one row is returned for each distinct salad type in the SALAD_TRAY table that hasn't yet been defined in the SALAD_TYPE table. You might think that you could use DISTINCT here, but you can't because salad tray descriptions are all different. The MAX function is applied to the SAMPLE_DESCRIPTION column to arbitrarily choose one salad tray description as the description for the new type being created. All of this data is returned to the INSERT statement, which inserts the new rows into the SALAD_TYPE table.

You can also use the subquery method of inserting to quickly generate large amounts of test data. You can do this by inserting a copy of a table's current data back into that table, repeating the process until you have the volume of data that you are after. Consider this example:

```
SQL> INSERT INTO client
  2     SELECT * FROM client;

9 rows created.

SQL> /

18 rows created.

SQL> /

36 rows created.
```

Each time the forward slash is used to execute the statement, the number of rows in the table is doubled.

Updating Existing Data

The UPDATE statement enables you to modify existing table data. There are two forms of the UPDATE statement. One form allows you to update a table and to explicitly provide new values for columns in rows being modified. The second form allows you to base the new values on a subquery. Both of these forms are described in this section.

Performing a standard update

The most common form of the UPDATE statement simply sets one or more columns to a new value. The basic format of the statement looks like this:

```
UPDATE tablename
SET columnname = expression,
    columnname2 = expression2,
    ...
WHERE conditions;
```

Replace *tablename* with your table's name and replace *columnname*, *columnname2*, and so forth, with the names of the columns you want to modify. The *expression* and *expression2* values represent the new values for those columns. These expressions may be a literal value, another column, or the result of any valid SQL expression. The datatype of the expression, of course, must be compatible with the column being changed. Replace the WHERE clause with any valid WHERE clause to specify which rows you want to modify. You can update all the rows in a table by omitting the WHERE clause entirely.

The following example demonstrates where you add *red* to the list of colors for a specific fish in the FISH table. The new value of the column is actually computed by an expression that references both the old value and a text constant.

```
UPDATE fish
SET colors = colors || ',red'
WHERE name_of_fish = 'Wesley';
```

You can set a column's value to null by using the NULL keyword as the new value. The following example sets DEATH_DATE to NULL for all rows in the FISH table:

```
UPDATE fish
SET death_date = NULL;
```

This statement updates every row in the table because no WHERE clause is supplied.

Using UPDATE statements based on subqueries

The second variation on the UPDATE statement has a great amount of flexibility because it uses a subquery—a query within the UPDATE statement. The basic format is shown in the following example:

```
UPDATE tablename
    SET (columnname, columnname2, ...) =
        (SELECT columnname3, columnname4, ...
         FROM tablename2
         WHERE conditions)
WHERE conditions;
```

Replace *tablename* with the table to be updated. Replace *columnname*, *columnname2*, and so forth, with a list of columns to be updated. The subquery is everything inside the parentheses after the equal sign. You can place any query inside the subquery as long as the columns in the subquery (*columnname3*, *columnname4*,...) match the columns in the UPDATE statement's column list.

A subquery used in the SET clause of an UPDATE statement may be correlated or noncorrelated. Correlated subqueries offer more flexibility and are often the reason that you want a subquery in the first place.

Note

> Whenever you use a subquery in the SET clause of an update statement, you must be sure that the subquery returns exactly one row. If the subquery returns no rows at all, then all the columns being updated will be set to null. If the subquery returns more than one row, Oracle will return an error.

Using a Noncorrelated Subquery Example

When you use a noncorrelated subquery in an UPDATE statement, the query will return the same value for each row being updated. This typically is useful only if just one row is being updated. The following example shows such an update. The MONHLY_SALES table is being updated to reflect the sales for the month of January 1996:

```
UPDATE MONTHLY_SALES
SET (SALES_AMOUNT) =
        (SELECT SUM(SALES_AMOUNT)
         FROM DAILY_SALES
         WHERE SALES_DATE BETWEEN
                TO_DATE('01-JAN-1996','DD-MON-YYYY')
                AND TO_DATE('31-JAN-1996','DD-MON-YYYY'))
WHERE SALES_MONTH = TO_DATE('JAN-1996','MON-YYYY');
```

Remember, for an update of this type to succeed, the row being updated must already exist. Don't confuse this with an INSERT...SELECT FROM statement.

Using Correlated Subqueries to Update Data

A subquery is said to be correlated when it references values from the table being updated. When this occurs, Oracle must execute the subquery once for each row that you are changing. This represents the most versatile use of subqueries in an UPDATE statement because it not only allows you to update a large number of rows, but it also allows you to use values from those rows to derive the new values for the columns that you are changing.

The following statement shows an example of a correlated subquery being used with an UPDATE statement. It goes through and changes the descriptions for all the salad tray records. The new description for each salad tray is taken from the record in the SALAD_TYPE table that corresponds to the type of salad tray being modified. Here's the UPDATE statement that does all this work for you:

```
UPDATE salad_tray tray
SET sample_description = (
        SELECT description_text
        FROM salad_type type
        WHERE type.salad_type = tray.salad_type)
WHERE tray.salad_type IS NOT NULL;
```

Notice the use of table aliases in this command. The SALAD_TRAY table is assigned the alias TRAY, and the SALAD_TYPE table is assigned the alias TYPE. These aliases are used in the WHERE clause of the subquery to qualify the column names being used. They make it clear which table each column belongs to. The WHERE clause in the main query restricts the update so that it is only applied to SALAD_TRAY rows that actually have an associated salad type code.

Using correlated UPDATE statements like this allows you to update a lot of data with one statement. The keys to doing this successfully lie in creating a set of rules for deriving the new values from existing data, and in writing WHERE clauses that can be used to correlate those new values with the proper rows in the table being modified.

Tip   If you're going to issue a correlated subquery like this to do a mass update of your data, be sure to think through thoroughly the implications of what you are doing. You might want to run some SELECTs first to be certain that you are selecting the right records to be updated. You might also run some SELECTs to verify that your subqueries are working properly. When doing a mass update like this, it's easy to overlook oddities in your data that can cause problems.

Deleting Data

You use the DELETE command to delete rows from a table. The basic form of the command is relatively simple and looks like this:

```
DELETE FROM tablename
WHERE condition;
```

Replace *tablename* with an actual table name. Replace *condition* with any valid WHERE clause conditions. These may be simple comparison expressions, or they may be nested subqueries.

The following DELETE statement uses a simple WHERE clause with no subqueries and deletes all fruit-salad trays from the SALAD_TRAY table:

```
DELETE
FROM salad_tray
WHERE salad_type = 'FRUIT';
```

Tip   Test your DELETE statements by creating SELECT statements using the same WHERE clause. Then, execute those SELECT statements. With this approach, you can see which rows are selected for deletion before you actually delete them.

You can use subqueries to good effect in DELETE statements. The following example uses a noncorrelated subquery to find and delete all salad types for which no trays exist:

```
DELETE
FROM salad_type
WHERE salad_type NOT IN (
    SELECT salad_type
    FROM salad_tray);
```

Note   You can test these DELETE statements against the sample database, but you might want to roll back the delete afterwards, so as not to delete all your sample data.

Correlated subqueries are useful as well. The following example shows a DELETE similar to the previous one, but it uses a correlated subquery. It will delete any salad tray records containing invalid salad-type values:

```
DELETE
FROM salad_tray tray
WHERE NOT EXISTS (
    SELECT *
    FROM salad_type type
    WHERE tray.salad_type = type.salad_type);
```

If you intend to add a foreign key constraint from the SALAD_TRAY table to the SALAD_TYPE table, you need to be sure that all the salad trays have valid types. Otherwise, Oracle won't allow you to add the constraint. A DELETE statement such as the one shown in the previous example allows you to delete any records that have invalid type codes, allowing you to create the constraint.

Tip   If you need to use DELETE for all the rows in a table and the table is very large, consider using the TRUNCATE command instead. Truncating a table goes much faster because Oracle doesn't allow a rollback to be done. The tradeoff is that your risk of losing data is increased, because if you truncate the wrong table by mistake, you can't roll back the transaction.

Substituting a Subquery for a Table Name

The actual table or view to be modified is usually listed in an INSERT, UPDATE, or DELETE command. However, you can use a subquery in place of the table or view name. When you do this, the subquery is treated as if it were a view. In fact, it represents an inline view. Therefore, the same rules apply here as when modifying a view. (See the sidebar "Modifying Data in a View" at the beginning of the chapter.)

Here's an example showing an INSERT into an inline view:

```
INSERT INTO
    (SELECT BREAD_NO, BREAD_NAME FROM BREAD)
    VALUES (10,'Poppy Seed');
```

Inline views are really used much more often in SELECT statements than in any of the INSERT, UPDATE, or DELETE statements.

Summary

In this chapter, you learned:

✦ The ability to write queries helps you write commands to modify data in tables and views.

✦ You are allowed to use only specific kinds of views when modifying data. When modifying data using a view, the underlying table's data actually gets modified.

✦ An UPDATE command modifies data in existing rows in a table or view. The UPDATE command has two basic variations: one using literals or expressions to set new values for the columns, and one using a subquery to perform that function.

✦ The INSERT command adds a new row (or set of new rows) to a table. You may insert one row at a time, or you may use a subquery to insert several rows at once.

✦ The DELETE command removes rows from a table. Use a WHERE clause to tell Oracle which rows you want to delete. If you leave off the WHERE clause, you'll delete all rows in a table.

✦   ✦   ✦

Oracle8i Tuning

Optimizers and Statistics

Choosing the correct optimizer and maintaining current statistics are two of the keys to getting good performance out of SQL queries that you execute against your database. Oracle supports two different optimizers; you have to choose which to use. Oracle also implements functionality that you can use to collect information about the data in your tables and indexes so that the optimizer can make intelligent decisions about how best to retrieve data for a query.

Comparing Cost-based and Rule-based Optimization

When you submit a SELECT query to be executed against your database, Oracle must provide some sort of algorithm to retrieve the data that you are after from the database. The part of Oracle that does this is called the *optimizer*. The algorithm for retrieving your data is referred to as an *execution plan*. Oracle supports two optimizers: One is rule-based, and the other is cost-based.

Examining the rule-based optimizer

The optimizer that Oracle first developed is rule-based. It looks at your query, checks for certain constructs such as joins, the use of indexed columns in the WHERE clause, and so forth, and then uses that information to determine an access path to the data. Oracle's rule-based optimizer looks only at the syntax of your SQL statements and at whether fields are indexed. That's it. It makes no attempt to compare the amount of disk I/O and CPU required for different execution plans.

As good as the rule-based optimizer is, in many cases it won't choose the best execution plan for a query. In part, this is because it doesn't look at the amount of I/O or CPU needed to execute any given plan; in part, it's because the plan chosen depends on how the SELECT statement is written. Something as simple as changing the order of the tables listed in the FROM clause can have a disastrous effect on performance.

Examining the cost-based optimizer

The cost-based optimizer represents Oracle's vision for the future. Introduced with the release of Oracle7, the cost-based optimizer chooses its execution plan based on the estimated cost of the various alternative approaches. This *cost* is determined largely by the amount of disk I/O and CPU resources that a given execution plan is expected to consume. Getting good performance out of the rule-based optimizer depends on getting programmers to structure their queries correctly based on their knowledge of the data being queried. The cost-based optimizer uses information about your data, such as how many rows are in a table, how many unique values are in an index, and so forth, to make intelligent decisions regardless of how a query is written. The key to getting good performance out of the cost-based optimizer is to gather statistics for your tables and keep them current.

Note   Actually, the cost-based optimizer isn't perfect either. It won't always choose the absolute best execution plan. Still, Oracle has improved it tremendously since its initial release.

Choosing the optimizer to use

You should use the cost-based optimizer. It's that simple. Oracle has not enhanced the rule-based optimizer at all since the cost-based optimizer was released. The cost-based optimizer is the future, and Oracle has clearly stated its intention to drop support for the rule-based optimizer at some as-yet-unspecified date. Only the cost-based optimizer contains support for relatively new features such as index-organized tables, star joins, and parallel execution. Oracle's future development efforts are all going into the cost-based optimizer.

When it first came out, many developers and database administrators were leery of using the cost-based optimizer because of the kinks in the early implementation. Because it was predictable, the rule-based optimizer offered a certain comfort level. The cost-based optimizer wasn't so predictable because the results are based on the characteristics of the data being queried, not the structure of the SQL state-ment. Database administrators and programmers often viewed this unpredictability negatively, and many chose to continue using the rule-based optimizer.

The only reason that you might consider using the rule-based optimizer now is if you are running an older application that was originally designed with that optimizer in mind. If all your SQL statements are tuned specifically for the rule-based optimizer, you may not be able to abruptly switch. In such a case, you may want to set your database to use the rule-based optimizer. However, you should also look at migrating your application. Until you do that, you won't be able to take advantage of the new features supported by the cost-based optimizer, and someday, the rule-based optimizer may disappear.

Choosing the Default Optimizer

You choose the optimizer for a database by placing an OPTIMIZER_MODE entry in the database parameter file. If you want to go with the cost-based optimizer, that entry would look like this:

```
OPTIMIZER_MODE = CHOOSE
```

OPTIMIZER_MODE has four possible values, which are described in the following list:

CHOOSE ✔	Enables cost-based optimization. Oracle will choose to use it if statistics are present.
RULE	Restricts Oracle to using the rule-based optimizer.
FIRST_ROWS	Enables cost-based optimization, with the goal of always returning the first few rows quickly, even if that leads to a higher overall cost.
ALL_ROWS	Enables cost-based optimization but with the goal of reducing overall cost. This is the same as CHOOSE.

With the optimizer mode set to CHOOSE, FIRST_ROW, or ALL_ROWS, the cost-based optimizer is used whenever statistics have been generated for at least one of the tables involved in the query. If no statistics have been gathered, no information exists for the cost-based optimizer to use, so Oracle falls back on the rule-based optimizer.

Note Whenever you change the OPTIMIZER_MODE parameter, you need to shut down and restart the database for that change to take effect.

The difference between FIRST_ROWS and ALL_ROWS is in the time it takes Oracle to begin returning rows from a query. If you are primarily running batch jobs, you will want to reduce overall I/O and CPU costs. In that case, specify ALL_ROWS or CHOOSE. The two are equivalent. If your queries are primarily generated by online users, you don't want them waiting and waiting for results to appear on their screens. Use FIRST_ROWS in this case to tell Oracle to optimize for quick response. When you use FIRST_ROWS, Oracle may choose a plan that takes longer overall but that gets a response back to the user quickly. Oracle may, for example, choose to use an index over a tablescan, even when the tablescan would take less I/O overall, because using the index allows a more immediate response.

Overriding the Optimizer Choice

You can override the optimizer choice both at the session level and at the statement level. To override the optimizer setting for the duration of your session, use the ALTER SESSION command, as shown in this example:

```
SQL> ALTER SESSION SET OPTIMIZER_MODE = FIRST_ROWS;

Session altered.
```

In this example, the statement was issued from SQL*Plus. You could also issue it from within a program. Changes you make with ALTER SESSION stay in effect until you disconnect from the database.

You can specify the optimizer mode at the individual statement level through the use of hints. For example, the following statement uses a hint to choose the cost-based optimizer and to specify that execution be optimized for overall throughput:

```
SELECT /*+ all_rows */ id_no, animal_name
FROM aquatic_animal
WHERE death_date IS NULL;
```

Hints are placed in SQL statements using a specific type of comment. The format for the comment looks like this:

```
/*+ hint */
```

The comment must begin with /*+, and it must end with */. Don't forget the plus sign (+). If you leave out the +, Oracle won't recognize the comment as a hint. Hints must also immediately follow the keyword beginning the statement.

Note   Using hints can be tricky because if you get the syntax wrong, Oracle treats the hint as a comment. No error message is generated. To be sure that a hint is working correctly, you can use EXPLAIN PLAN to view Oracle's execution plan for the statement. Chapter 19, "Tuning SQL Statements," shows you how to do this.

You can use four hints to choose optimizer modes. The hints are named to match the parameter setting, which are CHOOSE, FIRST_ROWS, ALL_ROWS, and RULE.

Generating Statistics

For the cost-based optimizer to function, it must have information about your data. It must know details such as how many rows are in a table, how big your indexes are, and how closely the order of the data in a table matches the order in an index.

Collectively, all the pieces of information that the cost-based optimizer uses are known as *statistics.*

Collecting and maintaining statistics for the optimizer entails some overhead. That overhead is much more than can be supported during normal operations such as inserting and updating rows in a table. Consequently, Oracle leaves it to you to decide when to incur this overhead. You have to kick off statistics collection manually, using the ANALYZE command.

You should have some idea of the types of statistics that are generated to know how to best use the ANALYZE command. Different statistics are generated for different types of objects. This section explains the types of statistics that are collected for tables, indexes, and columns.

Looking at table statistics

Table 18-1 shows the statistics that Oracle generates for a table. You can access these statistics via columns in the DBA_TABLES, ALL_TABLES, and USER_TABLES data dictionary views. The column names corresponding to the statistic are also shown in Table 18-1.

Table 18-1 Table Statistics	
Column Name	**Statistic**
NUM_ROWS	The number of rows in the table
BLOCKS	The number of data blocks currently being used for data
EMPTY_BLOCKS	The number of data blocks allocated to the table but that have never been used for data
AVG_SPACE	The average amount of free space, expressed in bytes, within each block
CHAIN_CNT	The number of chained rows
AVG_ROW_LEN	The average length of the rows in the table, in bytes
LAST_ANALYZED	The date on which the statistics for the table were generated

When you collect statistics for a table, unless you specify otherwise, Oracle also collects statistics for indexes on that table.

Looking at index statistics

Table 18-2 shows the statistics that Oracle generates for an index. Index statistics are returned by columns in the DBA_INDEXES, ALL_INDEXES, and USER_INDEXES data dictionary views.

Table 18-2	
Index Statistics	
Column Name	**Statistic**
BLEVEL	The depth of the index, or number of levels, from the index's root block to its leaf blocks
LEAF_BLOCKS	The number of leaf blocks, which are the blocks containing pointers to the rows in the table, in the index
DISTINCT_KEYS	The number of distinct index values
AVG_LEAF_BLOCKS_PER_KEY	The average number of leaf blocks containing entries for one value
AVG_DATA_BLOCKS_PER_KEY	The number of data blocks, on average, pointed to by one index value
CLUSTERING_FACTOR	A clustering factor, indicating how closely the order of rows in the table happens to match the ordering in the index
LAST_ANALYZED	The date on which the statistics for the index were generated

Looking at column statistics

Table 18-3 shows the statistics gathered for columns.

Table 18-3	
Column Statistics	
Column Name	**Statistic**
NUM_DISTINCT	The number of distinct values contained in the column
LOW_VALUE	The lowest value in the column, limited to the first 32 bytes of that value
HIGH_VALUE	The highest value in the column, limited to the first 32 bytes of that value

Column Name	Statistic
DENSITY	The column's density
NUM_NULLS	The number of rows that contain null values for the column
NUM_BUCKETS	The number of buckets in the column's histogram
LAST_ANALYZED	The date on which the statistics for the column were generated

Column statistics aren't always generated. By default, when you issue an ANALYZE TABLE command, only table and index statistics are generated. You have to specifically ask to generate column statistics.

The statistics shown in Table 18-3 aren't the only items generated when you generate column statistics. In addition to the items listed in the table, Oracle also generates histograms for the columns.

Displaying column histograms

Histograms are generated when you compute column statistics and indicate the distribution of data within a column. A histogram, if you aren't familiar with the term, is a type of graph. Figure 18-1 shows a histogram illustrating the distribution of tank numbers in the AQUATIC_ANIMAL table.

Tank #

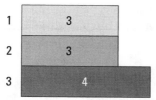

Figure 18-1: A histogram showing the distribution of tank numbers in the AQUATIC_ANIMAL table

The histogram shown in Figure 18-1 is called a width-balanced histogram, and it is the type most people are familiar with. However, it's not the type that Oracle uses. In a width-balanced histogram, the number of buckets is fixed and the length of the bars varies with the number of values that fall into each bucket. Oracle uses height-balanced histograms, where the length of the bars is fixed and the number of buckets is variable.

The concept of a height-balanced histogram can be difficult to grasp at first. Figure 18-1 represents a width-balanced histogram. There are three bars in the graph representing three different tank values. The height of each bar corresponds to the number of rows in the AQUATIC_ANIMAL table with the given tank number value. Each bar represents a distinct value for the TANK_NO column. When width-balanced histograms are used, the height of each bar varies, but the number of values represented by each bar is a constant. Height-balanced histograms work using the opposite behavior.

When generating a height-balanced histogram, Oracle first determines how many buckets to use. You can control the number of buckets, but for now, assume that two buckets will be used. Oracle divides the number of rows in the table (10) by the number of buckets (2) to get a value for the number of rows to place in each bucket: in this case, 10 / 2 = 5. Finally, Oracle divides the ten rows into two buckets and records the highest value in each bucket. Figure 18-2 illustrates a height-balanced histogram based on the same data used for the width-balanced histogram in Figure 18-1.

Tank #

1 - 2	5
2 - 3	5

Figure 18-2: Oracle generates height-balanced histograms to record the distribution of values within a column.

Keep in mind that the number of buckets may vary, but that the number of rows represented by each bucket is the same. You can see the histograms that Oracle generates in the ALL_TAB_HISTOGRAMS data dictionary view, where each bucket is represented by one row in the view.

Note   If the number of distinct values in a column is less than the number of buckets in the histogram that you create, Oracle actually creates a histogram more like the one shown in Figure 18-1, with one bucket for each distinct value. If you have more values than buckets, which is often the case, you'll get a histogram like the one shown in Figure 18-2.

Issuing the ANALYZE command

To actually get Oracle to generate all these statistics and histograms, you need to issue an ANALYZE command. Using the ANALYZE command, you can generate statistics for a table, its indexes, and its columns.

The ANALYZE command affects only one table at a time, which can be a bit inconvenient if you want to generate statistics for all the tables in a schema or for all the tables in your database. One approach to this problem is to generate a SQL*Plus script that does the job and to just invoke that script when you need it. Another approach is to use the DBMS_UTILITY package, which contains a procedure that allows you to analyze an entire schema with one command.

If you're using the cost-based optimizer, analyze your tables regularly. How frequently you do this depends on how fast your data changes. You may find, if you have extremely volatile tables, that it makes sense to analyze them more frequently than the others.

Analyzing a Table

When you analyze a table, you can choose between computing statistics exactly and estimating statistics based on a sampling of the rows in the table. Which approach you take depends on how much time you have and how large your table is. When you compute statistics exactly, Oracle is forced to read all the data in the table. With a large table, that can take quite some time. Even just a few minutes per table adds up if you have a lot of tables to go through. You can reduce the amount of time by choosing to estimate.

To analyze a table and all its indexes, issue an ANALYZE TABLE command, as shown in the following example:

```
ANALYZE TABLE tablename COMPUTE STATISTICS;
```

This command uses the COMPUTE keyword, which specifies to compute statistics exactly. To estimate statistics, use the ESTIMATE keyword, optionally followed by a SAMPLE clause, to indicate how large a sample to use. The following example shows statistics being generated for the AQUATIC_ANIMAL table based on a 5 percent sample:

```
SQL> ANALYZE TABLE aquatic_animal
  2  ESTIMATE STATISTICS SAMPLE 5 PERCENT;

Table analyzed.
```

As you can see, you won't get much feedback from this command. Oracle simply reads through the specified percentage of the table and the specified percentage of each index, and computes the statistics that you asked for.

You can use a FOR clause to control the scope of the statistics generation. By default, when you use ANALYZE TABLE, Oracle generates statistics for the table and for all indexes on the table. The FOR clause controls that behavior. The following two commands limit the analysis to just the table, and just the indexes, respectively:

```
ANALYZE TABLE aquatic_animal
   COMPUTE STATISTICS FOR TABLE;

ANALYZE TABLE aquatic_animal
   COMPUTE STATISTICS FOR ALL INDEXES;
```

The FOR clause also allows you to generate statistics for individual columns within the table.

Analyzing Columns and Generating Histograms

If you want to generate column statistics for a table, make sure that you've generated statistics for the table first. Any time that you generate table statistics, you wipe out any column statistics. The following example shows how you might issue two commands, one after the other, to generate statistics for a table and its indexed columns:

```
SQL> ANALYZE TABLE aquatic_animal COMPUTE STATISTICS;

Table analyzed.

SQL> ANALYZE TABLE aquatic_animal
  2  COMPUTE STATISTICS FOR ALL INDEXED COLUMNS;

Table analyzed.
```

In this example, statistics are generated only for the indexed columns. You also have the options of generating statistics for all columns or for a specific list of columns.

Note   It only makes sense to generate statistics for columns that are used in the WHERE clause of a query.

When you generate column statistics, Oracle creates histograms showing the distribution of data within those columns. By default, Oracle will use up to 75 buckets for each histogram. You can use the SIZE clause to specify a different limit, which can be anywhere from 1 to 254. The command in the following example specifies an upper limit of ten buckets and analyzes only the TANK_NO column:

```
SQL> ANALYZE TABLE aquatic_animal
  2  COMPUTE STATISTICS FOR COLUMNS tank_no SIZE 10;

Table analyzed.
```

Specifying a size of 10 doesn't mean that you will necessarily get ten buckets. Oracle may choose to use less depending on the number of rows in the table and the number of distinct values in the column being analyzed.

After analyzing a column, you can query the ALL_TAB_HISTOGRAMS view to see the histograms that Oracle generated. Consider this example:

```
SQL> SELECT endpoint_number,
  2          endpoint_value
  3  FROM all_tab_histograms
  4  WHERE owner = 'SEAPARK'
  5  AND table_name = 'AQUATIC_ANIMAL'
  6  AND column_name = 'TANK_NO'
  7  ORDER BY endpoint_number;

ENDPOINT_NUMBER ENDPOINT_VALUE
--------------- --------------
              3              1
              7              2
             10              3
```

In this example, there are only three distinct values and ten buckets, so Oracle creates a bucket for each value. You can see this because the first bucket has an endpoint greater than zero. The ENDPOINT_VALUE indicates the value represented in the bucket. The ENDPOINT_NUMBER indicates the cumulative number of rows:

✦ Three rows have a value of 1 for the tank number.

✦ Four rows (7–3) have a value of 2 for the tank number.

✦ Three rows (10–7) have a value of 3 for the tank number.

If you were to create a two-bucket histogram using SIZE 2, the results would look like the following:

```
ENDPOINT_NUMBER ENDPOINT_VALUE
--------------- --------------
              0              1
              1              2
              2              3
```

In this case, since the number of buckets is less than the number of distinct values in the column (two buckets is less than three distinct values), Oracle simply places five rows in each bucket. The following statements are true about this scenario:

✦ The bucket with an endpoint number of 0 is a special bucket that contains zero rows, and instead tells us the lowest value in the column. In this case, we see that the lowest tank number is 1.

✦ The endpoint number is used only to place the buckets in order and has no bearing on the cumulative number of rows in each bucket.

✦ Since there are ten rows in the table, buckets 1 and 2 have five rows each.

✦ There are five rows with tank numbers from 1 through 2.

✦ There are five rows with tank numbers from 2 through 3.

With this latter type of histogram, Oracle won't record duplicate buckets. You might, for example, see results like the following:

```
ENDPOINT_NUMBER ENDPOINT_VALUE
--------------- --------------
              0               1
              1               2
              4               3
```

Notice the gap between endpoints number 1 and 4. There are really three buckets containing an endpoint value of 3. Oracle is saving space here. You have to interpret these results as a shortened version of the following:

```
ENDPOINT_NUMBER ENDPOINT_VALUE
--------------- --------------
              0               1
              1               2
              2               3
              3               3
              4               3
```

Once generated, Oracle can use these statistics to determine how best to execute a query when that query contains references to the TANK_NO column in its WHERE clause. If you write a query specifying WHERE TANK_NO BETWEEN 1 AND 3, the optimizer looks at the histogram and quickly determines that the query returns all rows in the table. Using this information, the optimizer likely chooses to forgo using any indexes and just does a full tablescan to return all the rows.

Analyzing an Entire Schema

If you want to analyze all the tables in a particular schema, you can use the ANALYZE_SCHEMA procedure in the DBMS_UTILITY package. This is a built-in PL/SQL procedure that Oracle supplies.

Note   The DBMS_UTILITY package, together with all other built-in packages, is created when you run the catproc.sql script on a new database.

The syntax for calling DBMS_UTILITY.ANALYZE_SCHEMA is as follows:

```
DBMS_UTILITY.ANALYZE_SCHEMA (
    schema VARCHAR2,
    method VARCHAR2,
    estimate_rows NUMBER,
    estimate_percent NUMBER,
    method_opt VARCHAR2)
```

The following list describes each of the elements in this syntax:

✦ schema — The name of the schema for which you want to analyze a table.

✦ method — This is either ESTIMATE, COMPUTE, or DELETE, depending on whether you want to estimate statistics, compute them exactly, or delete them.

✦ estimate_rows — The number of rows to sample, if you're estimating. Omit this argument if you aren't estimating or if you are estimating based on a percentage.

✦ estimate_percent — The percentage of rows to sample, if you're estimating. Omit this argument if you aren't estimating or if you are estimating based on a specific number of rows.

✦ method_opt — This is the FOR clause that you want to use: for example, FOR TABLE, FOR ALL INDEXED COLUMNS, and so on.

The following example demonstrates how to use DBMS_UTILITY.ANALYZE_SCHEMA to analyze all tables and then all indexed columns owned by the user SEAPARK:

```
SQL> EXECUTE dbms_utility.analyze_schema ('SEAPARK','ESTIMATE',NULL,20,'');

PL/SQL procedure successfully completed.

SQL> EXECUTE dbms_utility.analyze_schema ('SEAPARK','ESTIMATE',NULL,20, -
>            'FOR ALL INDEXED COLUMNS');

PL/SQL procedure successfully completed.
```

Note The hyphens at the end of each line are SQL*Plus continuation characters. They must be preceded by at least one space.

A similar procedure in the DBMS_UTIL package, named ANALYZE_DATABASE, enables you to analyze all tables in all schemas in the database. The parameters are the same, except that ANALYZE_DATABASE doesn't require a schema name. The ANALYZE_DATABASE procedure takes only the other four parameters. You can read more about these and other procedures in the DBMS_UTILITY package, by reading the *Oracle8i Supplied Packages Reference* manual.

Deleting Statistics

Believe it or not, sometimes you may want to delete statistics that you have generated. For example, you might find that you have generated statistics by mistake. If the optimizer mode is set to CHOOSE, then generating statistics for a table will cause queries against that table to suddenly begin using the cost-based optimizer rather than the rule-based optimizer. This can have a drastic effect on performance.

You can delete statistics for one particular table by issuing the following command:

```
ANALYZE TABLE aquatic_animal DELETE STATISTICS;
```

You can delete the statistics for all tables in a schema by making a call to DBMS_UTILITY.ANALYZE_SCHEMA, as shown in the following example:

```
SQL> EXECUTE dbms_utility.analyze_schema ('SEAPARK', 'DELETE');

PL/SQL procedure successfully completed.
```

Remember, if no statistics are available for any of the tables involved in a query, Oracle will be forced to use the rule-based optimizer.

Discovering Chained Rows

When you analyze a table, Oracle counts the number of chained and migrated rows. You can access that count by selecting the CHAIN_CNT column from DBA_TABLES (or ALL_TABLE or USER_TABLES). Chained and migrated rows can become a significant performance issue if you access them frequently.

Chained rows are rows that are not entirely stored within one database block. When you access a chained row, Oracle reads the block containing the first part of the row, finds a pointer to a second block, reads the second block, picks up more of the row, possibly finds a pointer to a third block, and so on.

Migrated rows are those that have grown to the point where they will no longer fit in the block originally used to store the row. When that happens, Oracle may move the entire row to a new block, leaving a pointer to that new block in the original block.

Chained rows have two causes. If a row in a table is larger than the database block size, then it will never fit in one block and will always be chained. Row chaining can also occur whenever a row grows in size to the point where the size exceeds the free space in any available block assigned to the table. Row migration occurs when rows grow in size and require more space than remains in the block.

Chained and migrated rows present a performance problem because of the extra I/O involved. Instead of reading one block and getting an entire row, Oracle must read at least two blocks. If Oracle needs to read two rows from a block and both rows are chained, then one I/O turns into three I/Os.

Because of the potentially high I/O overhead involved, check for chained rows regularly. The simplest way to do this is to periodically run a report that lists chained row counts for all your tables. Listing 18-1 shows a query that lists the number of chained rows for each table in a user's schema.

Listing 18-1: **Listing chained row counts**

```
SQL> SELECT table_name, chain_cnt
  2  FROM user_tables
  3  ORDER BY chain_cnt DESC;

TABLE_NAME                       CHAIN_CNT
-------------------------------- ---------
AQUATIC_ANIMAL                          37
CARETAKER                                0
CHECKUP                                  0
CHECKUP_HISTORY                          0
PARK_REVENUE                             0
SEAPARK_STATISTICS                       0
TANK                                     0
```

For this query to provide accurate results, you must analyze the tables first. Once you discover chained rows, you can get rid of them in a couple of different ways. Depending on how much data you have in the table and on how much time you have, you can use either of the following methods:

✦ Export the table, delete the table, and import the table back again. This approach is the most disruptive, but it gives you a chance to adjust storage parameters on the table.

✦ Specify that the ANALYZE command lists the chained rows. This allows you to reinsert them into the table.

Chapter 8, "Using Oracle8i's Export Utility," and Chapter 9, "Using Oracle8i's Import Utility," show you how to use the Export and Import utilities, respectively. Refer to those chapters if you aren't already familiar with Export and Import. The rest of this section shows you how to list the chained rows and reinsert them without having to re-create the entire table.

Creating the CHAINED_ROWS table

Before you can use the ANALYZE command to get a list of chained rows in a table, you must create another table to hold that list. Oracle supplies a script named UTLCHAIN1.SQL that you can use for this purpose. You'll find UTLCHAIN1.SQL in your $ORACLE_HOME/rdbms/admin directory.

Note

For Oracle releases prior to 8.1.5 (8i), you must use UTLCHAIN.SQL. You can't use the CHAINED_ROWS table created by UTLCHAIN.SQL to hold a list of chained rows on an index-organized table (IOT).

Listing 18-2 shows you how to use UTLCHAIN1.SQL to create a chained rows table.

Listing 18-2: Creating the CHAINED_ROWS table

```
SQL> @e:\oracle\ora81\rdbms\admin\utlchain1.sql

Table created.

SQL> DESCRIBE CHAINED_ROWS
 Name                         Null?    Type
 ----------------------- -------- -------------
 OWNER_NAME                        VARCHAR2(30)
 TABLE_NAME                        VARCHAR2(30)
 CLUSTER_NAME                      VARCHAR2(30)
 PARTITION_NAME                    VARCHAR2(30)
 SUBPARTITION_NAME                 VARCHAR2(30)
 HEAD_ROWID                        UROWID
 ANALYZE_TIMESTAMP                 DATE
```

You do need the CREATE TABLE system privilege to create the CHAINED_ROWS table, but you don't need any special or unusual privileges besides that. The table name doesn't absolutely need to be CHAINED_ROWS. If you want a different name, you can use the ALTER TABLE command to rename it. You can place the table in any schema that you like, although it will be easiest to create it in the schema that you are analyzing.

Listing the chained rows

Having created a CHAINED_ROWS table, you can use the ANALYZE command to generate a list of chained rows for the table. You do this by adding a LIST CHAINED

ROWS clause to the command. The following example shows this being done for the AQUATIC_ANIMAL table:

```
SQL> ANALYZE TABLE aquatic_animal
  2  LIST CHAINED ROWS INTO chained_rows;

Table analyzed.
```

Now that you've listed the chained rows, you are ready to report on the results and reinsert the rows.

Viewing the results

The CHAINED_ROWS table will end up with one row for each chained row in the table that you analyzed. The most important piece of information contained in the CHAINED_ROWS table is the ROWID identifying the rows that are chained. Query the CHAINED_ROWS table, and you'll get results similar to the following:

```
SQL> SELECT * FROM chained_rows;

OWNER_NAME   TABLE_NAME       HEAD_ROWID            ANALYZE_T
-----------  ---------------  --------------------  ---------
SEAPARK      AQUATIC_ANIMAL   AAADViAAHAAADQ3AAS    10-SEP-99
SEAPARK      AQUATIC_ANIMAL   AAADViAAHAAADQ3AAT    10-SEP-99
SEAPARK      AQUATIC_ANIMAL   AAADViAAHAAADQ3AAU    10-SEP-99
SEAPARK      AQUATIC_ANIMAL   AAADViAAHAAADQ3AAW    10-SEP-99
SEAPARK      AQUATIC_ANIMAL   AAADViAAHAAADQ3AAX    10-SEP-99
```

As you can see, the schema name and table name are part of each record. That allows one CHAINED_ROWS table to contain information for multiple database tables. The HEAD_ROWID column contains the ROWIDs identifying the chained rows. You can use this information to delete and reinsert these rows, thus eliminating as much chaining as possible.

Reinserting chained rows

If you don't have the time or desire to export and import the entire table, you can still do something to eliminate chained rows. You can delete them and reinsert them by following these steps:

1. Copy the chained rows to a temporary work table.

2. Delete the chained rows from the main table.

3. Select the chained rows from the work table and reinsert them into the main table.

While using this method to eliminate chained rows, users will still be able to access the table, but after step 2, they won't be able to access any of the chained rows until the process is complete. Consider this as you decide when to do this.

Copying Chained Rows to a Work Table

You can use the ROWID in the CHAINED_ROWS table to identify the chained rows in the main table. An easy way to create a work table and populate it at the same time is to issue the CREATE TABLE statement using a subquery attached to it. The following example shows such a statement being used to create a work table to hold the chained rows from the AQUATIC_ANIMAL table:

```
SQL> CREATE TABLE aquatic_animal_chained
  2      AS SELECT *
  3          FROM aquatic_animal
  4          WHERE ROWID IN (
  5              SELECT head_rowid
  6              FROM chained_rows
  7              WHERE table_name = 'AQUATIC_ANIMAL'
  8              AND owner_name = 'SEAPARK'
  9              );

Table created.
```

At this point, the AQUATIC_ANIMAL_CHAINED table contains copies of all the chained rows from the AQUATIC_ANIMAL table.

Deleting Chained Rows from the Main Table

Once you've copied the chained rows into a work table, you need to delete them from the main table. You can use a DELETE statement to do this, together with the same subquery used in the previous CREATE TABLE statement. Consider this example:

```
SQL> DELETE FROM aquatic_animal
  2      WHERE ROWID IN (
  3          SELECT head_rowid
  4              FROM chained_rows
  5              WHERE table_name = 'AQUATIC_ANIMAL'
  6              AND owner_name = 'SEAPARK'
  7              );

37 rows deleted.
```

It's possible that deleting rows like this could lead to foreign key constraint violations. If so, you will need to disable those foreign key constraints using ALTER TABLE DISABLE CONSTRAINT commands, and reenable them after you've reinserted the rows.

Reinserting the Rows

Reinserting the chained rows is the easy part. All you need to do is select all the rows from the work table and insert them back into the main table, as shown in this example:

```
SQL> INSERT INTO aquatic_animal
  2     SELECT * FROM aquatic_animal_chained;

37 rows created.
SQL> COMMIT;
Commit complete.
```

When you insert rows into a table, Oracle always looks for a block large enough to hold the entire row. So, most of the chained rows should be made whole again. The exceptions will be those rows that are simply too large to fit in a single block.

Note   The only way to deal with rows that are too large to ever fit in one block is to re-create the entire database using a larger block size. This represents a serious amount of work. Think about it before you do it. Make sure that the potential performance gain is worth the effort you will expend. If only a few rows fall into the category of being too large for a block, it may not be worth the time and effort to re-create the database to eliminate the chaining.

After you've reinserted the rows back into the main table and you've committed the transaction, don't forget to reenable any constraints that you might have dropped to delete those rows. You may also want to drop the work table, delete the rows from the CHAINED_ROWS table, and reanalyze the main table to see the improvement that you made.

Importing and Exporting Statistics

Beginning with the 8i release, Oracle now contains support for exporting and importing statistics. You can use this feature to maintain several sets of statistics within one database, switching back and forth between them at will, or you can even use it to copy statistics between databases.

Why would you want to save and restore statistics? This feature is useful for several reasons:

✦ Before you reanalyze statistics for a schema, you can save the current statistics as a backup. If, after analyzing the tables to bring the statistics up to date, the optimizer starts generating wildly inefficient execution plans, you can ditch the new statistics and restore the previous set.

✦ If you have a good test environment, you may be able to generate a set of statistics there that results in efficient query execution plans from the optimizer. You can then transfer those statistics to your production database, ensuring that the same execution plans are generated there as well.

✦ If you are moving data from one database to another, you can move the statistics as well. This saves you the time and effort of reanalyzing the data after you've moved it.

Being able to save and restore statistics is convenient because the cost-based optimizer is a two-edged sword. It's great that it can adjust to changes in your data, but sometimes, those adjustments can lead to surprise performance problems. The ability to test new statistics before you apply them can help eliminate those surprises.

Using the DBMS_STATS package

The built-in DBMS_STATS package is the key to exploiting the new features that allow you to save and restore statistics and to transfer them between databases. The DBMS_STAT package contains procedures that perform the following functions:

✦ Export statistics from the data dictionary to a table

✦ Import statistics into the data dictionary from a table

✦ Gather new statistics, storing them in either a table or in the data dictionary

✦ Arbitrarily set values for specified statistics

To use DBMS_STATS, you must have been granted EXECUTE access on the package. The SYS user owns the package, so you must log on as SYS to grant yourself access to it.

Exporting statistics

Exporting statistics doesn't have quite the same meaning as when you use the Export utility to export data. The Export utility writes data from your tables to a flat file. When you export statistics, Oracle reads them from the data dictionary and writes them to a database table. You need the following to export statistics:

✦ A table in which to place the exported statistics

✦ A name for use in identifying the set of statistics created by a particular export

The table that is used to hold the exported statistics is referred to as the statistics table. A procedure in the DBMS_STATS package can create this table for you. As for the name you use to identify the statistics, it can be anything that you dream up. You can have several sets of exported statistics, and the name is used to differentiate between them.

Creating the Statistics Export Table

The DBMS_STATS.CREATE_STAT_TABLE procedure will create a statistics table. The procedure header appears as follows:

```
DBMS_STATS.CREATE_STAT_TABLE (
ownname IN VARCHAR2,
stattab IN VARCHAR2,
   tblspace IN VARCHAR2)
```

The following list describes the elements in this example:

✦ ownname — Identifies the schema in which you want the table to be created.

✦ stattab — The name that you want to give the table.

✦ tblspace — The tablespace in which you want the table placed. This is an optional argument. If omitted, the default tablespace is used.

You can create as many statistics tables as you like. Each table may also have as many sets of statistics as you want. The following example shows you how to create a statistics table named SEAPARK_STATISTICS in the SEAPARK schema:

```
SQL> EXECUTE DBMS_STATS.CREATE_STAT_TABLE ( -
>     'SEAPARK','SEAPARK_STATISTICS', 'USERS');

PL/SQL procedure successfully completed.
```

Once you have created a statistics table, you are ready to export some statistics.

Exporting Statistics from the Data Dictionary

You can export statistics for a particular schema, a specific table or index, or for the entire database. The DBMS_STATS.EXPORT_SCHEMA_STATS procedure exports statistics for an entire schema. The syntax appears as follows:

```
DBMS_STATS.EXPORT_SCHEMA_STATS (
    ownname IN VARCHAR2,
    stattab IN VARCHAR2,
    statid IN VARCHAR2,
    statown IN VARCHAR2)
```

The following list describes the elements in this example:

✦ ownname — The name of the schema for which you want to export statistics.

✦ stattab—The name of the statistics table.

✦ statid—A name that you want to use to identify this particular export.

✦ statown—The name of the schema containing the statistics table. If this is omitted, the table is assumed to exist in the same schema as you are exporting.

To actually export the statistics for a schema and place them into a statistics table, issue a command like that shown in the following example:

```
SQL> EXECUTE DBMS_STATS.EXPORT_SCHEMA_STATS ( -
>     'SEAPARK','SEAPARK_STATISTICS', -
>     'SEAPARK_990909', 'SEAPARK');

PL/SQL procedure successfully completed.
```

The command in this example exports statistics for all tables, indexes, and columns in the SEAPARK schema, placing them into a table named SEAPARK_STATISTICS. The entire set of statistics generated by this export can be identified using the name SEAPARK_990909.

With the statistics in a table like this, you now have the option of restoring them sometime later. You also have the option of exporting the table and transferring the statistics to another database.

Transferring statistics to another database

You can move statistics from one database to another by following these steps:

1. Export the statistics to a table in the source database.

2. Use the Export utility to export the statistics table to a flat file.

3. Use the Import utility to import the statistics table into the target database.

4. Make a call to DBMS_STATS to import the statistics from the table into the target database's data dictionary.

You've already seen that you can use the DBMS_STATS.EXPORT_SCHEMA_STATS procedure to accomplish step 1. In the next section, you see how to use DBMS_STATS.IMPORT_SCHEMA_STATS to accomplish step 4. You accomplish steps 2 and 3 by using the standard Export and Import utilities. Listing 18-3 shows the SEAPARK statistics being transferred from one database to another.

Listing 18-3: **Transferring statistics between databases**

```
$exp seapark/seapark@jonathan file=seapark_stats log=seapark_stats_exp tables=se
apark_statistics

Export: Release 8.1.5.0.0 - Production on Thu Sep 9 19:37:17 1999

(c) Copyright 1999 Oracle Corporation.  All rights reserved.


Connected to: Oracle8i Release 8.1.5.0.0 - Production
With the Partitioning and Java options
PL/SQL Release 8.1.5.0.0 - Production
Export done in WE8ISO8859P1 character set and WE8ISO8859P1 NCHAR character set

About to export specified tables via Conventional Path ...
. . exporting table              SEAPARK_STATISTICS          30 rows exported
Export terminated successfully without warnings.

$imp seapark/seapark@coin file=seapark_stats log=seapark_stats_imp tables=seapar
k_statistics ignore=y

Import: Release 8.1.5.0.0 - Production on Thu Sep 9 19:37:32 1999

(c) Copyright 1999 Oracle Corporation.  All rights reserved.


Connected to: Oracle8i Release 8.1.5.0.0 - Production
With the Partitioning and Java options
PL/SQL Release 8.1.5.0.0 - Production

Export file created by EXPORT:V08.01.05 via conventional path
import done in WE8ISO8859P1 character set and US7ASCII NCHAR character set
import server uses US7ASCII character set (possible charset conversion)
export server uses WE8ISO8859P1 NCHAR character set (possible ncharset conversio
n)
. importing SEAPARK's objects into SEAPARK
. . importing table             "SEAPARK_STATISTICS"         30 rows imported
Import terminated successfully without warnings.
```

In the Listing 18-3 example, the import was done using the ignore=y setting
because the SEAPARK_STATISTICS table already exists in the target database.

Importing statistics

Importing statistics works in reverse from exporting them. You make a call to DBMS_STATS, and the statistics that you request are read from the statistics table and loaded into the data dictionary. The DBMS_STATS.IMPORT_SCHEMA_STATS procedure is used to import statistics for a schema, and the syntax is as follows:

```
DBMS_STATS.IMPORT_SCHEMA_STATS
    ownname IN VARCHAR2,
    stattab IN VARCHAR2,
    statid IN VARCHAR2,
    statown IN VARCHAR2)
```

The following list describes the elements of this syntax:

✦ ownname — The schema for which you want to import statistics.

✦ stattab — The name of the statistics table.

✦ statid — The name identifying the set of statistics that you want to import.

✦ statown — The name of the schema containing the statistics table. If this is omitted, the table is assumed to exist in the same schema as the one you are importing.

The following example shows the set of statistics named SEAPARK_990909 being imported for the SEAPARK schema:

```
SQL> EXECUTE DBMS_STATS.IMPORT_SCHEMA_STATS ( -
>     'SEAPARK','SEAPARK_STATISTICS', -
>     'SEAPARK_990909', 'SEAPARK');

PL/SQL procedure successfully completed.
```

The command in this example replaces any existing statistics for the SEAPARK schema with ones from the set named SEAPARK_990909.

Using other DBMS_STATS procedures

A number of other useful procedures exist in the DBMS_STATS package than just the few that you've seen here. The DBMS_STATS package contains functionality that allows you to do the following:

✦ Import and export statistics for an entire database

✦ Import and export statistics for a schema

✦ Import and export statistics for individual tables and indexes

    ✦ Arbitrarily make up your own statistics for an object

    ✦ Create your own histograms

You can find more information about the DBMS_STATS package in the *Oracle8i Supplied Packages Reference.*

Summary

In this chapter, you learned:

    ✦ Oracle supports two optimizers: one rule-based and one cost-based. The rule-based optimizer chooses execution plans based largely on the manner in which you structure the SQL statements that you write. The cost-based optimizer, on the other hand, bases its decisions on the amount of I/O and CPU resources required to execute any given query. You are strongly encouraged to use the cost-based optimizer. It supports more of Oracle's newer functionality, such as index-organized tables, partitioning, and so forth.

    ✦ You can use the ALTER SESSION command to change the optimizer default for a session. Use optimizer hints to change the setting for one statement.

    ✦ The cost-based optimizer requires statistics about your data to make any type of intelligent decision about how to retrieve it. Therefore, if you are using the cost-based optimizer, analyze your tables regularly. In fact, if you have no statistics at all on tables being queried, Oracle will be forced to use the rule-based optimizer regardless of which optimizer you choose.

    ✦ You can use the ANALYZE command to generate optimizer statistics for tables and indexes. However, if you want to analyze all the tables in a schema or in the entire database, you may find it easier to use procedures in the DBMS_UTILITY package. You can use the DBMS_UTILITY.ANALYZE_SCHEMA procedure to analyze all objects in a schema, and you can use DBMS_UTILITY.ANALYZE_DATABASE to analyze all objects in a database.

    ✦ Chained rows represent those rows with data spread over more than one database block. Chaining and migration entail significant I/O overhead. Check periodically for the presence of chained rows, and if the number becomes great enough to impact performance, take steps to eliminate them.

    ✦ Oracle8i contains new functionality that allows you to export statistics from the data dictionary into a database table. This allows you to save statistics before analyzing your objects, and it also allows you to restore those old statistics in the event that the new ones result in poorly performing execution plans. The DBMS_STATS package contains the procedures used to import and export statistics.

✦   ✦   ✦

Tuning SQL Statements

If you want to get maximum performance from your applications, you need to tune your SQL statements. Tuning a SQL statement means discovering the execution plan that Oracle is using. Once you know the execution plan, you can attempt to improve it.

You can discover the execution plan for a statement in at least three ways. One is to issue an EXPLAIN PLAN statement from SQL*Plus. Another alternative is to use the SQL*Plus autotrace feature, and still another alternative is to use Oracle's SQL Trace feature. When you use SQL Trace, you can log statistics about statements as they are being executed, which is invaluable if you are trying to fix a poorly performing process.

You can attempt to improve the performance of a query in many ways. You can create indexes, you can increase the size of the buffer cache, and you can use optimizer hints. This chapter concentrates on the use of optimizer hints. *Hints* are instructions to the Oracle optimizer that are buried within your statement. You can use hints to control virtually any aspect of statement execution.

Using the Explain Plan Feature

Oracle's Explain Plan feature allows you to discover the execution plan for a SQL statement. You do this by using a SQL statement, not surprisingly named EXPLAIN PLAN, to which you append the query of interest. Consider this example:

```
EXPLAIN PLAN
SET STATEMENT_ID = 'q1'
FOR
SELECT *
FROM aquatic_animal;
```

After issuing this statement, you can query a special table known as the *plan table* to find the execution plan that Oracle intends to use for the query. Here's an example of an extremely simple execution plan, which happens to be the plan that Oracle would use for the preceding query:

```
TABLE ACCESS FULL AQUATIC_ANIMAL
```

There's not much to this plan, but it tells you that Oracle intends to read all the rows in the AQUATIC_ANIMAL table to satisfy your query.

The EXPLAIN PLAN statement is most often used from SQL*Plus, or from SQLPlus Worksheet. Before you can use EXPLAIN PLAN, you need to create a plan table to hold the results. You also need to know how to query that table.

Creating the plan table

When you issue an EXPLAIN PLAN statement, Oracle doesn't display the results on the screen. In fact, the Oracle database software has no way to directly write data to the display at all. Instead, when you issue an EXPLAIN PLAN statement, Oracle writes the results to a table known as the *plan table,* and it's up to you to create it.

The easiest way to create a plan table is to use the Oracle-supplied script named utlxplan.sql. You'll find that script in your $ORACLE_HOME/rdbms/admin directory. Listing 19-1 shows utlxplan.sql being invoked from SQL*Plus.

Listing 19-1: **Creating the plan table**

```
SQL> @e:\oracle\ora81\rdbms\admin\utlxplan

Table created.

SQL> DESCRIBE plan_table

 Name                 Null?    Type
 ------------------   -------- -----------------
 STATEMENT_ID                  VARCHAR2(30)
 TIMESTAMP                     DATE
 REMARKS                       VARCHAR2(80)
 OPERATION                     VARCHAR2(30)
 OPTIONS                       VARCHAR2(30)
 OBJECT_NODE                   VARCHAR2(128)
 OBJECT_OWNER                  VARCHAR2(30)
 OBJECT_NAME                   VARCHAR2(30)
 OBJECT_INSTANCE               NUMBER(38)
 OBJECT_TYPE                   VARCHAR2(30)
 OPTIMIZER                     VARCHAR2(255)
 SEARCH_COLUMNS                NUMBER
```

```
ID                      NUMBER(38)
PARENT_ID               NUMBER(38)
POSITION                NUMBER(38)
COST                    NUMBER(38)
CARDINALITY             NUMBER(38)
BYTES                   NUMBER(38)
OTHER_TAG               VARCHAR2(255)
PARTITION_START         VARCHAR2(255)
PARTITION_STOP          VARCHAR2(255)
PARTITION_ID            NUMBER(38)
OTHER                   LONG
DISTRIBUTION            VARCHAR2(30)
```

The name of the table created by the script is PLAN_TABLE. This is also the default table name used by the EXPLAIN PLAN statement. You can name the plan table something else if you want to, but then you have to supply that name every time you explain a plan.

Note   The structure of the plan table sometimes changes from one release of Oracle to the next. Consequently, when you upgrade, you may need to drop and re-create your plan tables.

It's normal to have more than one plan table in a database. In fact, it's quite typical for every user using the EXPLAIN PLAN feature to have his or her own plan table in his or her own schema.

Explaining a query

Having created a plan table, you are now in a position to explain the execution plan for a query. Say that you have the following SELECT statement:

```
SELECT a.id_no, a.animal_name, a.tank_no,
       NVL(c.caretaker_name, t.chief_caretaker_name)
FROM aquatic_animal a, tank t, caretaker c
WHERE a.tank_no = t.tank_no
AND c.caretaker_name (+) = t.chief_caretaker_name
ORDER BY a.tank_no, a.animal_name;
```

This statement contains two joins, one an inner join, and one an outer join. It also contains an ORDER BY clause, which results in a sort. If you want to know how Oracle is going to go about executing this query, you can use an EXPLAIN PLAN statement that looks like this:

```
EXPLAIN PLAN
SET STATEMENT_ID = 'user_supplied_name'
FOR query;
```

You're basically appending the keywords EXPLAIN PLAN ... FOR onto the front of your query and executing the result. You need to give the results a name so that you can query them later. That's what the SET STATEMENT_ID clause is for. Whatever text you supply as a statement ID is stored with the results in the plan table.

> **Note** Explaining a plan doesn't cause the SQL statement to be executed. Oracle determines the execution plan, nothing more.

Listing 19-2 shows EXPLAIN PLAN being used.

Listing 19-2: **Using the EXPLAIN PLAN statement**

```
SQL> DELETE
  2   FROM plan_table
  3   WHERE statement_id = 'caretakers';

6 rows deleted.

SQL>
SQL> EXPLAIN PLAN
  2   SET STATEMENT_ID = 'caretakers'
  3   FOR
  4   SELECT a.id_no, a.animal_name, a.tank_no,
  5          NVL(c.caretaker_name, t.chief_caretaker_name)
  6   FROM aquatic_animal a, tank t, caretaker c
  7   WHERE a.tank_no = t.tank_no
  8   AND c.caretaker_name (+) = t.chief_caretaker_name
  9   ORDER BY a.tank_no, a.animal_name;

Explained.
```

The delete is necessary because EXPLAIN PLAN always adds to the plan table. If any records happen to exist with a statement ID of 'caretakers', they play havoc with the EXPLAIN PLAN results. It's safest to do a delete first, to avoid any possibility of duplication.

> **Note** If you reuse a statement ID without deleting the plan table entries from the previous time, you'll get bizarre results when you query the plan table. This is especially true if you query the plan table using a CONNECT BY query. Instead of getting a five-line plan, for example, you might get 50+ lines, many of them duplicates of each other.

After you've explained a plan, you can query the PLAN TABLE to see the details of that plan.

Showing the execution plan for a query

The records in the plan table are related to each other hierarchically. Each record has an ID column and a PARENT_ID column. You execute a given SQL statement by performing a series of operations. Each operation, in turn, may consist of one or more operations. The most deeply nested operations are executed first. They, in turn, feed results to their parents. This process continues until only one result is left — the result of the query — which is returned to you.

Using the Plan Table Query

The three most significant columns in the plan table are named OPERATION, OPTIONS, and OBJECT_NAME. For each step, these tell you which operation is going to be performed and which object is the target of that operation.

You can use the following SQL query to display an execution plan once it has been generated:

```
SELECT id,
       LPAD(' ', 2*(level-1)) || operation
       || ' ' || options
       || ' ' || object_name
       || ' ' ||
       DECODE(id, 0, 'Cost = ' || position)
          step_description
FROM plan_table
START WITH id = 0 AND statement_id = 'statement_id'
CONNECT BY prior id = parent_id
AND statement_id = 'statement_id'
ORDER BY id, position;
```

You use the CONNECT BY clause to link each operation with its parent. The LPAD business is for indention so that if an operation has child rows, those rows will be indented underneath the parent.

Showing the Plan for the Caretakers Statement

Listing 19-3 shows the plan table being queried for the results of the EXPLAIN PLAN on the caretakers statement.

Listing 19-3: **Querying the plan table**

```
SQL> SELECT id,
  2         LPAD(' ', 2*(level-1)) || operation
  3         || ' ' || options
  4         || ' ' || object_name
  5         || ' ' ||
  6         DECODE(id, 0, 'Cost = ' || position)
  7            step_description
  8  FROM plan_table
  9  START WITH id = 0 AND statement_id = 'caretakers'
 10  CONNECT BY prior id = parent_id
 11  AND statement_id = 'caretakers'
 12  ORDER BY id, position;

 ID STEP_DESCRIPTION
---- ----------------------------------------------------
  0 SELECT STATEMENT    Cost = 9
  1   SORT ORDER BY
  2     HASH JOIN
  3       NESTED LOOPS OUTER
  4         TABLE ACCESS FULL TANK
  5         INDEX UNIQUE SCAN CARETAKER_PK
  6       TABLE ACCESS FULL AQUATIC_ANIMAL

7 rows selected.
```

To interpret this plan, you need to read your way outwards from the most deeply nested operations. For example:

1. The most deeply nested operations are 4 and 5. The parent operation is a nested loop (3). This means that Oracle will read all rows in the TANK table (4), and for each tank row, it will read the corresponding CARETAKER row (5). Oracle accesses the CARETAKER table via the primary key index named CARETAKER_PK.

2. The results of the join between TANK and CARETAKER are fed into a hash join process (2) that pulls in the corresponding rows from the AQUATIC_ANIMAL table. A full tablescan will be done on the AQUATIC_ANIMAL table, meaning that all the rows will be accessed.

3. The results of the hash join (2) are fed into a sort operation (1). This orders the results as requested by the query's ORDER BY clause. In this case, the results will be ordered by tank number and animal name.

4. The results of the sort (1) are fed back as the results of the SELECT statement (0), and are what you ultimately see.

The cost that you see, 9 in the previous example, is an arbitrary number used to give you some idea of the relative amount of I/O and CPU space required to execute a query. The *cost* of a query is derived from the POSITION column in the row containing operation ID zero. The plan table query shown here uses the DECODE function to display the cost when that row is encountered.

By itself, the number means nothing. You have to compare it to the cost for alternate execution plans. A plan with a cost of 9 will consume more or less half the resources as a plan with a cost of 18.

Note   The execution plan cost comes into play only when the cost-based optimizer is being used. Use the rule-based optimizer, and your cost will always be null.

Understanding Execution Plan Operations

To understand an execution plan like the one shown in the previous section, you need to understand the meanings of the different operations together with their options. Table 19-1 provides brief descriptions of each combination.

Table 19-1 Execution Plan Operations	
Operation + Option	**Description**
AND-EQUAL	Executes two child operations and returns only those rows that are returned by both
BITMAP CONVERSION TO ROWIDS	Converts a bitmap into a set of ROWIDs
BITMAP CONVERSION FROM ROWIDS	Converts a set of ROWIDs into a bitmap
BITMAP CONVERSION COUNT	Counts the number of entries in a bitmap
BITMAP INDEX SINGLE VALUE	Retrieves the bitmap that corresponds to a specific value in the column
BITMAP INDEX RANGE SCAN	Returns the bitmaps that correspond to a range of values in a column
BITMAP INDEX FULL SCAN	Scans a bitmapped index
BITMAP MERGE	Merges two bitmaps into one
BITMAP MINUS	Subtracts one bitmap from another
BITMAP OR	Merges two bitmaps into one

Continued

Table 19-1 *(continued)*

Operation + Option	Description
CONNECT BY	Retrieves rows hierarchically
CONCATENATION	Combines multiple rowsets into one
COUNT	Counts rows
FILTER	Filters a set of rows based on some condition in the WHERE clause
FIRST ROW	Returns only the first row of a query's results
FOR UPDATE	Indicates that the retrieved rows will be locked for subsequent updating
HASH JOIN	Joins two tables
INDEX UNIQUE	Uses an index to look up a specific value
INDEX RANGE SCAN	Uses an index to look up a range of values
INLIST ITERATOR	Performs an operation once for each value listed in an IN list
INTERSECTION	Looks at two rowsets and returns only those rows found in both
MERGE JOIN	Joins two tables
MERGE JOIN OUTER	Performs an outer join of two tables
MINUS	Subtracts one rowset from another
NESTED LOOPS	Executes one child operation for each row returned by another
PARTITION SINGLE	Executes an operation on one partition of a table or an index
PARTITION ITERATOR	Performs an operation on a list of partitions
PARTITION ALL	Performs an operation on all partitions of a table or an index
PARTITION INLIST	Performs an operation on partitions associated with an IN clause
PROJECTION	Returns a single set of records for a set of queries
REMOTE	Performs an operation on a remote database
SEQUENCE	Retrieves a value from an Oracle sequence
SORT AGGREGATE	Applies an aggregate function to a rowset
SORT UNIQUE	Sorts rows, eliminating duplicates
SORT GROUP BY	Sorts rows into groups
SORT JOIN	Sorts rows in preperation for a join
SORT ORDER BY	Sorts rows as specified by a query's ORDER BY clause
TABLE ACCESS FULL	Reads every row in a table

Operation + Option	Description
TABLE ACCESS CLUSTER	Reads every row in a table that matches a given cluster key
TABLE ACCESS HASH	Reads every row in a table that matches a given hash cluster key
TABLE ACCESS BY ROWID	Retrieves a row from a table using the ROWID
UNION	Performs a SQL union
VIEW	Executes the query for a view

Hinting for a better plan

Now that you know how Oracle is planning to execute the query, you can think about ways in which to improve performance. One way that you can change an execution plan that you don't like is to add optimizer *hints* to the query. These hints take the form of specially formatted comments and tell the optimizer how *you* want the query to be executed. They aren't really hints, either, even though Oracle refers to them as such. They're more like commands. It's true that Oracle will ignore hints that are contradictory or that are impossible to carry out, but you'll never see Oracle ignore a hint when it can be carried out.

Looking at a Hint Example

Recall that the execution plan for the caretakers query shown earlier looked like this:

```
0 SELECT STATEMENT    Cost = 9
1    SORT ORDER BY
2       HASH JOIN
3          NESTED LOOPS OUTER
4             TABLE ACCESS FULL TANK
5             INDEX UNIQUE SCAN CARETAKER_PK
6          TABLE ACCESS FULL AQUATIC_ANIMAL
```

Notice that an index retrieval is done on the CARETAKER table when it is joined to the TANK table. Suppose that, based on your knowledge of the data, a full tablescan would me more efficient than using an index. You could force that behavior by adding a hint to the query. Here's an example where three hints are used to force full tablescans on all the tables:

```
SELECT /*+ full(a) full(t) full(c) */
       a.id_no, a.animal_name, a.tank_no,
       NVL(c.caretaker_name, t.chief_caretaker_name)
FROM aquatic_animal a, tank t, caretaker c
WHERE a.tank_no = t.tank_no
AND c.caretaker_name (+) = t.chief_caretaker_name
ORDER BY a.tank_no, a.animal_name;
```

The three hints are: `full(a)`, `full(t)`, and `full(c)`. These tell Oracle to perform full tablescans on each of the three tables. The resulting execution plan looks like this:

```
0 SELECT STATEMENT    Cost = 11
1   SORT ORDER BY
2     HASH JOIN
3       HASH JOIN OUTER
4         TABLE ACCESS FULL TANK
5         TABLE ACCESS FULL CARETAKER
6       TABLE ACCESS FULL AQUATIC_ANIMAL
```

Voila! No more indexes. Notice that your cost has gone up from 9 to 11. This is Oracle's interpretation of the query cost. It may not reflect reality. The only way to be sure is through some real-world testing of the query.

Examining Hint Syntax

When you place a hint in a SQL statement, the comment needs to take a special form, and it needs to immediately follow the verb. For example:

```
SELECT /*+ hint comment hint hint comment ...*/
...
```

Notice the plus (+) sign immediately following the start of the comment. That plus sign tells Oracle that the comment contains hints. The comment may contain several hints, and you may have comments interspersed with your hints. You should separate hints from each other, and from any nonhint text, by at least one space.

Keep the following rules in mind when writing hints:

1. The comment with the hints must immediately follow the `SELECT`, `INSERT`, `UPDATE`, or `DELETE` keyword.

2. For Oracle to recognize the hints, the comment must start with `/*+`.

Note   As an alternative, you can use `--+` to start a comment containing hints. If you do this, the comment continues until the end of the line is reached. In practice, almost everyone uses `/*+ ... */`.

3. Several hints allow you to reference table names and/or index names. Table and index names are always enclosed within parentheses.

4. If you alias a table in your query, you must use that alias in any hints that refer to the table.

5. If you supply contradictory hints, Oracle will ignore at least one of them.

6. If your hints refer to indexes that don't exist, Oracle will ignore them.

7. If you want to control the execution of a subquery, you must place a hint in that subquery. Hints in the main query refer to the main query. Hints in a subquery refer to the subquery.

8. If you write a hint incorrectly, Oracle will ignore it.

9. Oracle never returns error messages for badly written hints. Hints are embedded within comments, and to comply with ANSI standards, error messages can't be returned for comments.

The last item, number 9, is particularly important. If you get a hint wrong, don't start the comment correctly, or put the comment in the wrong place, you won't get an error message. Therefore, you should always perform an explain plan on any queries containing hints to be sure that Oracle is recognizing those hints.

Understanding the Available Hints

Table 19-2 describes each of the hints that Oracle supports.

Table 19-2 Oracle's Optimizer Hints	
Hint	**Description**
ALL_ROWS	Produces an execution plan that optimizes overall resource usage.
AND_EQUAL(table_name index_name index name...)	Specifies to access a table by scanning two or more indexes and merging the results. You must specify at least two index names with this hint.
APPEND	Specifies not to reuse any free space that may be available in any extents allocated to a table. This hint applies only to INSERT statements.
CACHE (table_name)	Specifies to keep data from the named table in memory as long as possible.
CHOOSE	Specifies to use the cost-based optimizer if statistics exist for any of the tables involved.
CLUSTER(table_name)	Specifies to access the named table by scanning the cluster. This hint is valid only for clustered tables.
DRIVING_SITE (table_name)	Specifies which database to use as the driving site when joining tables from two different databases. The driving site will be the database in which the named table resides.
FIRST_ROWS	Produces an execution plan that optimizes for a quick initial response.
FULL(table_name)	Specifies to access the named table by reading all the rows.

Continued

Table 19-2 *(continued)*

Hint	Description
HASH(`table_name`)	Specifies to do a hash scan of the named table. This hint is valid only for hash-clustered tables.
HASH_AJ(`table_name`)	Specifies to do a hash anti-join of the specified table.
INDEX(`table_name` [`index_name`...])	Specifies to access the named table through an index. You may optionally specify a list of indexes from which to choose.
INDEX_ASC(`table_name` [`index_name`...])	Specifies an index to scan, the same as INDEX, but also specifies to scan the index in ascending order.
INDEX_COMBINE (`table_name` [`index_name`...])	Specifies to access the table using a combination of two indexes. You may optionally supply a list of indexes from which to choose.
INDEX_DESC(`table_name` [`index_name`...])	Specifies an index to scan, the same as INDEX, but also specifies to scan the index in descending order.
INDEX_FFS(`table_name` [`index_name`...])	Specifies to access rows in the table via a fast full index scan. You may optionally supply a list of indexes that Oracle can choose from.
MERGE_AJ(`table_name`)	Specifies to resolve a NOT IN subquery for the named table by performing a merge anti-join.
NO_MERGE	Specifies not to merge a query into a view's query. This hint applies only to queries against views.
NO_PARALLEL(`table_name`)	Specifies not to use any parallel processing features when accessing the named table.
NOAPPEND	Specifies to use free space in extents currently allocated to a table. This hint applies only to INSERT statements.
NOCACHE(`table_name`)	Specifies to remove data from memory from the named table as quickly as possible.
ORDERED	Specifies to join tables from left to right, in the same order in which they are listed in the FROM clause of the query.
PARALLEL(`table_name` [, `degree`[, `num_instances`]])	Specifies the degree of parallelism, and optionally the number of instances, to use when accessing the named table.
PARALLEL_INDEX (`table_name`, `index_name` [,`degree` [,`num_instances`]])	Specifies to access the named table via an index, and to use parallel processing features to scan that index. You may optionally specify the degree of parallelism and the number of instances to use.

Hint	Description
PUSH_SUBQ	Specifies to evaluate subqueries as soon as possible during query execution.
ROWID(table_name)	Specifies to access the named table using ROWIDs.
RULE	Specifies to use the rule-based optimizer.
STAR	Specifies to use a star query execution plan, if at all possible.
STAR_TRANSFORMATION	Specifies to transform the query into a star query, if at all possible.
USE_CONCAT	Specifies to convert a query with conditions into two or more queries unioned together.
USE_HASH(table_name)	Specifies to use a hash join whenever the named table is joined to any other table.
USE_MERGE(table_name)	Specifies to use a merge join whenever the named table is joined to any other table.
USE_NL(table_name)	Specifies to use a nested loop when joining the named table to any other table. The other table will always be the driving table.

Using SQL*Plus Autotrace

If you're using SQL*Plus release 3.3 or higher, you can take advantage of the autotrace feature to have queries explained automatically. The process is simple. You turn autotrace on using the SET command, and you issue the query as you normally would. SQL*Plus will execute the query and display the execution plan following the results. Listing 19-4 shows an example.

Listing 19-4: **Using the autotrace feature**

```
SQL> SET AUTOTRACE ON EXPLAIN
SQL> SELECT animal_name
  2  FROM aquatic_animal
  3  ORDER BY animal_name;

ANIMAL_NAME
----------------------------
Batty
Bopper
Flipper
Nosey
```

Continued

Listing 19-4: *(continued)*

```
Paintuin
Rascal
Shorty
Skipper
Snoops
Squacky

10 rows selected.


Execution Plan
-----------------------------------------------------------
   0      SELECT STATEMENT Optimizer=CHOOSE (Cost=3 Card=10
             Bytes=170)
   1    0   SORT (ORDER BY) (Cost=3 Card=10 Bytes=170)
   2    1    TABLE ACCESS (FULL) OF 'AQUATIC_ANIMAL' (Cost=1
             Card=10 Bytes=170)
```

Note   If you leave off the keyword EXPLAIN, and issue just the command SET AUTOTRACE ON, SQL*Plus will display execution statistics in addition to the execution plan. To do this, you must either be the DBA or have the PLUSTRACE role.

Using autotrace is convenient because you don't need to manually query the plan table. SQL*Plus does it for you automatically. However, SQL*Plus does execute the query. If a query generates a lot of I/O and consumes a lot of CPU, you won't want to kick it off just to see the execution plan. The EXPLAIN PLAN statement would be a better choice. If you don't mind executing the query but don't want to see the results, use the TRACEONLY setting. Consider this example:

```
SQL> SET AUTOTRACE TRACEONLY EXPLAIN
SQL> SELECT animal_name
  2  FROM aquatic_animal
  3  ORDER BY animal_name;

Execution Plan
-----------------------------------------------------------
   0      SELECT STATEMENT Optimizer=CHOOSE (Cost=3 Card=10 Bytes=170)
   1    0   SORT (ORDER BY) (Cost=3 Card=10 Bytes=170)
   2    1    TABLE ACCESS (FULL) OF 'AQUATIC_ANIMAL' (Cost=1 Card=10
             Bytes=170)
```

Note   Even when you use TRACEONLY, SQL*Plus still sends the query to the database where it is executed. The TRACEONLY setting just prevents SQL*Plus from pulling back the results.

When you are through using autotrace, you can turn the feature off by issuing the SET AUTOTRACE OFF command.

Using SQL Trace and TKPROF

Oracle includes a facility known as SQL Trace that is extremely useful for diagnosing performance problems on running systems. It logs information to an operating system file for all the queries executed by a specific session, or by all sessions. Later, you can review that information, find out which queries are consuming the most CPU or generating the most I/O, and take some corrective action. SQL Trace returns the following information for each SQL statement:

✦ A count of the times that the statement was executed

✦ The total CPU and elapsed time used by the statement

✦ The total CPU and elapsed times for the parse, execute, and fetch phases of the statement's execution

✦ The total number of physical reads triggered by the statement

✦ The total number of logical reads triggered by the statement

✦ The total number of rows processed by the statement

The information on physical I/O and CPU time is most helpful when it comes to identifying statements that are causing performance problems.

Taking care of prerequisites

Before you can use SQL Trace, you need to take care of some prerequisites. Three initialization parameters affect how SQL Trace operates. One of them points to the location in which Oracle writes the trace files. This is important because you need to know where to find a trace file after you generate it. You also need to know how Oracle names these files.

Checking Initialization Parameters

The three initialization parameters that affect SQL tracing are the following:

✦ TIMED_STATISTICS — Controls whether Oracle tracks CPU and elapsed time for each statement. Always set this parameter to TRUE. The overhead for that is minimal, and the value of the timing information is well worth it.

✦ MAX_DUMP_FILE_SIZE — Controls the maximum size of the trace file generated by the SQL Trace facility. These files get very large very fast, so Oracle allows you to limit their size.

✦ USER_DUMP_DEST — Points to the directory in which trace files are created. This parameter is important when you want to find trace files.

You can control the TIMED_STATISTICS parameter at the session level rather than at the database level. To turn timed statistics on for your session, issue this command:

```
ALTER SESSION SET TIMED_STATISTICS = TRUE;
```

You can't set the maximum file size at the session level. You must set it in the parameter file for the instance. You can specify the maximum file size in either bytes or operating- system blocks. If you specify the size using a raw number, Oracle interprets it to mean blocks. If you supply a suffix such as K or M, Oracle interprets it as kilobytes or megabytes. For example:

```
MAX_DUMP_FILE_SIZE=100        100 blocks
MAX_DUMP_FILE_SIZE=100K       100KB
MAX_DUMP_FILE_SIZE=100M       100MB
```

If you are tracing a long process and the size of the trace file reaches the limit specified by MAX_DUMP_FILE_SIZE, then Oracle will silently stop tracing. The process will continue to run.

The USER_DUMP_DEST parameter points you to the directory where the trace files are created. Knowing its value is critical to the task of finding the trace files that you generate.

Note   If you change any of these parameters in the database parameter file, you will need to stop and restart the instance for those changes to take effect.

Finding Your Trace Files

To find your trace files, you need to know the following: which directory they were written to, and their names. The USER_DUMP_DEST initialization parameter points to the directory. You can check the value of this parameter by looking in the database parameter file or by issuing this query:

```
SELECT value
FROM v$parameter
WHERE name = 'user_dump_dest';
```

Note   If you're not the DBA, you may not have access to the v$parameter view.

Finding the directory is the easy part. Figuring out which trace file is yours is a bit more difficult. Oracle generates trace file names automatically, and the names are based on numbers that aren't always easy to trace back to a session. A typical trace file name would be ORA00230.TRC.

So how do you find your trace file? One way is by looking at the timestamp. Write down the time of day when you enable tracing, and also the time at which you finish. Later, look for a trace file with a modification date close to the finish time. If you're not sure of your finish time, look at files with modification dates later than your starting time. Hopefully, there won't be so many people using the trace facility simultaneously that this becomes a difficult task. If you have multiple trace files all created around the same time, you may have to look at the SQL statements inside each file to identify the one that you generated.

Enabling the SQL Trace feature

You can turn on the SQL Trace feature in three ways:

1. Issue an ALTER SESSION command.

2. Make a call to DBMS_SYSTEM.SET_SQL_TRACE_IN_SESSION.

3. Set SQL_TRACE=TRUE in the database parameter file.

The method that you choose depends on whether you want to enable tracing for your session, for someone else's session, or for all sessions connected to the database.

Enabling SQL Trace for Your Session

If you're logging on through SQL*Plus to test a few SQL statements, you can turn tracing on by using the ALTER SESSION commands. The following two commands turn tracing on and then off:

```
ALTER SESSION SET SQL_TRACE = TRUE;
ALTER SESSION SET SQL_TRACE = FALSE;
```

In between these two commands, you should execute the SQL queries that you are interested in tracing.

Enabling SQL Trace for Another Session

Most often, you will want to enable tracing for some other session besides your own. You may have a batch process that is taking a long time to run or an online program that is responding slowly. In that case, you will need to follow these steps to trace the SQL statements being executed:

1. Start the batch process or online program that you are interested in tracing.

2. Start another session using SQL*Plus.

3. Issue a SELECT statement against the V$SESSION view to determine the SID and serial number of the session created in step 1 by the program that you want to trace.

4. Issue a call to DBMS_SYSTEM.SET_SQL_TRACE_IN_SESSION to turn tracing on for that session.

5. Collect the information that you need.

6. Issue a call to DBMS_SYSTEM.SET_SQL_TRACE_IN_SESSION to turn tracing off.

The DBMS_SYSTEM.SET_SQL_TRACE_IN_SESSION procedure requires that you identify the specific session that you want to trace by supplying both the session identifier (SID) and the serial #. You can get this information from the V$SESSION view, which tells you who is logged on to the database. Here's an example of the query to use:

```
SQL> SELECT username, sid, serial#
  2  FROM v$session;

USERNAME                              SID   SERIAL#
------------------------------- --------- ---------
...
SEAPARK                                 9       658
SYSTEM                                 11      1134
```

Once you have the SID and serial # of the session that you want to trace, you can enable and disable tracing, as shown in this example:

```
SQL> EXECUTE DBMS_SYSTEM.SET_SQL_TRACE_IN_SESSION (9,658,TRUE);

PL/SQL procedure successfully completed.

SQL> EXECUTE DBMS_SYSTEM.SET_SQL_TRACE_IN_SESSION (9,658,FALSE);

PL/SQL procedure successfully completed.
```

In this example, tracing was turned on for the SEAPARK user. The first call to DBMS_SYSTEM.SQL_TRACE_IN_SESSION included a value of TRUE to enable tracing. The second call included a value of FALSE to stop it.

Enabling SQL Trace for All Sessions

You can enable tracing for all sessions connecting to a database by placing the following entry in the database parameter file and then *bouncing* the database:

```
SQL_TRACE = TRUE
```

Note To *bounce* the database means to stop it and then restart it.

If you're running Oracle Parallel Server, this parameter will apply only to instances that read the parameter file that you change. If you bounce only one instance, then only sessions connected to that one instance will be traced.

Use care when you enable tracing on a database-wide basis like this. Some performance overhead is involved. Make sure that you really need database-wide statistics, and whatever you do, remember to turn it off later by setting SQL_TRACE = FALSE.

Using the TKPROF command

The raw trace files generated by Oracle aren't very readable. To view the results of a trace, you must run the TKPROF utility against the trace file that you generated. The TKPROF utility will read the trace file and create a new file containing the information in human readable form.

The TKPROF utility allows you to sort the queries in the output file based on a number of different parameters. For example, you can choose to have the queries that consumed the most CPU sorted to the front of the file. With large files, sorting the results makes it easier for you to quickly identify those queries most in need of work.

The TKPROF utility also provides you with the option of issuing an EXPLAIN PLAN for each statement in the trace file. The result here is that the output file will contain execution plans, in addition to the statistics, for each statement.

Using TKPROF Syntax

The TKPROF utility is a command-line utility. You run it from the command prompt, and you pass information to TKPROF using a series of command-line parameters. The syntax looks like this:

```
tkprof tracefile outputfile
       [explain=username/password]
       [table=[schema.]tablename]
       [print=integer]
       [aggregate={yes|no}]
       [insert=filename]
       [sys={yes|no}]
       [sort=option[,option...]]
```

The following list describes each of the elements in this syntax:

   ✦ tracefile — Specifies the name of the trace file to be formatted.

   ✦ outputfile — Specifies the name of the output file that you want to create. This file will contain the formatted trace output.

   ✦ explain=username/password — Causes TKPROF to issue an EXPLAIN PLAN for each SQL statement in the trace file. To do this, TKPROF will connect using the username and password that you specify.

✦ `table=[schema.]tablename`—Specifies an alternate plan table to use. When you use the explain option, TKPROF expects to find a plan table named `PLAN_TABLE`. If your plan table is named differently, use this option.

✦ `print=integer`—Causes TKPROF to generate output only for the first *integer* SQL statements found in the trace file.

✦ `aggregate=yes|no`—Controls whether TKPROF reports multiple executions of the same SQL statement in summary form. The default is yes. If you say no, your output file could be quite large, as each execution of each statement will be listed separately.

✦ `insert=filename`—Causes TKPROF to generate a file containing INSERT statements. These INSERT statements will contain the trace information and can be used to save the trace data in a database table.

✦ `sys={yes|no}`—Controls whether recursive SQL statements and SQL statements executed by the user SYS are included in the output file. The default value is yes.

✦ `record=filename`—Creates a SQL script in the specified file that contains all the user-issued SQL statements in the trace file. You can use this file to recreate and replay the events that were traced.

✦ `sort=option[, option...]`—Sorts the trace output on the options that you specify.

Table 19-3 describes the available sort options.

Table 19-3
TKPROF Sort Options

Sort Option	Description
prscnt	The number of times a statement was parsed
prscpu	The amount of CPU time used for parsing
prsela	The elapsed parse time
prsdsk	The number of physical disk reads necessary during parsing
prsqry	The number of buffers accessed for a consistent read during parsing
prscu	The number of buffers accessed for a current read during parsing
prsmis	The number of library cache misses when a statement was parsed
execnt	The number of times the statement was executed
execpu	The amount of CPU time used for statement execution
exeela	The elapsed statement execution time

Sort Option	Description
exedsk	The number of physical disk reads necessary during execution
exeqry	The number of buffers accessed for a consistent read during execution
execu	The number of buffers accessed for a current read during execution
exerow	The number of rows processed during statement execution
exemis	The number of library cache misses during statement execution
fchcnt	The number of fetches used to return data for the statement
fchcpu	The amount of CPU time spent on fetches
fchela	The elapsed time spent on fetches
fchdsk	The number of physical disk reads made during a fetch
fchqry	The number of buffers accessed for a consistent read during a fetch
fchcu	The number of buffers accessed for a current read during a fetch
fchrow	The total number of rows fetched

If you're ever uncertain of the syntax, you can get a quick reminder by invoking TKPROF without passing any arguments. The TKPROF utility will display a help screen in response that contains a brief syntax summary.

Executing TKPROF

The simplest way to execute TKPROF is to specify an input and an output file name, like this:

```
$tkprof ora00242.trc ora00242.lst

TKPROF: Release 8.1.5.0.0 - Production on Tue Sep 14 09:56:03 1999

(c) Copyright 1999 Oracle Corporation.  All rights reserved.
```

If your trace file contains a lot of SQL statements, you will want to sort the results. You'll likely find it beneficial to sort by the amount of CPU consumed when executing a statement. Consider this example:

```
$tkprof ora00242.trc ora00242.lst sort=execpu

TKPROF: Release 8.1.5.0.0 - Production on Tue Sep 14 09:57:41 1999

(c) Copyright 1999 Oracle Corporation.  All rights reserved.
```

It's usually wise to generate execution plans for each SQL statement in the file. If you look at the execution plan for a poorly performing statement, it can help you better understand the problem.

Explaining Plans

TKPROF's `explain` option allows you to generate execution plans for the SQL statements in the trace file. When you use the explain option, you must supply `TKPROF` with a username and password. `TKPROF` uses it to log on and explain the plans. The user that you specify must have access to the tables referenced by the queries in the trace file. The user should also own a plan table named `PLAN_TABLE`. However, if no plan table currently exists, and if the user has the `CREATE TABLE` privilege, `TKPROF` will create one temporarily. Here's an example of the explain option being used:

```
$tkprof ora00242.trc ora00242.lst sort=execpu explain=seapark/seapark

TKPROF: Release 8.1.5.0.0 - Production on Tue Sep 14 10:05:33 1999

(c) Copyright 1999 Oracle Corporation.  All rights reserved.
```

You'll notice that when you use the `explain` option, TKPROF's execution time is much longer than otherwise. This is due to the overhead involved in connecting to the database and issuing `EXPLAIN PLAN` statements for each query.

Note On UNIX systems, avoid passing a password on the command line. Any user issuing the `ps` command will be able to see it. Just pass in your username, and allow the utility that you are running to prompt you for your password.

One very important point about `TKPROF`'s `explain` option is that the plans are generated when you run `TKPROF`, not when the tracing is done. Consequently, the execution plan for a given statement may not reflect the plan that was actually used when the statement was executed. If you've created indexes in between the tracing and the running of `TKPROF`, or if you reanalyze the tables during that time, the plans that `TKPROF` generates may differ from those that were actually used when the trace was done.

Interpreting TKPROF's output

When you look at the file containing the `TKPROF` output, you'll see a section like the one shown in Listing 19-5 for each SQL statement.

Listing 19-5: **TKPROF output for a SQL statement**

```
SELECT a.id_no, a.animal_name, a.tank_no,
       NVL(c.caretaker_name, t.chief_caretaker_name)
FROM aquatic_animal a, tank t, caretaker c
WHERE a.tank_no = t.tank_no
AND c.caretaker_name (+) = t.chief_caretaker_name
ORDER BY a.tank_no, a.animal_name
```

```
call     count  cpu  elapsed disk query current rows
-------  -----  ---- ------- ---- ----- ------- ----
Parse       1  0.09    0.25    8  166      0    0
Execute     1  0.00    0.00    0    0      0    0
Fetch       2  0.00    0.03    7    6      8   10
-------  -----  ---- ------- ---- ----- ------- ----
total       4  0.09    0.28   15  172      8   10
```

Misses in library cache during parse: 1
Optimizer goal: CHOOSE
Parsing user id: 57   (SEAPARK)

```
Rows Row Source Operation
---- ---------------------------------------
  10 SORT ORDER BY
  10  HASH JOIN
   3   NESTED LOOPS OUTER
   4    TABLE ACCESS FULL TANK
   2    INDEX UNIQUE SCAN (object id 13669)
  10   TABLE ACCESS FULL AQUATIC_ANIMAL
```

```
Rows Execution Plan
---- ---------------------------------------------------------
   0 SELECT STATEMENT   GOAL: CHOOSE
  10  SORT (ORDER BY)
  10   HASH JOIN
   3    NESTED LOOPS (OUTER)
   4     TABLE ACCESS   GOAL: ANALYZED (FULL) OF 'TANK'
   2     INDEX   GOAL: ANALYZED (UNIQUE SCAN)
           OF 'CARETAKER_PK' (UNIQUE)
  10     TABLE ACCESS   GOAL: ANALYZED (FULL)
           OF 'AQUATIC_ANIMAL'
```

The major sections that you see here include the following:

✦ The SQL statement itself

✦ Statistics related to the execution of that SQL statement

✦ Information about the execution plan used for the statement

The statistics are often the key to diagnosing performance problems with specific SQL statements. To interpret this output, you need to understand what those statistics are telling you.

Understanding TKPROF's statistics

The first set of statistics that TKPROF displays for a statement is in tabular form. One row exists for each phase of SQL statement processing, plus a summary row at the bottom. The three phases of statement processing are:

✦ **The parse phase.** In this phase, Oracle takes a human-readable SQL statement and translates it into an execution plan that it can understand. This is where syntax is checked, object security is checked, and so forth.

✦ **The execution phase.** Most of the work occurs in this phase, especially for INSERT, UPDATE, and DELETE statements. With SELECT statements, the execution phase is where Oracle identifies all the rows that are to be returned. Any sorting, grouping, or summarizing takes place here.

✦ **The fetch phase.** This phase applies only to SELECT statements, and it is where Oracle sends the selected data to the application.

The columns that you see in the tabular statistics represent various counts and timings.

> **Note**
>
> If the TIMED_STATISTICS parameter is not TRUE, you will see zeros for all the timings.

The column descriptions are as follows:

✦ COUNT — Tells you the number of times that a SQL statement was parsed or executed. For SELECT statements, this tells you the number of fetches that were made to retrieve the data.

✦ CPU — Tells you the amount of CPU time spent in each phase.

✦ ELAPSED — Tells you the elapsed time spent in each phase.

✦ DISK — Tells you the number of database blocks that were physically read from disk in each phase.

✦ QUERY — Tells you the number of buffers that were retrieved in consistent mode (usually for queries) in each phase.

✦ CURRENT — Tells you the number of buffers that were retrieved in current mode in each phase.

Following the tabular statistics, TKPROF reports the number of library cache misses, the optimizer goal, and the numeric user ID of the user who parsed the statement. The sidebar describes what to look for when running a trace.

Key Items to Look for When Running a Trace

When I run a trace, it's usually in response to someone's complaint about poor performance. So I'm looking for statements that take a long time to execute, especially relative to the number of rows that they return. With that in mind, here are some important items to watch for:

✦ **A high CPU or elapsed time**. If you are tuning a two-hour batch process, don't waste your time on statements that account for only a few seconds of that process. Focus your efforts on those statements that consistently consume the most time.

✦ **A high number of disk reads relative to the number of reads in the query and current columns**. This could indicate that tablescans are occurring or that your database buffer cache isn't large enough. If the disk reads exceed 10 percent of `query+disk+current`, then you may have cause for concern. However, if a query is doing a tablescan and you want it to do a tablescan, then a high percentage of disk reads is not such a concern.

✦ **A high parse count**. Ideally, a SQL statement should be parsed only once. If your parse counts are consistently higher, consider increasing the size of your shared pool. A high parse count could also indicate that your SQL statements are not using bind variables. Check your programs to see if they are building a new SQL statement for each execution.

✦ **Library cache misses**. A high number of library cache misses also indicates that your shared pool size is too small.

Once you've used the statistics to identify potentially troublesome statements, you can look at the execution plan to determine what is causing the problem.

Summary

In this chapter, you learned:

✦ You can use the SQL*Plus `EXPLAIN PLAN` statement to find out the execution plan for a SQL statement. To use `EXPLAIN PLAN`, you must create a plan table to hold the results. The Oracle-supplied `Utlxplan.sql` script will create this table for you, and you can find it in the `$ORACLE_HOME/rdbms/admin` directory.

✦ Optimizer hints allow you to tell Oracle how to execute a SQL statement. Hints are embedded in comments. Comments containing hints must immediately follow the keyword beginning the SQL statement and must take the form `/*+ ... */`. Use hints sparingly, and make sure that your table and index statistics are kept up-to-date.

✦ The autotrace option of SQL*Plus provides another way to get at the execution plan for a query. It's more convenient to use than EXPLAIN PLAN but carries with it the disadvantage of actually having to execute the statement being explained. If you are dealing with a statement that generates a lot of I/O or that takes a long time, use EXPLAIN PLAN, not autotrace.

✦ To help yourself identify poor performing SQL queries, you can use SQL Trace. SQL Trace is an Oracle utility that captures statistics about SQL statements while they are running. Later, you can review these statistics, identify problem statements, and take corrective action.

✦ When you use SQL Trace, the statistics that it captures are written to a trace file. You must use the TKPROF utility to process that trace file before you can view the results.

✦   ✦   ✦

Tuning an Oracle Database

This chapter discusses some ways that you can monitor and tune the performance of a database instance. In addition to the topics listed above, you'll learn how to interpret the results you obtain from collecting statistics, and you'll learn some things that you can do to improve key performance metrics such as the buffer cache hit ratio.

Collecting Statistics

Oracle makes it easy for you to monitor a large number of database statistics by providing two well-known SQL scripts named UTLBSTAT and UTLESTAT. You can find these scripts in your $ORACLE_HOME/rdbms/admin directory.

Note   The UTLBSTAT and UTLESTAT scripts are both SQL scripts. The full file names have the .sql extension, and are utlbstat.sql and utlestat.sql.

The UTLBSTAT and UTLESTAT SQL scripts allow you to collect statistics showing what is happening with your database over a period of time. To use them, you follow these steps:

1. Run UTLBSTAT. This script creates several work tables, grabs a snapshot of current statistics from several dynamic performance views (the V$ views), and stores that snapshot in the work tables.

2. Wait however long you wish. The reason you need to wait is that these two scripts collect statistics over a period of time. The statistics generated by these scripts will tell you about database performance during this specific period.

3. Run UTLESTAT. This script grabs a snapshot of current statistics from dynamic performance views and compares it to the snapshot recorded earlier by UTLBSTAT. It then generates a report based on the differences between the two scripts.

The value of UTLBSTAT and UTLESTAT lie in their ability to report statistics for a specific period of time. The dynamic performance views and the associated statistics that these scripts reference are available to you in real-time. However, the information returned from those views is cumulative from the point in time that you started the database. If your database has been up continuously for months, you might not notice small day-to-day variations by looking only at the current values in the views.

For example, if the buffer cache hit ratio drops suddenly in one day, that may not affect the overall ratio you get when you query the performance views directly. However, if you've been running UTLBSTAT and UTLESTAT each day, and recording the buffer cache hit ratio, the sudden drop will be painfully obvious.

To get the most value from these statistics, enable Oracle's timed statistics feature. This allows Oracle to track the amount of time spent on various events. Enable timed statistics by placing the following line in your database parameter file:

```
TIMED_STATISTICS = TRUE
```

Collecting timed statistics involves a small amount of overhead, but the value of the information you get makes the overhead well worth it.

Note   No significant overhead is associated with the UTLBSTAT and UTLESTAT scripts themselves. Several short queries are executed when you run UTLBSTAT, and several more are executed when you run UTLESTAT. That's it. The scripts have no impact on database performance during the collection period.

Beginning the collection process

To begin the process of collecting statistics, you need to run UTLBSTAT to establish a baseline. The UTLBSTAT script connects to the database as the internal user, so historically, it has to be run from Server Manager. Beginning with the 8i release, you can also run the script from SQL*Plus.

When you run UTLBSTAT, it first drops and re-creates the working tables that it uses. If those tables don't happen to exist, you'll see several error messages scroll by on the screen. Don't be alarmed. It's okay if the DROP commands fail. The CREATE TABLE commands will succeed, and the work tables will be created.

After creating the work tables, several INSERT statements are issued to populate them. These INSERT statements grab a current snapshot of information from key performance views such as V$SYSSTAT, V$LATCH, and V$LIBRARYCACHE. This information is stored in the work tables for later comparison with the ending values grabbed by UTLESTAT.

Note

The most recent run of UTLBSTAT is always the starting point for the statistics generated by UTLESTAT. You can run UTLBSTAT many times in succession, but it is the last run that counts.

Listing 20-1 shows UTLBSTAT running against an Oracle8i database from SQL*Plus. The beginning and ending of the output is shown. Most of the middle has been omitted to save space.

Listing 20-1: **Running the UTLBSTAT script**

```
SQL> @utlbstat
SQL>
SQL> Rem **********************************************************************
SQL> Rem                       First create all the tables
SQL> Rem **********************************************************************
SQL>
SQL> drop table stats$begin_stats;
drop table stats$begin_stats
          *
ERROR at line 1:
ORA-00942: table or view does not exist


SQL> create table stats$begin_stats as select * from v$sysstat where 0 = 1;

Table created.

...

SQL> insert into stats$begin_stats select * from v$sysstat;

196 rows created.

SQL>
SQL> insert into stats$begin_lib select * from v$librarycache;

8 rows created.

SQL>
SQL> insert into stats$begin_latch select * from v$latch;

142 rows created.

SQL>
SQL> commit;

Commit complete.
```

Once UTLBSTAT has run, all you need to do is wait until the end of the time period for which you are collecting statistics, and then run UTLESTAT.

Note   If you stop and restart the database after running UTLBSTAT, that will reset all the values reported by the dynamic performance views and will invalidate your statistics. For valid results, the database must be up and running during the entire time, beginning when UTLBSTAT is executed up until the time when UTLESTAT is executed.

Ending the collection process

To end the process of gathering statistics, run the UTLESTAT script. This script gathers another snapshot of statistics from the dynamic performance views, compares that against the original snapshot saved by UTLBSTAT, and generates a text file named report.txt that contains the results. The UTLESTAT script also drops the work tables.

Note   If you run UTLESTAT without first running UTLBSTAT, you will get a lot of errors because the work tables won't exist. Any results that you get — and you probably won't get any — won't be valid.

Listing 20-2 shows UTLESTAT being executed.

Listing 20-2: **Running the UTLESTAT script**

```
SQL> @utlestat
SQL> rem
SQL> rem $Header: utlestat.sql 17-apr-98.15:26:01 kquinn Exp $ estat.sql

...

SQL> connect internal;
Connected.
SQL>
SQL> Rem ***************************************************************
SQL> Rem                  Gather Ending Statistics
SQL> Rem ***************************************************************
SQL>
SQL>
SQL> insert into stats$end_latch select * from v$latch;

142 rows created.

SQL> insert into stats$end_stats select * from v$sysstat;

196 rows created.
```

```
...

SQL> drop table stats$end_waitstat;

Table dropped.

SQL> drop table stats$waitstat;

Table dropped.
```

After running UTLESTAT, you can review the results by editing or printing the file named report.txt. The file will be created in whatever directory was your current directory at the time you ran UTLESTAT.

Tip   Each subsequent run of UTLESTAT will overwrite the report.txt file. You need to save or rename this file if you want to compare the results of two different runs.

Interpreting the results

The report.txt file will be several pages in size, and it will contain literally hundreds of different statistics. These will be divided into the following sections:

✦ Library cache statistics

✦ Database statistics

✦ The dirty buffer write queue length

✦ Systemwide wait events

✦ Latch statistics

✦ Buffer busy wait statistics

✦ Rollback segment statistics

✦ Current initialization parameter settings

✦ Dictionary cache statistics

✦ Tablespace and datafile input/output statistics

Let's examine what you will see in each of the different parts of the report.

Library Cache Statistics

The *library cache* is an area in the system global area (SGA) where Oracle caches execution plans and parse trees for recently issued SQL statements. The library cache also contains cached copies of PL/SQL code. The statistics indicate how well the cache is performing, and look like this:

```
LIBRARY       GETS GETHITRATI  PINS PINHITRATI RELOADS INVALID
------------  ---- ----------- ----- ---------- ------- -------
...
SQL AREA      9779       .916 29852       .969       4      62
TABLE/PROCED  4220       .892  8035       .882       9       0
TRIGGER         64       .656    74       .554       0       0
```

The LIBRARY column shows the different types of objects that Oracle is caching. The row for SQL AREA, for example, represents information about cached SQL statements. The GETS column refers to the number of times that Oracle looked up an object, while the PINS column refers to the number of times that Oracle executed it. The GETHITRATIO and PINHITRATIO columns (the names may be truncated in the report) indicate how often items were found in memory. In this example, pinned SQL statements were found in memory 96.9 percent of the time. The RELOADS column indicates the number of times an object had to be reloaded after being flushed from the cache.

Key items to look at here are the hit ratios and the reload counts. You want the number of reloads to be zero, if possible. If the reload counts are high, that's a good indication that you should increase the size of your shared pool. Low hit ratios might also be improved by a larger shared pool, or they may reflect an application that isn't issuing the same SQL statements over and over again. In this example, the PINHITRATIO for SQL statements is .969, which is considered good. (Anything .95 or higher is considered good.) For triggers, the PINHITRATIO is rather low, but given the low number of gets and pins, the low ratio could simply be the result of the triggers being loaded into the cache for the first time. As with most of the statistics, you'll get the most useful results after your database has been running for a while.

Database Statistics

The database statistics in the report summarize changes in a long list of system statistics during the period covered by UTLBSTAT and UTLESTAT. The results look like this:

```
Statistic              Total Per Transact Per Logon Per Second
--------------------- ------ ------------- --------- ----------
...
consistent gets       917670      9762.45   3855.76    1696.25
db block gets          20763       220.88     87.24      38.38
...
physical reads          3017        32.1      12.68       5.58
physical writes         2027       21.56       8.52       3.75
...
session logical reads 938433      9983.33      3943    1734.63
...
```

The statistic name is the name of the statistic as reported by the V$SYSSTAT view. The TOTAL column contains the difference in value for the statistic between the beginning and end of the period that was monitored. The other three columns break this difference down on a per-transaction, per-logon, and per-second basis.

One task you can perform with these statistics is to calculate the buffer cache hit ratio for the period being monitored. You can do that by using the following formula:

```
1 - physical reads / (consistent gets + db block gets)
```

Plugging the statistics shown here into this formula will get you a buffer cache hit ratio of .9967. This means that 99.67 percent of the time that Oracle went to read a database block, that block was already in memory. That's good. Buffer cache hit ratios are usually considered good if they are .90 or higher. A lower hit ratio is an indication that you may need to increase the size of the cache (by adjusting the db_block_buffers initialization parameter).

The Dirty Buffer Write Queue Length

The section of the report labeled "The dirty buffer write queue length" consists of only one number and indicates the average number of blocks that are waiting to be written at any given time. Lower values are better. If you find the value of this statistic is increasing, or if it is 10 or higher, you should probably look at reducing it. To reduce this value, you have to increase Oracle's write throughput. One possible way to do this is by increasing the db_block_simultaneous_writes parameter in your database parameter file. Another approach is to configure your database to have more database writer processes. You do this by increasing the db_writer_processes initialization parameter.

Systemwide Wait Events

Wait events are events that cause a process to wait. For example, a process might need to wait for a read to occur. Two sections contain information on wait events, one showing statistics for background processes and one showing statistics for nonbackground processes. Both sections look like this:

```
Event Name                    Count Total Time Avg Time
---------------------------- ----- ---------- --------
SQL*Net message from client   5256     418502    79.62
...
db file scattered read          93         43      .46
log file switch completion        2         41     20.5
single-task message               1         15       15
direct path write               162         14      .09
direct path read                 35         13      .37
control file sequential read     25         12      .48
...
```

The column titles are fairly self-explanatory. For each event, the report shows the total number of waits (the `Count` column), the total time spent waiting (`Total Time`), and the average wait time per event (`Avg Time`). The time is reported in hundredths of a second. For example, this report shows that 12/100ths of a second was spent waiting for a control file read to occur.

Obviously, the fewer the waits and the less time spent waiting, the better. Some values, such as the ones for the event named "SQL*Net message from client," will always be high. These don't represent a problem. However, you should investigate abnormally high values that aren't always high.

Latch Statistics

You'll find two sections containing latch statistics in the report. *Latches* represent locks on critical areas of memory, and *latch contention* can lead to significant performance problems. The first latch statistic section contains statistics for normal latch requests. The second section contains statistics for latch requests made in a `nowait` mode. The two sections are shown in Listing 20-3.

Listing 20-3: **Latch statistics appear in two sections**

LATCH_NAME	GETS	MISSES	HIT_RATIO	SLEEPS	SLEEPS/MISS
Active checkpoint	224	0	1	0	0
Checkpoint queue l	4907	0	1	0	0
Token Manager	126	0	1	0	0
cache buffer handl	234	0	1	0	0
cache buffers chai	1858071	0	1	0	0
cache buffers lru	8539	0	1	0	0
...					

LATCH_NAME	NOWAIT_GETS	NOWAIT_MISSES	NOWAIT_HIT_RATIO
cache buffers chai	4015	0	1
cache buffers lru	63	0	1
channel handle poo	25	0	1
...			

The first section contains columns with sleep statistics. When a process requests a latch and that latch isn't available, the process will enter a sleep state where it waits for the latch. The second section doesn't contain the two sleep-related columns because it represents statistics for those times when a process requested a latch only if it was available immediately. In other words, the process wasn't willing to wait.

Two key performance indicators here are the number of misses and the number of sleeps. Ideally, you want both to be zero, indicating that processes are always able to get latches when they need them. The hit ratio represents the ratio of successful *gets* to the total number of *gets*. It should be as close to 1 as possible. If your hit ratio drops much below 1 and the number of sleeps increases, you may be experiencing latch contention.

Buffer Busy Wait Statistics

The buffer busy wait statistics section of the Report.txt file is significant only when the "buffer busy waits" statistic in the wait events section is high. Normally, this section of the report will be empty and will look like this:

```
CLASS                  COUNT              TIME
-----------------  -----------------  ----------------
0 rows selected.
```

If the "buffer busy waits" count is significant, that indicates contention for latches on one or more types of blocks in the buffer cache. The CLASS column reports the type of blocks for which waits are occurring. The COUNT column reports the number of times a block couldn't be accessed when requested because contention was occurring. The UTLESTAT report gives some suggestions for resolving problems with buffer busy waits.

Rollback Segment Statistics

The rollback segment section of the report provides you with information about rollback segment usage during the period covered by the statistics. It looks somewhat like the following example:

UNDO_SEGMENT	TRANS_TBL_GETS	TRANS_TBL_WAITS	UNDO_BYTES_WRITTEN	SEGMENT_SIZE_BYTES	...	SHRINKS
					...	
0	3	0	0	407552	...	0
2	90	0	40008	612352	...	0
3	72	0	32984	612352	...	0

Note This sample output has been edited a bit to make it fit on one page. In the real report, the columns are much wider, and the column names aren't wrapped around onto two lines.

Two key values to look at here are TRANS_TBL_WAITS and the number of SHRINKS. The TRANS_TBL_WAITS column represents the number of times that a process had to wait to get a rollback segment. If this is more than a few percent of the value in the TRANS_TBL_GETS column, then consider adding more rollback segments to your database. The SHRINKS column represents the number of times that a rollback segment grew beyond its optimal size and was shrunk back again. There's a performance impact from shrinking a rollback segment, so a large number of shrinks isn't good. To reduce the number of shrinks, increase the optimal size setting for your rollback segments.

Current Initialization Parameter Settings

The current initialization parameter settings section provides you with a list of the parameter settings in effect when you run UTLESTAT. Only the nondefault settings are listed:

```
NAME                                            VALUE
----------------------------------------------  -------------------
audit_trail                                     DB
compatible                                      8.1.5
db_block_buffers                                8192
db_block_size                                   2048
...
```

There's nothing in this section that you really need to look for. It simply serves as a reference should you ever compare two different reports.

Dictionary Cache Statistics

The dictionary cache section of the report tells you how efficient the data dictionary cache is in terms of how often dictionary information needs to be read from disk vs. how often it is found already in memory. The dictionary cache section of the report looks like this:

```
NAME             GET_REQS GET_MISS SCAN_REQ SCAN_MIS ...
---------------  -------- -------- -------- -------- ...
dc_tablespaces        441       18        0        0 ...
dc_free_extents       411      134      110        0 ...
dc_segments           803      190        0        0 ...
dc_rollback_seg       107        0        0        0 ...
...
```

In the dictionary cache section, you need to check only the dictionary cache hit ratio. You can compute that ratio by using the following formula:

```
1 - SUM(GET_MISS) / SUM(GET_REQS)
```

You have to sum the GET_REQS and GET_MISS values for all dictionary elements. There's really no sense in looking at the hit ratios for any one element because you can't adjust them on such a fine basis. Using just the data in this example, the dictionary cache hit ratio ends up being 0.806. That's not very good. Hit ratios of 0.95 or more are considered ideal. If your hit ratio is low, you can attempt to improve it by increasing the size of the shared pool. The SHARED_POOL_SIZE initialization parameter controls the size of the shared pool.

Tablespace and Datafile Input/Output Statistics

The last two sections in the report show the amount of disk input and output on a per-tablespace basis and then on a per-file basis. Both sections contain the same I/O-related information, as shown in Listing 20-4.

Listing 20-4: The tablespace and datafile input/output section

TABLE_SPACE	READS	BLKS_READ	READ_TIME	WRITES	BLKS_WRT	...
CHECKUP_HISTORY	3	3	0	3	3	...
INDX	3	3	0	3	3	...
ITEM_DATA	3	3	0	3	3	...
ITEM_PHOTOS	3	3	0	3	3	...

TABLE_SPACE	FILE_NAME	READS	BLKS_READ	READ_TIME	...
CHECKUP_HISTORY	E:\ORACLE\ORA...	3	3	0	...
INDX	E:\ORACLE\ORA...	3	3	0	...
ITEM_DATA	E:\ORACLE\ORA...	3	3	0	...
ITEM_PHOTOS	E:\ORACLE\ORA...	3	3	0	...

The READS and WRITES columns show the number of physical reads and writes for each of the tablespaces and datafiles. The BLKS_READ column shows the number of database blocks that were read. The BLKS_WRT column shows the number of database blocks written. The READ_TIME and WRITE_TIME columns (not shown here because of the page width) show the time spent reading and writing, respectively. The times are in hundredths of a second.

The key point that you want to look at here is the distribution of your I/O load. You should avoid concentrating large amounts of I/O on any one disk, because you can end up requesting more throughput than that disk can provide. If you see high concentrations of I/O in any one tablespace or on any one disk, take steps to distribute that load over multiple disks.

Note In a UNIX environment, you need to be cognizant of your disk configuration and how your mountpoints have been set up when you interpret this section. What looks like one disk may in fact be several. The reverse could also be true.

This data also provides an indication of how much sequential I/O (possibly in the form of tablescans) is occurring. Reads that are the result of index lookups tend to bring back one block of data at a time. Tablescans, on the other hand, cause several blocks of data to be read in by each physical read. If the BLKS_READ value is high in relation to the READS value, that's an indication that tablescans may be taking place. It's not absolute proof, though, and tablescans aren't always negative. But if you see something that you aren't expecting, investigate it.

Tuning the SGA

The system global area (SGA) is a large block of memory that is shared by all the processes that make up an instance. It contains several key memory structures, including the database buffer cache, the shared pool, and the redo log buffer. These are illustrated in Figure 20-1.

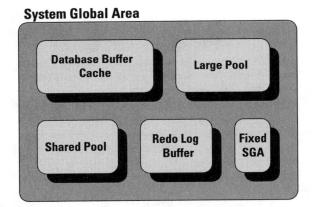

Figure 20-1: Memory structures in the SGA

The *database buffer cache,* often just referred to as the buffer cache, holds the most recently accessed database blocks in memory where Oracle can quickly access them if you need them again. The shared pool caches data dictionary information, PL/SQL code, and execution plans for SQL statements.

Note   If you need a quick recap of Oracle8i's memory architecture, see Chapter 3, "Oracle8i Architecture."

Properly sizing the buffer cache and the shared pool is key to optimizing an Oracle database's performance. Changing the size of these areas is easy: You just change some initialization parameters. Knowing when to change them is the trick. This section will show you two key statistics that you can monitor over time to be sure that you have a reasonable amount of memory allocated to each.

The buffer cache hit ratio

You can use the *buffer cache hit ratio* (often just called the cache hit ratio) to determine how much benefit you are getting from your database buffer cache. I/O activity in a database is often concentrated on a relatively small number of blocks in comparison to the total number on disk. Oracle takes advantage of this by holding the most recently used blocks in memory. If a block happens to be in memory and Oracle needs to access it again, you've just saved an I/O operation. The buffer cache hit ratio tells you how often this is happening.

Computing the Buffer Cache Hit Ratio

To compute the buffer cache hit ratio, use the following formula:

```
1 - (physical reads / (db block gets + consistent gets))
```

You can get the values that you need for this formula by querying the V$SYSSTAT dynamic performance view. For example:

```
SQL> SELECT name, value
  2  FROM v$sysstat
  3  WHERE name IN ('physical reads',
  4                 'db block gets',
  5                 'consistent gets');

NAME                       VALUE
-------------------- ---------
db block gets               1806
consistent gets            71765
physical reads              4133
```

Using these figures, the cache hit ratio is computed as follows:

```
0.94 = 1 - (4133 / (1806 + 71765))
```

As a rule of thumb, hit ratios are considered good if they are 0.90 or higher. That's not an ironclad rule, though. If you have an application that simply isn't hitting the same indexes or data from one query to the next, you may never achieve 0.90.

Note

The hit ratio that you get by querying V$SYSSTAT includes all activity since the instance was started. It may be better to run UTLBSTAT and UTLESTAT, and use the information from the resulting report to compute the cache hit ratio for a short period of time. You might, for example, choose a representative time during the day when the system is being used normally.

Improving the Cache Hit Ratio

If your hit ratio is low, you should at least attempt to improve it. The only way to improve it, short of possibly rewriting all your applications, is to increase the amount of memory allocated to the buffer cache. Tuning the cache hit ratio involves an iterative process consisting of these steps:

1. Compute the current hit ratio.

2. Increase the size of the buffer cache.

3. Compute the hit ratio again. If it improved, go back to step 2. If there was no improvement, then undo your change and stop.

The point of all this is that you should increase the size of your buffer cache only if each increase results in a significant improvement in the cache hit ratio. At some point, you will reach a size beyond which you see no improvement. That's the size you want for the buffer cache. Make it larger than that, and you are wasting memory that you could more profitably use for other purposes. You might, for example, increase the size of your shared pool so that it can accommodate more SQL statements.

Changing the Buffer Cache Size

The DB_BLOCK_BUFFERS initialization parameter controls the size of the buffer cache. You set this in your database parameter file, and it is read whenever you start the instance. The DB_BLOCK_BUFFERS parameter defines the buffer cache size in terms of the number of data blocks that it can hold. Here's a sample setting:

```
DB_BLOCK_BUFFERS = 1000
```

In this example, enough memory will be set aside in the SGA to hold 1,000 blocks. If your block size (DB_BLOCK_SIZE) is 8KB, then the total size of the buffer cache will be 1000 * 8KB, or 8,192,000 bytes.

Because the initialization parameter file is read only when you start an instance, changing the DB_BLOCK_BUFFERS parameter involves stopping and restarting the database. Follow these steps:

1. Change the DB_BLOCK_BUFFERS parameter in the initialization file.

2. Stop the instance.

3. Restart the instance.

By making the change first, you minimize the total downtime to just the few seconds that you need to type the SHUTDOWN and STARTUP commands.

The library cache hit ratio

Recall that the library cache is the area in memory where Oracle stores SQL statements in case they are needed again. Actually, it's not the SQL statements themselves that are so important, but rather, the parse trees and execution plans associated with those statements.

You may recall from Chapter 3 that most applications execute a relatively small number of distinctly different SQL statements. If you have 50 people banging away at an order-entry screen, the underlying SQL statements executed by the application are going to be the same from one order to the next. Oracle stores the execution plans for these statements in the library cache, checks each incoming SQL statement against the cached statements, and reuses execution plans whenever possible. The library cache hit ratio tells you how frequently reuse is occurring.

Deciding If Two SQL Statements Are the Same?

To gain the maximum benefit from the shared SQL area, you need to understand something about how Oracle decides if two SQL statements are the same. Here are the rules that Oracle follows when comparing two statements:

✦ The statement text must match exactly. Each character counts, and the comparison is case-sensitive.

✦ The objects referred to in the statement must be identical. If two statements select from a table named DATA, but the statements refer to tables owned by two different users, then they won't be considered the same.

Keep the first rule in mind when developing an application. For example, say that your developers code the following two statements into different screens of an order-entry application:

```
SELECT cust_name
FROM cust
WHERE cust_num = :1


SELECT cust_name FROM cust WHERE cust_num = :1
```

Because the line breaks are in different places, Oracle will see these as two distinctly different SQL statements. Both versions will end up being cached in the library cache. The impact on memory when just two versions of a SQL statement are used is minimal, but multiply this scenario by five or ten statements, with five or ten versions of each statement, and suddenly you are using 5–10 times the amount of memory that you really need. The more consistent your developers are when coding SQL statements, the better off you'll be.

One last issue worth mentioning is the use of bind variables in SQL statements. Both of the statements shown previously use bind variables named :1. Whether you name your bind variables with names or numbers doesn't matter, but it does matter that you use them.

Consider what would happen if our hypothetical order-entry system dynamically generated SQL statements for each customer lookup. You might get a series of statements like these:

```
SELECT cust_name FROM cust WHERE cust_num = 10332
SELECT cust_name FROM cust WHERE cust_num = 98733
SELECT cust_name FROM cust WHERE cust_num = 81032
SELECT cust_name FROM cust WHERE cust_num = 00987
```

Oracle will see each of these as a new statement, will parse it, and then will send it to the optimizer to generate an execution plan. Because bind variables aren't being used, you lose any benefit from the library cache. The moral of the story? Use bind variables whenever possible for frequently executed SQL statements.

Computing the Library Cache Hit Ratio

You can compute the library cache hit ratio by using the following formula:

```
SUM(pins - reloads) / SUM(pins)
```

You can get this information directly, by querying the V$LIBRARYCACHE dynamic performance view. For example:

```
SQL> SELECT SUM(pins - reloads) / SUM(pins)
  2  FROM v$librarycache;

SUM(PINS-RELOADS)/SUM(PINS)
---------------------------
                  .99972407
```

A hit ratio close to 1 is good. You certainly wouldn't need to worry about this result. If it's less than .99, you should try to improve it.

Note The hit ratio that you get by querying V$LIBRARYCACHE includes all activity since the instance was started. If your instance has been running for a long time (days or months), you may want to compute the hit ratio over a shorter period of time. You can use the values from a UTLBSTAT/UTLESTAT report to do that.

Improving the Library Cache Hit Ratio

If your hit ratio is low, or if it's lower than you would like, you can try to improve it by adding more memory to the shared pool. You do that by following an iterative process just like the one you use when you adjust the database buffer cache. The idea is to keep increasing the size of the shared pool until you reach the point where an increase has no effect on the hit ratio.

Before you increase the size of the shared pool, however, check to see how much of it is currently unused. You can do that by issuing this query:

```
SELECT * FROM v$sgastat WHERE name = 'free memory';
```

If it turns out that you have plenty of free memory in the shared pool already, then an increase in size probably won't improve the library cache hit ratio. If you have a lot of free space, the cause of a poor hit ratio is likely to be in the design of the applications that are running against your database.

Note If you're running a decision support system where each query is likely to be different no matter what you do, a low library cache hit ratio might just be a fact of life.

Changing the Shared Pool Size

You change the shared pool size by adjusting the value of the `shared_pool_size` initialization parameter. Chapter 3 discusses this parameter, but here are some sample values:

```
shared_pool_size = 50000000      50 million bytes
shared_pool_size = 10m           10 megabytes
shared_pool_size = 10k           10 kilobytes
```

You set this parameter in your database parameter file. When you change it, you need to stop and restart the instance for the change to take effect.

The dictionary cache hit ratio

The dictionary cache is stored in the shared pool and caches recently accessed data- dictionary information. Caching this information in memory greatly reduces the time and I/O necessary to parse SQL statements.

Note The dictionary cache is often referred to as the row cache.

You can determine the efficiency of the dictionary cache by computing the hit ratio. The following example shows how you can compute this ratio:

```
SQL> SELECT SUM(gets - getmisses - usage - fixed)
  2          / SUM(gets)
  3  FROM v$rowcache;

SUM(GETS-GETMISSES-USAGE-FIXED)/SUM(GETS)
-----------------------------------------
                               .91279688
```

A value of 0.85 or higher is generally considered acceptable. Of course, you can always try to improve on any results that you get! The process for tuning the dictionary cache hit ratio is exactly the same as for tuning the library cache hit ratio. You have to adjust the size of the shared pool. Oracle determines on its own how much of the shared pool memory to use for the dictionary cache.

Tuning Rollback Segments

Two points are important when tuning rollback segments: detecting contention and reducing shrinkage. Contention occurs when there are too few rollback segments in your database for the amount of updates that are occurring. When contention occurs, time is lost while processes wait their turn. Shrinkage occurs when you have defined an *optimal* size for a rollback segment (using the OPTIMAL keyword in the storage clause), and then the rollback segment grows beyond that size and is forced to shrink back again.

Detecting rollback segment contention

You can detect rollback segment contention by querying the V$ROLLSTAT. You're interested in the number of times that a process was forced to wait in relation to the number of times it attempted to access a rollback segment. The following query will tell you that:

```
SELECT SUM(gets), SUM(waits), SUM(waits)/SUM(gets)
FROM v$rollstat;
```

Contention is indicated by waits. Any nonzero value for waits indicates that contention is occurring. If the sum of the waits ever becomes greater than about 1 percent of the total gets, then the contention is severe enough that you ought to do something about it. You can lower contention by creating more rollback segments.

Because the query shown here reflects all activity that has occurred since the instance has started, you may want to consider marking off a period of time and executing the query twice: once at the beginning of the period and once at the end. That will tell you if contention is occurring *now* (now being defined as during that period). If you have a database that's been up for two weeks and you execute the query once, you have no way of knowing whether the contention problem still exists or whether it was last week's problem.

Detecting shrinkage

When you create a rollback segment, you can define an initial size, a maximum size, and an optimal size. For example:

```
CREATE ROLLBACK SEGMENT rbs21
    TABLESPACE rbs
    STORAGE (INITIAL 10K OPTIMAL 20K
             NEXT 10K MAXEXTENTS 8);
```

This statement creates a rollback segment with an initial size of 20KB (rollback segments always have at least two extents allocated) and an optimal size of 20KB. The rollback segment can grow beyond 20KB if necessary, up to a maximum size of 80KB (8 extents). However, if the rollback segment grows beyond 20KB, Oracle will shrink it back to 20KB in size when that extra space is no longer needed.

Shrinking entails quite a bit of overhead, and you don't want your rollback segments constantly growing and shrinking. You can check the amount of shrinking that is occurring by looking at the V$ROLLSTAT view. Consider this example:

```
SQL> SELECT name, shrinks
  2  FROM v$rollstat, v$rollname
  3  WHERE v$rollstat.usn = v$rollname.usn;

NAME                                   SHRINKS
---------------------------------    ---------
SYSTEM                                       0
RB1                                          0
RB2                                         25
```

If you're getting more than a small handful of shrinks per day, that's too much. You can reduce shrinkage by increasing the optimal size setting or by setting the optimal size to NULL. Setting the optimal size to NULL eliminates the problem of shrinkage entirely, because it tells Oracle never to shrink a rollback segment back to size at all. However, the NULL setting brings with it a potential new problem. If a segment grows to an extremely large size, it will stay that size forever. Ideally, you want the optimal size to be something that is exceeded only occasionally, maybe a few times per day.

Tuning the Redo Log Buffer

The redo log buffer is an area in memory to which processes write a record of the changes that they make to the data in the database. The log writer process eventually writes that record to the database redo log files. Changes must be recorded in the redo log before they can be committed. If user processes can't access the redo log buffer in a timely fashion, performance can suffer.

To tune the redo log buffer, you need to monitor for contention and take steps to reduce it when it is found. Multiple processes can write into the redo log buffer at the same time. When a process needs to write, it must first allocate some space in which to do that. If space is available, that's great. If no space is available because it is all being used by other processes, then you have contention.

The redo buffer allocation retries statistic tells you if contention for the redo log buffer is occurring. You can get the value for this statistic from V$SYSSTAT, as shown in this example:

```
SQL> SELECT name, value
  2  FROM v$sysstat
  3  WHERE name = 'redo buffer allocation retries';

NAME                                            VALUE
--------------------------------------------   ---------
redo buffer allocation retries                     39573
```

This statistic tells you the number of times a process had to wait for a slot to open up in the redo log buffer. To properly interpret this statistic, check its value more than once to see how much it is changing over time. Ideally, a process should never need to wait for a slot in the buffer, so if this number is growing consistently, consider increasing the redo log buffer size. You can do that by increasing the value of the LOG_BUFFER initialization parameter. Increasing the buffer size helps ensure that a space will be available when it is needed.

Summary

In this chapter, you learned:

✦ You can use two scripts, UTLBSTAT.SQL and UTLESTAT.SQL, to collect statistics telling you how efficiently your database is operating. These scripts allow you to measure those statistics over any arbitrary period of time that you desire.

✦ The GETHITRATIO and the PINHITRATIO are two key statistics that tell you how well the library cache is performing. The library cache contains recently executed SQL statements and PL/SQL program units. The greater the ratios, the more often Oracle is finding items in the cache as opposed to reading from disk.

✦ To improve the GETHITRATIO and PINHITRATIO, you can try increasing the size of the shared pool. Do that by increasing the value of the shared_pool initialization parameter.

✦ The buffer cache hit ratio tells you how often Oracle is able to avoid disk I/O because a needed data block was found in the database buffer cache. Buffer cache hit ratios of 90 percent or higher are generally considered to be good.

✦ If your buffer cache hit ratio is low, you can attempt to improve it by increasing the size of the cache. Increase the value for the db_block_buffers initialization parameter to do this.

✦ To detect contention for rollback segments, monitor the percentage of waits to gets found in the V$ROLLSTAT dynamic performance view. If the percentage of waits is high, perhaps higher than 1 percent of the gets, then consider adding more rollback segments.

✦ You should avoid excessive growth and shrinkage of rollback segments. If the number of shrinks reported by V$ROLLSTAT is high, then consider increasing the optimal size setting for the affected rollback segments.

✦ To check for redo log buffer contention, monitor the value of the redo buffer allocation retries statistic as reported by the V$SYSTAT view. If this value increases significantly over time, you are experiencing contention. You can reduce contention by increasing the size of the redo log buffer.

✦   ✦   ✦

Backup and Recovery

Oracle8i Backup

One of your most important responsibilities as a DBA is
to ensure that regular backups are performed and that
you can use them to recover the database in the event of a
hardware or software failure. You are the person responsible
for ensuring that the loss of a disk drive or the accidental
deletion of a file doesn't cause permanent loss of data. To
fulfill this responsibility, you have to understand how to back
up your database. You need to understand such concepts as
archive logging so that you can perform up-to-the-minute
recovery if data is lost. You also have to understand how to
protect your control files and the importance of protecting
your database redo log. In this chapter, you'll learn about
ARCHIVELOG mode and why it is important. You'll also learn
the difference between online and offline backups.

✦ ✦ ✦ ✦

In This Chapter

Running in
ARCHIVELOG
mode

Backing up a
database

Protecting control
files and redo log
files

Testing the integrity
of backup files

✦ ✦ ✦ ✦

Running in ARCHIVELOG Mode

Most Oracle production databases are run in ARCHIVELOG
mode. You'll hear that term a lot, so you need to know just
what it means. *ARCHIVELOG mode* is what enables you to
recover from a failure without losing any transactions that
were committed prior to the time when the failure occurred.
In the real world, this is almost always a requirement.

ARCHIVELOG mode is a mode wherein a copy is made of each
redo log file before the log writer process reuses it. Recall
from Chapter 3, "Oracle8i Architecture," that the log writer
cycles through the redo log files in a circular fashion, writing
first to one, then to another, and so on, for as long as the
database is running. Figure 21-1 illustrates this.

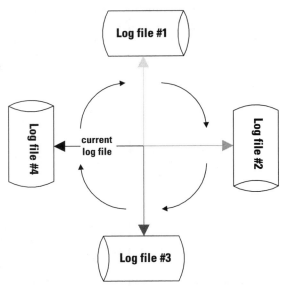

Figure 21-1: Redo log files are written to in a circular fashion.

Each time that the log writer makes another cycle through the redo log files, the previous contents of those files are overwritten. When used this way, you are said to be running in NOARCHIVELOG mode, and the redo log files provide protection only from instance or system crashes. Oracle makes sure that the redo log files always contain enough information to redo any changes that haven't yet been written to the datafiles.

Redo log files can also provide you with the means to recover a lost database, but only if you have saved all the redo log files generated since the most recent full backup. To ensure that all the redo log files are saved, you need to switch your database into ARCHIVELOG mode. When running in ARCHIVELOG mode, Oracle won't overwrite a redo log file until a permanent copy of that file has been created. The copy is called an archive log file, or sometimes an archived log file. Figure 21-2 shows the effect of running a database in archivelog mode.

When you run a database in ARCHIVELOG mode, you can choose to manually make copies of each redo log file as it is filled, or you can start an optional archiver process to automate that copying. Most DBAs end up starting the archiver process and going the automated route.

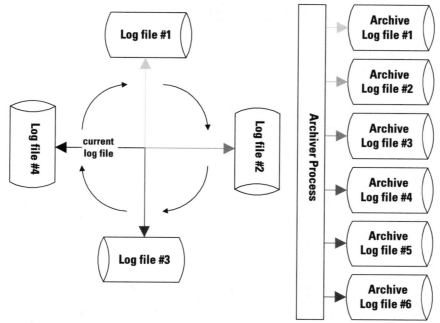

Figure 21-2: Running a database in archivelog mode

Issuing the ARCHIVE LOG LIST command

You can check the archiving status of your database by connecting with SQL*Plus or Server Manager and issuing the ARCHIVE LOG LIST command. Consider this example:

```
SQL> ARCHIVE LOG LIST
Database log mode              Archive Mode
Automatic archival             Enabled
Archive destination            d:\oradata\jonathan
Oldest online log sequence     303
Next log sequence to archive   306
Current log sequence           306
```

In this case, the database is running in ARCHIVELOG mode, and automatic archival has been enabled. That means an archiver process (usually named ARC0) is running in the background that automatically makes a copy of each redo log file as it is filled. The archiver process in this example is currently caught up because the values for "Current log sequence" and "Next log sequence to archive" are the same. The log sequence number is incremented each time Oracle fills one log file and switches to another.

Enabling ARCHIVELOG mode

To enable ARCHIVELOG mode on a database, you can do the following:

1. Set the archive log destination. This is the directory to which archived log files are copied.
2. Define the format of the archive log file names.
3. Check other archive log-related settings.
4. Place your database into archivelog mode.
5. Start the archiver process.

To place a database into ARCHIVELOG mode, you have to close it. Since you're likely to be changing several initialization file parameters, it's usually easiest to *bounce* the instance — in other words, to shut it down and start it up again.

Setting the Archive Log Destination

The archiver process needs to know where to place the archive log files that it creates. Oracle8i allows you to specify up to five archive log destinations. As each redo log file is filled, the archiver process will copy it to each destination that you specify. You use the following initialization parameters to specify the destinations:

log_archive_dest_1

log_archive_dest_2

log_archive_dest_3

log_archive_dest_4

log_archive_dest_5

For most cases, one archive log destination is enough. The destination should be the full path of a directory somewhere on disk. The following example shows an entry from a database parameter file for `log_archive_dest_1`:

```
log_archive_dest_1 = "location=d:\oradata\jonathan"
```

The `location` keyword is part of the specification, and it indicates that a directory name follows. You can use the other destination parameters, `log_archive_dest_2`, `log_archive_dest_3`, and so forth, as you choose. Setting them to a null string (" ") is the same as omitting them from the parameter file altogether.

Note Older releases of Oracle supported only one archive log destination, which was specified by the `log_archive_dest` parameter (no digit in the parameter name). The "`location=`" is not used when setting that parameter. Oracle8i supports either method, but you have to do everything one way or the other. Use either `log_archive_dest` or `log_archive_dest_1`, `log_archive_dest_2`, and so forth. You can't mix the two methods.

When you change your parameter file, you need to stop and restart the database for that change to take effect. If your database is running, you can use the ALTER SYSTEM command to temporarily change the archive log destination. Issue the command like this:

```
ALTER SYSTEM SET archive_log_dest_1 = 'LOCATION=path'
```

Replace *path* with the full path to the directory in which you want to place the archive log files. When you make a change using ALTER SYSTEM like this, remember that the next time the database starts, it will use whatever archive log destination is set in the parameter file. For changes to be permanent, they must be made to the parameter file.

Defining the Format of Archive Log File Names

Archive log files need to have names, and Oracle lets you control the format of those names. You specify the name format through the `log_archive_format` parameter. That parameter must be set to a string of characters that represents a valid file name on your system. You can use two special character sequences to make archive log file names unique. These character sequences are the following:

✦ `%s` — Gets replaced by the log sequence number, which increments with each file

✦ `%t` — Gets replaced by the redo log thread number

The "`%s`" string is a must have. It must be part of your archive log file name to make each file name unique. The "`%t`" string gets replaced by a thread number and is applicable to Oracle Parallel Server (OPS). Under OPS, each instance gets its own thread of redo. If two or more instances share an archive log destination, include the thread number as part of the redo log file name.

Note It's wise to always use `%t` and `%s` in the archive log file name.

The following example shows the parameter setting that you can use if you want the archive log files to start with `arch` and to contain the sequence number and thread numbers separated by underscores:

```
log_archive_format = "arch_%s.%t"
```

File names generated using this parameter setting take this form:

```
arch_1.1
arch_2.1
arch_3.1
...
```

You can use the `ALTER SYSTEM` command to change the `log_archive_format` parameter while the database is running, but such a change won't be permanent. Stopping and restarting the database will cause the archiver to revert back to the `log_archive_format` specified in the parameter file.

Placing Your Database in ARCHIVELOG Mode

Once you've defined an archive log destination and you've defined the archive log file name format, you are ready to place your database into archive log mode. You do that using the `ALTER DATABASE ARCHIVELOG` command. Your database must be closed to make this change. Because you're likely to be making initialization parameter changes at the same time that you are placing your database into ARCHIVELOG mode, it's usually best to shut down and restart everything. Listing 21-1 shows an example of a database being placed into archivelog mode:

Listing 21-1: **Placing a database into ARCHIVELOG mode**

```
SVRMGR> CONNECT / AS SYSDBA
Connected.
SVRMGR> SHUTDOWN
Database closed.
Database dismounted.
ORACLE instance shut down.
SVRMGR> STARTUP MOUNT
ORACLE instance started.
Total System Global Area              38322124 bytes
Fixed Size                               65484 bytes
Variable Size                         21405696 bytes
Database Buffers                      16777216 bytes
Redo Buffers                             73728 bytes
Database mounted.
SVRMGR> ALTER DATABASE ARCHIVELOG;
Statement processed.
SVRMGR> ALTER DATABASE OPEN;
Statement processed.
SVRMGR>
```

Here, the database was first shut down and then restarted. This causes any new settings for archive log-related parameters to take effect. You start the database using the MOUNT keyword, which prevents it from being opened. You use the ALTER DATABASE ARCHIVELOG command to place the database into ARCHIVELOG mode. Finally, you use the ALTER DATABASE OPEN command to open the database for general use. If you like, you can issue the ARCHIVE LOG LIST command to verify the new ARCHIVELOG status.

Starting the Archiver Process

If you don't want to manually archive each log file, and most people don't, you must start Oracle's archiver process. There are two ways to do this. One way is to issue the ARCHIVE LOG START command each time that you start the database. The other way is to set the log_archive_start initialization parameter.

You can issue the ARCHIVE LOG START command from SQL*Plus or Server Manager whenever you're logged on as INTERNAL, SYSDBA, or SYSOPER. The syntax is simple, and there is no output to speak of. You simply issue the command as shown in the following example:

```
SVRMGR> ARCHIVE LOG START;
Statement processed.
```

A corresponding ARCHIVE LOG STOP command also exists. If you would like the archiver process to start automatically whenever you start the database, you can place the following setting into your initialization parameter file:

```
log_archive_start = true
```

With this in place, every time you start the database, Oracle will automatically start the archiver process.

Managing archive log files

When you run a database in ARCHIVELOG mode, you must periodically purge old archive log files. Otherwise, the directory that is your archive log destination will fill up, the archiver won't be able to copy any more log files, and your database will grind to a halt. You must make two decisions when it comes to purging old archive log files:

✦ How long do you want to keep the files?

✦ How long do you want to keep the files online where they can be conveniently accessed?

At a minimum, you need to keep all the archive log files since your most recent full backup. If that's too many to keep online at once, you can periodically copy them to tape and delete them from disk, thus making room for more files. It's easier if you can manage to keep them all online. That way, restoring a datafile doesn't force you into having to retrieve a bunch of old archive log files from tape. Most DBAs end up writing shell scripts to periodically copy old archive log files to tape and delete them from disk.

Archiving a log file manually

If you're running the database in ARCHIVELOG mode but you don't have the archiver process running, then you will need to manually archive your log files. You can't do that just by copying them. You have to archive them in such a way that Oracle knows that they have been copied. That way, Oracle knows when it's safe to reuse a log file and when it isn't.

You can use the ARCHIVE LOG command to manually archive log files. You would normally use two forms of the command. The ARCHIVE LOG ALL command tells Oracle to copy all log files that have been filled but that haven't been copied yet. The ARCHIVE LOG NEXT command tells Oracle to archive just the one log file that is next in the sequence. The following example shows the ARCHIVE LOG ALL command being used to archive all filled redo log files that haven't been archived yet:

```
SVRMGR> archive log all
1 log archived.
SVRMGR>
```

Why would you want to manually archive log files, as opposed to letting the archiver do it for you automatically? If you're archiving to disk, it's probably better to let the archiver do it automatically. However, if you are archiving to tape or some other removable media device, then you may want to exert control over when the redo log files are copied. Having the archiver on automatic in such a case would require that you leave your tape (or other media) mounted all the time. It might not be feasible to do that. If you're manually archiving, then you only need to mount the tape while you issue the ARCHIVE LOG ALL command. Then you can dismount the tape until next time.

Note   If you are manually archiving, be sure to have enough redo log files and size them large enough so that you can go a reasonable length of time before having to archive. Consider sizing your redo log files to hold a day's worth of data. That way, you have to archive only once per day. Remember, if your redo log files all fill up, your database will stop.

Backing Up a Database

Backing up an Oracle database involves copying the files that make up the database to a backup storage medium. There are two types of backups to be aware of:

✦ Online backups, often referred to as *hot backups*

✦ Offline backups, often referred to as *cold backups*

The difference between an online and an offline backup is that you perform an online backup when the database is open; you perform an offline backup when the database is completely shut down — that is, closed and dismounted.

An Oracle database is composed of several types of files. When you back up a database, you should be sure to back up the following files:

✦ All the datafiles

✦ The control file (if an online backup is being performed, you can't just copy this file)

✦ The database initialization parameter file

✦ The archive log files

The only other file type you'll encounter is the online redo log file. Some DBAs back these up as well, but it's a dangerous practice. Oracle recommends against it. The reason you shouldn't back up redo log files is that there's really no reason to ever have to restore them. In fact, generally, if you do restore your online redo logs, you will lose data. If you are recovering a database, and you want to recover the database to the way it was at the moment that it was lost, you need the most current redo log files to do that. If you restore an older set of redo log files on top of your current files, you've just lost whatever data was in those files. You should protect redo log files by multiplexing, not by backing them up. The sidebar discusses the danger of restoring redo log files.

You should back up control files, but you still need to be careful about restoring them. If you are performing an offline backup, you can just copy your control files to tape. If you are performing an online backup, then Oracle has the control files open and you need to issue an ALTER DATABASE command to specify to make the copy for you.

Datafiles, initialization parameter files, and archive log files are always backed up by copying the files. If you are performing an online backup, you do have to specify when you are copying the datafiles.

The Danger in Restoring Redo Log Files

In the heat of battle, it's easy to slip up and restore the wrong files. When restoring from an online backup, if you want to roll forward and bring the database up to date, you generally don't want to restore either the control files or the redo log files. I was once going through a practice run of a large database restore where I did just that. There's nothing quite like that sinking feeling when you realize you've just shot yourself in the foot and trashed your database. Fortunately, it was only a test.

Backing up a database offline

Offline backups are the simplest to implement. You shut down the database, copy the files to tape, and then restart the database. Simple as they are to implement, offline backups do carry with them one big disadvantage: They require the database to be closed. In many shops today, 24x7 availability is required, so shutting down the database for a backup isn't an option.

If you can afford the downtime to do an offline backup each night, then that's probably the best way to go. Certainly, it's the simplest. Otherwise, you need to go with the approach of performing online backups. The process for performing an offline backup is simple. Just follow these steps:

1. Shut down the database.

2. Copy the datafiles, control files, initialization files, and archive log files to tape.

3. Restart the database.

In general, you will want to write scripts to automate this process. On small systems, such as an NT server, the offline backup can be part of the nightly operating system backup. To make that work, you need to write pre- and post-backup scripts to shut down the database before the backup and to restart it afterwards. Commercial backup software, such as Seagate's Backup Exec or Sterling Software's SAMS Alexandria, is capable of automatically executing scripts before and after a backup. Oracle's Recovery Manager Software (often referred to as RMAN) can be used to write backup scripts as well.

Note   If you are scheduling unattended offline backups, it is critical to periodically check to be sure that your scripts are in fact shutting down the database first. Many times, DBAs assume this is happening, when in fact it isn't.

Backing up a database online

Online backups, as the name suggests, are those performed while the database is open. That is also their primary advantage. Doing an online backup is a much more complex process than doing an offline backup. Ultimately, you end up copying the datafiles while the database is open. However, you must tell Oracle that you are doing so; otherwise, the backup won't be valid.

To perform online backups, your database must be running in ARCHIVELOG mode because restoring from an online backup always involves recovering transactions from the database log files. You have to be archiving redo log files to be sure of having them when you need them.

To perform an online backup, the procedure gets more complicated. Generally, you need to do the following:

1. Back up the control files.
2. Back up the datafiles for some or all of the tablespaces.
3. Archive the current online redo log files.
4. Back up the archive log files.

The first three steps require you to issue commands to the database. Step 2 can be especially complicated because you need to intersperse SQL statements with your file copies. You can write your own scripts to automate online backups, or you can use one of the commercial backup tools on the market. Oracle supplies Recovery Manager (RMAN), which is a utility that you can use to automate the backup process. Several third-party vendors also provide backup solutions that work with Oracle. One such vendor is Sterling Software (http://www.sterling.com), which markets an automated backup and tape management software package called SAMS Alexandria.

Backing Up Control Files

When you perform an online backup, by definition, the database is open. If you just copied the open control file using operating system commands, you wouldn't get a consistent version of the file.

When the database is open and you want to back up the control file, you need to issue an ALTER DATABASE command like this:

```
ALTER DATABASE BACKUP CONTROLFILE  TO 'filename';
```

Replace *filename* with the full directory path and file name to which you want Oracle to copy the control file.

In addition to making a binary copy of the control file, it can also be helpful to generate a file containing the SQL statements necessary to re-create one from scratch. Oracle will do that for you too. Just issue the following command:

```
ALTER DATABASE BACKUP CONTROLFILE TO TRACE;
```

When you issue this command, Oracle will write the commands necessary to re-create the control file to a trace file. Finding the trace file can be a bit tricky. Oracle writes it to your database's user_dump_dest directory (usually $ORACLE_BASE/admin/sid/udump) and names it ORAxxxxx.trc, where xxxxx is a five-digit number. To find the correct file in the user_dump_dest directory, you have to look at the file creation dates. Find the file or files created at about the time you issued the command—hopefully, there will be only one—and open each one to see if they contain a CREATE CONTROL file statement.

Having a trace file with commands to rebuild your control file comes in handy if you ever need to move your datafiles or if you are restoring your database and placing the files in different directories than they were in originally.

Backing Up Datafiles

When you perform an online backup of a database, you need to copy the datafiles one tablespace at a time. Before copying the files for a tablespace, you need to specify that you are doing so by issuing the following command:

```
ALTER TABLESPACE tablespace_name BEGIN BACKUP;
```

Replace tablespace_name with the name of the tablespace whose files you are going to copy. When you are done copying files for the tablespace, issue the following command:

```
ALTER TABLESPACE tablespace_name END BACKUP;
```

This specifies that you are done backing up the tablespace. Repeat this process for each tablespace that you back up. The reason for these BEGIN BACKUP and END BACKUP commands is that Oracle needs to maintain the datafile headers in a consistent state while they are being copied. When you issue the BEGIN BACKUP, Oracle stops updating the checkpoint in the file headers of the affected datafiles. During the time that the tablespace is in backup mode, Oracle records changes to the data in that tablespace by writing entire data blocks to the redo log files. In normal operation, Oracle just writes enough information to describe each change.

As an example, if you had a database with three tablespaces—SYSTEM, USERS, and TOOLS—your online backup sequence would look like this:

1. Issue an ALTER TABLESPACE system BEGIN BACKUP command.

2. Copy the files for the SYSTEM tablespace.

3. Issue an `ALTER TABLESPACE system END BACKUP` command.

4. Issue an `ALTER TABLESPACE users BEGIN BACKUP` command.

5. Copy the files for the USERS tablespace.

6. Issue an `ALTER TABLESPACE users END BACKUP` command.

7. Issue an `ALTER TABLESPACE tools BEGIN BACKUP` command.

8. Copy the files for the TOOLS tablespace.

9. Issue an `ALTER TABLESPACE tools END BACKUP` command.

Any script to do this will have to constantly be switching in and out of either Server Manager or SQL*Plus. You need to issue the `ALTER TABLESPACE` commands from one of those tools, but you need to issue the file copies by using operating system commands.

You also have to deal with the fact that the datafiles in a database change occasionally. If you had a shell script to do your online backups, you would need to modify the shell script each time a datafile was added or removed. Another option is to write one shell script that dynamically generates one or more other scripts based on information in the data dictionary. Because this can get complex, many sites will purchase a third-party tool to automate the backup process.

If you are not using an automated backup and recovery solution already, you might want to consider Oracle's Recovery Manager. It is discussed in the sidebar.

Recovery Manager

If you're not already using an automated backup and recovery solution, take a look at Oracle's Recovery Manager. Recovery Manager was introduced with Oracle8, and it has the following capabilities:

✦ It can automate the process of performing both offline and online backups.

✦ It compresses backups by only copying database blocks that are being used.

✦ It can optionally maintain a recovery catalog, contained in an Oracle database other the one being backed up, which records each backup and restore operation that you do.

✦ It has the ability to interface to third-party tape management software.

✦ It can perform incremental backups, backing up only data that has changed since the most recent backup prior to the one being taken.

Recovery Manager is a command-line utility, and some of the commands get rather complex, but Oracle Enterprise Manager implements a set of wizards that builds and executes Recovery Manager command files for you.

Archiving the Current Online Redo Log Files

After you finish backing up all the datafiles, you need to archive the current online redo log files because they are needed for recovery. Archiving them allows them to be backed up with all the other archive log files. To have Oracle archive the current redo log files, issue this command:

```
ALTER SYSTEM ARCHIVE LOG CURRENT;
```

This command causes Oracle to switch to a new log file. Oracle then archives all redo log files that have not yet been archived. Another approach to this same task is to issue the following two commands:

```
ALTER SYSTEM SWITCH LOGFILE;
ALTER SYSTEM ARCHIVE LOG ALL
```

The first command forces the log switch, and the second causes Oracle to archive all the redo log files that are full but that haven't been archived yet.

Backing Up Archive Log Files

Once you've archived your current online redo log files, the last step is to back up all of your archive log files. You'll need these to restore the database. You don't need to issue any special commands to Oracle to back up these files. Just copy them to tape using whatever commands are appropriate for your operating system.

Exporting databases

Database exports can be considered a form of backup. However, you should always consider exports a supplement to the other types of backup. Exports are good for restoring an object that you drop accidentally or for restoring the definition of such an object, but that's about it. The process for restoring an entire database from an export is cumbersome. Unlike a file-based backup, you can't use an export to recover a database up to the point of failure. When you restore from an export, you get only what is in the export file. You can't roll forward from that. Exports are not substitutes for database file backups.

Protecting Control Files and Redo Log Files

Control files and redo log files are necessary for recovery. You always need to have the latest versions of the files available, so you can't protect them by copying them to tape. Instead, you need to protect yourself from ever losing these files, and you do that by multiplexing them. To *multiplex* a file means to keep two or more copies of the file, and to always write the same information to both.

You can multiplex files using hardware, software, or a combination of both. Hardware solutions involve disk mirroring. You configure two disks so that the same information is always written to both. If one disk goes bad, the other disk takes over, and you don't lose any data. To multiplex using software, you specify that you have multiple files, and the Oracle software takes care of writing everything to each copy of the file.

Note

> If you depend totally on hardware mirroring, be aware that a corrupt write may end up corrupting the mirror as well as the primary copy of the file.

If you're particularly worried about losing data (and most DBAs probably are a bit paranoid about this), you can combine both methods. If you currently are not multiplexing your control and redo log files, you should begin doing so.

Multiplexing control files

If you want to increase the number of control file copies for your database, you need to follow these steps:

1. Shut down the database.

2. Copy one of the control files to a new location, on a separate disk drive.

3. Modify the control_files parameter in your database parameter file so that the new control file is included in the list of control files for your database.

4. Restart your database.

You actually do have to go through a shutdown-and-restart process to add a new control file. You can't use the ALTER DATABASE statement to make a copy of the control file while performing this procedure, as you could when you were just making a backup, because once the ALTER DATABASE command finishes, the control file copy rapidly gets out of sync with the original.

The control_files parameter in the initialization file lists all the control files for the database. Oracle looks at this list when you start a database. The parameter setting consists of a comma-delimited list of file names, and it looks like this:

```
control_files = ("E:\Oracle\oradata\jonathan\control01.ctl",
                 "F:\Oracle\oradata\jonathan\control02.ctl")
```

When you start a database, Oracle reads this parameter, opens the files that are listed, and writes the same information to each of the files as long as the database is mounted. If you're not sure how many control files you have in your current database, you can find out by querying the V$CONTROLFILE dynamic performance view. Consider this example:

```
SQL> SELECT * FROM v$controlfile;

STATUS  NAME
------- --------------------------------------------------
        E:\ORACLE\ORADATA\JONATHAN\CONTROL01.CTL
        F:\ORACLE\ORADATA\JONATHAN\CONTROL02.CTL
```

The STATUS field should normally be null. If it contains the string INVALID, then you have a problem with that control file. Always maintain at least two control files (three is better) for a database, and they should all be on separate disks. That way, the loss of any one disk doesn't compromise your database.

Multiplexing redo log files

You can add more redo log files to your database while it is running. You may recall from Chapter 3, "Oracle8i Architecture," that redo log files are organized into groups, each group having multiple members. Oracle writes the same information to all members of a group.

You can query the V$LOGFILE view to see how many redo log groups you have and to see how many members (files) are in each group. Consider this example:

```
SQL> SELECT * FROM v$logfile
  2  ORDER BY group#;

   GROUP# STATUS  MEMBER
--------- ------- --------------------------------------------
        1         E:\ORACLE\ORADATA\JONATHAN\RED004.LOG
        2         E:\ORACLE\ORADATA\JONATHAN\RED003.LOG
        3         E:\ORACLE\ORADATA\JONATHAN\RED002.LOG
        4         E:\ORACLE\ORADATA\JONATHAN\RED001.LOG
```

Note   If you are running Oracle Parallel Server, you can query the GV$LOGFILE view. It contains the same information as V$LOGFILE, but it also identifies the instance using each log file.

In this example, there are four groups, with one log file in each group. Unless hardware mirroring is being used, this is not an ideal situation. Loss of the E drive would result in the loss of data. You can add files to a redo log group by issuing the following ALTER DATABASE command:

```
ALTER DATABASE
    ADD LOGFILE MEMBER
        'filename'
    TO GROUP group_number;
```

Replace *group_number* with the number of the group to which you want to add a member. Replace *filename* with the fully qualified path and file name that you want to use for the new log file. Oracle will create the new log file and add it to the group. The four commands shown in Listing 21-2 add a log file to each of the four groups shown previously.

Listing 21-2: **Adding log files to groups**

```
ALTER DATABASE
    ADD LOGFILE MEMBER
        'F:\ORACLE\ORADATA\JONATHAN\RED004.LOG'
    TO GROUP 1;

ALTER DATABASE
    ADD LOGFILE MEMBER
        'F:\ORACLE\ORADATA\JONATHAN\RED003.LOG'
    TO GROUP 2;

ALTER DATABASE
    ADD LOGFILE MEMBER
        'F:\ORACLE\ORADATA\JONATHAN\RED002.LOG'
    TO GROUP 3;

ALTER DATABASE
    ADD LOGFILE MEMBER
        'F:\ORACLE\ORADATA\JONATHAN\RED001.LOG'
    TO GROUP 4;
```

There will now be two members per group, and the output from querying the V$LOGFILE view will look like this:

```
SQL> SELECT * FROM v$logfile
  2  ORDER BY group#;

  GROUP# STATUS  MEMBER
---------- ------- ----------------------------------------
       1          E:\ORACLE\ORADATA\JONATHAN\RED004.LOG
       1          F:\ORACLE\ORADATA\JONATHAN\RED004.LOG
       2          E:\ORACLE\ORADATA\JONATHAN\RED003.LOG
       2          F:\ORACLE\ORADATA\JONATHAN\RED003.LOG
       3          E:\ORACLE\ORADATA\JONATHAN\RED002.LOG
       3          F:\ORACLE\ORADATA\JONATHAN\RED002.LOG
       4          F:\ORACLE\ORADATA\JONATHAN\RED002.LOG
```

With two log files per group, and each file on a different drive, there is no longer a single point of failure.

Testing the Integrity of Backup Files

You can test the integrity of your backup files in a couple of different ways. One way is to use Oracle's DBVERIFY utility to see whether or not the physical structure of the data blocks within a backup datafile looks good. Another way to validate the integrity of your backup files is to attempt to restore them.

Using the DBVERIFY utility

The DBVERIFY utility is a command-line utility. The command to start it is dbv. Under Windows NT, with releases prior to 8i, the command will be dbverf80, dbverf73, and so forth. You can invoke the DBVERIFY utility by using the following syntax:

```
dbv parameter=value [parameter=value...]
```

The *parameter* element must be one of the items in the list that follows. The *value* element in the syntax should be replaced with a value appropriate for the parameter with which it's associated. The value for the FILE parameter, for example, should be a file name.

✦ FILE—Specifies the name of the database file to verify.

✦ START—Specifies the starting block number to verify. If START is not specified, DB_VERIFY assumes the first block in the file.

✦ END—Specifies the ending block number to verify. If END is not specified, DB_VERIFY assumes the last block in the file.

✦ BLOCKSIZE—Specifies the block size. A size of 2,048 is assumed if you don't specify otherwise.

✦ LOGFILE—Specifies the file to which DBVERIFY output should be written. (The default sends output to the terminal display.)

✦ FEEDBACK—Specifies whether DBVERIFY should display its progress on the screen while DB_VERIFY runs. The feedback is in the form of a dot that is displayed for every *n* blocks, where *n* is the value that you supply. For example, FEEDBACK=1000 results in a dot (.) being displayed for every 100 database blocks.

✦ HELP—Allows you to get help on these parameters. Use HELP=Y.

✦ PARFILE—Allows you to read DBVERIFY parameters from a file. This functions just like PARFILE does when used with the Import and Export utilities.

The example in Listing 21-3 shows DBVERIFY being run against a file named item_data.dbf. The feedback parameter has been set to 100, so a dot will display for each 100 blocks (or pages) that have been examined.

Note The DBVERIFY utility uses the term *pages* to mean blocks. A page and a database block are the same thing.

Listing 21-3: **Running DBVERIFY**

```
$dbv file=item_data.dbf feedback=100 blocksize=8096

DBVERIFY: Release 8.1.5.0.0 - Production on Thu Oct 7 15:57:52

(c) Copyright 1999 Oracle Corporation.  All rights reserved.

DBVERIFY - Verification starting : FILE = item_data.dbf
.......................................................
.......................................................
.......................................................
.......................................................
.......................................................
.......................................................
.......................

DBVERIFY - Verification complete

Total Pages Examined        : 51200
Total Pages Processed (Data) : 0
Total Pages Failing   (Data) : 0
Total Pages Processed (Index): 1
Total Pages Failing   (Index): 0
Total Pages Processed (Other): 5
Total Pages Empty           : 51194
Total Pages Marked Corrupt  : 0
Total Pages Influx          : 0
```

You can run the DBVERIFY utility only against datafiles. It can't check redo log files or archive log files.

Testing the restore process

One of the best favors you can do for yourself is to test your ability to restore your database from a backup. Although you can't do a trial restore on every backup that you take, you can certainly do a trial run once in awhile. If you can actually restore the database, then you know that all your database files are being backed up properly, that your ALTER TABLESPACE BEGIN BACKUP and ALTER TABLESPACE END BACKUP commands are being executed when they should, and so forth. Not only will a few trial restores bolster your confidence in your backup process, but they will also give you valuable practice for the real thing.

Summary

In this chapter, you learned:

✦ One of the most important tasks, if not *the* most important task, you'll need to do is to back up your database. It's critical that you plan for the eventual hardware and software problems that will cause you to lose datafiles, and that you ensure that you are always in a position to recover from those problems. No one else will worry about this for you.

✦ To enable up-to-the-minute recovery of a database, you must be running that database in archivelog mode, and you must save all the archived log files since the most recent full backup. That way, if you lose a file, you can restore it from the backup and then bring it up to date by applying any changes to it that have been recorded in the redo log files.

✦ Offline backups are those performed when the database is completely shut down. The process for doing them is simple. Shut down the database. Copy the files to tape. Restart the database.

✦ Online backups are those performed while the database is running. You must use the ALTER DATABASE BACKUP CONTROLFILE command to copy the control file. You must issue an ALTER TABLESPACE ... BEGIN BACKUP command before copying the files for a tablespace, and you must issue an ALTER TABLESPACE ... END BACKUP command afterwards. You must archive all online redo log files, which you can do by issuing an ALTER SYSTEM ARCHIVE LOG CURRENT command, and then you must back up all your archive log files.

✦ Redo log files and control files are critical to recovery, and you need to be sure that you always have the latest versions of those files available. Therefore, you should protect redo log files and control files by multiplexing them. Redo log files should not normally be backed up with the database files.

✦ If you're in doubt about the integrity of a backup datafile, you can run DBVERIFY against the file. The DBVERIFY utility does a check of the internal structure of the data blocks within the file, and it reports any problems that it finds.

✦   ✦   ✦

Recovering a database

The ability to recover your database is just as important as the ability to back it up. After all, a backup is no good if you can't restore from it. A lot of issues are involved in restoring an Oracle database. You have to know the difference between restoring a database that runs in NOARCHIVELOG mode and one that runs in ARCHIVELOG mode. You need to know how to handle the redo log files, and you need to understand media recovery. In this chapter, you learn how to restore lost datafiles, and then how to recover the database to the point in time at which the files were lost.

Requiring Recovery

Rarely would you ever lose an entire Oracle database. It's far more common to have a single drive go bad, causing you to lose just the files that are on that drive. How you recover from such a loss depends largely on whether your database is running in ARCHIVELOG mode. If you're not running in ARCHIVELOG mode and you lose a database file, your only option is to restore the entire database from the most recent backup.

Any changes made since the backup was performed are lost. In addition, you must shut down the entire database while it is being restored. Because it's usually not acceptable in a production setting to lose data or to shut down the database for an extended period, most Oracle production databases are run in ARCHIVELOG mode.

If you lose files from a database running in ARCHIVELOG mode, you recover from that loss by restoring the most recent versions of those files from tape and then performing media

recovery to bring those files up to date. You can do all this while the database is
running, and without any committed changes being lost.

In the context of Oracle, the term recovery has a very specific meaning. *Recovery*
refers to the process of reading redo log entries from archived and online redo log
files and applying those changes to a datafile to bring it up to date. Figure 22-1
illustrates this.

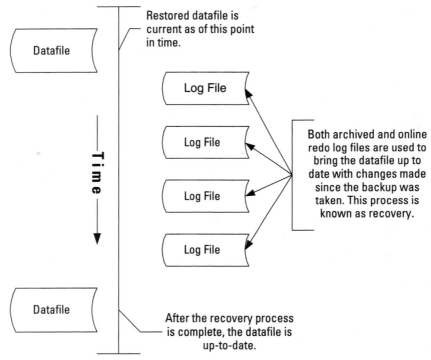

Figure 22-1: The recovery process

When you restore a file from a backup, the file represents the state of the database
at the time the file was backed up, not when it was lost. Usually, you want to
recover all the changes that were made during the interim — between the time the
file was backed up and the time it was lost. Because all changes are written to the
log files, it's possible to read those log files and apply the changes again to the file
that you restored. This is the core process on which all Oracle recovery operations
are based.

Restoring a NOARCHIVELOG Mode Database

Restoring a database running in NOARCHIVELOG mode represents the simplest possible case. Since no archived log files exist, no media recovery is possible. The entire operation essentially turns into an exercise in copying files. The process for restoring a NOARCHIVELOG mode database consists of the following steps:

1. Shut down the database, if the instance is still running.

2. Restore the control files and the datafiles from the most recent backup. If you have a backup control file, made with the `ALTER DATABASE BACKUP CONTROLFILE` command, use that. It will make step 4 easier.

3. Specify whether you've moved any of the files.

4. Reopen the database.

Shutting down the database

If your database is open when you lose the files, some or all of the background processes are likely to still be running, and the instance probably still has the remaining files open. Before restoring anything, make certain that all processes associated with the instance are stopped. You can do this with the `SHUTDOWN ABORT` command, as shown in this example:

```
$sqlplus /nolog

SQL*Plus: Release 8.1.5.0.0 - Production on Mon Oct 11 13:54:06 1999

(c) Copyright 1999 Oracle Corporation.  All rights reserved.

SQL> connect internal
Connected.
SQL> shutdown abort
ORACLE instance shut down.
```

With the instance completely shut down, you can proceed to restore the files.

Restoring the files

When you restore files for a database running in noarchivelog mode, you need to do the following:

✦ Restore all control files.

✦ Restore all datafiles.

✦ Do not restore the redo log files.

The reason that you have to restore all the control files and datafiles is that Oracle requires these files to be consistent with respect to each other. If you have one datafile that's a day older than another, that's not consistent. Since you have no archived logs, you won't be able to apply changes from those logs to make them consistent either. Your only option is to restore all the files.

Note　NOARCHIVELOG mode is suitable only in situations where you can afford to lose all the changes that you've made since the most recent backup. Development and test databases are often run in NOARCHIVELOG mode. Read-only databases may also be run in NOARCHIVELOG mode.

Specifying new file locations

If the loss of a disk forces you to restore files to different locations than they were in originally, you need to tell Oracle about that. Otherwise, when you try to restart the database, Oracle will look for the files, it won't be able to find them, and you'll see an error message like the following:

```
ORA-01157: cannot identify/lock data file 2 - see DBWR trace file
ORA-01110: data file 2: 'E:\ORACLE\ORADATA\JONATHAN\USERS01.DBF'
```

Oracle stores the names and locations of all database files in the control file. The reason you get an error like this is that Oracle is trying to open a file named in the control file, and that file cannot be found.

You can use two methods to tell Oracle that you have moved a database file. One approach is to issue an ALTER DATABASE RENAME FILE command. That command allows you to change the file names and locations recorded in the database control file. Another approach to the same task is to re-create the entire control file. Issuing ALTER DATABASE RENAME FILE commands is probably the safer approach. Creating a new control file allows you to rename all your files at once, but if you make a mistake, you could cause more problems, and you could lose data.

Using the ALTER DATABASE RENAME FILE Command

The ALTER DATABASE RENAME FILE command allows you to change the name and location of a file as recorded in the database control file. It accepts two parameters. One parameter is the original path and file name. The other parameter is the new value that you want Oracle to use in its place. The syntax looks like this:

```
ALTER DATABASE RENAME FILE
    'original_filename' TO 'new_filename';
```

Replace *original_filename* with the full path and file name that Oracle is currently using. Replace *new_filename* with the full path and file name representing where the file is currently located. The format for these strings, and whether they are case-sensitive, depends on the operating system. UNIX systems typically have case-sensitive file names. Windows NT systems do not.

To *rename* a database file, the database must be mounted but not open. It must be mounted because the changes need to be recorded in the control file. Oracle opens the control file when you mount the database. You can't rename a file when the database is open because the files would then be in use. You can't rename files that are currently open. Listing 22-1 shows the ALTER DATABASE RENAME FILE command being used to specify that you have renamed USERS01.DBF to USERS0199.DBF.

Listing 22-1: **Renaming database files**

```
SQL> CONNECT INTERNAL
Connected to an idle instance.
SQL> STARTUP MOUNT
ORACLE instance started.

Total System Global Area    38322124 bytes
Fixed Size                     65484 bytes
Variable Size               21405696 bytes
Database Buffers            16777216 bytes
Redo Buffers                   73728 bytes
Database mounted.
SQL> ALTER DATABASE RENAME FILE
  2      'E:\ORACLE\ORADATA\JONATHAN\USERS01.DBF' TO
  3      'E:\ORACLE\ORADATA\JONATHAN\USERS0199.DBF';

Database altered.
```

Note that this command changes the name and location of a file only as recorded in the database control file. It doesn't rename the file at the operating-system level, nor does it physically move the file to the new location. You must perform both of those tasks yourself. The ALTER DATABASE RENAME FILE command does a search and replace, taking the original file name that you provided and replacing it with the new file name.

To issue the ALTER DATABASE RENAME FILE command, you need to know what the original file names in your database are. How can you find that out? If your database is operational, you can query the V$DATAFILE view for this information. However, if you're restoring the database, it's not going to be operational, so consider generating a list of file names in advance. You may want to periodically run a SQL script such as the following:

```
SPOOL datafile_list
SELECT name FROM v$datafile;
SPOOL OFF
```

You can even run a slightly more complex script periodically that generates the ALTER DATABASE RENAME FILE commands for you. For example:

```
SET PAGESIZE 0
SPOOL rename_file_commands.sql
SELECT 'ALTER DATABASE RENAME FILE '
       || '''' || name || ''' TO ''''';'
FROM v$datafile;
SPOOL OFF
```

The result of executing this script will be a file containing an ALTER DATABASE RENAME FILE command for every datafile in your database. The contents will look like the following:

```
ALTER DATABASE RENAME FILE
'E:\ORACLE\ORADATA\JONATHAN\SYSTEM01.DBF' TO '';
ALTER DATABASE RENAME FILE
'E:\ORACLE\ORADATA\JONATHAN\USERS0199.DBF' TO '';
ALTER DATABASE RENAME FILE
'E:\ORACLE\ORADATA\JONATHAN\RBS01.DBF' TO '';
```

You could easily edit this file, type in new file names, and then execute it.

If all else fails and you don't have a list of original file names to work from, you can always attempt to open the database, get the file name from the error message, and then rename that file. You would have to repeat this process once for each file that you move.

Re-creating the Control File

If you're moving all or most of your datafiles at once, you may find it easier to re-create the control file. As part of that process, you can provide new names and locations for all database files. Re-creating the control file is a good idea only if you have previously been in the habit of generating control file backups using the following command:

```
ALTER DATABASE BACKUP CONTROLFILE TO TRACE;
```

This command actually generates a trace file containing the necessary CREATE CONTROLFILE command, together with other necessary commands. Although you could write the CREATE CONTROLFILE command yourself, it's not easy to do, especially if you don't have access to the database anymore. You also risk losing data if you get it wrong, so let Oracle generate it for you. Listing 22-2 provides an example of a script generated when you back up the control file to trace.

Listing 22-2: **Trace file contents for a control file backup**

```
STARTUP NOMOUNT
CREATE CONTROLFILE REUSE DATABASE "JONATHAN" NORESETLOGS
ARCHIVELOG
    MAXLOGFILES 32
    MAXLOGMEMBERS 2
    MAXDATAFILES 32
    MAXINSTANCES 16
    MAXLOGHISTORY 1630
LOGFILE
  GROUP 1 'E:\ORACLE\ORADATA\JONATHAN\REDO04.LOG'  SIZE 1M,
  GROUP 2 'E:\ORACLE\ORADATA\JONATHAN\REDO03.LOG'  SIZE 1M,
  GROUP 3 'E:\ORACLE\ORADATA\JONATHAN\REDO02.LOG'  SIZE 1M,
  GROUP 4 'E:\ORACLE\ORADATA\JONATHAN\REDO01.LOG'  SIZE 1M
DATAFILE
  'E:\ORACLE\ORADATA\JONATHAN\SYSTEM01.DBF',
  'E:\ORACLE\ORADATA\JONATHAN\USERS0199.DBF',
  'E:\ORACLE\ORADATA\JONATHAN\RBS01.DBF',
  'E:\ORACLE\ORADATA\JONATHAN\TEMP01.DBF',
  'E:\ORACLE\ORADATA\JONATHAN\OEMREP01.DBF',
  'E:\ORACLE\ORADATA\JONATHAN\INDX01.DBF',
  'E:\ORACLE\ORADATA\JONATHAN\USERS02.DBF',
  'E:\ORACLE\ORADATA\JONATHAN\CHECKUP_HISTORY.DBF',
  'E:\ORACLE\ORADATA\JONATHAN\LOCAL_UNIFORM.DBF',
  'E:\ORACLE\ORADATA\JONATHAN\LOCAL_AUTOALLOCATE.DBF',
  'E:\ORACLE\ORADATA\JONATHAN\LOCAL_UNIFORM_2.DBF',
  'E:\ORACLE\ORADATA\JONATHAN\ITEM_DATA.DBF',
  'E:\ORACLE\ORADATA\JONATHAN\ITEM_PHOTOS.DBF',
  'E:\ORACLE\ORADATA\JONATHAN\TEST_MIN_EXTENT_SIZE.DBF',
  'E:\ORACLE\ORADATA\JONATHAN\TEST_MIN_EXTENT_SIZE_2.DBF',
  'E:\ORACLE\ORADATA\JONATHAN\TEST_5.DBF',
  'E:\ORACLE\ORADATA\JONATHAN\TEST_5B.DBF',
  'E:\ORACLE\ORADATA\JONATHAN\TEST_LARGE.DBF',
  'E:\ORACLE\ORADATA\JONATHAN\TEST_LARGEB.DBF'
CHARACTER SET WE8ISO8859P1
;
# Recovery is required if any of the datafiles are restored
backups,
# or if the last shutdown was not normal or immediate.
RECOVER DATABASE
# Database can now be opened normally.
ALTER DATABASE OPEN;
# No tempfile entries found to add.
#
```

This script is meant to be executed from Server Manager. If you decide to execute it from SQL*Plus, you will need to change the pound signs (#) to a double dash (--), or delete the comment lines entirely, because SQL*Plus doesn't recognize pound signs as comment characters. You will also want to edit the trace file and remove all the messages that Oracle places before and after these commands.

> **Note**   You must be connected as SYSDBA or as INTERNAL to create a control file.

Also before you execute the script, be sure to edit it and change all the file names to reflect the new locations and names of the database files. If your original control files still exist, leave in the keyword REUSE, and the new files will be created over the top of the originals. Otherwise, remove the keyword REUSE to create totally new files. If you are restoring the database from a backup, you should delete the RECOVER DATABASE and ALTER DATABASE OPEN commands and open the database yourself.

Reopening the database

After restoring the datafiles and rebuilding the control file if necessary, you should open the database using the RESETLOGS option. This resets the log files to ensure that there won't be any conflicts between new entries and those left over from the previous incarnation of the database.

RESETLOGS is an option of the ALTER DATABASE OPEN command. One issue that you may run into when you try to use it is that Oracle will allow the option to be used only in two cases:

✦ An incomplete media recovery is performed.

✦ A backup control file is used to start the database.

Backup control files are those created with the ALTER DATABASE BACKUP CONTROLFILE command (but not using the TO TRACE option). Because restoring from an offline backup doesn't involve media recovery, to use the RESETLOGS option, you will need to use a backup control file. What if you don't have a backup control file? Fortunately, you can make one. Just follow these steps:

1. Start Server Manager (or SQL*Plus) and mount the database.

2. Use the ALTER DATABASE BACKUP CONTROLFILE command to make a backup control file.

3. Shut down the database.

4. Copy the backup control file over the original control files that you have restored.

With the backup control file in place, you are now ready to open the database using the RESETLOGS option.

Note This information applies only to Oracle8 and Oracle8i. Prior releases of Oracle did not allow you to use RESETLOGS on backup control files.

Listing 22-3 shows backup control files being created on a Windows NT server.

Listing 22-3: **Replacing control files with a backup control file**

```
E:\Oracle>svrmgrl

Oracle Server Manager Release 3.1.5.0.0 - Production

(c) Copyright 1997, Oracle Corporation.  All Rights Reserved.

Oracle8i Release 8.1.5.0.0 - Production
With the Partitioning and Java options
PL/SQL Release 8.1.5.0.0 - Production

SVRMGR> CONNECT INTERNAL
Connected.
SVRMGR> STARTUP MOUNT
ORACLE instance started.
Total System Global Area                   34451404 bytes
Fixed Size                                    65484 bytes
Variable Size                              17469440 bytes
Database Buffers                           16384000 bytes
Redo Buffers                                 532480 bytes
Database mounted.
SVRMGR> ALTER DATABASE BACKUP CONTROLFILE TO 'CONTROLXX.CTL';
Statement processed.
SVRMGR>
SVRMGR> EXIT
Server Manager complete.
E:\Oracle\ORADATA\orcl>copy controlxx.ctl control01.ctl
        1 file(s) copied.

E:\Oracle\ORADATA\orcl>copy controlxx.ctl control02.ctl
        1 file(s) copied.

E:\Oracle\ORADATA\orcl>copy controlxx.ctl control03.ctl
        1 file(s) copied.
```

The end result of this cumbersome process is that you replace your database control files with backup control files. You can now go back into Server Manager, start up the instance, and open the database using the RESETLOGS option. Consider this example:

```
SVRMGR> CONNECT INTERNAL
Connected.
SVRMGR> STARTUP MOUNT
ORACLE instance started.
Total System Global Area                    34451404 bytes
Fixed Size                                     65484 bytes
Variable Size                               17469440 bytes
Database Buffers                            16384000 bytes
Redo Buffers                                  532480 bytes
Database mounted.
SVRMGR> ALTER DATABASE OPEN RESETLOGS;
Statement processed.
```

Given the requirement that you issue RESETLOGS in conjunction with a backup control file, it's probably best if you routinely make backup control files as part of your backup process. Then you can use those backup control files when restoring the database, instead of having to go through the rather cumbersome process shown here.

Requiring Media Recovery

Media recovery is the process of reading changes from the redo log files and reapplying those changes to one or more datafiles that have been restored from a backup. The end result is that the datafiles are brought up to date and they reflect all changes made since the backup. The need to do media recovery is the reason you have a redo log in the first place.

The online redo log files allow Oracle to perform media recovery to recover from a system crash or the sudden failure of a database instance. Whenever you commit a transaction, Oracle makes certain that the changes from that transaction are written to the redo log files. The changes may not be written to the datafiles until later. If the system crashes before the changes can be written to the datafiles, Oracle will detect the crash when you restart the database, read the lost changes from the redo log files, and apply them to the datafiles. Media recovery, when performed in response to a crash like this, is referred to as *crash recovery*.

You know that Oracle cycles through the set of redo log files for a database, writing to each file in turn. Throughout all this, Oracle ensures that redo log entries are not overwritten until their changes have been written to the datafiles. This ensures that crash recovery can always be performed. Imagine, though, if redo log entries were kept indefinitely. You could use such a log to replay all the changes that took place over a period of days, weeks, or even months. Not only could you recover from a crash, but you could also recover from losing a file due to drive failure. This is where archived redo logs come into play.

When you run a database in ARCHIVELOG mode, Oracle makes a copy of each redo log file as it is filled. These copies, known as archived log files, together with any online redo log files that have not yet been copied, form a continuous record of all changes made to the database. If you lose a datafile and are forced to restore it from a backup, the information in the archived log files can be used to reapply all the changes to that file that were made since the backup took place. The net effect is that you suffer zero data loss.

How long archived log files are retained is up to you. In fact, if you're not using RMAN and an automated scheduling tool such as what Enterprise Manager provides, you will need to write your own scripts to purge old archived log files. As long as you have all the archived log files generated since the most recent full backup of a database file, you will always be able to recover that file.

Recovering from a Lost Datafile

The loss of a datafile, usually caused by the failure of a disk, is probably the most common recovery scenario that you'll encounter. If you're running in archivelog mode, you can restore just the files that you lost, recover them to the way they were at the point of failure, and do all this while the rest of the database is up and running.

Note   If the lost file is part of the SYSTEM tablespace, then you won't be able to keep the database open while it is being restored.

To restore a lost file, follow these steps:

1. Take the datafile offline if Oracle hasn't already done that for you.

2. Restore the file from the most recent backup.

3. Recover the file.

4. Bring the file back online.

The process is usually quite painless, especially if you have the necessary archived log files still on disk and in the directory pointed to by the ARCHIVE_LOG_DEST parameter.

Taking the lost datafile offline

Chances are, if a drive failure caused you to lose a datafile, Oracle will have already taken the file offline. Verify this, however, before proceeding further. To check the status of files in your database, issue the query shown in this example:

```
SQL> SELECT status, name FROM v$datafile;

STATUS  NAME
------- ----------------------------------------------------
SYSTEM  E:\ORACLE\ORADATA\JONATHAN\SYSTEM01.DBF
OFFLINE E:\ORACLE\ORADATA\JONATHAN\USERS0199.DBF
ONLINE  E:\ORACLE\ORADATA\JONATHAN\RBS01.DBF
```

In this case, you can see that the USERS0199.DBF file is offline. If the file that you've lost is not yet offline, you can take it offline by issuing this command:

```
ALTER DATABASE
    DATAFILE 'filename' OFFLINE;
```

Replace filename with the full path and name of the file, as reported by the v$datafile view. With the file safely offline, you can proceed to restore and recover it. Users of the database will still be able to do work that doesn't require access to the data in the file that you've taken offline.

Restoring the lost datafile

Before you can recover the file, you need to restore it. You should, of course, restore it from the most recent backup that you have available. If a drive failure forces you into restoring the file to a new location, you need to issue an ALTER DATABASE RENAME FILE command to record the new location in the database control file. See the section "Using the ALTER DATABASE RENAME FILE command" earlier in this chapter for details on doing this.

Recovering the lost datafile

After restoring the file, you need to recover it. You can use the SQL*Plus (or Server Manager) RECOVER command for this purpose. If you need to recover multiple files, you can recover them all at once by issuing this command:

```
RECOVER DATABASE
```

Using RECOVER DATABASE causes Oracle to check all the files and recover any that need recovering. A more surgical approach would be to use RECOVER DATAFILE and list the files that you specifically want to recover. The syntax for doing that is as follows:

```
RECOVER DATAFILE 'filename' [,'filename'...];
```

Replace *filename* with the path and name of a file that you want to recover. You can list multiple files in the command. Separate the file names with commas.

To recover a datafile, you must connect to the database as either SYSDBA, SYSOPER, or INTERNAL. For example:

```
SQL> CONNECT SYSTEM/MANAGER AS SYSDBA
Connected.
```

Once connected, you can issue the RECOVER command. As Oracle proceeds to recover the datafile, it will prompt you each time it needs to access an archived log file. You can respond to each prompt by pressing the Enter key, or you can use the keyword AUTO to specify that Oracle proceed without prompting you all the time. Listing 22-4 shows the use of RECOVER DATAFILE to bring the USERS0199.DBF file up to date.

Listing 22-4: **Recovering a datafile**

```
SQL> RECOVER DATAFILE 'E:\ORACLE\ORADATA\JONATHAN\USERS0199.DBF';
ORA-00279: change 3080219 generated at 10/07/99 19:20:50 needed for thread 1
ORA-00289: suggestion : D:\ORADATA\JONATHAN\ARCH_307.1
ORA-00280: change 3080219 for thread 1 is in sequence #307


Specify log: {<RET>=suggested | filename | AUTO | CANCEL}
AUTO
ORA-00279: change 3100373 generated at 10/08/99 08:56:17 needed for thread 1
ORA-00289: suggestion : D:\ORADATA\JONATHAN\ARCH_308.1
ORA-00280: change 3100373 for thread 1 is in sequence #308
ORA-00278: log file 'D:\ORADATA\JONATHAN\ARCH_307.1' no longer needed for this
recovery

...

ORA-00279: change 3181229 generated at 10/10/99 10:20:05 needed for thread 1
ORA-00289: suggestion : D:\ORADATA\JONATHAN\ARCH_312.1
ORA-00280: change 3181229 for thread 1 is in sequence #312
ORA-00278: log file 'D:\ORADATA\JONATHAN\ARCH_311.1' no longer needed for this
recovery


Log applied.
Media recovery complete.
```

In this example, the keyword AUTO is used as the response to the first prompt. This works because all the needed archived log files are still online, and they are still in the directory pointed to by the ARCHIVE_LOG_DEST parameter.

If the needed archived log files are on disk but not where Oracle expects them to be, you can respond to the prompt by supplying the correct path and file name for the archived log file that Oracle is seeking. If the needed archived log files aren't on disk but are instead on a backup medium such as a tape, you need to restore them to disk before you can recover the datafile. This is why many DBAs keep archived log files online long enough to cover the period since the most recent full backup.

Bringing the recovered file back online

The last task, after you've recovered the file, is to bring it back online. You can do that with the ALTER DATABASE command, as shown in this example:

```
SQL> ALTER DATABASE
  2     DATAFILE 'E:\ORACLE\ORADATA\JONATHAN\USERS0199.DBF'
  3     ONLINE;

Database altered.
```

Now you can sit back, relax, and have a coffee. The file has been recovered, it's back online, and the users can work as normal.

Terminating an Incomplete Recovery

When you recover a database, Oracle doesn't require you to recover all changes up to the moment when the database was lost. Usually you will want to do so, but sometimes you may want (or need) to terminate the recovery process earlier. When you do that, you are said to have performed an *incomplete recovery.*

You might perform an incomplete recovery for both voluntary and involuntary reasons. The involuntary reasons include the following:

✦ **Loss of an online redo log file.** The last part of the recovery process reads changes from the online redo log files and applies those changes to the files being recovered. If you've lost your online redo log files, then you can't recover the changes that were recorded in those files.

✦ **Loss of an archived log file.** If you lose an archived log file and you have no backups of that file, then you will be able to recover changes only up to the point in time represented by that file.

These two points illustrate the need to carefully protect your online redo logs and to back up your archived log files. The recovery process always proceeds from the oldest change forward, through the most recent change. If you get to a point where you are missing a file, that's where you have to stop.

Note The first point, that of losing online redo log files, is why Oracle recommends against backing up those files. If you get flustered in a recovery situation, and unthinkingly restore redo log files from a backup, you will have totally and utterly lost your ability to recover up to the point of failure.

You might voluntarily want to perform an incomplete recovery if either of the following applies:

✦ A processing error results in lost or damaged data and you want to rerun the process.

✦ A user error results in important data being deleted.

Both of these scenarios are really the same. Either way, something went wrong at a certain point in time, and data was corrupted or lost. You might, for example, have a billing process that runs each night. If a major error occurs, you may want to be able to rerun the entire billing process again. Incomplete recovery allows you to do that. You restore the entire database from the last backup and recover it up to the moment just prior to when the billing process was run. Then you can correct the source of the error and rerun the process.

Note Incomplete recovery doesn't always represent the ideal way to recover from process failures. If online transactions are taking place at the same time that a batch process is running, those transactions will be lost if you perform an incomplete recovery to rerun the batch process.

After performing an incomplete recovery, it's important to immediately perform another full backup of your entire database. After performing an incomplete recovery, you need to open your database with the RESETLOGS option. Doing that effectively prevents you from using the existing archive and redo logs to recover again.

Understanding the different types of incomplete recovery

When you voluntarily perform an incomplete recovery, you can approach it in three ways:

✦ You can recover up to a specific point in time.

✦ You can recover up to a specific change.

✦ You can recover one log file at a time until you decide to manually cancel the recovery operation.

You specify how you want to approach incomplete recovery when you issue the RECOVERY command.

Incomplete recovery is sometimes referred to as point-in-time recovery because it results in a database that reflects its state at some past point in time. You can't perform incomplete recovery on datafiles and tablespaces. To perform an incomplete recovery, you need to restore all the datafiles and roll everything forward to the desired point in time.

Note   Tablespace point-in-time recovery (TSPTR) is a complex process, and it involves cloning all or part of your database. It also requires you to manually deal with dependencies between objects in the tablespace that you are restoring and objects in the rest of that database.

Using the UNTIL clause

You use the `UNTIL` clause of the `RECOVERY` command to specify an incomplete recovery. The syntax for the `UNTIL` clause looks like this:

```
RECOVER DATABASE
    [UNTIL CANCEL]
    [UNTIL CHANGE scn]
    [UNTIL TIME 'datetime']
    rest_of_command;
```

The following list describes the elements of this syntax:

✦ `UNTIL CANCEL`—Specifies a cancel-based recovery.

✦ `UNTIL CHANGE`—Specifies recovery up to, but not including, a specific system change number (SCN).

✦ `scn`—Specifies the change number at which to stop the recovery process. This change number should be one higher than the one you want to recover through. In other words, to recover through change 919, specify `UNTIL CHANGE 920`.

✦ `UNTIL TIME`—specifies recovery up to a certain date and time.

✦ `datetime`—Specifies the date and time through which you want to recover the database. The format to use is `'YYYY-MM-DD:HH24:MI:SS'`. For example, to recover the database to where it was at 11:35 pm on December 29, 1988, use the string `'1988-12-29:23:35:00'`.

After performing an incomplete recovery, you must open the database using the `RESETLOGS` option. This defines a new incarnation of the database and tells Oracle that the data currently in the online redo log files is no longer needed for recovery.

Except for issuing the actual `RECOVER` command, the process for performing an incomplete recovery is the same as for a complete recovery. Restore the files, in this case, all of them; make sure the required archived log files are available; and issue the command. Listing 22-5 shows a database being restored to its state as of 8:00 am on October 10, 1999.

Listing 22-5: **Performing an incomplete recovery**

```
SQL> CONNECT INTERNAL
Connected to an idle instance.
SQL> STARTUP MOUNT
ORACLE instance started.

Total System Global Area     38322124 bytes
Fixed Size                      65484 bytes
Variable Size                21405696 bytes
Database Buffers             16777216 bytes
Redo Buffers                    73728 bytes
Database mounted.
SQL>  RECOVER DATABASE UNTIL TIME '1999-10-10:08:00:00'
ORA-00279: change 3080219 generated at 10/07/99 19:20:50 needed for thread 1
ORA-00289: suggestion : D:\ORADATA\JONATHAN\ARCH_307.1
ORA-00280: change 3080219 for thread 1 is in sequence #307


Specify log: {<RET>=suggested | filename | AUTO | CANCEL}
AUTO
ORA-00279: change 3100373 generated at 10/08/99 08:56:17 needed for thread 1
ORA-00289: suggestion : D:\ORADATA\JONATHAN\ARCH_308.1
ORA-00280: change 3100373 for thread 1 is in sequence #308
ORA-00278: log file 'D:\ORADATA\JONATHAN\ARCH_307.1' no longer needed for this
recovery


ORA-00279: change 3120735 generated at 10/08/99 20:56:26 needed for thread 1
ORA-00289: suggestion : D:\ORADATA\JONATHAN\ARCH_309.1
ORA-00280: change 3120735 for thread 1 is in sequence #309
ORA-00278: log file 'D:\ORADATA\JONATHAN\ARCH_308.1' no longer needed for this
recovery


ORA-00279: change 3140919 generated at 10/09/99 23:19:46 needed for thread 1
ORA-00289: suggestion : D:\ORADATA\JONATHAN\ARCH_310.1
ORA-00280: change 3140919 for thread 1 is in sequence #310
ORA-00278: log file 'D:\ORADATA\JONATHAN\ARCH_309.1' no longer needed for this
recovery


ORA-00279: change 3161072 generated at 10/09/99 23:38:49 needed for thread 1
ORA-00289: suggestion : D:\ORADATA\JONATHAN\ARCH_311.1
ORA-00280: change 3161072 for thread 1 is in sequence #311
ORA-00278: log file 'D:\ORADATA\JONATHAN\ARCH_310.1' no longer needed for this
recovery


Log applied.
Media recovery complete.
```

The database has now been brought back to the same state it was in at 8:00 am on October 10, 1999. All that remains is to open the database using the RESETLOGS option, as shown in this example:

```
SQL> ALTER DATABASE OPEN RESETLOGS;

Database altered.
```

The database is now ready for use.

Restoring a Database from an Export

You can use an export file to restore a database, although it's not something that you want to be in the position of having to do. It's much easier to restore a database from a file system backup. Restoring from an export has several disadvantages:

✦ The restore process takes a long time.

✦ You can't restore individual files.

✦ You can't perform media recovery, so you can't recover changes made after the export was taken.

Note   In addition to these disadvantages, if your database is a significant size to begin with, it may not be feasible to generate complete database exports in the first place.

In spite of all this, if all you have to work with is an export file, you can follow these steps to use an export file to recover your database to the way it was when the export was performed.

1. Remove all traces of the database that you are trying to recover. Delete all datafiles, log files, control files, and so forth.

2. Create a new database from scratch. Create only the SYSTEM tablespace and some rollback segments. Run the CATALOG.SQL and CATPROC.SQL scripts.

3. Import into the new database using the export file from the old database as the source. Specify IGNORE=Y on the import command line.

While importing, you may encounter some errors as the Import utility attempts to create objects owned by SYSTEM that are already present in the new database. The IGNORE=Y option tells the Import utility to ignore these errors. If everything else works well, the Import utility should create all your tablespaces, create all your schema objects, and load those with data.

For more information on the Import utility, see Chapter 9, "Using Oracle8i's Import Utility." For more information on the Export utility, see Chapter 8, "Using Oracle8i's Export Utility."

Summary

In this chapter, you learned:

✦ If your database is running in noarchivelog mode and you lose a file, your only recourse is to restore the entire database from the most recent backup. You will lose all changes made since the backup.

✦ By running your database in archivelog mode, you enable yourself to restore a file and recover all changes made up until the moment that the file was lost. Production databases should almost always be run in archivelog mode.

✦ When you restore a noarchivelog mode database, don't restore the redo log files. Instead, use the RESETLOGS option when reopening the database.

✦ If you have to restore a file to a new location as the result of a bad disk, have Oracle record the new location in the database control file. You can do this by issuing an ALTER DATABASE RENAME FILE command, or you can re-create the control file completely.

✦ To recover a file that you've restored, issue the RECOVER DATABASE command. For the recovery to be complete, all archived log files generated since the backup must be available, and you must have all online redo log files available as well. The last few changes to be applied will always come from the online redo log files, so it's important to preserve these.

✦ Crash recovery is the recovery process that Oracle employs after a system crash. Data is read from the redo log files and applied to the database files to restore any lost changes. Media recovery provides the same process, but the term media is used when you restore files from a backup and you recover using archived log files.

✦ Incomplete recovery is the process of recovering a database to the way it was at some point in time in the past. After performing incomplete recovery, use the RESETLOGS option when opening the database.

✦ ✦ ✦

Advanced Topics

Using PL/SQL

PL/SQL is Oracle's procedural language extension to SQL. SQL is a declarative language. You describe the results, and the database software decides how to procedure those results. Sometimes that works well; sometimes it doesn't. Some tasks don't lend themselves to being described by a single SQL statement. For those tasks, you can use PL/SQL.

Entire books have been written about PL/SQL. If you are serious about PL/SQL and expect to use it heavily, then check out at least one of those books. A good book to look at is *Oracle PL/SQL Programming* by Steven Feuerstein and Bill Pribyl, O'Reilly & Associates, 1997. This chapter gives you the condensed view of PL/SQL. It quickly covers all the basic aspects of the language and also shows you how you can get to SQL and your database's data from your PL/SQL code.

Examining Basic PL/SQL Language Concepts

This section talks about the basic PL/SQL language concepts. First, you'll learn about PL/SQL's relationship to SQL. Although they are tightly coupled, they are distinct from each other. Next, you'll learn the basic structure of a PL/SQL program. Finally, you'll learn about PL/SQL datatypes and variable declarations.

Comparing PL/SQL to SQL

SQL is an ANSI-standard declarative language that you use to manipulate data in a database. PL/SQL, on the other hand, is a proprietary procedural language that Oracle developed as an extension to SQL. Both run inside the database, as Figure 23-1 illustrates.

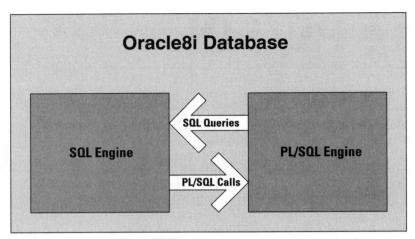

Figure 23-1: SQL and PL/SQL are both implemented in the database.

SQL and PL/SQL are tightly coupled. Both run in the database server, and you can freely call one from the other. PL/SQL programs can invoke SQL statements, and those same SQL statements can invoke other PL/SQL programs. In addition, PL/SQL supports the same set of datatypes as the database uses. PL/SQL supports NULLS, and PL/SQL supports all the standard built-in SQL functions. These attributes make it easy to read data from a table and manipulate it in PL/SQL.

Even though PL/SQL and SQL are tightly coupled, you shouldn't consider them to be the same. They are not. In fact, in some early releases of Oracle, PL/SQL was considered an optional component. Fortunately, that's no longer true because PL/SQL is too useful to be without. Remember, though, that SQL is the declarative language consisting of SELECT, INSERT, UPDATE, DELETE, and other such statements. PL/SQL is Oracle's procedural language.

Note With the release of 8i, PL/SQL is not the only choice you have for a procedural language. Oracle8i also supports Java within the database. You can read more about Java in Chapter 31, "Managing Oracle8i's Java Virtual Machine."

Studying PL/SQL's block structure

The designers of PL/SQL were strongly influenced by the defense department language known as Ada. The result is that PL/SQL is a language structured around what is termed a block. In PL/SQL, a *block* is a program unit consisting of the following elements:

✦ Variable declarations (optional)

✦ Program code

✦ Exception-handling code (optional)

The variable declarations and the exception-handling code are optional, but the syntax allows for them. Here's what the basic syntax of a PL/SQL block looks like:

```
DECLARE
...
BEGIN
...
EXCEPTION
...
END;
```

You would replace the ellipses (...) in each section by either program code or by variable declarations, depending on which part of the block you were working with.

Working with the Declaration Section

The declaration section of a PL/SQL block always comes first and is usually introduced by the keyword DECLARE. This is where you declare the variables, procedures, and functions needed by the code that executes within the block. Consider this example:

```
DECLARE
    id_no NUMBER(10);
    animal_name VARCHAR2(30);
    ...
```

The keyword DECLARE is usually used to introduce the declaration section. When you're writing a stand-alone block like this, DECLARE is always used this way. However, if you are writing a function or a procedure, the function or procedure header takes the place of DECLARE. Here's a quick example:

```
FUNCTION get_animal_name (id IN NUMBER) IS
    id_no NUMBER(10);
    animal_name VARCHAR2(30);
    ...
```

Most of the examples in this chapter show stand-alone blocks.

Working with the Executable Section

The executable section of a PL/SQL block always begins with BEGIN. That should be easy to remember, and certainly it makes intuitive sense. The BEGIN keyword always follows the declaration section, if there is a declaration section. Consider this example:

```
DECLARE
    id_no NUMBER(10);
    animal_name VARCHAR2(30);
BEGIN
    IF id_no IS NULL THEN
    ...
```

The keyword BEGIN marks the beginning of the code. When Oracle executes the block, it starts with the first line of code following BEGIN and works its way sequentially through the remainder of the block.

Since declarations are optional, it's entirely possible to have a PL/SQL block that starts off with the keyword BEGIN. Here's an example:

```
BEGIN
   IF TO_CHAR(SYSDATE,'Day') = 'Saturday' THEN
   ...
```

Blocks like this, with no variable declarations, are more often used when nesting blocks for exception-handling purposes than when writing stand-alone blocks. You'll read more about nesting blocks later in this chapter.

You can use the two keywords END and EXCEPTION to signal the end of the executable portion of a block. Use the END keyword to terminate the entire block. It follows the executable section if you aren't writing any exception handlers. If you are writing exception handlers, then you use the keyword EXCEPTION to mark where the executable section ends and the exception-handler section begins.

Working with the Exception-Handling Section

The exception section of a PL/SQL block is where execution will go if an error occurs during the execution of a block. This section of the block, identified by the keyword EXCEPTION, contains one or more WHEN statements. These WHEN statements are referred to as exception handlers. Consider this example:

```
DECLARE
   id_no NUMBER(10);
   animal_name VARCHAR2(30);
BEGIN
   IF id_no IS NULL THEN
   ...
EXCEPTION
   WHEN OTHERS THEN
   ...
```

Exception handlers allow you to group all the error-handling code for a block in one place, and they allow you to focus on just the program logic in the executable section. You'll learn more about handling exceptions later in the chapter.

Nesting Blocks

You can nest PL/SQL blocks, one inside the other. The two major reasons for doing this involve the need to handle exceptions and the need to control the scope of variable declarations. Nested blocks can occur within all three sections of a PL/SQL block. In the declaration section, nested blocks must always be in the form of a function or a procedure. In the executable and exception-handling sections, you can nest stand-alone blocks.

The trivial example shown in Listing 23-1, which you can actually execute, demonstrates a stand-alone PL/SQL block where each section contains one nested block.

Listing 23-1: **PL/SQL blocks may be nested, one inside the other**

```
DECLARE
    --Nested procedure declaration
    PROCEDURE DO_NOTHING IS
        BEGIN
            NULL;
        END;
BEGIN
    --Nested unnamed block in the
    --executable section
    BEGIN
        DO_NOTHING;
    END;
EXCEPTION
WHEN OTHERS THEN
    --Nested unnamed block in the
    --exception-handling section
    BEGIN
        NULL;
    END;
END;
/
```

To execute this code in SQL*Plus, type it exactly as it is shown here. The forward slash (/) shown at the end of the outer block is not a PL/SQL construct. The forward slash indicates to SQL*Plus (or SQLPlus Worksheet) that you are done entering the block and you want to execute it. If you're using SQL*Plus to experiment, you need to type the forward slash as the first character on a line by itself to have your PL/SQL block executed.

The NULL statement that you see throughout this code is a special PL/SQL statement that does absolutely nothing. You'll learn more about the NULL statement later—not that there's much more to learn about it. You'll learn more about why you might want to nest PL/SQL blocks in the sections "Understanding Variable Scope" and "Nesting Blocks."

Declaring variables

You declare variables in the first section of a PL/SQL block. While that section is optional, it's really unusual to be able to get any productive work done in PL/SQL without using at least a few variables. Declaring variables involves the following:

✦ Naming them properly

✦ Assigning the right datatypes

✦ Declaring scalar variables and record variables

✦ Controlling variable scope

To get the most out of PL/SQL, it is important to understand your options for declaring and using variables.

Naming Rules

The rules for naming PL/SQL variables are straightforward, and not surprisingly, they mirror the rules for naming database columns. Here's what you need to know:

✦ Variable names must start with a letter.

✦ After the first letter, variable names may consist of any combination of letters, digits (0–9), underscores (_), dollar signs ($), and pound signs (#).

✦ Variable names can be from 1 to 30 characters long.

✦ Variable names are not case-sensitive. For example, PL/SQL considers LAST_NAME and last_name to be the same.

✦ Variable names should not match any language keywords. You should not, for example, try to name a variable IF, because IF is a keyword that is part of the language syntax.

The same rules that apply to variables also apply to other identifiers such as datatype names, procedure names, and function names.

Looking at PL/SQL Datatypes

Because PL/SQL is closely tied to the Oracle database, you won't be surprised that for the most part, the PL/SQL datatypes mirror those that you can use in the database. This makes it easy for you to write code to manipulate data from the database. PL/SQL does, however, have a few datatypes all its own, and in a few cases, PL/SQL datatypes aren't 100-percent compatible with their database counterparts.

Table 23-1 provides a quick overview of the PL/SQL datatypes. Any differences between the PL/SQL implementation and the Oracle implementation are described in the notes column.

Table 23-1
PL/SQL Datatypes

Datatype	Notes
BFILE	An external binary file. It's the same as the database BFILE.
BINARY_INTEGER	A PL/SQL-specific type that can hold integer values. If you're working only with integers, this type would be more efficient than NUMBER.
BLOB	A binary large object. It's the same as the database BLOB.
BOOLEAN	A PL/SQL-specific type that can hold TRUE/FALSE values.
CHAR	A character string. This is the same as the database CHAR type, but PL/SQL CHAR variables can be up to 32,767 bytes long, whereas database CHAR values can be only 2,000 bytes long.
CLOB	A character large object. It's the same as the database CLOB.
DATE	A date. This is the same as the database DATE type.
LONG	A long character string. This is the same as the database LONG, but it is limited to 32,767 bytes.
LONG RAW	A LONG RAW type. This is the same as the database LONG RAW, but it is limited to 32,760 bytes.
NCHAR	A character string in the national character set. This is the same as the database NCHAR, but it may hold up to 32,767 bytes.
NCLOB	A character large object using the national character set. It's the same as the database NCLOB.
NUMBER	A number. This is the same as the database NUMBER type.
NVARCHAR2	A variable-length character string using the national character set. This is the same as the database NVARCHAR2, but it may hold up to 32,767 bytes.
PLS_INTEGER	A PL/SQL-specific type that implements integer values using a machine-specific representation. This provides better performance than a BINARY_INTEGER type.
RAW	A raw byte string. This is the same as the database RAW, but it may hold up to 32,767 bytes.
ROWID	A PL/SQL type used to hold database row ids. This type is now obsolete. You should use UROWID in all new code. ROWID is maintained only for purposes of backwards compatibility.
UROWID	A PL/SQL type used to hold Oracle8i universal row IDs.
VARCHAR2	A variable-length character string. This is the same as the database VARCHAR2, but it can hold up to 32,767 bytes.

In addition to the datatypes listed in Table 23-1, PL/SQL implements a number of subtypes. A *subtype* is an alternate name for a datatype that occasionally comes with some additional restrictions on the values that you can use. Table 23-2 lists the available PL/SQL subtypes.

Table 23-2 PL/SQL Subtypes		
Subtype	**Parent Datatype**	**Notes**
NATURAL	BINARY_INTEGER	Restricts values to natural numbers. The set of natural numbers consists of zero and all the positive integers.
NATURALN	BINARY_INTEGER	Restricts values to natural numbers and also cannot be null.
POSITIVE	BINARY_INTEGER	Restricts values to positive integers.
POSITIVEN	BINARY_INTEGER	Restricts values to positive integers and cannot be null.
SIGNTYPE	BINARY_INTEGER	Restricts values to -1, 0, or 1.
CHARACTER	CHAR	Allows for ANSI compatibility. It's the same as CHAR.
DEC	NUMBER	Allows for ANSI compatibility. It's the same as NUMBER.
DECIMAL	NUMBER	Allows for ANSI compatibility. It's the same as NUMBER.
DOUBLE PRECISION	NUMBER	Declares floating-point values with up to 126 bits of binary precision.
FLOAT	NUMBER	Declares floating-point values with up to 126 bits of binary precision.
INT	NUMBER	Declares integers.
INTEGER	NUMBER	Declares integers.
NUMERIC	NUMBER	Same as NUMBER. Provided for ANSI compatibility.
REAL	NUMBER	Declares floating-point values with up to 63 bits of binary precision.
SMALLINT	NUMBER	Declares integers.

Subtype	Parent Datatype	Notes
STRING	VARCHAR2	Allows for ANSI compatibility. It's the same as VARCHAR2.
VARCHAR	VARCHAR2	It's the same as VARCHAR2. However, Oracle recommends against using VARCHAR because its definition may change someday.

All subtypes are PL/SQL-specific. You use them just as you would a regular datatype, but what you are really getting is a variable of the parent datatype. Subtypes can be constraining or nonconstraining. A *constraining* subtype implements restrictions on the values that it can hold. The POSITIVE subtype is a good example of a constraining subtype. Variables of type POSITIVE are really BINARY_INTEGERS, but Oracle won't allow you to store anything other than positive values in those variables. The DECIMAL subtype is a good example of a *nonconstraining* datatype. It's simply an alternate name for NUMBER.

Declaring Variables

Variables are declared in the declaration section of a PL/SQL block, which usually follows the keyword DECLARE. The syntax to use follows:

```
variable_name datatype;
```

Replace variable_name with a valid name that conforms to the variable naming rules listed earlier. Replace datatype with one of the datatypes listed in Tables 23-1 and 23-2. In many cases, you also need to supply a length for the datatype. You do that the same way in PL/SQL as you do in Oracle. The following code illustrates several common types of variable declarations:

```
DECLARE
    last_name VARCHAR2(30); -- 30 characters for last name
    birth_date DATE;
    salary NUMBER(9,2); -- 9 digits. 7 to the left of the
                        -- decimal, and 2 to the right
    resume CLOB;
```

If you are working with database data, you can use %TYPE to declare a variable so that it automatically matches a given column definition. The syntax to do that is as follows:

```
variable_name [schema.]table_name.column_name%TYPE;
```

Here are some examples relevant to the SEAPARK schema used in the sample
database for this book:

```
a_name seapark.aquatic_animal.animal_name%TYPE;
b_date aquatic_animal.birth_date%TYPE;
```

The first declaration works in code compiled by any database user because it
explicitly identifies the SEAPARK schema in the declaration. The second declaration
can be used only in cases where the user compiling the code owns a table named
AQUATIC_ANIMAL.

Note   To use %TYPE to reference a table in another schema, you need to have at least
SELECT access to that table.

Although using %TYPE results in more typing on your part — the declarations are
usually longer — it helps insulate your code from changes to the underlying column
definition. Change a column from VARCHAR2(30) to VARCHAR2(40), for example,
and your code will recompile and continue to work just fine.

Declaring Records

A *record* is a composite variable that is made up of several related values. In
PL/SQL, records are most often used to hold the values returned by cursors and
SELECT statements. Using a record allows you to manipulate a row of data as a
single unit instead of having to treat each column separately.

To declare a record variable, you first must define a record type. The syntax for
defining a record type looks like this:

```
TYPE type_name IS RECORD (
    variable_name datatype[,
    variable_name datatype[,
    variable_name dataype]...]
);
```

Once you have a record type defined, you can use it as any other type when
declaring a record variable. The following example declares a record type that
matches the columns in the AQUATIC_ANIMAL table and then uses that type to
declare a record variable:

```
TYPE aquatic_animal_type IS RECORD (
    ID_NO                 NUMBER(10),
    TANK_NO               NUMBER(10),
    ANIMAL_NAME           VARCHAR2(30),
    MARKINGS_DESCRIPTION  VARCHAR2(30),
    BIRTH_DATE            DATE,
    DEATH_DATE            DATE
```

*Record: many rows
not same save typing
and eliminate "wrong
data assignment)*

```
);
animal aquatic_animal_type;
```

With the *animal* record declared, you can now reference the individual elements within that record by using a dot (.) to separate the variable name from the record name. For example:

```
...
animal.animal_name := 'Justin';
...
```

You'll see more of this in code examples as you read through the remainder of this chapter. You'll also see later how you can use records such as this to facilitate the retrieval and update of information contained in database tables.

The `aquatic_animal_type` shown in the prior example is declared in such a way as to exactly match the definition of the underlying `AQUATIC_ANIMAL` table. The need to declare record variables that match a table is so common that Oracle provides a shortcut for doing this. Instead of declaring a type to match the table and then declaring a variable based on that type, you can use the built-in `%ROWTYPE` keyword to reference the table's definition directly. The syntax for doing this is as follows:

```
variable_name [schema.]table_name%ROWTYPE;
```

The result is that now you can declare the `animal` record like this:

```
animal seapark.aquatic_animal%ROWTYPE;
```

The `%ROWTYPE` keyword works just like `%TYPE`, but for tables rather than individual columns. It generally results in less typing because you don't have to create a type to match the table, and like `%TYPE`, it helps insulate you from changes to the underlying table definition.

Understanding Variable Scope

A variable's *scope* refers to the visibility of that variable from your code. Recall that the PL/SQL language is structured in blocks. Any variable or type definitions are visible from the block in which they are declared. This includes any nested blocks. Take a look at the declarations in the following example for the variables named A and B.

```
DECLARE
    A NUMBER;
BEGIN
    ...
```

```
     DECLARE
         B NUMBER;
     BEGIN
     END;
     ...
 END;
 /
```

The variable A can be referenced throughout this code because it's declared in the outermost block. The variable B can be referenced only from within the innermost block. If you try to reference B in the outer block, you get an error when you compile the code.

Another important facet of scope that you need to understand is that a variable declaration in a nested block may destroy your access to a variable of the same name in the outer block. Consider this example:

```
DECLARE
    A NUMBER;
BEGIN
    ...
    DECLARE
        A VARCHAR2(40);
    BEGIN
        A := 'In here, A is a character string.';
    END;
    ...
END;
/
```

Both blocks in this example declare a variable named A. The outermost block declares A as a NUMBER, while the inner block declares A as VARCHAR2. These are two different variables. Any code in the inner block that refers to A will end up referencing the VARCHAR2 variable. Any code in the outer block that refers to A will end up referencing the NUMBER variable.

Using expressions

Expressions in PL/SQL are not much different than those in any other language. There is the usual assortment of arithmetic, string, comparision, and logical operators. You can string multiple operators and variables together to build expressions of any length. Each operator has a precedence that controls evaluation of long expressions, but like with most languages, you can use parentheses to override or clarify the default order.

Table 23-3 provides a list of the PL/SQL operators and their order of precedence when more than one operator is used in an expression.

Table 23-3
PL/SQL Operators and Their Precedence

Precedence	Operator	Description	Example
first	**	exponentiation	2 ** 3 = 8
	NOT	logical NOT	NOT TRUE = FALSE
second	+	identity	+5 = 5 -
	-	negtion	5 = -5 (5 below zero)
third	*	multiplication	15 * 14 = 210
	/	division	210 / 15 = 14
fourth	+	addition	1 + 2 = 3
	-	subtraction	4 - 2 = 4
	||	concentation	'Sharon' || ' ' || 'Rann' = 'Sharon Rann'
fifth	=	is equal to	if X = 5 then...
	!=, <>, ~=	is not equal to	if X <> 5 then...
	<	is less than	if X < 5 then...
	>	is greater than	if X > 5 then...
	<=	is less than or equal to is	if X <= 5 then...
	>=	greater than or equal to	if X >= 5 then...
	IS [NOT] NULL	tests to see if a value is null	IF X IS NULL THEN IF X IS NOT NULL THEN
	[NOT] LIKE	tests to see if a string matches a pattern	'Nate' LIKE 'N_te' = TRUE 'Nate' LIKE 'N*' = TRUE
	[NOT] BETWEEN		An underscore matches any one character, while an asterisk matches multiple characters.

Continued

		Table 23-3 *(continued)*	
Precedence	**Operator**	**Description**	**Example**
fifth (continued)		is one value between two others, inclusively?	5 BETWEEN 5 AND 10 = TRUE **This is the same as:** (5 >= 5) AND (5 <= 10).
	[NOT] IN	is a value contained in a list of values?	8 IN (10, 8, 100) = TRUE 20 NOT IN (10) = TRUE
sixth	AND	logical AND	(5 = 5) AND (5 != 10) = TRUE
seventh	OR	logical OR	(5 = 5) OR (5 = 10) = TRUE

Comparing variable- and fixed-length strings

When comparing two strings, trailing spaces may or may not affect the results. Fixed-length strings, those declared with the keyword CHAR, are compared using *blank-padded comparision semantics*. That's a fancy way of saying that trailing blanks do not matter where CHAR values are concerned. For example, in the following code, the two names are equal, even though one is longer than the other:

```
DECLARE
   name_1   CHAR(30) := 'Jonathan                      ';
   name_2   CHAR(10) := 'Jonathan';
BEGIN
   IF name_1 = name_2 THEN
      DBMS_OUTPUT.PUT_LINE('The strings are equal.');
   END IF;
END;
```

If you have worked with COBOL in the past, you will understand blank-padded comparision semantics quite well. Variable-length strings, on the other hand, such as those declared as VARCHAR2, are compared using *nonblank comparison semantics*—a fancy way of saying that trailing spaces do matter. If you take the code just shown and change the datatypes from CHAR to VARCHAR2, the strings will no longer be considered equal:

```
   name_1   VARCHAR2(30) := 'Jonathan                      ';
   name_2   VARCHAR2(10) := 'Jonathan';
```

This sort of makes sense because VARCHAR2 strings do contain a length component, while CHAR strings do not. The important point to remember, though, is that if even one string in a comparision is VARCHAR2, then nonblank comparison semantics are still used. In the following example, both strings are set to the same value, but they aren't equal:

```
name_1   CHAR(30) := 'Jonathan';
name_2   VARCHAR2(10) := 'Jonathan';
```

To deal with this, you may want to use the RTRIM function when comparing a fixed-length string to a variable-length string. The RTRIM function takes a string as an input and returns the same string less any trailing spaces. It should be used on the CHAR value, as shown in this example:

```
DECLARE
  name_1   CHAR(30) := 'Jonathan';
  name_2   VARCHAR2(10) := 'Jonathan';
BEGIN
  IF RTRIM(name_1) = name_2 THEN
    DBMS_OUTPUT.PUT_LINE('The strings are equal.');
  ELSE
    DBMS_OUTPUT.PUT_LINE('The strings are not equal.');
  END IF;
END;
```

In this example, the strings will be equal because RTRIM returns the value of name_1 less the 22 trailing spaces.

Interacting with the outside

The PL/SQL language was built to run inside the database. Unlike most languages such as C and Java, PL/SQL has no built-in mechanism for communicating with the outside world. Using pure PL/SQL, all you can do is retrieve data from the database, manipulate it, and store it back again.

Built-In Packages That Support I/O

While there are no built-in language features to do any type of I/O, Oracle has developed a set of standard built-in packages that can be used to communicate with the world outside of PL/SQL. The list of packages includes the following:

✦ DBMS_OUTPUT — Can be used to display output from PL/SQL when you are running PL/SQL code from SQL*Plus or SQLPlus Worksheet.

✦ UTL_FILE — Can be used to read and write files on the database server.

✦ DBMS_PIPE—Can be used to communicate with other processes running on the server. The DBMS_PIPE package, for example, can be used to send messages back and forth between a PL/SQL program unit being executed within the database and a C program being executed from the operating system prompt.

✦ DBMS_ALERT—Can be used to synchronize the actions of several processes.

✦ DBMS_AQ—Can be used to communicate with other processes in a distributed database environment. AQ stands for advanced queuing. This relatively new Oracle feature provides a robust and reliable messaging system for use in developing distributed applications.

Describing these packages in detail is well beyond the scope of this book. However, you should be aware that they exist. If you do ever need to make use of the features implemented by these packages, consult one of the several PL/SQL books on the market—Oracle's own reference material is not too shabby, either.

The DBMS_OUTPUT Package

The one package that you absolutely should know about if you are writing any amount of PL/SQL is the DBMS_OUTPUT package. The DBMS_OUTPUT package allows you to display output from PL/SQL using SQL*Plus or SQLPlus Worksheet. You can use three DBMS_OUTPUT procedures to generate output. These procedures are as follows:

✦ DBMS_OUTPUT.PUT_LINE—Allows you to display a line of text.

✦ DBMS_OUTPUT.PUT—Allows you to display some text but doesn't generate a newline character.

✦ DBMS_NEW_LINE—Generates a newline character. Use this after making one or more calls to DBMS_OUTPUT.PUT.

The DBMS_OUTPUT.PUT_LINE and DBMS_OUTPUT.PUT procedures each accept one argument, which may be a character string, a number, or a date. Whatever you pass in as an argument is written out to a buffer in memory. You can set SQL*Plus (and SQLPlus Worksheet) to check this buffer each time you execute a PL/SQL block or SQL statement and to display any data that it finds.

Listing 23-2 shows a PL/SQL block being executed from SQL*Plus. The block makes several calls to procedures in the DBMS_OUTPUT package. Notice that the first line contains the command SET SERVEROUTPUT ON. This is a SQL*Plus command that causes SQL*Plus to display the output that it finds in the buffer.

Listing 23-2: **Displaying output from SQL*Plus**

```
SQL> SET SERVEROUTPUT ON
SQL>
SQL> DECLARE
  2      x VARCHAR2 (40);
  3  BEGIN
  4      DBMS_OUTPUT.PUT_LINE('This is one line.');
  5
  6      x := 'The number is ';
  7      DBMS_OUTPUT.PUT(x);
  8      DBMS_OUTPUT.PUT(11);
  9
 10      DBMS_OUTPUT.NEW_LINE;
 11  END;
 12  /
This is one line.
The number is 11

PL/SQL procedure successfully completed.
```

The first call is to DBMS_OUTPUT.PUT_LINE, and it results in one line of output. The next two calls are to DBMS_OUTPUT.PUT. The two calls together result in one line. The DBMS_OUTPUT.NEW_LINE function has to be called to end the second line by writing a newline character. If this isn't done, you won't see the second line of output at all. Finally, notice that both variables and literals may be passed to these procedures. The first call to DBMS_OUTPUT.PUT passes a variable as an argument, while the second call passes in a constant. Either way is acceptable, depending on what you need to do.

Using DBMS_OUTPUT as shown here is fine if you just need to generate a small amount of output. However, if you need to write out large amounts of data, you will need to increase the size of the memory buffer that holds the data. By default, DBMS_OUTPUT can handle only 2,000 characters of output. You can specify a different buffer size when you issue the SET SERVEROUTPUT ON command (release 8 and above only), or you can make a call to DBMS_OUTPUT.ENABLE. To size the buffer using SET SERVEROUTPUT, issue the following command:

```
SET SERVEROUTPUT ON SIZE buffer_size
```

To size the buffer using DBMS_OUTPUT.ENABLE, call that procedure prior to any of the other DBMS_OUTPUT procedures. Pass the buffer size as an argument, as in this example:

```
DBMS_OUTPUT.ENABLE (buffer_size);
```

The maximum buffer size that you can set is 1,000,000 bytes, so that becomes the limit on the amount of output that you can generate using any one PL/SQL program unit. Also be aware of the following points relative to using DBMS_OUTPUT:

✦ Leading spaces are always removed from lines of output.

✦ Only complete lines are retrieved and displayed. Therefore, you usually use DBMS_OUTPUT.PUT_LINE. If you use DBMS_OUTPUT.PUT, you must be sure to end each line of output by making a call to DBMS_OUTPUT.NEW_LINE.

✦ SQL*Plus doesn't retrieve or display any data from the buffer until execution of the PL/SQL program unit is complete.

The first limitation can be frustrating if you want white space in your output. About the best you can do in that case is to use tab characters in your output. Tab characters can be generated by making a call to the CHR function. The CHR(9) function returns a tab, as shown in Listing 23-3.

Listing 23-3: **Using the CHR(9) function**

```
SQL> SET SERVEROUTPUT ON SIZE 10000
SQL>
SQL> BEGIN
  2     DBMS_OUTPUT.PUT_LINE('ONE');
  3     DBMS_OUTPUT.PUT_LINE(CHR(9) || 'TWO');
  4     DBMS_OUTPUT.PUT_LINE(CHR(9) || CHR(9) || 'THREE');
  5  END;
  6  /
ONE
     TWO
          THREE

PL/SQL procedure successfully completed.
```

The final item, that of output not being displayed until the PL/SQL program unit is complete, effectively prevents you from using DBMS_OUTPUT.PUT_LINE to implement any type of progress meter for a long-running PL/SQL block.

Using Different Statement Types

PL/SQL is a procedural language. It implements several types of statements that give you control over the path of execution through your code. These statement types fall into the following categories:

✦ Conditional branching

✦ Looping

✦ Exception handling

As with most languages, you use IF statements to implement conditional branches in PL/SQL. For looping, you have plain loops, FOR loops, and WHILE loops.

Using IF statements

The IF statement is the basis for all conditional logic in PL/SQL. The syntax for the IF statement is as follows:

```
IF expression THEN
    statements
[ELSIF expression
    statements]
[ELSE
    statements]
END IF;
```

Replace expression with any valid TRUE/FALSE expression. Replace statements with whatever PL/SQL statements you want to execute. The following example shows a simple IF statement:

```
IF x = 5 THEN
    DBMS_OUTPUT.PUT_LINE('x = 5');
END IF;
```

Using the ELSIF Clause

The ELSIF clause in an IF statement provides you with a way to test for a different condition if the first one is not true. An IF statement may have any number of ELSIF clauses. They are checked in the order in which they are written. When PL/SQL finds an ELSIF clause where the expression evaluates to TRUE, it executes the code associated with that clause. Control then passes out of the IF statement. Listing 23-4 demonstrates the use of the ELSIF clause.

Listing 23-4: **Using the ELSIF clause**

```
SQL> SET SERVEROUTPUT ON
SQL> DECLARE
  2      x NUMBER;
  3  BEGIN
  4      x := 3;
  5
  6      IF x = 1 THEN
  7          DBMS_OUTPUT.PUT_LINE('x = 1');
  8      ELSIF x = 2 THEN
  9          DBMS_OUTPUT.PUT_LINE('x = 2');
 10      ELSIF x = 3 THEN
 11          DBMS_OUTPUT.PUT_LINE('x = 3');
 12      ELSIF x > 2 THEN
 13          DBMS_OUTPUT.PUT_LINE('x > 2');
 14      END IF;
 15  END;
 16  /
x = 3

PL/SQL procedure successfully completed.
```

In the IF statement shown here, the first true expression encountered is x = 3. Since that is true, the corresponding DBMS_OUTPUT.PUT_LINE statement is executed. The expression x > 2 is also true, but that doesn't matter. Once one branch of an IF statement is taken, the others are ignored.

Note A common coding mistake is to write ELSEIF instead of ELSIF. There's no E in the middle. ELSIF is the correct spelling.

Using the ELSE Clause

The ELSE clause is an optional part of the IF statement, and it is used to identify code to be executed when none of the IF or ELSIF expressions are true, as shown in Listing 23-5.

Listing 23-5: **Using the ELSE clause**

```
SQL> SET SERVEROUTPUT ON
SQL>
SQL> DECLARE
  2      x NUMBER;
  3  BEGIN
  4      x := 3;
  5
  6      IF x = 4 THEN
```

```
 7          DBMS_OUTPUT.PUT_LINE('x = 4');
 8       ELSIF x > 4 THEN
 9          DBMS_OUTPUT.PUT_LINE('x > 4');
10       ELSE
11          DBMS_OUTPUT.PUT_LINE('x <> 4 and x < 4');
12       END IF;
13    END;
14    /
x <> 4 and x < 4

PL/SQL procedure successfully completed.
```

In this example, because none of the expressions listed in the IF statement are true, the code in the ELSE clause is executed.

Handling Nulls in Boolean Expressions

When writing IF statements, you must always be cognizant of the effect of null values on expressions. Unless you are using a function or operator such as NVL or IS NULL that is designed to detect null values, any null value in an expression will result in the expression also being null. That's a problem where Boolean expressions — the type used in IF statements — are concerned because null values are considered neither true nor false.

Most people think of an IF statement as having two paths, one to take if an expression is true and the other to take if an expression is false. Null values mess that up because a null expression also causes the ELSE path to be taken. This can lead to some strange results, as the code example in Listing 23-6 illustrates.

Listing 23-6: **The effect of a null on a Boolean expression**

```
SQL> DECLARE
  2      x NUMBER;
  3  BEGIN
  4      IF x = 2 THEN
  5         DBMS_OUTPUT.PUT_LINE('x = 2');
  6      ELSIF x <> 2 THEN
  7         DBMS_OUTPUT.PUT_LINE('x <> 2');
  8      ELSE
  9         DBMS_OUTPUT.PUT_LINE('x is null');
 10      END IF;
 11  END;
 12  /
x is null

PL/SQL procedure successfully completed.
```

Notice that neither the IF branch nor the ELSIF branch is taken here. The expression x = 2 is false, and so is the opposite expression x <> 2. Intuitively, most people wouldn't think that both of these statements can be false at the same time, but nulls make it possible for that to be the case.

In a way, it's too bad that IF statements weren't designed with some sort of built-in ELSIFNULL clause to which control would branch if an expression evaluates to null. Since that wasn't done, you have to think about the possibility of nulls each time you write an IF statement.

Here is a list of several ways that you can prevent your code from stumbling over null values when it executes:

✦ Be sure to initialize your variables. In the prior example, the variable x was null because it was never initialized to a value.

✦ Take advantage of the built-in NVL function to transform null values into usable, non-null values.

✦ Use the IS NULL and IS NOT NULL operators to explicitly test for null values.

✦ Write three-pronged IF statements, such as the one shown in the previous example, that relegate the ELSE clause to handling the case where the expression evaluates to null.

The last piece of advice in the previous list about writing three-pronged IF statements can become difficult to implement if the expression that you are evaluating becomes complex. Listing 23-7 shows a more robust approach to the same problem. It uses a Boolean variable to temporarily store the result of an expression. That variable is then used in an IF statement in such a way that any null value in the expression will cause the ELSE branch to be taken.

Listing 23-7: **Storing the result of an expression in a Boolean variable**

```
DECLARE
    b BOOLEAN;
    x NUMBER;
BEGIN
    --Assign the value of the expression to b
    b := (x = 2);

    --Now branch based on the result. There are
    --three possibilities: the expression was true,
    --it was false, or it was null.
    IF b = TRUE THEN
        DBMS_OUTPUT.PUT_LINE('The expression was true.');
```

```
        ELSIF b = FALSE THEN
            DBMS_OUTPUT.PUT_LINE('The expression was false.');
        ELSE
            DBMS_OUTPUT.PUT_LINE('The expression was null.');
        END IF;
    END;
    /
```

The important point to notice about this example is that it explicitly tested for both the truth and falsity of the expression. A typical IF statement would have tested for true and let control fall through to an ELSE clause in all other cases — the assumption being that not true is the same as false. The example shown here is more robust because it has three branches, one for each possibility: true, false, and null.

Writing loops

PL/SQL supports three different types of looping constructs. They are:

✦ The WHILE loop, which executes a set of statements while a condition is true

✦ The FOR loop, which executes a set of statements a specific number of times, incrementing a counter each time through

✦ The basic loop, which executes a set of statements repeatedly, and which won't stop until an EXIT statement is executed

Using the WHILE Loop

A WHILE loop executes a series of statements as long as a specified Boolean expression evaluates to true. The syntax for a WHILE loop looks like this:

```
WHILE expression LOOP
    statements
END LOOP;
```

Replace expression with any Boolean expression. Replace statements with one or more PL/SQL statements. When a WHILE loop is encountered, the expression is evaluated. If the expression evaluates to TRUE, the statements are executed. Then the expression is evaluated again. If it's still true, the statements are executed again. This process continues until the expression becomes *not true*. Note that a null expression is not true and will result in the termination of the loop. Here's a rather simple example of a WHILE loop:

```
DECLARE
    x NUMBER;
BEGIN
```

```
    x := 0;

    WHILE x <= 3 LOOP
        x := x+1;
    END LOOP;
END;
/
```

A WHILE loop is usually the best choice when you can base the decision about executing a loop on the results of an expression.

Using the FOR Loop

The FOR loop executes a series of statements a specific number of times and increments a counter for each pass through the loop. The syntax for a FOR loop is as follows:

```
FOR counter IN [REVERSE] start_value..end_value LOOP
    statements
END LOOP;
```

In this syntax, counter is the name that you want to give to the loop counter. The first time through the loop, the counter will take on the value specified by start_value. The second time through, the counter will take on the value start_value+1. This process will continue until the counter exceeds end_value. If the keyword REVERSE is used, the process is reversed—the counter will count down from start_value until end_value is reached.

> **Note**   The two dots between the starting and ending values are part of the syntax.

Here's a simple example of a FOR loop that will execute ten times:

```
BEGIN
    FOR x IN 1..10 LOOP
        null;
    END LOOP;
END;
/
```

Notice that there is no variable declaration for x. It's not necessary to declare the loop counters used in FOR loops. Their declaration is implicit. Related to this, it's worth pointing out that the scope of the loop counter in a FOR loop is limited to the statements in the body of the loop. You can't reference the loop counter, x in this example, from outside the loop.

Unlike many languages, PL/SQL doesn't allow you to control the increment used in a FOR loop. The counter is incremented by either 1 or -1, depending on whether REVERSE is used. Those are the only two possible choices.

Using the Basic Loop

The basic loop is a looping construct that has no built-in control mechanism. Instead, you have to write code into the loop body to terminate the loop. The syntax for a basic loop looks like this:

```
LOOP
    statements
END LOOP;
```

So how do you terminate this type of loop? The best way is to use either an EXIT statement or an EXIT WHEN statement.

The EXIT statement

The EXIT statement is a simple one-word statement that allows you to terminate a loop. If you're writing a basic loop, you can use EXIT from within an IF statement to terminate that loop. The code in Listing 23-8 simulates a REPEAT...UNTIL loop by using a combination of a basic loop and an EXIT statement:

Listing 23-8: **Simulating a REPEAT...UNTIL loop**

```
DECLARE
    x NUMBER;
BEGIN
    x := 0;
    LOOP
        x := x+1;

        IF x >= 3 THEN
            EXIT;
        END IF;
    END LOOP;
END;
/
```

This loop will always execute at least once because the termination condition is at the end of the loop, not the beginning. Of course, you could easily place the IF statement at the beginning of the loop if you like. It's best, however, to place it either at the beginning or the end, but not in the middle. Your code will be more readable that way.

The EXIT WHEN statement

The EXIT WHEN statement is a newer version of the EXIT statement that allows you to include the termination condition in the statement itself, thus removing the need for the enclosing IF statement. Here's the syntax for EXIT WHEN:

```
EXIT WHEN expression;
```

Replace *expression* with any Boolean expression. If it evaluates to TRUE, the loop will terminate. The following example is a reinterpretation of the previous loop, this time using EXIT WHEN:

```
DECLARE
    x NUMBER;
BEGIN
    x := 0;
    LOOP
        x := x+1;

        EXIT WHEN x >= 3;
    END LOOP;
END;
/
```

There's no difference between using EXIT WHEN and EXIT inside an IF statement, except that EXIT WHEN usually results in more readable code.

Note   You can also use both EXIT and EXIT WHEN with FOR and WHILE loops. However, if you do use either of the EXIT statements in a FOR or WHILE loop, make sure that you have a good reason for doing so because it will make your code more difficult to understand.

Using other statements

Some other PL/SQL statements are used less often than what you've seen so far. These are the NULL and GOTO statements. The NULL statement is useful as a place-holder during development. The GOTO statement is rarely used anymore, but you may encounter it, so you should know how it works.

Using the NULL Statement

The NULL statement is a statement that does absolutely nothing. You saw it used in one of the earlier code examples in this chapter. The syntax for NULL is painfully simple, and it looks like this:

```
NULL;
```

Pretty much the only reason to use NULL is as a placeholder when developing code. If you're writing an IF...THEN...ELSE statement, for example, and you want to test out the IF part before you've written the ELSE part, you might do the following:

```
IF x = 2 THEN
    DBMS_OUTPUT.PUT_LINE('x = 2');
ELSE
    NULL;
END IF;
```

This example is almost too simple, but the NULL statement here allows you to test this code for the case where x =2 without your having to write the code for the ELSE clause first.

Using the GOTO Statement

The GOTO statement has long been out of fashion. If you use it, you'll probably have a dozen people lecturing you on the merits of GOTO-less programming. Regardless of whether you agree with that viewpoint, the fact is that you will see very few GOTOs.

The GOTO statement allows you to branch to a specific statement in a block of PL/SQL code. The syntax looks like this:

```
GOTO label
```

In this syntax, label represents a statement label. You place labels in your code by enclosing them within double angle brackets. The code example shown in Listing 23-9 is yet another implementation of the REPEAT..UNTIL loop that you saw earlier for the EXIT statements. It uses GOTO, a statement label, and an IF statement to implement the loop.

Listing 23-9: Another way to use the REPEAT...UNTIL loop

```
DECLARE
    x NUMBER;
BEGIN
    x := 0;
<<repeat_loop>>
    x := x+1;
    DBMS_OUTPUT.PUT_LINE(X);
    IF x < 3 THEN
        GOTO repeat_loop;
    END IF;
END;
/
```

The statement label in this example is `repeat_loop`. Notice that it's enclosed within double-angle brackets (`<<` and `>`). That location marks the spot to which control goes when the `GOTO` statement is executed. Statement labels are subject to the same naming rules as any other PL/SQL identifier.

There are some limits to where you can jump using a `GOTO` statement. To start with, the label must precede an executable statement or block. The label must also be unambiguous. It's entirely possible to use the same label name twice in the same block, but if you do, the destination of the `GOTO` can't be resolved unambiguously, and your code will fail. You are not allowed to jump into the middle of a loop from outside the loop, nor can you jump into the middle of an `IF` statement or a nested block.

Handling Exceptions

Exceptions are handled in the last part of a PL/SQL block, which is identified by the keyword `EXCEPTION`. Any errors or unusual conditions that arise during execution of the code in the main part of the block will cause execution to branch immediately to the exception handlers in the `EXCEPTION` section. Exception handlers are defined using the `WHEN` statement, as shown in this example:

```
DECLARE
    x VARCHAR2(1);
BEGIN
    SELECT dummy
    INTO x
    FROM dual
    WHERE dummy <> 'X';
EXCEPTION
    WHEN NO_DATA_FOUND THEN
        DBMS_OUTPUT.PUT_LINE('No matching rows were found.');
END;
/
```

You can execute this code on any Oracle database, and the `SELECT` statement should fail, causing the exception handler to take over. The exception will be `NO_DATA_FOUND`, which is one of Oracle's standard exceptions, because the `DUAL` table should not have any rows that match the `WHERE` clause in this `SELECT`. If you're running the code from SQL*Plus, be sure to issue the `SET SERVEROUTPUT ON` command so that you can see the error message.

Note   If the code in this example succeeds, you have a problem with your database. The `DUAL` table should have only one row, with one column, and the value of that column should be `'X'`.

To effectively handle exceptions in your PL/SQL code, you need to understand the types of exceptions that may be thrown. You also need to understand how to catch those exceptions using the WHEN statement and how you can use nested PL/SQL blocks to fine-tune your exception-handling approach.

Examining standard PL/SQL exceptions

Oracle defines a number of standard PL/SQL exceptions such as the NO_DATA_FOUND exception that you just saw in the previous section. These exceptions allow you to tailor your exception-handling code to match the problem that occurred. Table 23-4 lists these standard exceptions.

Table 23-4
Standard PL/SQL Exceptions

Exception	ORA Number	SQLCODE	Description
ACCESS_INTO_NULL	ORA-06530	-6530	You tried to assign a value to an uninitialized object.
COLLECTION_IS_NULL	ORA-06531	-6531	You attempted to use an uninitialized nested table or varying array.
CURSOR_ALREADY_OPEN	ORA-06511	-6511	You tried to open a cursor that is already open.
DUP_VAL_ON_INDEX	ORA-00001	-1	You tried to insert a row into a table, and that row violated a unique index constraint.
INVALID_CURSOR	ORA-01001	-1001	You attempted a cursor operation, but you didn't provide a valid, open cursor.
INVALID_NUMBER	ORA-01722	-1722	A SQL statement failed in an attempt to convert a character string to a number.
LOGIN_DENIED	ORA-01017	-1017	You tried to connect to Oracle but didn't supply a valid username and password.

Continued

Table 23-4 *(continued)*

Exception	ORA Number	SQLCODE	Description
NO_DATA_FOUND	ORA-01403	+100	You issued a SELECT INTO statement for which no matching row was found.
NOT_LOGGED_ON	ORA-01012	-1012	You attempted a database call without first logging on to the database.
PROGRAM_ERROR	ORA-06501	-6501	An internal PL/SQL error occurred.
ROWTYPE_MISMATCH	ORA-06504	-6504	The return type of a PL/SQL cursor variable doesn't match the return type of the corresponding host cursor.
SELF_IS_NULL	ORA-30625	-30625	You attempted to invoke a method on an object instance, but the object instance was null.
STORAGE_ERROR	ORA-06500	-6500	PL/SQL has run out of memory.
SUBSCRIPT_BEYOND_COUNT	ORA-06533	-6533	You attempted to reference a nested table using an index that was larger than the number of elements in that table.
SUBSCRIPT_OUTSIDE_LIMIT	ORA-06532	-6532	You used a subscript with a varying array that is outside the range supported by that array's type declaration.
SYS_INVALID_ROWID	ORA-01410	-1410	You tried to convert a character string into a rowid, and the conversion failed.
TIMEOUT_ON_RESOURC	ORA-00051	-51	A timeout occurred while Oracle was waiting for a resource.

Exception	ORA Number	SQLCODE	Description
TOO_MANY_ROWS	ORA-01422	-1422	You executed a SELECT INTO statement, and that statement returned more than one row.
VALUE_ERROR	ORA-06502	-6502	You attempted to store a value into a variable that the variable couldn't hold. You get this exception if the value is too large, too long, or if it can't be converted into the correct type.
ZERO_DIVIDE	ORA-01476	-1476	You attempted to divide a number by zero.

In addition to these standard exceptions, it's also possible to define exceptions of your own. That's beyond the scope of this book, and it's more than you're likely to need unless you are a full-time PL/SQL programmer. However, if you do run across code containing exceptions not listed in Table 23-4, that's probably why — the programmer created his or her own exceptions.

Using the WHEN statement

You use the WHEN statement in the exception section of a PL/SQL block so that you can write code specific to each exception that you are interested in handling. The exception part of a PL/SQL block consists entirely of a series of WHEN statements, each one supplying code for a different type of exception.

The WHEN Statement Syntax

The syntax for WHEN is as follows:

```
WHEN exception [OR exception...] THEN
    statements
WHEN exception [OR exception...] THEN
    statements
WHEN OTHERS THEN
    statements
```

Each WHEN statement is referred to as an *exception handler*. You can have as many WHEN statements in a block as you need. The WHEN OTHERS statement allows you to define a catchall exception handler that gets executed when none of the other WHEN statements apply. You can have only one WHEN OTHERS in a block, and it must be the final WHEN statement.

Within the WHEN statement, you have access to the built-in SQLCODE function that returns a numeric value corresponding to the specific error that occurred. See Table 23-7 for a listing of SQLCODE values that correspond to each exception. If you're writing a WHEN statement for each exception type, then SQLCODE is redundant. It's useful, though, if you are handling two types of exceptions with one WHEN statement. Then you can use SQLCODE from within that WHEN statement to determine exactly which exception occurred.

An Example of Exception Handling

The PL/SQL stored function shown in Listing 23-10 contains three exception handlers. Each handler returns an error message appropriate for the exception that triggers it.

Listing 23-10: A PL/SQL stored function with three exception handlers

```
CREATE OR REPLACE FUNCTION get_animal_name (
    animal_id IN NUMBER)
RETURN VARCHAR2 IS
    animal_name VARCHAR2(20);
BEGIN
    SELECT animal_name
    INTO get_animal_name.animal_name
    FROM aquatic_animal
    WHERE id_no = animal_id;

    RETURN animal_name;
EXCEPTION
WHEN NO_DATA_FOUND OR TOO_MANY_ROWS THEN
    RETURN 'Non-existent or non-unique ID';
WHEN VALUE_ERROR THEN
    RETURN 'Animal name too long';
WHEN OTHERS THEN
    RETURN 'Name could not be determined';
END;
/
```

The first handler takes care of two exceptions: NO_DATA_FOUND and TOO_MANY_ROWS. The same message is returned for both. The second handler takes care of only the VALUE_ERROR exception. The final handler is coded using WHEN OTHERS, and consequently handles any other exception that might occur.

When to Use the WHEN Statement

When should you write exception handlers, and when shouldn't you? As a general rule, you write them when you can't afford to have processing come to a halt because an error occurred. You can also write them to allow a process to terminate gracefully in the event of an error. If neither of these applies, save yourself the trouble; you probably don't need to write any exception handlers.

Certain types of PL/SQL coding constructs are more prone to exceptions than others. Consider writing exception handlers to trap errors produced by any of the following:

✦ SELECT INTO statements. Exceptions will occur if a SELECT INTO statement returns less than one row or if it returns more than one row.

✦ Any other type of SQL statement such as INSERT, UPDATE, or DELETE.

✦ Any type of cursor processing statement such as OPEN, CLOSE, and FETCH.

✦ The use of nested tables and varrays. When you use these types of objects, exceptions can be caused if you use invalid index values, fail to initialize the object, and access null elements.

In theory, just about any PL/SQL statement can cause exceptions. In practice, you can avoid a lot of problems through careful coding. If you are getting exceptions because you are fetching from cursors that aren't open or because you are accessing arrays using indexes outside the range that you defined for those arrays, then you are probably being a bit sloppy in the way that you write your code.

Most exceptions tend to occur when interacting with the database because that's when you don't really have any control over what comes back. Someone may have changed a table, for example, causing you to get larger values back than you originally thought possible, in turn causing VALUE_ERROR exceptions in your code. That's why it is particularly important to check for exceptions when you are interacting with the database using SQL statements and cursors.

Using nested blocks and exceptions

You can fine-tune the scope of your exception-handling code by taking advantage of PL/SQL's ability to nest blocks. You aren't locked into having just one set of exception handlers for a program unit. Instead, you can give important statements their own excepting handlers by enclosing those statements in their own block.

Consider the get_tank_info procedure shown in Listing 23-11. Given a tank number, this procedure retrieves both the tank's name and a count of the number of animals residing in the tank.

Listing 23-11: A procedure to retrieve tank and animal information

```
CREATE OR REPLACE PROCEDURE get_animal_info (
    animal_id IN NUMBER,
    animal_name OUT VARCHAR2,
    tank_name OUT VARCHAR2)
IS
    a_name aquatic_animal.animal_name%TYPE;
    t_name tank.tank_name%TYPE;
    t_no tank.tank_no%TYPE;
BEGIN
    --Retrieve the animal's name and tank #
    SELECT animal_name, tank_no
    INTO a_name, t_no
    FROM aquatic_animal
    WHERE id_no = animal_id;

    --Retrieve the tank name
    SELECT tank_name
    INTO t_name
    FROM tank
    WHERE tank_no = t_no;

    --Pass the values back to the calling program.
    animal_name := a_name;
    tank_name := t_name;
END;
/
```

Currently, this procedure has no exception handlers. If a tank isn't found, the procedure will simply abort with an error message. That's not a very robust approach, and if you were writing this procedure, you might want to add in some error handling. The problem is that one error handler might not be able to do everything that you need it to do. Do you really want an error in the first SQL statement to be handled the same as an error in the second SQL statement? Even if you can't get the tank's name, you may still want to retrieve the count of animals within that tank. You really want to treat errors differently for each of the two SQL statements, and the secret to doing that is to nest each SQL statement within its own block. By doing that, each statement can have its own set of exception handlers.

Listing 23-12 shows the get_tank_info procedure after some error-handling code has been added. Notice that each SQL statement is placed within its own block. Further, notice that even if an error occurs with the first SQL statement and a tank isn't found, the second statement will still execute to count the number of animals in the tank.

Listing 23-12: **The get_tank_info procedure with added exception-handling code**

```
CREATE OR REPLACE PROCEDURE get_tank_info (
    tank_no IN NUMBER,
    tank_name OUT VARCHAR2,
    animal_count OUT VARCHAR2)
IS
    t_name tank.tank_name%TYPE;
    a_count NUMBER;
BEGIN
    --Retrieve the tank name
    BEGIN
        SELECT tank_name
        INTO t_name
        FROM tank
        WHERE tank_no = get_tank_info.tank_no;
    EXCEPTION
        WHEN NO_DATA_FOUND THEN
            t_name := 'Missing tank record';
        WHEN TOO_MANY_ROWS THEN
            t_name := 'More than one tank';
        WHEN OTHERS THEN
            t_name := 'Error retrieving tank name';
    END;

    --Count the animals in the tank
    BEGIN
        SELECT COUNT(*)
        INTO a_count
        FROM aquatic_animal
        WHERE tank_no = get_tank_info.tank_no;
    EXCEPTION
        WHEN OTHERS THEN
            a_count := 0;
    END;

    --Pass the values back to the calling program.
    tank_name := t_name;
    animal_count := a_count;
END;
/
```

If the first SELECT fails, the tank name will be set to one of three messages, depending on which exception handler is invoked. Control will then pass out of that nested block, back to the main block. Because the nested block will have handled the error, processing in the outer block continues as normal. The second SELECT will always be executed in an attempt to retrieve a count of the animals assigned to the particular tank.

The second SELECT is also enclosed in its own block, but this time there is only one exception handler, a WHEN OTHERS handler. If any error occurs, regardless of what that error might be, the animal count will be reported as zero. The end result is that this procedure will always return values to the caller. Any errors will be trapped inside the nested blocks and will never be seen outside the procedure.

You can nest blocks to any depth that you like, and the ability to do that is key to writing good, robust exception handlers. It allows you to fine-tune your exception-handling code on a statement-by-statement basis, rather than writing one generic set of exception handlers that attempts to handle all cases.

Raising exceptions

PL/SQL allows you to raise your own exceptions if you need to. For example, you can raise an exception from a trigger to prevent the execution of a SQL statement. The built-in PL/SQL procedure named raise_application_error provides one way of manually raising an exception. The raise_application_error procedure is called as follows:

```
raise_application_error (error_number, message);
```

Replace error_number with any number between -20,000 and -20,999. Those are the numbers reserved for user-defined errors. Replace message with a text message of your choice. Messages may be up to 2,048 bytes long.

The following listing shows a trigger designed to prevent the deletion of any live animals from the SEAPARK database. It uses the raise_application_error procedure to signal the error, thus causing the SQL statement doing the delete to fail.

```
CREATE OR REPLACE TRIGGER delete_check
BEFORE DELETE ON AQUATIC_ANIMAL
FOR EACH ROW
BEGIN
    IF :old.death_date IS NULL THEN
        --the animal is alive
        raise_application_error (-20000,
                'Animal ' || :old.id_no
                || ' is alive and cannot be deleted.');
    END IF;
END;
/
```

This simple trigger checks the death date before allowing the animal's record to be deleted. If no death date has been recorded, the animal is presumed to be alive and an error is raised, preventing the deletion of the record. Oracle will display the message passed to `raise_application_error`. The following example shows you how this looks from SQL*Plus:

```
SQL> delete from aquatic_animal where id_no = 100;
delete from aquatic_animal where id_no = 100
                   *
ERROR at line 1:
ORA-20000: Animal 100 is alive and cannot be deleted.
ORA-06512: at "SEAPARK.DELETE_CHECK", line 4
ORA-04088: error during execution of trigger 'SEAPARK.DELETE_CHECK'
```

You can see that the error number passed to `raise_application_error` shows up here as `ORA-20000`, and it's displayed along with the text of the message parameter. The message makes it very clear just what went wrong. Since the error was raised from a trigger, Oracle also reports the name of the trigger involved.

Executing SQL from PL/SQL

Oracle has several options for getting at the data in your database from PL/SQL. One of the easiest mechanisms to use is the cursor `FOR` loop. A cursor `FOR` loop is one that is based on a `SELECT` statement rather than an arbitrary range of values. PL/SQL automatically executes the code in the loop once for each database row returned by the `SELECT` statement.

Cursor `FOR` loops provide the functionality needed for most applications, but if you need to go beyond the predefined model of looping through the results of a SQL `SELECT` statement, you can always fall back on standard cursor processing.

Using the cursor FOR loop

A cursor `FOR` loop is a special type of `FOR` loop that executes once for each row returned by a SQL query. It provides a convenient way to select and process a SQL result set from PL/SQL. There are a couple of ways to write one, but the simplest approach is as follows:

```
FOR record_name IN (select_statement) LOOP
    statements
END LOOP;
```

The `record_name` in the syntax serves much the same purpose as the loop counter in a standard `FOR` statement. Through the record name, you access the values in the rows returned by the SELECT statement. Replace *select_statement* with any valid SELECT statement, and replace *statements* with whatever PL/SQL statements you want executed as part of the loop.

The body of a cursor FOR loop is executed once for each record returned by the associated SELECT statement. On the first iteration, *record_name* will point to the first row returned. Each iteration through the loop advances to the next row until the end is reached and the loop terminates. The following example opens a cursor on the AQUATIC_ANIMALS table and displays the name of each animal in the database:

```
BEGIN
    FOR animal IN (
        SELECT animal_name
        FROM aquatic_animal
        ORDER BY animal_name)
    LOOP
        DBMS_OUTPUT.PUT_LINE(animal.animal_name);
    END LOOP;
END;
/
```

Note   If you execute this example from SQL*Plus, be sure to execute the SET SERVER-OUTPUT ON command first so that SQL*Plus will display the output for you to see.

Cursor FOR loops provide an easy and convenient way to retrieve and process data from a database table.

Using standard cursor processing

Standard cursor processing is more complex than using a cursor FOR loop. To retrieve and process the results in a SQL query, you must:

1. Declare a cursor in the declaration section of your PL/SQL block.

2. Open the cursor using the OPEN statement.

3. Issue one or more FETCH statements to retrieve the results of the cursor's SELECT statement.

4. Close the cursor by issuing a CLOSE statement.

When you write a cursor FOR loop, all this is done for you automatically. There's a cursor, but it's implicit, and you never need to worry about it. When you do standard cursor processing, you are said to be working with an *explicit cursor* because you have to declare it yourself.

Declaring a Cursor

You declare a cursor in the declaration section of a PL/SQL block using the following syntax:

```
CURSOR cursor_name
    [(parameter_name [IN] datatype [{:= | DEFAULT} value]
    [,parameter_name [IN] datatype [{:= | DEFAULT} value]...])]
        [RETURN returntype] IS select_statement;
```

The following list describes the elements of this syntax:

✦ *cursor_name* — The name you want to give the cursor.

✦ *parameter_name* — The name of a parameter in the cursor's SELECT statement.

✦ *datatype* — The datatype of the parameter.

✦ *value* — A default value for the parameter.

✦ *returntype* — The return type of the cursor. You don't need to supply this. If you do, the type must match a database table definition.

✦ *select_statement* — The SQL SELECT statement to be executed when the cursor is opened.

Declaring a cursor isn't as complicated as this statement makes it look. The following example shows a cursor being declared for a SELECT statement where no parameters are used:

```
CURSOR animal_list IS
    SELECT animal_name
    FROM aquatic_animal
    ORDER BY animal_name;
```

If you want to execute the same SELECT statement more than once but you want to use different criteria for the WHERE clause each time, you can define a cursor with parameters. The following example defines a cursor that returns the names of all animals in a given tank:

```
CURSOR animal_list (
    tank_number NUMBER)
IS
    SELECT animal_name
    FROM aquatic_animal
    WHERE tank_no = tank_number
    ORDER BY animal_name;
```

The parameter in this example is `tank_number`. When you open this cursor, you will need to pass in a number as a parameter. That number is then bound to the `tank_number` parameter in the `SELECT` statement.

Opening a Cursor

Before you can use a cursor that you've declared, you need to open it. You do that using PL/SQL's `OPEN` statement, and the syntax looks like this:

```
OPEN cursor_name [(parameter_value[, parameter_value...])];
```

The following list describes the elements of this syntax:

✦ `cursor_name` — The name of the cursor that you want to open

✦ `parameter_value` — A value that you want to pass as a parameter to the cursor

When you open a cursor, the SQL statement associated with that cursor is passed to Oracle and executed. If you pass parameters to the cursor, the values of those parameters are bound to the corresponding parameters in the cursor's SQL statement.

The following two examples show you how to open each of the two cursors shown in the previous section:

```
OPEN animal_list;

OPEN animal_list (1);
```

The first example opens the version of the `animal_list` cursor that didn't take parameters. The second example works for the version of the `animal_list` cursor that did take a parameter, and it returns a list of all animals living in tank number 1.

Fetching from a Cursor

You use the `FETCH` statement to retrieve data from a cursor. The `FETCH` statement returns one row at a time. Each time you fetch, PL/SQL advances to the next row returned by the cursor's query and returns the values for that row. The syntax for the `FETCH` statement is as follows:

```
FETCH cursor_name
INTO {record_name|variable_name[, variable_name...]};
```

The following list describes the elements of this syntax:

✦ `cursor_name` — The name of the cursor from which you want to fetch.

✦ `record_name`—A record with a type that exactly matches the data being returned by the cursor's SELECT statement.

✦ `variable_name`—The name of a variable. If you aren't fetching into a record, you must supply one variable for each column returned by the cursor's SELECT statement.

A typical FETCH statement is as follows:

```
FETCH animal_list INTO animal_name;
```

To know whether you have reached the end of the query's result set, you must check the cursor's status after each fetch. You can do that by looking at either of the %FOUND or %NOTFOUND parameters. You reference these attributes by appending their names onto the name of the cursor. Fetches are usually done in the context of some sort of loop. The following example shows a loop based on using %NOTFOUND:

```
...
LOOP
   FETCH animal_list INTO animal_name;
   EXIT WHEN animal_list%NOTFOUND;
END LOOP;
```

The %NOTFOUND attribute will be FALSE so long as rows are being returned by the FETCH statement. When you fetch past the end of the result set, %NOTFOUND becomes TRUE. The %FOUND attribute works in exactly the reverse manner. It is TRUE so long as rows are being fetched, and it becomes FALSE when you fetch past the end of the result set. The following loop shows a solution based on using %FOUND:

```
FETCH animal_list INTO animal_name;
WHILE animal_list%FOUND LOOP
   ...
   FETCH animal_list INTO animal_name;
END LOOP;
```

Neither %FOUND nor %NOTFOUND will return a valid value until after the first fetch from a cursor. Between the time the cursor is opened and the first fetch is made, both of these attributes will be null.

Closing a Cursor

When you're done with a cursor, you should close it to free up resources. The syntax for closing a cursor looks like this:

```
CLOSE cursor_name;
```

Replace `cursor_name` in this syntax with the name of the cursor that you want to close.

Reviewing an Example of Standard Cursor Processing

So far, all you've seen are code snippets illustrating the various statements used in cursor processing. It's time now to see all the pieces working together. The code example shown in Listing 23-13 shows a cursor being used to retrieve a list of animals from the database. The cursor accepts a tank number as a parameter. If you run this code from SQL*Plus (remember to execute SET SERVEROUTPUT ON first), you will see these results displayed on your screen.

Listing 23-13: **Using PL/SQL cursors**

```
DECLARE
    CURSOR animal_list (
        tank_number NUMBER)
    IS
        SELECT animal_name, birth_date
        FROM aquatic_animal
        WHERE tank_no = tank_number;

    animal_name aquatic_animal.animal_name%TYPE;
    birth_date aquatic_animal.birth_date%TYPE;
BEGIN
    --Open the cursor for tank #1
    OPEN animal_list (1);

    --Fetch and display data for each animal
    LOOP
        FETCH animal_list INTO animal_name, birth_date;
        EXIT WHEN animal_list%NOTFOUND;

        DBMS_OUTPUT.PUT_LINE (
            animal_name || ' born '
            || TO_CHAR(birth_date, 'dd-Mon-yyyy'));
    END LOOP;

    --Close the cursor
    CLOSE animal_list;
END;
/
```

The procedural part of this block starts off with an OPEN statement that opens the cursor, passing a 1 as the value for the tank number parameter. Next comes a loop that fetches and displays information about each animal until %NOTFOUND becomes true. The last statement in the block closes the cursor.

Using non-SELECT statements

You can also execute data manipulation statements, such as INSERT, UPDATE, and DELETE, from within PL/SQL. They are simply written inline as part of your PL/SQL code. You may also use transaction control statements such as COMMIT, ROLLBACK, and SET TRANSACTION. Listing 23-14 contains PL/SQL code that shows you how easy this is to do.

Listing 23-14: **Using data manipulation and transaction control statements**

```
BEGIN
  --Explicitly start the transaction
  SET TRANSACTION READ WRITE;

  --Demonstrate INSERT, UPDATE, and DELETE from PL/SQL.
  INSERT INTO aquatic_animal
    (id_no, tank_no, animal_name,
markings_description, birth_date)
    VALUES (300,1,'Swampy','none',
TO_DATE('26-Dec-1995','dd-mon-yyyy'));
  UPDATE aquatic_animal
    SET markings_description = 'cranky and aggressive'
  WHERE id_no = 300;
  DELETE
    FROM aquatic_animal
  WHERE id_no = 300;

  --End this transaction
  COMMIT;
END;
/
```

Data definition statements, such as CREATE USER, CREATE INDEX, and so on, can't be coded directly in PL/SQL. If you need to execute these types of statements, read up on the DBMS_SQL package or on the new native dynamic SQL support that came out with Oracle8i. The DBMS_SQL package is a PL/SQL package, provided by Oracle, that allows you to execute SQL statements that you build at runtime. Native dynamic SQL is a new, easier-to-use feature that allows you to perform the same task. Using dynamic SQL, you can execute any SQL statement that you want, including DDL statements.

Using singleton SELECT statements

A *singleton SELECT* is a SELECT statement that fetches exactly one record from the database and stores the result in one or more PL/SQL variables. It uses the keyword INTO to specify a list of variables that will hold the results. The syntax is as follows:

```
SELECT column[, column...] INTO variable[, variable...]
  FROM remainder_of_statement;
```

The following list describes the elements of this syntax:

✦ *column* — A column name from one of the tables in the FROM clause. This may also be a SQL function, a PL/SQL stored function, or a literal.

✦ *variable* — A PL/SQL variable. The value in the first column is stored in the first variable, the value from the second column is stored in the second variable, and so on.

✦ *remainder_of_statement* — Except for the INTO clause, this SELECT statement looks just like any other.

You have to be careful with singleton selects because a runtime error will occur if they return more than one row. A runtime error will also occur if they return less than one row. The following situations are when you should consider using a singleton SELECT:

✦ You are selecting summary information, such as SELECT COUNT(*), where you know only one value will be returned.

✦ You are selecting one record, and you are specifying either the primary key or the Oracle rowid in the WHERE clause.

The following code contains an example of a singleton SELECT:

```
DECLARE
    num_of_animals NUMBER;
BEGIN
    SELECT COUNT(*) INTO num_of_animals
    FROM aquatic_animal;
END;
/
```

This code retrieves a count of the number of records in the AQUATIC_ANIMALS table and places that count into the num_of_animals variable. If you issue a singleton SELECT and it returns more than one row or less than one row, you will receive either the TOO_MANY_ROWS exception or the NO_DATA_FOUND exception, respectively.

Summary

In this chapter, you learned:

✦ PL/SQL is a robust procedural language developed by Oracle as an extension to SQL. Use PL/SQL to write procedural code that executes within the database. This includes stand-alone PL/SQL blocks as well as stored procedures, stored functions, and triggers.

✦ PL/SQL is a block-structured language, with each block having three sections: a declaration section, an executable section, and an exception-handler section. These sections are identified by the keywords DECLARE, BEGIN, and EXCEPTION, respectively. PL/SQL blocks end with the keyword END.

✦ PL/SQL blocks may be nested to control variable scope or to provide fine-tuned exception handling.

✦ PL/SQL datatypes, used when declaring variables, mostly match the datatypes used within the database. You can use the %TYPE and %ROWTYPE keywords to declare variables that match a specific column, or to declare records that match a specific table.

✦ The easiest way to retrieve data from a database from within PL/SQL is to use the cursor FOR loop. With only minimal coding, you can define both a query to be executed and a sequence of PL/SQL statements to operate on each row returned by that query.

✦ When more complex processing is required, you can manually declare cursors and use PL/SQL's OPEN, FETCH, and CLOSE statements to open those cursors, retrieve data, and close the cursors. When using FETCH, always check %FOUND ... u reached the end of the result set ... uery.

✦

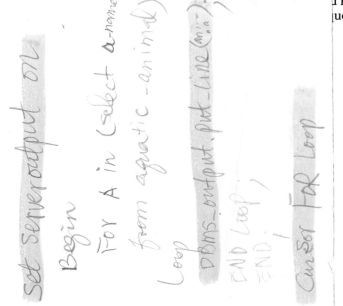

Using Procedures, Packages, Functions, and Triggers

Oracle allows you to store PL/SQL code in the database so that you can execute it repeatedly without having to reload it each time. Stored code is organized into procedures, functions, packages, and triggers. In this chapter, you'll learn how to create and maintain these types of stored program units.

This chapter builds on the information in Chapter 23, "Using PL/SQL," which covered how to write PL/SQL. Now you will learn how to save your PL/SQL code in the database so that you and others can easily execute it again. You'll also learn how to use triggers, which allow you to execute PL/SQL and SQL before or after you insert, update, or delete data from a table.

Understanding Stored Code

Most of the PL/SQL blocks shown in the previous chapter were anonymous. An *anonymous block* is a PL/SQL block that has no name and isn't stored in the Oracle data dictionary. You can execute anonymous blocks only when they are compiled and loaded into memory as the result of a call from an application.

Stored procedures, functions, packages, and triggers within the Oracle world are also known as *subprograms*. You can express business- or database-related tasks through the use of logically grouped SQL and PL/SQL statements within these subprograms.

Stored subprograms are kept in a user's schema in a compiled format known as *pseudocode (p-code)*. That way, they don't have to be recompiled each time they are called. When a subprogram is called, Oracle loads it into the shared pool in the system global area (SGA). Then the PL/SQL engine and SQL executors collaborate to process the statements within that object.

The diagram shown in Figure 24-1 conceptually illustrates how a stored subprogram is executed from a client application.

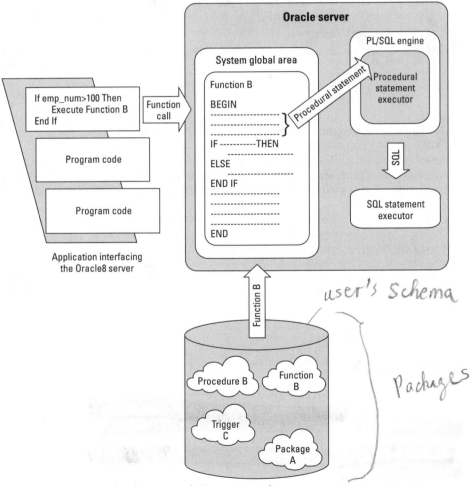

Figure 24-1: A stored subprogram being executed

Looking at Oracle stored subprograms

In today's world of distributed processing, stored procedures, functions, and packages make sense. While residing in the database, these subprograms can execute extremely quickly in a compiled format and without the network traffic that would be involved were you to execute the same code from a client application.

Business object design is becoming the norm in the development of mission-critical applications. Objects are required to be extensible, modular, reusable, maintainable, and abstracted. Oracle-stored subprograms provide the capability to embrace all of these business object requirements for the following reasons:

✦ You can use the PL/SQL language to write code tailored to your business needs.

✦ Using stored packages, you can break programs down into manageable, well-defined modules.

✦ Once created and tested, you can use stored subprograms with confidence. You can usually modify well-designed, loosely coupled subprograms without affecting the rest of the component architecture.

✦ To use stored subprograms, you must know what they do, not how they work. Therefore, you can design business applications without worrying about specific implementation details.

Procedures and functions enable you to use PL/SQL to combine the ease and flexibility of SQL with the procedural functionality of a structured programming language. The major difference between an Oracle stored procedure and an Oracle function is that a function has to return a value.

Packages are a group of logically related procedures and functions encapsulated together as a single unit. Each exposed procedure or function within a package can be called independently. One important aspect of Oracle procedures and functions residing in packages is that you can overload them. You'll learn more about overloading later in this chapter in the section "Overloading Package Interfaces."

Following the chapter case study

This chapter contains several examples of stored PL/SQL program units. All the examples revolve around a library scenario in which the main purpose is to keep track of books as they are borrowed and returned. The tables in the library scenario are as follows:

STUDENTS	Contains a list of all students
BOOKS	Contains a list of library books
BOOKS_LOANED	Contains a list of books on loan to students

DEPARTMENT	Contains a list of departments
BOOKS_RESERVED	Contains a list of books reserved by students
STUDENTS_FINES	Contains a list of students who have book fines

If you run the script to load the sample data for this book, these tables will exist in user AMY's schema.

A student can go to the library and either request any book in the system or request a list of books recommended by a particular department. If the books are available, the student can borrow them for three weeks. The student can renew the books during the loan period if the books aren't reserved while on loan. If the student returns the books after the loan period, he or she accumulates daily charges on the books due.

Using Stored Procedures

Stored procedures can be instrumental in moving business logic from your client application to the database server. The database server is likely to be faster and more robust than any client PC, thus possessing the capability to process most business tasks quickly and securely. At the same time, using stored procedures can reduce the network traffic between the client and the Oracle server because instead of making several calls to execute a series of SQL statements, only one call is made to invoke the stored procedure.

Creating stored procedures by example

You create stored procedures by using the CREATE PROCEDURE statement. The typical structure of that statement looks like this:

```
CREATE PROCEDURE procedure_name argument_list
    Variable Declaration Section
BEGIN
    PL/SQL Code
EXCEPTION
    PL/SQL Exception Handling Code
END;
/
```

Note   The semicolon at the end isn't really part of the CREATE PROCEDURE syntax. However, if you're executing the CREATE PROCEDURE statement from SQL*Plus, you will need to use the semicolon to tell SQL*Plus to execute the statement that you have just entered.

Now let's look at a simple stored procedure that enables a student to borrow a book. (See Listing 24-1.) The stored procedure receives a student ID to identify the student and a book ID to identify the book requested for loan. The stored procedure then returns the result of the book loan operation back to the caller.

Listing 24-1: A stored procedure for borrowing a book

```
CREATE OR REPLACE PROCEDURE loan_book(
    student_num IN INTEGER,
    book_num IN INTEGER,
    loan_status IN OUT VARCHAR2 )
AS
    loan_key INTEGER;
    reserve_key INTEGER;
    book_due DATE;
    book_wait INTEGER;
    reserved_loaned EXCEPTION;
BEGIN
    /*Check if the book is on loan or reserved */
    SELECT reserved_id INTO reserve_key
    FROM books_reserved
    WHERE reserved_book_id = book_num;

    SELECT book_loan_id INTO loan_key
    FROM BOOKS
    WHERE book_id = book_num;

    IF loan_key > 0 OR reserve_key > 0 THEN
        IF loan_key > 0 THEN -- Get the due back date of the book
                        SELECT bl_loan_date INTO book_due
                        FROM BOOKS_LOANED
                        WHERE bl_loan_id = loan_key;
        END IF;
        IF reserve_key > 0 THEN -- Get the wait list on the book
                        SELECT reserved_wait_no INTO
                            book_wait
                        FROM BOOKS_RESERVED
                        WHERE reserved_id = reserve_key;
        END IF;
        RAISE reserved_loaned;
    ELSE -- Book is available to be loaned
        INSERT INTO BOOKS_LOANED
        VALUES ( books_on_loan.nextval,
        book_num, student_num, SYSDATE, 0);


        UPDATE BOOKS
          SET book_loan_id = books_on_loan.currval
          WHERE book_id = book_num;
```

Continued

Listing 24-1: *(continued)*

```
END IF;
EXCEPTION
   WHEN NO_DATA_FOUND THEN
   loan_status :=
   'The book could not be found in the Library System.';
   WHEN reserved_loaned THEN
      IF loan_key > 0 THEN
         loan_status :=
   'The book is currently on loan and is due for return on '
   || (book_due + 30) || '.';
      END IF;
      IF reserve_key > 0 THEN
         Loan_status :=
         loan_status || ' ' ||
         'The book is reserved with a waiting list of '
         || book_wait || ' persons ';
      END IF;
END;
/
```

Listing 24-1 contains the CREATE PROCEDURE command with parameter definitions, a variable declaration section, a procedure body containing PL/SQL and SQL statements, and an exception-handing section. The exception handlers in the exception-handling section are invoked when someone tries to borrow a book that is already on loan or that is on reserve.

The CREATE PROCEDURE Syntax

As with all database objects, you must create stored procedures before you can use them. You use the CREATE PROCEDURE command for that purpose. The syntax is as follows:

```
CREATE [OR REPLACE] PROCEDURE procedure_name
  [(parameter [{IN | OUT | IN OUT}] datatype
     [{:= | DEFAULT} expression]
  [,(parameter [{IN | OUT | IN OUT}] datatype
     [{:= | DEFAULT} expression]...]]
[AUTHID {CURRENT_USER | DESIGNER}]
{IS | AS}
   [declarations]
BEGIN
   code
[EXCEPTION
   exception_handlers]
END
```

The following list describes the elements of this syntax:

- ✦ OR REPLACE — A keyword that instructs Oracle to overwrite any existing procedure with the same name.

- ✦ *procedure_name* — The name of the procedure that you are creating.

- ✦ *parameter* — A parameter to the procedure.

- ✦ IN | OUT | INOUT — A keyword indicating whether the parameter is an input, an output, or both. The default is IN.

- ✦ *datatype* — The datatype of an argument, which can be any valid Oracle datatype.

- ✦ DEFAULT *expression* — A default value for a parameter.

- ✦ AUTHID CURRENT_USER — A keyword indicating that the procedure will execute using the invoker's rights model. Access to database objects depends on the privileges held by the invoker.

- ✦ AUTHID DESIGNER — A keyword indicating that the procedure will execute using the definer's rights model. Access to database objects depends on the privileges held by the definer.

- ✦ *declarations* — Where you declare PL/SQL variables.

- ✦ *code* — The PL/SQL code for the procedure.

- ✦ *exception_handlers* — The set of exception handlers for the procedure.

A stored procedure is comprised of two parts: the declaration and the body. The *declaration* defines the stored procedure name and the formal parameters required to execute it, and it indicates whether the procedure should execute using invoker's rights or definer's rights. The *body* of the stored procedure is essentially a PL/SQL block. It contains declarations, code, and exception handlers.

The Declaration Section

When creating a stored procedure, the declaration serves to mark the beginning of the block. In a sense, it replaces the need for DECLARE. Any variable declarations, type declarations, record declarations, and so forth, should follow the procedure declaration.

The declaration section is where you define parameter datatypes and parameter modes. It is also where you optionally indicate which rights model to use.

Parameter datatypes

The datatype defines the PL/SQL datatype of a formal parameter. Unlike when you declare a variable, when you define the datatype for a parameter to a procedure, you don't constrain the type by specifying a length. Use types like VARCHAR2 or

NUMBER, but don't attempt to use VARCHAR2(10) or NUMBER (4). If you specify a length for a parameter, you will get an error when you try to create the procedure.

If your procedure parameters need to match a table definition or a column definition, you can use %ROWTYPE and %TYPE in the declaration. These two keywords are discussed in Chapter 23, "Using PL/SQL." They allow you to declare a parameter such that it matches a specified table or column. For example, the following procedure definition uses %TYPE to make the STUDENT_NUM parameter match the STUDENT_ID column in the STUDENTS table:

```
CREATE OR REPLACE PROCEDURE loan_book(
    student_num students.student_id%TYPE
```

Because %TYPE has been used, an alteration of the underlying column definition doesn't necessitate a change to the procedure's declaration. The %ROWTYPE attribute creates a record with fields that match a table. Use %ROWTYPE if you want your parameter to be a record.

Parameter modes

Formal parameters have modes, which describe their behavior in the definition of a stored procedure or a function. The mode of a parameter indicates whether it is modified when the procedure is executed. The three valid modes are IN, OUT, and IN OUT.

IN	Defines the formal parameter as an input variable to the stored subprogram. This type of formal parameter is read-only and cannot be assigned a value within the subprogram body. The actual parameter can be a constant or a variable.
OUT	Defines the formal parameter used as a container for returning a value from the procedure. You can't reference OUT values from within a procedure. You can only assign them a value. The OUT parameters must be variables because they must be able to hold a return value.
IN OUT	Defines the formal parameter as both an input and an output. This type of parameter must be a variable because it must be capable of holding an output value.

The following LOAN_BOOK procedure provides an example of parameter modes being used:

```
CREATE OR REPLACE PROCEDURE loan_book(
    student_num IN INTEGER,
    book_num IN INTEGER,
    loan_status IN OUT VARCHAR2)
```

Because they are input only, the formal parameters STUDENT_NUM and BOOK_NUM can be constants or variables. Any attempt to return a value through these parameters results in a compile error. The LOAN_STATUS parameter, however, is an IN OUT parameter. You can use it both as an input and as a way to return a value from the procedure.

Default parameter values

You can use the DEFAULT keyword to specify a default value for IN and IN OUT parameters. Doing so allows the procedure to be invoked with an incomplete parameter list. For any parameters that aren't specifically supplied, the default values will be used. The following parameter declaration declares a STUDENT_ID parameter with a default value of 134.

```
student_num IN students.student_id%TYPE DEFAULT 134;
```

As an option, instead of using the keyword DEFAULT, you can choose to use the assignment operator (:=) instead. The following example also declares a STUDENT_ID parameter with a default value of 134:

```
student_num IN students.student_id%TYPE := 134;
```

There is no particular advantage to using DEFAULT over the := operator. The choice of which to use is up to you. Use whichever you believe to be the most readable.

Positional and named notation methods of passing parameters

When you invoke a stored procedure, you can pass parameters to that procedure using either positional or named notation. *Positional notation* refers to the method of listing the actual parameters in the same order in which they are defined in the procedure declaration. *Named notation* refers to a method whereby you specify parameter values by name. When named notation is used, you can specify the parameters in any order. The following example invokes the LOAN_BOOK procedure and illustrates positional notation:

```
DECLARE
    msg VARCHAR2;
BEGIN
    loan_book(1,5,msg);
END;
/
```

Notice that three values were passed to LOAN_BOOK. These three values match up to the procedure's three parameters. The matching is done based on the order of the parameters in the procedure's declaration, so you have a book ID of 1, a student ID of 5, and a text variable to hold the results.

Named notation allows you to pass the parameters by name. When you use named notation, the order isn't important. PL/SQL will look at the names that you supply. Each name must match up with a formal parameter in the procedure declaration. To specify a name for a parameter, you can use the following syntax in the procedure call:

```
formal_name=>value
```

Replace *formal_name* with the formal parameter name as found in the procedure declaration. Replace *value* with either a constant or a variable name. For example, the following code also calls the LOAN_BOOK procedure, and with the same values as before. Named notation is used this time, and the parameter order doesn't match that in the procedure's declaration:

```
DECLARE
    msg VARCHAR2;
BEGIN
    loan_book(loan_status=>msg,
              student_num=>5,
              book_num=>1,);
END;
/
```

Named notation requires a lot more typing; therefore, it's not used often. It can prove handy, however, when you are calling a procedure that has a large number of arguments, and where you want to take the defaults for all but one or two of those arguments. In such a case, using named notation may be easier than trying to supply a value for each argument using positional notation.

The Procedure Body

The procedure body is a PL/SQL block where business- and data-related tasks are defined using PL/SQL and SQL statements. As noted earlier, the keyword DECLARE isn't used because the CREATE PROCEDURE statement is sufficient to mark the start of the block.

In addition to the procedure code, the procedure body can contain an error-handling section. The keyword EXCEPTION marks the beginning of the error-handling section, which is where you would place the PL/SQL WHEN statements used to handle exceptions.

Maintaining stored procedures

You can drop a stored procedure by using the DROP PROCEDURE statement. For example:

```
DROP PROCEDURE loan_book;
```

If you want to change the code behind a stored procedure, you must drop the procedure and re-create it. As a shortcut to doing that, you can issue the `CREATE OR REPLACE PROCEDURE` command, telling Oracle to replace the existing procedure.

Seeing the errors

When you compile a stored procedure or any other type of stored code, you risk receiving a compilation error. If your code doesn't compile, Oracle will tell you, but it won't automatically display details about the error. To get the details, you can use the SQL*Plus `SHOW ERRORS` command, or you can query the data dictionary. The `SHOW ERRORS` command is a SQL*Plus command that usually provides a convenient way to get an error listing for a procedure that you are trying to compile. The syntax to use follows:

```
SHOW ERRORS {PROCEDURE|FUNCTION|PACKAGE} [schema].name
```

The following list describes the elements of this syntax:

✦ `PROCEDURE`—Indicates that you want to see the error listing for a stored procedure.

✦ `FUNCTION`—Indicates that you want to see the error listing for a function.

✦ `PACKAGE`—Indicates that you want to see the error listing for a package.

✦ `schema`—Specifies the owner of the procedure, function, or package. If you are the owner, you don't need to specify this.

✦ `name`—Specifies the name of the procedure, function, or package.

The `SHOW ERRORS` command gets its information from the data dictionary. You can go straight to that source yourself if you need to. The following three data dictionary views provide information about compilation errors:

`USER_ERRORS`	For program units that you own
`ALL_ERRORS`	For program units that you own, or to which you have been granted access
`DBA_ERRORS`	For all program units in the database

The `SHOW ERRORS` command, as well as the data dictionary views listed here, apply equally to functions and packages as well as to stored procedures. You'll read about functions and packages later in this chapter.

Retrieving the source code

Oracle retains the source code for stored program units that you load into the database. If necessary, you can retrieve the source code for a program unit from one of these views:

USER_SOURCE	For program units that you own
ALL_SOURCE	For program units that you own and to which you have been granted access
DBA_SOURCE	For all program units in the database

Even though Oracle keeps the source code in the data dictionary, you'll find it best to maintain your own copy outside of the database. If you use stored procedures extensively, consider using a third-party source-code control system that implements check-in/check-out capabilities.

Creating Functions

Functions are similar to stored procedures except that they are required to return a value. For example, we could have easily defined the LOAN_BOOK procedure as a function. Instead of returning the text message through an output parameter, it could have been returned as the result of the function.

The syntax for creating a function is almost the same as for a stored procedure. The major difference is the addition of a RETURN clause. This clause is used to specify the datatype of the value returned by the function. For example, the function in Listing 24-2 returns a single value indicating the total fines accrued by a student.

Listing 24-2: **Using a function to return a value**

```
CREATE OR REPLACE FUNCTION student_fines (
    student_num IN INTEGER)
RETURN REAL AS
    book_fine     REAL;
    total_fine    REAL := 0;
    CURSOR scroll_fines (student_key INTEGER)
        IS
        SELECT bl_fine
        FROM BOOKS_LOANED
        WHERE bl_student_id = student_key;
BEGIN
    OPEN scroll_fines(student_num);
    LOOP
```

```
            FETCH scroll_fines INTO book_fine;
            EXIT WHEN scroll_fines%NOTFOUND;
            total_fine := total_fine + book_fine;
        END LOOP;
        CLOSE scroll_fines;
        RETURN total_fine;
    END;
    /
```

Notice that the declaration includes the clause RETURN REAL, which defines the datatype of the value to be returned by the function. The PL/SQL RETURN statement right before the end of the PL/SQL block is what specifies the value to be returned. The RETURN statement may be anywhere in the block, and you can code more than one. For example, you might write an IF statement that chooses between two different values to return. Regardless, once the RETURN statement is executed, control passes out of the function back to the code that called it.

If you want to execute the STUDENT_FINES function shown here, you can do that by invoking it in a SQL statement. The following example shows STUDENT_FINES being used to retrieve the total fines owed by student number 5:

```
SQL> SELECT student_fines (5) FROM dual;

STUDENT_FINES(5)
----------------
              10

1 row selected.
```

As a general rule, if you have just one value that you are returning, consider using a function. This is especially true if you intend to use that value in an expression or in a SQL statement, as shown previously.

You use the CREATE FUNCTION statement to create a stored function. The syntax is shown in Listing 24-3.

Listing 24-3: **Creating a stored function**

```
CREATE [OR REPLACE] FUNCTION function_name
    [(parameter [{IN | OUT | IN OUT}] datatype
        [{:= | DEFAULT} expression]
    [,(parameter [{IN | OUT | IN OUT}] datatype
        [{:= | DEFAULT} expression]...]]
RETURN returntype
```

Continued

Listing 24-3: *(continued)*

```
[AUTHID {CURRENT_USER | DESIGNER}]
{IS | AS}
    [declarations]
BEGIN
    code
[EXCEPTION
    exception_handlers]
END
```

The following list describes the elements in this syntax:

- ✦ OR REPLACE—A keyword that instructs Oracle to overwrite any existing function with the same name.

- ✦ *function_name*—The name of the function that you are creating.

- ✦ *parameter*—A parameter to the function.

- ✦ IN | OUT | INOUT—A keyword indicating whether the parameter is an input, an output, or both. The default is IN.

- ✦ *datatype*—The datatype of an argument, which can be any valid Oracle datatype.

- ✦ DEFAULT *expression*—A default value that you may optionally specify for a parameter.

- ✦ RETURN *returntype*—The datatype of the value returned by the function.

- ✦ AUTHID CURRENT_USER—A keyword indicating that the function will execute using the invoker's rights model. Access to database objects depends on the privileges held by the invoker.

- ✦ AUTHID DESIGNER—A keyword indicating that the function will execute using the definer's rights model. Access to database objects depends on the privileges held by the definer.

- ✦ *declarations*—Where you declare PL/SQL variables.

- ✦ *code*—The PL/SQL code for the function.

- ✦ *exception_handlers*—The set of exception handlers for the function.

The components found in a function declaration are the same as those found in a procedure declaration. The only difference is that a function has a return value, and the datatype of that return value is specified by the RETURN clause.

Creating Packages

A *package* is a group of related PL/SQL procedures and functions. Packages may also contain package-level variables that the procedures and functions in the package can use and whose values persist throughout a user's session.

Packages consist of two distinct parts: a specification and a body. The specification consists of a list of declarations for the procedures and functions in the package. You have to create the specification before you create the body. However, subsequent changes to the package body don't require changes to the specification. The only time you need to change a package specification is when one of the declarations needs to be changed.

You create a package's specification and body with two different statements. The CREATE PACKAGE statement creates the specification, while the CREATE PACKAGE BODY statement creates the body. Listing 24-4 shows the statement needed to create a specification for a package named LIBRARY_MANAGEMENT, which encapsulates a number of routines, including the LOAN_BOOK procedure shown earlier in this chapter.

Listing 24-4: **Creating a package specification**

```
CREATE OR REPLACE PACKAGE library_management AS
    PROCEDURE loan_book    (
        student_num IN INTEGER,
        book_num IN INTEGER,
        loan_status IN OUT VARCHAR2
        ) ;
    PROCEDURE reserve_book (
        student_num IN INTEGER,
        book_num IN INTEGER
        );
    PROCEDURE return_book (
        student_num IN INTEGER,
        book_num IN INTEGER,
        book_status OUT INTEGER,
        fine_info OUT VARCHAR2
        );
END library_management;
/
```

This package specification contains declarations for three procedures: LOAN_BOOK, RESERVE_BOOK, and RETURN_BOOK. The actual code for these procedures needs to reside in a package body, which you create separately (see Listing 24-5).

Listing 24-5: **Creating a package body**

```
CREATE OR REPLACE PACKAGE BODY library_management AS
    FUNCTION book_reserved (book_num IN INTEGER)
        RETURN INTEGER
        AS
        wait_no INTEGER := 0;
    BEGIN
        SELECT MAX(reserved_wait_no) INTO wait_no
        FROM books_reserved
        WHERE reserved_book_id = book_num;
        RETURN wait_no;
    EXCEPTION
        WHEN NO_DATA_FOUND THEN
            RETURN wait_no;
    END book_reserved;

    PROCEDURE loan_book (
        student_num IN INTEGER,
        book_num IN INTEGER,
        loan_status IN OUT VARCHAR2 )
    AS
        loan_key          INTEGER;
        reserve_key       INTEGER;
        book_due          DATE;
        book_wait         INTEGER;
        reserved_loaned EXCEPTION;
    BEGIN
        /*Check if the book is on loan or reserved */
        reserve_key := book_reserved(book_num);
        SELECT book_loan_id INTO loan_key
        FROM BOOKS
        WHERE book_id =  book_num;
        IF loan_key > 0 OR reserve_key > 0 THEN
            IF loan_key > 0 THEN -- Get the due back date
                SELECT bl_loan_date INTO book_due
                FROM BOOKS_LOANED
                WHERE bl_loan_id = loan_key;
            END IF;
            IF reserve_key > 0 THEN -- Get the wait list
                SELECT reserved_wait_no INTO book_wait
                FROM BOOKS_RESERVED
                WHERE reserved_id = reserve_key;
            END IF;
            RAISE reserved_loaned;
        ELSE -- Book is available to be loaned
            INSERT INTO BOOKS_LOANED
            VALUES ( books_on_loan.nextval,
                    book_num, student_num,
                    SYSDATE, 0);
```

```
            COMMIT;
            UPDATE BOOKS
            SET book_loan_id = books_on_loan.currval
            WHERE book_id = book_num;
            COMMIT;
        END IF;
    EXCEPTION
            WHEN NO_DATA_FOUND THEN
    loan_status :=
    'The book could not be found in the library system.';
            WHEN reserved_loaned THEN
                IF loan_key > 0 THEN
    loan_status :=
'The book is currently on loan and is due for return on '
        || (book_due + 30) || '.';
                END IF;
                IF reserve_key > 0 THEN
    Loan_status := loan_status || ' ' ||
        'The book is reserved with a waiting list of '
        || book_wait || ' persons ';
                END IF;
    END loan_book;

    PROCEDURE reserve_book (
        student_num IN INTEGER,
        book_num    IN INTEGER)
    AS
        wait_no INTEGER;
    BEGIN
        wait_no := book_reserved(book_num) + 1;
        INSERT INTO books_reserved VALUES
        (books_on_reserve.nextval,
         book_num, student_num, wait_no);
    END reserve_book;

    PROCEDURE Update_book_fines(
        student_num IN INTEGER)
    AS
    BEGIN
        UPDATE books_loaned
        SET bl_fine = (SYSDATE - (bl_loan_date + 30)) * .5
        WHERE bl_student_id = student_num
        AND ((bl_loan_date + 30) < SYSDATE);
    END Update_book_fines;

    FUNCTION student_fines (student_num IN INTEGER)
    RETURN REAL
    AS
        book_fine   REAL;
        total_fine  REAL := 0;
    CURSOR  scroll_fines (student_key INTEGER)
```

Continued

Listing 24-5: *(continued)*

```
                IS
                SELECT bl_fine
                FROM BOOKS_LOANED
                WHERE bl_student_id = student_key;
        BEGIN
            OPEN scroll_fines(student_num);
            LOOP
                FETCH scroll_fines INTO book_fine;
                EXIT WHEN scroll_fines%NOTFOUND;
                total_fine := total_fine + book_fine;
            END LOOP;
            CLOSE scroll_fines;
            dbms_output.put_line(TO_CHAR(total_fine));
            UPDATE students_fines
            SET sf_fine = total_fine
            WHERE sf_student_id = student_num;
            RETURN total_fine;
        END student_fines;

        PROCEDURE return_book(
            student_num IN  INTEGER,
            book_num    IN  INTEGER,
            book_status OUT INTEGER,
            fine_info   OUT VARCHAR2)
        AS
            loan_key         INTEGER;
            student_fine     REAL := 0;
        BEGIN  .
            -- Get the loan information
            SELECT book_loan_id INTO loan_key
            FROM books
            WHERE book_id = book_num;
            -- Get the fines due for the student
            student_fine := student_fines(student_num);
            -- Update the BOOKS table
            UPDATE books
            SET book_loan_id = 0
            WHERE book_id = book_num;
            -- Delete the loan Record
            DELETE books_loaned WHERE bl_loan_id = loan_key;
            COMMIT;
            book_status := 1;
            fine_info :=
                'The student has a remaining fine of $'
                || student_fine;
        END return_book;
    END library_management;
/
```

This package body implements the three procedures defined in the package specifications. If you look closely, you'll see that it also implements three functions that aren't in the package specification: BOOK_RESERVED, UPDATE_BOOK_FINES, and STUDENT_FINES. These functions are internal to the package. They can be called from other program units in the same package, but they can't be called from outside the package. Only the program units listed in the package specification are visible to the world outside the package body.

Examining package creation syntax

The preceding examples showed you the syntax used when creating package specifications and package bodies. However, the formal syntax is described in the next two sections. The syntax used for creating a package specification is shown in Listing 24-6.

Listing 24-6: **The syntax for CREATE PACKAGE**

```
CREATE [OR REPLACE] PACKAGE [schema.]package_name
[AUTHID {CURRENT_USER|DEFINER}] [FORCE]
{IS|AS}
    {function_declaration
    |procedure_declaration
    |variable_declaration
    |type_declaration
    |cursor_declaration
    |exception_declaration}

    {function_declaration
    |procedure_declaration
    |variable_declaration
    |type_declaration
    |cursor_declaration
    |exception_declaration}
...
END [package_name];
```

The following list describes the elements in this syntax:

✦ schema — The owner of the package. You need the CREATE ANY PROCEDURE system privilege to create a package in someone else's schema.

✦ package_name — The name that you want to give the package.

✦ AUTHID CURRENT_USER—A keyword indicating that you want the package to run under the invoker's rights model.

✦ AUTHID DEFINER—A keyword indicating that you want the package to run under the definer's rights model. This is the default.

✦ FORCE—A keyword that causes the package to be dropped and re-created even if there are existing dependencies. This can be used only if you have also specified REPLACE, and only if the existing specification was created with PRAGMA repeatable. A pragma is a directive to the PL/SQL compiler.

✦ function_declaration—A function declaration.

✦ procedure declaration—A procedure declaration.

✦ variable_declaration—A variable declaration.

✦ type_declaration—A type declaration.

✦ cursor_declaration – A cursor declaration.

✦ exception_declaration—An exception declaration.

The name of a package must be unique in a given schema, and both the package specification and body must share the same name. The package specification objects can use similar names if object overloading is being used. See the section "Overloading Package Interfaces" later in this chapter.

PL/SQL objects declared in the package specification are global—they can be called or used by external users who have EXECUTE privileges on the package or who have EXECUTE ANY PACKAGE privileges. The arguments defined for each procedure or function listed in a package specification must match those defined for the corresponding procedures and functions in the package body.

By default, packages are created using a definer's rights model. That means that any user who is executing code in the package temporarily inherits the database access of the package owner. By specifying AUTHID CURRENT_USER, you can create a package where the invoker's rights model is used. In that case, users invoking the package execute the package code with their own privileges.

Examining the CREATE PACKAGE BODY syntax

The CREATE PACKAGE BODY command defines the PL/SQL code for all the program units in the package. This includes the public routines declared in the package specification, and it also includes private routines that are declared only in the body. The syntax for CREATE PACKAGE BODY is shown in Listing 24-7.

Listing 24-7: **The syntax for CREATE PACKAGE BODY**

```
CREATE [OR REPLACE] PACKAGE BODY [schema.]package_name
{IS|AS}
    {function
    |procedure
    |variable
    |type
    |cursor
    |exception}

    {function
    |procedure
    |variable
    |type
    |cursor
    |exception}
...
BEGIN
    initialization_code
EXCEPTION
    exception_handlers
END [package_name];
```

The following list describes the elements of this syntax:

✦ schema — The owner of the package.

✦ package_name — The name of the package.

✦ function — A function definition.

✦ procedure — A procedure definition.

✦ variable — A variable declaration.

✦ type — A type declaration.

✦ cursor — A cursor declaration.

✦ exception — An exception declaration.

✦ initializiation_code — The code to initialize package variables. This code is executed the very first time in a database session that a package is referenced.

✦ exception_handlers — The exception-handling code for the package's initialization code.

In the package body, procedure and function definitions must include the code as well as the declaration. If a procedure or function is listed in the package specification, the declaration in the package body must match that in the package specification.

A package body can't be compiled if its respective package specification isn't already in place. The package body can be debugged, enhanced, or replaced without recompiling the package specification.

Following the declaration of the public and private subprograms in the package body, you can define an initialization section. You can use this section to initialize package variables. You can't pass parameters to the initialization section, and it is run only once, when you first call the package, in any given database session.

Executing packages

When you call a package, you actually reference one of its procedures or functions. To reference a packaged procedure or function, use dot notation. For example, use the syntax in the following example to call the RESERVE_BOOK procedure within the LIBRARY_MANAGEMENT package:

```
DECLARE
    student_id NUMBER := 1;
    book_id NUMBER := 43;
BEGIN
    library_management.reserve_book(student_id, book_id)
END;
/
```

Notice that the procedure is referenced by using both the package name and the procedure name, with the names being separated by a dot.

Overloading package interfaces

Overloading enables procedures and functions in a package to share the same name as long as their formal parameters differ in number, order, or datatype. This functionality is useful if you want to provide flexibility in terms of the arguments that you must pass to a procedure or a function when you invoke it. If, for example, you have a function that takes a date as an argument, perhaps you want to allow that date to be passed as both a DATE variable or as a character variable. Overloading allows you to do that.

Here's an example of overloading. The INSERT_LOAN_DATE function in this example is declared twice, once with a parameter of type DATE, and once with a parameter of type VARCHAR2:

```
CREATE OR REPLACE PACKAGE overload_example AS
   FUNCTION insert_loan_date
       (book_id IN INTEGER, loan_date IN DATE );
       RETURN REAL
FUNCTION insert_loan_date
       (book_id IN INTEGER, loan_date IN VARCHAR2 );
       RETURN REAL
END overload_example.
```

The fact that a function named INSERT_LOAN_DATE is declared twice means that you really have two completely different functions. When you invoke INSERT_LOAN_DATE, the datatype of the parameters that you pass determines which function actually gets executed. You need to write code for both versions in the package body.

Dropping packages

You can use the DROP PACKAGE statement to drop both the specification and the body or just the body of a package. The syntax for DROP_PACKAGE is as follows:

```
DROP PACKAGE [BODY] [schema.]package_name [FORCE];
```

The following list describes the elements in this syntax:

- ✦ BODY — Specifies that just the package body be dropped. The specification will remain.

- ✦ schema — Specifies the owner of the package. The default is the name of the currently logged-on user.

- ✦ package_name — The name of the package to drop.

- ✦ FORCE — Applies only to packages created with the pragma REPEATABLE, and forces those to be dropped even if other database objects depend on them.

To drop a package, you must either be the owner or you must have been granted the DROP ANY PROCEDURE privilege.

Using Triggers

Traditionally, triggers have been stored in PL/SQL blocks executed in response to data manipulation language (DML) statements on a table. Using triggers, you could write code to be executed in response to INSERT, UPDATE, or DELETE statements on a table. That code could then do some or all of the following:

- ✦ Prevent invalid data transactions

- ✦ Implement complex security
- ✦ Enforce referential integrity (RI) across nodes in a distributed database
- ✦ Create strategic and complex business rules
- ✦ Provide auditing
- ✦ Maintain synchronous tables
- ✦ Gather statistics on frequently modified tables

DML triggers are an old feature of Oracle and probably represent the most widely used type of trigger. Oracle8i implements some relatively new types of triggers as well. These include the following:

Instead-of triggers	Allow you to write code that is invoked when a user tries to insert, update, or delete through a view
Database event triggers	Allow you to write code that is invoked in response to database events such as startup and shutdown
DDL triggers	Allow you to write code that is invoked in response to data definition language (DDL) statements issued by a user

This section talks about the traditional DML triggers first and then covers the newer types of triggers that are now available.

Using DML triggers

DML triggers are those that fire in response to a data manipulation statement on a table. You use the CREATE TRIGGER statement to create DML triggers. Before creating a trigger, think through the following questions:

- ✦ To what table should the trigger be attached?
- ✦ For what event, or events, should the trigger fire?
- ✦ Should the trigger fire once for each row touched by the triggering DML statement, or should it fire once for each statement?
- ✦ Should the trigger fire before the event occurs or after it occurs?

The last three questions determine the basic type of a trigger.

Trigger Types

A trigger is said to *fire* when the defined event occurs on the table to which the trigger is attached. Three DML events, or statements, if you prefer, may cause a trigger to fire. The three statements are INSERT, UPDATE, and DELETE. In addition, you can also specify whether a trigger fires before the statement is executed or after. Triggers that execute prior to the triggering statement are called *before triggers*. Triggers that execute subsequent to the triggering statement are called *after triggers*. Finally, you can control whether the trigger fires once for each row affected by the statement in question. *Statement-level triggers* fire once per statement, regardless of how many rows are affected by that statement. *Row-level triggers* fire once for each row that the statement affects.

Row-level triggers are the only ones that have access to the data in the rows being changed. If your purpose in writing the trigger is to audit changes to the data in a table or to enforce business rules or referential integrity, or if it otherwise depends on the actual data in the affected rows, you should write a row-level trigger. Otherwise, consider a statement-level trigger.

Before triggers allow you to take action before an event occurs. For example, you can use a before-delete trigger to check whether a deletion should be allowed. The trigger can raise an error if there is a reason to disallow the deletion, and the statement will fail.

You can use an after trigger to perform the same function, but why let Oracle do all the work of deleting the record first, only to have to roll back the change afterwards? In general, use before triggers when you are enforcing business rules, when you are enforcing referential integrity, or when you want to modify data before it is changed. Use after triggers when you simply want to log or record changes that have occurred.

A DML Trigger

Let's use the library scenario to develop a trigger. Say that you have a business rule that disallows a student from borrowing a book if his or her book fines accrue to an amount greater than $10. That rule would be difficult, if not impossible, to enforce using Oracle's built-in referential integrity constraints. However, it's easy to enforce with a trigger.

The STUDENTS table in the sample database has a column named STUDENT_BL_STATUS. The purpose of this column is to indicate whether a given student is allowed to borrow a book. If the column contains a T, then the student can borrow books. If the column contains an F, then the student is prevented from borrowing books. The trick is to properly maintain that column using a trigger.

The following provides an example of the logic that you can go through when writing a trigger to maintain the STUDENT_BL_STATUS column:

✦ Because the value of STUDENT_BL_STATUS depends on the student's outstanding fine amount, the trigger should be attached to the STUDENTS_FINES table.

✦ The amount of the fine determines whether the status should be T or F. Because access to specific data is needed, the trigger must be a row-level trigger.

✦ The trigger isn't trying to prevent updates on the STUDENTS_FINES table. Rather, it's going to maintain a value in another table in harmony with a value in STUDENTS_FINES. Therefore, the trigger should be an after trigger. There's no point in modifying the STUDENTS table until after the changes have been successfully made to STUDENTS_FINES.

The trigger shown in Listing 24-8 will properly maintain the value of the STUDENT_BL_STATUS field in the STUDENTS table in response to changes in each student's outstanding fine amount.

Listing 24-8: **A trigger for maintaining a value**

```
CREATE OR REPLACE TRIGGER update_student_loan_status
AFTER INSERT OR UPDATE ON STUDENTS_FINES
FOR EACH ROW
BEGIN
    IF :NEW.sf_fine > 10 THEN
        UPDATE students
        SET student_bl_status ='F'
        WHERE students.student_id = :NEW.sf_student_id;
    ELSE
        UPDATE students
        SET student_bl_status ='T'
        WHERE students.student_id = :NEW.sf_student_id;
    END IF;
END;
/
```

Note   This trigger handles only insertions or updates, not deletes.

The code in this trigger is fairly straightforward. If the new fine is greater than $10, the STUDENT_BL_STATUS field for the student in question is set to F, thus preventing that student from borrowing any more books. When the outstanding fine drops back below $10, the flag will be set to T.

Notice the use of :NEW in the trigger's code. The :NEW parameter is a table alias automatically created by Oracle that allows you to access the new values for the row being changed. If you need to access the old values, you use :OLD.

Using instead-of triggers

Instead-of triggers were introduced in Oracle8 and allow you to write code that executes in response to a DML statement issued against a view. The words "instead of" are used to describe the trigger because the DML statement is never actually executed. The trigger's code takes its place. The result is that many views that you could previously use only in SELECT statements are now usable in INSERT, UPDATE, and DELETE statements as well. Like any other type of trigger, you create instead-of triggers by using the CREATE TRIGGER statement.

Nonupdateable Views

The problem of nonupdateable views is an old one. Views are often used to provide database security. Views are created that limit a user's access to the data in the underlying table, and the user is granted access only to the view and not the table. In cases where a user needs to update the table, and hence needs to update the view, that can cause problems. Not all views are updateable, meaning that not all views can be used in INSERT, UPDATE, or DELETE statements, at least not without writing instead-of triggers.

If you have a simple view on a single table, chances are that you will be able to insert records into that view, delete records through that view, and update through that view. These types of views are said to be inherently updateable, and you can't use them in any INSERT, UPDATE, or DELETE statement. Other types of views, however, are not inherently updateable. Specifically, any view containing one or more of the following constructs is not updateable:

- ✦ Aggregate functions such as AVG and COUNT
- ✦ A GROUP BY clause
- ✦ The DISTINCT keyword
- ✦ The CONNECT BY or START WITH clauses
- ✦ Certain types of joins

not updateable → instead of trigger (Ins. upd.)

With the release of Oracle8, Oracle relaxed the prohibitions against updating join views, and there are now many cases where you can update a join view without writing an instead-of trigger. If you have a join view, you can check the data dictionary to see which columns in that view, if any, are updateable. The data dictionary views to look at are USER_UPDATABLE_COLUMNS, ALL_UPDATABLE_COLUMNS, and DBA_UPDATABLE_COLUMNS. These give you information about your views, views to which you have been granted access, and all views in the database, respectively.

If you have a view that contains one of the constructs listed in this section and you still want to update it, you need to create an instead-of trigger. This trigger provides code that Oracle executes in place of whatever DML statement you issue.

An Instead-of Trigger Example

The following SQL creates a view that joins three tables: STUDENTS, BOOKS, and BOOKS_LOANED. It returns a list of all students, together with any books that they may have borrowed. The SQL does an outer join between STUDENTS and

BOOKS_LOANED so that all students show in the view, regardless of whether they have borrowed a book.

```
CREATE OR REPLACE VIEW students_and_books AS
SELECT student_id, first_name, last_name,
       bl_book_id, book_title
FROM students, books_loaned, books
WHERE student_id = bl_student_id(+)
AND bl_book_id = book_id(+);
```

If you create this view, you can check USER_UPDATABLE_COLUMNS to see if it is updateable. For this view, none of the columns will be updateable. Here's how you check:

```
SQL> SELECT column_name, updatable, insertable, deletable
  2  FROM user_updatable_columns
  3  WHERE table_name='STUDENTS_AND_BOOKS';

COLUMN_NAME                        UPD INS DEL
-------------------------------    --- --- ---
STUDENT_ID                         NO  NO  NO
FIRST_NAME                         NO  NO  NO
LAST_NAME                          NO  NO  NO
BL_BOOK_ID                         NO  NO  NO
BOOK_TITLE                         NO  NO  NO
```

Now let's say that you want to allow deletions to be made from this view. Your first task, then, is to decide just what it means to delete a record from this view. Does it mean to delete the student, the book, or just the loan?

For purposes of our example, let's assume that a deletion from the STUDENTS_AND _BOOKS view should be interpreted as a deletion of the loan. To delete the record of a loan, you need to do the following:

✦ Delete the loan record from the BOOKS_LOANED table.

✦ Delete the loan ID from the BOOKS table.

The instead-of trigger shown in Listing 24-9 will accomplish these tasks and will fire in response to a DELETE against the STUDENTS_AND_BOOKS view.

Listing 24-9: An instead-of trigger for deleting a loan ID and record

```
CREATE OR REPLACE TRIGGER students_and_books_delete
INSTEAD OF DELETE ON students_and_books
REFERENCING OLD AS old NEW AS new
```

```
BEGIN
   --First, delete the loan data from BOOKS.
   UPDATE books
      SET book_loan_id = NULL,
          book_due = NULL
   WHERE book_id = :old.bl_book_id;

   --Then delete the actual loan record.
   DELETE FROM books_loaned
   WHERE bl_book_id = :old.bl_book_id;
END;
/
```

This trigger turns a delete from the STUDENTS_AND_BOOKS view into two operations: an update of BOOKS and a delete from BOOKS_LOANED. By using instead-of statements like this, you can control the meaning of DML statements issued against a view.

Using database event triggers

Oracle8i lets you write triggers that fire in response to certain database events. These allow you to write code that executes automatically in response to a user logon, database startup, and so forth.

 Caution   Be very careful when experimenting with database event triggers. They affect all database users, and if you create one with errors, it can affect all database users. A logon trigger that doesn't compile correctly will prevent all database users from connecting. The only way to log on and drop such a trigger is to connect as INTERNAL or as SYSDBA.

Supported Events

Five events are supported for use in event triggers:

SERVERERROR	You can write triggers that fire after a server error has occurred.
LOGON	You can write triggers that fire after a user logs on to the database.
LOGOFF	You can write triggers that fire before a user logs off the database.
STARTUP	You can write triggers that fire immediately after the database is opened.
SHUTDOWN	You can write triggers that fire whenever an instance is shut down.

Note that triggers defined for the events listed here can be either before triggers or after triggers, but not both. Which type you can have depends on the event. For example, it would be pretty difficult to have a before startup trigger because the database must be running before a trigger can even be executed.

You can apply the LOGON and LOGOFF trigger types to specific database users. You can define the other triggers only for the database as a whole.

Database Event Attributes

To make these triggers more useful, you can reference several predefined attributes from the code that a trigger executes. These attributes, some of which are event-specific, allow you to determine who the current user is, what specific error occurred, and so forth. Table 24-1 lists these attributes.

Table 24-1
Database Event Attributes

Attribute	Description
sys.sysevent	Valid in all event triggers. Returns a 20-character string containing the name of the event that caused the trigger to fire.
sys.instance_num	Valid in all event triggers. Returns a number identifying the instance causing the trigger to fire.
sys.database_name	Valid in all event triggers. Actually returns the database *brand* name, not the database name. This will be "ORACLE."
sys.server_error (stack_position)	Valid in SERVERERROR triggers. Returns the error number from the specified position in the error stack. The most recent error will be in position 1.
is_servererror (error_number)	Valid in SERVERROR triggers. Returns TRUE if the specified error number is in the error stack. Otherwise, returns FALSE. This is a function and is not preceded by sys.
sys.login_user	Valid in all event triggers. Returns the name of the user causing the trigger to fire.

You can use these so-called attributes in your PL/SQL code much like you would use a function. For example, you might use sys.login_user in an IF statement so that you can execute user-specific code in a logon trigger:

```
IF sys.login_user = 'SYSTEM' THEN
   ...
```

The error stack referred to in the descriptions for sys.server_error and is_servererror refers to the fact that when an error occurs, it is usually reported at several levels. The following error, taken from some SQL*Plus output, illustrates this:

```
ERROR at line 1:
ORA-01722: invalid number
ORA-06512: at "AMY.STUDENTS_AND_BOOKS_DELETE", line 5
ORA-04088: error during execution of trigger
'AMY.STUDENTS_AND_BOOKS_DELETE'
```

This message actually lists three errors, and this is fairly typical of how Oracle works. As an error percolates its way up from a deeply nested procedure, more messages keep getting placed onto the stack. You can use the is_servererror function, available in SERVERERROR triggers, to check the entire stack for a specific error. You can use the sys.servererror function to retrieve errors one at a time from the stack.

An Event Trigger Example

To create a trigger on a database event, you must have the ADMINISTER_DATABASE_TRIGGER system privilege. Normally, that's conferred on database administrators as a result of having been granted the DBA role, but it can also be granted separately.

One possible use of a database event trigger is to pin frequently used PL/SQL packages into memory so that they will already be loaded when users invoke them. The following database startup trigger automatically pins the package named DBMS_STANDARD:

```
CREATE TRIGGER pin_packages
AFTER STARTUP ON DATABASE
BEGIN
    dbms_shared_pool.keep('sys.dbms_standard');
END;
/
```

Note You must create the DBMS_SHARED_POOL package before creating this trigger. To do that, you must run the script in $ORACLE_HOME/rdbms/admin named DBM-SPOOL.SQL while logged on as the user named SYS. Once created, you must grant EXECUTE on that package to the user creating the database startup trigger.

Pinning packages into memory at startup ensures that they are already loaded when they are needed and that they stay in memory for as long as the database is up and running. Pinning frequently used packages improves performance if it prevents them from having to be constantly reread from disk each time they are used.

Using DDL triggers

DDL triggers are triggers that execute in response to CREATE, ALTER, or DELETE statements that affect schema objects. You can define DDL triggers to fire either before or after one of these events.

You create DDL triggers using the CREATE TRIGGER statement, but the syntax is a bit unusual as compared to that used for the other trigger types. When you create a DDL trigger, you can define the scope to be the entire database, or you can define the scope to be one schema or a list of schemas. The ON clause of the CREATE TRIGGER statement takes this form:

```
ON {DATABASE|schema_name.SCHEMA}
```

The DATABASE keyword causes the trigger to fire in response to the specified DDL event regardless of the schema that is affected. The *schema_name*.SCHEMA syntax is a little unusual. The word SCHEMA here is a keyword, and it follows the actual schema name. You separate the schema name and the keyword SCHEMA by a dot. For example, if you want a trigger to fire whenever an object is created in the AMY schema, you would specify ON amy.SCHEMA in the CREATE TRIGGER statement.

Note   Users can create DDL triggers on their own schema as long as they have the CREATE TRIGGER privilege.

DDL Event Attributes

As with database event triggers, DDL event triggers can also use various attributes to determine which event fired the trigger, which object is being affected, in which schema the object resides, and so forth. Table 24-2 describes these attributes.

Table 24-2 DDL Event Attributes	
Attribute	**Description**
sys.sysevent	Valid in all event triggers. Returns a 20-character string containing the name of the event that caused the trigger to fire.
sys.instance_num	Valid in all event triggers. Returns a number identifying the instance causing the trigger to fire.
sys.database_name	Valid in all event triggers. Actually returns the database *brand* name, not the database name. This will be "ORACLE."

Attribute	Description
sys.login_user	Valid in all event triggers. Returns the name of the user causing the trigger to fire.
sys.dictionary_obj_type	Valid in DDL event triggers. Returns the type of object that was created, altered, or dropped.
sys.dictionary_obj_name	Valid in DDL event triggers. Returns the name of the object that was created, altered, or dropped.
sys.dictionary_obj_owner	Valid in DDL event triggers. Returns the name of the object's owner.

The second example in the next section shows how you can use these attributes in your code.

A DDL Trigger Example

The following example shows a simple DDL trigger that will help prevent someone from accidentally dropping objects owned by the user SYSTEM:

```
CREATE OR REPLACE TRIGGER no_drop
BEFORE DROP
ON system.SCHEMA
BEGIN
   raise_application_error(
      -20000,'Can''t drop objects owned by SYSTEM.');
END;
/
```

This trigger was created using ON system.SCHEMA, and it is a BEFORE DROP trigger. All it needs to do is raise an error. The trigger definition ensures that it fires at the right time.

Note   While interesting exercises, the triggers shown here don't absolutely prevent the possibility of accidentally deleting an object. For one thing, the trigger owner can always disable the trigger with a command like the following:

```
ALTER TRIGGER no_drop DISABLE;
```

In fact, to delete one of these triggers, you need to disable it first. Also, event triggers are never fired when you are logged on as SYS, INTERNAL, or SYSDBA.

Here is an alternative solution that uses a database-level trigger to accomplish the same feat. To ensure that it is protecting the right schema, the code references the `sys.dictionary_obj_owner` attribute:

```
CREATE OR REPLACE TRIGGER no_drop
BEFORE DROP
ON DATABASE
BEGIN
    IF sys.dictionary_obj_owner = 'SYSTEM' THEN
        raise_application_error(
            -20000,'Can''t drop objects owned by SYSTEM.');
    END IF;
END;
/
```

Note   You will need to drop the first version of the NO_DROP trigger before you can cre-ate the second. If you create the NO_DROP trigger while logged on as the user SYSTEM, you will either need to disable it first or you will need to log on as SYS, INTERNAL, or SYSDBA to delete it.

Summary

In this chapter, you learned:

✦ Using stored procedures allows you to develop and deploy well-tested code in the database. Applications can then call upon this code as needed. Having the code stored in the database also helps minimize network traffic.

✦ Stored procedures don't return a value, and you create them by using the CREATE PROCEDURE statement. Stored functions do return a value, and you create them using the CREATE FUNCTION statement.

✦ Packages provide a way to group related procedures and functions into one unit. Packages also provide for the separation of the code from the interface specification.

✦ Oracle8i supports four types of triggers: DML triggers, instead-of triggers, database event triggers, and DDL triggers. DML triggers are those that execute in response to INSERT, UPDATE, and DELETE statements on a table. You use instead-of triggers to make views updateable by providing code that gets executed when a user updates the view. Database event triggers allow you to have PL/SQL code executed in response to significant database events such as startup and shutdown. DDL triggers execute in response to CREATE, ALTER, and DROP statements when those statements affect objects that a user owns.

✦ Use extreme care when creating database event triggers, especially those involving the logon event. A logon trigger with an error can prevent everyone from logging on to the database.

✦   ✦   ✦

Using Oracle8i's Auditing Features

In today's high-data-transaction environments, there is always a requirement to monitor what is going on within a system. You must know more than who is connected, and from which host. You may need to gather statistics, monitor data access, or watch for potentially suspicious activity. You can do all of these things using Oracle8i's auditing features.

Oracle8i's auditing features allow you to track access to tables, the use of privileges, and the use of specific SQL statements. In addition, because the Internet has become a popular method of implementing a three-tier system, Oracle8i now provides a way to track middle-tier connections made on behalf of end users. This chapter provides a detailed exploration of Oracle8i's auditing concepts and audit implementation techniques.

Oracle8i Auditing Concepts

With all the auditing features available in Oracle8i, it is easy to get carried away auditing too much. The result can be an overwhelmingly detailed audit log, one so detailed that you never bother to look at it. When considering a database audit, first clarify the reason — or reasons — for the audit in conjunction with the types of auditing facilitated by the Oracle8i server. Then, limit your auditing effort to the minimum required to achieve your goals.

Why audit a database?

Auditing a database involves the recording and analysis of information, which is based on selected database operations executed by users. The motives for auditing user activity fall into two main categories:

✦ **Monitoring errant or unauthorized user activity.** Organizational data is the backbone of any company. If you modify data or drop tables important to the operation of internal systems, the database provides erroneous results. The database security administrator must provide solutions to such scenarios, and without a database audit trail, the root of such situations could remain a mystery.

✦ **Monitoring database statistics.** Auditing certain database operations provides an essential understanding of how the database is used. These statistics enable database designers to enhance the database's physical design or even answer some database root-cause analysis problems. The amount of information gathered from such monitoring feeds the data/information/knowledge cycle.

Auditing options offered by Oracle8i

Oracle8i permits three types of auditing: statement, privilege, and schema object. These types provide a flexible approach to implementing any auditing scenario. All three types of auditing are implemented using various forms of the AUDIT statement.

Statement Auditing

Statement auditing allows you to audit specific SQL statements executed by users. It offers no provision for tracking the schema objects referenced by those statements. The basic syntax for this kind of auditing command follows:

```
AUDIT option, option,
[BY [ username | proxy_name [ ON BEHALF OF [ ANY | username ] ]
] ]
[BY [ SESSION | ACCESS]]
[WHENEVER [NOT] SUCCESSFUL]
```

Use statement auditing on these two groups of SQL statements:

✦ DDL statements, with respect to specific database object types, not specific objects. For example, the following audit command audits all CREATE TABLE and DROP TABLE statements:

```
AUDIT TABLE;
```

✦ DML statements, with respect to a particular type of database object operation, but not specifically an operation on a named object. For example, the following audit command initiates auditing for all SELECT FROM TABLE statements, irrespective of the table on which the SQL statement executes:

```
AUDIT SELECT TABLE;
```

Statement auditing can be broad or focused in scope; use statement auditing to audit activities of all users or a selected subset of users.

Privilege Auditing

Privilege auditing audits the use of system privileges such as CREATE TABLE or SELECT ANY TABLE. You can audit the use of any system privilege. The general syntax for this form of auditing is as follows:

```
AUDIT [option | ALL ]
ON [username.]objectname
[BY [SESSION|ACCESS]]
[WHENEVER [NOT] SUCCESSFUL]
```

Privilege auditing is more focused than statement auditing because each option audits only specific types of system privileges, not a related set of statements. For example, the statement audit option AUDIT TABLE audits the CREATE TABLE, DROP TABLE, and ALTER TABLE SQL statements, while the privilege audit option CREATE TABLE audits only CREATE TABLE SQL statements. The privilege audit option for monitoring the creation of all tables follows:

```
AUDIT CREATE TABLE;
```

Note If similar statement and privilege audit options are set — for example, the AUDIT TABLE statement audit option and the AUDIT CREATE TABLE privilege audit option — only a single record is generated in the audit trail when an event falls into both categories.

You can set privilege auditing to audit system privilege activities of a selected user or all users of a database.

Schema Object Auditing

Schema object auditing audits specific DML statements on a specified schema object. You can audit SQL statements that reference the following object types: tables, views, sequences, stored procedures, functions, and packages. Schema object auditing is implemented using the following syntax:

```
AUDIT [option | ALL ]
ON [username.]objectname
[BY [SESSION|ACCESS]]
[WHENEVER [NOT] SUCCESSFUL]
```

The following list shows the DML statements that will be recorded as the result of schema object auditing:

```
ALTER
AUDIT
COMMENT
DELETE
EXECUTE
```

```
GRANT
INDEX
INSERT
LOCK
RENAME
SELECT
UPDATE
```

For example, `AUDIT SELECT ON` tablename audits all SQL `SELECT` statements executed against the specified table. If objects are indirectly referenced by synonyms, clusters, or indexes, they can be audited by setting schema object audit statements on their respective base tables.

Note If schema object auditing is set on a table and its view, a `SELECT` operation on the view generates two audit records.

Because it only audits a specific DML statement on a schema object, schema object auditing is very focused. Schema object auditing always applies to all users of the database.

Focusing the Auditing Options

Oracle8i enables you to focus statement, privilege, and schema object auditing with the following techniques:

✦ You may limit your auditing to successful SQL statement executions, unsuccessful SQL statement executions, or both.

✦ You may specify that SQL statement executions are recorded once per user session or every time the SQL statement is executed.

Auditing successful or unsuccessful SQL execution

This type of constraint focuses the Oracle8i auditing efforts on SQL operations that are successful, unsuccessful, or both. An unsuccessful SQL operation is a valid SQL statement that fails due to a lack of permissions to execute completely or a reference to a nonexistent schema object. The syntax for implementing this audit focus strategy involves using one of the two following clauses with your `AUDIT` command:

```
WHENEVER SUCCESSFUL
WHENEVER NOT SUCCESSFUL
```

If neither line is mentioned in the audit syntax, both successful and unsuccessful SQL statement executions are audited.

Session and access auditing

The `BY SESSION` and `BY ACCESS` auditing type constraints dictate when audit records should be generated. The `BY SESSION` constraint setting inserts only one audit record in the audit trail for each audit option execution during the user's session.

For example, the following auditing command audits `SELECT` commands for the `BOOKS_LOANED` table:

```
AUDIT SELECT ON AMY.BOOKS_LOANED BY SESSION;
```

User `TONY` connects to the database and executes five `SELECT` statements on the `BOOKS_LOANED` table. Oracle8i generates only one audit record because you specified the `BY SESSION` option. The `BY ACCESS` constraint setting generates an audit record into the audit trail for each audit option execution. For example, if you set `BY ACCESS` for the previous example, `TONY` generates five audit records into the audit trail. You can only set the following audit operations using the `BY ACCESS` audit option constraint:

✦ All statement audit options that audit DDL operations

✦ All privilege audit options that audit DDL statements

For all other audit options, `BY SESSION` is the default.

Auditing by user

Statement and privilege auditing options permit auditing on SQL statements issued by a specific or general user in a database. You can use the `BY USER` auditing constraint to minimize the number of audit records generated. For example, use the following syntax to enforce the statement auditing option on the `SELECT` statement by the users `TONY` and `KRISTY`:

```
AUDIT SELECT TABLE by TONY, KRISTY
```

Schema object auditing options cannot be constrained to specific users.

Auditing by proxy

A new feature of Oracle8i is the ability to audit by proxy. A *proxy* is a new feature of Oracle8i that allows middleware (such as an application server) to log on as a user without passing the user's password to the database. Sending passwords to the database is a possible security leak, especially if the transaction is done across the Internet.

Before you can audit by proxy, you must set up a user and the middleware with a proxy relationship. The `ALTER USER` command has a new parameter for this. The syntax is as follows:

```
ALTER USER user_name GRANT  CONNECT THROUGH proxy_name
[ WITH ROLE [ALL EXCEPT ] role_name ]
```

The `user_name` is the end user. The `proxy_name` parameter specifies the name of the Oracle user with which the middleware (application server) logs on to the database. Omitting the `WITH ROLE` clause gives the proxy the same roles as the user.

For example, a Web-database application server logs on as `WEBAPP`. The end user named `JOHN` logs on to the Web application and queries the database. The application server queries the database as the proxy of `JOHN`. As the proxy, the application is able to query all the tables that `JOHN` is allowed to query. To tell the database to use `WEBAPP` as `JOHN`'s proxy, issue the following command:

```
ALTER USER JOHN GRANT CONNECT THROUGH WEBAPP;
```

The middleware verifies the user's identity by requiring a name and password, or any other sort of validation it wants. It then acts as the user's proxy (or representative) when accessing the database. The database validates the identity of the middleware and assumes that the middleware is a familiar and trustworthy entry point into the database.

Even though the user logged on to Oracle is named `WEBAPP`, Oracle knows that it is really `JOHN` on the other side of the application. The application has many end users for which it is a proxy. The auditing thread between the end user and the database activity would be lost without new functionality to take proxies into account.

Oracle8i has added the `BY PROXY` clause into the `AUDIT` command for handling these new forms of activity. The syntax is as follows:

```
AUDIT option BY PROXY [ ON BAHALF OF [ ANY | user_name ] ];
```

Continuing with our example, let's say you want to audit all the query activity that user `JOHN` has done through the `WEBAPP` proxy. The command for auditing would be as follows:

```
AUDIT SELECT TABLE BY WEBAPP ON BEHALF OF JOHN;
```

To stop the auditing, use the `NOAUDIT` command, as shown here:

```
NOAUDIT SELECT TABLE BY WEBAPP ON BEHALF OF JOHN;
```

To end the proxy relationship between the proxy and the user, use the `ALTER USER` command, as follows:

```
ALTER USER JOHN REVOKE CONNECT THROUGH WEBAPP;
```

Implementing Oracle8i Auditing

Now that you have seen the basics of Oracle8i auditing concepts, let's implement auditing in an Oracle8i database. Implementing Oracle8i auditing involves enabling auditing at the database level using an initialization parameter. Then you begin enabling and disabling auditing options on statements, privileges, or schema objects. The statement, privilege, and schema object auditing options can be enabled or disabled using the `AUDIT` command.

Enabling Oracle8i auditing

To enable auditing, you must modify the AUDIT_TRAIL initialization parameter in the database parameter file. This modification controls whether Oracle8i generates audit records into the audit trail, regardless of whether statement, privilege, and schema object auditing have been defined. By default, auditing is completely disabled and the parameter is set to NONE. The following list contains valid AUDIT_TRAIL parameter values:

✦ DB — Enables database auditing and directs all audit records to the database audit trail

✦ OS — Enables database auditing by directing audit records to the operating system audit trail

✦ NONE — Disables auditing (the default value)

Enabling auditing options

Use the AUDIT command to enable statement, privilege, and schema object auditing. To set statement and privilege audit options, you must have the AUDIT SYSTEM system privilege. To set auditing for schema object auditing, you must own the object or have the AUDIT ANY system privilege. You can use the following audit constraints in conjunction with the AUDIT command to limit the audit scope:

```
WHENEVER SUCCESSFUL/ WHENEVER NOT SUCCESSFUL
BY SESSION/BY ACCESS
```

When a session is created, the current auditing options are retrieved from the data dictionary. These auditing options exist for the life of the session. Setting or modifying audit options causes all subsequent sessions to use the new options, while existing sessions still continue to use the audit options in place at their creation. In contrast, changes to schema object audit options are immediately effective for current sessions.

Note   The AUDIT command only activates auditing options; it does not enable Oracle8i auditing as a whole.

To audit all unsuccessful connections to the database BY SESSION, regardless of user, use the following command:

```
AUDIT SESSION WHENEVER NOT SUCCESSFUL;
```

To audit all unsuccessful connections to the database by a specified user (TONY), use the following command:

```
AUDIT SESSION BY TONY WHENEVER NOT SUCCESSFUL;
```

To audit all unsuccessful INSERT, DELETE, and DROP ANY TABLE system privileges on all tables, use BY ACCESS, which requires two statements, as follows:

```
AUDIT INSERT TABLE, DELETE TABLE
    BY ACCESS
    WHENEVER NOT SUCCESSFUL;
AUDIT DROP ANY TABLE
    BY ACCESS
    WHENEVER NOT SUCCESSFUL;
```

To audit all successful DELETE commands on the STUDENTS table, use BY ACCESS as follows:

```
AUDIT DELETE ON AMY.STUDENTS
    BY ACCESS
    WHENEVER SUCCESSFUL;
```

Disabling audit options

The NOAUDIT command disables existing enabled auditing options. It can include the BY USER constraint to disable auditing of certain users selectively. You can also use the constraint WHENEVER to limit the disable scope to the constraint — not the entire audit option. Some examples of the NOAUDIT command follow:

```
NOAUDIT SESSION;
NOAUDIT DELETE ANY TABLE;
NOAUDIT DELETE ON AMY.STUDENTS
    WHENEVER NOT SUCCESSFUL;
```

The Oracle8i Audit Trail

Audit records can be stored in the database, in a table owned by the user SYS, or in an operating system file. The Oracle8i audit trail table is the table named AUD$ in the SYS schema of each Oracle8i database. Several views allow you to query and report on this information.

The generation and insertion of an audit trail record is independent of a user's transaction. If a user rolls back a transaction, the audit record is still generated and committed. Audit records are never generated by sessions established for the user SYS or as INTERNAL. The following events are always audited, and are logged on the database alert log, regardless of whether Oracle8i auditing is enabled: instance startup, instance shutdown, and administrative connections.

Each audit trail record can contain different types of information, depending on the DML and DDL SQL operations audited and the auditing constraints set. The following information is always recorded:

✦ The user's name

✦ The session identifier

- ✦ The terminal identifier
- ✦ The name of the schema object accessed
- ✦ The operation performed or attempted
- ✦ The completion code of the operation
- ✦ The date and timestamp
- ✦ The system privileges used

Either Oracle8i or the operating system (OS) audit trail can store all the database audit records. Let's look at the advantages of using each audit storage mechanism.

Operating system audit trail

The OS audit trails enable you to consolidate auditing information from your environment and other applications, not just from Oracle8i. This consolidation can provide a bigger picture of the system operations under observation. However, you may need to write custom software to report on it. The following codes are encoded in an operating system audit trail and need to be decoded for interpretation:

- ✦ Action Code describes the operation performed. The AUDIT_ACTIONS data dictionary table contains a list of codes and their respective descriptions.
- ✦ Privileges Used describes system privileges used to perform an action. The table SYSTEM_PRIVILEGE_MAP lists all of these codes and their respective descriptions.
- ✦ Completion Code describes the result of an attempted operation. A successful operation returns a value of 0, while unsuccessful operations return the respective Oracle8i error code describing why the operation was unsuccessful.

The database audit trail

With the database audit trail, Oracle8i provides several predefined views that allow Oracle8i to report audit information in many ways. You can use database tools such as Oracle Reports, PowerBuilder, or even SQL*Plus to generate custom audit reports.

Note   The database audit trail does not store information about data values that may have been changed by a SQL statement.

Implementing the Oracle8i Audit Trail Views

Oracle8i provides several predefined views to interpret the audited information back to users in a more meaningful way. To implement these views, connect to the Oracle8i database as the SYS user and run the CATAUDIT.SQL script with the SQL*Plus or the Oracle SQLPlus Worksheet tools.

Executing the CATAUDIT.SQL script creates the views shown in Listing 25-1. For those views that are the most useful to you, a short description follows the view name.

Listing 25-1: Views created by running the CATAUDIT.SQL script

```
ALL_DEF_AUDIT_OPTS
AUDIT_ACTIONS - A list of code numbers and their meaning.
                The codes appear in the AUD$ table.
DBA_AUDIT_EXISTS
DBA_AUDIT_OBJECT - Audit trail for objects.
DBA_AUDIT_SESSION - Audit trail for user sessions.
DBA_AUDIT_STATEMENT - Audit trail for statements.
DBA_AUDIT_TRAIL - All audit trail records.
DBA_OBJ_AUDIT_OPTS - Current auditing settings for objects.
DBA_STMT_AUDIT_OPTS - Current auditing settings for DML and
                      DDL statements STMT_AUDIT_OPTION_MAP.
USER_AUDIT_OBJECT
USER_AUDIT_SESSION
USER_AUDIT_SESSION
USER_AUDIT_STATEMENT
USER_AUDIT_TRAIL - audit trail for a user.
USER_OBJ_AUDIT_OPTS
USER_TAB_AUDIT_OPTS
```

Querying the Oracle8i Audit Trail Views

Using the views listed above and the SYS.AUD$ and SYS.AUDIT_OPTIONS tables, you should be able to report on any portion of the audit trail you need. For example, if you want to look at the audit trail for the user named PREM, you can use the query shown in Figure 25-1, which illustrates the results set produced from executing a SELECT statement on the USER_AUDIT_TRAIL view during an audit of the BOOKS_LOANED table. Access the views by executing SQL statements against them in the SQL*Plus or Oracle SQL Worksheet tools.

```
SQLWKS> SELEC OWNER,OBJ_NAME
2> ACTION, ACTION_NAME, SESSIONID, ENTRYID, RETURNCODE
3> FROM SYS.USER_AUDIT_TRAIL
4>WHEREOBJ_NAME='BOOKS_LOANED'
5>
```

OS_USERNAME	USERNAME	TERMINAL	TIMESTAMP	OWNER	OBJ_NAME	ACTION	ACTION_NAME	SESSIONID	ENTRYID	RETURNCODE
Sulaco	PREM	SULACO	29-Oct-97	PREM	BOOKS_LOANED	2	INSERT	132	1	2291
Sulaco	PREM	SULACO	29-Oct-97	PREM	BOOKS_LOANED	2	INSERT	137	1	0
Sulaco	PREM	SULACO	29-Oct-97	PREM	BOOKS_LOANED	2	INSERT	137	2	0
Sulaco	PREM	SULACO	29-Oct-97	PREM	BOOKS_LOANED	2	INSERT	137	3	0
Sulaco	PREM	SULACO	29-Oct-97	PREM	BOOKS_LOANED	2	INSERT	137	4	0
Sulaco	PREM	SULACO	29-Oct-97	PREM	BOOKS_LOANED	7	DELETE	138	2	0
Sulaco	PREM	SULACO	29-Oct-97	PREM	BOOKS_LOANED	4	DELETE	138	3	0

7 rows selected

Figure 25-1: Audit trail records contain user, session, object, and other identifiers.

The following query looks at all your auditing records, listing them in descending order by date and time:

```
SELECT TO_CHAR(TIMESTAMP#,'MM/DD/YY HH:MI:SS') TIMESTAMP,
USERID,  AA.NAME ACTION,
OBJ$CREATOR||'.'||OBJ$NAME OBJECT_NAME
FROM SYS.AUD$ AT, SYS.AUDIT_ACTIONS AA
WHERE AT.ACTION# = AA.ACTION
ORDER BY TIMESTAMP# DESC;
```

If you disable Oracle8i auditing as a whole, you can use the CATNOAUD.SQL script to remove the preceding audit views.

Managing the audit trail

Although the whole auditing process is relatively inexpensive, strictly follow these audit guidelines to avoid fragmented auditing and uncontrolled growth of the system tablespace:

1. Audit generally and then audit specifically. The accumulation of some foundation information provides a better framework for auditing options and constraints.

2. Archive audit records and purge the audit trails to stop the SYSTEM tablespace from filling up.

3. Turn off unrequired audit options to focus the audit, or try other audit options.

Controlling the Growth of the Audit Trail

If the audit trail becomes completely full and no more audit records can be inserted, audited statements cannot successfully execute until you purge the audit trail. The database security administrator must control the growth of the database audit trail. The database audit trail grows in accordance with two factors:

✦ The number of audit options turned on (such as BY SESSION or BY ACCESS)

✦ The frequency of executed audited statements

The maximum size of the audit trails is predetermined at the time of database creation. To maintain the SYS.AUD$ table, you cannot move it to another tablespace as a means of controlling growth. You can modify the initial storage parameter accordingly, however.

Purging the Audit Records from the Audit Trail

To free the SYSTEM tablespace and manage the audit trail, you need to purge the SYS.AUD$ table at set times in respect to its growth pattern. There are several ways to purge audit records, as described here. To delete all audit trail records, execute the following command:

```
DELETE FROM SYS.AUD$;
```

You can also delete specific records, such as all records for the STUDENTS table, as follows:

```
DELETE FROM SYS.AUD$ WHERE objname = 'STUDENTS';
```

You can also archive the audit records by exporting them to an operating system file or using the following statement:

```
INSERT INTO audit_temp SELECT * FROM SYS.AUD$;
```

Note   Only the SYS user, who holds the DELETE ANY TABLE system privilege, and any user granted the DELETE privilege on SYS.AUD$ by the user SYS can delete records.

If the audit trail fills and an auditing option is enabled BY SESSION, users will not be able to connect to the database. In this situation, the SYS user must connect and delete the records. The SYS user is not audited and can make space available.

Reducing the Size of the Audit Trails

As with any database table, used extents remain after records are deleted from the audit trail, thus causing the SYS.AUD$ to show an incorrect size. The following procedures enable you to reduce the size of the SYS.AUD$ table and provide better management of the audit trail:

1. Copy or export the data out of the SYS.AUD$ table.

2. Connect to the database with administrative privileges.

3. Truncate the SYS.AUD$ table using the TRUNCATE TABLE command.

4. Reload the archived audit trail records into the SYS.AUD$ table.

Note   SYS.AUD$ is the only SYS schema object you can modify directly.

Protecting the Audit Trail

To protect the integrity of the audit records and guarantee accuracy of the audit trail, put the following procedures in place:

◆ Grant the DELETE ANY TABLE system privilege to system administrators only.

◆ Audit changes to the audit trail by using the following:

```
AUDIT INSERT, UPDATE, DELETE ON SYS.AUD$ BY ACCESS;
```

Using Triggers to Implement Auditing

You can use triggers to supplement Oracle8i's auditing features. Triggers record detailed information about the data used in the SQL statements, and triggers give you more control over what gets audited. Triggers are most useful when you need to audit changes to the data in a table, because triggers allow you to record both the before and after images of rows that are changed. You can't do that using Oracle's built-in auditing features.

Generally, when using triggers to audit changes to data, you should use AFTER triggers. That way you don't waste time and I/O resources recording changes, only to have them rolled back in the event that the triggering statement fails.

Setting up trigger auditing

Conduct the following tasks before creating a trigger for auditing:

1. Identify the data values that need to be audited — constrained by the preceding points.

2. Create a table to contain the audit trail based on the data values modified by the audit trigger.

Note   Create the audit trail table in a different schema to allow better tablespace management and data segregation from the audited tables.

You have to set the triggering event on the audit trigger appropriately to capture the necessary actions on the audited table.

Creating audit triggers by example

Let's use the preceding framework to implement trigger auditing on the BOOKS_LOANED table owned by the user AMY. The following data columns need to be audited in the BOOKS_LOANED table:

✦ BL_BOOK_ID

✦ BL_STUDENT_ID

✦ BL_LOAN_DATE

✦ BL_FINE

Create a table to contain the BOOKS_LOANED audit data using the following command:

```
CREATE TABLE AUDIT_BOOKS_LOANED (
AUDIT_ID              NUMBER(5) PRIMARY KEY,
AUDIT_BOOK_ID         NUMBER(5) ,
AUDIT_STUDENT_ID      NUMBER(5) ,
AUDIT_LOAN_DATE       DATE ,
AUDIT_BOOK_FINE       NUMBER(5,2),
AUDIT_ACTION          VARCHAR2(10),
AUDIT_DATE            DATE  DEFAULT (SYSDATE));
```

Now, create a trigger that will record INSERT, UPDATE, and DELETE operations on the BOOKS_LOANED table, as shown in Listing 25-2.

Listing 25-2: Creating a trigger to record operations on the BOOKS_LOANED table

```
CREATE OR REPLACE TRIGGER rt_Audit_books_loaned
BEFORE INSERT OR UPDATE OR DELETE ON BOOKS_LOANED
FOR EACH ROW
DECLARE
Trigger_action      VARCHAR2(10);
BEGIN
IF UPDATING THEN
    Trigger_action:= 'Update';
    INSERT INTO AUDIT_BOOKS_LOANED
    VALUES (AUDIT_BOOKS_LOANED_SEQ.nextval,:old.BL_BOOK_ID,
    :old.BL_STUDENT_ID,:old.BL_LOAN_DATE,:new.BL_FINE,
    Trigger_action, SYSDATE);
END IF;
IF DELETING    THEN
    Trigger_action:= 'Delete';
    INSERT INTO AUDIT_BOOKS_LOANED
     VALUES
     (AUDIT_BOOKS_LOANED_SEQ.nextval,:old.BL_BOOK_ID,:old.BL_
     STUDENT_ID, :old.BL_LOAN_DATE,:old.BL_FINE,Trigger_action,
     SYSDATE);
END IF;
IF INSERTING THEN
    Trigger_action:= 'Insert';
    INSERT INTO AUDIT_BOOKS_LOANED
    VALUES
    (AUDIT_BOOKS_LOANED_SEQ.nextval,:new.BL_BOOK_ID,:new.BL_
    STUDENT_ID, :new.BL_LOAN_DATE,:new.BL_FINE, Trigger_action,
    SYSDATE);
END IF;
END;
```

Summary

In this chapter, you learned:

✦ The audit feature within Oracle8i can monitor potentially suspicious user activity as well as provide statistics on how the database is being accessed and used.

✦ Oracle8i can audit database operations at the following levels: SQL statement, system privilege, and schema object.

✦ You can narrow the focus of Oracle8i auditing by capturing only successful events or only unsuccessful events. You can also choose between having audited SQL statements recorded once per session or once per use. You can further focus your auditing efforts by auditing specific users rather than all users.

✦ The audit trail can be accessed through a number of views using the AUD$ system table.

✦ The AUD$ table requires growth management and should be archived and purged at regular intervals.

✦ Triggers provide a way to capture changes to the data in a table — something you can't do using the built-in auditing features of Oracle8i.

✦   ✦   ✦

Introducing WebDB

One of the important features added to Oracle8i is really more than just a feature—it's a complete product called WebDB. As the name implies, *WebDB* is a tool that helps you to take the data in your Oracle database and make it available to users on the Web. Although WebDB comes with Oracle8i, you can also download the product for no cost from the Oracle Technical Network at `http://technet.oracle.com`.

This chapter is meant to be a brief introduction to WebDB, which is a comprehensive product. It provides an overview of the makeup of WebDB, an example of using WebDB to create a report to familiarize you with the product, and some information on how you can perform basic administrative functions for WebDB, since this will quite possibly be a part of your overall job.

Cross-Reference If you want to learn considerably more about WebDB, we recommend that you consult *The Oracle WebDB Bible* by Rick Greenwald and James Milbery (IDG Books Worldwide, Inc.).

An Overview of WebDB and Internet Computing

WebDB is a tool that has been designed to create Internet computing application systems. *Internet computing* is a term that applies to an infrastructure that uses a Web browser as the key user interface on the client and a server on the back end. Unlike client/server computing, Internet computing uses a different communication protocol, HTTP, and a different display interface, HTML, and typically implements stateless transactions. *Stateless transactions* are complete within each page of data exchanged.

WebDB not only creates information systems that run in the Internet computing environment, but the product itself is an Internet computing application. This means that all of the advantages of Internet computing apply to the actual process of building applications with WebDB as well as to the applications created with WebDB.

This chapter uses the term *WebDB site* somewhat interchangeably with the term *WebDB application system.* In fact, a WebDB application system is much like a normal Web site. In WebDB, a *site* is a collection of a variety of information, from standard static HTML pages and data-driven dynamically constructed pages to interactive forms and any datatype supported by a browser, including graphics and sound. WebDB gives users and developers the ability to freely add new information to a site, such as late-breaking news related to the site.

Understanding the architecture of a WebDB site

Before you learn about the components of WebDB, you should have a basic understanding of how a WebDB site is implemented. A WebDB system has three basic pieces, with each serving a specific function. Not surprisingly, these match up with the components of Internet computing described previously. The three pieces that make up a WebDB system are as follows:

✦ **Client software.** The only client software that WebDB requires is a Web browser capable of using HTML version 3. This includes all of the major Web browsers.

✦ **Communications.** The WebDB client uses HTTP to communicate with the server. This typically means that TCP/IP will be the underlying communications protocol between the client and the server machines. Note that the communications protocol is *not* an Oracle communications protocol, so SQL*Net or Net8 aren't required for WebDB clients.

✦ **Server software.** WebDB needs two different types of server software: a listener, which will pick up the HTTP requests from the client, and an Oracle server capable of executing the WebDB application code.

The client component acts as the user interface to information stored in a WebDB site. The use of the browser as the client environment means that all WebDB content will take the form of an HTML page. The page can be static, or it can be generated dynamically. It can include different media types, including graphics, and it can act as a way to collect information from the user through the use of a form. But at its core, it is still an HTML page—nothing more, nothing less. This concept will help you to understand the framework of a WebDB information system.

The communications component passes requests for pages to the server component and receives the HTML pages that are returned from the server.

Examining WebDB components

WebDB has a number of different components that help you to create, deploy, and maintain a WebDB application system. These components are organized around four basic functions, which are the four choices from the top-level WebDB menu, as shown in Figure 26-1:

✦ Browsing application components and data in the Oracle database used for WebDB

✦ Building WebDB components, database objects, and sites

✦ Administering WebDB components, sites, and configuration parameters

✦ Monitoring the operation of your WebDB system

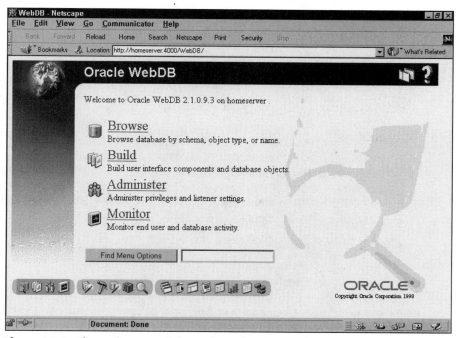

Figure 26-1: The main page of the WebDB development environment

When you first enter WebDB, you choose one of these areas before moving on to working on your own WebDB components. The top-level menu is accessible from any location within the WebDB environment, so it acts as a basic context switcher for the development environment. Let's look at the options available on this top-level menu.

Browsing Application Components

As explained previously, the WebDB environment is, in effect, hosted by an Oracle database. All the static information that WebDB and WebDB applications use is contained within the Oracle database. The data that is used as the source of information for dynamically built WebDB content is typically kept in the Oracle database. The code that makes up both the WebDB product itself and the components built with WebDB are all contained in PL/SQL packages, which are typically executed by the Oracle database.

WebDB's Browse functionality gives you the ability to examine the different types of objects and data in the Oracle database that acts as the host for WebDB. You can use different options in the Browse section of WebDB to examine the WebDB components stored in the database, as well as standard database objects, such as tables, indexes, and a variety of other more specific database objects. Regular end users can also use WebDB's browsing capabilities to access their own data in the Oracle database, since all data access through WebDB is controlled by standard database security.

Building WebDB Components

The WebDB component builders are where your development effort will normally start. This area lets you build the WebDB user interface components and construct Web sites using these components.

You will no doubt be spending most of your time building user interface components in WebDB. Four basic types of user interface objects exist, each of which uses one or more of the following builders:

   ✦ Read-only, which includes the builders for reports, charts, and calendars

   ✦ Read-write, which includes the builder for forms

   ✦ HTML, which includes the builders for dynamic HTML pages and frame drivers

   ✦ Organization, which includes the builders for menus and hierarchies

When you access the User Interface Components section of the WebDB development environment, you gain access to all of the builders through the menu shown in Figure 26-2.

You can access the user interface builders from a shortcut menu bar that is at the bottom of almost all of the tools in WebDB, as shown at the bottom of Figure 26-2. Table 26-1 describes each of the builders.

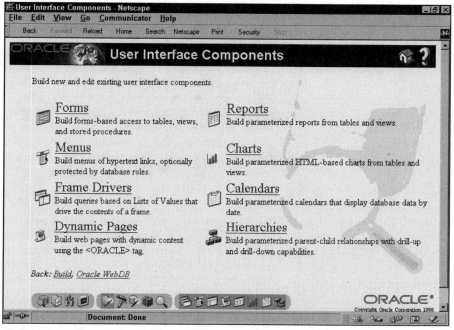

Figure 26-2: The User Interface Components main page

Table 26-1
Component Builders

Button	Name	Description
	Reports	The Reports builder in WebDB leads you through the process of creating reports. A *report* is a dynamic HTML page that is created from a query on data in the Oracle database. The Reports builder can create HTML reports, ASCII preformatted data, and Microsoft Excel spreadsheets directly from database data.
		You can create reports that accept parameters to produce dynamic reports based on selection criteria. When you create a report with parameters, WebDB automatically creates a parameter entry form for you. You or your users can also apply a number of default parameters to every report to control attributes such as sort order.

Continued

Table 26-1 *(continued)*

Button	Name	Description
	Charts	Sometimes information can be more clearly understood if it is presented in the graphical format of a chart. WebDB's Charts builder makes it easy to create charts based on data in the Oracle database. Charts builder isn't intended to replace sophisticated data analysis tools, but rather, to provide a quick and easy graphical display of results for database data. WebDB itself uses WebDB's chart-building capability throughout the system. All of the graphs that are provided by the monitoring tools are built with the Charts component.
	Calendars	WebDB's Calendars builder is used for information that can be categorized by a calendar date. The Calendars builder automatically creates a calendar graphic and inserts the relevant data into the appropriate place in the calendar. A sample calendar application is shown in Figure 26-3.
	Forms	WebDB's Forms builder can create forms based on tables, views, and stored procedures. You can create simple single-table forms, query-by-example forms, and even master/detail forms. Forms builder allows you to add client-side validations and lists of values, which can be represented in a variety of ways, such as a list box or series of radio buttons in the form.
	Dynamic pages, HTML with SQL	Reports builder, described previously, helps you to create standard reports based on the data in the Oracle database. You can also create HTML pages that are more freeform and that don't necessarily adhere to the more rigid structure of a report but still blend dynamic data from the Oracle database with standard HTML elements. These dynamic HTML pages are stored in the Oracle database, just like other WebDB components.
	Frame drivers	One of the standard elements of HTML pages is the use of frames. WebDB includes frame drivers that help you to construct frames for your WebDB site and also provides built-in frame management.
	Menus	WebDB's Menus builder helps you to construct menus and hierarchies of menus that can access the objects that you build with WebDB's other tools. Menus can also be used to create navigation paths for users. WebDB's menus can link to their own components as well as to any other Web objects that you can reach via a URL.

Button	Name	Description
	Hierarchies	WebDB's Hierarchies builder automatically navigates through nested relationships in your database (like the classic employee-manager hierarchy). The Hierarchies builder makes it easy to create complex linked applications by joining different WebDB components based on data values.
		You can also include normal HTML links to any URL as part of the user interface components in a WebDB application.

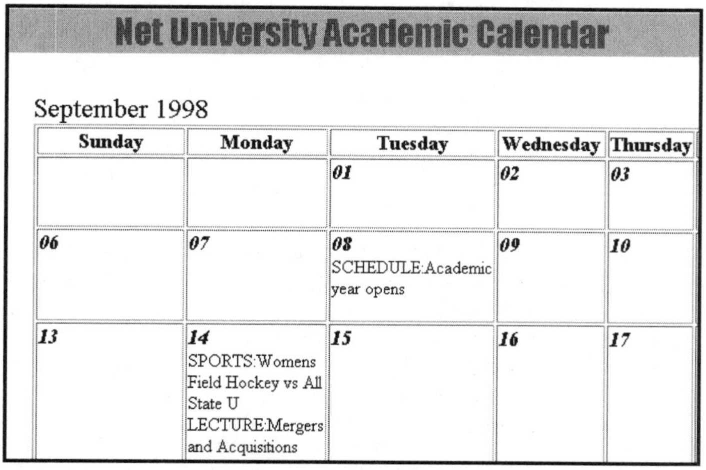

Net University Academic Calendar

September 1998

Sunday	Monday	Tuesday	Wednesday	Thursday
		01	*02*	*03*
06	*07*	*08* SCHEDULE:Academic year opens	*09*	*10*
13	*14* SPORTS:Womens Field Hockey vs All State U LECTURE:Mergers and Acquisitions	*15*	*16*	*17*

Figure 26-3: A calendar created with Calendars builder

Administering WebDB's Applications

WebDB not only gives developers an environment to create application systems, but it also provides equally powerful tools to help administer the resulting applications. Table 26-2 describes WebDB's administrative capabilities.

	Table 26-2 **Administrative Tools**	
Button	**Name**	**Description**
	Manage Users and Privileges	All WebDB applications exist within a security matrix. When users access a WebDB application, they log on with a username and password. You can limit access to different WebDB components and data, based on the identity of a user.

Continued

Table 26-2 *(continued)*

Button	Name	Description
		WebDB provides tools that allow you to create security roles, which can designate security for multiple users and reduce the burden of assigning and maintaining security.
	Component Finder	As you build more and more WebDB applications, you will find that your Oracle database will start to contain hundreds of components. Component Finder can search for components across component types and creators, making it easy to find that certain piece whose name just happens to have slipped your mind. Component Finder can be used from many different WebDB builders.
	Utilities	The WebDB utilities provide the capability to move content between applications and sites. A site administrator can quickly export both content and data, which can be copied onto a second system. Content can also be automatically replicated using the Oracle database's built-in replication facilities. WebDB even provides a utility for creating your own component builders if you need to repeatedly create similar components.
	Shared Component Library	One of the most powerful WebDB features is the ability to build components that can be reused by multiple applications or application components. These components can be logical entities, such as lists of values or JavaScript programs; multimedia objects, such as image files; links that provide navigation between different WebDB components; or even advanced components, such as translations for WebDB pages. The Shared Component Library provides a powerful productivity boost by allowing you to create these components once and then reuse them throughout your WebDB site. The Shared Component Library not only reduces development time by allowing for object reuse, but more importantly, it also allows you to reduce maintenance by having only a single copy of these reused components.

Monitoring WebDB Components

To ensure that your WebDB system is running optimally, WebDB provides a set of monitoring tools that allows you to check on a variety of system usage statistics. You can use WebDB's monitoring tools to track the usage of individual content and manage performance. WebDB automatically keeps track of content usage and performance statistics. You can use the monitors to view system usage, to set logging options, and to monitor performance of a WebDB site in real time.

Building a WebDB Site

The final capability of WebDB is the ability to create a WebDB site. A WebDB site is similar to a standard Web site, but with WebDB, you can create a site through a set of wizards, which are referred to as site builders, just as you can build components. Figure 26-4 shows the home page of a typical WebDB site.

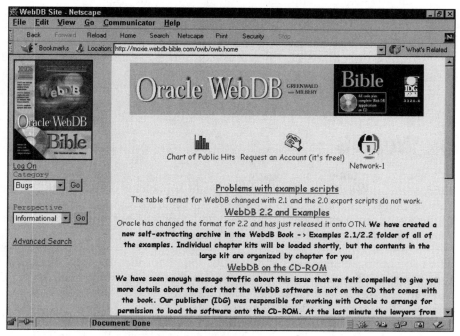

Figure 26-4: A standard WebDB site home page

You can see a navigation bar on the left of the page, a header at the top of the page, and a series of links on the main body of the page. These links represent either individual items or *folders,* which, as the name implies, are simply collections of items. Each item is a URL link, so each item can point to any location on the Web, to a WebDB component, or to any component that can be referenced through a URL.

Creating WebDB application systems

From even this brief introduction, you can see that WebDB gives you the ability to perform many, many tasks. You might begin to fear the possible complexity of actually creating all of these components. Fear not. WebDB is a wizard-driven environment, which means that you will not have to write any code at all.

WebDB is a *declarative* development environment. This means that instead of writing lots of procedural code, you merely have to supply a set of values that describe the functionality of your WebDB component. Each WebDB builder has a wizard that prompts you for the appropriate parameters and can supply online help about the parameters. After you supply these parameters, WebDB generates the underlying PL/SQL code that will actually build your application's HTML pages.

You don't need to know much about PL/SQL to create applications with WebDB. If you want to change an application, you merely edit the values you originally supplied to the wizards.

Note   You can, however, use JavaScript on the client or PL/SQL procedures on the server to extend the functionality inherent in your WebDB application system. Because of this, you can do almost anything you want with WebDB, within the limitations of HTML's static nature.

Using WebDB

As you no doubt understand by now, WebDB is a fairly broad product, capable of building and managing many different types of application components and data. This section walks you through the process of creating a simple report with WebDB. You will get a feel for the WebDB development environment, although you won't be going very deeply into the entire full-bodied product.

When you build a component with WebDB, you go through a series of pages in the appropriate builder, which prompt you for the component's characteristics. To illustrate the way you can create application modules with WebDB, let's use the example of a simple report based on the TANK, AQUATIC_ANIMALS, and CARETAKER tables in the demo database for this book. The user HAROLD will be building the report, which will simply list the animals in each tank, with the tanks sorted by their caretakers' names.

In the interest of efficiency, we won't go through the entire installation process for WebDB or spend time setting up a user profile for HAROLD. Instead, we'll assume that these tasks have been completed and that we are ready to build our first report. Since WebDB is a completely wizard-driven interface, this example includes plenty of screen images.

Since HAROLD will be building a report, you navigate from the home page of WebDB directly to the report-building section of the product, shown in Figure 26-5. You get there through a series of menu pages or by using the Reports command on the shortcut menu at the bottom of most WebDB pages.

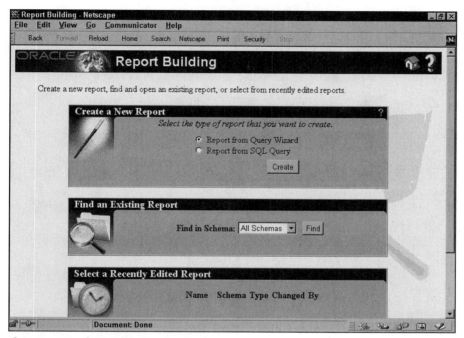

Figure 26-5: The main Reports page

You have three basic choices on the Report Building page:

1. You can build a new report, with the use of either the Query wizard or a SQL query.

2. You can find an existing report.

3. You can select from a list of recently edited reports, which is empty since this is the first report HAROLD is building.

You use the Query wizard to create a brand-new report by clicking the Create button in the top panel. The first page of the Query wizard appears, as shown in Figure 26-6.

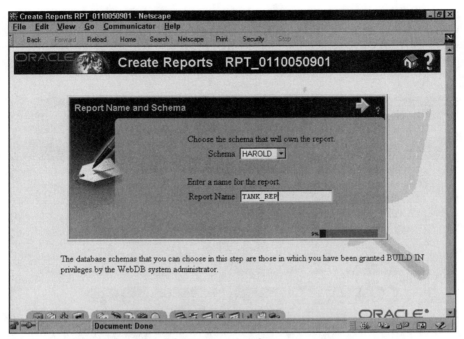

Figure 26-6: The first page of the Query wizard

You build the report as a PL/SQL package in a particular schema — in this case, HAROLD's schema. You also give the report a descriptive name on this page, such as TANK_REP in the lower entry box.

At the top of each wizard page, you will generally see three icons — a left-pointing arrow to take you back a step, a right-pointing arrow to move you to the next step, and a checkered flag to complete the component with the default choices for any untouched wizard pages. The first wizard page has no left arrow; similarly, the last wizard page has no right arrow.

On the next page of the wizard, you can choose the tables you wish to include in the report. For this report, select the AQUATIC_ANIMAL, CARETAKER, and TANK tables from the SEAPARK schema, as shown in Figure 26-7.

The next page prompts you for the join conditions for the table. WebDB automatically finds the relationship between the TANK table and the AQUATIC_ANIMAL table, as shown in Figure 26-8, since a foreign key constraint is on the AQUATIC_ANIMAL table.

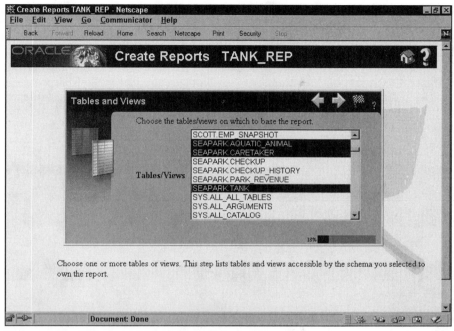

Figure 26-7: Selecting tables to include in the report

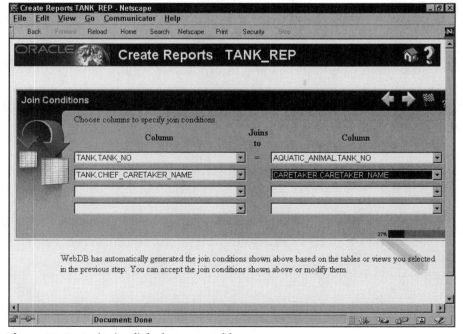

Figure 26-8: Assigning links between tables

You have to add the join condition between the CHIEF_CARETAKER_NAME column in the TANK table and the CARETAKER_NAME in the CARETAKER table before you move to the next page in the builder.

The next page, shown in Figure 26-9, allows you to select the columns you want displayed in the report. For this report, select the CARETAKER_NAME from the CARETAKER table, TANK_NAME and CAPACITY_GALLONS from the TANK table, and ANIMAL_NAME, MARKINGS_DESCRIPTION, and BIRTH_DATE from the AQUATIC_ANIMALS table.

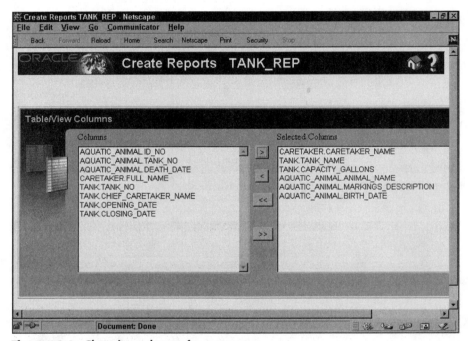

Figure 26-9: Choosing columns for a report

The next wizard page, shown in Figure 26-10, allows you to assign conditions to limit the data in the report. These conditions are automatically imposed each time the report is run — they don't require any user interaction.

You want to show only animals that are alive in this report, so you add a condition for the DEATH_DATE to be NULL. The next wizard page, shown in Figure 26-11, lets you modify how the selected columns will be displayed.

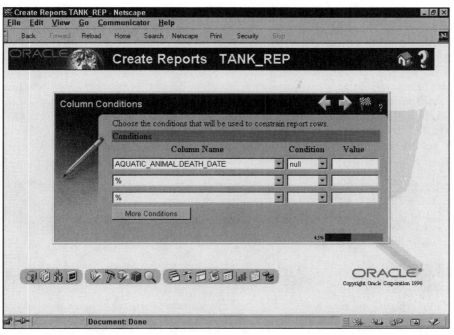

Figure 26-10: Adding a condition

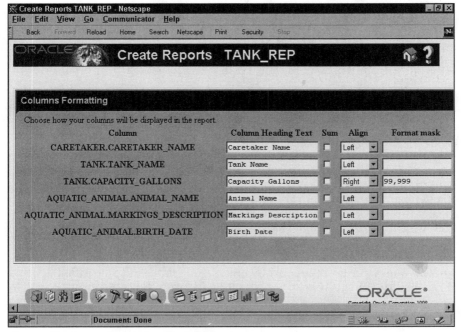

Figure 26-11: Modifying the display of columns

The headings for each column are taken from the column names, with any underscores replaced by spaces and the first letter of each individual word capitalized. You can also add formatting, and for this report, it makes sense to add a format mask of "99,999" for the CAPACITY_GALLONS column.

The next page of the wizard, shown in Figure 26-12, contains many display options. To produce a more attractive report, you should set several of the display options. You first change the way that null values are displayed from the default, the text string "(null)," to a simple dash. The second change you make on the Display Options page is to set break columns in the report on the right-hand side of the page.

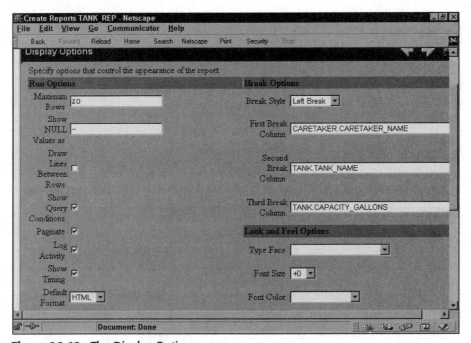

Figure 26-12: The Display Options page

When you specify a break column, WebDB automatically suppresses the display of any repeating values for the break column. Your report will look better if you list the CARETAKER_NAME, the TANK_NAME, and the CAPACITY_GALLONS only once for each value, so these columns have been added to the list of break columns.

Adding break columns to your report doesn't guarantee any type of sort order, so you will want to order the report by CARETAKER_NAME and TANK_NAME for the sake of readability. For this report, you should also order the animals in the tank from the youngest to the oldest, so add the BIRTH_DATE column and sort it in descending order. The next wizard page, shown in Figure 26-13, lets you add parameters to your report.

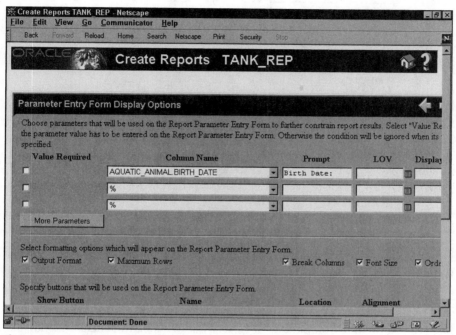

Figure 26-13: The Parameter Entry Form Display Options page

You can use these parameters to constrain the rows that are included in the report and that are entered by users when they run the report. For this report, it would be useful to allow users to limit the animals shown to a certain age, so you select the BIRTH_DATE from the list box of columns and assign a prompt of "Birth Date:." The final two columns in the parameter specification, labeled "LOV" and "Display LOV As," allow you to add a list of values for any parameters so that your user can get some online help for selecting valid values. The next page in the wizard, shown in Figure 26-14, lets you add text and a format to the report.

In the upper-left corner of the Add Text page, a list box allows you to specify a template for the report. You can add a template for any of the components that you will build with WebDB to ensure a consistent appearance for all the modules you build. WebDB comes with its own set of templates, although you can also create your own templates. For the purposes of this report, choose PUBLIC.TEMPLATE_6.

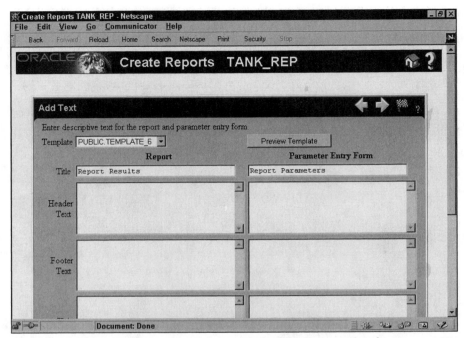

Figure 26-14: The Add Text page of the report-building Query wizard

The Query wizard for building this report has a couple more pages, but you don't have to use them to complete your report. Simply click the checkered flag on the top of the page to complete the report.

But what are you doing when you complete the report? Until you click the checkered flag or the OK button that comes in the final panel of all of the WebDB component builders, all you have been doing is adding values to a set of internal tables maintained by WebDB. When you complete your specifications for the component, WebDB actually builds the PL/SQL package that is used to create the report at run time. Once you've generated the report, WebDB presents you with the Manage Component page, as shown in Figure 26-15.

Click the Run link at the bottom of the page to run the report. This link actually calls a PL/SQL procedure inside the generated PL/SQL package for the report that generates the report from the data in the Oracle database. The report will run and be returned to you in all its glory, as shown in Figure 26-16.

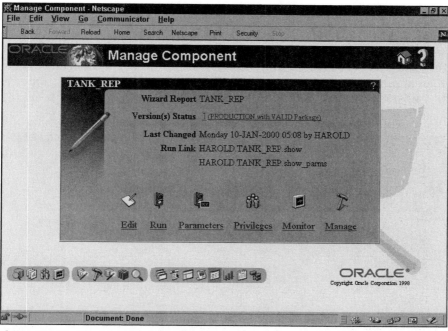

Figure 26-15: The Manage Component page

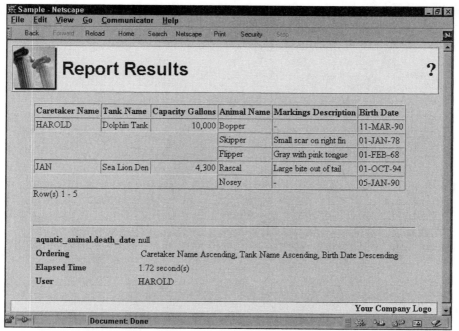

Figure 26-16: Your first report

When you ran the report, you weren't given the opportunity to add selection parameters for it. You can test this capability by returning to the WebDB development environment with the Back button of the browser. Then select the Parameters menu command on the Manage Components page to open the automatically generated report parameters form. This menu command calls a different procedure in the report package, a procedure that generates the report parameters form shown in Figure 26-17.

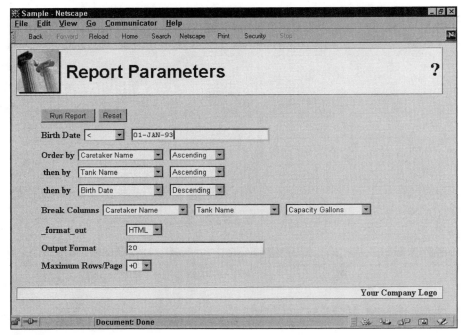

Figure 26-17: The Report Parameters form

Note that the report parameters form uses the same template as the standard report. Also notice that the form not only contains a line where you can enter a condition for the parameter, but it also allows a user to change many other facets of the report, including the sort order, break columns, and the output format. You can also see that WebDB has automatically included the column headings you specified for each column, rather than the column names, in the belief that these headings will be more comprehensible to the people running the report. The report parameters form for this report is a default version of the form. You can suppress the display of these other options in the Parameter Form Display Options page of the Reports builder.

For this version of the report, you want to see only some of the older animals in the tank, so you can enter the less-than (<) selection operator and a value of 01-JAN-93, respectively. Once you have entered these parameters, you can click the Run Report button to open the new report, as shown in Figure 26-18.

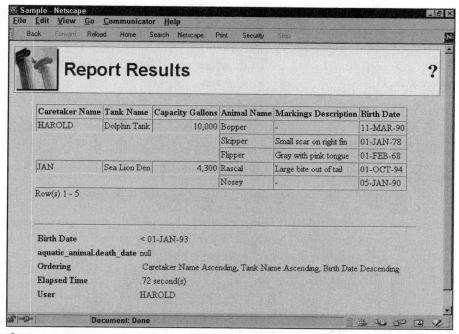

Figure 26-18: Your new report

You can also edit any of the attributes you have assigned to your report through the Reports builder. Once you edit these values, you regenerate the report's PL/SQL package.

This section presented a whirlwind tour of WebDB's report-building capabilities; now you have a taste of what this powerful new Oracle8i option can do. The final sections of this chapter cover some of the maintenance issues that you may confront when WebDB components are a part of your Oracle database installation.

Administering WebDB

So far, this chapter has introduced you to the WebDB product and given you a taste of what it's like to create a report with WebDB. In fact, you may not be using WebDB itself, but you may have the responsibility of maintaining the Oracle database that is used to host WebDB. Therefore, this chapter closes with some information on how to administer WebDB, including finding out about components and their attributes with Component Finder, managing components, and importing and exporting WebDB components and schemas.

Using Component Finder

Component Finder is the basic tool you use to retrieve information about your WebDB components. The basic user interface page for Component Finder is shown in Figure 26-19.

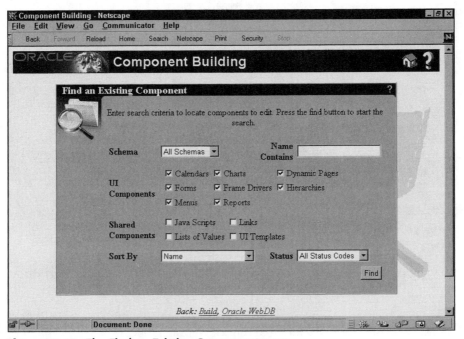

Figure 26-19: The Find an Existing Component page

The list of components includes some basic information about each entry, including the type of component, the schema the component is stored in, the name of the component, who created and last modified the component and when, and the current status of the most recent version of the component. The name of the component acts as a hot link to the Component Manager page.

When you use Component Finder to select components, such as a list of all available report modules, you will get a listing such as the one shown in Figure 26-20.

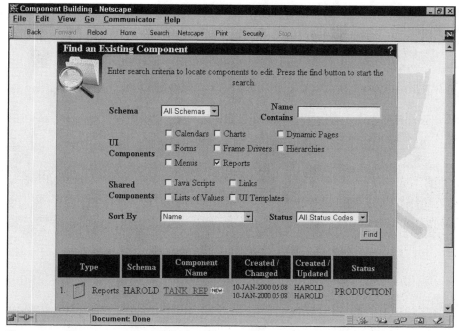

Figure 26-20: A component listing returned in Component Finder

Notice in the figure that you can see the report component, the TANK_REP report; its creation was discussed in the previous section.

Managing components

When you created a report module in the previous section, you were introduced to the WebDB's Manage Component page. You can change the parameters that control the generation of your WebDB component through the Edit link, and you can run your component directly or with parameters through the Run and Parameter links, respectively.

Other functions are also available to you when you select the Manage link on the Manage Component page. The new page will have six links represented by icons in the middle of the page and four additional choices at the bottom of the page.

About

The About link gives you some basic information about the current versions of a component and a complete listing of the values of all the parameters that you have assigned for the creation of a component, as shown in the data returned in Figure 26-21.

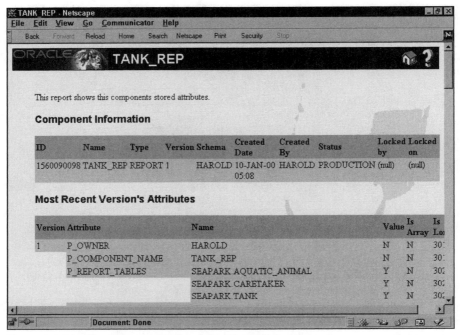

Figure 26-21: The Return page from the About link

The information presented on the About page is essentially a recap of all of the information about the component stored in the WebDB data tables. All of the values you entered through the pages of the Query wizard to build the report are listed, with the prefix "P_" attached to a descriptive name.

When you look at the values returned on the About page, you get to see the inside of WebDB. It's helpful to get to know the type of parameters used for a particular component, since many of them can be passed to your component if you are calling the PL/SQL package from a link from another PL/SQL package or directly from a browser. You will learn about these last two options later in this chapter.

Copy

When you click the Copy link, WebDB delivers the Copy Component page, as shown in Figure 26-22. This page allows you to create a copy of the *current* version of a component under another name or in another schema. The copied version of the component is given a version number of 1, since it's a brand-new component. You can use this ability to create explicit versions of a component with meaningful names, as described in the sidebar "Version Maintenance." When you take this approach to versioning, every released version of a component will have a version number of 1, so it will be easy to identify if a component is actively part of the development process.

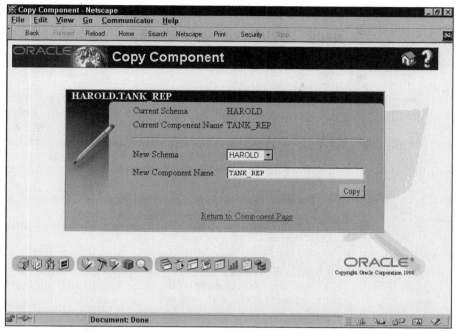

Figure 26-22: The Copy Component page

Rename

When you click the Rename link, WebDB allows you to rename an existing component. The Rename process differs from the Copy process in two ways. First of all, renaming a component maintains all the existing versions of the component, not just the current one. Secondly, the new name for the component is applied directly to the component, so it has the effect of *deleting* the current name of the component.

Generate

You should be familiar with the generate process by now. You generate the PL/SQL package that is your run-time component when you click the OK button at the end of a WebDB wizard process or if you click the Finish button at the end of an editing session. Since these are typically the last tasks that you do in your development process, why would you ever want to use the Generate link?

Typically, you won't ever need to use it, but sometimes you might import the data in the WebDB tables but not the packages created from that data. In these situations, it may be faster for you to use the Generate link rather than entering Edit mode for a particular component. When you use WebDB to export your components, the SQL script that is created includes a call to the generate procedure, so the script will automatically generate the component.

You will have to explicitly call the generate procedure once. When you generate a component, the code to explicitly implement shared components, such as links, is included in the generated component. So if you change a shared component, the changes in that component won't appear in other WebDB components until they are regenerated.

If you select the Generate link for an existing component and return to the Manage Component page, you will see that there is no new version number for the component. This is the case even though you may have heard the whirring of a disk drive that led you to believe that WebDB was creating a new package. WebDB did create a new PL/SQL package, but since it had the exact same characteristics of the current version, there was no need to increment the version number.

Keep in mind that a version is defined by a new set of parameters in the WebDB database, not a new copy of the resulting package.

Drop

When you click the Drop link, WebDB opens the Drop Component page, as shown in Figure 26-23. You are given the opportunity to drop each individual version of a component. By default, all the versions are selected for deletion as shown by the check marks in the check boxes in front of their names. Unless you want to completely delete a component, you should be careful to deselect at least one of the boxes.

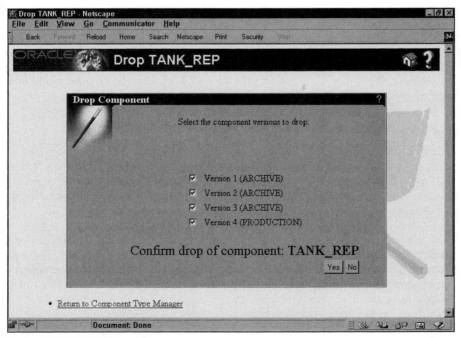

Figure 26-23: The Drop Component page

Version Maintenance

In an iterative development environment, it's easy to end up with a lot of versions for a component. In fact, since it's so easy to change a WebDB component, it is almost inevitable that you will end up with many versions of a component. The WebDB built-in versioning feature is great from the standpoint of always being able to cancel out changes by returning to a previous version, but it is less than great for identifying which version is which, since the only identifier is a version number.

You can avoid version overload in two basic ways. The first is to be fairly ruthless about cleaning up versions during the development and release process. While your component is in developmental flux, you can just keep modifying the component and creating more versions. But as soon as you attain a steady state, you have to remember to go back to the Manage Component page and drop all the interim versions. This will reduce the number of versions that you have for a particular component, but you will still have multiple versions of a component with holes in the version numbering scheme.

The second method is to make a fresh copy of each new version of a component that you want to keep. You can give each copy a name that is more descriptive, which can help to administer the different versions of a component.

In either case, it's good practice to add some type of version indicator to your component, either in the header or footer of the component, or if your users object to seeing the version number on a page as a hidden field. Having version numbers isn't that useful if you have no way of knowing which version is being run at any particular time.

As you can probably guess at this point, dropping a version means that WebDB deletes the rows that contain the parameters for that version of the component. Even if you drop all the versions of a component, any generated PL/SQL packages will still exist. You will have to delete them through SQL*Plus or some other maintenance tool if you want to eliminate the actual component. The sidebar discusses version maintenance.

The one management choice not yet covered is the Export choice. You actually have two different methods available to you if you want to export a WebDB component, so this choice is covered in the next section.

Additional Manage Component page options

The bottom of the Manage Component page has some additional links. These links don't specifically relate to the management of a component, but they are very useful, especially for understanding what is happening under the covers in your WebDB-generated components and in the WebDB development environment.

Show SQL Query Info

Selecting the Show SQL Query Info link displays the SQL statement that was used to generate the HTML page at the top of the page. If you select the Show SQL Query Info link, the next time you return to the Manage Component page, this option will toggle to Hide SQL Query Info.

PL/SQL Code

The PL/SQL links allow you to take a look at the actual code that WebDB generates for you. You can either view the *package specification,* (package spec) which lists the procedures that are a part of the package and the parameters these procedures accept, or the *package body,* which includes all the PL/SQL code that is actually used to implement the procedures.

For the most part, looking at the package body isn't really that helpful. There is a mass of code, much of which just calls other PL/SQL procedures. If you're curious and have a good understanding of PL/SQL, the package body can give you some insight into how WebDB components actually work.

The package spec can also be of use. Since you may have occasion to call the PL/SQL package from some other environment or PL/SQL package, you must know the details of the package spec if you want to use any of the procedures in the package correctly.

You can see that, for a report, the only procedure that has very many parameters is the SHOW procedure, and that the parameters for that procedure look a lot like the parameters that are set from the Parameter form for the report.

There are two timestamps in the PL/SQL package specification for a component. The first is at the top of the code, which indicates when a package was initially created. The timestamp that comes below the CREATE or REPLACE PACKAGE code is the time that the current version was created. If you were to use the Generate link for a component, even though the specifications for the component had not changed, you would still see a new timestamp in this part of the code, since the package was regenerated by the Generate link.

Call Interface

The call interface provides a sample URL that describes how to call the procedure at run time. You can see all of the arguments that are passed by the display options panel, which you can also include in the calling URL.

Show Locks

This chapter assumes that you will be the only user working on a particular component at a particular time. But since your Oracle database supports the ability to have many, many users at the same time, WebDB also allows you to have many different developers simultaneously. But just as no two users can write to the same row of data at the same time, no two WebDB developers can modify the same component at the same time. Although the component locks aren't actual locks on the underlying rows in the WebDB host database, the logical locking imposed by WebDB serves the same purpose as the database locks implemented by the Oracle database.

When one developer is working on a component, the component is locked. You may occasionally see a status description for a version in the Manage Component page that says something like "PRODUCTION locked by *username*," where *username* identifies the database user who is actively modifying the parameters for a component.

When the component is locked, you will be unable to edit it or perform any administrative tasks on the component. You may, however, be able to run the package generated by the component, since this package is independent of the data rows that have been locked by another developer.

Occasionally, you may find that a lock is held on a component in error. You can explicitly release the lock on a component through the Utilities menu in WebDB, which is described in more detail in the next section.

Exporting and Importing WebDB Components

One of the great advantages of WebDB is that all the components you build with WebDB are stored in an Oracle database. The parameters that control how a component is built are also stored within database tables and used to build the PL/SQL packages that are the actual components.

Several benefits derive from this architecture. Your components are kept in a single secure location. When you back up the Oracle database that hosts your WebDB application system, you are also backing up the components that make up the system. And you can use the existing import and export capabilities of an Oracle database to move components from one Oracle database to another.

Exporting user interface components

You can easily export individual user interface components. Clicking the Export link on the Manage page for the report you are viewing returns a page that contains the text of a SQL script, as shown in Figure 26-24.

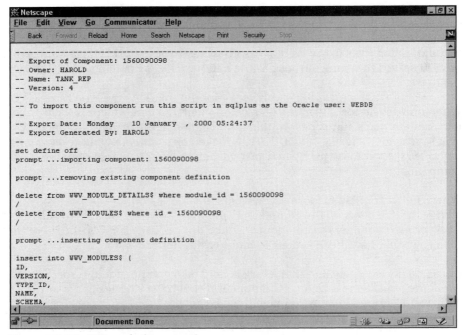

Figure 26-24: SQL code for exporting a component

The generated export code is set up to do the following three basic tasks:

✦ Remove any existing copies of the component, which is identified by a unique number, by deleting from the `WWV_MODULES$` and the `WWV_MODULE_DETAILS$` tables any rows associated with that unique number. These two tables are the internal data tables used by WebDB to hold the parameters used to generate components.

✦ Add the rows into these same tables that will define the *most current* version of the component.

✦ Generate the PL/SQL package for the component by calling the `build_procedure` for the component.

To create a SQL script, select all of the text in your browser and save it to a file, typically with an extension of .sql. You can run this script in SQL*Plus to load the component into an Oracle database and generate the PL/SQL package for the component by using the following command at the SQL*Plus prompt:

```
@filename
```

In the command above, *filename* is the name of the file to which you saved the export file.

Notice that the comments at the top of the script instruct you to run the script as the WEBDB user, who is the owner of the WebDB system and data tables. The WebDB system user is normally the only user with access to the internal WebDB data tables and will always have access to the schema that will hold the generated components.

Caution You will have to use the user account for the owner of the WebDB installation, which, by default, is the WEBDB user.

Exporting shared components

Shared components are different from standard user interface components in a number of ways. First of all, they don't belong to a particular schema in the Oracle database. They are stored in data tables that are part of the schema that owns WebDB, which is typically called WEBDB. Secondly, shared components aren't generated at all. Generated user interface components simply include the shared components within the HTML pages that are generated by the component at run time.

Consequently, a different mechanism exists for exporting shared components. To use the Export utility, you will have to be logged on as the owner of WebDB. When you log on as the owner, you will get an additional menu page of WebDB utilities. You can use the Export Shared Components link on that page to open the page shown in Figure 26-25.

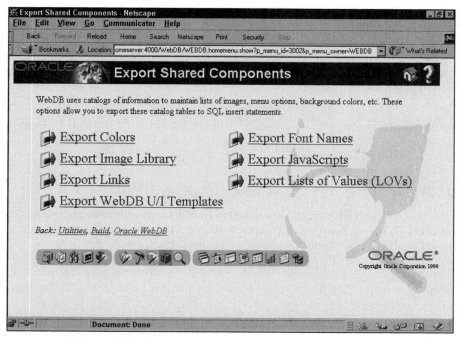

Figure 26-25: Exporting shared components

When you click any of the Export Shared Components links, you will see a page showing a SQL script, just like you did when you exported an individual component. Once the script is displayed in your browser, you can copy and paste the script to a text file with a .sql file extension, as you did with the scripts for the user interface components.

You may want to create a standard set of shared components that you will use across multiple WebDB development machines. All you have to do is to make sure that a particular WebDB installation contains only the shared components that you want to include in the library and then export those components to SQL scripts. When you install a new WebDB site, all you have to do is use SQL*Plus to load the scripts containing the standard shared components to reproduce them to the new server.

Importing WebDB components

The end result of exporting either type of WebDB component is the same: a script file with the SQL statements needed to add the data back into the Oracle database that acts as the host for WebDB. The easiest way to do this is to use SQL*Plus.

To import a file, simply start SQL*Plus, making sure that you log on as the appropriate user — the owner of WebDB installation, who is typically called WEBDB. Once you start SQL*Plus, simply enter the at sign (@), which indicates a script file, and then the complete path and file name of the SQL file, and SQL*Plus will run the commands listed in the script file. If you set the start directory for the SQL*Plus shortcut icon to the directory that contains the script file, you don't need to indicate the path name.

If you want to run a SQL script named rep1.sql that exists in the C:\ directory, you can start SQL*Plus and log on as the owner of the WebDB environment. Then enter the following line of code:

```
@c:\REP1.SQL
```

The script runs, and the component loads.

Using Oracle's Import and Export utilities

The standard, recommended way to export and import components in WebDB is to export each individual user interface component to its own SQL script file and to export each type of shared component into its own SQL script file.

There is a lot to be said for this practice. Once you have completed work on a component, exporting it to a script file ensures that it is safe. Even in the highly improbable event of an unrecoverable corruption of your Oracle database, you can still re-create the component from the script file.

As you build more and more complex systems with WebDB, however, you will eventually end up with more and more export files. If you want to load an entire system, you will find yourself running a lot of scripts in SQL*Plus. Since each of the scripts is self-contained, you can combine all the individual export files into one larger file, or you can write a batch file to run each of the scripts in turn.

However, this seems like a lot of work to go through for a fairly straightforward task — moving an entire WebDB environment, including all the shared and user interface components, to another Oracle database. There is instead a more direct way to accomplish this task. You can turn to the standard Export utility for Oracle8i.

Using the Export Utility to Export a WebDB Database

Since all the data and procedures that make up a WebDB application system reside in two separate schemas, you can use the Export utility to dump the contents of these schemas to a binary file that can be used to re-create the environment on another machine.

You can use the Export utility, as described in Chapter 8, "Using Oracle8i's Export Utility," through a command-line interface or interactively. The first step to exporting your WebDB environment is to export the schema or schemas that contain your application components.

Once you have exported the schema that contains the WebDB environment, you can go through the same process with the schema that contains the WebDB application system, which, by default, is WEBDB. You use the Export utility to accomplish this.

Using the Import Utility to Import a WebDB Database

You can use the Import utility to import the dump files you create with the Export utility. Just as you can use a single command to export a dump file, you can use a corresponding single command to import the file using Oracle's Import utility.

The end result of this approach is that loading a dump file into an existing schema won't replace any existing components with the newer versions in the dump file. Since the dump file is the complete schema, it makes sense to simply delete the target schema before loading the dump file.

Now that you know two ways to export and import WebDB components, which one should you use in which situation?

Choosing an export method

Which export method should you use? Before exploring this topic, it's worth spending a little time to understand the differences between the two methods. In the WebDB export process, each individual component is exported to a SQL script, which you can copy and save to a text file. The script is fully functional — from dropping any existing versions of a component to regenerating the component from the data files you have just loaded — and easily readable. The WebDB process exports components and libraries as logical entities.

When you use the standard Oracle Export utility, the entire schema for the WebDB development environment and the schema that owns the application are exported to binary files. These files aren't easily readable and must be handled by the Oracle Import utility. This type of export process is more like a physical process; the actual tables, the data they contain, and the stored procedures created from them are all exported to dump files. When the files are reloaded, there is no recompilation of the components. The stored procedures are simply reloaded back into the schema that owns them.

In most cases, the choice should be pretty clear. Using the standard Oracle Export utility is referred to as the "large mallet" approach: You dump and restore everything that is needed in the WebDB environment and as part of your development environment. If you are moving a complete WebDB site, using the Export utility will give you what you want, all at once. Of course, if you are moving a complete Oracle database that contains a WebDB application, it makes perfect sense to simply dump and reload the entire database, or to add the schemas relevant to your WebDB application to any batch file you would create for the operation.

But this method treats the entire schema as a single entity — you have no ability to handle a single component or group of components separately. You can't really exclude any components when you use this method. About all you can do is not load a particular application schema or load more than one application schema that used the same shared components.

If you want to selectively load components as they are changed, you will have to use the export scripts created for you with the WebDB export choice. The granularity for this type of export is a single component or library of shared components, which are much more flexible to work with.

In general, the choice of an export method is pretty easy. You will either be copying an entire WebDB environment, which you can do with the Oracle Export utility, or you won't be, which will require you to use the standard WebDB export choices.

We recommend using the standard WebDB export choice for each individual component and for the libraries of shared components. Making individual export files for each component may seem like a lot of work from this vantage point. However, the first time you attempt to find an individual component when access to the host Oracle database is difficult, you will realize the following: that any effort made to make export files seems trivial compared to the time spent trying to reload an entire dump file to its own schema and then export the component. Besides, if you have implemented a good programming scenario, the completion of a component calls for several actions, including cleaning up any earlier revisions, so adding the small task of exporting the component won't require much more time.

The bottom line is simple: Using the WebDB-provided Export utility gives you the security and flexibility you need, without much additional work in a good development environment. Besides, the Export utility is not officially supported as a way of transferring WebDB components, so you may find yourself all alone if a problem occurs when using it.

Combining multiple WebDB sites

Right now, you're probably concentrating on a single WebDB application, but down the road, you may want to create new WebDB sites that use preexisting components already created in a different WebDB development environment.

You can accomplish this by simply creating an export file or files from each site and loading them into the combined site. If you choose to use the Export utility to move one of the sites to the new location, you will have to use the standard WebDB export scripts to load the other set of components, since the Export utility won't overwrite existing data structures in the target database.

A more likely scenario is when you want to load the shared components from multiple sites into a new WebDB site. You can accomplish this easily by creating an export file for each shared component library from each of the parent WebDB sites and then loading these .sql files using SQL*Plus.

Caution

WebDB uses a fairly sophisticated scheme to assign a unique ID to all components. There is very little chance that loading more than one shared component library or set of components could create a situation where one component could write over another component. Nonetheless, we recommend extensive testing whenever you combine multiple sites into a single WebDB environment.

Summary

In this chapter, you learned:

✦ WebDB is a powerful tool that you can use to dynamically access data in your Oracle database. You can build reports, forms, and a variety of other components. These components are built and used from any standard Web browser.

✦ You can build reports or any other WebDB component by using a WebDB wizard, which walks you through the process of specifying the options for the report. Once you have finished your specification, WebDB generates a PL/SQL package that will produce the final report. You can edit the report specification and regenerate the PL/SQL packages.

✦ WebDB gives you a variety of ways to manage your components, including exporting and importing them.

✦   ✦   ✦

Partitioning with Oracle8i

This chapter shows you how to create and manage partitioned tables and indexes. As you work with the information presented here, keep in mind that the design of these objects affects the efficiency of queries and DML commands. As your database grows in size, efficient, localized (within a single partition) queries become more important to keep response times reasonable. Partitioning data across logical boundaries that match common query patterns gives you the best performance improvements for your efforts.

Introducing Very Large Databases

Very large databases (VLDB) are a rapidly growing trend in the enterprise world. Oracle has kept up with this trend and has greatly increased its support over the years for large databases. One of the key features that Oracle has developed to make large amounts of data manageable is the ability to partition your data. This chapter talks about partitioning, what it means, and how it is implemented. Very large databases can be categorized into two types:

✦ Online Transaction Processing (OLTP) databases

✦ Data warehouses

Online Transaction Processing databases support a large concurrent user population. The database transactions usually follow the simple Create, Read, Update, and Delete (CRUD) matrix. Data warehouses, on the other hand, have an infrastructure that supports both OLTP and Decision Support Systems (DSS). The segregation of data within the data warehouse makes this type of database unique.

A data warehouse is usually built to store historical data, often in a summarized or aggregated format. With an Oracle8i database, you can create both your OLTP and data warehouse in one database. The element of time splits the OLTP and DSS

portions of the database. A data warehouse might store all credit card transactions for the past five years, if you have the space to hold this enormous amount of data. If storage space is an issue, the data warehouse might store only the aggregated summaries of credit card transactions for the past five years. The data is used to analyze purchasing
trends, for instance.

Partitioning Database Objects

A VLDB often contains a few large database objects (such as tables and indexes) with their respective sizes from the gigabyte to the terabyte range. A database is rarely identified as a VLDB based solely upon the number of database objects it constitutes.

Oracle8i partitioning addresses the implementation of VLDBs by allowing large database objects to be split into smaller, more manageable units. These smaller units, or partitions, can only be created for tables and indexes. Figure 27-1 illustrates the concept of partitioning.

When you partition large tables and indexes into smaller chunks, you gain the following advantages:

✦ Reduced database downtime for maintenance

✦ Reduced database downtime due to media failure

✦ Improved query performance

✦ Better distribution of disk access

✦ Partition transparency

Reducing database downtime

If you split database objects into smaller, more manageable partitions, you can perform maintenance on individual units of the database objects, as opposed to the whole database object. Also, if you place the object within its own tablespace, you can bring the tablespace offline for maintenance while the database is still operational. The key advantage here is that while you are performing maintenance on one partition of an object, all the other partitions can be available for users to use.

If the database experiences media (disk) failure, the database must be recovered. Recovery involves restoring the respective database files, using the SQL RECOVER command to recover the lost data, and finally bringing the respective datafiles and tablespaces online. Most VLDBs are mission-critical, and database failures waste valuable data processing time. Most failures do not involve losing the entire database, but rather only one or more disks. If one of the failed disks is used to store a nonpartitioned table, that entire table will be unavailable until you complete the recovery process. If the table is partitioned, on the other hand, only the affected partitions are unavailable. Partitions are unaffected if they don't use the disk (or disks) that failed.

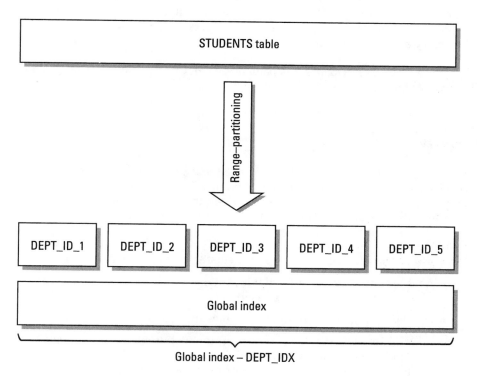

Figure 27-1: Partitioning

Query performance

Because partitions can be created based on ranges of certain columns, queries that require a full tablescan can focus on a particular partition rather than a range of partitions. This focus drastically reduces the search time necessary to satisfy the data requirements of a SQL query.

Disk access

Partitions allow a flexible physical implementation of a database object. Partitions can be created on separate tablespaces, which you can, in turn, place on their own physical disks. Having a dedicated disk controller permits faster searches on partitions. Database design can specify that high-hit-rate database objects have their own dedicated disks.

Partition transparency

In today's complex application development environment, the developer certainly does not want physical constraints on data access. Partition implementation is transparent to end users. Users or developers do not need to be aware of the physical implementation of the database objects — that capability is available for query and I/O optimization.

Note

The Cost Based Optimizer is partition-aware, while the Rule Based Optimizer is not partition-aware.

Creating Table Partitions

Designing VLDBs is a complex task. The database architect must be aware of the fundamental concepts of Oracle8i partitioning. You must forecast certain tables to be potentially partitionable, but every table cannot be partitioned. The following guidelines provide a validation framework for whether a potential logical table is a partition candidate:

✦ A table existing within an Oracle8i cluster cannot be partitioned.

✦ A table cannot be partitioned if it contains LONG or LONG RAW columns. These datatypes are being phased out.

✦ Oarcle8i supports partitioning of tables that contain LOB columns.

✦ An index-organized table can be partitioned, but only when the partitioning key (the list of columns that are used to determine partitions) is a subset of the table's primary key. The ability to partition an index-organized table is a new feature of Oracle8i.

✦ An index-organized table stores data sorted on the primary key.

Use the CREATE TABLE command with the PARTITION BY range to create a partitioned table. The PARTITION BY clause is added to the end of the CREATE TABLE command. There are three variations on the PARTITION BY clause, which are explained here:

✦ **Partitioning by range.** The table rows are divided into different partitions based on a list of value ranges for a list of columns.

✦ **Partitioning by hash.** The table rows are divided evenly into a specified number of partitions based on values in a list of columns. The range in each partition is calculated by the database using a hash function to provide equal distribution of rows across each partition.

✦ **Partitioning by composite.** The table rows are first partitioned by range and then, within each range, partitioned again by hash values. Hash partitioning can use a different list of columns than range partitioning. This allows for even greater division of the table's data.

Partitioning by range

Partitioning by range tells Oracle8i to separate the table into sections based on the value of one or more columns. Up to 16 columns are allowed in the list of columns for partitioning by range. The syntax of the PARTITION BY RANGE clause within the CREATE TABLE command is:

```
[PARTITION BY RANGE (column list)
(PARTITION [ part_name] VALUES LESS THAN (values list),  ...)]
[ENABLE | DISABLE ROW MOVEMENT ]
```

The partition name is optional. If omitted, the system assigns a name beginning with the SYS_ prefix. The ENABLE ROW MOVEMENT clause is a new clause introduced in Oracle8i. This allows the partition key of a partitioned table to be modified, which in effect allows the row to move from one partition to another if needed. The default setting is DISABLE ROW MOVEMENT, which does not allow any changes to the partition key. Previous releases of Oracle did not allow rows to move between partitions.

For example, the CREATE TABLE statement in Listing 27-1 creates a STUDENTS table with five partitions. Each partition's description specifies a partition name and physical attributes for the partition.

Listing 27-1: **Creating a table with five partitions**

```
CREATE Table STUDENTS
(
    STUDENT_ID              NUMBER                  NOT Null,
    STUDENT_FIRST_NAME   VARCHAR2(25)            Null    ,
    STUDENT_LAST_NAME    VARCHAR2(25)            Null    ,
    STUDENT_DEPT_ID      NUMBER                  Null    ,
    STUDENT_ADDRESS      VARCHAR2(50)            Null    ,
    STUDENT_CITY         VARCHAR2(25)            Null    ,
    STUDENT_STATE        VARCHAR2(15)            Null    ,
    STUDENT_ZIP          VARCHAR2(10)            Null    ,
    STUDENT_BL_STATUS    CHAR                    Null,
CONSTRAINT              DEPT_ID_PK Primary Key(STUDENT_DEPT_ID)
)
PARTITION BY RANGE (STUDENT_DEPT_ID)
(    PARTITION DEPT_ID_1 VALUES LESS THAN (100)
         TABLESPACE OM1,
     PARTITION DEPT_ID_2 ValueS LESS THAN (250)
         TABLESPACE OM2,
     PARTITION DEPT_ID_3 ValueS LESS THAN (500)
         TABLESPACE OM3,
     PARTITION DEPT_ID_4 ValueS LESS THAN (750)
         TABLESPACE OM4,
     PARTITION DEPT_ID_5 ValueS LESS THAN (MAXVALUE)
         TABLESPACE OM5)
DISABLE ROW MOVEMENT;
```

Figure 27-2 illustrates the partitioned STUDENTS table.

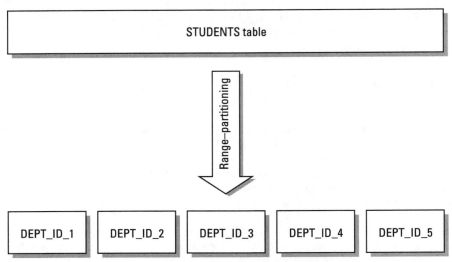

Figure 27-2: The STUDENTS table after range-partitioning

Each partition can have its own storage characteristics allowing tables to span multiple tablespaces. The STUDENTS table is partitioned based on the STUDENTS_DEPT_ID column values. Five partitions are created in this example. These partitions have the following names and range values:

- ✦ DEPT_ID_1 — Range 0 to 99
- ✦ DEPT_ID_2 — Range 100 to 249
- ✦ DEPT_ID_3 — Range 250 to 499
- ✦ DEPT_ID_4 — Range 500 to 749
- ✦ DEPT_ID_5 — Range 750 to MAXVALUE

The MAXVALUE keyword is used to allow for any rows that do not fit into the other partition range to be allocated within the last partition. The MAXVALUE keyword is usually reserved for the very last partition and is used to indicate that there is no upper limit to the values in that partition.

The STUDENTS table can also be partitioned using Oracle8i's Schema Manager. Schema Manager provides a visual interface to create, maintain, split, and drop the partitions of a table. Figure 27-3 illustrates the STUDENTS table partitions in the Oracle8i Schema Manager.

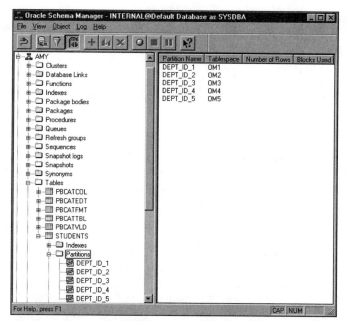

Figure 27-3: Partitions through the Oracle8i Schema Manager

Table Partition Attributes

Oracle8i implements horizontal partitioning using range partitioning. Range partitioning maps rows to partitions based on the range of the partition column values. Implement range partitioning by using the following clauses in the CREATE TABLE statement:

```
PARTITION BY Range ( Column_list )
VALUES LESS THAN ( Value_list )
```

The PARTITION BY RANGE Clause

The PARTITION BY RANGE clause defines the columns used to partition the table. The column_list is also known as the partitioning columns. The following statement specifies this clause:

```
PARTITION BY Range (STUDENT_DEPT_ID)
```

The VALUES LESS THAN Clause

The VALUES LESS THAN clause for a table partition specifies the upper-bound values for the partitioned columns. The lower-bound value is always derived. The lower-bound value for one partition is the upper-bound value of the previous partition. Each partition in the list when you create a table must have an upper-bound value that is greater than that specified for the previous partition in the list. For example, the partition DEPT_ID_2 has an upper-bound key value of 250, which is greater than the upper-bound value for the previous partition DEPT_ID_1:

```
PARTITION DEPT_ID_1 ValueS LESS THAN (100)
    TABLESPACE OM1
PARTITION DEPT_ID_2 ValueS LESS THAN (250)
    TABLESPACE OM2
```

Note If the partitioning column contains null key values, Oracle8i sorts them greater than the other partition key values, but less than the MAXVALUE. Thus, in partitioning a table on columns that contain null values, the last partition's bounds should specify the MAXVALUE keyword. Otherwise, Oracle8i will not be able to place the respective null rows in any of the defined partition ranges, and an error will occur for that transaction.

Using Multiple Columns to Partition Tables

If more than one column is defined for the partition, Oracle8i treats the partition key values as vectors to decide in which partition a row will be placed. For example, the following statement defines a multicolumn partition for the STUDENTS table:

```
PARTITION BY Range (STUDENT_ID, STUDENT_DEPT_ID)
(    PARTITION DEPT_ID_1 ValueS LESS THAN (1000, 100)
        TABLESPACE OM1,
     PARTITION DEPT_ID_2 ValueS LESS THAN (2000, 250)
        TABLESPACE OM2,
     PARTITION DEPT_ID_3 ValueS LESS THAN (3000, 500)
        TABLESPACE OM3,
     PARTITION DEPT_ID_4 ValueS LESS THAN (4000, 750)
        TABLESPACE OM4,
  PARTITION DEPT_ID_5 ValueS LESS THAN (MAXVALUE,MAXVALUE)
        TABLESPACE OM5);
```

If a row is inserted with the keys (2500, 150), the row is inserted into the DEPT_ID_3 partition because key (2500, x) is less than (3000, x) and greater than (2000, x). Multicolumn partitions are sometimes used to help divide data evenly across the defined partitions.

Partition Names

You should identify every partition by a name. If you do not specify a name, Oracle will assign one for you. Each partition's name must be unique in respect to the other partitions defined for the same parent table or index. This unique naming scheme enables you to refer to the partitions directly in data manipulation, import, export, and maintenance operations. For example, the following SELECT statement only returns rows that exist in the DEPT_ID_1 partition.

```
SQL> SELECT STUDENT_FIRST_NAME, STUDENT_DEPT_ID
 2 FROM AMY.STUDENTS Partition (DEPT_ID_1);
STUDENT_FIRST_NAME          STUDENT_DEPT_ID
- - - - - - - - - - - - - - - - - - - - - - - -
Amy                              50
Sampson                          25
Einstein                         68
Cortney                          99
Patrick                          54
Chandi                           10
6 Rows selected.
```

Hash partitioning

Hash partitioning is a new way to partition data that was introduced in Oracle8i. Instead of distributing rows to partitions based on the range that a column value falls into, hash partitioning uses a hashing function on a column value to evenly distribute rows between multiple partitions. You can use hash partitioning to evenly distribute a table's data across two or more tablespaces, which in turn can be mapped to different disks. The syntax follows:

```
[PARTITION BY HASH (column list)
(PARTITION partition_name [ TABLESPACE tablespace_name] , ... )
     -- or --
( PARTITIONS number_partitions [ STORE IN tablespace_name,  ...
] )

[ENABLE | DISABLE ROW MOVEMENT ]
```

You can choose two different ways to specify the partitions for hash partitioning:

✦ List each partition by name and then (optionally) name the tablespace in which each partition is stored. This gives you a great deal of control over the name and location of the partitions that are created.

✦ Specify a number of partitions and then optionally list one or more tablespaces in which the partitions are stored. If you specify more partitions than tablespaces, the database cycles through the tablespaces as many times as needed to create the specified number of partitions.

Regardless of which method you use for hash partitioning, it is recommended that you end up with a total number of partitions that is a power of two (2, 4, 8, 16, and so on) for optimum performance.

The ENABLE ROW MOVEMENT clause can be used with this format of partitioning to allow rows to migrate from one partition to another if the row's data warrants it.

Following is an example in which a table is partitioned into four specifically named hash partitions:

```
CREATE TABLE BOOKSTORE
(BOOKSTORE_ID NUMBER PRIMARY KEY,
STATE VARCHAR2(20) NOT NULL,
ZIP_CODE VARCHAR2(11) NOT NULL)
PARTITION BY HASH (STATE, ZIP_CODE)
(PARTITION BKPART_A TABLESPACE BOOKSTORE_A ,
 PARTITION BKPART_B TABLESPACE BOOKSTORE_B ,
 PARTITION BKPART_C TABLESPACE BOOKSTORE_A ,
 PARTITION BKPART_D TABLESPACE BOOKSTORE_B)
ENABLE ROW MOVEMENT;
```

In the previous example, the BOOKSTORE table is partitioned into four partitions named BKPART_A through BKPART_D. Two tablespaces are used to store the partitions: BOOKSTORE_A and BOOKSTORE_B. Partitioning is based on the STATE and ZIP_CODE columns.

Composite partitioning

A table created with composite partitioning gives you a two-step partitioning plan. First, the table is partitioned the same as a range partitioned table. Then, each partition is subsequently partitioned using hash partitioning. The syntax for this combination, or composite partitioned table, is as follows:

```
[PARTITION BY RANGE (column list)
(SUBPARTITION BY HASH (column list)
 SUBPARTITIONS number_partitions [ STORE IN tablespace_name,
 ... ]
)
(PARTITION [ part_name] VALUES LESS THAN (values list) , ...)]
[ENABLE | DISABLE ROW MOVEMENT ]
```

The syntax of this method combines the syntax of both the range and the hash partition syntax. The formulation of the composite partitioned table can be broken into three steps:

1. Define the list of columns for the range partitioning.

2. Define the hash partitioning for your subpartitions: You define the column list for hash partitioning and the number of subpartitions and (optionally) the tablespaces where the subpartitions are stored.

3. Complete the definition of the range partitions.

As an example, let's create a table called BOOKSALES that is composite partitioned. The range partition will be on the BOOK_SALE_AMOUNT column. The hash subpartition will be on the SALES_DATE column. Listing 27-2 shows the CREATE TABLE command:

Listing 27-2: Using the CREATE TABLE command to create BOOKSALES

```
CREATE TABLE BOOKSALES
    (BOOKSALES_ID NUMBER,
     SALES_DATE DATE,
     BOOK_SALE_AMOUNT NUMBER,
     SALES_REP_NAME VARCHAR2(30),
     CUSTOMER_ID NUMBER)
PARTITION BY RANGE (BOOK_SALE_AMOUNT)
    (SUBPARTITION BY HASH (SALES_DATE)
     SUBPARTITIONS 8 STORE IN BK_STORAGE_A, BK_STORAGE_B)
(PARTITION SMALL_SALE VALUES LESS THAN (150),
 PARTITION MEDIUM_SALE VALUES LESS THAN (450),
 PARTITION LARGE_SALE VALUES LESS THAN (MAXVALUE));
```

As you look at the example, you can see that there are three range partitions (SMALL_SALE, MEDIUM_SALE, and LARGE_SALE). Within each of these partitions, there are eight subpartitions divided by the values found in the SALES_DATE column. These subpartitions are stored in two tablespaces: STORAGE_A and STORAGE_B.

This kind of partitioning is obviously aimed at very large tables. In addition, the partition you design must match the query activity for the table. When you do this, you are taking advantage of Oracle8i's enhanced optimization for partitioned tables and indexes.

Equi-partitioning

When you create indexes on a partitioned table, you can choose to also partition the indexes that you are creating. However, you do not need to partition your indexes to match your table. If you do choose to define your index partitions to match your table partitions, then your index partitions are said to be equi-partitioned. Equi-partitioning also applies when two or more related tables are partitioned on the same set of columns.

For example, if the STUDENTS table is partitioned using STUDENT_ID and STUDENT_DEPT_ID, and the STUDENT_HOUSING table also uses the same partition columns, the two tables are equi-partitioned. The equi-partition of tables has the following advantages:

✦ Oracle8i improves the partitioned table's execution plan in complex JOIN and SORT operations.

✦ Media recovery time is reduced, as dependent tables or indexes can be recovered to the same time.

✦ You can achieve table and index equi-partitioning using local indexes.

Creating Index Partitions

The Oracle Optimizer can take advantage of partitioned indexes just like it does for partitioned tables. You can create two different types of partitioned indexes (local or global), depending on what you need. These two types of partitioned indexes are described in this section, along with a summary of recommendations for partitioning indexes. These two types of range partitioned indexes can be created:

✦ **Local indexes** — an index that covers each table partition individually

✦ **Global indexes** — An index that spans all the table partitions.

Both types of indexes abide by the following index partitioning rules:

✦ A partitioned index cannot be applied on cluster tables.

✦ A bitmap index on a partitioned table must be a local index.

✦ Partitioned and nonpartitioned indexes can be applied to partitioned and nonpartitioned tables.

✦ Bitmap indexes on nonpartitioned tables cannot be range partitioned.

Local indexes

Local indexes contain partition keys that only map to rows stored in a single named partition. If a local index is created for the STUDENTS table, five indexes are created — one for each partition. You can create a local index on a partition by issuing the CREATE INDEX command using the local attribute. For example, the following CREATE INDEX statement creates a local index called DEPT_IDX on the STUDENTS table:

```
CREATE Index DEPT_IDX ON STUDENTS (STUDENT_DEPT_ID)
LOCAL
(    PARTITION DEPT_ID_1 TableSPACE OM1,
     PARTITION DEPT_ID_2 TableSPACE OM2,
     PARTITION DEPT_ID_3 TableSPACE OM3,
     PARTITION DEPT_ID_4 TableSPACE OM4,
     PARTITION DEPT_ID_5 TableSPACE OM5);
```

Figure 27-4 illustrates the local index DEPT_IDX.

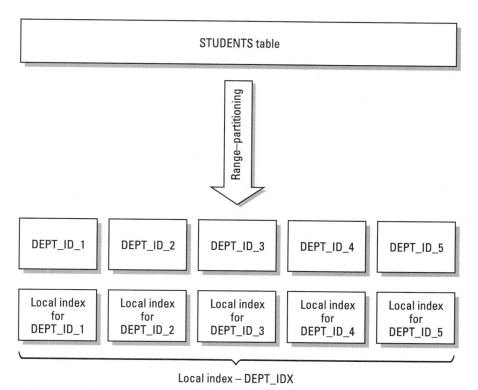

Local index – DEPT_IDX

Figure 27-4: The local index — DEPT_IDX

Every local index is equi-partitioned with respect to the underlying table. If the index is created using the same partition columns and range partition keys as the underlying partitioned table, the local index is called a local prefixed index. If a local index is created using columns that are not in the partition key of the underlying table, the index is called a local nonprefixed index. Local indexes have the following advantages:

✦ Only the local index is affected if a single partition is involved in DML statements.

✦ Partition independence is supported. If, for example, a different partition fails, the partition's index is unaffected.

✦ Only local indexes can support individual partition import and export routines.

✦ Oracle8i ensures better query access plans. Once the Optimizer has eliminated partitions, only the local indexes within the remaining partitions are used for index lookups.

✦ Incomplete recovery is simplified because the partition and the respective local index can be recovered to the same time.

✦ Local indexes can be rebuilt individually.

✦ Bitmap indexes are supported only as local indexes.

There are two types of local indexes:

✦ **Local prefixed indexes.** A local prefixed index uses the partition columns in its index. For example, the STUDENTS index DEPT_IDX is a local prefixed index.

✦ **Local nonprefixed indexes.** A local nonprefixed index does not contain any partition columns in its index. For example, if the STUDENTS table has an index based on ZIPCODE, the index would be a local nonprefixed index. Local nonprefixed indexes are very useful in historical tables because they provide fast access to data required for reporting and other DSS requirements.

Note   A nonprefixed index scan is more expensive than a prefixed index scan.

Global indexes

A global index contains keys that refer to more than one partition of an underlying table. You create a global index by using the global attribute of the CREATE INDEX command. A global index is not usually equi-partitioned with its underlying partitioned table. In general, all nonpartitioned indexes are treated as global prefixed indexes. For example, the DEPT_IDX index on the STUDENTS table can be created as a global index with the following CREATE INDEX statement:

```
CREATE Index DEPT_IDX ON STUDENTS (STUDENT_DEPT_ID)
GLOBAL PARTITION BY Range (STUDENT_DEPT_ID)
  (PARTITION DEPT_ID_1 ValueS LESS THAN (1000, 100)
        TABLESPACE OM1,
    PARTITION DEPT_ID_2 ValueS LESS THAN (2000, 250)
        TABLESPACE OM2,
    PARTITION DEPT_ID_3 ValueS LESS THAN (3000, 500)
        TABLESPACE OM3,
    PARTITION DEPT_ID_4 ValueS LESS THAN (4000, 750)
        TABLESPACE OM4,
  PARTITION DEPT_ID_5 ValueS LESS THAN (MAXVALUE,MAXVALUE)
        TABLESPACE OM5);
```

Figure 27-5 illustrates the global index DEPT_IDX.

Global partitions can be created with different partition bounds than the underlying table's partitions. But even if you define the bounds identically to the underlying table, Oracle8i does not treat global indexes as equi-partition indexes. As a result, global indexes require more maintenance than local indexes.

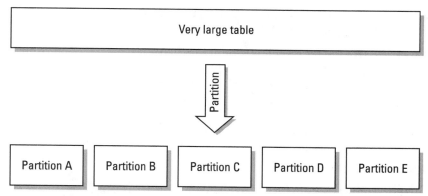

Figure 27-5: The global index — DEPT_IDX

Note   When using global indexes, use the MAXVALUE keyword for the highest bound on the last partition. This keyword takes all respective values into account in the underlying table.

Maintaining global indexes on a very large table is time consuming because of the following reasons:

✦ If the underlying partition is removed or moved, the global index is immediately affected because it spans all partitions of the underlying table. You need to rebuild the global index with the time proportional to the size of the table — not the partition directly affected by the operation.

✦ If the partition needs to be recovered to a time, the partition and the global index need to be resynchronized to the same time. Thus, the global index will need to be rebuilt.

Guidelines for partitioning indexes

Implementing the correct type of index on a very large table affects the performance of the respective DML commands against the table as well as any necessary maintenance operations. The following points provide a guide in selecting the proper index for a large table:

✦ If the table requires regular maintenance, local indexes are recommended.

✦ If the table is historical, query performance can be improved by using local nonprefixed indexes.

✦ If the table requires regular maintenance, use local indexes. If the partition resides on its own tablespace, you can still access the underlying table while the partition is brought offline for maintenance.

✦ The downtime for a partition is proportional to the size of the partition — not to the size of the underlying table.

Changing Partition Attributes

You can use the ALTER TABLE command to modify certain aspects of partitions. In fact, looking at the syntax explanation in Oracle8i documentation, there are 15 different variations on the ALTER TABLE command just for modifying partitioning. Here are a few of the modifications you can make to partitions:

✦ Move a partition from one tablespace to another.

✦ Add another partition.

✦ Rename a partition.

✦ Modify storage clauses for range and composite partitions.

✦ Split partitions.

✦ Merge partitions.

The following list of ALTER commands manage and maintain partition tables:

✦ MODIFY PARTITION — Modifies the real physical attributes of the partition.

✦ RENAME PARTITION — Renames a partition to another name.

✦ MOVE PARTITION — Moves a partition to another segment.

✦ COALESCE PARTITION — Moves the data of a specified partition into remaining partitions and then drops the partition. This applies only to hash partitions.

✦ ADD PARTITION — Adds a new partition to the table. It is usually added after the highest partition.

✦ DROP PARTITION — Removes a partition and its data from the table.

✦ MERGE PARTITION — Merges partitions into a single partition.

✦ TRUNCATE PARTITION — Efficiently removes all rows in a partition.

✦ SPLIT PARTITION — Creates a new partition from an old partition.

✦ EXCHANGE PARTITION — Exchanges the data between a partition and a nonpartitioned table.

Following is an example of a command to move one partition (BKPART_D) of the BOOKSTORE table to the tablespace named BOOKSTORE_D.

```
ALTER TABLE BOOKSTORE
MODIFY PARTITION BKPART_D TABLESPACE BOOKSTORE_D);
```

Splitting a partition

Splitting a partition allows you to readjust the partitioning and create new partitions out of an old partition. This might be needed when one partition in a table grows significantly larger than the others. Using the STUDENTS table as an example, let's say we have defined several partitions, and the final two partitions defined in the CREATE TABLE command look like the following:

```
...
PARTITION DEPT_ID_4 VALUES LESS THAN (750),
PARTITION DEPT_ID_5 VALUES LESS THAN (MAXVALUE)
```

Now you want to divide the final partition (DEPT_ID_5) into two partitions. You want one partition to have an upper-bound of 950 and the other partition to hold all values from 950 on up. Consider this command:

```
ALTER TABLE STUDENTS SPLIT PARTITION DEPT_ID_5 AT (950) INTO
PARTITION DEPT_ID_5 VALUES LESS THAN (950)
PARTITION DEPT_ID_6 VALUES LESS THAN (MAXVALUE);
```

Whenever you use the ALTER TABLE command to modify partition information, only the partitions that you specify in the command are changed. The specifications for the other partitions remain the same.

Merging partitions

Merging partitions is a way to consolidate space, and it allows you to drop a partition that you have emptied without losing any data. When you merge partitions, you must always merge two adjacent partitions. Merging does the opposite of splitting. The resulting new partition inherits the upper-bound of the higher partition. Here is the syntax for merging partitions:

```
ALTER TABLE table_name
MERGE PARTITIONS partition_1, partiton_2 INTO PARTITION
new_partition;
```

This is a valid command only for range partitioned tables. One exception applies: You cannot merge partitions in index-organized tables, even if those tables are range partitioned.

Exchanging data between a partition and a table

If you have a partitioned table that contains historical data in a data warehouse, there are times when you want to load all your current data into the historical table. You can do this with a new feature called EXCHANGE PARTITION. This new feature gives you a fast and efficient method of moving data into a partitioned table, one partition at a time. You specify a nonpartitioned table and a partition, and the two objects exchange data.

To accomplish a data exchange, use the `ALTER TABLE` with the `EXCHANGE PARTITON` clause. (This can also be done with subpartitions in exactly the same way.) The syntax is as follows:

```
ALTER TABLE partitioned_table_name
EXCHANGE partition_name WITH TABLE non_partitioned_table_name
[INCLUDING | EXCLUDING INDEXES ]
[ WITH | WITHOUT VALIDATION ]
[ EXCEPTIONS INTO exception_table_name ];
```

The basic example shown below moves the data in a table named `CURRENT_DEPARTMENT` into the `STUDENTS` table's `DEPT_ID_6` partition. All the current data in the `DEPT_ID_6` partition is moved to the `CURRENT_DEPARTMENT` table as part of this same process.

```
ALTER TABLE STUDENTS
EXCHANGE DEPT_ID_6 WITH TABLE CURRENT_DEPARTMENT;
```

Dropping partitions

If you drop a partition, all the data in that partition is removed as well. If you want to preserve the data, you should merge the data into other partitions before dropping the partition. The syntax to drop a partition is as follows:

```
ALTER TABLE partitioned_table_name DROP PARTITION
partition_name;
```

You cannot use this command if there is only one partition in the table. You must drop the table instead.

Using the ALTER INDEX command

The `ALTER INDEX` command may be used to modify partitioned indexes. The following options are available to you:

✦ `REBUILD PARTITION`—Rebuilds one partition of an index

✦ `DROP PARTITION`—Removes a partition from a global index

✦ `SPLIT PARTITION`—Splits a global partition into two partitions

✦ `UNUSABLE`—Marks the index as unusable

✦ `RENAME PARTITION`—Renames a partitioned index

The syntax for the `ALTER INDEX` command is similar to the `ALTER TABLE` command for the corresponding action on a partitioned table.

Partitions and the data dictionary

You can find out about partitioned tables and indexes in your database by querying the data dictionary. Use the following views to access information on the implemented partitions in a database. Remember that DBA, USER, and ALL are prefixes on these views that narrow or broaden the scope of objects covered in the view. The USER-prefixed views report only partitions owned by the user logged on to the database when executing the query. The DBA prefix reports all partitions and is available to DBA-level users. The ALL prefix reports partitions you own or that you have been granted privileges to view.

✦ DBA_IND_PARTITIONS—Returns one row for each index partition in the database

✦ DBA_TAB_PARTITIONS—Returns one row for each table partition in the database

✦ DBA_PART_COL_STATISTICS—Returns statistics such as the low and high values in the partition and when it was last analyzed.

✦ USER_TAB_PARTITIONS

✦ USER_PART_COL_STATISTICS

✦ USER_IND_PARTITIONS

✦ ALL_TAB_PARTITIONS

✦ ALL_IND_PARTITIONS

✦ ALL_PART_COL_STATISTICS

Here is an example of a query and the resulting data using the USER_TAB_PARTITIONS view:

```
SQL> SELECT PARTITION_NAME, NUM_ROWS,
  2 BLOCKS, AVG_ROW_LEN
  3 FROM USER_TAB_PARTITIONS
  4 WHERE TABLE_NAME = 'STUDENTS_PART'
  5 /
PARTITION_NAME                   NUM_ROWS    BLOCKS AVG_ROW_LEN
-------------------------------- ---------- ---------- -----------
DEPT_ID_2                                 3          1          12
DEPT_ID_3                                 0          0           0
DEPT_ID_4                                 3          1          13
DEPT_ID_5                                 0          0           0
DEPT_ID_1                                 0          0           0
```

Summary

In this chapter, you learned:

✦ With the lowering of hardware prices and the escalation of data use, the database must store more complex and large data, such as video, movies, graphic images, and sound (wav) files.

✦ The term VLDB refers to databases of a terabyte in size. This chapter has addressed the design, implementation, and management of VLDBs through the use of Object Partitioning and Large Objects (LOBs).

✦ Commonly, certain database implementations only contain a few extremely large tables that qualify the database as VLDB. These objects can be partitioned into smaller and more manageable units.

✦ Partitioned units are transparent to users.

✦ The PARTITION BY RANGE clause used within a CREATE TABLE statement creates a partitioned table.

✦ The PARTITION BY RANGE clause permits the horizontal partitioning of data in a custom or equi-partitioned fashion.

✦ The following indexes can be created for partitioned tables: local prefixed, local nonprefixed, and global.

✦ Partitioning a very large table has the following advantages: reduction of database downtime, increased query performance, and better disk access.

✦   ✦   ✦

Using Large Object Types

CHAPTER

28

Gone are the days when business applications dealt only with highly structured numeric and text fields. Today's applications tackle a wide variety of complex and large datatypes including video, graphic images, sound, and documents. A Web commerce application might need to store pictures for a Web store. A Web site delivering the news must be able to serve up sound and video. Any database backing such an application must be capable of storing these types of data. Oracle8i delivers that capability through its support of large objects (LOBs). This chapter explains the large object types available with Oracle8i, shows you how to create tables with large object columns, and then shows you how to use the built-in DBMS_LOB package to manipulate those large objects.

What Are Large Objects?

The definition of a large object might depend on your definition of *large*. Where Oracle is concerned, a *large object* is an item that potentially may contain large amounts of binary or text data. The data may have a structure, but the structure will be opaque to Oracle. For example, a compressed GIF image certainly has a structure to it (or else how could your browser display it?), but Oracle sees only a stream of bytes.

Oracle allows large objects to be up to 4GB in size. That's ample room to store most files that people work with today. Oracle frequently uses the acronym LOB, which is derived from *Large OB*ject, to refer to large objects in general.

Oracle supports two major types of large objects: internal LOBs and external LOBs. The distinction between the two categories is based on whether the datatype is stored internally or externally with respect to the Oracle8i database. An internal LOB is one that is stored inside the database files. An external LOB is one that is stored in a file outside of Oracle.

Internal LOBs

Internal LOBs are those that are stored inside the database. They can be defined as columns in a table or as attributes of an object type. Oracle8i supports the following three datatypes for internal LOBs:

✦ BLOB (binary data)

✦ CLOB (single-byte character data)

✦ NCLOB (Multibyte national character data)

Storing LOBs internally has a couple of benefits. Operations on internal LOBs participate fully in transactions. You can make changes to an internal LOB and then roll back or commit those changes. Internal LOBs also get backed up with the database, and you can use normal database recovery operations to restore them.

External LOBs

The BFILE type is an external LOB type. An *external LOB* is one that is stored outside the database. BFILE is the only external LOB type that Oracle8i supports. The BFILE type defines a LOB that is really just a pointer to an operating system file. The actual LOB data is then stored in that file. Unlike the internal LOBs, BFILEs are read-only. You can't create them using Oracle. You need to get them from some other source. Also, unlike internal LOBs, BFILEs don't participate in transactions.

The BFILE type may seem a bit odd at first, but it can be useful if you are dealing with files that are normally accessed by external programs and that only occasionally need to be retrieved through the database. If you have a set of GIF files supporting a Web site, you may want to store them as BFILEs. That way, you eliminate the overhead of loading them all into the database.

Creating a Table with LOBs

To create a table with LOB columns, you first need to decide on the column names and the datatypes to use. Then you need to give some thought to how you want to store those objects. Creating a table with large object columns can be as simple as choosing a LOB datatype and defining a column based on it. Consider this example:

```
CREATE TABLE student (
   student_id          INTEGER,
   student_history     CLOB
);
```

That's not a very robust approach, though. LOBs can get quite large, and they can impact the performance of queries against a table. You're wiser if you take a little time to think about how you want to store them. You can specify almost as many storage options for a LOB column as you can for the table itself. You also need to think about how you want to initialize the LOB columns.

Listing 28-1 provides a more robust example of how to create a table with LOB columns, which also includes appropriate storage clauses. The example includes three LOB columns, including one BLOB, one CLOB, and one BFILE.

Listing 28-1: **Creating a table with LOB columns**

```
CREATE TABLE STUDENT
(
    STUDENT_ID          INTEGER,
    STUDENT_FIRST_NAME  VARCHAR2(25),
    STUDENT_LAST_NAME   VARCHAR2(25),
    STUDENT_PICTURE     BLOB default EMPTY_BLOB(),
    STUDENT_HISTORY     CLOB default EMPTY_CLOB(),
    STUDENT_REPORT      BFILE,
    CONSTRAINT STUDENT_PK
      Primary Key (STUDENT_ID)
) TABLESPACE users
  STORAGE (INITIAL 10K NEXT 10K)
  LOB (STUDENT_PICTURE) STORE AS (
     DISABLE STORAGE IN ROW
     TABLESPACE student_pictures
     STORAGE (INITIAL 1M NEXT 1M)
  ),
  LOB (STUDENT_HISTORY) STORE AS (
     ENABLE STORAGE IN ROW
     TABLESPACE users
     Storage (INITIAL 200K NEXT 100K)
  );
```

Here are some specific items worth noting about this example:

✦ The CLOB and BLOB columns each have an associated LOB clause that specifies both a tablespace and storage characteristics.

✦ The LOB clause for the STUDENT_PICTURE column specifies DISABLE STORAGE IN ROW. The LOB clause for STUDENT_HISTORY, on the other hand, specifies ENABLE STORAGE IN ROW.

✦ The CLOB and BLOB columns both have default values assigned. These defaults are `EMPTY_CLOB()` and `EMPTY_BLOB()`, respectively.

All of these items are significant and will be explained in this chapter.

Setting storage parameters for large object columns

When you create a table with LOB columns, you need to think about the following:

✦ The storage of LOB data, whether you want it to be stored inline with each row of the table

✦ The tablespace in which you want to store the data

✦ The storage parameters that you want to use for the LOB

Oracle treats LOB columns almost as if they were another table. Both tables and LOBS are stored in segments. A *segment* is a set of extents that has been allocated for a data structure. As with any other segment, you can assign a LOB segment to a tablespace, and you can specify storage parameters such as the initial and next extent sizes.

Tip   Consider storing LOB data in a separate tablespace from the main table data. That way, queries that aren't accessing the LOB columns won't have to read past them.

You specify the storage parameters for a large object column by adding a LOB clause to the `CREATE TABLE` statement. The earlier example included two such clauses. The syntax for the LOB clause looks like this:

```
LOB (name[,name...]) STORE AS [segment_name]
    [(lob_param[, lob_param...])])]
```

The following list describes the parameters for this LOB clause:

✦ *name* — The name of a LOB column in the table. One LOB clause can be used for multiple columns. If you list multiple columns here, then you can't specify a segment name.

✦ *segment_name* — A name for the segment. This name will appear in DBA_ SEGMENTS and other data dictionary views that return segment names. If you don't specify a name, Oracle will generate one for you. You can specify a segment name only when the LOB clause is for exactly one LOB column.

✦ *lob_param* — One of the large object parameters described in Table 28-1.

Table 28-1
LOB Parameter Descriptions

Parameter	Description
PCTVERSION *integer*	Controls the percentage of LOB storage space that Oracle uses to hold old versions of LOBs for purposes of read consistency. When you modify a LOB, Oracle tries to preserve the old version for other transactions that might need it. It does this by making new copies of the LOB blocks that you modify. However, if Oracle doesn't eventually overwrite the old versions of those blocks, you'll run out of disk space.
	The PCTVERSION value limits the amount of space that can be used for old versions of LOB blocks. For infrequently modified LOBS, you can make this percentage very low, perhaps even as low as 5 percent. The default value is 10 percent. If you update your LOB columns frequently, consider raising it to 20 percent or even 30 percent.
CACHE / NOCACHE	Specifies whether to cache the LOB values in memory after use. Caching the LOB increases the speed with which a LOB can be accessed a second time. Be sure to specify the CACHE option if you plan to access the LOB frequently; otherwise, use NOCACHE.
LOGGING / NOLOGGING	Specifies that Oracle record all operations on the LOB in the database redo log files. The NOLOGGING option does the opposite. The NOLOGGING option improves performance, but at the risk of your not being able to fully recover the LOB data in the event of a drive failure. Consider NOLOGGING only if you can easily reload the LOBs from an external source.
CHUNK *integer*	Specifies the chunk size to use when manipulating a LOB. This is how much data Oracle reads in from disk at one time when you are accessing the LOB. Oracle always rounds the chunk size up to the nearest even multiple of the database block size. The chunk size can't be larger than either the initial extent size or the next extent size.
	For example, if you specify CHUNK 8 and the data block size is 2KB, a 16KB chunk will be read each time the LOB is accessed.

Continued

	Table 28-1 *(continued)*	
Parameter	**Description**
ENABLE / DISABLE STORAGE IN ROW	Specifies whether the LOB may be stored inline (in the same segment) with the rest of the table data when the LOB size is relatively small. If you use ENABLE STORAGE IN ROW, the LOB column will be stored inline with the table data subject to a 4,000-byte limit. If more than 4,000 bytes (including overhead) are needed to store the LOB, then it will always be stored in its own segment.
	When rows are being accessed directly via an index, inline LOBs can be retrieved faster than out-of-line LOBs because the act of retrieving the row results in the LOB being retrieved as well. However, inline LOB storage may severely decrease the performance of queries doing full tablescans. That's because the inline LOBs can add significantly to the amount of data being scanned.
TABLESPACE *name*	Identifies the tablespace in which you want data for the LOB column to be stored. This can be different from the tablespace used for the table's non-LOB columns.
STORAGE (...)	Specifies storage parameters for the LOB. This is a standard storage clause like that used when creating tables and indexes.

Initializing internal LOBs

When a column doesn't have a value, you're probably used to thinking of that column as being null. LOB columns may also be null. However, LOB columns have the added ability to be empty as well, and being empty isn't the same as being null.

Internally, Oracle manages LOBs using what is called a locator. A *locator* is a structure that contains information about a LOB and that points to where the data making up the LOB is stored. When you store a LOB out of line, it is the locator that tells Oracle where the data really is. Locators are always inline. A *null LOB* is one that doesn't have a locator. An *empty LOB* is one that has a locator but no data.

Before you can work with a LOB — for example, by writing data into it — you must initialize it so that it has a locator. Oracle has two functions that return locators: EMPTY_BLOB() and EMPTY_CLOB().

Each of these functions returns a locator corresponding to the type of LOB indicated by the function name. You can use these functions when inserting data into a table, to be sure that your LOBs are initialized. Consider this example:

```
INSERT INTO STUDENT
(STUDENT_ID, STUDENT_FIRST_NAME, STUDENT_LAST_NAME,
```

```
      STUDENT_PICTURE,
      STUDENT_HISTORY,
      STUDENT_REPORT)
VALUES
(1003, 'AMY','CHANDI', EMPTY_BLOB(), EMPTY_CLOB(), NULL);
```

Another approach to initializing LOBs is to specify default values for the LOB columns when you create the table. For example:

```
STUDENT_PICTURE      BLOB default EMPTY_BLOB(),
STUDENT_HISTORY      CLOB default EMPTY_CLOB(),
```

Initializing the LOB with a locator saves Oracle from having to expand the row to accommodate it later. It also saves work later, because to work with a LOB, you must have a locator that you've selected from a table. In other words, you must have already saved the record with the LOB locator in it.

Using BFILEs

A *BFILE* is a LOB that is stored in operating system files external to the database. Typically, a BFILE is a file stored on disk, but it could also be stored on a CD-ROM, a network drive, or any other external media devices connected to the Oracle8i server.

Before you can use BFILEs, you need to create a DIRECTORY object. The DIRECTORY object is used as an alias for the physical operating system directory that contains the BFILE object. Use the CREATE DIRECTORY command to create DIRECTORY objects. For example, the following statement associates an alias, AMY_ALIAS, with the path e:\jonathan\oracle_bible\amy_files:

```
CREATE DIRECTORY AMY_ALIAS
    AS 'E:\JONATHAN\ORACLE_BIBLE\AMY_FILES';
```

Note   You must have the CREATE ANY DIRECTORY system privilege to create a directory. Also, creating a directory in Oracle doesn't do anything at the operating-system level. You must create the corresponding operating system directory yourself.

For users to be able to use the directory, you have to grant them read access. The following grant gives the user AMY access to the AMY_ALIAS directory:

```
GRANT READ ON DIRECTORY AMY_ALIAS TO AMY;
```

Note   If you create the directory, you automatically get read privileges on it. You don't need to grant them to yourself.

Having read access to a directory in Oracle doesn't mean anything as far as the operating system is concerned. The Oracle software must be given access to the directory at the operating-system level.

With a directory created, you can use the BFILENAME function to insert a value into a table's BFILE columns. This function maps the BFILE column to the physical file. For example, the following statement inserts the file AMY_REPORT.DOC into the STUDENT table:

```
INSERT INTO STUDENT
(STUDENT_ID, STUDENT_FIRST_NAME, STUDENT_LAST_NAME,
 STUDENT_PICTURE,
 STUDENT_HISTORY,
 STUDENT_REPORT)
VALUES
(1003, 'AMY','CHANDI',
 EMPTY_BLOB(),
 EMPTY_CLOB(),
 BFILENAME('AMY_ALIAS', 'AMY_REPORT.DOC')
);
```

Remember, the contents of a BFILE aren't stored in the database. Only the file name and directory are recorded. For the data to be accessible to applications, the file must remain available on disk.

Manipulating LOBs

Once you create a table with a LOB column, you need to be able to insert data into that column. You also need to be able to retrieve it again, and to manipulate it. Oracle8i supports several mechanisms for accessing LOB data. These include the following:

✦ The PL/SQL DBMS_LOB package

✦ The Oracle Call Interface (OCI)

✦ Pro*C/C++

✦ Pro*COBOL

✦ Oracle Objects for OLE (OO4O)

✦ JDBC

The remaining part of this chapter focuses on manipulating LOBs using the DBMS_LOB package from PL/SQL.

Selecting a LOB from a table

Before you can use a LOB in any capacity, you must retrieve its locator. For example, the following PL/SQL retrieves the STUDENT_PICTURE locator:

```
DECLARE
    STUDENT_PIC        BLOB;
BEGIN
    SELECT STUDENT_PICTURE INTO STUDENT_PIC
    FROM STUDENT
    WHERE STUDENT_ID = 1003;
END;
/
```

It's the locator that is stored in the STUDENT_PIC variable, not the entire LOB itself. Once you have the LOB in memory, you can use the routines in the DBMS_LOB package to operate on it.

Writing into a LOB

Two procedures allow you to write data into a LOB. One is DBMS_LOB.WRITEAPPEND. The other is DBMS_LOB.WRITE. The WRITEAPPEND procedure provides an easy way to add data onto the end of a LOB. The WRITE procedure, on the other hand, allows you to write data anywhere into a LOB.

The PL/SQL block shown in Listing 28-2 uses the DBMS_LOB.WRITEAPPEND procedure to write 30 characters to the STUDENT_HISTORY column. Notice that the LOB locator must be retrieved before any writing is done. Notice also that FOR UPDATE is used when retrieving the LOB locator. This is done to lock the row; otherwise, you won't be allowed to update the LOB.

Listing 28-2: Writing data into a LOB column

```
DECLARE
    stud_hist CLOB;
BEGIN
    --Fetch the LOB locator
    SELECT student_history INTO stud_hist
    FROM student
    WHERE student_id = 1003
    FOR UPDATE;

    --The LOB is empty to start with. Append 10 characters
    --onto the end.
    DBMS_LOB.WRITEAPPEND (stud_hist, 10, '1234567890');

    --Do the same thing twice more, giving
    --us a total of 30 characters.
    DBMS_LOB.WRITEAPPEND (stud_hist, 10, '1234567890');
    DBMS_LOB.WRITEAPPEND (stud_hist, 10, '1234567890');
END;
/
```

After executing this PL/SQL block, the LOB in question should contain the following value:

```
12345678901234567890123456 7890
```

The DBMS_LOB.WRITE procedure is a bit more complex than DBMS_LOB.WRITEAPPEND, but with that complexity comes versatility. Using DBMS_LOB.WRITE, you can write anywhere into the LOB by specifying an offset and a length. The PL/SQL block shown in Listing 28-3 replaces characters 11–20 of the LOB created by the previous example.

Listing 28-3: **Replacing data in a LOB column**

```
DECLARE
    stud_hist CLOB;
BEGIN
    --Fetch the LOB locator
    SELECT student_history INTO stud_hist
    FROM student
    WHERE student_id = 1003
    FOR UPDATE;

    --Replace the middle set of 10 characters.
    DBMS_LOB.WRITE (stud_hist, 10, 11, 'abcdefghij');
END;
/
```

The call to DBMS_LOB.WRITE shown in this example specifies 10 as the number of characters to write and 11 as the offset at which to start writing. The value of the LOB after executing this code will be:

```
1234567890abcdefghij1234567890
```

When working with CLOBs, you specify the offset in characters, together with the number of characters to write. When working with BLOBs, you specify these offsets and lengths in terms of bytes.

Note CLOBs and BLOBs participate in transactions. Be sure to commit your changes if you want to make them permanent.

Reading from a LOB

You use the DBMS_LOB.READ function in the DBMS_LOB package for all LOB read operations. For example, the code shown in Listing 28-4 reads the STUDENT_HISTORY column from the STUDENT table for a student with an ID of 1003:

Listing 28-4: **Reading data from a LOB**

```
DECLARE
    STU_HISTORY CLOB;
    HISTORY_LEN BINARY_INTEGER:= 2000;
    OFFSET INTEGER:= 1;
    BUFFER_VAR VARCHAR2(2000);
BEGIN
    SELECT STUDENT_HISTORY INTO STU_HISTORY
    FROM STUDENT
    WHERE STUDENT_ID = 1003;

    DBMS_LOB.READ(STU_HISTORY,
                  HISTORY_LEN,
                  OFFSET,
                  BUFFER_VAR);

    DBMS_OUTPUT.PUT_LINE(BUFFER_VAR);
END;
/
```

When reading a LOB, you may not want to read the entire LOB at once. Instead, you can read a piece at a time. The offset argument to the READ procedure determines the location within the LOB's data stream that reading begins. The first character of a CLOB has an offset of 1, the second character has an offset of 2, and so forth. For BLOBs, the offset is in bytes. The length argument, HISTORY_LEN in this example, tells the READ procedure how many characters (or bytes) that you want to read, beginning from the offset.

Using the DBMS_LOB Package Reference

The DBMS_LOB package contains routines that access BLOBs, CLOBs, NCLOBs, and BFILEs. Each routine requires a LOB locator as input to manipulate or even read a LOB value. Thus, you need a SELECT statement to read the locator for a LOB value into a PL/SQL variable initially. You then pass that locator to the various DBMS_LOB procedures that you call to manipulate the LOB.

Routines that modify BLOBs, CLOBs, and NCLOBs

Several procedures in the DBMS_LOB package are used to modify LOB values. They allow you to write, copy, and erase data. The procedure names are as follows:*

APPEND   Appends the contents of the source LOB to a
                  destination LOB

COPY	Copies all or part of the source LOB to a destination LOB
ERASE	Erases all or part of a LOB
LOADFROMFILE	Loads a BFILE's data into an internal LOB
TRIM	Trims a LOB value to the specified shorter length
WRITE	Writes data to a LOB from a specified offset position

APPEND(*dest_lob, src_lob*)

The APPEND(dest_lob, src_lob) routine appends the source LOB to the destination LOB. The arguments are as follows:

✦ dest_lob — Identifies the LOB to be appended

✦ src_lob — Identifies the LOB to be read and appended to the destination

Both arguments are locators. The row containing the destination LOB must be locked using the SELECT FOR UPDATE statement.

COPY(*dest_lob, src_lob, amount, dest_offset, src_offset*)

The COPY(dest_lob, src_lob, amount, dest_offset, src_offset) routine copies all or part of a source LOB to a destination LOB and takes the following arguments:

✦ dest_lob — Specifies the locator of the destination LOB

✦ src_lob — Specifies the locator of the source LOB

✦ num_bytes — Specifies the number of bytes to copy

✦ dest_offset — Specifies the offset of where to copy into the destination

✦ src_offset — Specifies the offset into the source LOB at which copying begins

The row containing the destination LOB must be locked using the SELECT FOR UPDATE statement.

ERASE(*lob_loc, amount, offset*)

The ERASE(lob_loc, amount, offset) procedure erases all or part of a LOB. The number of bytes erased is returned in the amount parameter. The arguments are as follows:

✦ lob_loc — Specifies the locator of the LOB to be erased

✦ amount — Specifies the number of bytes to be erased

✦ offset — Specifies the offset of LOB to be erased

The row containing the destination LOB must be locked using the SELECT FOR UPDATE statement.

LOADFROMFILE(*dest_lob, src_file, amount, dest_offset, src_offset*)

The LOADFROMFILE(*dest_lob, src_file, amount, dest_offset, src_offset*) procedure copies all or part of an external LOB to an internal LOB and takes the following arguments:

- ✦ *dest_lob*—Specifies the locator of the destination LOB
- ✦ *src_lob*—Specifies the locator of the external source LOB (a BFILE) to be loaded to the destination
- ✦ *num_bytes*—Specifies the number of bytes to copy from the BFILE
- ✦ *dest_offset*—Specifies the offset to use when copying into the destination
- ✦ *src_offset*—Specifies the offset into the source LOB at which copying begins

A BFILE LOB must be successfully opened using the DBMS_LOB.FILEOPEN routine before it can be loaded. After loading the BFILE, you must close it using the DBMS_LOB.FILECLOSE routine.

TRIM(*lob_loc, newlen*)

The TRIM(*lob_loc, newlen*) routine trims the value of the internal LOB to a specified length and takes the following arguments:

- ✦ *lob_trim*—Specifies the locator of the LOB to be trimmed.
- ✦ *newlen*—Sets the new length of the LOB. Oracle will delete any parts of the LOB beyond this point.

WRITE(*lob_loc, amount, offset, buffer*)

The WRITE(*lob_loc, amount, offset, buffer*) routine writes an amount of data into a LOB from the offset position to a specified length. Any data already contained in that space is overwritten. The WRITE procedure takes the following arguments:

- ✦ *lob_write*—Specifies the locator of the LOB to be written
- ✦ *amount*—Specifies the number of bytes to write into the LOB
- ✦ *offset*—Specifies the offset at which the writing is to begin
- ✦ *buffer*—Specifies the input buffer for the write operation

WRITEAPPEND(*lob_loc, amount, buffer*)

The WRITEAPPEND(*lob_loc, amount, buffer*) routine appends data onto the end of a LOB. The WRITEAPPEND procedure takes the following arguments:

- ✦ *lob_write*—Specifies the locator of the LOB to be written
- ✦ *amount*—Specifies the number of bytes to append onto the LOB
- ✦ *buffer*—Specifies the input buffer for the write operation

Routines that read or examine BLOBs, CLOBs, and NCLOBs

The DBMS_LOB procedures described in this section allow you to read data from LOB columns, to compare two LOBs, and to search a LOB for a specific string:

COMPARE	Compares two similar LOB types
GETCHUNKSIZE	Retrieves the chunk size for the LOB
GETLENGTH	Retrieves the length of the LOB
INSTR	Returns the matching position of the nth occurrence of a specified pattern in the LOB
READ	Reads data from the LOB starting at a specified offset position
SUBSTR	Returns part of the LOB value starting at a specified offset position

COMPARE(*lob_1, lob_2, amount, offset_1, offset_2*)

The COMPARE(lob_1, lob_2, amount, offset_1, offset_2) function compares two LOBs of the same datatype. Zero is returned if the two LOBs match exactly; otherwise, a nonzero integer is returned. This routine takes the following arguments:

- ✦ lob_1 — Specifies the locator of the first LOB to compare
- ✦ lob_2 — Specifies the locator of the second LOB to compare
- ✦ amount — Specifies the number of bytes to compare
- ✦ offset_1 — Specifies the offset into LOB #1 at which to begin comparing
- ✦ offset_2 — Specifies the offset into LOB #2 at which to begin comparing

If two BFILE LOBs are being compared, the BFILEs must first be opened using the DBMS_LOB.FILEOPEN routine. Afterwards, the BFILEs must be closed using the DBMS_LOB.FILECLOSE routine.

GETCHUNKSIZE(*lob_loc*)

The GETCHUNKSIZE(lob_loc) routine returns the chunk size of a LOB and takes the following argument:

- ✦ lob_loc — Specifies a LOB locator

The length of an empty LOB is zero.

GETLENGTH(*lob_loc*)

The GETLENGTH(`lob_loc`) routine returns the length of a LOB and takes the following argument:

> ✦ `lob_loc` — Specifies a LOB locator

For BLOBs, the chunk size is in bytes. For CLOBs, it is in characters.

INSTR(*lob_loc, pattern, offset, nth*)

The INSTR(`lob_loc, pattern, offset, nth`) function searches a LOB for a specified pattern of data. The function's return value identifies the starting position of the pattern, if the pattern was found. The DBMS_LOB.INSTR function takes the following arguments:

> ✦ `lob_loc` — Specifies a locator of the LOB to be matched with a pattern
>
> ✦ `pattern` — Specifies the pattern that needs to be located in the LOB
>
> ✦ `offset` — Specifies the offset of where to start the pattern matching operation
>
> ✦ `nth` — Specifies the occurrence number to find

The pattern and the LOB value must be from the same character set.

READ(*lob_loc, amount, offset, buffer*)

The READ(`lob_loc, amount, offset, buffer`) routine reads a specific portion of a LOB into a buffer. The number of bytes read is returned through the amount parameter. DBMS_LOB.READ takes the following arguments:

> ✦ `lob_loc` — Specifies the locator of the LOB to read
>
> ✦ `amount` — Specifies the number of bytes to read
>
> ✦ `offset` — Specifies the offset into the LOB where reading is to begin
>
> ✦ `buffer` — Specifies the buffer to store the output of the read operation

If you attempt to read past the end of the LOB, a NO_DATA_FOUND exception will occur.

SUBSTR(*lob_loc, amount, offset*)

The SUBSTR(`lob_loc, amount, offset`) function extracts a specified amount of data from a LOB and returns it to the calling application. This routine takes the following arguments:

> ✦ `lob_loc` — Specifies the locator of the LOB from which to extract data
>
> ✦ `amount` — Specifies the number of bytes to extract from the LOB
>
> ✦ `offset` — Specifies the offset at which to start the extract operation

OPEN and CLOSE routines

The DBMS_LOB package implements the following procedures and functions for opening and closing a LOB:

CLOSE   Closes a LOB

OPEN   Opens a LOB

ISOPEN   Checks to see if a LOB is open

Opening and closing a LOB is optional and allows you to treat several LOB operations as if they were one. This can affect when triggers on a table are fired.

CLOSE(*lob_loc*)

The CLOSE(*lob_loc*) procedure closes a previously opened LOB. The parameter is as follows:

✦ *lob_loc* — Specifies the locator of the LOB to close

OPEN(*lob_loc, open_mode*)

The OPEN(*lob_loc, open_mode*) procedure opens a LOB. The parameters are as follows:

✦ *lob_loc* — Specifies the locator of the LOB to open.

✦ *open_mode* — Specifies the mode in which you want to open the LOB. Use DBMS_LOB.LOB_READONLY if you want to read data only from the LOB; otherwise, use DBMS_LOB.LOBREADWRITE.

Opening a LOB prior to working with it is optional, but if you do open a LOB, you must remember to close it when you're finished.

ISOPEN(*lob_loc*)

The ISOPEN(*lob_loc*) function can be used to see if a specific LOB is currently open. The one argument is as follows:

✦ *lob_loc* — Specifies the locator of the LOB that you want to check

A value of 1 is returned if the LOB is open; otherwise, 0 is returned.

Read-only routines for BFILEs

The DBMS_LOB package also includes a number of routines that you can use to retrieve data from BFILEs. Remember that BFILEs are stored in operating system files, and that they are external to the database. Because of that, Oracle only allows you to read from BFILEs.

FILECLOSE	Closes the BFILE
FILECLOSEALL	Closes all previously opened BFILEs
FILEEXISTS	Verifies if a specific BFILE exists on the operating system file system
FILEGETNAME	Retrieves the directory alias and file name for a BFILE
FILEISOPEN	Verifies if a BFILE is open
FILEOPEN	Opens a BFILE

FILECLOSE(*file_loc*)

The FILECLOSE(*file_loc*) routine closes a successfully opened external LOB (BFILE) file and takes the following argument:

✦ *file_loc*—Specifies the locator of the BFILE to close

FILECLOSEALL()

The FILECLOSEALL() procedure closes all open BFILEs for a session. It takes no arguments, and is called like this:

```
DBMS_LOB.FILECLOSEALL;
```

FILEEXISTS(*file_loc*)

The FILEEXISTS(*file_loc*) function verifies that a BFILE locator actually points to a valid file on the operating system's file system. This routine takes the following argument:

✦ *file_loc*—Specifies the locator of the BFILE to verify

If the file exists, a 1 is returned; otherwise, a 0 is returned.

FILEGETNAME(*file_loc, dir_alias, filename*)

The FILEGETNAME(*file_loc, dir_alias, filename*) procedure returns the directory alias and physical file name of a specific BFILE locator. The arguments are as follows:

✦ *file_loc*—Specifies the BFILE locator

✦ *dir_alias*—Specifies the variable to hold the alias directory

✦ *filename*—Specifies the variable to hold the physical file name

FILEISOPEN(*file_loc*)

The `FILEISOPEN(file_loc)` function verifies whether a specific `BFILE` is open and takes the following argument:

✦ `file_loc` — Specifies the `BFILE` locator

If the file is open, a 1 is returned; otherwise, a 0 is returned.

FILEOPEN(*file_loc, open_mode*)

The `FILEOPEN(file_loc, open_mode)` procedure opens a `BFILE` for read-only access. No other operations are permitted on the `BFILE` because it is stored externally with respect to the database. The arguments are as follows:

✦ `file_loc` — Specifies the locator of the `BFILE` LOB

✦ `open_mode` — Specifies the mode in which to open the `BFILE`

Currently, the mode can be set only to `DBMS_LOB.FILE_READONLY`. Oracle may extend the `BFILE` manipulation capabilities later, but for now, you can only read.

Routines for use with temporary LOBs

Oracle8i introduces a new feature known as the *temporary LOB*. These are LOBs that you can create that aren't part of any table. The following `DBMS_LOB` procedures and functions work with temporary LOBs:

`CREATETEMPORARY`	Creates a temporary LOB
`FREETEMPORARY`	Gets rid of a temporary LOB
`ISTEMPORARY`	Checks to see if a LOB is temporary

While they exist, temporary LOBs are stored in your temporary tablespace. Only two types of temporary LOB are supported, BLOB and CLOB.

CREATETEMPORARY(*lob_loc, cache, dur*)

The `CREATETEMPORARY(lob_loc, cache, dur)` procedure creates a temporary BLOB or CLOB. The arguments are as follows:

✦ `lob_loc` — Specifies a LOB locator.

✦ `cache` — Specifies whether you want Oracle to read the temporary LOB into the buffer cache. This is a `TRUE/FALSE` value.

✦ `dur` — Specifies the duration of the LOB's existence. Use either `DBMS_LOB.SESSION` or `DBMS_LOB.CALL`, depending on whether you want the LOB to last for the duration of your session or just for one call.

If you don't specify a duration, the default is for the LOB to remain for the entire session.

FREETEMPORARY(*lob_loc*)

The `FREETEMPRARY(lob_loc)` function gets rid of a temporary LOB that you created earlier. The argument is as follows:

✦ *lob_loc* — Specifies a LOB locator pointing to the temporary LOB to be freed

ISTEMPORARY(*lob_loc*)

The `ISTEMPORARY(lob_loc)` function indicates whether a LOB is a temporary LOB. The argument is as follows:

✦ *lob_loc* — Specifies a LOB locator

A value of 1 is returned if the LOB is temporary; otherwise, a 0 is returned.

DBMS_LOB exceptions

The `DBMS_LOB` package raises exceptions that you can trap using the exception keyword in a PL/SQL block. The following exceptions can be raised:

INVALID_ARGVAL	Occurs if the DBMS_LOB routine arguments are either null or out of range
ACCESS_ERROR	Occurs if a read or write operation by a DBMS_LOB routine exceeds the LOB size bounds
NO_DATA_FOUND	Occurs if no data is found in the LOB
VALUE_ERROR	Occurs if the DBMS_LOB routine accepts an invalid input argument.

Summary

In this chapter, you learned:

✦ With the lowering of hardware prices and the escalation of data use, databases are fast becoming the central repository for all data in an enterprise. As a result, databases must store large and complex data such as video, graphic images, and sound. Oracle8i enables you to store these types of data through the use of large objects, or LOBs.

✦ Oracle8i supports four large object types: BLOB, CLOB, NCLOB, and BFILE. The BLOB type is designed for storing large binary objects. The CLOB type is for storing large amounts of character data. The NCLOB type is for character data in the national character set. The BFILE type allows you to store pointers to external operating system files.

✦ The maximum amount of data that you can store in a LOB is 4GB.

✦ The DBMS_LOB package is a built-in PL/SQL package containing procedures and functions for manipulating LOBs.

✦ Oracle8i implements a new type of LOB known as a temporary LOB. Temporary LOBs are stored in a user's temporary tablespace and are not part of any table. A temporary LOB may exist for the duration of the user's session or for just one database call.

✦　　　✦　　　✦

Using Oracle8i's Object Features

O racle8i is an object-relational database. In addition to allowing you to store data in the form of tables, as any relational database should, Oracle8i also allows you to work with objects. Object-oriented design is fast becoming the standard way to develop software. It only makes sense for database technology to follow that trend. Oracle8i's object-oriented features allow you to carry that design paradigm into the database. This chapter provides a brief introduction to Oracle8i's object-oriented technology. You'll learn how to:

✦ Define objects by creating object types

✦ Define order and map methods, allowing you to compare two objects

✦ Store objects in object tables

✦ Store objects as columns in a relational table

Introducing Oracle8i Object Technology

In a nutshell, Oracle8i's object-oriented features allow you to define object types, and then to instantiate objects based on those types. An object type in Oracle is what the rest of the world refers to as a class. It's a collection of attributes, procedures, and functions that are combined into one unit. Attributes are like variables. The procedures and functions are referred to as methods.

Typically, in an object-oriented environment, the methods of an object serve as an interface to the underlying attributes.

The methods manipulate an object, while the attribute records the object's state. Figure 29-1 shows this.

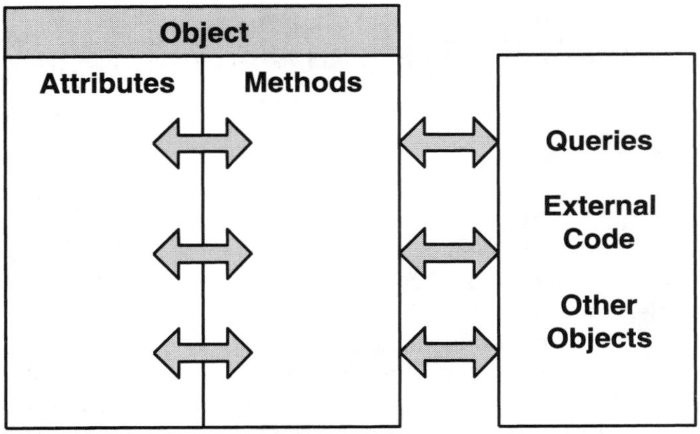

Figure 29-1: Methods are used to manipulate an object.

Figure 29-1 shows the attributes of an object being accessed through its methods. This doesn't always have to be the case. Oracle8i also allows you to directly manipulate the attributes of an object.

Important terms

To work with Oracle8i objects, you need to understand the following terms:

- **Object type.** A template on which a class of objects is based. (This is what most people refer to as an object class.) As you'll see later, object type definitions bear a striking resemblance to PL/SQL packages.
- **Attribute.** A variable that is part of the object type definition.
- **Method.** A procedure or function that is part of the object type definition.
- **Map method.** A method used to determine a numerical value for use in comparing two objects.
- **Order method.** A method used to directly compare two objects, returning a value to indicate whether an object is less than, equal to, or greater than another object.
- **Object table.** A relational table that is defined to match an object type. Such a table will have one column for each object attribute.

Not True

✦ **Object column.** An object column in a relational table.

✦ **Object view.** A view that makes relational data from one or more relational tables appear as if it were really an object table.

Limitations of Oracle8i's object implementation

As innovative as Oracle8i's object implementation is, it does suffer from some limitations. For example:

not True in 10g
X

✦ There is no provision for inheritance. You can't extend one object type to create newer, more complex types.

✦ You can't define private attributes. *Private attributes* are those that are not accessible from outside the object's methods.

✦ You can't define your own constructor for an object.

From an object-oriented standpoint, these are serious limitations. The inability to write your own constructors and to define private attributes prevents you from completely protecting the integrity of an object's attributes. In any true object-oriented language, custom constructors are often used to prevent an object from being instantiated with an invalid set of attribute values. In Oracle8i, there's no way to prevent that from happening. Likewise, because private attributes aren't supported, even if you have a valid set of attributes to start with, there's no way to maintain that. Any piece of code can bypass an object's methods in favor of directly manipulating its attributes.

Understanding Oracle8i Object Types

Object types are the foundation of Oracle8i's object technology. Before you can create an object, or otherwise work with objects, you need to define a type. An object type definition includes the following:

✦ A type name
✦ Attributes definitions
✦ Method definitions

After creating a type, you can create, manipulate, and store objects based on that type.

Defining an object type

The definition for an object type strikingly resembles that of a PL/SQL package definition. Like a package, types are defined in two parts: the type and the type body. The *type* contains definitions for all the attributes and declarations for all the methods. The *type body* contains the code to implement those methods.

Creating a Type

You can use the CREATE TYPE statement to create an object type. Listing 29-1 shows you how to create an object type for the aquatic animals in the Seapark database.

Listing 29-1: **Creating an object type**

```
CREATE OR REPLACE TYPE a_animal AS OBJECT (
    ID_NO                   NUMBER(10),
    TANK_NO                 NUMBER(10),
    ANIMAL_NAME             VARCHAR2(30),
    MARKINGS_DESCRIPTION    VARCHAR2(30),
    BIRTH_DATE              DATE,
    DEATH_DATE              DATE,

    MEMBER PROCEDURE set_tank_no (new_tank_no IN NUMBER),
    MEMBER FUNCTION get_animal_name RETURN VARCHAR2,
    MEMBER PROCEDURE animal_has_died (died_on IN DATE)
);
/
```

Note   You need the CREATE TYPE privilege to create an object type.

The code shown here simply defines the type. It doesn't contain the code to actually implement the three methods. That needs to be done as part of the type body. Were the type to consist only of attributes, you could stop here; there would be no need for a type body. However, since methods are involved, you need to create a type body with code for those methods.

Creating a Type Body

You can use the CREATE TYPE BODY statement to create a type body. The type body in Listing 29-2 contains an implementation of the three methods defined for the a_animal type.

Listing 29-2: **Creating a type body**

```
CREATE OR REPLACE TYPE BODY a_animal AS
    MEMBER PROCEDURE set_tank_no (new_tank_no IN NUMBER) IS
    BEGIN
        tank_no := new_tank_no;
    END;

    MEMBER FUNCTION get_animal_name RETURN VARCHAR2 IS
    BEGIN
        RETURN animal_name;
    END;

    MEMBER PROCEDURE animal_has_died (died_on IN DATE) IS
    BEGIN
        IF death_date IS NOT NULL THEN
            --the animal can't die twice
            RAISE_APPLICATION_ERROR (-20000,
                'Animal ' || TO_CHAR(id_no)
                || ' is already dead.');
        ELSE
            --We only want the date, not the time.
            death_date := TRUNC(died_on);

            --If the animal is dead, it is no longer in a tank.
            tank_no := NULL;
        END IF;
    END;
END;
/
```

The set_tank_no method is a simple method that directly assigns a new value to the tank_no attribute. In object-oriented terms, this is a mutator method. *Mutator methods* are those that are used to change the values of an object's attributes. The get_animal_name method, on the other hand, is an accessor method. *Accessor methods* return the values of attributes.

The animal_has_died method is a bit more interesting. It records the death of an animal. It's interesting because it isn't a method that directly sets an attribute. Rather, it's a method that implements the business rules for a real-life event. When an animal dies, not only must the date of death be recorded, but also the animal must be (hopefully) removed from its tank. The animal_has_died method provides an interface to these business rules. Should the rules change, the method can be modified to reflect the changes. That's the true power of object-oriented programming. Code that interacts with the a_animal object doesn't need to know how to record a death. That's built into the object's definition.

Using constructor methods

A *constructor method* is one that creates an actual instance of an object that you have defined. Constructor methods always have the same name as the object type, and their definition is implied. Whenever you create a type using the CREATE TYPE statement, Oracle automatically creates a constructor method for that type. The method is always defined such that all of the type's attributes are passed as parameters. With respect to the a_animal type, the automatically defined constructor would look like the following:

```
METHOD PROCEDURE a_animal (
    id_no IN NUMBER,
    tank_no IN NUMBER,
    animal_name IN VARCHAR2,
    markings_description IN VARCHAR2,
    birth_date IN DATE,
    death_date IN DATE
)
```

Note that the order in which the attributes are passed as parameters always matches the order in which you declare them in the CREATE TYPE statement.

True object-oriented languages such as C++ or Smalltalk allow you to define your own constructors for an object class. By doing that, you can write validation code that ensures that objects are never created using an invalid set of attribute values. Oracle doesn't support this. With Oracle, you have only one constructor. It allows all attributes to be set and imposes no restrictions on the values.

Instantiating an object

Having defined an object type, you can instantiate an object of that type by calling its constructor. The PL/SQL code in Listing 29-3 creates an object of type a_animal and then makes a call to each of the three methods.

Note If you run this example from SQL*Plus and you want to see the output, be sure to execute the command SET SERVEROUTPUT ON first.

Listing 29-3: **Instantiating and using an object**

```
DECLARE
    animal_one a_animal;
BEGIN
    --Call the constructor to instantiate an object.
    animal_one := a_animal (501, 2, 'Jed',
                            'none',
```

```
                              TO_DATE('1-Jan-2000','dd-mon-yyyy'),
                              null);

      --Change the tank number.
      animal_one.set_tank_no (3);

      --Get the animal name and display it.
      DBMS_OUTPUT.PUT_LINE(animal_one.get_animal_name);

      --Record the animal's death.
      animal_one.animal_has_died (
         TO_DATE('1-Jan-2001','dd-mon-yyyy')
         );
   END;
   /
```

The code in Listing 29-3 shows you how to create an object and use its methods. Later in this chapter, you'll learn how you can save objects in a table.

Using map and order methods

Oracle provides two special types of methods for use in comparing objects with each other. Comparing two objects for equality is fairly easy; you can just compare each of the attributes. However, comparing two objects to see which is *greater* than the other is a more complex problem. You have to define what *greater* means. In terms of animals, does it mean longer, heavier, older, or wider? Answering that question is where map and order methods come into play. They allow you to define the manner in which two objects of the same type are ordered with respect to each other.

Map Methods

Map methods allow you to compute a single scalar value that represents the value of an object in a comparison. You may return a NUMBER, DATE, or VARCHAR2 value.

Map methods are identified using the MAP keyword, which must be the first keyword in the declaration. The version of the a_animal type shown in Listing 29-4 includes a map function that returns a character value.

Listing 29-4: **The a_animal type with a map method**

```
CREATE OR REPLACE TYPE a_animal AS OBJECT (
    ID_NO                      NUMBER(10),
    TANK_NO                    NUMBER(10),
```

Continued

Listing 29-4: *(continued)*

```
ANIMAL_NAME               VARCHAR2(30),
MARKINGS_DESCRIPTION      VARCHAR2(30),
BIRTH_DATE                DATE,
DEATH_DATE                DATE,

MEMBER PROCEDURE set_tank_no (new_tank_no IN NUMBER),
MEMBER FUNCTION get_animal_name RETURN VARCHAR2,
MEMBER PROCEDURE animal_has_died (died_on IN DATE),

MAP MEMBER FUNCTION compare RETURN VARCHAR2
);
/
```

In the type body, you need to write code to implement the map method. Listing 29-5 shows an implementation of the a_animal type's map method that returns an uppercase version of the animal's name for comparison purposes.

Listing 29-5: The implementation for the a_animal type's map method

```
CREATE OR REPLACE TYPE BODY a_animal AS
    MEMBER PROCEDURE set_tank_no (new_tank_no IN NUMBER) IS
    BEGIN
        tank_no := new_tank_no;
    END;

    ...

    MAP MEMBER FUNCTION compare RETURN VARCHAR2 IS
    BEGIN
        RETURN UPPER(animal_name);
    END;
END;
/
```

With a map method defined, you can write SQL queries that sort results based on object columns. You can also write code that compares two a_animal objects. All you have to do is reference the two objects in a comparison expression, and Oracle invokes the map methods automatically. The values returned by the map methods are then used to determine which object is greater than the other, as shown in Listing 29-6.

Listing 29-6: Comparing two a_animal objects

```
DECLARE
    animal_one a_animal;
    animal_two a_animal;
BEGIN
    --Call the constructor to instantiate animal_one
    animal_one := a_animal (501, 2, 'Jed',
                        'none',
                        TO_DATE('1-Jan-2000','dd-mon-yyyy'),
                        null);

    --Call the constructor to instantiate animal_two
    animal_two := a_animal (502, 2, 'Zeeke',
                        'none',
                        TO_DATE('1-Jan-1999','dd-mon-yyyy'),
                        null);

    --Now, compare the two objects
    IF animal_two > animal_one THEN
        DBMS_OUTPUT.PUT_LINE ('Zeeke is greater than Jed');
    ELSIF animal_two < animal_one THEN
        DBMS_OUTPUT.PUT_LINE ('Zeeke is less than Jed');
    ELSE
        DBMS_OUTPUT.PUT_LINE ('Zeeke is equal to Jed');
    END IF;
END;
/
```

Not all object types lend themselves to representation as a simple scalar value. As an alternative to the map method, you can write an order method that performs a more sophisticated comparison.

Note   You can't use both map and order for the same type. An object type can have only one such function defined. You need to choose between the two depending on how you want the objects to be compared.

Order Methods

To implement more complex comparison semantics, you can use an order method. An *order method* is defined for an object type and takes another object of the same type as a parameter. The order method returns an integer value signifying whether the object passed as a parameter is greater than, less than, or equal to the object whose order method has been invoked.

Listing 29-7 shows a version of the a_animal object type with an order method defined.

Listing 29-7: An a_animal object with an order method

```
CREATE OR REPLACE TYPE a_animal AS OBJECT (
    ID_NO                 NUMBER(10),
    TANK_NO               NUMBER(10),
    ANIMAL_NAME           VARCHAR2(30),
    MARKINGS_DESCRIPTION  VARCHAR2(30),
    BIRTH_DATE            DATE,
    DEATH_DATE            DATE,

    MEMBER PROCEDURE set_tank_no (new_tank_no IN NUMBER),
    MEMBER FUNCTION get_animal_name RETURN VARCHAR2,
    MEMBER PROCEDURE animal_has_died (died_on IN DATE),

    ORDER MEMBER FUNCTION compare (other_animal IN a_animal)
    RETURN INTEGER;
);
/
```

Listing 29-8 shows the corresponding type body showing the code for the order method.

Listing 29-8: The implementation for the a_animal type's order method

```
CREATE OR REPLACE TYPE BODY a_animal AS
    MEMBER PROCEDURE set_tank_no (new_tank_no IN NUMBER) IS
    BEGIN
        tank_no := new_tank_no;
    END;

    ...

ORDER MEMBER FUNCTION compare (other_animal IN a_animal)
    RETURN INTEGER IS
    BEGIN
        IF animal_name > other_animal.animal_name THEN
            RETURN 1;
        ELSIF animal_name < other_animal.animal_name THEN
            RETURN -1;
        ELSE
            RETURN 0;
        END IF;
    END;
END;
/
```

The method that you use doesn't affect the code that you write to compare objects. The same example used to demonstrate the map method will work for the order method. The difference is in how Oracle internally does the comparison.

Using order methods is generally less efficient than map methods. This is especially true when you are referencing the object in the ORDER BY clause of a SQL query. When map methods are used, Oracle can call the map method once for each row returned by the query and then sort the results. When an order method is used, Oracle must call that method multiple times for each object as it sorts the results.

Storing Objects in the Database

You can store objects in the database in one of two ways. You can create an object table and store objects as rows in that table, or you can create an object column in a standard, relational table. Each solution has its set of advantages and disadvantages. Object tables are perhaps a bit more versatile because they also let you look at the data relationally. Storing objects as columns, on the other hand, allows you to embed multiple objects in one record.

Using object tables

An *object table* is one in which the attributes of an object type are mapped to columns in the table. Each row in the table then represents one object. Because object tables are like other tables in that they have rows and columns, they can be treated just as if they were any other relational table. You can, for example, write object-oriented code that treats the table as a table of objects, and at the same time use reporting tools that treat the table as a relational table.

Creating an Object Table

To create an object table, you use a special form of the CREATE TABLE command. Instead of supplying a list of columns for the table, you supply a type name instead. For example, Listing 29-9 demonstrates how you can create an object table for the a_animal type.

Listing 29-9: Creating an object table by supplying a type name

```
SQL> CREATE TABLE a_animal_table OF a_animal;

Table created.
```

Continued

Listing 29-9: *(continued)*

```
SQL> DESCRIBE a_animal_table
 Name                           Null?    Type
 ------------------------------ -------- -------------
 ID_NO                                   NUMBER(10)
 TANK_NO                                 NUMBER(10)
 ANIMAL_NAME                             VARCHAR2(30)
 MARKINGS_DESCRIPTION                    VARCHAR2(30)
 BIRTH_DATE                              DATE
 DEATH_DATE                              DATE
```

Notice that when you describe the table afterwards, it looks just like any other table. It's not, really. Oracle does know that you've created the table based on the `a_animal` object. Because it's an object table, you won't be allowed to add or modify any of the columns. In fact, you won't be able to re-create the type anymore either, because that would invalidate the table.

When you create a table like this on an object type, Oracle automatically generates a hidden field to contain an object ID. Oracle then generates unique object IDs for each object that you insert into the table. You won't see the object column when you describe the table, but you will see it if you look at the constraints. Oracle generates a unique constraint on the hidden object ID column.

If you prefer object IDs to be based on the primary key, you can define the table using the syntax shown in this example:

```
CREATE TABLE a_animal_table_2 OF a_animal
    (id_no PRIMARY KEY)
    OBJECT ID PRIMARY KEY;
```

Here, the table named A_ANIMAL_TABLE_2 has been created for the `a_animal type`. The ID_NO column has been defined as the primary key, and the OBJECT_ID clause has been used to cause OBJECT ID to be based on the primary key.

Having created an object table, you can create indexes on that table just as if it were any other table. You can also define constraints on an object table just as if it were any other table.

Note

Oracle is very inflexible in regards to handling object type dependencies. Once you have created a dependency on an object type, whether that dependency is an object table or an object column, Oracle won't allow you to drop, modify, or re-create the object type. If you want to add an attribute or a method to the object type, you have to drop all the dependencies first, then make your changes, and then re-create all the dependent objects. If you have data in those dependent objects, you have to save it first and restore it afterwards.

Inserting Data into an Object Table

You can insert data into an object table in two ways. One way is to use the traditional INSERT statement, as shown here:

```
SQL> INSERT INTO a_animal_table
  2  (id_no, tank_no, animal_name,
  3   markings_description, birth_date)
  4  VALUES (503,2,'Happy','Bent fin',
  5          TO_DATE('1-Jan-1999','dd-mon-yyyy'));

1 row created.
```

Another way to insert rows into an object table is to call the object's constructor to instantiate an object, and then pass that object in the VALUES clause. Here's an example:

```
SQL> INSERT INTO a_animal_table
  2      VALUES (a_animal (504,1,'Lucky','No markings',
  3              TO_DATE('1-jan-1999','dd-mon-yyyy'),
  4              NULL)
  5      );

1 row created.
```

Since the a_animal constructor was called, values had to be supplied for each of the six attributes. This includes the death_date attribute, which in this case was set to null.

Note   The examples in the subsequent sections on retrieving and updating data will not function unless you insert these two records for animals #503 and #504 into the object table.

Retrieving Data from an Object Table

You can retrieve data from an object table in two ways. You can issue a standard SELECT statement against the table to retrieve data relationally, or you can use the VALUE operator to return objects from the table. The following SELECT statement retrieves the name of animal #504 in the standard relational manner:

```
SQL> SELECT animal_name
  2  FROM a_animal_table
  3  WHERE id_no = 504;

ANIMAL_NAME
------------------------------
Lucky
```

To retrieve a row from an object table and have it come back as an object, you need to use the SQL VALUE operator. The VALUE operator takes a correlation variable as an argument, so you must write your query to include one. A correlation variable is an alternate name that you provide for a table listed in the FROM clause of a SELECT query.

Listing 29-10 shows a PL/SQL block that retrieves the a_animal object for animal #504 from the database. Notice that the a_animal_table has been given the correlation name a_a in the query's FROM clause, and that the correlation name is then used with the VALUE operator.

Listing 29-10: **Retrieving an object from an object table**

```
SQL> SET SERVEROUTPUT ON
SQL>
SQL> DECLARE
  2      animal_504 a_animal;
  3  BEGIN
  4      --Retrieve the object from the table.
  5      SELECT VALUE (a_a) INTO animal_504
  6      FROM a_animal_table a_a
  7      WHERE id_no = 504;
  8
  9      DBMS_OUTPUT.PUT_LINE (animal_504.get_animal_name);
 10  END;
 11  /
Lucky

PL/SQL procedure successfully completed.
```

Using the VALUE operator with the correlation name tells Oracle to return the row for the table in question as an object, not as a collection of columns.

Note   The use of a correlation name as an argument to VALUE is necessary. If you supply the table name instead, you will receive an error. The error will most likely be a PLS-00334 error.

Updating an Object in an Object Table

As with inserting and selecting, you can update data in an object table in one of two ways. You can use the standard SQL UPDATE statement to set new values for one or more columns, or you can use a modified form of the UPDATE statement that replaces one object with another.

Using the standard relational UPDATE statement, you could change animal #504's name from Lucky to Unlucky like this:

```
SQL> UPDATE a_animal_table
  2     SET animal_name = 'Unlucky'
  3     WHERE id_no = 504;

1 row updated.
```

If you want to update the entire object, then you need to use the following syntax:

```
UPDATE tablename tn
   SET tn = object
   ...
```

As with the SELECT statement, a correlation name is necessary when updating an object table in this manner. The correlation name is used as the target of a SET clause that places a new object into the row. Listing 29-11 shows an example that retrieves the object for animal #504, changes the animal name to Unlucky, and saves the entire object back into the object table.

Listing 29-11: **Updating an object in a table**

```
SQL> SET SERVEROUTPUT ON
SQL>
SQL> DECLARE
  2      animal_504 a_animal;
  3  BEGIN
  4      --Retrieve the object from the table.
  5      SELECT VALUE (a_a) INTO animal_504
  6      FROM a_animal_table a_a
  7      WHERE id_no = 504;
  8
  9      --Change the name
 10      animal_504.animal_name := 'Unlucky';
 11
 12      --Store the object back into the table
 13      UPDATE a_animal_table a_a
 14      SET a_a = animal_504
 15      WHERE id_no = 504;
 16  END;
 17  /

PL/SQL procedure successfully completed.
```

As when you are selecting an object, you need to be sure that you use a correlation name when updating an object in an object table.

Using object columns

As an alternative to storing an object in an object table, you can store an object as a column of a relational table. The following somewhat contrived example shows how you would create a table with an object column:

```
CREATE TABLE a_animals (
    animal a_animal);
```

This table has one column, but it could just as well have several. In this case, the one column in the table is an object column of type a_animal.

Inserting Data into an Object Column

To insert data into an object column, you must supply an object for that column. You can do this by calling the constructor in the INSERT statement or by passing an object in the VALUES list. The following example inserts a row into the a_animals table, invoking the a_animal object's constructor to create an object for the animal column:

```
SQL> INSERT INTO a_animals (animal)
  2     VALUES (a_animal (505, 1, 'Barney',
  3                  'No markings',
  4                  TO_DATE('1-Jan-2000','dd-mon-yyyy'),
  5                  NULL));

1 row created.
```

Because the animal column is an object column, any value inserted into that column must also be an object. In this example, the constructor was called to create an object as part of the INSERT statement. If you are writing a PL/SQL code, you can pass an object variable instead. See Listing 29-12.

Listing 29-12: **Storing an object variable into an object column**

```
SQL> DECLARE
  2       animal_one a_animal;
  3  BEGIN
  4       --Instantiate an object.
  5       animal_one := a_animal (506, 1, 'Harry',
  6                  'No markings',
  7                  TO_DATE('1-Jan-2000','dd-mon-yyyy'),
  8                  NULL);
  9
 10       --Insert a row into the a_animals table.
 11       INSERT INTO a_animals (animal)
 12           VALUES (animal_one);
 13  END;
```

```
14  /

PL/SQL procedure successfully completed.
```

In this example, an object variable is first instantiated. Then, that object variable is passed to the INSERT statement as one of the values in the VALUES list.

Selecting Data from an Object Column

When dealing with object columns, you can either select the entire column as an object or you can select individual attributes from the object column. If you're selecting the entire column as an object and you're using SQL*Plus to do that, SQL*Plus will display all attributes of the column as a call to the constructor. Consider this example:

```
SQL> select animal from a_animals;

ANIMAL(ID_NO, TANK_NO, ANIMAL_NAME, MARKINGS_DESCRIPTION, BIR
------------------------------------------------------------
A_ANIMAL(505, 1, 'Barney', 'No markings', '01-JAN-00', NULL)
A_ANIMAL(506, 1, 'Harry', 'No markings', '01-JAN-00', NULL)

2 rows selected.
```

If you're writing PL/SQL code, you can use the INTO clause of the SELECT statement to place the resulting object into an object variable. See Listing 29-13.

Listing 29-13: **Retrieving an object from an object column**

```
SQL> SET SERVEROUTPUT ON
SQL> DECLARE
  2       animal_one a_animal;
  3  BEGIN
  4       --Retrieve the object for animal 506.
  5       SELECT animal INTO animal_one
  6       FROM a_animals a
  7       WHERE a.animal.id_no = 506;
  8
  9       --Display the animal name
 10       DBMS_OUTPUT.PUT_LINE(animal_one.animal_name);
 11  END;
 12  /
Harry

PL/SQL procedure successfully completed.
```

In this example, the animal's object is first retrieved into a variable, and then the `DBMS_OUTPUT.PUT_LINE` procedure is used to display the name of the animal.

If you want to select only certain attributes from an object column, you can do that. First, you need to supply a correlation name for the table. Then reference the column and attribute using dot notation, as shown in the following example:

```
correlation.column.attribute
```

The `SELECT` statement in the following example selects the `id_no` and `animal_name` attributes from the `animal` column in the `a_animals` table:

```
SQL> SELECT a.animal.id_no, a.animal.animal_name
  2  FROM a_animals a;

ANIMAL.ID_NO ANIMAL.ANIMAL_NAME
------------ -----------------------------
         505 Barney
         506 Harry

2 rows selected.
```

When you select attributes this way, the correlation name is required. If you leave it off, you'll receive an error.

Updating Data in an Object Column

You can update an object column in one of two ways. You can update the entire column by supplying a new version of the object, or you can update specific attributes. Listing 29-14 presents an example that uses PL/SQL to create an object variable, which is then used to update an object column.

Listing 29-14: **Updating an object column**

```
SQL> DECLARE
  2      animal_one a_animal;
  3  BEGIN
  4      --Retrieve the object for animal 506.
  5      SELECT animal INTO animal_one
  6      FROM a_animals a
  7      WHERE a.animal.id_no = 506;
  8
  9      --Change the animal's name.
 10      animal_one.animal_name := 'Blurry';
 11
 12      --Update the table with the new version of the object.
 13      UPDATE a_animals a
 14      SET a.animal = animal_one
```

```
15      WHERE a.animal.id_no = 506;
16  END;
17  /

PL/SQL procedure successfully completed.
```

If you don't want to write PL/SQL, or you don't want to deal with objects, you can write an UPDATE statement that updates individual attributes in the column. The following shows an alternative way of changing an animal's name:

```
SQL> UPDATE a_animals a
  2  SET a.animal.animal_name = 'Blurry'
  3  where a.animal.id_no=506;

1 row updated.
```

As always, when manipulating objects through SQL, you must use a correlation name for the table in your query.

Using object views

Object views provide you with a way to make existing relational data appear as if it were in an object table. Like a relational view, an object view is based on a SELECT statement. Additionally, object views have an associated object type. The SELECT statement is used to define the source of the data for the type.

The following CREATE VIEW statement defines an object view named animals that allows you to work with the rows in the aquatic_animals table as if they were objects:

```
CREATE OR REPLACE VIEW animals OF a_animal
    WITH OBJECT OID (id_no)
    AS SELECT id_no,
              tank_no,
              animal_name,
              markings_description,
              birth_date,
              death_date
       FROM aquatic_animal;
```

The WITH OBJECT OID (id_no) clause tells Oracle that the id_no column uniquely identifies an object in the object table. This is a requirement when creating object views. When you create an object table, Oracle automatically creates a behind-the-scenes identifier to uniquely identify each object in the table. No such identifier exists for data that you select from relational tables, so you must specify which columns uniquely identify an object in the view.

Once you've created an object view, you can use it as you would an object table. If the view is an updateable view, you can insert, update, and delete through the view. Otherwise, you will need to write instead-of triggers if you want to perform those functions.

 Cross-Reference　See Chapter 15, "Working with Views, Synonyms, and Sequences," for information on what makes a view updateable.

Summary

In this chapter, you learned:

✦ Oracle8i is an object-relational database. It is a hybrid that allows you to slowly move towards working with data in an object-oriented manner while still retaining compatibility with relational applications.

✦ Oracle8i's object support has three major limitations: lack of support for inheritance, inability to define private attributes, and inability to write constructor methods.

✦ To work with objects, you must first create an object type. An object type consists of attribute (variable) and method (procedure and function) definitions. Like PL/SQL packages, object types have both a type definition and a type body. The type definition defines the attributes for the type and also defines the interfaces to the methods. The type body contains the PL/SQL code to implement the type methods.

✦ You can store objects in object tables or as object columns in relational tables. In addition, you can create object views to make relational data appear as if it were an object.

✦ To allow for the comparison and ordering of objects, you may define map and order methods. Map methods assign a single, scalar value to represent an object's order in a sorted list. Order methods compare two objects and enable you to implement complex comparison semantics.

✦　✦　✦

Implementing Resource Management

Resource management is a new feature in Oracle8i that allows you to apportion CPU resources amongst various users and groups of users. The potential for one user or group of users to consume an inordinate amount of resources has always existed. In prior releases of Oracle, you could attempt to address such problems through user profiles, but user profiles are limited. They can cut off a user after that user consumes a certain amount of CPU or I/O, but they can't do the same for a group of users. Also, user profiles cannot meter resources such that a user can spread the effort of executing a large query out over a larger period of time.

Oracle8i's resource management feature brings flexibility to the table. You can apportion CPU time to different user groups on a percentage basis, and you can identify some groups as having a higher priority than others. By doing this, you can ensure that users who are performing critical functions always have the necessary CPU resources available, regardless of what other users may be doing at the same time. In this chapter, you'll learn how to create and manage resource plans in a database.

How Resource Management Works

Resource management works by dividing users into groups based on common resource requirements. A resource plan is then put into place that allocates CPU time amongst the groups that have been defined. This allows you to ensure that no single user, or group of users, uses up all the processing capacity.

Understanding plans, directives, and consumer groups

The resource plan is the basis for resource management in a database. A *resource plan* functions at the instance level, and it consists of a number of resource directives that control how CPU time is allocated to the users connected to that instance. You may define several resource plans for a database, but only one plan can be in effect for an instance at any given time.

Resource plans are made up of resource directives. A *resource directive* is a statement giving a user or a named group of users a specific allotment of CPU time. This allotment is expressed as a percentage of the whole. Resource directives also perform two other functions. You can use them to prioritize groups of consumers, and you can use them to place limits on the degree of parallelism available to a consumer group.

Finally, at the bottom of all this is the resource consumer group. A *resource consumer group* is a named group of users who each have similar resource requirements. For example, you may have a decision support consumer group and a customer care consumer group.

The diagram shown in Figure 30-1 illustrates how you can use the directives for a resource plan to apportion CPU resources to the various consumer groups in a database.

Figure 30-1 shows two consumer groups: the decision support group and the customer care group. The decision support group consists of users who are executing long-running, CPU-intensive, ad hoc queries. The customer care group is composed of users responding to phone calls and other client inquiries. They tend to execute short, predefined queries. Recognizing that it's more important to respond quickly to a customer, 80 percent of the CPU resources have been dedicated to the customer care group. Only 20 percent can be used by the decision support users.

Understanding priority

In addition to allocating CPU by percentage, you can also prioritize those allocations into as many as eight levels. By assigning priorities, you can further subdivide CPU capacity. With respect to the example shown previously in Figure 30-1, you could subdivide the decision support users into two groups: one for vice presidents and one for other executives. Figure 30-2 illustrates this, showing that the vice presidents get most of the decision support CPU capacity.

Here, the customer care group gets 80 percent of CPU allocation. This is just as before. The remaining 20 percent still goes to the decision support users, but that 20 percent has been divided between two distinct subgroups. Vice presidents get 70 percent of the 20 percent allocated to decision support, while all other executives get 30 percent of that 20 percent.

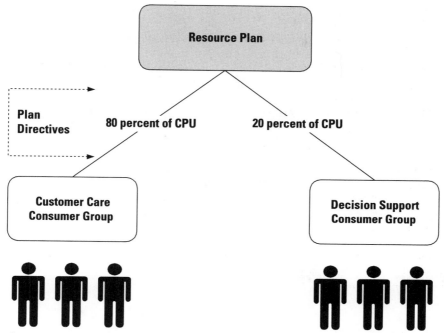

Figure 30-1: Resource directives apportion CPU resources to consumer groups.

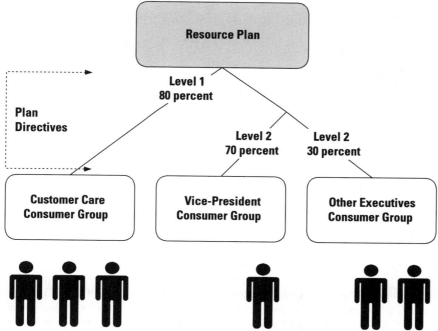

Figure 30-2: Decision support users will get bumped by the higher-priority customer care users.

Nesting plans

Resource plans may also be nested. You can divide one plan into two or more subplans. As with resource priorities, you can also use nested plans to divide and subdivide CPU allocation between various groups and subgroups. However, when a system is not fully loaded, Oracle distributes extra CPU time differently depending on whether plans or priorities are involved. Figure 30-3 shows another way of dividing the CPU time among the three consumer groups shown earlier.

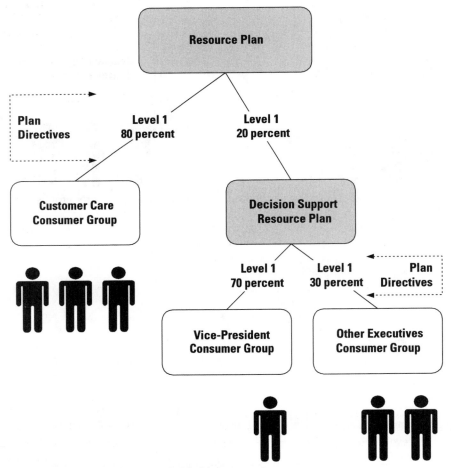

Figure 30-3: CPU allocation divided between three consumer groups

At first glance, it appears that the results of using nested resource plans are the same as you get when you prioritize CPU time. A difference does exist, though, and it's an important one. The key to understanding the difference lies in understanding that extra CPU time is allocated to other users in the same plan based on the priority of those users.

With a single plan, such as that shown in Figure 30-2, any extra CPU time is allocated to users on a priority basis. So if the vice presidents aren't using all of their allotted CPU time, Oracle will reallocate that CPU time on a priority basis. Thus, it might go to the customer care users because they are priority 1 before it would go to the priority 2 users.

The rules change, however, when a resource plan contains one or more subplans. As long as there is at least one user for a subplan, the subplan gets all of its CPU allotment. With respect to Figure 30-3, if there was only one decision support user, that user would be able to use all of the CPU allocated to the decision support plan. In other words, excess CPU allocation within the decision support group goes to other decision support users. Only if no decision support users are logged on at all will that 20 percent become available to the customer care users.

How to Create a Resource Plan

In order to use Oracle8i's resource management features, you need to create a resource plan for your database. The resource plan identifies the consumer groups and allocates resources among them. The process for creating and implementing a resource plan for a database looks like this:

1. Create a work area for use in building the new plan.

2. Create the plan.

3. Create resource consumer groups.

4. Create resource plan directives.

5. Validate the plan.

6. Move the plan from the work area.

7. Set the active plan for the instance.

The work area used to build new resource plans is known as the *pending area*. The process for defining a plan can get fairly complex if you have a lot of different priorities and subplans. The pending area gives you a place to create and revise a plan at your leisure, without having to worry that your partially built plan will affect database operations. This becomes especially important if you happen to be revising the plan that is currently active.

Two built-in PL/SQL packages are used for creating and managing resource plans. You use the DBMS_RESOURCE_MANAGER package to create plans, plan directives, and consumer groups. You use the DBMS_RESOURCE_MANAGER_PRIVS package to grant privileges related to resource plans.

Prerequisites

To work with resource plans, you need to hold a special privilege known as
ADMINISTER_RESOURCE_MANAGER. This privilege is not a standard system privilege,
nor is it a role. It's a privilege that exists only within the context of resource
management.

Granting the ADMINISTER_RESOURCE_MANAGER Privilege

The SYSTEM user and the DBA role each hold the ADMINISTER_RESOURCE_MANAGER
privilege by default. The SYSTEM user, or a user with the DBA role, can grant the
ADMINISTER_RESOURCE_MANAGER privilege to other users by making a call to the
GRANT_SYSTEM_PRIVILEGE procedure in the DBMS_RESOURCE_MANAGER_PRIVS
package. For example, the following call grants this privilege to the user SEAPARK:

```
DBMS_RESOURCE_MANAGER_PRIVS.GRANT_SYSTEM_PRIVILEGE (
    'SEAPARK', 'ADMINISTER_RESOURCE_MANAGER', FALSE);
```

The third argument indicates whether the user getting the privilege is allowed to
further grant that privilege to others. A value of TRUE allows the user to do that. A
value of FALSE prevents the user from further granting the privilege. This is exactly
like the WITH ADMIN OPTION of SQL's GRANT command.

Note   Granting someone the ADMINISTER_RESOURCE_MANAGER privilege allows him
or her to create and manage plans, but it doesn't provide access to the system
views that return information about resource plans. You need to grant SELECT
access to those views as a separate operation.

Determining Who Has the ADMINISTER_RESOURCE_MANAGER Privilege

If you want to find out which users hold the ADMINISTER_RESOURCE_MANAGER
privilege, you can query the DBA_RSRC_MANAGER_SYSTEM_PRIVS view. This view
returns one row for each user with the privilege. Consider this example:

```
SQL> SELECT *
  2  FROM dba_rsrc_manager_system_privs;

GRANTEE              PRIVILEGE                        ADMIN_OPTION
-------------------- -------------------------------- -------------
CTXSYS               ADMINISTER RESOURCE MANAGER      NO
DBA                  ADMINISTER RESOURCE MANAGER      YES
EXP_FULL_DATABASE    ADMINISTER RESOURCE MANAGER      NO
IMP_FULL_DATABASE    ADMINISTER RESOURCE MANAGER      NO
MDSYS                ADMINISTER RESOURCE MANAGER      NO
SYSTEM               ADMINISTER RESOURCE MANAGER      YES
```

The USER_RSRC_MANAGER_SYSTEM_PRIVS view returns the same information, but
only for the current logged-on user. You can query from that if you just want to
check whether you have the privilege yourself.

The DBA_SYS_PRIVS view also shows who has the ADMINISTER RESOURCE MANAGER privilege. That's rather odd, because you can't use the standard GRANT and REVOKE commands to manage it.

Creating the pending area

The first step in the process of creating a new resource plan is to create a pending area. Do that with a call to DBMS_RSRC_MANAGER.CREATE_PENDING_AREA. Consider this example:

```
SQL> EXECUTE DBMS_RESOURCE_MANAGER.CREATE_PENDING_AREA();

PL/SQL procedure successfully completed.
```

Everything else that you do now will be done in the pending area. When the new plan is defined as you want it to be, you can commit the pending changes.

Creating the plan

You create a plan by making a call to the DBMS_RESOURCE_MANAGER package's CREATE_PLAN procedure. All you need is a name for the plan and a comment describing the plan.

The examples in this chapter show you how to implement the scenario shown in Figure 30-3. In that scenario, there was a plan and a subplan. The following example creates these two plans. The top-level plan is named NORMAL, while the plan for decision support users is named DECISION.

```
BEGIN
    DBMS_RESOURCE_MANAGER.CREATE_PLAN (
        'NORMAL',
        'Use this plan for normal operations.');

    DBMS_RESOURCE_MANAGER.CREATE_PLAN (
        'DECISION',
        'The decision support subplan.');
END;
/
```

Creating these plans really gives you nothing more than two names. For those plans to mean anything, you need to define consumer groups and then create plan directives to allocate resources among those groups. Also, the link between the two plans is defined using a plan directive. You'll see how this is done later in this chapter.

Creating resource consumer groups

Before you can create plan directives, you need to create consumer groups. Only after you have your plans and consumer groups defined can you link the two using directives.

To create a consumer group, you need a name and a comment. With that information, you make a call to the CREATE_CONSUMER_GROUP procedure in the DBMS_RESOURCE_MANAGER package. Listing 30-1 shows the code needed to create the three consumer groups shown in Figure 30-3.

Listing 30-1: **Creating consumer groups**

```
BEGIN
    DBMS_RESOURCE_MANAGER.CREATE_CONSUMER_GROUP (
        'Customer Care',
        'Customer care users take phone calls from clients.'
        );

    DBMS_RESOURCE_MANAGER.CREATE_CONSUMER_GROUP (
        'VP DSS Users',
        'Vice-President decision support users'
        );

    DBMS_RESOURCE_MANAGER.CREATE_CONSUMER_GROUP (
        'Other DSS Users',
        'Other decision support users'
        );
END;
/
```

The next step is to link your newly created consumer groups to your resource plans.

Creating resource plan directives

With the consumer groups and resource plans created, now you can create resource plan directives to allocate resources between them. You use the DBMS_RESOURCE_MANAGER package's CREATE_PLAN_DIRECTIVE procedure to do this.

A directive always links a resource plan with either another resource plan or with a consumer group. Every plan has a certain percentage of database resources to allocate. The top-level plan has 100 percent of those resources. The directives for each plan must then further allocate the resources that have been assigned to that plan. In our case (refer back to Figure 30-3), the first split involves giving 80 percent of database resources to the customer care group and 20 percent to the decision support group. The code in Listing 30-2 makes this initial 80/20 split.

Listing 30-2: **Creating the directives for an 80/20 resource split**

```
BEGIN
    DBMS_RESOURCE_MANAGER.CREATE_PLAN_DIRECTIVE (
        'NORMAL',
        'Customer Care',
        'Resource allocation for customer care group.',
        cpu_p1 => 70
        );

    DBMS_RESOURCE_MANAGER.CREATE_PLAN_DIRECTIVE (
        'NORMAL',
        'DECISION',
        'Resource allocation for decision support users.',
        cpu_p1 => 20
        );
END;
/
```

The first call to CREATE_PLAN_DIRECTIVE allocates 70 percent of CPU time to the customer care group under the normal plan. The second call allocates 20 percent of CPU time to the decision support group. Why a 70/20 split instead of the 80/20 split called for in our scenario? The missing 10 percent is for a special group called OTHER_GROUPS. Oracle requires that some resources be set aside for users and groups for which you have not explicitly allocated resources.

To further subdivide the decision support group's 20 percent, you execute the code shown in Listing 30-3.

Listing 30-3: **Subdividing resource allocation**

```
BEGIN
    DBMS_RESOURCE_MANAGER.CREATE_PLAN_DIRECTIVE (
        'DECISION',
```

Continued

Listing 30-3 *(continued)*

```
        'VP DSS Users',
        'For the vice-presidents.',
        cpu_p1 => 70
        );

    DBMS_RESOURCE_MANAGER.CREATE_PLAN_DIRECTIVE (
        'DECISION',
        'Other DSS Users',
        'For the other executives.',
        cpu_p1 => 30
        );
END;
/
```

The first parameter to the CREATE_PLAN_DIRECTIVE procedure is the plan name. This time, the plan name given is DECISION. That's because this 70/30 split applies to the decision support group.

Finally, assign that 10 percent that we held back earlier to the OTHER_GROUPS group. Here is the code to do this. Notice that the 10 percent comes from the plan named NORMAL. It could come from any plan, but NORMAL is where we held back the 10 percent, so we'll use this 10 percent.

```
BEGIN
    DBMS_RESOURCE_MANAGER.CREATE_PLAN_DIRECTIVE (
        'NORMAL',
        'OTHER_GROUPS',
        'For users not part of any group.',
        cpu_p1 => 10
        );
END;
/
```

The OTHER_GROUPS parameter is a group name that Oracle recognizes automatically. You don't have to create that group. You just have to create a plan directive that allocates resources to it.

Submitting the pending area

After you have created the resource plan and the consumer groups, and after you have created the plan directives necessary to apportion resources amongst the various groups, you are ready to make your changes permanent. This involves two steps: validating the pending area and submitting the pending area.

Validating the Pending Area

Before you make the changes in the pending area permanent, you need to validate them using the VALIDATE_PENDING_AREA procedure in the DBMS_RESOURCE_ MANAGER package. The VALIDATE_PENDING_AREA procedure verifies that the following statements are true:

✦ Consumer group names and plan names referenced by plan directives really exist.

✦ Plans have directives.

✦ Plans are not nested in such a way that circular references exist.

✦ You have not deleted a plan that is currently being used as the top-level plan by a running database instance.

✦ Your percentages don't add up to more than 100 percent.

✦ You don't have a plan and a resource group with the same name.

✦ Somewhere, you have a plan directive that allocates resources to a group named OTHER_GROUPS. This is for users who haven't specifically been assigned to a group in the currently active plan.

The call to VALIDATE_PENDING_AREA is simple, and it looks like this:

```
BEGIN
    DBMS_RESOURCE_MANAGER.VALIDATE_PENDING_AREA();
END;
/
```

If validation fails, you will receive an error message. The following message shows the error message that you will receive if you forget to allocate resources for OTHER_GROUPS:

```
ERROR at line 1:
ORA-29382: validation of pending area failed
ORA-29377: consumer group OTHER_GROUPS is not part of top-plan NORMAL
ORA-06512: at "SYS.DBMS_RMIN", line 249
ORA-06512: at "SYS.DBMS_RESOURCE_MANAGER", line 254
ORA-06512: at line 2
```

If you receive an error, you need to fix it and then retry the validation. The DBMS_ RESOURCE_MANAGER package does implement procedures for updating and deleting resource plans, consumer groups, and plan directives. These procedures are described later in this chapter.

Submitting the Pending Area

If you can successfully validate the pending area, then it's time to submit your changes and make them permanent. The call to the SUBMIT_PENDING_AREA procedure in the following code takes the changes from the pending area and puts them into effect:

```
BEGIN
    DBMS_RESOURCE_MANAGER.SUBMIT_PENDING_AREA();
END;
/
```

If all you've done is modify existing plans and directives, you can probably stop here. If you are implementing resource management for the first time, you will now need to assign users to the new consumer groups that you've created. After that, you will need to issue an ALTER SYSTEM command to activate your new plan.

Note   The SUBMIT_PENDING_AREA procedure makes an implicit call to VALIDATE_PENDING_AREA. Changes are always validated prior to being submitted.

Placing users into groups

You can place users only into groups that exist in the permanent area. If you have a new consumer group that you've created and it exists only in the pending area, you will need to wait until after submitting your changes to assign users to that group.

Before placing a user into a consumer group, you must grant that user switch privileges on the group. The *switch privilege* allows a user to switch into a consumer group. It's a strange-sounding name, but that's what Oracle chose to use.

Granting Switch Privileges

To grant a user switch privileges on a group, use the GRANT_SWITCH_CONSUMER_GROUP procedure in the DBMS_RESOURCE_MANAGER_PRIVS package. The code in the following example grants the user SEAPARK access to the customer care consumer group:

```
BEGIN
    DBMS_RESOURCE_MANAGER_PRIVS.GRANT_SWITCH_CONSUMER_GROUP (
        'SEAPARK', 'Customer Care', FALSE);
END;
/
```

You can actually grant a user switch privileges on several consumer groups, enabling that user to switch back and forth between groups at will. That can be useful if you have one user who runs two different types of applications. If you've written the applications in-house, you can program the applications to automatically switch the user to the appropriate consumer group.

Tip If you don't want users changing their consumer group setting, then grant them switch privileges only on one group, and make that group their initial group. They won't be able to switch out of it.

Setting a User's Initial Consumer Group

To set a user's initial consumer group, which is the one assigned when the user first connects to an instance, use the SET_INITIAL_CONSUMER_GROUP procedure. The following example sets the initial group for the SEAPARK user to be the customer care group:

```
BEGIN
    DBMS_RESOURCE_MANAGER.SET_INITIAL_CONSUMER_GROUP (
        'SEAPARK', 'Customer Care');
END;
/
```

Once logged on, users can switch themselves to other consumer groups, providing they have been granted access to those groups, by using the DBMS_RESOURCE_ MANAGER package's SWITCH_CURRENT_CONSUMER_GROUP procedure. You can also change groups for a user by using the SWITCH_CURRENT_CONSUMER_GROUP_FOR_ SESS and SWITCH_CURRENT_CONSUMER_GROUP_FOR_USER procedures. You'll read more about these procedures later in this chapter.

Setting the plan for an instance

Finally, you need to set your new plan as the current plan for the instance. You can do that in one of two ways. You can set the resource plan for an instance dynamically by using the ALTER SYSTEM command, or you can set a parameter in the instance's parameter file.

Note You need the ALTER SYSTEM system privilege to issue the ALTER SYSTEM command.

The RESOURCE_MANAGER_PLAN parameter defines the current resource plan for an instance. The following ALTER SYSTEM command sets it to the plan created in this chapter, which is named NORMAL:

```
ALTER SYSTEM
    SET resource_manager_plan = normal;
```

To set the plan used when you first start the instance, you can place a line like the following in your instance's initialization parameter file:

```
resource_manager_plan = normal
```

Using the `ALTER SYSTEM` command, you can change resource plans at will. You can use one plan during the day and a different plan at night. One plan might tilt the balance of resources towards online users, while the other might favor decision support users. The possibilities are endless. Oracle8i's resource management feature gives you a great deal of flexibility in controlling how a database is used.

Note Remember that you must stop and restart your database before any changes that you make in your initialization parameter file take effect.

Using multilevel plans

The preceding example implemented the scenario described in Figure 30-3. This scenario contained two plans, each with one level of resource allocation. Figure 30-2 illustrated an alternate scenario containing one plan and two levels of resource allocation underneath that plan. The difference between the two approaches lies in how excess CPU time for a plan is allocated. The code shown in Listing 30-4 implements the scenario shown in Figure 30-2.

Listing 30-4: Implementing a multi-lever resource plan

```
BEGIN
    --Create one plan.
    DBMS_RESOURCE_MANAGER.CREATE_PLAN (
        'NORMAL',
        'Use this plan for normal operations.');

    --Create the three consumer groups.
    DBMS_RESOURCE_MANAGER.CREATE_CONSUMER_GROUP (
        'Customer Care',
        'Customer care users take phone calls from clients.'
        );

    DBMS_RESOURCE_MANAGER.CREATE_CONSUMER_GROUP (
        'VP DSS Users',
        'Vice-President decision support users'
        );

    DBMS_RESOURCE_MANAGER.CREATE_CONSUMER_GROUP (
        'Other DSS Users',
        'Other decision support users'
        );

    --Create the plan directives to allocate
    --resources to the three groups.
    DBMS_RESOURCE_MANAGER.CREATE_PLAN_DIRECTIVE (
        'NORMAL',
```

```
          'Customer Care',
          'Resource allocation for customer care group.',
          cpu_p1 => 70
          );

     DBMS_RESOURCE_MANAGER.CREATE_PLAN_DIRECTIVE (
          'NORMAL',
          'VP DSS Users',
          'Resource allocation for the vice presidents',
          cpu_p2 => 70
          );

     DBMS_RESOURCE_MANAGER.CREATE_PLAN_DIRECTIVE (
          'NORMAL',
          'Other DSS Users',
          'Resource allocation for the other executives',
          cpu_p2 => 30
          );

     --Don't forget the special case of OTHER_GROUPS.
     DBMS_RESOURCE_MANAGER.CREATE_PLAN_DIRECTIVE (
          'NORMAL',
          'OTHER_GROUPS',
          'For users not part of any group.',
          cpu_p1 => 10
          );

END;
/
```

Notice that this listing contains only one plan: the Normal plan. Three consumer groups are defined — the same as in the previous scenario. The major difference is in how resources are allocated to those groups. The customer care group is allocated 70 percent of CPU resources at level 1. That leaves 30 percent for the other two groups. That 30 percent is allocated between the other groups using the CPU_P2 parameter. Level 1 users take priority over any level 2 users, so if the vice presidents aren't using all of their CPU allocation, the customer care users, not the other executives, will get first crack at it.

Making changes

To make changes to resource plans, consumer groups, and plan directives, you need to follow this procedure:

1. Create a pending area.

2. Make whatever changes you need to make.

3. Validate the pending area.

4. Commit the changes in the pending area.

This procedure is not very different from the one used to create a resource plan in the first place. The key difference is that here you are making modifications. The DBMS_RESOURCE_MANAGER package contains a number of routines that can be used to modify consumer groups and plan directives, and the interface to these routines is very similar to the various create routines that you've read about so far. For example, Listing 30-5 shows two plan directives being modified. Ten percent is taken from the customer care group and given over to the special group named OTHER_GROUPS.

Listing 30-5: **Modifying resource plan directives**

```
SQL> EXECUTE DBMS_RESOURCE_MANAGER.CREATE_PENDING_AREA();

PL/SQL procedure successfully completed.

SQL>
SQL> EXECUTE DBMS_RESOURCE_MANAGER.UPDATE_PLAN_DIRECTIVE -
>         ('NORMAL','CUSTOMER CARE',NEW_CPU_P1=>60);

PL/SQL procedure successfully completed.

SQL>
SQL> EXECUTE DBMS_RESOURCE_MANAGER.UPDATE_PLAN_DIRECTIVE -
>         ('NORMAL','OTHER_GROUPS',NEW_CPU_P1=>20);

PL/SQL procedure successfully completed.

SQL>
SQL> EXECUTE DBMS_RESOURCE_MANAGER.VALIDATE_PENDING_AREA;

PL/SQL procedure successfully completed.

SQL>
SQL> EXECUTE DBMS_RESOURCE_MANAGER.SUBMIT_PENDING_AREA;

PL/SQL procedure successfully completed.
```

In the same manner, you can also update consumer groups, delete consumer groups, delete plan directives, and even delete resource plans.

The DBMS_RESOURCE_MANAGER Reference

The DBMS_RESOURCE_MANAGER package has entry points for creating, updating, and deleting resource plans, plan directives, and consumer groups. You've seen most of the create procedures in this chapter's examples. Each of those create procedures has corresponding update and delete procedures. All of these procedures are described in this section.

How to reference a procedure

The procedures described in this section are all part of the DBMS_RESOURCE_ MANAGER package. For simplicity, the package name has been omitted from the procedure definitions. Whenever you use a procedure, you must preface it with the package name, as shown in the following example:

```
DBMS_RESOURCE_MANAGER.CREATE_PENDING_AREA;
```

Notice the period separating the package name from the procedure name. The use of a period for that purpose is standard within PL/SQL.

Optional parameters

Many of the procedures in the DBMS_RESOURCE_MANAGER package have optional parameters in their interfaces. An optional parameter is one that you don't have to pass when you call the procedure. The nature of these procedures is such that it's quite common to omit a number of parameters, so passing parameters using named notation rather than position notation is often convenient.

You use positional notation to pass parameters by position, as shown in the following example:

```
DBMS_RESOURCE_MANAGER.CREATE_PLAN_DIRECTIVE (
    'my plan', 'my group', null, null, 80);
```

In this example, the first parameter that is listed in the procedure call corresponds to the first formal parameter defined for the procedure, the second parameter that is listed corresponds to the second formal parameter, and so forth. The 80 in this example corresponds to the CPU_P2 parameter. The two NULL parameters correspond to the COMMENT and CPU_P1 parameters. Nulls need to be passed in as placeholders here, to make the value of 80 correspond with the fifth formal parameter, which is CPU_P2.

An easier way to skip parameters is to use named notation. By naming each param-eter explicitly, you relieve yourself of the burden of passing nulls for parameters that you want to skip. You can even mix positional and named location if you like. The following example uses positional notation for the first two param-eters and then switches to named notation for the third:

```
DBMS_RESOURCE_MANAGER.CREATE_PLAN_DIRECTIVE (
    'my plan', 'my group', CPU_P2=>80);
```

No values at all were specified for the COMMENT and CPU_P1 parameters, which has the same effect as passing in nulls.

Note   With named notation, your parameters don't need to be passed in any particular order. With positional notation, the order determines the correspondence between the actual and formal parameters.

The pending area

Oracle requires that resource plan changes be made in the pending area, not to the live plan being used for the instance. Only after the changes have been validated can they be put into effect.

Creating the Pending Area

To create a pending area and begin a new round of changes, use the CREATE_ PENDING_AREA procedure. This is shown as follows:

```
CREATE_PENDING_AREA;
```

There are no parameters for this procedure.

Validating the Pending Area

After you've made changes to resource plans, consumer groups, and resource plan directives, validate those changes before committing them. Use the VALIDATE_ PENDING_AREA procedure for that purpose:

```
VALIDATE_PENDING_AREA;
```

There are no parameters for this procedure. If the procedure detects any problems with the changes that you've made in the pending area, you will receive an error message. Fix the problem identified by the error message, and try the validation again. If you have multiple problems, you may have to iterate through this process several times.

Submitting the Pending Area

To submit the changes in the pending area, use the SUBMIT_PENDING_AREA procedure:

```
SUBMIT_PENDING_AREA;
```

There are no parameters for this procedure. Note that a call to SUBMIT_PENDING_ AREA implies a call to VALIDATE_PENDING_AREA as well. Oracle won't allow the changes to be submitted if a validation error occurs.

Erasing the Pending Area

If you are in the middle of making changes and decide that you don't want to make them, you can erase the pending area by calling the CLEAR_PENDING_AREA procedure:

```
CLEAR_PENDING_AREA;
```

There are no parameters for this procedure. Clearing the pending area gets rid of it completely. If you want to make changes afterwards, you will need to issue another call to CREATE_PENDING_AREA.

Resource plans

Resource plans describe how a database is to allocate resources. The DBMS_ RESOURCE_MANAGER package contains procedures for creating, updating, and deleting these plans.

Creating Resource Plans

Use the CREATE_RESOURCE_PLAN procedure to create a resource plan:

```
CREATE_PLAN (
    plan                        IN VARCHAR2,
    comment                     IN VARCHAR2,
    cpu_mth                     IN VARCHAR2
                        DEFAULT 'EMPHASIS',
    max_active_sess_target_mth IN VARCHAR2
        DEFAULT 'MAX_ACTIVE_SESS_ABSOLUTE',
    parallel_degree_limit_mth   IN VARCHAR2
            DEFAULT 'PARALLEL_DEGREE_LIMIT_ABSOLUTE');
```

The following list describes the parameters in this syntax:

✦ plan—A name for the plan that you are creating. This may be up to 30 characters long.

✦ comment — A comment describing the plan. This may be up to 2,000 characters long.

✦ cpu_mth — The method to use in allocating CPU resources. The default is 'EMPHASIS'.

✦ max_active_sess_target_mth — The method to use in allocating the maximum number of sessions. The default is 'MAX_ACTIVE_SESS_ABSOLUTE'.

✦ parallel_degree_limit_mth — The method to use in limiting the degree of parallelism. This defaults to 'PARALLEL_DEGREE_LIMIT_ABSOLUTE', which is currently the only supported method.

Modifying Resource Plans

Use the UPDATE_RESOURCE_PLAN procedure to update a resource plan, as follows:

```
UPDATE_PLAN (
    plan                           IN VARCHAR2,
    new_comment                    IN VARCHAR2 DEFAULT NULL,
    new_cpu_mth                    IN VARCHAR2 DEFAULT NULL,
    new_max_active_sess_target_mth IN VARCHAR2 DEFAULT NULL,
    new_parallel_degree_limit_mth  IN VARCHAR2 DEFAULT NULL);
```

See the CREATE_RESOURCE_PLAN procedure for descriptions of these parameters. When updating a plan, identify the plan by name and pass in only those parameters whose values you want to change. To change a plan's comment, for example, identify the plan by using the PLAN parameter and pass the new comment in the COMMENT parameter.

Note You can't change a plan's name. If you don't like the name, you must delete and re-create the plan.

Deleting Resource Plans

Use the DELETE_RESOURCE_PLAN procedure to delete a plan, as follows:

```
DELETE_PLAN (
    plan IN VARCHAR2);
```

Pass a resource plan name, using the plan parameter, to identify the plan that you want to delete. If you want to delete not only a resource plan but also any plan directives, consumer groups, and subplans associated with the plan, you can use the following DELETE_RESOURCE_PLAN_CASCADE procedure:

```
DELETE_PLAN_CASCADE (
    plan IN VARCHAR2);
```

Use the `plan` parameter to pass in the name of the plan that you want to delete. When using `DELETE_PLAN_CASCADE`, be sure that you really do want to delete all the consumer groups and subplans that fall under the plan that you are deleting.

Resource plan directives

Resource plan directives form the real meat of any resource plan. Resource plans can have one or more directives, and it is these directives that describe exactly how resources are to be allocated to the various consumer groups.

Creating Plan Directives

Use the `CREATE_PLAN_DIRECTIVE` procedure to create a resource plan directive. See Listing 30-6.

> ### Listing 30-6: **Syntax for the CREATE_PLAN_DIRECTIVE procedure**
>
> ```
> CREATE_PLAN_DIRECTIVE (
>     plan                      IN VARCHAR2,
>     group_or_subplan          IN VARCHAR2,
>     comment                   IN VARCHAR2,
>     cpu_p1                    IN NUMBER    DEFAULT NULL,
>     cpu_p2                    IN NUMBER    DEFAULT NULL,
>     cpu_p3                    IN NUMBER    DEFAULT NULL,
>     cpu_p4                    IN NUMBER    DEFAULT NULL,
>     cpu_p5                    IN NUMBER    DEFAULT NULL,
>     cpu_p6                    IN NUMBER    DEFAULT NULL,
>     cpu_p7                    IN NUMBER    DEFAULT NULL,
>     cpu_p8                    IN NUMBER    DEFAULT NULL,
>     max_active_sess_target_p1 IN NUMBER    DEFAULT NULL,
>     parallel_degree_limit_p1  IN NUMBER    DEFAULT NULL);
> ```

The following list describes the parameters for this procedure:

✦ `plan` — The name of the resource plan to which you want the directive to be attached.

✦ `group_or_subplan` — The name of a group or another plan. This directive specifies the amount of resources to be allocated to the group or plan that you name.

✦ `comment` — A comment about this directive.

✦ cpu_p1 — A value from 0–100 specifying the percentage of CPU to allocate to the named group or plan. This is a priority 1 allocation, with 1 being the highest priority.

✦ cpu_p2 — A value from 0–100 specifying the percentage of CPU to allocate to the named group or plan. This is a priority 2 allocation.

✦ cpu_p3 — A value from 0–100 specifying the percentage of CPU to allocate to the named group or plan. This is a priority 3 allocation.

✦ cpu_p4 — A value from 0–100 specifying the percentage of CPU to allocate to the named group or plan. This is a priority 4 allocation.

✦ cpu_p5 — A value from 0–100 specifying the percentage of CPU to allocate to the named group or plan. This is a priority 5 allocation.

✦ cpu_p6 — A value from 0–100 specifying the percentage of CPU to allocate to the named group or plan. This is a priority 6 allocation.

✦ cpu_p7 — A value from 0–100 specifying the percentage of CPU to allocate to the named group or plan. This is a priority 7 allocation.

✦ cpu_p8 — A value from 0–100 specifying the percentage of CPU to allocate to the named group or plan. This is a priority 8 allocation.

✦ max_active_sess_target_p1 — A target for the maximum number of sessions. This parameter is currently ignored. Oracle plans to add this functionality sometime in the future.

✦ parallel_degree_limit_p1 — A limit on the degree of parallelism that users who fall under this particular directive can use.

Modifying Plan Directives

Use the UPDATE_PLAN_DIRECTIVE procedure to modify the settings for an existing directive. See Listing 30-7.

Listing 30-7: Syntax for the UPDATE_PLAN_DIRECTIVE procedure

```
UPDATE_PLAN_DIRECTIVE (
    plan                        IN VARCHAR2,
    group_or_subplan            IN VARCHAR2,
    comment                     IN VARCHAR2,
    cpu_p1                      IN NUMBER   DEFAULT NULL,
    cpu_p2                      IN NUMBER   DEFAULT NULL,
    cpu_p3                      IN NUMBER   DEFAULT NULL,
    cpu_p4                      IN NUMBER   DEFAULT NULL,
    cpu_p5                      IN NUMBER   DEFAULT NULL,
    cpu_p6                      IN NUMBER   DEFAULT NULL,
```

```
cpu_p7                      IN NUMBER   DEFAULT NULL,
cpu_p8                      IN NUMBER   DEFAULT NULL,
max_active_sess_target_p1   IN NUMBER   DEFAULT NULL,
parallel_degree_limit_p1    IN NUMBER   DEFAULT NULL);
```

See the `CREATE_PLAN_DIRECTIVE` procedure for parameter descriptions. To update a directive, pass in the `plan` and `group_or_subplan` parameters to identify the directive. Then pass in values only for those parameters that you wish to change.

Deleting Plan Directives

Use the `DELETE_PLAN_DIRECTIVE` procedure to delete a plan directive:

```
DELETE_PLAN_DIRECTIVE (
    plan              IN VARCHAR2,
    group_or_subplan  IN VARCHAR2);
```

Together, the `plan` and `group_or_subplan` parameters identify the directive that you want to delete.

Consumer groups

Consumer groups represent groups of users who share a common need for resources. Rather than allocating resources to each user individually, you assign each user to an appropriate group and allocate resources to that group.

Creating Consumer Groups

Use the `CREATE_CONSUMER_GROUP` procedure to create a new consumer group, as follows:

```
CREATE_CONSUMER_GROUP (
    consumer_group IN VARCHAR2,
    comment IN VARCHAR2,
    cpu_mth IN VARCHAR2 DEFAULT 'ROUND-ROBIN');
```

The following list describes the parameters for this procedure:

✦ `consumer_group` — The name of the consumer group that you want to create.

✦ `comment` — A comment describing the consumer group.

✦ `cpu_mth` — The CPU resource allocation method to use for this consumer group. The default method is `'ROUND-ROBIN'`, which is also the only method currently supported.

Modifying Consumer Groups

Use the UPDATE_CONSUMER_GROUP procedure to modify the settings for a consumer group, as follows:

```
UPDATE_CONSUMER_GROUP (
    consumer_group IN VARCHAR2,
    new_comment    IN VARCHAR2 DEFAULT NULL,
    new_cpu_mth    IN VARCHAR2 DEFAULT NULL);
```

See the CREATE_CONSUMER_GROUP procedure for the parameter descriptions. To update a consumer group, identify the consumer group by name using the consumer_group parameter, then pass in new values for the other parameters that you want to change.

Deleting Consumer Groups

Use the DELETE_CONSUMER_GROUP procedure to delete a consumer group, as follows:

```
DELETE_CONSUMER_GROUP (
    consumer_group IN VARCHAR2);
```

Pass the consumer group name in the consumer_group parameter to identify the group that you want to delete.

Consumer group assignments

The DBMS_RESOURCE_MANAGER package implements three procedures that allow you to assign a user to a consumer group. You can set a user's initial group assignment, and you can switch users to new groups while they are connected to the database.

Setting a User's Initial Consumer Group

To set the consumer group to which a user is first assigned after connecting to the database, use the SET_INITIAL_CONSUMER_GROUP procedure, as follows:

```
SET_INITIAL_CONSUMER_GROUP (
    user           IN VARCHAR2,
    consumer_group IN VARCHAR2);
```

The following list describes the parameters for this procedure:

✦ user — The name of the user

✦ consumer_group — The name of the consumer group to which you want to assign the user

For a user to be part of a consumer group, that user must be granted switch privileges on that group. Use the DBMS_RESOURCE_MANAGER_PRIVS package, described later in this chapter, to grant access to a consumer group.

Switching a Session to Another Group

You can switch an active session to another consumer group at any time by using the SWITCH_CONSUMER_GROUP_FOR_SESS procedure, as follows:

```
SWITCH_CONSUMER_GROUP_FOR_SESS (
    session_id     IN NUMBER,
    session_serial IN NUMBER,
    consumer_group IN VARCHAR2);
```

The following list describes the parameters for this procedure:

✦ session_id — The session ID number for the session that you want to switch

✦ session_serial — The session serial number for the session that you want to switch

✦ consumer_group — The new consumer group assignment for that session

Together, the session_id and session_serial parameters identify the session that you want to switch. You can get a list of active sessions, including IDs and serial numbers, by querying the v$session view.

Switching a User to Another Group

You can switch an active user to another consumer group at any time by using the SWITCH_CONSUMER_GROUP_FOR_USER procedure, as follows:

```
SWITCH_CONSUMER_GROUP_FOR_USER (
    user           IN VARCHAR2,
    consumer_group IN VARCHAR2);
```

The following list describes the parameters for this procedure:

✦ user — The user that you want to switch

✦ consumer_group — The new consumer group assignment for that user

When you issue a call to the SWITCH_CONSUMER_GROUP_FOR_USER procedure, all current sessions for the specified user will be switched.

Note

The SWITCH_CONSUMER_GROUP_FOR_USER procedure doesn't change the user's initial setting. The next time the user connects, the user will be assigned to the group specified as his or her initial group. To change the initial group, use the SET_INITIAL_CONSUMER_GROUP procedure.

The DBMS_RESOURCE_MANAGER_PRIVS Reference

The DBMS_RESOURCE_MANAGER_PRIVS package contains four procedures that allow you to control what a user can do using the DBMS_RESOURCE_MANAGER package. Using DBMS_RESOURCE_MANAGER_PRIVS, you can identify users who will be allowed to create and change resource plans for a database. You can also grant users the privilege of changing their own consumer group assignments.

Note   The procedures described in this section are all part of the DBMS_RESOURCE_ MANAGER_PRIVS package. Remember that when referencing a procedure, you must prepend the package name to the procedure name. You reference GRANT_ SYSTEM_PRIVILEGE, for example, by writing the following:

```
DBMS_RESOURCE_MANAGER_PRIVS.GRANT_SYSTEM_PRIVILEGE
```

The ADMINISTER_RESOURCE_MANAGER privilege

The ADMINISTER_RESOURCE_MANAGER privilege gives you the ability to create and manage resource plans for a database. It also gives you the ability to place users into consumer groups. To grant and revoke this privilege, you must hold it with the admin option. The default DBA role that you get when you create a database gives you this.

Granting the ADMINISTER_RESOURCE_MANAGER Privilege

You can use the GRANT_SYSTEM_PRIVILEGE procedure to grant the ADMINISTER_RESOURCE_MANAGER privilege to a user or a role, as follows:

```
GRANT_SYSTEM_PRIVILIGE (
    grantee_name    IN VARCHAR2,
    privilege_name IN VARCHAR2
                    DEFAULT 'ADMINISTER_RESOURCE_MANAGER',
    admin_option    IN BOOLEAN);
```

The following list describes the parameters for this procedure:

✦ grantee_name — The name of the user or role to which you want to grant the privilege.

✦ privilege_name — The name of the privilege to grant. Currently, the only privilege that you can grant is ADMINISTER_RESOURCE_MANAGER.

✦ admin_option — A TRUE condition allows the grantee to grant this privilege to other users. A FALSE condition does not.

Revoking ADMINISTER_RESOURCE_MANAGER

You use the REVOKE_SYSTEM_PRIVILEGE procedure to revoke the ADMINISTER_RESOURCE_MANAGER privilege from a user or a role, as follows:

```
REVOKE_SYSTEM_PRIVILIGE (
    grantee_name   IN VARCHAR2,
    privilege_name IN VARCHAR2
                   DEFAULT 'ADMINISTER_RESOURCE_MANAGER');
```

The following list describes the parameters for this procedure:

✦ grantee_name — The name of the user or role from which you want to revoke a privilege.

✦ privilege_name — The name of the privilege to revoke. Currently, this must be ADMINISTER_RESOURCE_MANAGER.

Switch privileges

Switch privileges are issued to users to allow them to switch themselves to a resource consumer group. If you assign a default resource consumer group to a user, you must at least grant the user switch privileges to that group. If you want the user to be able to choose from among several resource groups, you must grant switch privileges for each of those groups.

> **Note**   To restrict a user to just one consumer group, grant switch privileges to the user of the group and make the group the user's default consumer group.

Granting Switch Privileges

To grant switch privileges to a user or to a role, use the GRANT_SWITCH_CONSUMER_GROUP procedure, as follows:

```
GRANT_SWITCH_CONSUMER_GROUP (
    grantee_name    IN VARCHAR2,
    consumer_group  IN VARCHAR2,
    grant_option    IN BOOLEAN);
```

The following list describes the parameters for this procedure:

✦ grantee_name — The name of the user or role to which you want to grant the privilege.

✦ consumer_group — The name of a consumer group. This is the group to which the privilege applies.

✦ grant_option—The grant option flag. This may be either TRUE or FALSE, and it works like the WITH GRANT OPTION of the SQL GRANT command. A TRUE condition allows the user to further grant the identical switch privilege to other users. A FALSE condition does not.

Revoking Switch Privileges

To revoke switch privileges from a user or role, use the REVOKE_SWITCH_ CONSUMER_GROUP procedure, as follows:

```
REVOKE_SWITCH_CONSUMER_GROUP (
    grantee_name    IN VARCHAR2,
    consumer_group  IN VARCHAR2);
```

The following list describes the parameters for this procedure:

✦ grantee_name—The name of the user or role from which you want to revoke the privilege

✦ consumer_group—The name of a consumer group

Resource Management and the Data Dictionary

You can query a number of data dictionary views to find information relative to resource management in a database. These views are described in Table 30-1.

Table 30-1	
Resource Manager Data Dictionary Views	
View Name	*Description*
DBA_RSRC_CONSUMER_GROUP_PRIVS	Shows you the switch privileges that have been granted to users and roles for the various consumer groups in a database.
DBA_RSRC_CONSUMER_GROUPS	Returns information about all the consumer groups in a database.
DBA_RSRC_MANAGER_SYSTEM_PRIVS	Tells you who has been granted the ADMINISTER_RESOURCE_MANAGER privilege.
DBA_RSRC_PLAN_DIRECTIVES	Returns information about all resource plan directives.
DBA_RSRC_PLANS	Returns information about all resource plans.

View Name	Description
DBA_USERS	Returns information about all users in the database. The INITIAL_RSRC_CONSUMER_GROUP column shows you the initial consumer group assignment for each user.
USER_RSRC_CONSUMER_GROUP_PRIVS	Tells you to which consumer groups you have access.
USER_RSRC_MANAGER_SYSTEM_PRIVS	Tells you whether you have been granted the ADMINISTER_RESOURCE_MANAGER privilege.
V$PARALLEL_DEGREE_LIMIT_MTH	Returns information about available parallel degree limit methods.
V$RSRC_CONSUMER_GROUP	Returns information about all currently active resource consumer groups.
V$RSRC_CONSUMER_GROUP_CPU_MTH	Returns information about available CPU allocation methods for consumer groups.
V$RSRC_PLAN	Returns the names of all currently active resource plans.
V$RSRC_PLAN_CPU_MTH	Returns information about available resource allocation methods.
V$SESSION	Returns information about all active database sessions. The RESOURCE_CONSUMER_GROUP column shows you the consumer group to which each session currently belongs.

As with most data dictionary views, the column names are fairly self-explanatory. In the following example, the DBA_RSRC_CONSUMER_GROUP_PRIVS view is queried to see a list of switch privileges held by the users:

```
SQL> SELECT *
  2  FROM dba_rsrc_consumer_group_privs
  3  ORDER BY grantee, granted_group;

GRANTEE          GRANTED_GROUP            GRANT INI
---------------- ------------------------ ----- ---
PUBLIC           DEFAULT_CONSUMER_GROUP YES    YES
PUBLIC           LOW_GROUP                NO     NO
SEAPARK          CUSTOMER CARE            NO     YES
SYSTEM           SYS_GROUP                NO     YES
```

The INITIAL column in this view indicates the default consumer group assignment.

Summary

In this chapter, you learned:

✦ Resource management is a new Oracle feature that allows you to allocate CPU resources among users and groups of users.

✦ Resource management requires that users be divided into groups called consumer groups. A resource plan is then put into effect for the database. That plan contains plan directives that specify how CPU resources are to be allocated among the various consumer groups. For added versatility, subplans may also be used.

✦ Resource plan changes are always made in a pending area, which you must first create using DBMS_RESOURCE_MANAGER.CREATE_PENDING_AREA. After completing your changes, validate them by calling DBMS_RESOURCE_MANAGER.VALIDATE_PENDING_AREA. If validation succeeds, submit the changes by calling the DBMS_RESOURCE_MANAGER.SUBMIT_PENDING_AREA procedure. Submitting the changes makes them permanent.

✦ To manage resource plans and consumer groups, you need to hold the ADMINISTER_RESOURCE_MANAGER privilege. This isn't quite the same as a system privilege, and it's granted using the DBMS_RESOURCE_MANAGER_PRIVS.GRANT_SYSTEM_PRIVILEGE procedure.

✦　　✦　　✦

Managing Oracle8i's Java Virtual Machine

One of the most talked about new features of Oracle8i is the inclusion of a Java Virtual Machine (JVM) within the database. Oracle8i's JVM gives you the ability to run Java in the database on an equal footing with PL/SQL. You use Oracle8i's `loadjava` utility to load Java code into the database. To call Java code from PL/SQL, you need to publish the methods that you want to use. You accomplish this with a new variation of the `CREATE PROCEDURE` and `CREATE FUNCTION` statements. In this chapter, you will learn about Oracle8i's Java architecture and the Java-specific initialization parameters. Next, you will learn how to load Java code into your database and how to invoke that Java code from PL/SQL.

Examining Oracle8i's Java Architecture

Oracle uses the term JServer to talk about the Java-enabled database. When you hear the term JServer, think of an Oracle8i database. However, don't think of it as just a database. Think of it in terms of its Java functionality. Oracle uses the term JServer to collectively refer to all the Java technology built into Oracle8i. JServer consists of the following major components:

✦ A Java Virtual Machine named Aurora

✦ Support for Java database connectivity (JDBC)

✦ Support for SQLJ, a SQL precompiler for Java

✦ A CORBA-compliant object request broker (ORB) referred to as the Aurora ORB

Oracle's JVM runs in the database on an equal footing with PL/SQL and SQL. Figure 31-1 illustrates this. The Java engine, the PL/SQL engine, and the SQL statement executor all have equal access to the shared pool, the database buffer cache, and other critical memory structures.

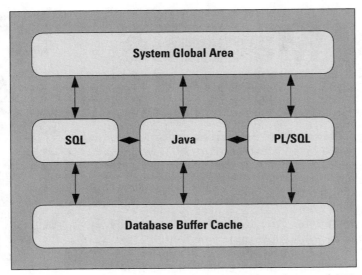

Figure 31-1: Aurora is on an equal footing with PL/SQL and SQL.

For Java to be useful in the database, you need to have easy access to the data in your database from the Java methods that you write. Oracle supports both JDBC and SQLJ. *JDBC* is an industry standard set of Java classes that are used for database access. *SQLJ* is a Java precompiler that allows you to embed SQL statements in your Java code. When the precompiler runs, your SQLJ statements are translated to standard JDBC calls. SQLJ is much easier to write than JDBC, and the inclusion of this precompiler makes database access very convenient for the programmer.

In addition to JDBC and SQLJ, Oracle also supports CORBA applications. CORBA is often used together with Enterprise Java Beans to allow client applications access to a database. Figure 30-2 shows how JDBC, SQLJ, and the other components comprising JServer are layered on top of Oracle8i's JVM.

You can see in Figure 31-2 that Oracle has supplied all the pieces necessary to write robust Java applications that run within the Oracle8i database.

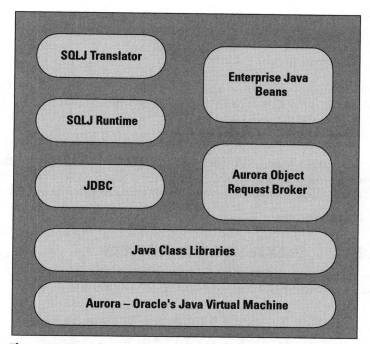

Figure 31-2: Major components in Oracle8i's Java environment

Configuring the Java Engine

To set up your Oracle8i database to use Java, you must first initialize the JServer engine by running an Oracle-supplied script that creates the standard Java runtime classes, the Java and SQLJ compilers, the JDBC classes, and the Aurora ORB. Then you must set three initialization parameters.

JServer initialization

You initialize JServer by executing the script named initjvm.sql while logged on as the user SYS. You'll find initjvm.sql in the $ORACLE_HOME/javavm/install directory. The script creates the following within the database:

✦ The Java compiler.

✦ The SQLJ precompiler.

✦ The standard Java runtime class libraries. This includes java.lang, java.net, and so forth.

✦ JDBC support.

✦ The Aurora ORB.

✦ Enterprise Java Beans runtime support.

If you're using the seed database created when you first installed Oracle8i, or if you used Oracle's Database Configuration Assistant to create your database, this script will already have been run. If you used your own scripts to create your database, you will need to invoke initjvm.sql yourself.

Note
The initjvm.sql script requires a shared pool size of at least 50MB to run. If the script fails because your shared pool is too small, just increase the shared pool size and rerun the script. You can shrink it back to a smaller size after the script has finished.

JServer-related initialization parameters

Three initialization parameters are specific to JServer. In addition, a couple of others affect how (or whether) JServer operates. Table 31-1 lists these parameters.

<table>
<tr><td colspan="2" align="center">Table 31-1
Initialization Parameters that Affect JServer</td></tr>
<tr><td>*Parameter*</td><td>*Description*</td></tr>
<tr><td>java_pool_size</td><td>Controls the amount of memory available to the Java pool. This memory is used for the in-memory representation of Java classes and methods, as well as for each session's copy of any static variables. The Java Pool is separate from the shared pool. Oracle recommends a setting of at least 20MB.</td></tr>
<tr><td>java_soft_sessionspace_limit</td><td>Sets a warning threshold for the amount of Java Pool pool memory that may be consumed by any single user for use by static variables. The default setting is 1MB. If a user uses more than the amount specified by this parameter, then a warning is written to a database trace file.</td></tr>
<tr><td>java_max_sessionspace_size</td><td>Sets a hard limit on the amount of Java pool memory that may be consumed by any single user. The default for this is zero, which means that no limit is enforced. If this limit is exceeded, the user's session will be terminated.</td></tr>
</table>

Parameter	Description
`compatible`	Sets the release number with which the instance will be compatible. This must be set to at least 8.1.5 for JServer to be used.
`shared_pool_size`	Sets the amount of shared pool space for the instance. The shared pool is used when loading or compiling Java classes. Shared pool space is also used when executing the `initjvm.sql` script. At least 50MB of shared pool space is required to run `initjvm.sql`.

Loading Java Classes into Oracle8i

You can load Java classes into your database using the `loadjava` utility. This utility allows you to load any of the following:

- ✦ Java source code
- ✦ SQLJ source code
- ✦ Java class files

If you load Java source code (from `.java` files), `loadjava` will call on Oracle8i's built-in Java compiler to compile that code for you. Likewise, if you load SQLJ code (from `.sqlj` files), Oracle8i's built-in SQLJ compiler will be called. Neither of these is well-suited for use in developing and debugging Java code. If you're doing extensive development work, you're better off using an integrated development environment (IDE) such as JDeveloper to debug and test your code, and then load it into Oracle when you are certain that it works. You can even load just the `.class` files, if you like, and do all your compiling in an IDE.

Setting the CLASSPATH environment variable

If you are going to use `loadjava` to load SQLJ code into your database, you need to define an environment variable named `CLASSPATH` and make sure that it points to a file named `translator.zip`. Consider this example:

```
$ORACLE_HOME\sqlj\lib\translator.zip
```

Note   Replace `$ORACLE_HOME` with the name of your top-level Oracle directory.

The Oracle8i installer is supposed to set up CLASSPATH for you, but the 8.1.5 Windows NT version doesn't do it properly. You won't be able to run the SQLJ compiler without the setting shown here.

To check the CLASSPATH setting on a Windows NT installation, open a Command Prompt window and issue the SET CLASSPATH command shown in the following example:

```
C:\>set classpath
CLASSPATH=e:\oracle\ora81\sqlj\lib\translator.zip
```

To set the CLASSPATH variable on Windows NT, right-click the My Computer icon and select Properties from the pop-up menu. Click the Environment tab to see the options shown in Figure 31-3.

Figure 31-3: Setting the CLASSPATH variable in Windows NT

To define a CLASSPATH variable, fill in the Variable and Value fields as shown in Figure 31-3, and then click the Set button.

Using the loadjava command

The loadjava utility loads a Java source file or class file into the database. The syntax for loadjava appears as follows:

```
loadjava {-user | -u} username/password[@database]
         [-option [-option ...]]
         filename [ filename...]
```

The following list describes the parameters for this syntax:

✦ *username/password* — Your username and password. The Java objects are loaded into the schema identified by *username*.

✦ *database* — A Net8 service name identifying the database to which you want to connect.

✦ *filename* — A file that you want to load. You may load multiple files using one command. You may load Java class files, Java source files, and SQLJ source files using the extensions .class, .java, and .sqlj, respectively.

✦ *option* — One of the options described in Table 31-2. In most cases, an option may be identified by either its full name or by a single-letter abbreviation. For example, either -help or -h may be used to get a short help summary. Abbreviations and option names are case-sensitive.

Table 31-2
The loadjava Command Options

Option	Abbr	Description
andresolve	a	Resolves each class as it is loaded. This is not normally used.
debug	N/A	Causes loadjava to generate debug information.
definer	d	Creates the classes so that they execute with definer's rights. In other words, the class methods execute with the privileges of the class owner and not of the user invoking the methods.
encoding *encoding_schema*	e	Specifies a standard JDK encoding scheme, which must match that used in the files being loaded. The default is latin1.
force	f	Forces Java class files to be loaded regardless of whether they have already been loaded. Caveat: You can't force the loading of a class if you have previously loaded the source for that class.
grant {username|rolename} [{username|rolename}...]	g	Grants execute privileges to the listed users for any classes being loaded.
help	h	Causes loadjava to display a short summary of these options.

Continued

Table 31-2 *(continued)*		
Option	**Abbr**	**Description**
oci8	o	Causes the OCI JDBC driver to be used when communicating with Oracle. This is the default behavior. See the -thin option.
oracleresolver	N/A	Causes Oracle to resolve object references by looking first at the user's schema and then at public objects.
resolve	r	Causes Oracle to resolve all external references for classes that are loaded immediately after all the classes have been compiled. Otherwise, the resolving doesn't happen until runtime.
resolver "resolver_spec"	R	Specifies a resolver specification to use that controls how references to other classes are resolved.
schema *schema*	S	Specifies a schema into which loadjava is to load the objects read from files listed on the command line. The default is to load objects into the schema of the user invoking the loadjava utility.
synonym	s	Causes loadjava to create public synonyms for all classes that it loads. You must have the CREATE PUBLIC SYNONYM privilege to use this option.
thin	t	Causes loadjava to use the thin JDBC driver to connect to the database. See the -oci8 option.
verbose	v	Causes loadjava to display progress messages as each file is loaded.

Most of the time, you can leave all the options at their default settings. As an example, let's work through the process of loading a simple Java class into the database. Listing 31-1 shows how the AquaticAnimal class implements a getCaretaker method that returns the name of the caretaker for a specified animal.

Listing 31-1: **The AquaticAnimal class**

```
import sqlj.runtime.*;
import sqlj.runtime.ref.*;

#sql iterator AnimalCaretaker (String caretakerName);

public class AquaticAnimal {

   public static String getCaretaker(int animalID) throws
Exception {

     /* Declare an iterator (cursor)*/
     AnimalCaretaker iterAnimalCaretaker;

     /* Get the caretaker's name */
     #sql iterAnimalCaretaker={
                     SELECT chief_caretaker_name AS
caretakerName

                     FROM tank, aquatic_animal
                     WHERE aquatic_animal.tank_no =
tank.tank_no

                     AND aquatic_animal.id_no = :animalID
                     };

     /* Return the caretaker's name */
     if (iterAnimalCaretaker.next())
       {
       return iterAnimalCaretaker.caretakerName();
       }
     else
       {
       return "There is no caretaker";
       }
   }
}
```

You can load this class into an Oracle8i database using the following command:

```
loadjava -user seapark/seapark AquaticAnimal.sqlj
```

In this case, since the .sqlj file is loaded, loadjava will call on Oracle8i's built-in SQLJ compiler to compile the SQLJ code.

Note

In this case, the database username and password are both seapark. If you are executing this command, be sure to use the password that you chose for the SEAPARK user in your database.

Publishing Java Methods for Use by PL/SQL

After loading Java code into your database, you won't immediately be able to execute that code from PL/SQL or SQL. If you have a Java method that you intend to use from PL/SQL, you must *publish* that method. Publishing a method makes it visible to PL/SQL and to SQL.

To publish a Java method, you use either the CREATE FUNCTION or the CREATE PROCEDURE statements. Use CREATE FUNCTION if your Java method returns a value. Use CREATE PROCEDURE if your Java method returns void. The syntax for the version of CREATE FUNCTION and CREATE PROCEDURE used to publish a Java method is shown in Listing 31-2.

Listing 31-2: **Publishing a Java method**

```
CREATE [OR REPLACE] FUNCTION function_name
[(function_parameter_list)]
RETURN datatype
[AUTHID {CURRENT_USER|DEFINER}]
[PARALLEL_ENABLE] [DETERMINISTIC] {IS|AS}
LANGUAGE JAVA
NAME
'class.method ([java_type[, java_type...]]) return java_type';
/

CREATE [OR REPLACE] PROCEDURE procedure_name
[(procedure_parameter_list)]
[AUTHID {CURRENT_USER|DEFINER}]
[PARALLEL_ENABLE] [DETERMINISTIC] {IS|AS}
LANGUAGE JAVA
NAME 'class.method ([java_type[, java_type...]])';
/
```

The following list describes the parameters for this syntax:

✦ LANGUAGE JAVA—Indicates that you are publishing a Java method.

✦ NAME—Identifies the Java method to which this PL/SQL function or procedure is linked.

✦ *class*—Specifies the class name.

✦ *method*—Specifies the method name.

✦ *java_type*—Specifies a Java type. You must list the Java types for each parameter in the Java method. The PL/SQL parameters are mapped onto the Java parameters, with Oracle converting between PL/SQL and Java types as necessary.

✦ return *java_type*—Identifies the return type of the method. This must be a Java type. It should be compatible with the PL/SQL return type. The keyword return here is case-sensitive and must be lowercase.

The following CREATE FUNCTION statement publishes the getCaretaker method of the AquaticAnimal class in our example. Note the forward slash that terminates the statement. The forward slash must be on a line by itself, and it must be the first character on that line.

```
CREATE OR REPLACE FUNCTION get_caretaker
    (animal_id IN NUMBER) RETURN VARCHAR2
    AS LANGUAGE JAVA NAME
    'AquaticAnimal.getCaretaker(int) return java.lang.String';
/
```

Once the method is published, you can invoke it from either SQL or PL/SQL. Listing 31-3 shows it both ways.

Listing 31-3: **Invoking a Java method from PL/SQL and SQL**

```
SQL> SET SERVEROUTPUT ON
SQL> BEGIN
  2     DBMS_OUTPUT.PUT_LINE (
  3         get_caretaker(100));
  4  END;
  5  /
HAROLD

PL/SQL procedure successfully completed.

SQL> SELECT get_caretaker(100)
  2  FROM dual;

GET_CARETAKER(100)
-------------------------------------------
HAROLD

1 row selected.
```

Once a Java method has been published, you can use it as if it were a regular PL/SQL function.

Java and PL/SQL Datatype Compatibility

To facilitate publishing Java methods so that they are visible from PL/SQL, Oracle8i will automatically convert between the Java and PL/SQL datatypes shown in Table 31-3. When publishing a Java method, each Java parameter should correspond to a compatible PL/SQL parameter as defined here.

Table 31-3 Java and PL/SQL Datatypes	
Java Datatype	*PL/SQL Datatype*
oracle.sql.NUMBER	NUMBER
byte	
short	
int	
long	
float	
double	
java.lang.Byte	
java.lang.Short	
java.lang.Integer	
java.lang.Long	
java.lang.Float	
java.lang.Double	
java.lang.BigDecimal	
oracle.sql.CHAR	VARCHAR2
java.lang.String	CHAR
java.lang.Date	NVARCHAR2
java.lang.Time	NCHAR

Java Datatype	PL/SQL Datatype
java.sql.Timestamp	LONG
byte	
short	
int	
long float	
double	
java.lang.Byte	
java.lang.Short	
java.lang.Integer	
java.lang.Long	
java.lang.Float	
java.lang.Double	
java.lang.BigDecimal	
oracle.sql.DATE	DATE
java.lang.Date	
java.lang.Time	
java.sql.Timestamp	
java.lang.String	
oracle.sql.CHAR	ROWID
oracle.sql.ROWID	
java.lang.String	
oracle.sql.BFILE	BFILE
oracle.sql.BLOB oracle.jdbc2.Blob	BLOB
oracle.sql.CLOB	CLOB
oracle.jdbc2.Clob	NCLOB
oracle.sql.STRUCT	OBJECT
oracle.jdbc2.Struct	
oracle.sql.REF	REF
oracle.jdbc2.Ref	
oracle.sql.ARRAY	TABLE
oracle.jdbc2.Array	VARRAY

Getting Information About Java Classes in Your Database

To get information about the Java classes in your database, you can query the DBA_OBJECTS view. The DBA_OBJECTS view returns a row for each database object. If you aren't the DBA and you don't have access to DBA_OBJECTS, you can query ALL_OBJECTS or USER_OBJECTS instead. The ALL_OBJECTS view returns one row for each object to which you have access, while USER_OBJECTS returns one row for each object that you own.

Java classes

You can get a list of Java classes by querying DBA_OBJECTS for objects with a type of 'JAVA CLASS'. To see all Java-related objects, query for all types beginning with 'JAVA'. The following query, for example, will list all Java objects owned by the user named SEAPARK:

```
SELECT object_name, object_type, status
FROM dba_objects
WHERE owner='SEAPARK'
AND object_type LIKE 'JAVA%'
ORDER BY object_name;
```

The object name returned by the DBA_OBJECTS view may or may not represent the full name of the Java object. Java names can be longer than standard Oracle object names, so Oracle must use some special methods to compensate for this.

Long names vs. short names

Names used for traditional Oracle objects such as tables and views are limited to 31 characters. The names of Java objects may be much longer than that. This is particularly true when the path to the class is considered to be part of the name. For example, the SQLJ class named sqlj/runtime/profile/util/CustomizerHarnessBeanInfo is longer than 30 characters, and it can't be used outside of the Java engine. To deal with this issue, Oracle generates a short name that uniquely identifies each class and makes that short name visible to SQL and PL/SQL.

When you query DBA_OBJECTS for a list of Java class names, Oracle returns the short name for each object. To see the full name, you must call on a built-in PL/SQL package named DBMS_JAVA. The DBMS_JAVA.LONGNAME function accepts a short name as a parameter and returns the full Java name as a result. See Listing 31-4.

Listing 31-4: **Retrieving the long name for a Java class**

```
SQL> SELECT object_name,
  2  DBMS_JAVA.LONGNAME(object_name) long_object_name
  3  FROM dba_objects
  4  WHERE object_type = 'JAVA CLASS'
  5  AND object_name <> DBMS_JAVA.LONGNAME(object_name);

OBJECT_NAME                      LONG_OBJECT_NAME
-------------------------------  -------------------------------
/10076b23_OraCustomDatumClosur   oracle/sqlj/runtime/OraCustomDa
                                 tumClosure

/10322588_HandlerRegistryHelpe   com/visigenic/vbroker/intercept
                                 or/HandlerRegistryHelper

/10739900_GenericURLDirContext   com/sun/jndi/url/jndi/GenericUR
                                 LDirContext
...
```

The query shown in Listing 31-5 returns a list of Java classes with long names that differ from their short names. In cases where the full Java name is not more than 31 characters, the short and long names will be the same. Such is the case with the AquaticAnimal class loaded earlier in this chapter.

Note   Oracle also implements a DBMS_JAVA.SHORTNAME function that does the reverse of DBMS_JAVA.LONGNAME. It takes the long name of a Java class and returns the corresponding short name.

Dropping Java Classes

To drop a set of Java classes from your database, you can use a utility named dropjava. The dropjava utility functions similarly to loadjava. You invoke it by passing in various command-line parameters and file names. In response, dropjava reads through the files and drops any objects from the database that loadjava would have created. The syntax for invoking dropjava is as follows:

```
dropjava {-user | -u} username/password[@database]
         [-option [-option ...]]
         filename [ filename...]
```

The following list describes the parameters for this syntax:

✦ *username/password* — Your username and password. The Java objects are dropped from the schema identified by *username*.

✦ *database* — The Net8 service name identifying the database to which you want to connect.

✦ *filenam* — The name of the file containing Java objects that you want to drop. You may list more than one file. dropjava will read the file (or files) and drop any objects that loadjava would have created. The files themselves will not be changed or deleted.

✦ *option* — One of the options described in Table 31-4. As with loadjava, an option may be identified by either its full name or by a single-letter abbreviation. For example, either -help or -h may be used to get a short help summary. Abbreviations and option names are case-sensitive.

Table 31-4
The dropjava Utility Options

Option	*Abbr*	*Description*
help	h	Causes dropjava to display a short summary of these options.
oci8	o	Causes the OCI JDBC driver to be used when communicating with Oracle. This is the default behavior, and it requires that the Oracle client software be installed and configured. See the -thin option.
schema *schema*	S	Specifies a schema from which dropjava is to drop the objects read from files listed on the command line. The default is to drop objects from the schema of the user invoking the dropjava utility.
thin	t	Causes dropjava to use the thin JDBC driver to connect to the database. The thin JDBC driver does not depend on the Oracle client software being installed. See the -oci8 option.
verbose	v	Causes dropjava to display progress messages as each file is loaded.

At first glance, dropjava may seem like a strange sort of utility, but it's actually rather convenient in practice. Executing loadjava on a file can result in several Java class and resource objects being loaded into the database. Usually, you want to treat these as a unit, loading them and dropping them together. The dropjava utility allows you to do that. Think of it as an "undo" for loadjava.

For example, the following command drops all the Java objects created when the `AquaticAnimal.sqlj` file was loaded into the database:

```
dropjava -u seapark/seapark AquaticAnimal.sqlj
```

You can see that this command is practically the same as the one used to load the objects in the first place. The only difference is that `dropjava` was used instead of `loadjava`.

Note   Bear in mind that `dropjava` only drops classes from the database. It doesn't delete, or in any way alter, the files listed as arguments.

Summary

In this chapter, you learned:

✦ Oracle8i now includes a Java engine that runs within the database. Oracle refers to its Java-enabled database as JServer. JServer includes not only the Java engine, but also support for CORBA, SQLJ, and JDBC. Oracle's Java engine is named Aurora.

✦ To configure the Java engine for a new database, you need to run a script named `initjvm.sql`. That script can be found in the `$ORACLE_HOME/javavm` directory. To run `initjvm.sql`, you should have at least 50MB of shared pool space.

✦ Three initialization parameters directly affect JServer's operation: `java_pool_size`, `java_soft_sessionspace_limit`, and `java_sessionspace_limit`. The `java_pool_size` parameter defines the amount of memory available for storing a Java session state. This includes each session's copy of static variables, and also the in-memory representation of Java classes and methods. The `java_soft_sessionspace_limit` parameter defines a warning threshold for the amount of space used by a session. The `java_sessionspace_limit` parameter defines a hard limit. If a user attempts to use more session space than the limit specifies, the user's session will be terminated.

✦ You can use the `loadjava` utility to load Java classes into an Oracle database. The `loadjava` utility can load Java source files, SQLJ source files, and compiled Java class files. The `dropjava` utility is the exact opposite of `loadjava`. The `dropjava` utility reads the same file and drops the objects that `loadjava` loaded.

✦ Java methods may be used from PL/SQL, but first you must publish those methods using a special form of the `CREATE FUNCTION` statement. To publish a Java method that returns `void`, use the `CREATE PROCEDURE` statement.

✦   ✦   ✦

The SQL Syntax Reference

This appendix describes the Oracle 8i SQL syntax, including all main SQL statements and their clauses. The aim of this appendix is to provide a concise and complete description of the SQL syntax. Please refer to the other chapters in this book for an explanation of the Oracle concepts and techniques.

The SQL Syntax Reference

The SQL notation used in this appendix is best explained according to an example. Consider the following:

```
SELECT [ALL|DISTINCT] {*|column} FROM
data_source[,data_source...]

data_source := [schema.]{table|view}
```

SELECT	Words in capitals denote command syntax.
column	Words in italics, lowercase are user-defined items or separately specified clauses like *data_source* in the example.
[ALL|DISTINCT]	Square brackets denote an optional choice, with the choices delimited by a vertical line. In the example, you may choose ALL, DISTINCT, or nothing.
{* | *column* }	Curly brackets denote a mandatory choice, with the choices delimited by a vertical line. In the example, you must choose between * or *column*.

`data_source[,` `data_source...]`	Repetitions are indicated by repeating the item between square brackets, adding an optional delimiter and three trailing dots at the end. In the example, you specify one or more data sources each delimited by a comma.
`data_source :=`	Often clauses are specified separately. In the example, you specify the *data_source* clause separately.

ALTER RESOURCE COST

You use `ALTER RESOURCE COST` to specify the parameters Oracle uses to calculate the total resource cost for a session. Four parameters can be weighted into the calculation. If a parameter is omitted, it won't be taken into account at all. The `ALTER RESOURCE COST` command's syntax follows:

```
ALTER RESOURCE COST
{ CPU_PER_SESSION integer
| CONNECT_TIME integer
| LOGICAL_READS_PER_SESSION integer
| PRIVATE_SGA integer
}
```

The following list explains all of the elements used in the `ALTER RESOURCE COST` command syntax:

`CPU_PER_SESSION`	Specifies the weight assigned to the amount of CPU time (in hundredths of a second) used by a session. The default value is 0, which means it isn't taken into account in the calculation.
`CONNECT_TIME`	Specifies the weight assigned to the elapsed connection time (in minutes) of a session. The default value is 0, which means it isn't taken into account in the calculation.
`LOGICAL_READS_PER_SESSION`	Specifies the weight assigned to the number of data block reads during a session. The default value is 0, which means it isn't taken into account in the calculation.
`PRIVATE_SGA`	Specifies the weight assigned to the private size of the SGA (in bytes) used by a session. The default value is 0, which means it isn't taken into account in the calculation.

ALTER SESSION

You can use the ALTER SESSION command to change session options. Listing A-1 provides the syntax for the ALTER SESSION command.

Listing A-1: **ALTER SESSION syntax**

```
ALTER SESSION
{ ADVISE {COMMIT|ROLLBACK|NOTHING}
| CLOSE DATABASE LINK dblink
| {ENABLE|DISABLE} COMMIT IN PROCEDURE
| {ENABLE|DISABLE|FORCE} PARALLEL
   {DML|DDL} [PARALLEL integer]
| SET session_option[,session_option...]
}

session_option :=
{ CONSTRAINT[S] = {IMMEDIATE|DEFERRED|DEFAULT}
| CREATE_STORED_OUTLINES = {TRUE|FALSE|'category_name'}
| CURRENT_SCHEMA = schema
| DB_BLOCK_CHECKING = {TRUE|FALSE}
| DB_FILE_MULTIBLOCK_READ_COUNT = integer
| FAST_START_IO_TARGET = integer
| FLAGGER = {ENTRY|IMMEDIATE|FULL|OFF}
| GLOBAL_NAMES = {TRUE|FALSE}
| HASH_AREA_SIZE = integer
| HASH_JOIN_ENABLED = {TRUE|FALSE}
| HASH_MULTIBLOCK_IO_COUNT = integer
| INSTANCE = integer
| ISOLATION_LEVEL = {SERIALIZABLE|READ COMMITTED}
| LOG_ARCHIVE_DEST_n =
    { null_string
    | { LOCATION = pathname | SERVICE = servicename }
      [MANDATORY|OPTIONAL]
      [REOPEN [=retry_time]]
    }
| LOG_ARCHIVE_DEST_STATE_n = {ENABLE|DEFER}
| LOG_ARCHIVE_MIN_SUCCEED_DEST = integer
| MAX_DUMP_FILE_SIZE = {size|UNLIMITED}
| NLS_CALENDAR = 'text'
| NLS_COMP = 'text'
| NLS_CURRENCY = 'text'
| NLS_DATE_FORMAT = 'format'
| NLS_DATE_LANGUAGE = language
| NLS_ISO_CURRENCY = 'text'
| NLS_LANGUAGE = language
| NLS_NUMERIC_CHARACTERS = 'text'
| NLS_SORT = {sort|BINARY}
| NLS_TERRITORY = territory
```

Continued

Listing A-1: *(continued)*

```
NLS_DUAL_CURRENCY = 'text'
OBJECT_CACHE_MAX_SIZE_PERCENT = integer
OBJECT_CACHE_OPTIMAL_SIZE = integer
OPTIMIZER_INDEX_CACHING = integer
OPTIMIZER_INDEX_COST_ADJ = integer
OPTIMIZER_MAX_PERMUTATIONS = integer
OPTIMIZER_MODE = {ALL_ROWS|FIRST_ROWS|RULE|CHOOSE}
OPTIMIZER_PERCENT_PARALLEL = integer
OPTIMIZER_SEARCH_LIMIT = integer
PARALLEL_BROADCAST_ENABLED = {TRUE|FALSE}
PARALLEL_INSTANCE_GROUP = 'text'
PARALLEL_MIN_PERCENT = integer
PARTITION_VIEW_ENABLED = {TRUE|FALSE}
PLSQL_V2_COMPATABILITY = {TRUE|FALSE}
REMOTE_DEPENDENCIES_MODE = {TIMESTAMP|SIGNATURE}
QUERIES_REWRITE_ENABLED = {TRUE|FALSE}
QUERIES_REWRITE_INTEGRITY =
{ENFORCED|TRUSTED|STALE_TOLERATED}
SESSION_CACHED_CURSORS = integer
SKIP_UNUSABLE_INDEXES = {TRUE|FALSE}
SORT_AREA_RETAINED_SIZE = integer
SORT_AREA_SIZE = integer
SORT_MULTIBLOCK_READ_COUNT = integer
SQL_TRACE = {TRUE|FALSE}
STAR_TRANSFORMATION_ENABLED = {TRUE|FALSE}
TEXT_ENABLE = {TRUE|FALSE}
TIMED_STATISTICS = {TRUE|FALSE}
USE_STORED_OUTLINES = {TRUE|FALSE|'category_name'}
}
```

The following list explains all of the elements used in the ALTER SESSION command syntax:

ADVISE COMMIT	Sends advice to a remote database (into the DBA_2PC_PENDING view) to commit the transaction when it becomes in doubt.
ADVISE ROLLBACK	Sends advice to a remote database (into the DBA_2PC_PENDING view) to roll back the transaction when it becomes in doubt.
ADVISE NOTHING	Sends advice to a remote database (into the DBA_2PC_PENDING view) to not end the transaction when it becomes in doubt.

CLOSE DATABASE LINK *dblink*	Specifies that the database link *dblink* is to be closed for the current session.
COMMIT IN PROCEDURE	Specifies that PL/SQL commits in stored functions or procedures are enabled or disabled.
ENABLE PARALLEL	Specifies that statements in a session will be run in parallel.
DISABLE PARALLEL	Specifies that statements in a session will be run serially.
FORCE PARALLEL	Specifies that statements in a session will be run in parallel, overriding the parallel clause if specified in the statements themselves.
DML	Specifies that DML statements are executed with the default or specified degree of parallelism.
DDL	Specifies that DML statements are executed with the default or specified degree of parallelism.
PARALLEL *integer*	Specifies the degree of parallelism, overriding the parallel clause in the statements.
SET	Specifies new values for session options.
CONSTRAINT[S]	Specifies when the conditions specified by deferrable constraints are enforced.
IMMEDIATE	Specifies that the conditions of deferrable constraints are checked immediately after each DML statement.
DEFERRED	Specifies that the conditions of deferrable constraints are checked when the transaction is committed.
DEFAULT	Specifies that the deferrable constraints are reset to their initial values: either IMMEDIATE or DEFERRED.
CREATE_STORED_OUTLINES	Enables or disables the automatic creation of outlines when queries are performed.
'category_name'	Enables the creation of stored outlines and specifies the name of the category created for the stored outlines.

CURRENT_SCHEMA *schema*	Specifies the schema that is to be used for the current session.
DB_BLOCK_CHECKING	Specifies whether data block checking is done.
DB_FILE_MULTIBLOCK_READ_COUNT	Specifies the maximum number of block reads in one I/O operation in a sequential scan.
FAST_START_IO_TARGET	Specifies the target number of I/O operations to or from the buffer cache when performing a recovery.
FLAGGER	Specifies that an error message should be generated when the SQL statement isn't compliant with the ANSI SQL92 standard. This is called *FIPS flagging*.
ENTRY	Specifies that FIPS flagging should be turned on.
IMMEDIATE	Specifies that FIPS flagging should be turned on.
FULL	Specifies that FIPS flagging should be turned on.
OFF	Specifies that FIPS flagging should be turned off.
GLOBAL_NAMES	Specifies whether global names resolution should be enforced when remote objects are referenced in SQL statements.
HASH_AREA_SIZE	Specifies the size in bytes of the memory used for hash operations in queries.
HASH_JOIN_ENABLED	Specifies whether hash joins are allowed in queries.
HASH_MULTIBLOCK_IO_COUNT	Specifies the number of data block reads/writes to perform when doing a hash join operation.
INSTANCE	Specifies the instance of the database to use.
ISOLATION_LEVEL	Specifies how transactions in which data is manipulated are handled.
SERIALIZABLE	Specifies that statements will fail if they update rows that are changed by another uncommitted transaction.

`READ COMMITTED`	Specifies that update statements will wait when they try to change rows that are updated by another uncommitted transaction, until the row locks are freed by that session.
`LOG_ARCHIVE_DEST_n`	Specifies up to 5 (*n* = 1..5) path or service names as destinations for archive redo log file groups.
`LOG_ARCHIVE_DEST_STATE_n`	Enables or defers any associated destination for archiving corresponding to the `LOG_ARCHIVE_DEST_n` option.
`LOG_ARCHIVE_MIN_SUCCEED_DEST`	Specifies the minimum number of destinations that must succeed for the online redo log file to be available for reuse.
`MAX_DUMP_FILE_SIZE size`	Specifies the maximum size of the trace dump file in blocks.
`UNLIMITED`	Specifies that no maximum is set for the size of the trace dump file.
`NLS_CALENDAR 'text'`	Specifies the name of a new calendar type.
`NLS_COMP 'text'`	Specifies that linguistic comparison is to be used according to the NLS_SORT parameter.
`NLS_CURRENCY 'text'`	Specifies the local currency symbol.
`NLS_DATE_FORMAT 'format'`	Specifies the default date format model.
`NLS_DATE_LANGUAGE language`	Specifies the language to use for names and abbreviations of date format elements.
`NLS_ISO_CURRENCY 'text'`	Specifies the name of the territory whose ISO currency symbol should be used.
`NLS_LANGUAGE language`	Specifies the name of the language Oracle will use to display messages in.
`NLS_NUMERIC_CHARACTERS 'dg'`	Specifies the new digital separator symbol (*d*) and group separator symbol (*g*) to be used.
`NLS_SORT=sort`	Specifies the name of the linguistic sort sequence to be used for the sorting of character sequences.

`NLS_SORT=BINARY`	Specifies that a binary sort will be used for the sorting of character sequences.
`NLS_TERRITORY territory`	Specifies the name of the territory to use.
`NLS_DUAL_CURRENCY 'text'`	Specifies a dual currency symbol.
`OBJECT_CACHE_MAX_SIZE_PERCENT`	Specifies the percentage to which the object cache can grow beyond its optimal size.
`OBJECT_CACHE_OPTIMAL_SIZE`	Specifies the size of the object cache in kilobytes. When the object cache reaches its maximum size it is reduced to the size specified.
`OPTIMIZER_INDEX_CACHING`	Specifies the percentage of index blocks assumed to be in the cache.
`OPTIMIZER_INDEX_COST_ADJ`	Specifies a percentage that indicates the importance the optimizer attaches to index paths as opposed to full tablescans.
`OPTIMIZER_MAX_PERMUTATIONS`	Specifies the number of permutations of the tables in a query that the optimizer will consider.
`OPTIMIZER_MODE`	Specifies the mode of the optimizer.
`ALL_ROWS`	Specifies that the optimizer will use the cost-based approach. Throughput is optimized.
`FIRST_ROWS`	Specifies that the optimizer will use the cost-based approach. Response time is optimized.
`RULE`	Specifies that the optimizer will use the "rule based" approach.
`CHOOSE`	Specifies that the optimizer will choose an optimization approach on the basis of statistics stored in the data dictionary.
`OPTIMIZER_PERCENT_PARALLEL`	Specifies the percentage of parallelism the optimizer will use in its cost functions.
`OPTIMIZER_SEARCH_LIMIT`	Specifies the search limit for the optimizer.
`PARALLEL_BROADCAST_ENABLED`	Enables or disables performance during hash and merge joins.

PARALLEL_INSTANCE_GROUP *'text'*	Specifies the instance group to be used for executing parallel query slaves.
PARALLEL_MIN_PERCENT	Specifies the minimum percentage of threads required for parallel queries.
PARTITION_VIEW_ENABLED	Specifies that unnecessary table accesses in a partition view are skipped.
PLSQL_V2_COMPATABILITY	Enables or disables compatibility of Oracle8i PL/SQL (PL/SQL version 3) with the previous version of PL/SQL.
REMOTE_DEPENDENCIES_MODE	Specifies how dependencies of remote stored procedures are handled.
TIMESTAMP	Specifies that procedures are executed only when the timestamps match.
SIGNATURE	Specifies that the procedures are executed when the signatures are considered safe.
QUERIES_REWRITE_ENABLED	Enables or disables query rewrites on materialized view.
QUERIES_REWRITE_INTEGRITY	Specifies the integrity of query rewrites.
SESSION_CACHED_CURSORS	Specifies the number of cursors that can be retained in the cache.
SKIP_UNUSABLE_INDEXES	Enables or disables error reporting of indexes that are marked UNUSABLE and enables or disables the usage of DML.
SORT_AREA_RETAINED_SIZE	Specifies the maximum amount of memory in bytes each sort operation will retain after the first fetch.
SORT_AREA_SIZE	Specifies the maximum amount of memory in bytes used for each sort operation.
SORT_MULTIBLOCK_READ_COUNT	Specifies the number of blocks to be read when a sort performs a read from a temp segment.
SQL_TRACE	Enables or disables SQL tracing.
STAR_TRANSFORMATION_ENABLED	Enables or disables the use of the "cost based" query transformation that will be applied to star queries.

TIMED_STATISTICS	Specifies whether the server requests the operating system time when generating time-related statistics.
USE_STORED_OUTLINES	Enables or disables the use of stored outlines to generate execution plans.
'category_name'	Specifies the name of a different category than the default category from which to use outlines.

ALTER SYSTEM

You can use the ALTER SYSTEM command to change settings dynamically in the Oracle instance. The settings will be lost when the database is unmounted. Listing A-2 provides the syntax for the ALTER SYSTEM command:

Listing A-2: ALTER SYSTEM syntax

```
ALTER SYSTEM
{ CHECKPOINT [GLOBAL|LOCAL]
| CHECK DATAFILES [GLOBAL|LOCAL]
| DISCONNECT SESSION 'SID,Serial#' POST_TRANSACTION
| {ENABLE|DISABLE} DISTRIBUTED RECOVERY
| {ENABLE|DISABLE} RESTRICTED SESSION
| FLUSH SHARED_POOL
| KILL SESSION 'SID,Serial#'
| SWITCH LOGFILE
| {SUSPEND|RESUME}
| SET parameter = value [parameter = value...]
| ARCHIVE LOG [THREAD integer]
  { STOP
  | { SEQUENCE integer
    / CHANGE integer
    / CURRENT
    / GROUP integer
    / LOGFILE 'filename'
    / NEXT
    / ALL
    / START
    }
    TO 'location'
  }
}
```

The following list explains all of the elements used in the ALTER SYSTEM command syntax:

CHECKPOINT	Causes Oracle to perform a checkpoint. All changes made by committed transactions will be written to disk.
GLOBAL	Performs the action in all instances that have opened the database when running in an Oracle parallel server environment.
LOCAL	Performs the action only for the current instance of the database when running in an Oracle parallel server environment.
CHECK DATAFILES	Causes the SGA to be updated with the current details of the data files.
DISCONNECT SESSION	Causes the session to be disconnected after the current transaction is ended.
POST_TRANSACTION	Allows any ongoing transactions to end before the session is disconnected.
'SID,Serial#'	Specifies the session to be killed or disconnected. Refer to the V$SESSION view for the values of SID and SERIAL#.
DISTRIBUTED RECOVERY	Specifies whether distributed recovery is enabled.
RESTRICTED SESSION	Specifies whether only users with the RESTRICTED SESSION privilege can log on or whether all users are allowed to log on.
FLUSH SHARED_POOL	Specifies that all the data in the shared pool of the SGA is cleared.
KILL SESSION	Kills the session specified. Uncommitted transactions are rolled back and all locks are released.
SWITCH LOGFILE	Forces Oracle to start writing to a new redo log file group.
SUSPEND	Specifies that all I/O and queries will be suspended.
RESUME	Reverses the SUSPEND command.
SET parameter = value	Assigns a value to a system parameter.
ARCHIVE LOG	Specifies that the redo log files are manually archived or it enables or disables automatic archiving.

THREAD *integer*	Specifies the thread in which the redo log files are to be archived.
STOP	Disables automatic archiving of redo log file groups.
SEQUENCE *integer*	Specifies that the online redo log file identified by the sequence number is to be archived manually.
CHANGE *integer*	Specifies that the online redo log file containing the redo log entry identified by the specified system change number (SCN) is to be archived manually.
CURRENT	Specifies that the current online redo log file group is to be archived manually.
GROUP *integer*	Specifies that the online redo log files in the specified redo log file group are to be archived manually.
LOGFILE '*filename*'	Specifies that the online redo log file identified by the specified file name is to be archived manually.
NEXT	Specifies that the next full online redo log file that is not yet archived is to be archived manually.
ALL	Specifies that all full online redo log files that aren't yet archived are to be archived manually.
START	Enables automatic archiving of redo log file groups.
TO '*location*'	Specifies the location to which the redo log files are archived.

ANALYZE

You can use the ANALYZE command to collect or delete statistics about a database object to validate its structure, to identify migrated and chained rows, or to validate and update object references. The results are stored in the data dictionary so they are available for the Oracle optimizer. Listing A-3 provides the syntax for the ANALYZE command.

Listing A-3: **ANALYZE syntax**

```
ANALYZE {INDEX|TABLE|CLUSTER}
schema.{cluster
       |index [PARTITION(partition_name)]
       |table [PARTITION(partition_name)]
       }
[ COMPUTE  STATISTICS    for_clause[ for_clause...]
| ESTIMATE STATISTICS    for_clause[ for_clause...]
[SAMPLE integer [ROWS|PERCENT]]

| DELETE   STATISTICS
| VALIDATE REF UPDATE [SET DANGLING TO NULL]
| VALIDATE STRUCTURE [CASCADE] {INTO {schema.}table}
| LIST CHAINED ROWS {INTO {schema.}table}
]

for_clause :=
{ FOR TABLE
| FOR ALL {INDEXED} COLUMNS {SIZE integer}
| FOR COLUMNS {SIZE integer}
[ (column    {SIZE integer}
[,column    {SIZE integer}...])
| (attribute {SIZE integer}
[,attribute {SIZE integer}...])
]
| FOR ALL {LOCAL} INDEXES
}
```

The following list explains all of the elements used in the ANALYZE command syntax:

INDEX index	Identifies the index to be analyzed. FOR clause cannot be used.
TABLE table	Identifies the table to be analyzed. Also collects statistics for indexes when no FOR clauses are used.
CLUSTER cluster	Identifies the cluster to be analyzed. Also collects statistics for tables and indexes when no FOR clauses are used.
PARTITION(partition_name)	Identifies the partition to be analyzed. This clause can only be used with partitioned objects, and results in only the portion of the object in the named partioned being analyzed. This clause cannot be used when analyzing clusters.

COMPUTE STATISTICS	Computes statistics about the specified objects.
ESTIMATE STATISTICS	Estimates statistics about the specified objects.
SAMPLE	Use a sample of the data to perform the analysis. Default value is 1064 rows; if more than half of the data is specified, all the data will be used.
integer ROWS	Use *integer* rows to collect statistics.
integer PERCENT	Use *integer* percent of the data to collect statistics.
DELETE STATISTICS	Deletes statistics stored in the data dictionary for the specified object.
VALIDATE REF UPDATE	Validates references in the specified table and corrects the rowid part of the reference if necessary. Can only be used for tables.
VALIDATE STRUCTURE	Validates the structure for the specified object. Also validates the structure of tables if this clause is specified for a cluster.
INTO *table*	Allows you to specify a table in which to collect the rowids of the partitions that are not succesfully validated. Default value for *table* is INVALID_ROWS (created by utlvalid.sql)
CASCADE	Cascade into tables and indexes associated with the analyzed object. When a table is analyzed CASCADE will cause Oracle to also analyze the table's indexes. When a cluster is analyzed, Oracle will also analyze the cluster index and the clustered tables and associated indexes.
LIST CHAINED ROWS	Lists migrated and chained rows of the analyzed object. Cannot be used when analyzing indexes.
INTO *table*	Allows you to specify a table in which to collect the migrated and chained rows. Default value for *table* is CHAINED_ROWS (created by utlchain.sql).
SET DANGLING TO NULL	Specifies that any REFs that point to an invalid or nonexistent object will be set to NULL.

The following elements are only applicable when analyzing tables:

FOR TABLE	Collect statistics for a table
FOR ALL COLUMNS	Collect statistics for all columns in a table
INDEXED	Collect statistics for all indexed columns in a table
FOR COLUMNS	Collect statistics for specific columns of a table
FOR ALL INDEXES	Collect statistics for all indexes on the table.
FOR ALL LOCAL INDEXES	Collect statistics for all local indexes on the table.
SIZE *integer*	Specifies the maximum number of partitions. Default value is 75 (minimum is 1, maximum is 254)

AUDIT (schema objects)

With the AUDIT command, you specify schema objects on which to perform auditing. Auditing keeps an audit trail of the operations performed on the object. In the audit trail, information is kept about the type of operation, the objects involved, the time of operation, and the user who performed the operation. You can use the audit trail to review database activity. The following is the syntax for the AUDIT command:

```
AUDIT {ALL|object_option[,object_option...]} ON
{ DEFAULT
| DIRECTORY directory_name
| [schema.]object
}
[ BY {SESSION|ACCESS} ]
[ WHENEVER [NOT] SUCCESSFUL ]
```

The following list explains all of the elements used in the AUDIT command syntax:

object_option	Specifies an operation to audit. See Table A-5 in the section "Reference Tables" for all options and the objects for which they apply.
ALL	Specifies that all object options applicable to the object will be audited.
schema.object	Specifies the object chosen for auditing. Schema is optional and may be omitted.
DIRECTORY *directory_name*	Specifies the directory chosen for auditing.

DEFAULT	Specifies that any newly created object will be audited using the options set. When using the default, audit options on current objects aren't changed.
BY SESSION	Specifies that only one audit record will be created for each operation type on an object in the same session.
BY ACCESS	Specifies that an audit record is created every time the audited operation is executed.
WHENEVER SUCCESSFUL	Audits only successful SQL statements.
WHENEVER NOT SUCCESSFUL	Audits only unsuccessful SQL statements.

AUDIT (SQL statements)

You use the AUDIT command to specify specific SQL statements for auditing. Auditing creates an audit trail of operations performed by the users. Auditing stores information about the type of operation, the objects involved, the time of operation, and the user who performed the operation. You can use the audit trail to review database activity. Listing A-4 provides the syntax for the AUDIT command:

Listing A-4: **AUDIT syntax**

```
AUDIT option[,option...]
[BY { user[,user...]
    | proxy [ON BEHALF OF
        { ANY
        | user[,user...]
        }
    }
]
[BY {SESSION|ACCESS}]
[WHENEVER [NOT] SUCCESSFUL]

option :=
{statement_option|system_privilege}
```

The following list explains all of the elements used in the AUDIT command syntax:

statement_option	Specifies specific SQL statements for auditing. See Tables A-1 and A-2 in the section "Reference Tables" for allowed statement options, and see Table A-3 for available shortcuts.

system_privilege	Specifies SQL statements for auditing that are authorized by the system privilege. See Table A-4 in the section "Reference Tables" for available system privileges.
BY *user*	Specifies that only statements issued by the specified user are audited. If this clause is omitted, all users' statements will be audited.
BY *proxy*	Specifies that only SQL statements that are executed by the specified proxy are audited.
ON BEHALF OF	Specifies that only statements executed on behalf of specified user(s) are audited.
ANY	Specifies that statements executed on behalf of any user are audited.
BY SESSION	Specifies that only one audit record is produced for each type of SQL statement in the same session.
BY ACCESS	Specifies that only one audit record is created per statement. If *statement_options* or *system_privileges* are specified for DDL statements, the BY SESSION clause is ignored and auditing is performed BY ACCESS by default. Otherwise, BY SESSION is the default clause.
WHENEVER SUCCESSFUL	Audits only successful SQL statements.
WHENEVER NOT SUCCESSFUL	Audits only unsuccessful SQL statements.

CALL

You can use the CALL command to execute a function, procedure, or method. The executed object may reside in a user-defined type, in a package in the local database, or in a remote database. The following is the syntax for the CALL command:

```
CALL [ [schema.]type.function[@dblink]
     | [schema.]type.procedure[@dblink]
     | [schema.]type.method[@dblink]
     | [schema.]package.function[@dblink]
     | [schema.]package.procedure[@dblink]
     | [schema.]package.method[@dblink]
     ] (expression[,expression...])
[INTO :host_variable]
```

The following list explains all of the elements used in the `CALL` command syntax:

schema	Specifies the schema in which the called object resides. (Optional.)
type	Specifies the type in which to call the function, procedure, or method.
package	Specifies the package in which to call the function, procedure, or method.
function	Specifies the function that is to be called in a type or package.
procedure	Specifies the procedure that is to be called in a type or package.
method	Specifies the method that is to be called in a type or package.
dblink	Specifies that a remote object is called and specifies the database link that points to the remote database.
expression	Specifies an argument supplied to the function, procedure, or method.
`INTO` :*host_variable*	Specifies in which host variable to store the return value.

COMMENT

Use `COMMENT` to add comments to a table, view, or snapshot. Comments are stored in the data dictionary and can be viewed by querying `ALL_COL_COMMENTS` or `USER_COL_COMMENTS` for column comments and `ALL_TAB_COMMENTS` or `USER_TAB_COMMENTS` for table comments. The following is the syntax for the `COMMENT` command:

```
COMMENT ON
{ TABLE   [schema.]{table|view|snapshot}
| COLUMN [schema.]{table|view|snapshot}.column
} IS 'text'
```

The following list explains all of the elements used in the `COMMENT` command syntax:

`TABLE`	Comments on a table, view, or snapshot.
`COLUMN`	Comments to a column in a table, view, or snapshot
`IS` `'text'`	Specifies the comment text.

schema	Specifies the schema in which the table, view, or snapshot resides. (Optional.)
table	Specifies the name of the table to add comments to.
view	Specifies the name of the view to add comments to.
snapshot	Specifies the name of the snapshot to add comments to.

COMMIT

The COMMIT command ends the current transaction and makes permanent all the changes performed in the transaction. In addition, it will clear all savepoints and remove all locks created in the transaction. By using the FORCE clause, you can manually commit in-doubt transactions. Note that the FORCE clause isn't allowed in PL/SQL. The following is the syntax for the COMMIT command:

```
COMMIT [WORK]
   [ COMMENT 'text'
   | FORCE   'text' [,SCN]
   ]
```

The following list explains all of the elements used in the COMMIT command syntax:

COMMIT WORK	Equivalent to COMMIT. The purpose for the WORK keyword is compliance with the SQL standard.
COMMENT 'text'	Adds an optional comment to the transaction. This comment is stored in the data dictionary view DBA_2PC_PENDING if the transaction becomes in doubt, together with the transaction ID.
FORCE 'text',SCN	Forces the commit of an in-doubt distributed transaction where *text* specifies the transaction ID. You can look up the transaction ID in the DBA_2PC_PENDING view. You may also specify *SCN* as the system change number. If omitted, the current system change number is used.

CREATE/ALTER/DROP CLUSTER

Clusters are schema objects that contain tables that all have one or more columns in common. Use the CREATE/ALTER/DROP CLUSTER commands to create new clusters, alter parameters of existing clusters, or remove clusters. The following is the syntax for the CREATE CLUSTER command:

```
CREATE CLUSTER [schema.]cluster
(column data_type[,column data_type...])
[ [physical_attributes]
```

```
[SIZE integer [K|M]]
[ INDEX
| [SINGLE TABLE] HASHKEYS integer [HASH IS expression]
]
]
[parallel_clause]
[CACHE|NOCACHE]
```

The following is the syntax for the ALTER CLUSTER command:

```
ALTER CLUSTER [schema.]cluster
{ [physical_attributes]
[SIZE      integer [K|M]]
[deallocate_unused_clause]
[allocate_extent_clause]
}
[parallel_clause]
```

The following is the syntax for the DROP CLUSTER command:

```
DROP CLUSTER [schema.]cluster
[INCLUDING TABLES [CASCADE CONSTRAINTS]]

allocate_extent_clause := ALLOCATE EXTENT
[ ( { [SIZE      integer [K|M]]
     [DATAFILE 'filename']
     [INSTANCE integer]    } ) ]

deallocate_unused_clause := DEALLOCATE UNUSED
[KEEP integer [K|M]]
```

The following list explains all of the elements used in the CREATE/ALTER/DROP CLUSTER command syntax:

schema.cluster	Specifies the name of the cluster to be altered, created, or dropped.
column	Specifies the name of the column in the cluster key.
data_type	Specifies the datatype of the column in the cluster key. All datatypes are allowed except for the LONG and LONG RAW datatypes. When the HASH IS clause is specified, you can't use the NUMBER or INTEGER datatypes with scale 0.
INDEX	Creates an indexed cluster. INDEX is the default value.
SINGLE TABLE	Specifies that the hash cluster contains only one table.

HASHKEYS *integer*	Creates a hash key cluster with *integer* hash values that are a minimum of 2.
HASH IS *expression*	Specifies that the *expression* is to be used as the hash function. If this clause is omitted, the internal Oracle hash function will be used.
parallel_clause	See the section "Common Clauses" for details.
CACHE	Specifies that blocks retrieved in a full tablescan are stored at the most recently used end of the LRU list in the buffer cache. This is recommended for small static tables.
NOCACHE	Specifies that blocks retrieved in a full tablescan are stored at the least recently used end of the LRU list in the buffer cache. NOCACHE is the default.
INCLUDING TABLES	Drops all tables within the cluster.
CASCADE CONTRAINTS	Drops all referential integrity constraints from tables outside the cluster to prevent integrity constraint errors when dropping the cluster. Note that only constraints are dropped that reference unique or primary keys in the tables in the cluster.
SIZE *integer* [K|M]	Specifies that *integer* bytes are used to store all rows with the same cluster key value or hash key value. Use *K* to denote kilobytes or *M* for megabytes.
ALLOCATE EXTENT	Specifies that a new extent will be created to accommodate the cluster.
DATAFILE '*filename*'	Specifies the data file in the tablespace to contain the new extent. If this clause is omitted, Oracle will choose a data file.
INSTANCE *integer*	Specifies that the extent will be made available to instance *integer*. If this clause is omitted, the extent is available to all instances. The INSTANCE clause is applicable only when running in parallel mode.
physical_attributes	See the section "Common Clauses" for details.
DEALLOCATE UNUSED	Specifies that space at the end of the object is explicitly freed and made available to other objects in the tablespace.
KEEP *integer*	Specifies to keep *integer* bytes of space above the high water mark but free the remaining unused space.

CREATE CONTROLFILE

You can use the CREATE CONTROLFILE command to create a new control file for the database. Before using this statement, create a full backup of the database files. Listing A-5 provides the syntax for the CREATE CONTROLFILE command.

Listing A-5: **CREATE CONTROLFILE syntax**

```
CREATE CONTROLFILE [REUSE] [SET] DATABASE database
LOGFILE [GROUP integer] file_spec
         [,[GROUP integer] file_spec...]
{RESETLOGS|NORESETLOGS}
DATAFILE file_spec[,file_spec...]
[ [MAXLOGFILES integer]
| [MAXLOGMEMBERS integer]
| [MAXLOGHISTORY integer]
| [MAXDATAFILES integer]
| [MAXINSTANCES integer]
| [ARCHIVELOG|NOARCHIVELOG]
]
[CHARACTER SET character_set]
```

The following list explains all of the elements used in the CREATE CONTROLFILE command syntax:

REUSE	Specifies that existing control files are reused, overwriting the existing data in them.
SET DATABASE database	Specifies that the name of the database should be changed to database.
DATABASE database	Specifies the database for which to create a new control file.
LOGFILE	Specifies the redo log file groups for the database. You have to specify all the redo log file groups.
GROUP integer	Specifies the log file group in which the log file is placed.
RESETLOGS	Specifies that the contents of the files specified in the LOGFILE clause should be ignored.
NORESETLOGS	Specifies that the contents of the files specified in the LOGFILE clause are expected to be exactly the same as the configuration at the moment that the database was shut down.

DATAFILE	Specifies all the data files in the database.
MAXLOGFILES *integer*	Specifies the maximum number of redo log file groups allowed to be used for the database.
MAXLOGMEMBERS *integer*	Specifies the maximum number of members, or copies, of a redo log file group.
MAXLOGHISTORY *integer*	Specifies the maximum number of archived redo log file groups.
MAXDATAFILES *integer*	Specifies the maximum number of data files to be used for the database.
MAXINSTANCES *integer*	Specifies the maximum number of instances of the database.
ARCHIVELOG	Specifies that the mode of archiving is established. The ARCHIVELOG clause prepares the database for the possibility of recovery in case of a media or instance failure.
NOARCHIVELOG	Specifies that the mode of archiving isn't established. This is the default.
file_spec	See the "Common Clauses" section for details.
CHARACTER SET	Specifies the name of the character set.

CREATE/ALTER DATABASE

You can use the CREATE/ALTER DATABASE commands to create, modify, maintain, or recover a database. Listing A-6 provides the syntax for the CREATE DATABASE command.

Listing A-6: **CREATE DATABASE syntax**

```
CREATE DATABASE [database]
{ [CONTROLFILE REUSE]
| [LOGFILE [GROUP integer] file_spec
            [,[GROUP integer] file_spec...]
  ]
| [MAXLOGFILES integer]
  [MAXLOGMEMBERS integer]
  [MAXLOGHISTORY integer]
  [MAXDATAFILES integer]
  [MAXINSTANCES integer]
  [ARCHIVELOG|NOARCHIVELOG]
  [CHARACTER SET character_set]
  [NATIONAL CHARACTER SET character_set]
| [DATAFILE file_spec [autoextend_clause]]
            [,file_spec [autoextend_clause]...]]
}
```

Listing A-7 provides the syntax for the ALTER DATABASE command.

Listing A-7: **ALTER DATABASE syntax**

```
ALTER DATABASE database
{ MOUNT {STANDBY|CLONE} DATABASE
| CONVERT
| OPEN [ READ ONLY
        | [READ WRITE] {RESETLOGS|NORESETLOGS}
      ]
| ACTIVATE STANDBY DATABASE
| recover_clause
| RENAME GLOBAL NAME TO database.domain[.domain...]
| RENAME FILE 'filename'[,'filename'...] TO
               'filename'[,'filename'...]
| RESET COMPATIBILITY
| ENABLE [PUBLIC] THREAD integer
| DISABLE THREAD integer
| CHARACTER SET character_set
| NATIONAL CHARACTER SET character_set
| DATAFILE 'filename'[,'filename'...]
      { ONLINE
      | OFFLINE [DROP]
      | RESIZE integer [K|M]
      | autoextend_clause
      | END BACKUP
      }
| CREATE DATAFILE 'filename'[,'filename'...] [AS file_spec]
| TEMPFILE 'filename'[,'filename'...]
      { ONLINE
      | OFFLINE
      | DROP
      | RESIZE integer [K|M]
      | autoextend_clause
      }
| ARCHIVELOG
| NOARCHIVELOG
| ADD LOGFILE [THREAD integer] [GROUP integer] file_spec
        [,[GROUP integer] file_spec...]
| ADD LOGFILE MEMBER add_logfile_spec[,add_logfile_spec...]
| DROP LOGFILE       file_list[,file_list...]
| DROP LOGFILE MEMBER 'filename'[,'filename'...]
| CLEAR [UNARCHIVED] LOGFILE file_list[,file_list...]
   [UNRECOVERABLE DATAFILE]
| CREATE STANDBY CONTROLFILE AS 'filename' [REUSE]
| BACKUP CONTROLFILE
  { TO 'filename' [REUSE]
  | TO TRACE [RESETLOGS|NORESETLOGS]
  }
```

```
}

add_logfile_spec := 'filename' [REUSE]
                          [,'filename' [REUSE]...] TO
{ GROUP integer
| 'filename'
| ('filename'[,'filename'...])
}

autoextend_clause := AUTOEXTEND
[ OFF
| ON [NEXT integer [K|M]]
| MAXSIZE {UNLIMITED|integer [K|M]}
]

file_list :=
{ GROUP integer
| 'filename'
| ('filename'[,'filename'...])
)

recover_clause := [AUTOMATIC] [FROM 'location']
[ CANCEL
| CONTINUE [DEFAULT]
| LOGFILE 'filename'
| DATAFILE 'filename'[,'filename'...]
| TABLESPACE table space[,table space...]
| [STANDBY] DATABASE
  [ [UNTIL CANCEL]
    [UNTIL TIME date]
    [UNTIL CHANGE integer]
    [USING BACKUP CONTROLFILE]
  ]
] [parallel_clause]
```

The following list explains all of the elements used in the CREATE/ALTER DATABASE command syntax:

database	Specifies the name of the database to create or alter.
CONTROLFILE REUSE	Specifies that existing control files are reused, overwriting the existing data in them.
LOGFILE	Specifies one of more log files to be used when creating the database. When used in the recover_clause, LOGFILE specifies that only the specified log files are recovered.

file_spec	See the "Common Clauses" section for details.
MAXLOGFILES *integer*	Specifies the maximum number of redo log file groups allowed to be used for the database.
MAXLOGMEMBERS *integer*	Specifies the maximum number of members, or copies, of a redo log file group.
MAXLOGHISTORY *integer*	Specifies the maximum number of archived redo log file groups.
MAXDATAFILES *integer*	Specifies the maximum number of data files to be used for the database.
MAXINSTANCES *integer*	Specifies the maximum number of instances of the database.
ARCHIVELOG	Specifies that the mode of archiving is established. The ARCHIVELOG clause prepares the database for the possibility of recovery in case of a media or instance failure.
NOARCHIVELOG	Specifies that the mode of archiving is not established. This is the default.
CHARACTER SET	Specifies the name of the character set the database uses to store data.
NATIONAL CHARACTER SET	Specifies the name of the character set the database uses to store data in NCHAR, NVARCHAR2, or NCLOB columns.
MOUNT	Specifies that the database will be mounted.
STANDBY DATABASE	Specifies that the standby database will be mounted. If used in the *recover_clause*, it will recover the standby database using the primary database's control file and redo log files.
CLONE DATABASE	Specifies that the clone database will be mounted.
CONVERT	Converts the Oracle7 data dictionary when migrating from Oracle7 to Oracle8.
OPEN	Specifies that the database is to be opened for normal use.
READ ONLY	Specifies that the database is to be opened for read-only use.

READ WRITE	Specifies that the database is to be opened for read-write use. The READ WRITE parameter is the default value.
RESETLOGS	Specifies that any data in the redo log files are to be ignored during recovery.
NORESETLOGS	Specifies that the redo log files will be left in the state in which they already exist.
ACTIVATE STANDBY DATABASE	Specifies that the standby database will be changed to the active database.
RENAME GLOBAL NAME TO	Specifies that the global name of the database will be changed to *database.domain*.
RENAME FILE	Specifies to rename data files, tempfiles, or redo log file members in the control file.
RESET COMPATIBILITY	Specifies that the database will be reset to an earlier version of Oracle.
ENABLE THREAD *integer*	Specifies the thread of redo log file groups that are to be enabled.
PUBLIC	Specifies that the thread will be made available publicly.
DISABLE THREAD *integer*	Specifies the thread of redo log file groups that are to be disabled.
ONLINE	Specifies that the data file or temp file is brought online.
OFFLINE	Specifies that the data file or temp file is taken offline.
RESIZE *integer* [K|M]	Specifies that the data file or temp file is resized to *integer* bytes. Use *K* or *M* to denote kilobytes or megabytes.
AUTOEXTEND OFF	Specifies that data files are not automatically extended when space runs out.
AUTOEXTEND ON	Specifies that data files are automatically extended when space runs out.
NEXT *integer* [K|M]]	Specifies the extra space assigned to the data file when the tablespace is enlarged.
MAXSIZE	Specifies the maximum size of the data file.
UNLIMITED	Specifies that the data file has no maximum limit.

END BACKUP	Specifies that media recovery will not be performed after a system failure or instance failure during a backup operation.
CREATE DATAFILE	Specifies that a new empty data file is created. See the section "Common Clauses" for details on *file_spec*.
TEMPFILE *'filename'*	Specifies that a new file is to be used as the temporary data file.
ADD LOGFILE	Specifies that one or more redo log files are added to a group or thread.
ADD LOGFILE MEMBER	Specifies that one or more members are added to redo log file groups.
DROP LOGFILE	Specifies that all members of a redo log file group are dropped.
DROP LOGFILE MEMBER	Specifies that one or more members of a redo log file group are dropped.
THREAD *integer*	Specifies the thread to which to add log files.
GROUP *integer*	Specifies the log file group in which the log file is placed.
CLEAR LOGFILE	Specifies that the redo log file is reinitialized.
UNARCHIVED	Specifies that a redo log file is reinitialized that wasn't archived.
UNRECOVERABLE DATAFILE	Specifies that an offline redo log file that is needed to recover the database is reinitialized.
CREATE STANDBY CONTROLFILE AS	Specifies that a control file is created for the standby database.
REUSE	Specifies that an existing control file is used.
BACKUP CONTROLFILE TO *'filename'*	Specifies that the control file is backed up to the specified file name.
TO TRACE	Specifies that SQL statements will be written to the trace file and that no control file will be created.
AUTOMATIC	Specifies that Oracle will decide which archived redo log file to take next during recovery.

FROM `'location'`	Specifies the location from which the redo log file is read.
CANCEL	Specifies that the recovery is to be terminated.
CONTINUE	Specifies that a recovery operation is continued.
CONTINUE DEFAULT	Equivalent to AUTOMATIC; however, no prompt for a file name is displayed.
LOGFILE `'filename'`	Specifies that only the specified log file will be recovered in the recovery operation.
DATAFILE `'filename'`	Specifies that only the specified data files will be recovered in the recovery operation. When used in the CREATE command, it specifies which data file to use with the database. When used in the ALTER command, it specifies which data file to bring online, take offline, resize, or autoextend.
TABLESPACE `table space`	Specifies that only the specified tablespaces will be recovered in the recovery operation.
STANDBY DATABASE	Specifies that the standby database is mounted.
DATABASE	Specifies that the whole database is to be recovered. The DATABASE parameter is the default value in the `recover_clause`.
UNTIL CANCEL	Specifies that the recovery will be performed until the ALTER DATABASE RECOVER statement is issued with the RECOVER CANCEL clause.
UNTIL TIME `date`	Specifies that the recovery will be performed until the date and time specified.
UNTIL CHANGE `integer`	Specifies that the recovery will be performed until the point where a change was found with the system change number specified by *integer*.
USING BACKUP CONTROLFILE	Specifies that a backup control file will be used and not the current control file, during the recovery operation.
`parallel_clause`	See the section "Common Clauses" for details.

CREATE/DROP DATABASE LINK

The CREATE/DROP DATABASE LINK command allows you to create or drop a database link. Database links can be used to access database objects in a remote database. To reference objects in the remote database, qualify the object with the database link name (for example, select * from emp@remote_database). The following is the syntax for the CREATE DATABASE LINK command:

```
CREATE [SHARED] [PUBLIC] DATABASE LINK dblink
[ CONNECT TO
    { CURRENT USER
    | user IDENTIFIED BY password
        [AUTHENTICATED BY user IDENTIFIED BY password]
    }
| AUTHENTICATED BY user IDENTIFIED BY password
]
[USING 'connect_string']
```

The following is the syntax for the DROP DATABASE LINK command:

```
DROP [PUBLIC] DATABASE LINK dblink
```

The following list explains all of the elements used in the CREATE/DROP DATABASE LINK command syntax:

SHARED	Specifies that a single network connection to create a public database link can be shared among multiple users. Available only with the multithreaded server configuration.
PUBLIC	Specifies that the database link to create or drop is available to all users. By default, this clause is omitted and private database links are created.
dblink	Specifies the name of the database link to be created or dropped.
CONNECT TO	Specifies the details to connect to the remote database.
CURRENT USER	Specifies the username in the remote database. When using global user authentication, you can use this clause to create a current user database link.

user IDENTIFIED BY*password*	Specifies the username and password for the user in the remote database. You may omit this clause and use the username and password of the current local session. This is referred to as *connected user database link* as opposed to *fixed user database link* when you specify this clause.
USING '*connect_string*'	Specifies the service name of the remote database.
AUTHENTICATED BY *user* IDENTIFIED BY *password*	Specifies the username and password on the remote instance. When using the SHARED option, this clause is mandatory.

CREATE/ALTER/DROP DIMENSION

You can use the CREATE/ALTER/DROP DIMENSION commands to create, alter, or drop dimension database objects. Dimension database objects define parent-child relationships between columns from the same and/or from other tables. No data storage is associated with dimension database objects. The following is the syntax for the CREATE DIMENSION command:

```
CREATE [FORCE|NOFORCE] DIMENSION [schema.]dimension
level_clause[level_clause...]
{hierarchy_clause|attribute_clause}
  [{hierarchy_clause|attribute_clause}...]
```

The following is the syntax for the ALTER DIMENSION command:

```
ALTER DIMENSION [schema.]dimension
{ COMPILE
| drop_clause[drop_clause...]
| add_clause[add_clause...]
}
```

Listing A-8 provides the syntax for the DROP DIMENSION command.

Listing A-8: **DROP DIMENSION syntax**

```
DROP DIMENSION [schema.]dimension

add_clause := ADD
{ level_clause
| hierarchy_clause
| attribute_clause
}
```

Continued

Listing A-8: *(continued)*

```
attribute_clause := ATTRIBUTE level DETERMINES
{ dependent_column
| ( dependent_column[,dependent_column...] )
}

drop_clause := DROP
{ LEVEL level [RESTRICT|CASCADE]
| HIERARCHY hierarchy
| ATTRIBUTE level
}

hierarchy_clause := HIERARCHY hierarchy (child_level)
    CHILD OF parent_level[CHILD OF parent_level...]
    [join_clause[join_clause...]]

join_clause := JOIN KEY
{ child_key_column
| ( child_key_column[,child_key_column...] )
}
REFERENCES parent_level

level_clause := LEVEL level IS
{ table.column
| ( table.column[,table.column...] )
}
```

The following list explains all of the elements used in the CREATE/ALTER/DROP DIMENSION commands syntax:

FORCE	Specifies that the creation of the dimension will succeed even if referenced tables do not exist.
NOFORCE	Specifies that the creation of the dimension will fail if referenced tables do not exist. The NOFORCE parameter is the default value.
schema.dimension	Specifies the name of the dimension to create, alter, or drop. The schema name is optional and may be omitted.
COMPILE	Specifies that the dimension is to be explicitly compiled when used in the ALTER DIMENSION command.
ATTRIBUTE level DETERMINES dependent_column	Specifies that the column level is uniquely identified by the column dependent_column.

LEVEL *level*	Defines the name of a level in the dimension.
table.column	Specifies a column in the level. You may specify multiple column names.
RESTRICT	Levels are prevented from being dropped from the dimension when they are referenced.
CASCADE	Specifies that all attributes and/or hierarchies that reference the level are dropped as well.
HIERARCHY *hierarchy*	Defines the name of a hierarchy in the dimension.
child_level	Specifies the name of a child level.
CHILD OF *parent_level*	Specifies to which parent level the child level relates.
JOIN KEY *child_key_column* REFERENCES *parent_level*	Specifies the join relationship between one or more *child_key_column* columns and the name of the parent level when columns are referenced in multiple tables.

CREATE/DROP DIRECTORY

You can use the CREATE/DROP DIRECTORY commands to create or drop a directory database object that represents a file system directory. A DIRECTORY object can be seen as an alias for a file system directory. You can use the DIRECTORY objects to store objects of the BFILE type. The following is the syntax for the CREATE DIRECTORY command:

```
CREATE [OR REPLACE] DIRECTORY directory_name AS 'path_name'
```

The following is the syntax for the DROP DIRECTORY command:

```
DROP DIRECTORY directory_name
```

The following list explains all of the elements used in the CREATE/DROP DIRECTORY commands' syntax:

OR REPLACE	If a directory is already present with the name *directory_name*, it will be replaced by the newly created directory. Effectively, it changes the definition of the directory object, and all grants to this directory object will remain in place.

directory_name	Specifies the name of the directory to be created or dropped.
AS '*path_name*'	Points to a directory in the file system on the server.

CREATE/ALTER/DROP FUNCTION

You can use the CREATE/ALTER/DROP FUNCTION commands to create, alter, or drop stored function database objects. You may define the function in PL/SQL or in another language. The difference between a stored FUNCTION and a stored PROCEDURE is that the function returns a value, whereas a procedure does not. The following is the syntax for the CREATE FUNCTION command:

```
CREATE [OR REPLACE]
FUNCTION schema.function {argument_list}
RETURN data_type
[AUTHID {CURRENT_USER|DEFINER}]
[DETERMINISTIC]
[PARRALEL_ENABLE]
{IS|AS}
{ function_body
| LANGUAGE JAVA NAME 'string'
| LANGUAGE c_declaration
}
```

The following is the syntax for the ALTER FUNCTION command:

```
ALTER FUNCTION schema.function COMPILE [DEBUG]
```

The following is the syntax for the DROP FUNCTION command:

```
DROP FUNCTION schema.function

argument_list :=
( argument {IN|OUT|IN OUT} [NOCOPY]     datatype
    [,argument {IN|OUT|IN OUT} [NOCOPY] datatype...]
)

c_declaration := C [NAME name]
LIBRARY library [WITH CONTEXT] [PARAMETERS (parameters)]
```

The following list explains all of the elements used in the CREATE/ALTER/DROP FUNCTION commands' syntax:

OR REPLACE	If a function is already present with the same name, it will be replaced. Effectively, it changes the definition of the function object, and all grants to this function will remain in place.

schema.function	Specifies the name of the function to be created, altered, or dropped. The schema name may be omitted.
RETURN *data_type*	Specifies the datatype of the function return value.
AUTHID	Specifies a method to obtain privileges at execution of the function CURRENT_USER or DEFINER.
CURRENT_USER	Specifies that the privileges for the function at execution time are the same as those for the user who calls the function.
DEFINER	Specifies that the privileges for the function at execution time are the same as for the owner of the schema in which the function resides.
DETERMINISTIC	Increases the performance of deterministic functions. When a function always returns the same value for the input parameters specified, this clause can be used to tell the optimizer to use a saved copy of the return value, if available, from the last time the function was executed.
PARRALEL_ENABLE	Specifies that the function can be executed from a parallel server.
function_body	Specifies the body of the function containing the implementation of it.
LANGUAGE	Specifies the language of the implementation of the function when no PL/SQL function body is specified.
COMPILE	Specifies that the function is going to be recompiled.
COMPILE DEBUG	Same as COMPILE, but also creates debug information for the PL/SQL debugger.
argument	Specifies one of the arguments passed to the function. You may pass PL/SQL variables, bind variables, constants, and literals depending on the mode of the argument (IN, OUT, and IN OUT).
IN	Specifies that the argument is an input variable, constant, or literal. The argument has to be specified when calling the function.

OUT	Specifies that the argument is an output variable. A variable needs to be specified to receive the value when the execution of the function is finished. No constants or literals are allowed as arguments.
IN OUT	Specifies that the argument is both an input and an output variable. A variable has to be specified. When the procedure is called, the value of the variable is taken. When the procedure is finished, the changed value is returned to the calling program. No constants or literals are allowed as arguments.
NOCOPY	Specifies that the argument is passed by reference and not by value. This may enhance performance when large arguments are used.
datatype	Specifies the datatype of the argument.
JAVA NAME *'string'*	Specifies the name of a Java function.
C NAME *name*	Specifies the name of a C function.
LIBRARY *library*	Specifies the name of the library in which the C routine can be found.
WITH CONTEXT	Specifies that the context pointer is passed to the external function.
PARAMETERS (*parameters*)	Specifies the position and parameters passed to the external function.

CREATE/ALTER/DROP INDEX

You can use the CREATE/ALTER/DROP INDEX commands to create, alter, or drop index database objects. Use the CREATE and ALTER commands to specify a number of options and parameters for the index. Furthermore, you can use the ALTER command to split index partitions and to modify or rebuild an index subpartition.

An index is a database object that provides direct access to a row via one or more indexed columns. Indexes can be created on tables and clusters. Listing A-9 provides the syntax for the CREATE INDEX command:

Listing A-9: **CREATE INDEX syntax**

```
CREATE [UNIQUE|BITMAP] INDEX [schema.]index ON
{ CLUSTER [schema.]cluster
    index_attributes
| [schema.]table table_alias (index_column[,index_column...])
    { INDEXTYPE IS indextype [PARAMETERS ('string')]
    | [ GLOBAL PARTITION BY RANGE
```

```
                (column_list)
    (global_partition_clause[,global_partition_clause...])
            index_attributes
        / LOCAL
            [ ( on_range_table[,on_range_table..] )
            / { store_in_clause
            | ( on_hash_table[,on_hash_table...] )
            }
            / store_in_clause
            [ (on_composite_table[,on_composite_table..]) ]
            ]
            index_attributes
        ]
    }
}
```

Listing A-10 provides the syntax for the ALTER INDEX command.

Listing A-10: **ALTER INDEX syntax**

```
ALTER INDEX [schema.]index
{ COALESCE
| RENAME TO new_index_name
| UNUSABLE
| PARAMETERS ('string')
| REBUILD { { PARAMETERS ('string')
            | {REVERSE|NOREVERSE}
            }
        | [PARTITION partition|SUBPARTITION subpartition]
        index_attributes
        }
| partitioning_clauses
| {ENABLE|DISABLE}
| [ parallel_clause
    | physical_attributes_clause
    | {LOGGING|NOLOGGING}
    | { ALLOCATE EXTENT ( { [INSTANCE integer]
                            [DATAFILE 'filename']
                            [SIZE integer [K|M]]
                        }
                    )
    | DEALLOCATE UNUSED [KEEP integer [K|M]]
    }
]
}
```

Listing A-11 provides the syntax for the DROP INDEX command:

Listing A-11: **DROP INDEX syntax**

```
DROP INDEX [schema.]index [FORCE]

global_partition_clause := PARTITION partition
VALUES LESS THAN (value_list)
[physical_attributes_clause]
[LOGGING|NOLOGGING]

index_attributes :=
[ [parallel_clause]
  [ONLINE]
  [COMPUTE STATISTICS]
  [physical_attributes_clause]
  [COMPRESS integer|NOCOMPRESS]
  [LOGGING|NOLOGGING]
  [TABLESPACE {tablespace|DEFAULT}]
  [NOSORT|REVERSE]
]

index_column := {column|column_expression} [ASC|DESC]

on_range_table :=
PARTITION [ partition [segment_attributes_clause]]

on_hash_table :=
PARTITION [partition [TABLESPACE table space]]

on_composite_table :=
PARTITION
[ partition
  [segment_attributes_clause]
  { store_in_clause
  | (subpartition[,subpartition...])
  }
]

partitioning_clauses :=
{ MODIFY DEFAULT ATTRIBUTES [FOR PARTITION partition]
  { [physical_attributes_clause]
    [TABLESPACE {tablespace/DEFAULT}]
    [LOGGING|NOLOGGING]
  }
| MODIFY PARTITION partition
  { UNUSABLE
  | COALESCE
  | { [physical_attributes_clause]
```

```
            [LOGGING|NOLOGGING]
            [ allocate_extent_clause
            |   DEALLOCATE UNUSED [KEEP integer [K|M]]
            ]
          }
        }
      }
/ RENAME {PARTITION|SUBPARTITION} current_name TO new_name
/ DROP PARTITION partition_name
/ SPLIT PARTITION partition_name_old AT (value_list)
  [INTO (partition_descr,partition_descr)]
  [parallel_clause]
/ MODIFY SUBPARTITION subpartition
  { UNUSABLE
  | allocate_extent_clause
  / DEALLOCATE UNUSED [KEEP integer [K|M]]
  }
}

partition_description := PARTITION
[partition [ [segment_attributes_clause]
              [COMPRESS integer|NOCOMPRESS]
            ]
]

segment_attributes_clause :=
[ [physical_attributes_clause]
  [TABLESPACE table space]
  [LOGGING|NOLOGGING]
]

store_in_clause :=
STORE IN ( {DEFAULT|tablespace[,table space...]} )

subpartition :=
SUBPARTITION [subpartition [TABLESPACE table space]]
```

The following list explains all of the elements used in the CREATE/ALTER/DROP INDEX commands' syntax:

UNIQUE
: Specifies that the columns on which the index is based must be unique.

BITMAP
: Specifies that the index will be created as a bitmap.

schema.index
: Specifies the index name to create, alter, or delete. The schema name may be omitted.

`ON CLUSTER cluster`	Specifies the cluster for which to create the index.
`table table_alias`	Specifies the table on which to create the index. A table alias may be specified.
`INDEXTYPE IS indextype`	Specifies the name of the domain index.
`PARAMETERS ('string')`	Specifies the string that is passed to the domain index routine.
`GLOBAL PARTITION BY RANGE`	Specifies that the index is partitioned in a different way as the underlying table. The global index is partitioned by the values of the columns in `column_list`.
`column_list`	Specifies the list of columns used to partition the index.
`LOCAL`	Specifies that the index is partitioned in the same way as the underlying table.
`RENAME TO new_index_name`	Renames the index and specifies a new name.
`UNUSABLE`	Marks the index, index partitions, or index subpartitions as unusable.
`REBUILD`	Specifies that the index or index partitions/subpartitions are rebuilt.
`REVERSE`	Specifies that the bytes in the index block are to be stored in reverse order.
`NOREVERSE`	Specifies that the bytes in the index block are not reversed when the index is rebuilt.
`PARTITION partition`	Specifies the partition of the index to rebuild.
`SUBPARTITION subpartition`	Specifies the subpartition of the index to rebuild.
`ENABLE`	Specifies that a function-based index will be made unavailable.
`DISABLE`	Specifies that a function-based index will be made available.
`parallel_clause`	See the section "Common Clauses" for details.

physical_attributes_clause	See the section "Common Clauses" for details.
LOGGING	Specifies that insert operations from SQL Loader will be logged in the redo log file.
NOLOGGING	Specifies that insert operations from SQL Loader will not be logged in the redo log file.
ALLOCATE EXTENT	Specifies that a new extent is created for the index.
INSTANCE *integer*	Specifies the instance for which the extent is made available.
DATAFILE *'filename'*	Specifies a data file in which to create the extent.
SIZE *integer*	Specifies the size of the extent. Use *K* for kilobytes and *M* for megabytes.
DEALLOCATE UNUSED	Specifies that free space allocated to the index will be made available for other segments to use.
KEEP *integer*	Specifies how many bytes of free space above the high water mark should be retained for the index.
FORCE	Specifies that a domain index will be dropped even if the indextype routine returns errors. In this case the index will be marked as LOADING.
VALUES LESS THAN *value_list*	When partitioning a global index, specifies the upper bound for the current partition. The values in *value_list* are comma separated and ordered. They correspond to the column names in the *column_list* in the GLOBAL PARTITION BY RANGE clause.
TABLESPACE *table space*	Specifies the name of the tablespace that stores the index, index partition, or index subpartition.
ONLINE	Specifies that during the building of the index, DML operations are allowed to run against the table.

COMPUTE STATISTICS	Specifies that statistics for the use of the Oracle optimizer will be collected during the creation of the index.
COMPRESS *integer*	Specifies the number of prefix columns to use in key compression.
NOCOMPRESS	Specifies that key compression is not used.
DEFAULT	Specifies that the index partitions or subpartitions are stored in the same way as the underlying table.
NOSORT	Can be used only in CREATE statements.
column	The name of one of the columns on which the index is based.
column_expression	Evaluates to one of the columns on which the index is based.
ASC	Specifies that the index is created in ascending order.
DESC	Specifies that the index is created in descending order.
MODIFY DEFAULT ATTRIBUTES	Specifies new values for the default attributes of a partitioned index.
FOR PARTITION *partition*	Specifies for which subpartition of the index the default attributes should be set.
MODIFY PARTITION *partition*	Specifies a set of options for the index partition *partition*.
COALESCE	Specifies that all free space in index blocks is collected, merged, and made available for reuse.
RENAME*current_name* TO *new_name*	Specifies that a partition or subpartition is renamed from *current_name* to *new_name*.
DROP PARTITION *partition_name*	Specifies that the partition *partition_name* is to be removed from a global partitioned index.
SPLIT PARTITION	Specifies that the partition is to be split into two partitions.

AT (*value_list*)	Specifies the upper bound for the first partition.
INTO (*partition_descr, partition_descr*)	Specifies the names for the two new partitions.
MODIFY SUBPARTITION	Specifies that a subpartition is to be made UNUSABLE or (de)allocates storage for the subpartition of the index.
DEALLOCATE UNUSED	Specifies that space above the high water mark at the end of the subpartition is to be made available for other segments in the tablespace.
STORE IN	Specifies how the index partitions or subpartitions are stored in tablespaces.

CREATE/DROP INDEXTYPE

You can use the CREATE/DROP INDEXTYPE commands to create or drop *indextype* database objects. The *indextype* objects manage application-specific indexes called domain indexes. *Domain indexes* are used for indexing operations on complex data. The *indextype* database object binds to an implementation type that implements user-defined index functions and procedures. The following is the syntax for the CREATE INDEXTYPE command:

```
CREATE INDEXTYPE [schema.]indextype
FOR for_list_item[,for_list_item...]
USING [schema.]implementation_type
```

The following is the syntax for the DROP INDEXTYPE command:

```
DROP INDEXTYPE [schema.]indextype [FORCE]

for_list_item :=
[schema.]operator(parameter_type[,parameter_type...])
```

The following list explains all of the elements used in the CREATE/DROP INDEXTYPE command syntax:

schema.indextype	Specifies the name of the *indextype* to create or drop. Schema is optional and may be omitted.
FOR	Specifies a list of operators that are supported by the *indextype*.

USING *schema.implementation_type*	Specifies the type that implements the Oracle Data Cartridge Interface. Schema is optional and may be omitted. (For more information on the Oracle Data Cartridge Interface, see the documentation that comes with the Oracle software.)
FORCE	Specifies that the indextype is dropped even if it is referenced by domain indexes. Those domain indexes will be invalidated.
schema.operator	Specifies the operator supported by the indextype.
parameter_type	Specifies one of the parameter types to the operator.

CREATE/DROP LIBRARY

You can use the commands CREATE/DROP LIBRARY to create or drop library database objects. Libraries can be regarded as synonyms for DLLs on the database server. You can use subroutines in these DLLs in PL/SQL using the EXTERNAL clause. The following is the syntax for the CREATE LIBRARY command:

```
CREATE [OR REPLACE] LIBRARY [schema.]library_name
{IS|AS} file_spec
```

The following is the syntax for the DROP LIBRARY command:

```
DROP LIBRARY library_name
```

The following list explains all of the elements used in the CREATE/DROP LIBRARY commands' syntax:

OR REPLACE	If a library is already present with the same name, it will be replaced. Effectively, it changes the definition of the library object, and all grants to this library will remain in place.
schema.library_name	Specifies the name of the library to create or drop. The schema name is optional and may be omitted.
IS	Synonym for AS.
AS	Synonym for IS.

file_spec   Specifies the DLL that implements the library.
                             The full path on the file system of the server is
                             required. See the "Common Clauses" section for
                             details.

CREATE/ALTER/DROP MATERIALIZED VIEW/SNAPSHOT

You can use the commands CREATE/ALTER/DROP MATERIALIZED VIEW/SNAPSHOT
to create, alter, or drop materialized views. Snapshot is synonymous with
materialized view. Materialized views can be used to summarize, replicate, and
distribute data. Listing A-12 provides the syntax for the CREATE MATERIALIZED
VIEW command.

Listing A-12: **CREATE MATERIALIZED VIEW syntax**

```
CREATE {MATERIALIZED VIEW|SNAPSHOT}
[schema.]materialized_view/snapshot
{ { [ physical_attributes]
    [LOB_storage_clause]
    [LOGGING|NOLOGGING]
    [CACHE|NOCACHE]
  }
| CLUSTER cluster (column[,column...])
}
[partitioning_clauses]
[parallel_clause]
[ BUILD {IMMEDIATE|DEFERRED}
| ON PREBUILT TABLE [ {WITH|WITHOUT} REDUCED PRECISION ]
]
[USING INDEX [physical_attributes]
[REFRESH refresh_clause|NEVER REFRESH]
[FOR UPDATE]
[ {DISABLE|ENABLE} QUERY REWRITE ]
AS subquery
```

Listing A-13 provides the syntax for the ALTER MATERIALIZED VIEW command.

Listing A-13: **ALTER MATERIALIZED VIEW syntax**

```
ALTER {MATERIALIZED VIEW|SNAPSHOT}
[schema.]materialized_view/snapshot
[ physical_attributes_clause
```

Continued

Listing A-13: *(continued)*

```
|  LOB_storage_clause[,LOB_storage_clause...]
|  modify_LOB_storage_clause[,modify_LOB_storage_clause...]
|  partitioning_clauses
|  parallel_clause
|  {LOGGING|NOLOGGING}
|  {CACHE|NOCACHE}
]
[USING INDEX physical_attributes]
[refresh_clause]
[ COMPILE
| ENABLE  QUERY REWRITE
| DISABLE QUERY REWRITE
]
```

The following is the syntax for the DROP MATERIALIZED VIEW command:

```
DROP {MATERIALIZED VIEW|SNAPSHOT}
[schema.]materialized_view/snapshot

refresh_clause :=
[FAST|COMPLETE|FORCE]
[ON DEMAND|ON COMMIT]
[START WITH date|NEXT date]
[WITH {PRIMARY KEY|ROWID}]
[ USING DEFAULT {MASTER|LOCAL} ROLLBACK SEGMENT
| USING {MASTER|LOCAL} ROLLBACK SEGMENT rollback_segment
]
```

The following list explains all of the elements used in the CREATE/ALTER/DROP MATERIALIZED VIEW/SNAPSHOT command syntax:

MATERIALIZED VIEW	Synonym for snapshot.
SNAPSHOT	Synonym for materialized view.
schema.materialized_view/snapshot	Specifies the name for the materialized view. The schema name is optional and may be omitted.
physical_attributes	See the "Common Clauses" section for details.
LOGGING	Specifies that insert operations from SQL Loader will be logged in the redo log file.
NOLOGGING	Specifies that insert operations from SQL Loader will not be logged in the redo log file.

CACHE	Specifies that when a full tablescan is performed, the blocks retrieved are placed at the most recently used end of the LRU list in the buffer cache.
NOCACHE	No caching is performed when a full tablescan is performed.
CLUSTER *cluster*	Specifies in which cluster the materialized view is to be created.
column	Name of the column in the cluster key.
partitioning_clauses	See *partitioning_clauses* in the section, "CREATE/ALTER/DELETE/ LOCK TABLE," for details.
parallel_clause	See the section "Common Clauses" for details.
BUILD IMMEDIATE	Specifies that the materialized view is immediately populated with data. The BUILD IMMEDIATE parameter is the default.
BUILD DEFERRED	Specifies that the materialized view initially populated at the next refresh operation.
ON PREBUILT TABLE	Specifies that an existing table with the same name as the materialized view is to be used. The table will be optionally maintained by the materialized view refresh mechanism.
WITHOUT REDUCED PRECISION	Specifies that the precision of the columns in the table must exactly match that of the columns in the materialized view.
WITH REDUCED PRECISION	Specifies that loss of precision resulting from differences in column precisions of the table and the materialized view is authorized
USING INDEX *physical_attributes*	Specifies the physical attributes for the indexes created for the materialized view. See the common clauses section for details about *physical_attributes*.

REFRESH *refresh_clause*	Specifies how Oracle will automatically refresh the materialized view.
NEVER REFRESH	Specifies that Oracle will not allow a refresh of the materialized view.
FAST	Specifies that the fast refresh mode is to be used. The fast refresh mode will perform incremental refreshes.
COMPLETE	Specifies that the *subquery* is re-executed to refresh the materialized view.
FORCE	Specifies that a fast refresh should be done if possible; otherwise, a complete refresh will be done. The FORCE parameter is the default option if FAST, COMPLETE, and FORCE are omitted.
ON DEMAND	Specifies that the materialized view is not automatically refreshed. A refresh can be initiated by using the dbms_mview procedures.
ON COMMIT	Specifies that the materialized view is to be refreshed at the next commit operation.
START WITH *date*	Specifies the first date for an automatic refresh operation.
NEXT *date*	Specifies the next date for an automatic refresh operation. Note that the interval between NEXT date and START WITH date is used to determine subsequent refreshes.
WITH PRIMARY KEY	Specifies that a primary key materialized view is to be created. The WITH PRIMARY KEY parameter is the default value.
WITH ROWID	Specifies that a rowid materialized view is to be created.
USING DEFAULTROLLBACK SEGMENT	Specifies that Oracle will choose a remote rollback segment for a refresh operation.
MASTER	Specifies the remote master rollback segment for the materialized view.

LOCAL	Specifies the remote rollback segment to be used for the local refresh group containing the materialized view.
FOR UPDATE	When the advanced replication option is used, this clause allows the materialized view to be updated. The changes will be propagated to the master tables.
DISABLE QUERY REWRITE	Disables the materialized view for query rewrites.
ENABLE QUERY REWRITE	Enables the materialized view for query rewrites.
AS *subquery*	Specifies the query to create the materialized view.
COMPILE	Specifies that the materialized view is to be revalidated. If objects referenced in the *subquery* are not accessible or if they are changed, the materialized view is invalidated for query rewrites.
LOB_storage_clause	See the *LOB_storage_clause* in the section, "CREATE/ALTER/DELETE/ LOCK TABLE," for details.
modify_LOB_storage_clause	See the *modify_LOB_storage_ clause* in the ALTER TABLE command section for details.
rollback_segment	Specifies the name of the rollback segment that is to be used.

CREATE/ALTER/DROP MATERIALIZED VIEW LOG/SNAPSHOT LOG

You can use the CREATE/ALTER/DROP MATERIALIZED VIEW LOG/SNAPSHOT LOG commands to create, alter, and drop materialized view log database objects. Oracle uses materialized view log objects to store information about changes in the master table of a materialized view. The materialized view log object is used when a fast refresh procedure is performed for the materialized view. The following is the syntax for the CREATE MATERIALIZED VIEW LOG command:

```
CREATE {MATERIALIZED VIEW|SNAPSHOT} LOG ON [schema.]table
[ [physical_attributes]
  [LOGGING|NOLOGGING]
  [CACHE|NOCACHE]
```

```
]
[partitioning_clauses]
[parallel_clause]
[WITH {ROWID|PRIMARY KEY|ROWID,PRIMARY KEY|PRIMARY KEY,ROWID}
  [(filter_column[,filter_column...])
]
[INCLUDING NEW VALUES|EXCLUDING NEW VALUES]
```

The following is the syntax for the ALTER MATERIALIZED VIEW LOG command:

```
ALTER {MATERIALIZED VIEW|SNAPSHOT} LOG ON [schema.]table
[ [physical_attributes]
  [partitioning_clauses]
  [parallel_clause]
  [LOGGING|NOLOGGING]
  [CACHE|NOCACHE]
]
[ADD {ROWID|PRIMARY KEY} [(filter_column[,filter_column...])]]
[INCLUDING NEW VALUES|EXCLUDING NEW VALUES]
```

The following is the syntax for the DROP MATERIALIZED VIEW LOG command:

```
DROP {MATERIALIZED VIEW|SNAPSHOT} LOG ON [schema.]table
```

The following list explains all of the elements used in the CREATE/ALTER/DROP MATERIALIZED VIEW LOG/SNAPSHOT LOG commands' syntax:

MATERIALIZED VIEW LOG	Synonym for SNAPSHOT LOG.
SNAPSHOT LOG	Synonym for MATERIALIZED VIEW LOG.
ON schema.table	Specifies the name of the master table of the materialized view. Schema is optional and may be omitted.
physical_attributes	See the section "Common Clauses" for details.
partitioning_clauses	See partitioning_clauses in the ALTER TABLE command section for details.
parallel_clause	See the section "Common Clauses" for details.
LOGGING	Specifies that insert operations from SQL Loader will be logged in the redo log file.
NOLOGGING	Specifies that insert operations from SQL Loader will not be logged in the redo log file.
CACHE	Specifies that when a full tablescan is performed, the blocks retrieved are placed at the most recently used end of the LRU list in the buffer cache.

NOCACHE	No caching is performed when a full tablescan is performed.
WITH ROWID	Specifies that the rowid of changed rows are to be stored in the materialized view log.
WITH PRIMARY KEY	Specifies that the primary key values of changed rows are to be stored in the materialized view log.
filter_column	Specifies that the values of these columns (specified as a comma-separated list) of the changed rows are to be stored in the materialized view log.
INCLUDING NEW VALUES	Specifies that both the old and the new values are to be stored in the materialized view log.
EXCLUDING NEW VALUES	Specifies that only the old values are to be stored in the materialized view log.
ADD ROWID	Specifies that the rowid of changed rows is to be stored in the materialized view log.
ADD PRIMARY KEY	Specifies that the primary key values of changed rows are to be stored in the materialized view log.

CREATE/DROP OPERATOR

You can use the CREATE/DROP OPERATOR commands to create or drop operator database objects. Database operator objects can be used in index types, DML, and queries. The following is the syntax for the CREATE OPERATOR command:

```
CREATE [OR REPLACE] OPERATOR [schema.]operator
BINDING binding_clause[,binding_clause...]
```

The following is the syntax for the DROP OPERATOR command:

```
DROP OPERATOR [schema.]operator [FORCE]

binding_clause := ( parameter_type[,parameter_type...] )
RETURN return_type
[ ANCILLARY TO
    primary_operator( parameter_type[,parameter_type...] )
      [,primary_operator( parameter_type[,parameter_type...]
)...]
| WITH INDEX CONTEXT,SCAN CONTEXT implementation_type
    [COMPUTE ANCILLARY DATA]
]
USING [schema.][package.|type.]function_name
```

The following list explains all of the elements used in the CREATE/DROP OPERATOR commands' syntax:

OR REPLACE	If an operator is already present with the same name, it will be replaced.
schema.operator	Specifies the name of the operator to create or drop. Schema is optional and may be omitted.
FORCE	Specifies that the operator is dropped even if it is still referenced. The objects that reference it will be made invalid.
BINDING	Specifies one or more parameter types that bind the operator to a function.
parameter_type	Specifies the datatype of one of the parameters.
RETURN return_type	Specifies the return datatype for the binding.
ANCILLARY TO	Specifies that the operator binding is ancillary to another operator binding— the primary operator binding.
primary_operator	Specifies the name of the primary operator.
WITH INDEX CONTEXT, SCAN CONTEXT implementation_type	Specifies the name of the type that is used by the function as scan context.
COMPUTE ANCILLARY DATA	Specifies that the operator binding computes the ancillary data.
USING	Specifies the function that implements the binding.
package	Specifies the package in which the function resides.
type	Specifies the type in which the function resides.
function_name	Specifies the name of the function that implements the binding.

CREATE/ALTER/DROP PACKAGE

You can use the CREATE/ALTER/DROP PACKAGE commands to create, alter, or delete packages in the database. Package specifications and bodies can be created, altered, or deleted separately. The following is the syntax for the CREATE PACKAGE and CREATE PACKAGE BODY commands:

```
CREATE [OR REPLACE] PACKAGE [BODY] [schema.]package
[AUTHID {CURRENT_USER|DEFINER}]
{IS|AS}
{package_specification|package_body}
```

The following is the syntax for the ALTER PACKAGE command:

```
ALTER PACKAGE [schema.]package
COMPILE [DEBUG] [PACKAGE|SPECIFICTION|BODY]
```

The following is the syntax for the DROP PACKAGE command:

```
DROP PACKAGE [BODY] [schema.]package
```

The following list explains all of the elements used in the CREATE/ALTER/DROP PACKAGE commands' syntax:

OR REPLACE	If a package is already present with the same name, it will be replaced. Effectively, it changes the definition of the package object, and all grants to this package will remain in place.
schema.package	Specifies the package. The schema identifier is optional.
IS	A synonym for AS.
AS	A synonym for IS.
package_specification	PL/SQL code for the package specification. In the specification, the function and procedure prototypes are coded as well as other publicly accessible objects.
package_body	PL/SQL code for the implementation of the functions and procedures in the package specification as well as the implementation of private code.
COMPILE PACKAGE	Specifies that the package is about to be compiled. Compiling the package will cause both the specification and the package body to be compiled.
COMPILE BODY	Specifies that the package body is about to be compiled. The package header will remain valid unless the package body will compile unsuccessfully.

COMPILE SPECIFICATION	Specifies that the package specification is about to be compiled.
COMPILE DEBUG	Same as COMPILE, but also creates debug information for the PL/SQL debugger.
AUTHID	Specifies a method to obtain privileges at execution of the package: CURRENT_USER or DEFINER. Applicable only to package specifications.
CURRENT_USER	Specifies that the privileges for the package at execution time are the same as those for the user that calls the package.
DEFINER	Specifies that the privileges for the package at execution time are the same as for the owner of the schema in which the package resides.

CREATE/ALTER/DROP PROCEDURE

You can use the CREATE/ALTER/DROP PROCEDURE commands to create, alter, or delete procedure database objects. You can also use the CREATE PROCEDURE command to register external procedures (3GL stored in a shared library). The following is the syntax for the CREATE PROCEDURE command:

```
CREATE [OR REPLACE] PROCEDURE
[schema.]procedure [(argument_spec[,argument_spec...])]
[AUTHID {CURRENT_USER|DEFINER}]
{IS|AS}
{ procedure_body
| LANGUAGE JAVA NAME 'string'
| LANGUAGE c_declaration
}
```

The following is the syntax for the ALTER PROCEDURE command:

```
ALTER PROCEDURE [schema.]procedure COMPILE [DEBUG]
```

The following is the syntax for the DROP PROCEDURE command:

```
DROP PROCEDURE [schema.]procedure

argument_spec := argument [IN|OUT|IN OUT] [NOCOPY] data_type

c_declaration := C [NAME name]
LIBRARY library [WITH CONTEXT] [PARAMETERS (parameters)]
```

The following list explains all of the elements used in the CREATE/ALTER/DROP PROCEDURE commands' syntax:

OR REPLACE	If a procedure is already present with the same name, it will be replaced. Effectively, it changes the definition of the procedure object, and all grants to this procedure will remain in place.
schema.procedure	Specifies the procedure object to be created, altered, or deleted. The schema identifier is optional and may be omitted.
IS	A synonym for the keyword AS.
AS	A synonym for the keyword IS.
procedure_body	PL/SQL code that implements the procedure body.
COMPILE	Specifies that the procedure is about to be compiled.
COMPILE DEBUG	Same as COMPILE, but also creates debug information for the PL/SQL debugger.
argument	Specifies the name of an argument in the argument_spec.
IN	Specifies that the argument is an input variable, constant, or literal. The argument has to be specified when calling the procedure.
OUT	Specifies that the argument is an output variable. A variable needs to be specified to receive the value when the execution of the procedure is finished. No constants or literals are allowed as arguments.
IN OUT	Specifies that the argument is both an input and an output variable. A variable has to be specified. When the procedure is called, the value of the variable is taken. When the procedure is finished, the changed value is returned to the calling program. No constants or literals are allowed as arguments.
NOCOPY	Specifies that the argument is passed by reference and not by value. This may enhance performance when large arguments are used.
data_type	Specifies the data type of the argument.
AUTHID	Specifies a method to obtain privileges at execution of the procedure: CURRENT_USER or DEFINER.

CURRENT_USER	Specifies that the privileges for the procedure at execution time are the same as those for the user that calls the procedure.
DEFINER	Specifies that the privileges for the procedure at execution time are the same as for the owner of the schema in which the procedure resides.
LANGUAGE	Specifies the language of the implementation of the function when no PL/SQL function body is specified.
JAVA NAME 'string'	Specifies the name of a Java function.
C NAME name	Specifies the name of a C function.
LIBRARY library	Specifies the name of the library in which the C routine can be found.
WITH CONTEXT	Specifies that the context pointer is passed to the external function.
PARAMETERS	Specifies the position and parameters passed to the external function.

CREATE/ALTER/DROP PROFILE

You can use the CREATE/ALTER/DROP PROFILE commands to create, alter, or drop profile database objects. You can assign a profile to a user to limit the usage of database resources. The following is the syntax for the CREATE PROFILE command:

```
CREATE PROFILE profile LIMIT
profile_option[profile_option...]
```

The following is the syntax for the DROP PROFILE command:

```
DROP PROFILE profile [CASCADE];
```

Listing A-14 provides the syntax for the ALTER PROFILE command:

Listing A-14: **ALTER PROFILE syntax**

```
ALTER PROFILE profile LIMIT profile_option[profile_option...]

profile_option :=
{ PRIVATE_SGA          {UNLIMITED|DEFAULT| integer {K|M}}
| SESSION_PER_USER     {integer|UNLIMITED|DEFAULT}
| CPU_PER_CALL          {integer|UNLIMITED|DEFAULT}
| CPU_PER_SESSION       {integer|UNLIMITED|DEFAULT}
| CONNECT_TIME          {integer|UNLIMITED|DEFAULT}
| IDLE_TIME           {integer|UNLIMITED|DEFAULT}
```

```
| COMPOSITE_LIMIT            {integer|UNLIMITED|DEFAULT}
  LOGICAL_READS_PER_SESSION    {integer|UNLIMITED|DEFAULT}
  LOGICAL_READS_PER_CALL      {integer|UNLIMITED|DEFAULT}
  PASSWORD_VERIFY_FUNCTION      {function|NULL|DEFAULT}
  { FAILED_LOGIN_ATTEMPTS      {expression|UNLIMITED|DEFAULT}
  | PASSWORD_LIFE_TIME       {expression|UNLIMITED|DEFAULT}
  | PASSWORD_LOCK_TIME       {expression|UNLIMITED|DEFAULT}
  | PASSWORD_GRACE_TIME      {expression|UNLIMITED|DEFAULT}
  | PASSWORD_REUSE_TIME      {expression|UNLIMITED|DEFAULT}
  | PASSWORD_REUSE_MAX       {expression|UNLIMITED|DEFAULT}
  }
}
```

The following list explains all of the elements used in the CREATE/ALTER/DROP PROFILE commands' syntax:

function	Specifies the password verification function to be used.
profile	Specifies the name of the profile.
COMPOSITE_LIMIT	Specifies the limit on the total resource cost for a session, expressed in service units.
CONNECT_TIME	Specifies the total elapsed time limit for a session in minutes.
CPU_PER_CALL	Specifies the CPU time limit per call in hundredths of a second.
CPU_PER_SESSION	Specifies the session CPU time limit in hundredths of a second.
FAILED_LOGIN_ATTEMPTS	Specifies the number of failed logon attempts the user can make before the account is locked.
IDLE_TIME	Specifies the total continuous idle time during a session in minutes.
LOGICAL_READS_PER_CALL	Specifies the total number of datablocks read from memory and disk per call to process a SQL statement.
LOGICAL_READS_PER_SESSION	Specifies the total number of datablocks read from memory and disk per session.
PASSWORD_VERIFY_FUNCTION	Specifies which password verification function should be used.
PASSWORD_GRACE_TIME	Specifies the number of days that logon is still allowed, but a warning is given that the password is due to expire.

PASSWORD_LIFE_TIME	Specifies the number of days the same password can be used for a user.
PASSWORD_LOCK_TIME	Specifies the number of days an account will be locked after a number of consecutive failed logon attempts.
PASSWORD_REUSE_MAX	Specifies the number of password changes required before an old password may be reused.
PASSWORD_REUSE_TIME	Specifies a number of days in which a password may not be reused.
PRIVATE_SGA	Specifies the size of the private SGA.
SESSION_PER_USER	Specifies the limit of *integer* concurrent sessions for a user.
CASCADE	Specifies that when a profile is dropped, it is deallocated from all users that were assigned this profile.
UNLIMITED	Specifies that no limit has been set for the parameter.
DEFAULT	Specifies that the limit is used as it is specified in the default profile for the user.
NULL	Specifies that no password verification is performed.

CREATE/ALTER/DROP ROLLBACK SEGMENT

You can use the CREATE/ALTER/DROP ROLLBACK SEGMENT commands to create, alter, and drop rollback segments. The ALTER ROLLBACK SEGMENT command can be used to manage the rollback segment. They can be brought online or offline, the storage parameters can be changed, and the rollback segment can be changed in size. The following is the syntax for the CREATE ROLLBACK SEGMENT command:

```
CREATE ROLLBACK SEGMENT rollback_segment
[TABLESPACE table space]
[storage_clause]
```

The following is the syntax for the ALTER ROLLBACK SEGMENT command:

```
ALTER ROLLBACK SEGMENT rollback_segment
{ ONLINE
| OFFLINE
| storage_clause
| SHRINK [TO integer [K|M]]
}
```

The following is the syntax for the DROP ROLLBACK SEGMENT command:

```
DROP ROLLBACK SEGMENT rollback_segment
```

The following list explains all of the elements used in the CREATE/ALTER/DROP ROLLBACK SEGMENT command syntax:

TABLESPACE table space	Specifies the tablespace in which the rollback segment is to be created.
storage_clause	See the section "Common Clauses" for details.
ONLINE	Specifies that the tablespace will be brought online.
OFFLINE	Specifies that the tablespace will be brought offline. When a tablespace is used for transactions, new transactions will be allocated to other tablespaces and the tablespace will be brought offline when no transactions use it anymore.
SHRINK	Specifies that the rollback segment will be shrunk to an optimal size or to the size specified in the TO clause.
TO integer K	Specifies that the rollback segment will be shrunk to integer KB.
TO integer M	Specifies that the rollback segment will be shrunk to integer MB.

CREATE SCHEMA

You can use the CREATE SCHEMA command to create multiple tables and views and issue multiple grants in one go. All the create and grant statements used should not end with a semicolon (;). If one of the statements fails, all of the statements will be rolled back. The following is the syntax for the CREATE SCHEMA command:

```
CREATE SCHEMA AUTHORIZATION schema
{ [create_table_statement]
  [create_view_statement]
  [grant_statement]
}
```

The following list explains all of the elements used in the CREATE SCHEMA command syntax:

schema Specifies the name of the schema to be created.

create_table_statement	Specifies a CREATE TABLE statement. See the section, "CREATE/ALTER/DELETE/LOCK TABLE," for details.

create_view_statement	Specifies a `CREATE VIEW` statement. See the section, "CREATE/ALTER/DROP VIEW," for details.
grant_statement	Specifies a `GRANT` statement. See the sections, "GRANT Object Privileges," and "GRANT System Privileges and Roles," for further details.

CREATE/ALTER/DROP SNAPSHOT

The `CREATE/ALTER/DROP SNAPSHOT` commands are synonymous with the `CREATE/ALTER/DROP MATERIALIZED VIEW` commands. See the section, "CREATE/ALTER/DROP MATERIALIZED VIEW," for details.

CREATE/ALTER/DROP SNAPSHOT LOG

The `CREATE/ALTER/DROP SNAPSHOT LOG` commands are synonymous with the `CREATE/ALTER/DROP MATERIALIZED VIEW LOG` commands. See the sections, "CREATE/ALTER/DROP MATERIALIZED VIEW/SNAPSHOT," and "CREATE/ALTER/DROP MATERIALIZED VIEW LOG/SNAPSHOT LOG," for details.

CREATE/ALTER/DROP/LOCK TABLE

You can use the `CREATE/ALTER/DROP/LOCK TABLE` commands to create, alter, drop, or lock table database objects. In the `CREATE LOCK TABLE` and `ALTER LOCK TABLE` commands, many clauses can be used to specify options ranging from referential integrity rules to storage parameters. You can use the `LOCK TABLE` command to explicitly lock a whole table to prevent other sessions from changing the data or structure of the table. The following is the syntax for the `CREATE TABLE` command for relational tables:

```
CREATE [GLOBAL TEMRORARY] TABLE [schema.]table
(relational_properties)
[ON COMMIT {DELETE|PRESERVE} ROWS]
[physical_properties]
[table_properties]
```

The following is the syntax for the `CREATE TABLE` command for object tables:

```
CREATE [GLOBAL TEMRORARY] TABLE [schema.]table
OF [schema.]object_type [(object_properties)]
[ON COMMIT {DELETE|PRESERVE} ROWS]
[OID_clause]
[OID_index_clause]
[physical_properties]
[table_properties]
```

Listing A-15 provides the syntax for the ALTER TABLE command:

```
ALTER TABLE [schema.]table
{ RENAME TO new_name
| records_per_block_clause
| alter_overflow_clause
| partitioning_clauses
| { [ADD (add_column_options)]
    [MODIFY (modify_column_options)]
    [move_table_clause]
    [physical_attributes]
    [LOGGING|NOLOGGING]
    [modify_collection_retrieval_clause
       [modify_collection_retrieval_clause...]
    [storage_clauses]
    [MODIFY CONSTRAINT constraint constraint_state]
    [drop_constraint_clause]
    [drop_column_clause]
    [allocate_extent_clause|deallocate_unused_clause]
    [CACHE|NOCACHE]
    [MONITORING|NOMONITORING]
  }
}
[parallel_clause]
[en/disable[en/disable...]]
```

The following is the syntax for the DROP TABLE command:

```
DROP TABLE [schema.]table [CASCADE CONSTRAINTS]
```

Listing A-16 provides the syntax for the LOCK TABLE command:

```
LOCK TABLE [schema.]{table|view}
[ @dblink
| PARTITION (partition)
| SUBPARTITION (subpartition)
]
IN lockmode MODE [NOWAIT]

add_column_options := add_column_option[,add_column_option...]
```

Continued

Listing A-16: *(continued)*

```
add_column_option :=
{ column datatype [DEFAULT expression]
    [column_ref_constraint]
    [column_constraint[column_constraint...]]
| table_constraint
| table_ref_constraint
}
[LOB_storage_clause]
[(partition_LOB_storage_clause[,partition_LOB_storage_clause...
])]

add_hash_partition_clause := ADD PARTITION
[ partition [TABLESPACE table space]
  [ [LOB_storage_clause]
    [varray_storage_clause]
  ]
  [parallel_clause]
]

add_overflow_clause := ADD OVERFLOW [segment_attributes_clause]
[ ( PARTITION [segment_attributes_clause]
    [,PARTITION [segment_attributes_clause]...]
  )
]

add_range_partition_clause :=
ADD PARTITION [partition] VALUES LESS THAN (value_list)
[partition_description]

add_subpartition_clause :=
ADD SUBPARTITION [subpartition [subpartition_description]]

allocate_extent_clause := ALLOCATE EXTENT
( [INSTANCE integer]
  [DATAFILE 'filename']
  [SIZE integer [K|M]]
)

alter_overflow_clause :=
{ overflow_clause
| add_overflow_clause
| [PCTTHRESHOLD integer]
  [INCLUDING column]
}

coalesce_partition_clause := COALESCE PARTITION
[parallel_clause]

column_constraint := CONSTRAINT constraint
{ [NOT] NULL
```

```
    |  {UNIQUE|PRIMARY KEY}
    |  {REFERENCES [schema.]table[(column)]
      [ON DELETE {CASCADE|SET NULL}]
    |  CHECK (condition)
    }
constraint_state

column_ref_constraint    :=
{ SCOPE FOR ( {ref_column|ref_attribute} )
    IS [schema.]scope_table
  | REF ( {ref_column|ref_attribute} ) WITH ROWID
  | [CONSTRAINT constraint]
    FOREIGN KEY ( {ref_column|ref_attribute} ) references_clause
}

composite_partitioning_clause :=
PARTITION BY RANGE (column_list)
[subpartition_clause]
( partition_definition[,partition_definition...] )

compression_clause := {NOCOMPRESS|COMPRESS [integer]}

constraint_state :=
[ { [ [NOT] DEFERRABLE ]
      [ INITIALLY {IMMEDIATE|DEFERRED} ]
    | [ INITIALLY {IMMEDIATE|DEFERRED} ]
      [ [NOT] DEFERRABLE ]
  }
]
[RELY|NORELY]
[USING INDEX [ [physical_attributes_clause]
               [NOSORT]
               {LOGGING|NOLOGGING}
             ]
[ENABLE|DISABLE]
[VALIDATE|NOVALIDATE]
[EXCEPTIONS INTO [schema.]table]

deallocate_unused_clause := DEALLOCATE UNUSED
[KEEP integer [K|M]]

drop_column_clause :=
{ DROP {UNUSED COLUMNS|COLUMNS CONTINUE} [CHECKPOINT integer]
| DROP {COLUMN ( column[,column...] )
    [CASCADE CONSTRAINTS]
    [INVALIDATE]
    [CHECKPOINT integer]
| SET UNUSED {COLUMN column|( column[,column...] )}
    [CASCADE CONSTRAINTS]
    [INVALIDATE]
}
```

Continued

Listing A-16: *(continued)*

```
drop_constraint_clause := DROP
{ CONSTRAINT constraint
| PRIMARY [CASCADE]
| UNIQUE ( column[,column...] ) [CASCADE]
}

drop_partition_clause := DROP PARITION partition

en/disable :=
{ enable_disable_clause
| {ENABLE|DISABLE} {TABLE LOCK|ALL TRIGGERS}
}

enable_disable_clause :=
{ENABLE|DISABLE}
[VALIDATE|NOVALIDATE]
{ UNIQUE ( column[,column...] )
| PRIMARY KEY
| CONSTRAINT constraint
}
[using_index_clause]
[EXCEPTION INTO [schema.]table]
[CASCADE]

exchange_partition/subpartition_clause :=
EXCHANGE {PARTITION partition|SUBPARTITION subpartition}
WITH TABLE nonpartitioned_table
[ {INCLUDING|EXCLUDING} INDEXES ]
[ {WITH|WITHOUT} VALIDATION ]
[ EXCEPTIONS INTO [schema.]table ]

foreign_key_clause := FOREIGN KEY ( column[,column...] )
REFERENCES [schema.]table[( column[,column...] )]
[ON DELETE {CASCADE|SET NULL}]

hash_partitioning_clause :=
PARTITION BY HASH (column_list)
[ { PARTITIONS quantity
    [STORE IN ( table space[,table space...] )]
  | ( PARTITION
        [ partition partitioning_storage_clause
                    [partitioning_storage_clause...]
        ]
    )
  }
]

index_organized_overflow_clause :=
[INCLUDING column] OVERFLOW [segment_attributes_clause]
```

```
index_organized_table_clause :=
{ [segment_attributes_clause] [index_organized_overflow_clause]
  [PCTTHRESHOLD integer]      [index_organized_overflow_clause]
  [compression_clause]        [index_organized_overflow_clause]
}

LOB_parameters :=
{ [TABLESPACE table space]
  [{ENABLE|DISABLE} STORAGE IN ROW]
  [storage_clause]
  [CHUNK integer]
  [PCTVERSION integer]
  [CACHE|NOCACHE [LOGGING|NOLOGGING]]
}

LOB_storage_clause := LOB
{ ( LOB_item[,LOB_item...] ) STORE AS (LOB_parameters)
| (LOB_item) STORE AS
  { (LOB_parameters)
  | LOB_segname
  | LOB_segname (LOB_parameters)
  }
}

merge_partitions_clause :=
MERGE PARTITIONS partition_1,partition_2
[INTO PARTITION [new_partition [partition_description]]]

modify_collection_retrieval_clause :=
MODIFY NESTED TABLE collection_item
RETURN AS {LOCATOR|VALUE}

modify_column_options :=
   modify_column_option[,modify_column_option...]

modify_column_option :=
{ column [datatype] [DEFAULT expression]
    column_constraint[column_constraint...]
| {VARRAY|NESTED TABLE}
    collection_item
    [RETURN AS {LOCATOR|VALUE}]
}

modify_default_attributes_clause :=
MODIFY DEFAULT ATTRIBUTES [FOR PARTITION partition]
segment_attributes_clause
[PCTTHRESHOLD integer]
[COMPRESS|DECOMPRESS]
[overflow_clause]
[ LOB LOB_item LOB_parameters[LOB LOB_item LOB_parameters...] ]
```

Continued

Listing A-16: *(continued)*

```
modify_LOB_storage_clause :=
MODIFY LOB (LOB_item) (modify_LOB_storage_parameters)

modify_LOB_storage_parameters :=
[storage_clause]
[PCTVERSION integer]
[CACHE|NOCACHE {LOGGING|NOLOGGING}]
[allocate_extent_clause]
[deallocate_unused_clause]

modify_partition_clause := MODIFY PARTITION partition
{ partition_attributes
| add_subpartition_clause
| COALESCE SUBPARTITION [parallel_clause]
| [REBUILD] UNUSABLE LOCAL INDEXES
}

modify_subpartition_clause := MODIFY SUBPARTITION subpartition
{ [REBUILD] UNUSABLE LOCAL INDEXES
| {allocate_extent_clause|deallocate_unused_clause}
| LOB LOB_item modify_LOB_storage_parameters
    [LOB LOB_item modify_LOB_storage_parameters...]
}

modify_varray_storage_clause := MODIFY VARRAY varray_item
[modify_LOB_storage_parameters]

move_partition_clause := MOVE PARTITION partition
[partition_description]
[parallel_clause]

move_subpartition_clause :=
MOVE SUBPARTITION subpartition subpartition_description

move_table_clause := MOVE [ONLINE]
{segment_attributes_clause|index_organized_table_clause}
[LOB_storage_clause[LOB_storage_clause...]]

nested_table_storage_clause :=
NESTED TABLE nested_item STORE AS storage_table
[((object_properties) physical_properties)]
[RETURN AS {LOCATOR|VALUE}]

object_properties :=
{ {table_constraint|table_ref_constraint}
| {column|attribute}
    [DEFAULT expression]
    [column_ref_constraint]
```

```
        [column_constraint[column_constraint...]]
}

OID_clause := OBJECT IDENTIFIER IS
{ SYSTEM GENERATED
| PRIMARY KEY
}

OID_index_clause := OIDINDEX [index]
( [physical_attributes_clause]
  [TABLESPACE table space]
)

overflow_clause := OVERFLOW
[physical_attributes_clause]
[allocate_extent_clause]
[deallocate_unused_clause]
[LOGGING|NOLOGGING]

partition_attributes :=
[physical_attributes_clause]
[LOGGING|NOLOGGING]
[allocate_extent_clause|deallocate_unused_clause]
[OVERFLOW physical_attributes_clause]
[ LOB LOB_item modify_LOB_storage_parameters
    [LOB LOB_item modify_LOB_storage_parameters...]
]

partition_LOB_storage_clause := PARTITION partition
LOB_storage_clause[LOB_storage_clause...]
[(SUBPARTITION subpartition
   LOB_storage_clause[LOB_storage_clause...]
 )
]

partitioning_clauses :=
{ modify_default_attributes_clause
| modify_partition_clause
| modify_subpartition_clause
| move_partition_clause
| move_subpartition_clause
| {add_range_partition_clause|add_hash_partition_clause}
| coalesce_partition_clause
| drop_partition_clause
| rename_partition/subpartition_clause
| truncate_partition/subpartition_clause
| split_partition_clause
| merge_partitions_clause
| exchange_partition/subpartition_clause
| row_movement_clause
}
```

Continued

Listing A-16: *(continued)*

```
partitioning_storage_clause :=
[TABLESPACE table space]
[ [LOB_storage_clause]
  [varray_storage_clause]
]

partition_definition := PARTITION partition
VALUES LESS THAN (value_list)
[ [segment_attributes_clause]
  [COMPRESS|DECOMPRESS]
]
[OVERFLOW [segment_attributes_clause]]
[ [LOB_storage_clause]
  [varray_storage_clause]
]
[partition_level_subpartitioning]

partition_description := segment_attributes_clause
[compression_clause]
[OVERFLOW [compression_clause]]
[ [LOB_storage_clause]
  [varray_storage_clause]
]
[partition_level_subpartitioning]

partition_level_subpartitioning :=
{ SUBPARTITIONS quantity
    [STORE IN ( table space[,table space...] )
| ( SUBPARTITION [subpartition partitioning_storage_clause]
    [SUBPARTITION [subpartition
partitioning_storage_clause],...]
  )
}

partitioning_storage_clause :=
[TABLESPACE table space]
[ [LOB_storage_clause]
  [varray_storage_clause]
]

physical_properties :=
[ segment_attributes_clause
| ORGANIZATION { INDEX index_organized_table_clause
               | HEAP [segment_attributes_clause]
               }
| CLUSTER cluster ( column[,column...] )
]
[ [LOB_storage_clause]
  [varray_storage_clause]
  [nested_table_storage_clause]
]
```

```
range_partitioning_clause :=
PARTITION BY RANGE (column_list)
( partition_definition[,partition_definition...] )

records_per_block_clause :=
{MINIMIZE|NOMINIMIZE} RECORDS_PER_BLOCK

references_clause := REFERENCES [schema.]object_table
[ON DELETE {CASCADE|SET NULL}]
[constraint_state]

relational_properties :=
  relational_property[,relational_property...]

relational_property :=
{ [ column datatype
      [DEFAULT expression]
      [column_ref_constraint]
      [column_constraint[column_constraint...]]
  ]
  [ {table_constraint|table_ref_constraint} ]
}

rename_partition/subpartition_clause :=
RENAME {PARTITION|SUBPARTITION} current_name TO new_name

row_movement_clause := {ENABLE|DISABLE} ROW MOVEMENT

segment_attributes_clause :=
[ [physical_attributes_clause]
  [LOGGING|NOLOGGING]
]

split_partition_clause :=
SPLIT PARTITION partition_name_old AT (value_list)
[INTO (partition_descr,partition_descr)]
[parallel_clause]

storage_clauses :=
{ modify_LOB_storage_clause[,modify_LOB_storage_clause...]
| varray_storage_clause[,varray_storage_clause...]
| modify_varray_storage_clause[modify_varray_storage_clause...]
| nested_table_storage_clause[,nested_table_storage_clause...]
}

subpartition_clause :=
SUBPARTITION BY HASH ( column_list[,column_list...] )
[SUBPARTITIONS quantity
  [STORE IN ( table space[,table space...] )
]
```

Continued

Listing A-16: *(continued)*

```
subpartition_description :=
[TABLESPACE table space]
[ [LOB_storage_clause]
  [varray_storage_clause]
]
[parallel_clause]

table_constraint      := CONSTRAINT constraint
{ {UNIQUE|PRIMARY KEY} (column[,column...])
| foreign_key_clause
| CHECK (condition)
}
constraint_state

table_ref_constraint     :=
{ SCOPE FOR ( {ref_column|ref_attribute} ) IS
[schema.]scope_table
| REF ( {ref_column|ref_attribute} ) WITH ROWID
| [CONSTRAINT constraint]
  FOREIGN KEY ( {ref_column|ref_attribute} ) references_clause

table_properties :=
[ range_partitioning_clause      [row_movement_clause]
| hash_partitioning_clause       [row_movement_clause]
| composite_partitioning_clause  [row_movement_clause]
]
[CACHE|NOCACHE]
[MONITORING|NOMONITORING]
[parallel_clause]
[enable_disable_clause[enable_disable_clause...]]
[AS subquery]

truncate_partition/subpartition_clause :=
TRUNCATE {PARTITION partition|SUBPARTITION subpartition}
[ {DROP|REUSE} STORAGE ]

using_index_clause := USING INDEX
[ [PCTFREE integer]
  [INITRANS integer]
  [MAXTRANS integer]
  [TABLESPACE table space]
  [storage_clause]
  [NOSORT]
  [LOGGING|NOLOGGING]
]

varray_storage_clause := VARRAY varray_item STORE AS LOB
{ LOB_segname (LOB_parameters)
```

```
|   LOB_segname
|   (LOB_parameters)
}
```

The following list explains all of the elements used in the
CREATE/ALTER/DROP/LOCK TABLE commands' syntax:

GLOBAL TEMRORARY	Specifies that a temporary table is to be created. The table will be visible to all sessions.
schema.table	Specifies the name of the table to create, drop, alter, or lock. Schema is optional and may be omitted.
ON COMMIT	When creating a temporary table, specifies whether the table is session (PRESERVE ROWS) or transaction specific (DELETE ROWS).
DELETE ROWS	Specifies that rows are removed from the temporary table as soon as the transaction is committed.
PRESERVE ROWS	Specifies that rows are removed from the temporary table when the session is closed.
OF schema.object_type	Specifies that an object table is to be created of type object_type.
RENAME TO new_name	Specifies that the table is to be renamed to new_name in the ALTER TABLE command.
ADD	Specifies that a new column or integrity constraint is to be added to the table.
MODIFY	Specifies that the details for an existing column are to be modified.
physical_attributes_clause	See the section "Common Clauses" for details.
LOGGING	Specifies that insert operations from SQL Loader will be logged in the redo log file.
NOLOGGING	Specifies that insert operations from SQL Loader will not be logged in the redo log file.

`MODIFY CONTRAINT constraint`	Specifies that the state of the constraint is to be changed.
`CACHE`	Specifies that blocks retrieved for this table are stored at the most recently used end of the LRU list in the buffer cache. Recommended for small static tables.
`NOCACHE`	Specifies that blocks retrieved for this table are stored at the least recently used end of the LRU list in the buffer cache. `NOCACHE` is the default.
`MONITORING`	Specifies that statistics will be collected for DML statements on the table.
`NOMONITORING`	Specifies that statistics will not be collected for DML statements on the table.
`parallel_clause`	See the section "Common Clauses" for details.
`view`	Specifies the name of the view to lock.
`@dblink`	Specifies the name of the database link pointing to the remote database when a table is to be locked in a remote database, `dblink`.
`PARTITION partition`	Specifies the name of the partition.
`SUBPARTITION subpartition`	Specifies the name of the subpartition.
`IN lockmode MODE`	Specifies the `lockmode` of the lock when a table, a view, or a subpartition of a table or view is to be locked.
`NOWAIT`	Specifies that when the table is already locked by another session, the control is immediately returned with an error. If `NOWAIT` is not specified, the session will block until the locking user gives up the lock on the table.
`column`	Specifies the name of the column to be added when used in `add_column_ option, column`. Specifies the column to be dropped or to be set to `UNUSED` when used in `drop_column_clause, column`. The unique constraint on the column is to be dropped when used in `drop_constraint_clause`. The

	unique constraint on the column is to be enabled or disabled when used in *enable_disable_clause*. Specifies the column to be modified when used in *modify_column_option, column*. Specifies the column for which to specify the properties when used in *object_properties, column*. Specifies the cluster columns when used in *physical_properties, column*.
datatype	Specifies the datatype of the column.
DEFAULT *expression*	Specifies a default column value.
TABLESPACE *table space*	Specifies the name of the tablespace.
ADD OVERFLOW	Specifies that an overflow datasegment is added to the table.
PARTITION	When used in the *add_overflow_clause*, PARTITION may be used to specify different physical attributes for each partition of the overflow segment.
ADD PARTITION	Specifies that a new partition is to be added to the table.
VALUES LESS THAN *value_list*	Specifies the upper bound for the new partition that is to be created.
ADD SUBPARTITION	Specifies that a new subpartition is to be added to the table.
ALLOCATE EXTENT	Specifies that a new extend has to be allocated.
INSTANCE *integer*	Specifies the instance to which the newly allocated extend will be made available.
DATAFILE *'filename'*	Specifies the data file in which to create the new extent.
SIZE *integer*	Specifies the size of the newly allocated extend in bytes. Use *K* for kilobytes and *M* for megabytes.
PCTTHRESHOLD *integer*	For index-organized tables, specifies the percentage of space reserved in an index block. The *integer* parameter must be between 1 and 50.

INCLUDING *column*	For index-organized tables, specifies the division point. The columns before this column are regarded as the index portion; the other columns are regarded as the overflow portion of the row.
COALESCE PARTITION	Specifies that the contents of a hash partition are distributed into one or more other partitions and that the partition is to be dropped.
PARTITION BY RANGE	Specifies that the table is partitioned by the values of the columns in *column_list*.
column_list	Specifies the list of columns to which to partition the table.
COMPRESS *integer*	Specifies the number of prefix columns to use in key compression.
NOCOMPRESS	Specifies that key compression is not used.
DEALLOCATE UNUSED	Specifies that free space allocated to the table will be made available for other segments to use.
KEEP *integer*	Specifies how many bytes of free space above the high water mark should be retained for the table.
DROP UNUSED COLUMNS	Specifies that all columns marked as UNUSED are to be dropped.
DROP COLUMNS CONTINUE	Specifies that the operation of a previously submitted and interrupted drop columns statement is to be resumed.
DROP COLUMN	Specifies the columns that are to be removed from the table together with all the values for these columns in each row of the table.
CHECKPOINT *integer*	Specifies that a checkpoint will be applied after dropping *integer* rows from the column. This clause can be used to prevent running out of undo log space.
CASCADE CONSTRAINTS	Specifies that all referential integrity constraints referring to the dropped columns are to be dropped as well.

`INVALIDATE`	Specifies that all objects that depend on the table are to be invalidated.
`SET UNUSED`	Specifies that one or more columns are to be marked `UNUSED`.
`DROP PRIMARY CASCADE`	Specifies the primary key constraint of a table. The `CASCADE` parameter is optional and specifies that all integrity constraints that depend on the dropped primary key are to be dropped as well.
`DROP UNIQUE CASCADE`	Specifies the unique key constraint of a table on the specified columns. The `CASCADE` parameter is optional and specifies that all integrity constraints that depend on the dropped unique key are to be dropped as well.
`DROP PARITION`	Specifies that the partition of the table with all its contents are to be dropped.
`ENABLE TABLE LOCK`	Enables table locking for DML and DDL statements when running in parallel server mode.
`DISABLE TABLE LOCK`	Disables table locking for DML and DDL statements when running in parallel server mode.
`ENABLE ALL TRIGGERS`	Specifies that all triggers on the table are to be enabled.
`DISABLE ALL TRIGGERS`	Specifies that all triggers on the table are to be disabled.
`ENABLE VALIDATE`	Enables the constraint and specifies that all old data complies with the constraint.
`ENABLE NOVALIDATE`	Enables the constraint and specifies that all new data has to comply with the constraint, whereas it doesn't ensure that old data complies with it.
`DISABLE VALIDATE`	Disables the constraint and drops the index on the constraint while keeping the data valid.
`DISABLE NOVALIDATE`	Disables the constraint, drops the index on the constraint, and doesn't ensure that the data will comply with the constraint.

PRIMARY KEY	Specifies that the primary key constraint on the table will be enabled or disabled.
CONSTRAINT *constraint*	Specifies the constraint that is to be used.
EXCEPTION INTO *schema.table*	Specifies the name of the table in which information about the rows that violate the constraint are placed. Schema is optional and may be omitted.
CASCADE	Specifies that constraints depending on the disabled constraint are disabled as well when disabling a constraint.
EXCHANGE	Specifies that a partition or sub-partition is converted into a nonpartitioned table and the nonpartitioned table is converted into a partition or subpartition, by exchanging their data.
WITH TABLE *nonpartitioned_table*	Specifies the name of the table with which to exchange the partition or subpartition's data.
INCLUDING INDEXES	Specifies that index partitions or subpartitions are also exchanged.
EXCLUDING INDEXES	Specifies that index partitions or subpartitions are not exchanged.
WITH VALIDATION	Specifies that the mapping of rows in the exchanged tables is checked. Oracle will raise an error when the columns don't map correctly.
WITHOUT VALIDATION	Specifies that the mapping of rows in the exchanged tables isn't checked.
EXCEPTIONS INTO *table*	Specifies the name of the table in which all rowids of rows violating the constraint(s) are put.
PARTITION BY HASH *column_list*	Specifies that the created table is to be partitioned using the hash method. The *column_list* parameter specifies the partitioning key.
PARTITIONS *quantity*	Specifies the default amount of subpartitions in each partition of a table.

OVERFLOW	Specifies the data segment in which the overflow data is stored.
ENABLE STORAGE IN ROW	Specifies that if the LOB value is less than approximately 4,000 bytes, the value is stored in the row.
DISABLE STORAGE IN ROW	Specifies that the LOB value is stored outside of the row.
storage_clause	See the "Common Clauses" section for details.
CHUNK integer	Specifies the number of bytes that will be allocated for LOB manipulation.
PCTVERSION integer	Specifies the maximum percentage of space that is used to store new versions of the LOB data.
LOB LOB_item	Specifies the name of the LOB item.
STORE AS LOB_segname	Specifies the name of the LOB data segment to store the LOB value in.
STORE AS LOB_parameters	Specifies a set of options according to which the LOB columns are stored.
MERGE PARTITIONS partition_1, partition_2 INTO PARTITION new_partition	Specifies that the partitions partition_1 and partition_2 are merged into a new partition new_partition, after which the partitions partition_1 and partition_2 are dropped.
MODIFY NESTED TABLE	Specifies what is returned when a collection item is queried.
collection_item	Specifies the name of the collection item: a nested table or a varying array.
RETURN AS LOCATOR	Specifies that the unique locator is returned for the collection item.
RETURN AS VALUE	Specifies that the values of the collection item are returned.
MODIFY DEFAULT ATTRIBUTES	Specifies new values for the attributes of the table.
FOR PARTITION	Specifies new values for the attributes in a specific partition of a table.
MODIFY LOB	Specifies new values for LOB storage parameters for a LOB item.

`MODIFY PARTITION`	Specifies the physical attributes for a partition of a table.
`COALESCE SUBPARTITION`	Specifies that the contents of a hash subpartition is distributed into one or more other subpartitions and that the subpartition is to be dropped.
`UNUSABLE LOCAL INDEXES`	Specifies that all local indexes associated with the partition are marked `UNUSABLE`.
`REBUILD`	Specifies that all local indexes associated with the partition that are marked UNUSABLE are rebuilt.
`MODIFY SUBPARTITION`	Specifies the physical attributes for a subpartition of a table.
`MODIFY VARRAY varray_item`	Specifies the storage parameters for a LOB in which a varying array is stored.
`MOVE PARTITION`	Specifies that the partition is to be moved to another segment.
`MOVE SUBPARTITION`	Specifies that the subpartition is to be moved to another segment.
`MOVE`	Specifies that the data of a nonpartitioned table is to be moved to another segment.
`ONLINE`	Specifies that DML operations on the table are allowed during the moving of the table.
`NESTED TABLE nested_item`	Specifies storage parameters for the nested table `nested_item`.
`STORE AS storage_table`	Specifies the name of the table in which the rows of the nested table `nested_item` reside.
`attribute`	Specifies the name of the attribute.
`OBJECT IDENTIFIER IS`	Specifies how the object identifier is determined.
`SYSTEM GENERATED`	Specifies that the object identifier is system generated. This is the default.
`PRIMARY KEY`	Specifies that the object identifier is based on the primary key.
`OIDINDEX index`	Specifies an index on the hidden object indentifier column when the object identifier is `SYSTEM GENERATED`.

SUBPARTITIONS *quantity*	Specifies the default amount of sub-partitions in each partition of a table.
STORE IN *table space*	Specifies the default tablespace in which the subpartitions of each partition of the table are to be stored.
ORGANIZATION INDEX	Specifies that the table should be organized as an index table.
ORGANIZATION HEAP	Specifies that the table should be organized as a regular table.
RECORDS_PER_BLOCK	Specifies whether Oracle restricts the number of records in a block.
MINIMIZE	Specifies that the number of records in a block will be restricted when they are created in future insert statements. This feature keeps bitmap indexes as compressed as possible.
NOMINIMIZE	Specifies that Oracle will not restrict the number of records in a block.
RENAME PARTITION	Specifies that the partition is renamed.
RENAME SUBPARTITION	Specifies that the subpartition is renamed.
current_name TO *new_name*	Specifies the old and new names when renaming a partition or subpartition.
ENABLE ROW MOVEMENT	Specifies that a row is allowed to move to a new partition when key values change.
DISABLE ROW MOVEMENT	Specifies that a row isn't allowed to move to a new partition when key values change.
SPLIT PARTITION	Specifies that the partition is to be split into two partitions.
AT (*value_list*)	Specifies the upper bound for the first partition.
INTO (*partition_descr, partition_descr*)	Specifies the names for the two new partitions.
SUBPARTITION BY HASH	Specifies that the partitions of the table are to be partitioned by hash.
AS *subquery*	Specifies a query on which to base the new table. See the section, "SELECT statement," for details on how to build the subquery statement.

`TRUNCATE`	Removes all rows from the partition or subpartition.
`DROP STORAGE`	Specifies that space is freed and made available to other objects when the partition or subpartition is truncated.
`REUSE STORAGE`	Specifies that space is freed and is kept for usage for the partition or subpartition when they are truncated.
`PCTFREE integer`	See the *physical_attributes* clause in the section "Common Clauses" for details.
`INITRANS integer`	See the *physical_attributes* clause in the section "Common Clauses" for details.
`MAXTRANS integer`	See the *physical_attributes* clause in the section "Common Clauses" for details.
`VARRAY varray_item`	Specifies the name of the varying array for which to define storage parameters.
`STORE AS LOB`	Specifies that the varying array will be stored as a LOB.
`DEFERRABLE`	Specifies that `SET CONSTRAINT` can be used to defer the checking of the constraint until the end of the transaction.
`NOT DEFERRABLE`	Specifies that the checking of the constraint can't be deferred in a transaction.
`INITIALLY IMMEDIATE`	Specifies that the constraint is checked at the end of the DML statement. This is the default.
`INITIALLY DEFERRED`	Specifies that the constraint is checked at the end of the transaction by default.
`RELY`	Specifies that the constraint is enabled without being enforced.
`NORELY`	Specifies that the constraint is enabled and enforced.
`USING INDEX`	Specifies the parameters for the index that Oracle uses for a primary key or unique key constraint.
`NOSORT`	Specifies that no ordering of the index has to be performed on creation because all the rows are already stored in ascending order.

NOT NULL	Specifies a constraint that doesn't allow NULL values in the column.
NULL	Specifies that the column can contain NULL values. No constraint is actually created.
UNIQUE	Designates one column or a combination of columns that are to be used as a unique key.
PRIMARY KEY	Designates one column or a combination of columns that are to be used as the primary key.
REFERENCES schema.table (column)	Specifies that the column is a foreign key and points to the column or columns in the parent table that make up the referenced key. Schema is optional and may be omitted. If no column is specified, the primary key columns are used.
ON DELETE CASCADE	Specifies that when a unique or primary key is deleted, all rows referencing it will also be deleted.
ON DELETE SET NULL	Specifies that when a unique or primary key is deleted, all rows referencing it will be set to NULL.
CHECK (condition)	Specifies a condition that each row in the table must satisfy.
SCOPE FOR	Specifies that the scope for a REF column is restricted to the table scope_table.
ref_column	Specifies the name of the REF column of a table.
ref_attribute	Specifies the name of an embedded REF attribute in an object column of a table.
IS schema.scope_table	Specifies the name of the table to which the scope of the REF column is restricted.
REF WITH ROWID	Specifies that the ROWID is stored with the REF column. The default is not to store the ROWID along with the REF column.
FOREIGN KEY	Specifies the foreign key.

REFERENCES *schema.*   Specifies that the column points to the
object_table   specified object table. Schema is
                                 optional and may be omitted.

CREATE/ALTER/DROP TABLESPACE

You use the CREATE/ALTER/DROP TABLESPACE commands to create, alter, and drop
tablespaces. Tablespaces are the logical storage units that make up a database. A
tablespace provides the storage for database objects. These objects can be stored
in one or more data files. You can specify the storage parameters and management
options using the CREATE and ALTER statements. The following is the syntax for the
CREATE TABLESPACE command:

```
CREATE TABLESPACE table space DATAFILE
    file_spec [autoextend_clause]
      [file_spec [autoextend_clause]...]
{ [TEMPORARY|PERMANENT]
  [ONLINE|OFFLINE]
  [MINIMUM EXTENT integer [K|M]]
  [DEFAULT storage_clause]
  [extent_management_clause]
}
```

The following is the syntax for the ALTER TABLESPACE command:

```
ALTER TABLESPACE table space
{ [COALESCE]
  [TEMPORARY]
  [PERMANENT]
  [READ ONLY|READ WRITE]
  [BEGIN BACKUP|END BACKUP]
  [ONLINE]
  [OFFLINE [NORMAL|TEMPORARY|IMMEDIATE|FOR RECOVER]]
  [MINIMUM EXTENT integer [K|M]]
  [DEFAULT storage_clause]
  [datafile_tempfile_clauses]
}
```

Listing A-17 provides the syntax for the DROP TABLESPACE command:

Listing A-17: **DROP TABLESPACE syntax**

```
DROP TABLESPACE table space
[INCLUDING CONTENTS [CASCADE CONSTRAINTS]]

autoextend_clause := AUTOEXTEND
```

```
{ OFF
| ON
  [NEXT integer [K|M]]
  [MAXSIZE {UNLIMITED|integer [K|M]}]
}

datafile_tempfile_clauses :=
{ ADD {DATAFILE|TEMPFILE}  file_spec [autoextend_clause]
                                    [file_spec
[autoextend_clause]...]
| RENAME DATAFILE 'filename'[,'filename'...]
  TO  'filename'[,'filename'...]
}

extent_management_clause := EXTENT MANAGEMENT
{ DICTIONARY
| LOCAL { AUTOALLOCATE
        | UNIFORM [SIZE integer [K|M]]
        }
}
```

The following list explains all of the elements used in the CREATE/ALTER/DROP TABLESPACE commands' syntax:

table space	Specifies the name of the tablespace to create, alter, or drop.
DATAFILE file_spec	Specifies the tablespace's data files. See the section "Common Clauses" for details on file_spec.
TEMPORARY	Specifies that the tablespace will be used only to hold temporary database objects.
PERMANENT	Specifies that the tablespace will be used to hold permanent database objects. The PERMANENT parameter is the default.
MINIMUM EXTENT integer	Specifies that each free extend in the data file is at least as large as integer bytes.
DEFAULT storage_clause	Specifies the default storage parameters that are used when objects are created in the tablespace.
COALESCE	Specifies that all free space in the data files is collected and recreated in larger contiguous extends.
READ ONLY	Specifies that the tablespace will be made read-only.

READ WRITE	Specifies that the tablespace will be made read-write.
BEGIN BACKUP	Denotes that an open backup is to be started while users can still access the tablespace.
END BACKUP	Denotes that the open backup is finished.
ONLINE	Specifies that the tablespace is brought online.
OFFLINE	Specifies that the tablespace is brought offline.
NORMAL	Specifies that before the tablespace is brought offline, all blocks in the data files are taken from the SGA. The NORMAL parameter is the default option.
TEMPORARY	Specifies that when the tablespace is brought offline, a checkpoint is performed for all online data files. This process doesn't ensure that all the data is written to the data files.
IMMEDIATE	Specifies that the tablespace is brought offline without performing a checkpoint. This process doesn't ensure that all the data is written to the data files.
FOR RECOVER	Specifies when the tablespace is brought offline for point-in-time recovery.
INCLUDING CONTENTS	Specifies that all the objects in the tablespace will be dropped.
CASCADE CONSTRAINTS	Dropping the tablespace INCLUDING CONTENTS may fail when referential integrity constraints from tables outside the tablespace exist. The CASCADE CONSTRAINTS clause may be used to drop these referential integrity constraints so the tablespace can be dropped.
AUTOEXTEND	When creating or altering the tablespace, AUTOEXTEND may be used to specify if and how the tablespace is automatically extended when space runs out.
OFF	Specifies that the tablespace is not automatically extended.
ON	Enables the automatic extension of the tablespace.
NEXT	Specifies the extra space assigned to the data file when the tablespace is enlarged.

MAXSIZE	Specifies the maximum size of the data file.
UNLIMITED	Specifies that there is no maximum limit in size for the data file.
ADD DATAFILE	Specifies the details of a new data file that is to be added to the tablespace.
ADD TEMPFILE	Specifies the details of a new temp file that is to be added to the tablespace.
RENAME DATAFILE	Renames one or more data files in the offline tablespace.
'filename'	Specifies the current name or the new name of the data file in the RENAME DATAFILE clause file name data file.
EXTENT MANAGEMENT	Specifies how the extends in the tablespace are managed: locally or in the database dictionary.
DICTIONARY	Specifies that the extends are managed using the database dictionary. The DICTIONARY parameter is the default value.
LOCAL	Specifies that the extends are managed locally. Each data file will contain and maintain a bitmap to keep track of free space within the data file.
AUTOALLOCATE	Specifies that Oracle manages the extend size automatically when managing the tablespace extends locally.
UNIFORM	Specifies the extend size to use when managing the tablespace extends locally. The default value is 1M.
SIZE integer	Specifies the extend size to use.

CREATE TEMPORARY TABLESPACE

You can use the common CREATE TEMPORARY TABLESPACE command to create a temporary tablespace. A temporary tablespace may be used to store database objects for the duration of a session. You can improve performance if you use temporary tablespaces for sort operations including ORDER BY, JOINS, and GROUP BY.

Temporary tablespaces can store only temporary objects. These may be temporary tables or they may be temporary segments created by Oracle while processing certain DML or DDL statements. There is a significant performance gain if temporary segments are stored in a temporary tablespace.

Note A temporary tablespace can only be a locally managed tablespace; whereas, you can also create a temporary tablespace using the CREATE TABLESPACE command and specify TEMPORARY as an attribute. In that case you can then use dictionary managed storage.

The following is the syntax for the CREATE TEMPORARY TABLESPACE command:

```
CREATE TEMPORARY TABLESPACE table space TEMPFILE file_spec
[autoextend_clause]
[EXTEND MANAGEMENT LOCAL]
[UNIFORM [SIZE integer [K|M]]]

autoextend_clause := AUTOEXTEND
{ OFF
| ON [NEXT integer [K|M]
    [MAXSIZE {UNLIMITED|integer [K|M]}]
}
```

The following list explains all of the elements used in the CREATE TEMPORARY TABLESPACE command syntax:

table space	Specifies the name of the temporary tablespace to create.
TEMPFILE file_spec	Specifies the temp files for the temporary tablespace. See the section "Common Clauses" for details on file_spec.
EXTEND MANAGEMENT LOCAL	Specifies that the extends are managed locally. Each data file will contain and maintain a bitmap to keep track of free space within the data file.
UNIFORM	Specifies the extend size to use. The default extent size is 1M.
SIZE integer	Specifies the extend size to use.
AUTOEXTEND	Specifies if and how the temporary tablespace is automatically extended when space runs out.
OFF	Specifies that the temporary tablespace is not automatically extended.
ON	Enables the automatic extension of the temporary tablespace.
NEXT	Specifies the extra space assigned to the data file when the temporary tablespace is enlarged.

MAXSIZE	Specifies the maximum size of the data file.
UNLIMITED	Specifies that there is no maximum limit in size for the data file.

CREATE/ALTER/DROP TRIGGER

The CREATE and DROP TRIGGER commands allow you to create or delete triggers for events in the database. You can use the ALTER TRIGGER command to enable or disable the trigger and to compile the trigger code. Listing A-18 provides the syntax for the CREATE TRIGGER command:

Listing A-18: **CREATE TRIGGER syntax**

```
CREATE [OR REPLACE] TRIGGER [schema.]trigger
{ BEFORE
| AFTER
| INSTEAD OF
}
{ dml_event[OR dml_event...]
| [ ddl_event[OR ddl_event...]
  | database_event[OR database_event...]
  ]
  ON { DATABASE | [schema.]table }
}
[referencing_clause]
[WHEN (condition)]
{ trigger_block
| call_procedure_statement
}
```

The following is the syntax for the ALTER TRIGGER command:

```
ALTER TRIGGER [schema.]trigger
{ ENABLE
| DISABLE
| COMPILE [DEBUG]
}
```

Listing A-19 provides the syntax for the DROP TRIGGER command.

Listing A-19: **DROP TRIGGER syntax**

```
DROP TRIGGER [schema.]trigger

database_event := {SERVERERROR|LOGON|LOGOFF|STARTUP|SHUTDOWN}

ddl_event := {CREATE|ALTER|DROP}

dml_event :=
{ DELETE
| INSERT
| UPDATE [OF column[,column...]]
} ON
{ [schema.]table
| [NESTED TABLE nested_table_column OF]
    [schema.]view
}

referencing_clause := REFERENCING
{ OLD [AS] old
| NEW [AS] new
| PARENT [AS] parent
}
[FOR EACH ROW]
```

The following list explains all of the elements used in the CREATE/ALTER/DROP TRIGGER commands' syntax:

OR REPLACE	Replaces a trigger if one is already present with the same name. Effectively, it changes the definition of the trigger.
schema.trigger	Specifies the trigger to be created, altered, or dropped. Specifying the schema name is optional and may be omitted.
BEFORE	Specifies that the trigger will fire BEFORE the triggering event is executed.
AFTER	Specifies that the trigger will fire AFTER the triggering event has completed its execution.
INSTEAD OF	Specifies that the trigger will replace the triggering event. By default, INSTEAD OF triggers are row triggers and fire FOR EACH ROW.

`ON DATABASE`	Specifies that the trigger is defined on the whole database.
`ON schema.table`	Specifies the table on which the trigger is defined. Schema is optional and may be omitted.
`WHEN (condition)`	Specifies a condition that specifies when the trigger will fire. If the condition evaluates to `TRUE`, the trigger will fire; otherwise, it will not fire. You may specify this clause only for row triggers (`FOR EACH ROW`); you can't use it for `INSTEAD OF` triggers.
`trigger_block`	PL/SQL code that implements the trigger.
`call_procedure_statement`	Specifies that a stored procedure is called instead of a trigger block. The syntax for this is the same as for the `CALL` statement. However, you may not use the `INTO` clause; use bind variables. You also may not reference columns of the table on which the trigger is defined. Use `:old` and `:new` instead.
`ENABLE`	Specifies that the trigger will be enabled.
`DISABLE`	Specifies that the trigger will be disabled. You can use this clause to temporarily stop the trigger from executing.
`COMPILE`	Specifies that the trigger will be compiled regardless of whether it is valid or invalid.
`COMPILE DEBUG`	Same as `COMPILE`, but also creates debug information for the PL/SQL debugger.
`ON schema.table`	Specifies on which table the trigger will be created. You may omit the schema name and default to the current schema.
`ON NESTED TABLEnested_table _column OF schema.view`	Specifies that the trigger will be created on a nested table column of a view. You may omit the schema name.
`OLD AS old`	Specifies that columns in the old row can be referenced in the trigger code in `trigger_block` as `:old.column` or `old.column`.

`NEW AS new`	Specifies that columns in the new row can be referenced in the trigger code in `trigger_block` as `:new.column` or `new.column`.
`PARENT AS parent`	Specifies that columns in the current row of the parent table can be referenced in the trigger code in `trigger_block` as `parent.column`.
`FOR EACH ROW`	Specifies that the trigger is a row trigger. If this clause is omitted, the trigger is created as a statement trigger. A statement trigger fires once per SQL statement; a row trigger fires for each row hit by the SQL statement.

CREATE/ALTER/DROP TYPE

You can use the CREATE/ALTER/DROP TYPE commands to create, alter, or drop user-defined type database objects. The user defined types may be any of the following types:

+ **Object type.** Contains member variables and member functions.

+ **Varying array type.** An ordered set of elements.

+ **Nested table type.** A table inside a master table for each row in the master table.

You may also create an incomplete type, which is a forward definition of the type. This can be used when creating types that reference each other. The following is the syntax for the CREATE TYPE command for incomplete types:

```
CREATE [OR REPLACE] TYPE [schema.]type_name
```

The following is the syntax for the CREATE TYPE command for object types:

```
CREATE [OR REPLACE] TYPE [schema.]type_name
[AUTHID CURRENT USER|AUTHID DEFINER]
{IS|AS}
OBJECT
( attribute datatype[,attribute datatype...]
  , {MEMBER|STATIC} {func_spec|proc_spec} [,pragma_clauses]
      [, {MEMBER|STATIC} {func_spec|proc_spec}
[,pragma_clauses]...]
)
[, {MAP|ORDER} MEMBER func_spec]
```

The following is the syntax for the CREATE TYPE command for varying array types:

```
CREATE [OR REPLACE] TYPE [schema.]type_name
{IS|AS}
{VARRAY|VARYING ARRAY}
(limit) OF datatype
```

The following is the syntax for the CREATE TYPE command for nested table types:

```
CREATE [OR REPLACE] TYPE [schema.]type_name
{IS|AS} TABLE OF datatype
```

The following is the syntax for the ALTER TYPE command:

```
ALTER TYPE [schema.]type_name
{ COMPILE [DEBUG] [SPECIFICATION|BODY]
| REPLACE AS OBJECT
  ( attribute datatype[,attribute datatype...]
    ,{MEMBER|STATIC} {func_spec|proc_spec} [,pragma_clauses]
    [,{MEMBER|STATIC} {func_spec|proc_spec}
[,pragma_clauses]...]
  )
  [, {MAP|ORDER} MEMBER func_spec]
}
```

Listing A-20 provides the syntax for the DROP TYPE command:

Listing A-20: **DROP TYPE syntax**

```
DROP TYPE [schema.]type_name [FORCE]


C_declaration := C [NAME name] LIBRARY library
[WITH CONTEXT]
[PARAMETERS(parameters)]

directive := {RNDS|WNDS|RNPS|WNPS|TRUST}

func_spec := FUNCTION name
(argument datatype[,argument datatype...])
RETURN datatype
[ {IS|AS}
  LANGUAGE {Java_declaration|C_declaration}
]

Java_declaration := JAVA NAME 'string'

pragma_clauses := pragma_clause[pragma_clause...]
```

Continued

Listing A-20: *(continued)*

```
pragma_clause := PRAGMA RESTRICT_REFERENCES
( {method_name|DEFAULT}, directive[,directive...] )

proc_spec := PROCEDURE name
(argument datatype[,argument datatype...])
[ {IS|AS}
  LANGUAGE {Java_declaration|C_declaration}
]
```

The following list explains all of the elements used in the CREATE/ALTER/DROP TYPE commands' syntax:

OR REPLACE	If a type is already present with the same name, it will be replaced. Effectively, it changes the definition of the type, and all grants to this type will remain in place.
schema.type_name	Specifies the name of the incomplete type, object type, varying array type, or nested table type to create, alter, or drop.
AUTHID	Specifies a method to obtain privileges at execution of the function: CURRENT_USER or DEFINER.
CURRENT_USER	Specifies that the privileges for the type at execution time are the same as those for the user that calls the type.
DEFINER	Specifies that the privileges for the type at execution time are the same as for the owner of the schema in which the type resides.
IS	Synonym for AS.
AS	Synonym for IS.
OBJECT	Specifies that an object type is created.
attribute datatype	When creating or altering object types, attribute specifies the name of the object attribute and datatype specifies the datatype of the object attribute.
MEMBER	Specifies that a function or procedure is called when the attribute is referenced. In the body of the routine, the keyword SELF can be used to reference the calling object.

STATIC	Specifies that a function or procedure is called when the attribute is referenced. The use of SELF is prohibited in the routine body.
MAP MEMBER *func_spec*	Specifies that the function *func_spec* is used when a sort operation is performed. The function will map the object to values of a predefined scalar type. The function is called only once per sort operation.
ORDER MEMBER *func_spec*	Specifies that the function *func_spec* is implicitly called when a sort operation is performed. The return value of the function is used to determine the relative position of the object in the sort. The function is called for each comparison performed in the sort operation.
VARRAY	Specifies that a varying array type is created.
VARYING ARRAY	Synonym for VARRAY.
limit	Specifies the maximum number of elements in the varying array.
OF *datatype*	Specifies the datatype for the nested table or varying array.
TABLE	Specifies that a nested table is created.
COMPILE	Specifies that the type is to be compiled regardless of whether the type is valid or invalid. By default, both the specification and the body of the type are compiled.
SPECIFICATION	Specifies that only the type specification is to be compiled.
BODY	Specifies that only the type body is to be compiled.
COMPILE DEBUG	Same as COMPILE, but also creates debug information for the PL/SQL debugger.
REPLACE AS OBJECT	Specifies that for object types, the definition of the object is to be changed by adding new member functions.
FORCE	Specifies that the type will be dropped even if objects exist that reference it. Referencing columns will be marked as UNUSED, making all the data in them inaccessible. It is not recommended to use FORCE.

C NAME *name*	Specifies the name of the C routine to call.
LIBRARY *library*	Specifies the name of the library in which the C routine can be found.
WITH CONTEXT	Specifies that the context pointer is passed to the external function.
PARAMETERS(*parameters*)	Specifies the position and parameters passed to the external function.
PRAGMA RESTRICT_REFERENCES	Compiler directive that specifies how functions access the database tables or packaged variables.
RNDS	Specifies that no tables are read (Reads No Database State).
WNDS	Specifies that no tables are modified (Writes No Database State).
RNPS	Specifies that no packaged variables are read (Reads No Package State).
WNPS	Specifies that no packaged variables are modified (Writes No Package State).
TRUST	Specifies that the restrictions specified are trusted to be true and are not to be enforced.
FUNCTION *name*	Specifies the name of the function to be used.
argument	Specifies one of the arguments passed to the function or procedure.
datatype	Specifies the datatype of the argument.
RETURN *datatype*	Specifies the datatype of the routine return value.
LANGUAGE	Specifies the language of the implementation of the type.
JAVA NAME '*string*'	Specifies the name of a Java routine.
method_name	Specifies the name of the MEMBER function or procedure to which the pragma compiler directives are being applied.
DEFAULT	Specifies that the PRAGMA compiler directives should be applied to all MEMBER functions of the type.
PROCEDURE *name*	Specifies the name of the procedure to be used.

CREATE/DROP TYPE BODY

You can use the CREATE/DROP TYPE BODY commands to create, replace, or drop the body of a user-defined object type. Together with the specification of the type, the type body defines the object type database object. Use CREATE/DROP TYPE to create or drop the type specification. The following is the syntax for the CREATE TYPE BODY command:

```
CREATE [OR REPLACE] TYPE BODY [schema.]type_name
{IS|AS}
{MEMBER|STATIC} {func_spec|proc_spec}
  [{MEMBER|STATIC} {func_spec|proc_spec}
[{MAP|ORDER} MEMBER func_spec]
END
```

Listing A-21 provides the syntax for the DROP TYPE BODY command:

Listing A-21: DROP TYPE BODY syntax

```
DROP TYPE BODY [schema.]type_name

C_declaration := C [NAME name] LIBRARY library
[WITH CONTEXT]
[PARAMETERS(parameters)]

func_spec := FUNCTION name
(argument datatype[,argument datatype...])
RETURN datatype
{IS|AS}
{ function_body
|   LANGUAGE {Java_declaration|C_declaration}
}

Java_declaration := JAVA NAME 'string'

proc_spec := PROCEDURE name
(argument datatype[,argument datatype...])
{IS|AS}
{ procedure_body
| LANGUAGE {Java_declaration|C_declaration}
}
```

The following list explains all of the elements used in the CREATE/DROP TYPE BODY commands' syntax:

OR REPLACE   If a type body is already present with the
                                              same name, it will be replaced.

`schema.type_name`	Specifies the name of the type to create, replace, or drop. Schema is optional and may be omitted.
`IS`	Synonym for `AS`.
`AS`	Synonym for `IS`.
`MEMBER`	Specifies that a function or procedure is called when the attribute is referenced. In the body of the routine, the keyword `SELF` can be used to reference the calling object.
`STATIC`	Specifies that a function or procedure is called when the attribute is referenced. The use of `SELF` is prohibited in the routine body.
`MAP MEMBER func_spec`	Specifies that the function `func_spec` is used when a sort operation is performed. The function will map the object to values of a predefined scalar type. The function is only called once per sort operation.
`ORDER MEMBER func_spec`	Specifies that the function `func_spec` is implicitly called when a sort operation is performed. The return value of the function is used to determine the relative position of the object in the sort. The function is called for each comparison performed in the sort operation.
`END`	Marks the end of the create type body statement.
`C NAME name`	Specifies the name of the C routine to call.
`LIBRARY library`	Specifies the name of the library in which the C routine can be found.
`WITH CONTEXT`	Specifies that the context pointer is passed to the external function.
`PARAMETERS(parameters)`	Specifies the position and parameters passed to the external function.
`FUNCTION name`	Specifies the name of the function to be used.
`argument`	Specifies one of the arguments passed to the function or procedure.
`datatype`	Specifies the datatype of the argument.
`RETURN datatype`	Specifies the datatype of the routine return value.

function_body	Specifies PL/SQL code that implements the function.
LANGUAGE	Specifies the language of the implementation of the type.
JAVA NAME *'string'*	Specifies the name of a Java routine.
PROCEDURE *name*	Specifies the name of the procedure to be used.
procedure_body	Specifies PL/SQL code that implements the procedure.

CREATE/ALTER/DROP VIEW

You can use the CREATE/ALTER/DROP VIEW commands to create, alter, or drop view database objects. *Views* are table-like structures that are based on a query on one or more tables or views. A view doesn't contain the data itself. Views can also be created on object tables or object views.

Listing A-22 provides the syntax for the CREATE VIEW command:

Listing A-22: **CREATE VIEW syntax**

```
CREATE [OR REPLACE] [[NO] FORCE] VIEW[schema.]view
[ (alias[,alias...])
| OF [schema.]type_name
    WITH OBJECT IDENTIFIER
    { DEFAULT
    | (attribute[,attribute...])
    }
]
AS subquery
[WITH { READ ONLY
     | CKECK OPTION [CONSTRAINT constraint]
     }
]
```

The following is the syntax for the ALTER VIEW command:

```
ALTER VIEW [schema.]view COMPILE
```

The following is the syntax for the DROP VIEW command:

```
DROP VIEW [schema.]view
```

The following list explains all of the elements used in the `CREATE/ALTER/DROP VIEW` commands' syntax:

`OR REPLACE`	If a view with the same name already exists, it will be replaced. Effectively, it changes the definition of the view object, and all grants to this view will remain in place.
`NO FORCE`	Specifies that the view will be created only when the following conditions are met: the referenced tables, views, and object types exist; and the user has privileges on the tables, views, and object types.
`FORCE`	Specifies that the view will be created even if the referenced objects don't exist, or if the user doesn't have sufficient privileges on them.
`schema.view`	Specifies the name of the view to be created. The schema name is optional and may be omitted.
`alias`	Specifies an alias for the column retrieved by the subquery. Aliases can't be used for object views.
`OF schema.type_name`	Specifies that the object view will be created of type `type_name`. Schema is optional and may be omitted.
`WITH OBJECT IDENTIFIER`	Specifies the method that is used to uniquely identify each row in the object view/table. It can be based on the object ID (`DEFAULT`) or on a custom list of type attributes (`attribute`).
`DEFAULT`	Specifies that the object identifier of the object table/view is used to uniquely identify each row.
`attribute`	Specifies the attributes of the object type to uniquely identify each row.
`AS subquery`	Specifies the `SELECT` statement with which to create the view.
`WITH READ ONLY`	Specifies that a read-only view is to be created. No DML statements may be issued against the view.
`WITH CKECK OPTION`	Specifies that all DML statements issued against the view must result in rows that can be retrieved by the `VIEW` query.

CONSTRAINT *constraint*	Specifies the CHECK OPTION constraint. If omitted, Oracle will generate a check option constraint automatically.

DELETE

You use the DELETE command to remove some or all rows from a table or view. Listing A-23 provides the syntax for the DELETE command:

Listing A-23: **DELETE syntax**

```
DELETE [hint] [FROM]
{ TABLE (collection_expression) [(+)]
| (subquery [WITH { READ ONLY
                  | CHECK OPTION [CONSTRAINT constraint]
                  }
            ]
  )
| [schema.]table[@dblink]
| [schema.]table PARTITION(partition_name)
| [schema.]table SUBPARTITION(subpartition_name)
| [schema.]table SAMPLE [BLOCK] (percent)
| [schema.]view[@dblink]
| [schema.]snapshot[@dblink]
} [alias]
[WHERE condition]
[RETURNING (expression[,expression...])
 INTO (data_item[,data_item...])
]
```

The following list explains all of the elements used in the DELETE command syntax:

hint	Specifies instructions for the optimizer. Hints are specified in comments.
collection_expression	Specifies that the *collection_expression* should be used as a table in the update statement.
PARTITION(*partition_name*)	When a table is divided into partitions, you can use this clause to delete only rows from a particular partition of the table.
SUBPARTITION	Specifies the subpartition of the table from which to delete rows. (Optional.)
schema.view	Specifies the view from which to delete rows.
schema.table	Specifies the table from which to delete rows.

schema.snapshot	Specifies the snapshot from which to delete rows.
@dblink	Points to the remote database, if rows are to be deleted from a remote database.
alias	Specifies an alternative name for the table, view, or subquery so it can be referenced more easily in the where clause. (Optional).
subquery	Specifies a query with which data is selected for deletion.
WHERE *condition*	Specifies that only rows satisfying the *condition* are deleted.
RETURNING *expression*	Specifies which columns are retrieved from rows that are deleted.
INTO *data_item*	Specifies a PL/SQL variable or bound variable that stores the value retrieved by the expression.
SAMPLE *percent*	Specifies that not all rows but the specified percentage of rows, chosen at random, are to be deleted.
SAMPLE BLOCK	Specifies random block sampling instead of random row sampling.
WITH READ ONLY	Specifies that the subquery can't be updated.
WITH CHECK OPTION	Specifies that changes to the table aren't allowed that would produce rows not selected in the subquery.
CONSTRAINT *constraint*	Specifies a name for the check option constraint. If omitted, Oracle will assign a name for the check option constraint.

EXPLAIN PLAN

You can use the EXPLAIN PLAN command to generate the Oracle execution plan for a SQL statement. The execution plan shows the operations Oracle performs internally to execute the SQL statement. The output of EXPLAIN PLAN is stored in an output table for which the details are specified in the list that follows. If you use the cost-based optimization, EXPLAIN PLAN also determines the cost of executing the statement. The following is the syntax for the EXPLAIN PLAN command:

```
EXPLAIN PLAN [SET STATEMENT_ID = 'text']
[INTO [schema.]table[@dblink]]
FOR statement
```

The following list explains all of the elements used in the EXPLAIN PLAN command syntax:

SET STATEMENT_ID = 'text'	Specifies the value of the statement_id column in the output table. The default value is null.
INTO table	Specifies the output table. See more details about the output table later in this section.
@dblink	Specifies the name of the database link if the output table resides on a remote database.
schema	Specifies the name of the schema in which the output table resides.
FOR statement	Specifies the SQL statement for which to generate the execution plan.

The output table in which the output from the EXPLAIN PLAN command is collected is usually called plan_table and can be created using the utlxplan.sql file. The following table provides the table description:

Column Name	Data Type
STATEMENT_ID	VARCHAR2(30)
TIMESTAMP	DATE
REMARKS	VARCHAR2(80)
OPERATION	VARCHAR2(30)
OPTIONS	VARCHAR2(30)
OBJECT_NODE	VARCHAR2(128)
OBJECT_OWNER	VARCHAR2(30)
OBJECT_NAME	VARCHAR2(30)
OBJECT_INSTANCE	NUMBER(38)
OBJECT_TYPE	VARCHAR2(30)
OPTIMIZER	VARCHAR2(255)
SEARCH_COLUMNS	NUMBER
ID	NUMBER(38)
PARENT_ID	NUMBER(38)
POSITION	NUMBER(38)

Continued

Column Name	Data Type
COST	NUMBER(38)
CARDINALITY	NUMBER(38)
BYTES	NUMBER(38)
OTHER_TAG	VARCHAR2(255)
PARTITION_START	VARCHAR2(255)
PARTITION_STOP	VARCHAR2(255)
PARTITION_ID	NUMBER(38)
OTHER	LONG

GRANT object privileges

With the GRANT command privileges on objects can be given to users and roles. To remove privileges from users and roles, use the REVOKE command. Listing A-24 provides the syntax for the GRANT command.

Listing A-24: **GRANT syntax**

```
GRANT privilege[,privilege...]
ON { [schema.]object_name
   | { DIRECTORY directory_name
     | JAVA   SOURCE [schema.]object
     | JAVA RESOURCE [schema.]object
     }
   }
TO object[object...]
[WITH GRANT OPTION]

object := {user|role|PUBLIC}

privilege := {object_privilege|ALL [PRIVILEGES]}
            [(column[,column...])]
```

The following list explains all of the elements used in the GRANT command syntax:

WITH GRANT OPTION	Specifies that the grantee can grant the object privileges to other users or roles.
object_privilege	Specifies the object privilege to be granted. See Table A-5 in the section "Reference Tables" for all object privileges.

ON *object*	Specifies the database object on which to grant the privileges.
DIRECTORY	Specifies the name of the directory database object on which to grant privileges.
JAVA SOURCE	Specifies the name of the Java source database object on which to grant privileges.
JARA RESOURCE	Specifies the name of the Java resource database object on which to grant privileges.
ALL PRIVILEGES	Grants all privileges on the object specified. Note that only privileges that are granted to the current user with the WITH GRANT OPTION can be granted to other users.
column	Specifies the columns on which the privileges are granted.
user	Specifies the user to grant the privileges to.
role	Specifies the role to grant the privileges to.
PUBLIC	Specifies that the privileges are granted to all users.

GRANT system privileges and roles

With the GRANT command, system privileges and roles can be granted to users and roles. To remove privileges from users and roles, use the REVOKE command. The following is the syntax for the GRANT command:

```
GRANT privilege[,privilege...]
TO object[,object...]
[WITH ADMIN OPTION]

object := {user|role|PUBLIC}

privilege := {system_privilege|role}
```

The following list explains all of the elements used in the GRANT command syntax:

WITH ADMIN OPTION	Specifies that the grantee can grant/revoke the role to/from another user or role. Also, the grantee can alter and drop the role.
system_privilege	Specifies the system privilege to be granted. See Table A-4 in the section "Reference Tables" for all system privileges.
user	Specifies the user to grant the privileges to.
role	Specifies the role to grant or the role to grant the privileges to.
PUBLIC	Specifies that the privileges are granted to all users.

INSERT

You use the INSERT statement to insert data into a table, a view, or an inline view. The data to insert may be specifies as a list of values or a subquery. Listing A-25 provides the syntax for the INSERT command.

Listing A-25: **INSERT syntax**

```
INSERT
{ TABLE (collection_expression) [(+)]
| (subquery [WITH { READ ONLY
                  | CHECK OPTION [CONSTRAINT constraint]
                  }
           ]
  )
| [schema.]table[@dblink]
| [schema.]table PARTITION(partition_name)
| [schema.]table SUBPARTITION(subpartition_name)
| [schema.]table SAMPLE [BLOCK] (percent)
| [schema.]view[@dblink]
| [schema.]snapshot[@dblink]
} [alias]
[(column[,column...])]
{ [sub_query]
  [VALUES (expression[expression...])
    [RETURNING (expression[,expression...])
     INTO (data_item[,data_item...]
  ]
}
```

The following list explains all of the elements used in the INSERT command syntax:

hint	Specifies instructions for the optimizer. Hints are specified in comments.
schema.table@dblink	Specifies the table to insert data into. You may omit the schema name and database link name to denote a table in the local schema in the local database.
schema.view@dblink	Specifies the view to insert data into. You may omit the schema name and database link name to denote a table in the local schema in the local database.
PARTITION	Specifies the name of the partition of the table into which to insert the data.

SUBPARTITION	Specifies the subpartition of the table into which to insert the data. (Optional.)
column	Specifies the column name of the view or table into which to insert data.
sub_query	Specifies a subquery to return rows that are to be inserted. Note that the order of the columns returned needs to match the order of the column list of the insert statement.
VALUES	Specifies a range of values of the row to be inserted. The order of these values needs to match the order of the column list of the insert statement.
RETURNING	Specifies that the rows affected by the insert statement are retrieved.
INTO	Specifies that the values of the retrieved rows are to be stored in the *data_items* specified.
data_item	Specifies a PL/SQL variable or bind variable
collection_expression	Specifies that the *collection_expression* should be used as a table in the update statement.
SAMPLE *percent*	Specifies that not all rows, but the specified percentage of rows chosen at random, are to be deleted.
SAMPLE BLOCK	Specifies random block sampling instead of random row sampling.
WITH READ ONLY	Specifies that the subquery can't be updated.
WITH CHECK OPTION	Specifies that changes to the table are not allowed that would produce rows not selected in the subquery.
CONSTRAINT *constraint*	Specifies a name for the check option constraint. If omitted, Oracle will assign a name for the check option constraint.

NOAUDIT (schema objects)

With NOAUDIT, you specify schema objects on which to stop auditing. To start auditing again, use the AUDIT command. The following is the syntax for the NOAUDIT command:

```
NOAUDIT object_option[,object_option...] ON
{ DEFAULT
| DIRECTORY directory_name
```

```
|  [schema.]object
}
[ BY {SESSION|ACCESS} ]
[ WHENEVER [NOT] SUCCESSFUL ]
```

The following list explains all of the elements used in the NOAUDIT command syntax:

object_option	An operation for auditing. See Table A-5 in the section "Reference Tables" for all options and the objects for which they apply.
schema	The schema in which the object resides that will no longer be audited.
object	The object that will no longer be audited.
DIRECTORY directory_name	The directory that will no longer be audited.
DEFAULT	Any newly created object will not be audited using the options set.
WHENEVER SUCCESSFUL	Stops auditing SQL statements that complete successfully.
WHENEVER NOT SUCCESSFUL	Stops auditing failing SQL statements.

NOAUDIT (SQL statements)

Use NOAUDIT to stop auditing specific SQL statements. To start auditing again, use the AUDIT command. The following is the syntax for the NOAUDIT command:

```
NOAUDIT option[,option...]
[BY { user[,user...]
    | proxy [ON BEHALF OF
        { ANY
        | user[,user...]
        }
    }
]
[WHENEVER [NOT] SUCCESSFUL]

option :=
{statement_option|system_privilege}
```

The following list explains all of the elements used in the NOAUDIT command syntax:

statement_option	Specifies specific SQL statements for which auditing should be stopped. See Tables A-1 and A-2 in the section "Reference Tables" for allowed statement options and Table A-3 for available shortcuts.

`system_privilege`	Specifies to stop auditing SQL statements that are authorized by the specified system privilege. See Table A-4 in the section "Reference Tables" for available system privileges.
BY `user`	Only statements issued by *user* are stopped from auditing. If this clause is omitted, all users' statements will not be audited.
BY `proxy`	Specifies that only SQL statements that are issued by the specified proxy are stopped from auditing.
ON BEHALF OF	Specifies that only statements executed on behalf of specified user(s) are stopped from auditing.
ANY	Specifies that statements executed on behalf of any user are stopped from auditing.
WHENEVER SUCCESSFUL	Stops auditing only successful SQL statements.
WHENEVER NOT SUCCESSFUL	Stops auditing only unsuccessful SQL statements.

REVOKE object privileges

With the REVOKE command, privileges on objects can be revoked, or taken away, from users and roles. To grant privileges to users and roles, use the GRANT command. Listing A-26 provides the syntax for the REVOKE command:

Listing A-26: **REVOKE syntax**

```
REVOKE privilege[,privilege...]
ON { [schema.]object_name
   | { DIRECTORY directory_name
     | JAVA    SOURCE [schema.]object
     | JAVA RESOURCE [schema.]object
     }
   }
FROM object[object...]
[CASCADE CONSTRAINTS]
[FORCE]

object := {user|role|PUBLIC}

privilege := {object_privilege|ALL [PRIVILEGES]}
```

The following list explains all of the elements used in the REVOKE command syntax:

CASCADE CONSTRAINTS	When the REFERENCES privilege or ALL PRIVILEGES are revoked, this clause specifies that all referential integrity constraints that the revokee defined using the REFERENCES privilege are to be dropped.
FORCE	When revoking EXECUTE object privileges on user-defined types that have table or type dependencies, this clause has to be specified.
object_privilege	Specifies the object privilege to be revoke. See Table A-5 in the section "Reference Tables" for all object privileges.
ON object	Specifies the database object from which to revoke the privileges.
DIRECTORY	Specifies the name of the directory database object from which to revoke privileges.
JAVA SOURCE	Specifies the name of the Java source database object from which to revoke privileges.
JARA RESOURCE	Specifies the name of the Java resource database object from which to revoke privileges.
ALL PRIVILEGES	Revokes all privileges from the object specified.
user	Specifies the user to revoke the privileges from.
role	Specifies the role to revoke the privileges from.
PUBLIC	Specifies that the privileges are revoked from all users.

REVOKE system privileges and roles

With the REVOKE command, system privileges and roles can be revoked, or taken away, from users and roles. To grant privileges to users and roles, use the GRANT command. The following is the syntax for the REVOKE command:

```
REVOKE privilege[,privilege...]
FROM object[,object...]

privilege := {system_privilege|role}

object := {user|role|PUBLIC}
```

The following list explains all of the elements used in the REVOKE command syntax:

system_privilege	Specifies the system privilege to be revoked. See Table A-4 in the section "Reference Tables" for all system privileges.

user	Specifies the user to revoke the privileges from.
role	Specifies the role to revoke or the role to revoke from users or other roles.
PUBLIC	Specifies that the privileges are revoked from all users.

SELECT

You can use the SELECT command to retrieve data from the database. Data can be retrieved from tables, object tables, views, object views, and materialized views or snapshots. Listing A-27 provides the syntax for the SELECT command:

Listing A-27: **SELECT syntax**

```
SELECT [hint] [ALL|{DISTINCT|UNIQUE}]
{*|select_item[,select_item...]}
FROM data_source[,data_source...]
[WHERE {condition|outer_join}]
[ [ [START WITH] condition CONNECT BY condition ]
  [ GROUP BY { expression[,expression...]
             | CUBE    (expression[,expression...])
             | ROLLUP  (expression[,expression...])
             }
      HAVING condition
  ]
]
[UNION|UNION ALL|INTERSECT|MINUS] (subquery)]
[ ORDER BY order_item[,order_item...] ]
[ FOR UPDATE [OF update_column[,update_column...]] [NOWAIT] ]

data_source :=
{ TABLE (collection_expression) [(+)]
| (subquery [WITH { READ ONLY
                  | CHECK OPTION [CONSTRAINT constraint]
                  }
           ]
  )
| [schema.]table[@dblink]
| [schema.]table PARTITION(partition_name)
| [schema.]table SUBPARTITION(subpartition_name)
| [schema.]table SAMPLE [BLOCK] (percent)
| [schema.]view[@dblink]
| [schema.]snapshot[@dblink]
} table_alias

order_item :=
{ expression [ASC|DESC]
```

Continued

Listing A-27: *(continued)*

```
|  position [ASC|DESC]
|  column_alias [ASC|DESC]
}

outer_join := table1.column
{ = table2.column (+)
|  (+) = table2.column
}

select_item :=
[ expression [AS] column_alias
|  { [schema.]table.*
   | [schema.]table.column
   | [schema.]view.*
   | [schema.]view.column
   | [schema.]snapshot.*
   | [schema.]snapshot.column
   }
]

update_column :=
{ [schema.]table.column
|  [schema.]view.column
}
```

The following list explains all of the elements used in the SELECT command syntax:

hint	Specifies instructions for the optimizer. Hints are specified in comments.
ALL	Specifies that all rows are returned.
DISTINCT	Specifies that only the unique rows are returned.
UNIQUE	Synonym for DISTINCT.
FROM	Specifies the data sources from which to retrieve rows.
WHERE condition	Specifies a condition that each retrieved row must satisfy.
START WITH condition	Specifies the rows to be used as roots when performing a hierarchical query. They are the rows matching the condition specified.

`CONNECT BY condition`	Specifies the relationship between parent and child records when performing a hierarchical query.
`GROUP BY expression`	Specifies that the returned data should be grouped together according to the expression specified. A single row of summary information is displayed per group.
`ROLLUP`	Specifies that super aggregate rows are produced.
`CUBE`	Specifies that cross-tabulation values are produced.
`HAVING condition`	Specifies a condition for the group rows returned after the `GROUP BY` clause. Only group rows satisfying the condition should be returned.
`UNION`	Combines the rows retrieved by the `SELECT` statement with the rows retrieved by the *subquery*. The `UNION` parameter returns all unique roles.
`UNION ALL`	Combines the rows retrieved by the `SELECT` statement with the rows retrieved by the *subquery*. The `UNION ALL` parameter returns all rows including duplicates.
`INTERSECT`	Combines the rows retrieved by the `SELECT` statement with the rows retrieved by the *subquery* but returns only the common rows.
`MINUS (subquery)`	Specifies that the rows that are also retrieved by *subquery* should not be displayed.
`ORDER BY order_item`	Orders the rows returned by the `SELECT` statement. As *order_item* you have to specify one or more column names, column aliases, or column positions.
`FOR UPDATE OF update_column`	Locks the selected rows. Other users can't lock the rows until the current transaction is ended.
`NOWAIT`	Specifies that if the `SELECT` statement tries to lock a row that is already locked by another user, the control is returned to the user.

schema	Specifies the schema name.
table	Specifies the table name.
dblink	Optionally specifies the database link that points to the database in which the object resides that is to be queried.
PARTITION(partition_name)	Specifies the partition of the table in which to perform the query. (Optional.)
SUBPARTITION (subpartition_name)	Specifies the subpartition of the table in which to perform the query. (Optional.)
view	Specifies the view name.
snapshot	Specifies the snapshot name.
table_alias	Specifies an optional alias for the table.
ASC	Specifies that ordering is to be performed in ascending order.
DESC	Specifies that ordering is to be performed in descending order.
position	Specifies the position of the *select_item* column in the select list to which ordering should be performed.
column_alias	Specifies the column alias for the column to which ordering should be performed.
table1.column	Specifies column1 in the *outer_join* clause.
table2.column	Specifies column2 in the *outer_join* clause.
expression	Specifies a column to select.
AS column_alias	Specifies an alias for the column to select.
*	Specifies that all columns of the object are selected.
collection_expression	Specifies that the *collection_ expression* should be used as a table in the select statement.
SAMPLE *percent*	Specifies that not all rows but the specified percentage of rows, chosen at random, are to be selected.
SAMPLE BLOCK	Specifies random block sampling instead of random row sampling.

WITH READ ONLY	Specifies that the subquery cannot be updated.
WITH CHECK OPTION	Specifies that changes to the table are not allowed that would produce rows not selected in the subquery.
CONSTRAINT *constraint*	Specifies the name of the check constraint.

SET TRANSACTION

You can use the SET TRANSACTION command to alter the transaction settings. You can set the transaction to be read only or read/write, and you can control how Oracle handles DML statements that try to modify data that is currently modified in other, uncommitted transactions. You can also use SET TRANSACTION to explicitly specify the rollback segment. If omitted, Oracle will choose a rollback segment for the transaction. The following is the syntax for the SET TRANSACTION command:

```
SET TRANSACTION
{ READ ONLY
| READ WRITE
| ISOLATION LEVEL {SERIALIZABLE|READ COMMITTED}
| USE ROLLBACK SEGMENT rollback_segment
}
```

The following list explains all of the elements used in the SET TRANSACTION command syntax:

READ ONLY	Specifies that the current transaction is read only. This statement can be used to establish read consistency between all queries executed in the current transaction (until a commit or rollback is performed).
READ WRITE	Specifies that the current transaction is read/write. This is the default setting.
ISOLATION LEVEL	Specifies how DML statements are handled in the current transaction: SERIALIZABLE or READ COMMITTED.
SERIALIZABLE	Specifies that in the current transaction DML statements will fail, while in other uncommitted transactions, the same data is changed.
READ COMMITTED	Specifies that in the current transaction, DML statements will wait until row locks held by transactions made in other uncommitted transactions are released. This is the default Oracle behavior.

USE ROLLBACK SEGMENT	Specifies the rollback segment to be used for the current transaction. This has to be the first statement executed in a transaction. If omitted, Oracle will choose a rollback segment to use for the duration of the transaction.

UPDATE

You can use the UPDATE command to update rows in tables, views, and snapshots. Listing A-28 provides the syntax for the UPDATE command:

Listing A-28: **UPDATE syntax**

```
UPDATE [hint] table_expression[,table_expression...]
SET assignment_expression[,assignment_expression...]
[WHERE condition]
[RETURNING expression[,expression...] INTO
          data_item[,data_item...]
]


assignment_expression :=
{ column = {expression|(subquery)}
| (column[,column...]) = (subquery[,subquery...])
}

table_expression :=
{ TABLE (collection_expression) [(+)]
| (subquery [WITH { READ ONLY
                  | CHECK OPTION [CONSTRAINT constraint]
                  }
            ]
  )
| { [schema.]view[@dblink]
  | [schema.]snapshot[@dblink]
  | [schema.]table[@dblink]
  | [schema.]table
      { SAMPLE [BLOCK] (percent)
      | {PARTITION (partition)|SUBPARTITION (subpartition)}
      }
  }
} table_alias
```

The following list explains all of the elements used in the UPDATE command syntax:

hint	Specifies instructions for the optimizer. Hints are given in comments.

`WHERE condition`	Specifies a condition that each updated row must satisfy.
`RETURNING expression INTO data_item`	Retrieves the rows affected by the update. The value of the columns specified in `expression` will be assigned to the variables specified in `data_item`.
`column`	Specifies the name of the column to update.
`subquery`	Specifies a query with which to retrieve one or more values that will be assigned to a column. The number of columns returned by the subquery should match the number of columns in the `assignment_expression`.
`TABLE collection_expression`	Specifies what to update: a table, a snapshot, a view, or an inline view. To update the latter, specify a subquery in the `table_expression`. You may update an object in a different schema by specifying `schema`, and you may update a remote object by specifying the database link that points to the remote database.
`WITH READ ONLY`	Specifies that the rows returned by `subquery` cannot be updated.
`WITH CHECK OPTION`	Specifies that the rows returned by `subquery` can be updated only if the updated row would be returned by `subquery`.
`CONSTRAINT constraint`	Specifies a name for the check option constraint. If omitted, Oracle will assign a name for the check option constraint.
`schema`	Optionally, specifies the schema in which the object resides that is to be updated.
`dblink`	Optionally, specifies the database link that points to the database in which the object resides that is to be updated.
`view`	Specifies the name of the view to be updated.
`snapshot`	Specifies the name of the snapshot to be updated.

SAMPLE percent	Specifies that not all rows but the specified percentage of rows, chosen at random, are to be updated.
SAMPLE BLOCK	Specifies random block sampling instead of random row sampling.
PARTITION partition	Specifies the partition of the table in which to perform the updates. It is optional to specify this clause when updating a table.
SUBPARTITION subpartition	Specifies the subpartition of the table in which to perform the updates. It is optional to specify this clause when updating a table.
table_alias	Specifies an alias for the object to update. You may want to refer to this table alias in the condition in the where clause.

Common clauses

This section describes clauses that many commands use.

The *file_spec* Clause

The following is the syntax for the file_spec clause:

```
file_spec := { 'filename' | ('filename'[,'filename'...] }
[ SIZE integer [K|M] ] [REUSE]
```

The following list explains all of the elements used in the file_spec clause syntax:

'filename'   Specifies the name of the file.

SIZE integer Specifies the size of the file in bytes. Use *K* for kilobytes and *M* for megabytes.

REUSE   Specifies that Oracle may reuse the file.

The *parallel_clause* Clause

The following is the syntax for the parallel_clause clause:

```
parallel_clause :=
{ NOPARALLEL
| PARALLEL [integer]
}
```

The following list explains all of the elements used in the *parallel_clause* clause syntax:

NOPARALLEL	Specifies serial execution. This is the default.
PARALLEL	Specifies parallel execution. Oracle will select the degree of parallelism.
PARALLEL *integer*	Specifies parallel execution with *integer* threads of execution.

The *physical_attributes* Clause

The following is the syntax for the *physical_attributes* clause:

```
physical_attributes :=
[PCTUSED    integer]
[PCTFREE    integer]
[INITRANS   integer]
[MAXTRANS   integer]
[SIZE       integer [K|M]]
[TABLESPACE table space]
[storage_clause]
```

The following list explains all of the elements used in the *physical_attributes* clause syntax:

PCTUSED *integer*	Specifies that the limit used to determine when addtional rows can be added to a cluster's data block is *integer* %, where *integer* = 0...99 with a default value of 40.
PCTFREE *integer*	Specifies that *integer* % of the space in the cluster's data block is reserved for future expansion, where *integer* = 0...99 with a default value of 10 percent.
INITRANS *integer*	Specifies that initially, *integer* concurrent transaction entries are allocated within each data block, where *integer* = 1...255 with a default value of 2.
MAXTRANS *integer*	Specifies that at maximum, *integer* concurrent transactions can update the data block, where *integer* = 1...255 with a default value of the MAXTRANS value used for the tablespace.
TABLESPACE *table space*	Specifies the tablespace in which the cluster resides.

The *storage_clause* Clause

The following is the syntax for the *storage_clause* clause:

```
storage_clause := STORAGE
( [INITIAL      integer [K|M]]
  [NEXT         integer [K|M]]
  [MINEXTENTS   integer]
  [MAXEXTENTS  {integer|UNLIMITED}]
  [PCTINCREASE integer]
  [FREELISTS    integer]
  [FREELIST GROUPS integer]
  [OPTIMAL [NULL|integer [K|M] ]]
  [BUFFER_POOL {KEEP|RECYCLE|DEFAULT}
)
```

The following list explains all of the elements used in the *storage_clause* clause syntax:

INITIAL *integer*	Specifies the size of the object's first extend in bytes. Use *K* for kilobytes or *M* for megabytes.
NEXT *integer*	Specifies the size of the object's next extends in bytes. Use *K* for kilobytes or *M* for megabytes.
MINEXTENTS *integer*	Specifies the number of extends to allocate when the object is created.
MAXEXTENTS *integer*	Specifies the maximum number of extends allowed for the object.
MAXEXTENTS UNLIMITED	Specifies that extends will be allocated as needed.
PCTINCREASE *integer*	Specifies the percentage with which the size of the third and subsequent extends will grow.
FREELISTS *integer*	Specifies the number of free lists for each of the free list groups.
FREELIST GROUPS *integer*	Specifies the number of free list groups.
OPTIMAL NULL	Use *K* for kilobytes or *M* for megabytes.
OPTIMAL *integer*	Use *K* for kilobytes or *M* for megabytes.
BUFFER_POOL KEEP	Specifies that a cache is used for an object and that the object is to be retained in memory to avoid I/O operations.

| BUFFER_POOL RECYCLE | Specifies that a cache is used for an object and that the object is removed from memory when it is no longer needed. |
| BUFFER_POOL DEFAULT | Specifies that a cache is used for an object without specifying KEEP or RECYCLE. |

Reference tables

Tables A-1 through A-5 provide information about statement options, shortcuts for statement privileges, system privileges, and object options and types.

Table A-1 Statement Options	
statement_option	**Statements and Operations**
CLUSTER	{AUDIT|CREATE|DROP|TRUNCATE} CLUSTER
CONTEXT	{CREATE|DROP} CONTEXT
DATABASE LINK	{CREATE|DROP} DATABASE LINK
DIMENSION	{ALTER|CREATE|DROP} DIMENSION
DIRECTORY	{CREATE|DROP} DIRECTORY
INDEX	{ALTER|CREATE|DROP} INDEX
NOT EXISTS	**Audits failing SQL statements when an object specified in the SQL does not exist**
PROCEDURE	{CREATE|DROP} FUNCTION
	{CREATE|DROP} LIBRARY
	CREATE|DROP} PACKAGE'
	{CREATE|DROP} PROCEDURE
	CREATE PACKAGE BODY
PROFILE	{ALTER|CREATE|DROP} PROFILE
PUBLIC DATABASE LINK	{CREATE|DROP} PUBLIC DATABASE LINK
PUBLIC SYNONYM	{CREATE|DROP} PUBLIC SYNONYM
ROLE	{ALTER|CREATE|DROP|SET} ROLE
ROLLBACK STATEMENT	{ALTER|CREATE|DROP} ROLLBACK SEGMENT
SEQUENCE	{CREATE|DROP} SEQUENCE
SESSION	**Audits logons**

Continued

Table A-1 *(continued)*

statement_option	Statements and Operations
SYNONYM	{CREATE|DROP} SYNONYM
SYSTEM AUDIT	AUDIT
	NOAUDIT **only when auditing SQL statements**
SYSTEM GRANT	GRANT
REVOKE	**Only when used with system privileges and roles**
TABLE	{COMMENT ON
	|CREATE
	|DELETE FROM
	|DROP
	|TRUNCATE} TABLE
TABLESPACE	{ALTER|CREATE|DROP} TABLESPACE
TRIGGER	{ALTER|CREATE|DROP} TRIGGER
	ALTER TRIGGER **only when** ENABLE **and** DISABLE **options are specified**
	ALTER TABLE **only when** ENABLE ALL TRIGGERS **or** DISABLE ALL TRIGGERS **clauses are used**
TYPE	{ALTER|CREATE|DROP} TYPE
	{CREATE|DROP} TYPE BODY
USER	{ALTER|CREATE|DROP} USER
VIEW	{CREATE|DROP} VIEW

Table A-2
Additional Statement Options

statement_option	Statements and Operations
ALTER SEQUENCE	ALTER SEQUENCE
ALTER TABLE	ALTER TABLE
COMMENT TABLE	COMMENT ON
	{ TABLE {table|view|snapshot}

statement_option	Statements and Operations
	| COLUMN { table.column
	| view.column
	| snapshot.column
	}
	}
DELETE TABLE	DELETE FROM {table|view}
EXECUTE PROCEDURE	**Audits whenever any package, procedure, function or library is referenced; for example: executing a function inside a package, a reading, or setting a variable inside a package**
GRANT DIRECTORY	{GRANT|REVOKE} privilege ON directory
GRANT PROCEDURE	{GRANT|REVOKE} privilege ON {procedure|function|package}
GRANT SEQUENCE	{GRANT|REVOKE} privilege ON sequence
GRANT TABLE	{GRANT|REVOKE} privilege ON {table|view|snapshot}
GRANT TYPE	{GRANT|REVOKE} privilege ON TYPE
INSERT TABLE	INSERT INTO {table|view}
LOCK TABLE	LOCK TABLE {table|view}
SELECT SEQUENCE	**Audits whenever CURRVAL or NEXTVAL is used in a statement**
SELECT TABLE	SELECT FROM {table|view|snapshot}
UPDATE TABLE	UPDATE {table|view}

Table A-3
Shortcuts for Statement Privileges

Shortcut	Equivalent
CONNECT	CREATE SESSION

Continued

Table A-3 *(continued)*

Shortcut	Equivalent
RESOURCE	ALTER SYSTEM
	CREATE CLUSTER
	CREATE DATABASE LINK
	CREATE PROCEDURE
	CREATE ROLLBACK SEGMENT
	CREATE SEQUENCE
	CREATE SYNONYM
	CREATE TABLE
	CREATE TABLESPACE
	CREATE VIEW
DBA	AUDIT SYSTEM
	CREATE PUBLIC DATABASE LINK
	CREATE PUBLIC SYNONYM
	CREATE ROLE
	CREATE USER
ALL	All the privileges in Table A-1 but not the privileges in Table A-2
ALL PRIVILEGES	All privileges in Table A-1 and Table A-2

Table A-4
System Privileges

system_privilege	Operations Authorized to Grantee
ANALYZE ANY	Analyze any table, cluster, or index in any schema.
AUDIT ANY	Audit any schema object using AUDIT statements.
{ ALTER ANY | CREATE [ANY] | DROP ANY } CLUSTER	Alter, create, or drop any cluster in any schema. When ANY is omitted after the CREATE clause, only private clusters can be created.

system_privilege	Operations Authorized to Grantee
{ CREATE ANY | DROP ANY} CONTEXT	Create or drop any context namespace.
{ CREATE PUBLIC | DROP [PUBLIC] } DATABASE LINK	Create or drop public database links. When PUBLIC is omitted after the DROP clause, only private database links can be dropped.
ALTER DATABASE	Change database settings.
{ ALTER ANY | CREATE [ANY] | DROP ANY} DIMENSION	Create, alter, or drop dimensions. When ANY is omitted, only private dimensions can be created.
(CREATE|DROP} ANY DIRECTORY	Create or drop any directory in any schema.
{ALTER ANY |CREATE [ANY] |DROP ANY} INDEX	Alter, create, or drop indexes. When ANY is omitted, only private indexes can be created.
{ CREATE [ANY] | DROP ANY | EXECUTE ANY} INDEXTYPE	Create, drop, or reference indextypes. When ANY is omitted, only private indextypes can be created.
{ CREATE [ANY] | DROP [ANY] } LIBRARY	Create or drop any procedures, functions, and libraries in any schema. When ANY is omitted after the DROP clause, only private libraries can be dropped.
{ ALTER ANY | CREATE [ANY] | DROP ANY} MATERIALIZED VIEW	Create, alter, or drop materialized views. When ANY is omitted, only private materialized views can be created.
{ CREATE [ANY] | DROP ANY | EXECUTE ANY} OPERATOR	Create, drop, or execute operators. When ANY is omitted, only private operators/bindings can be created.
{ALTER|CREATE|DROP} ANY OUTLINE	Create, alter, or drop any outlines in any schema.
GRANT ANY PRIVILEGE	Grant any system privileges to other users and roles.
{ ALTER ANY | CREATE [ANY] | DROP ANY | EXECUTE ANY } PROCEDURE	Alter, create, drop, or execute any stored procedure, function, or package in any schema. When ANY is omitted after the CREATE clause, only private procedures can be dropped.
{ALTER|CREATE|DROP} PROFILE	Alter, create, or drop profiles.
ALTER RESOURCE COST	Specify a formula to calculate the total cost of resources used by a session.

Continued

Table A-4 (continued)	
system_privilege	*Operations Authorized to Grantee*
{ ALTER ANY | CREATE | DROP ANY | GRANT ANY } ROLE	Alter, create, drop, or grant roles.
{ALTER|CREATE|DROP} ROLLBACK SEGMENT	Alter, create, or drop rollback segments.
{ ALTER ANY | CREATE [ANY] | DROP ANY | SELECT ANY } SEQUENCE	Alter, create, drop, or select any sequence in any schema. When ANY is omitted after the CREATE clause, only private sequences can be created.
RESTRICTED SESSION	Log on to the database after it is started using the STARTUP RESTRICT command.
{ALTER|CREATE} SESSION	For ALTER, issue alter session commands. For CREATE, log on to the database.
{ ALTER ANY | CREATE [ANY] | DROP ANY} SNAPSHOT	Alter, create, or drop any snapshot in any schema. When ANY is omitted after the CREATE clause, only private snapshots can be created.
{ CREATE [ANY] | CREATE PUBLIC | DROP ANY | DROP PUBLIC } SYNONYM	Create or drop synonyms. When ANY is specified, synonyms may be created or dropped in any schema. When PUBLIC is specified, public synonyms may be created or dropped.
SYSDBA	Perform the following Server Manager commands: ALTER DATABASE {OPEN|MOUNT|BACKUP} ARCHIVELOG CREATE DATABASE RECOVERY SHUTDOWN STARTUP The SYSDBA privilege also includes the RESTRICTED SESSION privilege.

system_privilege	*Operations Authorized to Grantee*
SYSOPER	Perform the following Server Manager commands: ALTER DATABASE {OPEN|MOUNT|BACKUP} ARCHIVELOG RECOVERY SHUTDOWN STARTUP The SYSDBA privilege also includes the RESTRICTED SESSION privilege.
{ALTER|AUDIT} SYSTEM	Issue ALTER SYSTEM commands or issue AUDIT SYSTEM commands to audit SQL statements.
{ ALTER ANY | BACKUP ANY | CREATE [ANY] | DELETE ANY | DROP ANY | INSERT ANY | LOCK ANY | UPDATE ANY | SELECT ANY} TABLE	Alter, back up, create, delete rows from, drop, insert rows into, lock, update, or select rows from any table in any schema. When ANY is omitted after the CREATE clause, only private tables may be created.
COMMENT ANY TABLE	Add comments to any table in any schema.
{ALTER|CREATE|DROP|MANAGE} TABLESPACE	Alter, create, or drop tablespaces. When MANAGE is used, the grantee can bring tablespaces online and offline and do tablespace backups.
UNLIMITED TABLESPACE	Use an unlimited amount of tablespace regardless of quotas specified for the tablespaces. You may not grant this privilege to roles.
FORCE [ANY] TRANSACTION	Force the commit or rollback in the local database of distributed in-doubt transactions. If ANY is omitted, only own (not distributed) in-doubt transactions may be committed or rolled back.

Continued

Table A-4 *(continued)*	
system_privilege	***Operations Authorized to Grantee***
{ ALTER ANY | CREATE [ANY] | DROP ANY } TRIGGER	Alter, create, or drop any trigger in any schema. If ANY is omitted after the CREATE clause, only private triggers can be created.
{ ALTER ANY | CREATE [ANY] | DROP ANY | EXECUTE ANY } TYPE	Alter, create, or drop any object type and object type bodies in any schema. When EXECUTE ANY is used, any type may be used and referenced, and methods of any type may be executed in any schema. The EXECUTE ANY option may not be granted to a role.
{ALTER|CREATE|DROP} USER	Alter, create, or drop users and set or change the parameters for a user including tablespace quotas, set default and temporary tablespaces, and set default roles; assign a profile.
BECOME USER	Become another user. This privilege is required when doing a full database import.
{ CREATE [ANY] | DROP ANY } VIEW	Create or drop any view in any schema.
[GLOBAL] QUERY REWRITE	Rewrite using a materialized view. Create function-based indexes. When GLOBAL is specified, the objects may be created in any schema.

Table A-5
Object Options and the Object Types to Which They Are Applicable

object_ option	Directory	Library	Sequence	Snapshot	Table	View	Procedure Function Package
ALTER			✓	✓	✓		
AUDIT	✓		✓	✓	✓	✓	✓
COMMENT			✓	✓	✓	✓	
DELETE			✓	✓	✓	✓	
EXECUTE		✓					✓

object_option	Directory	Library	Sequence	Snapshot	Table	View	Procedure Function Package
GRANT	✓	✓	✓	✓	✓	✓	✓
INDEX			✓	✓	✓		
INSERT			✓	✓	✓	✓	
LOCK			✓	✓	✓	✓	
READ	✓						
RENAME			✓	✓	✓	✓	✓
SELECT			✓	✓	✓	✓	
UPDATE			✓	✓	✓	✓	

object_option	Materialized View/ Snapshot	Directory	User-Defined Type	Operator	Index Type
ALTER					
AUDIT					
COMMENT					
DELETE	✓				
EXECUTE			✓	✓	✓
GRANT					
INDEX					
INSERT	✓				
LOCK					
READ		✓			
RENAME					
SELECT	✓				
UPDATE	✓				

✦   ✦   ✦

SQL Built-in Function Reference

This appendix describes the many built-in functions that are available from SQL and PL/SQL. Before presenting the list of functions, numeric format elements and date format elements are described. Then the functions are presented in alphabetical order.

Numeric Format Elements

Several of the SQL functions that will be described in this appendix, most notably the TO_CHAR function, involve the conversion of numeric values to character values, or vice versa. These functions all use the numeric format elements shown in Table B-1 to specify the format of the numbers when they are displayed in character form.

	Table B-1 Numeric Format Elements	
Element	**Sample**	**Description**
,	999,999	Marks the location of the comma in a formatted number.
G	999G999	Returns the group separator (usually a comma in the U.S.) as specified by the NLS_NUMERIC_CHARACTER setting. This is a language-dependent value.

Continued

Table B-1 *(continued)*

Element	Sample	Description
.	9.99	Marks the location of the decimal point in a formatted number.
D	9D99	Marks the location of the decimal point as specified by the NLS_NUMERIC_CHARACTER setting. This is a language-dependent value.
$	$999,999.99	Marks the location of a leading dollar sign in a formatted number.
C	C999,999.99	Marks the location of the currency symbol as specified by the NLS_ISO_CURRENCY parameter. This is a language-dependent value.
L	L999,999.99	Marks the location of the currency symbol, as specified by the NLS_CURRENCY parameter.
U	U999,999.99	Marks the location of the union currency symbol, as specified by the NLS_UNION_CURRENCY parameter.
0	0999	Marks a location in the number at which you want to begin displaying leading zeros.
9	9.99	Marks the location of a digit. Note that if no sign is specified in a number format, positive numbers will be formatted with one leading space to allow for a negative sign.
EEEE	999.9EEEE	Causes a number to be formatted using scientific notation.
FM	fm9.99	Formats a number with no leading or trailing blanks.
MI	999,999MI	Formats negative numbers with a trailing negative sign, and positive numbers with a trailing blank.
PR	999pr	Formats negative numbers within $\langle$ and $\rangle$ characters.
RN	RN	Formats a number in uppercase Roman numerals.
rn	rn	Formats a number in lowercase Roman numerals.
S	s999,999 999,999s	Formats both negative and positive values with a leading – or + sign. The *S* may also be placed at the end of the number, in which case the sign becomes a trailing sign.
TM	TM9 TME	Formats a number using the minimum amount of text characters (TM = Text Minimum). TM9 results in fixed notation being used, while TME results in scientific notation being used. If TM9 results in a string that is more than 64 characters long, scientific notation is used anyway.
X	XXXX xxxx	Returns the hexadecimal value of a number. The case of the hexadecimal characters A–F will match that of the format string. Use X for uppercase hexadecimal characters and x for lowercase.

Element	Sample	Description
V	999v999	Multiplies a value by 10 raised to the power specified by the number of 9s trailing the V character.

Date Format Elements

The elements shown in Table B-2 are used by TO_CHAR and TO_DATE to facilitate the conversion of date values to character strings and character strings to dates. All format elements may be used when formatting dates for display; however, not all may be used when translating the character representation of a date to a DATE type. An X in the TO_DATE? column indicates that the element may be used with the TO_DATE function.

Table B-2
Date Format Elements

Element	Example	TO_DATE?	Description
-/,.;:	mm/dd/yy	X	Places punctuation in a date. Any of these characters can be used as punctuation when formatting a date.
AD A.D. BC B.C.	YYYY AD yyyy bc YYYY B.C.	X	Marks the location of the AD/BC indicator. You can place this in a date with or without periods. The case of the indicator matches the case used for the format element.
AM A.M. PM P.M.	hh:mi am hh:mi a.m. hh:mi AM	X	Marks the location of the AM/PM indicator. You can place this in a date with or without periods. The case of the indicator matches the case used for the format element
PM P.M.	hh:mi pm hh:mi P.M.		Marks the location of the AM/PM indicator. This is the same as AM and A.M., but may not be used with TO_CHAR.

Continued

Table B-2 (continued)

Element	Example	TO_DATE?	Description
CC SCC	CC SCC		Returns the century value. The S is used to prefix BC dates with a negative sign. The year 2000 corresponds to the 20th century. The year 2001 corresponds to the 21st century.
D	D	X	Returns a number from 1–7 indicating the day of the week. Sunday is counted as day 1.
DAY	Day dd-Mon-yyyy	X	Returns the full name of the weekday in a nine-character-wide field.
DY	Dy dd-Mon-yyyy	X	Returns the abbreviated name of the weekday.
DD	dd-Mon-yyyy		Returns the day of the month.
DDD	ddd yyyy		Returns the day of the year.
E	E		Returns the abbreviated name of the era. This can be used only with calendars that support eras, such as the Japanese Imperial calendar.
EE	EE		Returns the full name of the era.
HH	HH:MI	X	Returns the hour as a value from 1–12.
HH12	hh12:mi:ss		Returns the hour as a value from 1–12.
HH24	HH24:MI	X	Returns the hour as a value from 0–23.
IW	IW		Returns the week of the year as defined by the ISO standard.
IYYY IYY IY I	dd-Mon-IY dd-Mon-IYYY		Returns one or more digits of the ISO year. IYYY returns the full four-digit year. IY returns the last two digits of the year.
J	J	X	Returns a value corresponding to the number of days since 1-Jan-4712 BC.
MI	hh:mi:ss	X	Returns the minute value.

Element	Example	TO_DATE?	Description
MM	mm/dd/yy	X	Returns the month number.
MON	dd-Mon-yyyy	X	Returns the abbreviated name of the month.
MONTH	Month dd, yyyy	X	Returns the full name of the month in a nine-character field.
Q	Q		Returns a number corresponding to the quarter of the year. Jan–Mar is quarter 1, Apr–Jun is quarter 2, and so forth.
RM	RM	X	Returns the month number in Roman numerals.
RR	dd-Mon-rr	X	Interprets a two-digit year based on a sliding window. If the year number is less than 50, and the current year is greater than or equal to 50, then the year will be interpreted as belonging to the next century. For example, in 1999, a date such as 1-Jan-30 will be interpreted as 1-Jan-2030.
RRRR	dd-Mon-rrrr	X	Similar to RR, but also allows a four-digit year to be input. If a four-digit year is used, it is unchanged. If a two-digit year is used, the same rules apply as apply for RR.
SS	hh:mi:ss	X	Returns the seconds.
SSSSS	sssss	X	Returns the number of seconds past midnight.
WW	WW		Returns a number corresponding to the week of the year.
W	W		Returns a number corresponding to the week of the month.
Y,YYY	Mon dd, Y,YYY	X	Returns the year with a comma following the thousands digit.
YEAR SYEAR	Mon dd, YEAR		Returns the year spelled out in words. The *S* causes BC years to be prefixed with a negative sign.

Continued

Table B-2 *(continued)*			
Element	**Example**	**TO_DATE?**	**Description**
YYYY SYYY YYY YY Y	Mon dd, YYYY	X	Returns from one to four digits of the year. Use YYYY to see all four digits, use YY to see only the last two digits, and so forth. The S causes BC years to be prefixed by a negative sign.

In general, date format elements are not case-sensitive. However, when formatting dates for display, the case does matter when the element being formatted is a text element. Using the month name as an example, note the effect of case on the following results:

```
TO_CHAR(SYSDATE,'MONTH') = NOVEMBER
TO_CHAR(SYSDATE,'Month') = November
TO_CHAR(SYSDATE,'month') = november
```

When the entire word MONTH is capitalized, the resulting month name is formatted in all caps. Otherwise, the capitalization of the first letter of the format string determines whether the first character of the month name is capitalized. These same rules also apply to the following format elements: AD, AM, PM, BC, DAY, DY, MON, RM, and YEAR.

SQL's Built-in Functions

The remainder of this appendix lists SQL's functions in alphabetical order. The following example illustrates the notation used in the syntax diagrams:

```
SELECT [ALL|DISTINCT] {*|column}
FROM table_name[,table_name...];
```

Each syntax diagram is followed by a list describing each element, as follows:

SELECT	Words in capitals denote syntax, usually the function names.
column	Lowercase italics represent items that you must supply when you invoke the function.
[ALL|DISTINCT]	Square brackets denote an optional choice, with the choices delimited by a vertical line. In this example, you may choose ALL, DISTINCT, or nothing.

{* | *column* }   Curly brackets denote a mandatory choice, with the choices delimited by a vertical line. In this example, you have to choose between * or *column*.

table_name[,table_name...]   Repetitions are indicated by repeating the item between square brackets and adding an optional delimiter and three trailing dots at the end. In this example, specify one or more data sources, each delimited by a comma.

Note   SQL's aggregate functions are different in nature from the functions described in this appendix. The aggregate functions are described in Chapter 16, "Selecting Data with SQL," and are not described again here.

ABS

The ABS function returns the absolute value of a number. The absolute value represents the value with any negative sign removed. Following is its syntax:

    ABS(*number*)

Its argument is described as follows:

> *number*   The number for which you want the absolute value

The ABS function strips the sign off of a number, as shown in this example:

    ABS (5) = 5
    ABS (-5) = 5

The absolute value of both 5 and –5 is 5.

ACOS

The ACOS function returns the arc cosine of a number. The result is expressed in radians and will be between 0 and pi, inclusively. Following is its syntax:

    ACOS(*number*)

Its argument is described as follows:

> *number*   This must be a value between –1 and 1.

The following examples show the arc cosines of 1 and –1, respectively:

    ACOS (1) = 0
    ACOS (-1) = 3.1415927 (pi)

ADD_MONTHS

The ADD_MONTHS function adds a specified number of months to a date. The day of the month is usually left unchanged. However, if the starting date represents the last day of its month, then the result will be adjusted so that it also represents the last day of the month. Also, if the resulting month has fewer days than the starting month, then the day may be adjusted downwards to come up with a valid date. Following is its syntax:

```
ADD_MONTHS(date, months)
```

Its arguments are described as follows:

date	A date value.
months	The number of months to add. To subtract months, use a negative value.

The following examples illustrate the use of the ADD_MONTHS function:

```
ADD_MONTHS(TO_DATE('15-Nov-1961','dd-mon-yyyy'), 1)
    = '15-Dec-1961
ADD_MONTHS(TO_DATE('30-Nov-1961','dd-mon-yyyy'), 1)
    = '31-Dec-1961
ADD_MONTHS(TO_DATE('31-Jan-1999','dd-mon-yyyy'), 1)
    = '28-Feb-1999'
```

Note that in the third example, the day of the month had to be adjusted downwards from 31 to 28 because February 1999 has only 28 days. In the second example, the date was adjusted upwards from 30 to 31 because of the need to maintain the date equal to the last day of the month.

ASCII

The ASCII function returns the decimal representation of the first character of whatever string you pass to it. This may or may not be an actual ASCII value. If your database character set is seven-bit ASCII, then you'll get an ASCII value back. The value returned will correspond to the character set being used.

```
ASCII(string)
```

Its argument is described as follows:

string	A string, or more usually a single character

The following examples illustrate the use of the ASCII function:

```
ASCII('J') = 74
ASCII('Jeff') = 74
```

As you can see from the second example, if you pass in a multicharacter string, the ASCII function ignores all but the first character.

ASIN

The ASIN function returns the arc sine of a number. The result is expressed in radians and will range in value from –(pi/2) to (pi/2). Following is its syntax:

```
ASIN(number)
```

Its argument is described as follows:

> number   This must be a value between –1 and 1.

The arc sines of 1 and -1, respectively, are:

```
ASIN (1) = 1.57
ASIN (-1) = -1.57
```

ATAN

The ATAN function returns the arc tangent of a number. The result is expressed in radians and ranges between –(pi/2) and (pi/2). Following is its syntax:

```
ATAN(number)
```

Its argument is described as follows:

> number   This must be a value between –1 and 1.

The following examples provide the arc tangents of 1 and –1, respectively:

```
ATAN (1) = 0.7854
ATAN (-1) = -0.7854
```

ATAN2

The ATAN2 function returns the arc tangent of two numbers. The results are expressed in radians. Following is its syntax:

```
ATAN2(first, second)
```

Its arguments are described as follows:

> first   The first value
>
> second   The second value

`ATAN2(first, second)` is the equivalent of `ATAN(first/second)`.

The following examples provide the arc tangents of 1 and –1, respectively:

```
ATAN2 (1,.5)) = 1.107
ATAN (1/.5) = 1.107
```

BFILENAME

The `BFILENAME` function returns a `BFILE` locator that points to a physical file on disk. Following is its syntax:

```
BFILENAME(directory, filename)
```

Its arguments are described as follows:

directory	A string specifying the directory containing the file. This is a directory created using the `CREATE DIRECTORY` command. It is not an operating system directory.
filename	The name of the file in the directory that you want the `BFILE` to point to. The file doesn't need to exist for you to create the `BFILE` locator.

The following example illustrates the use of the `BFILENAME` function:

```
BFILENAME('gif_dir', 'book_photo.gif')
```

CEIL

The `CEIL` function takes a number as input, which could be a noninteger value, and returns the lowest valued integer greater than or equal to the input value. Following is its syntax:

```
CEIL(number)
```

Its argument is described as follows:

number	Any numeric value, including decimal values

The following examples illustrate the use of the `CEIL` function:

```
CEIL(5.1) = 6
CEIL(-5.1) = -5
```

Note the result of using `CEIL` on a negative value. The lowest valued integer greater than or equal to –5.1 is actually –5. Mathematically, that makes sense, but it may seem counterintuitive at first.

CHARTOROWID

The CHARTOROWID function converts a character string to a rowid type. Following is its syntax:

```
CHARTOROWID(string)
```

Its argument is described as follows:

> string **A string that evaluates to a valid** rowid

The following examples illustrate the use of the CHARTOROWID function:

```
SQL> SELECT ROWID FROM dual;

ROWID
------------------
AAAADCAABAAAAVUAAA

SQL> SELECT * FROM dual
  2  WHERE ROWID = CHARTOROWID('AAAADCAABAAAAVUAAA');

D
-
X
```

CHR

The CHR function returns the character associated with a specific numeric value according to the database's character set. For example, given an ASCII value, CHR could be used to return the corresponding character. Following is its syntax:

```
CHR(integer [USING NCHAR_CS])
```

Its arguments are described as follows:

integer	An integer value representing a character in the database's character set
USING NCHAR_CS	Causes the character to be determined based on the database's national character set

The following examples illustrate the use of the CHR function:

```
CHR(10) = a tab character
CHR(65) = 'A'
```

These examples assume an ASCII-based character set.

CONCAT

The CONCAT function takes two strings as input, combines them together into one string, and returns the result. Following is its syntax:

```
CONCAT(string_1, string_2)
```

Its arguments are described as follows:

string_1   The first string.

string_2   The second string. This will be concatenated onto the end of the first string.

The following example illustrates using the CONCAT function:

```
CONCAT('This is ', 'a test') = 'This is a test'
```

 Note   It's often easier to concatenate strings using the || operator: for example, 'This is ' || 'a test'.

CONVERT

The CONVERT function converts a character string from one character set to another. Following is its syntax:

```
CONVERT (string, dest_char_set[, source_char_set])
```

Its arguments are described as follows:

string   The string to convert.

dest_char_set   The destination character set.

source_char_set   The source character set. If omitted, this defaults to the database's character set.

The following examples illustrate the use of the CONVERT function:

```
CONVERT('Jonathan','WE8EBCDIC37C','US7ASCII')
CONVERT('Jonathan','WE8ROMAN8')
```

The first example converts from the US7ASCII character set. The second example converts from the database's character set.

COS

The COS function returns the cosine of an angle. The result is expressed in radians. Following is its syntax:

```
COS(angle)
```

Its argument is described as follows:

angle   The value of an angle, expressed in radians

The following examples illustrate the use of the COS function:

```
COS(90 * 3.14/180) = .000796
COS(0) = 1
```

Note   You can convert an angle from degrees to radians using the following formula: radians = degrees * pi/180.

COSH

The COSH function returns the hyperbolic cosine of an angle. Following is its syntax:

```
COSH(angle)
```

Its argument is described as follows:

angle   The value of an angle, expressed in radians

The following examples illustrate the use of the COSH function:

```
COSH(0) = 1
COSH(90*3.14/180) = 2.507
```

See the COS function for information on converting from degrees to radians.

DECODE

The DECODE function serves as an inline IF statement. It takes an input value, compares it to a list of value/result pairs, and returns the result corresponding to the input value. There is a provision for a default result in case none of the value/result pairs match. Unlike other SQL functions, the DECODE function can recognize and operate with null values. Following is its syntax:

```
DECODE(input_value,
       value, result[,
       value, result...][,
       default_result]);
```

Its arguments are described as follows:

input_value	The value that you want to evaluate. The DECODE function compares this value to the various value/result pairs to determine the result to return.
value	A value in a value/result pair. If the input value matches this, then the corresponding result is returned. The NULL keyword may be used for a value to specify a result for a null input.
result	The result in a value result pair.
default_result	A default result that is returned if none of the values in the value/result pairs matches the input value.

The following example shows how the DECODE flag can be used to supply human readable terms for the values in the BLOOD_TEST_FLAG column of the SEAPARK user's CHECKUP table:

```
SELECT checkup_type,
       DECODE(blood_test_flag,
              'Y','Yes',
              'N','No',
                NULL,'None',
              'Invalid')
  FROM checkup;
```

This SQL statement demonstrates all the basic functionality of DECODE. The input to the function is the BLOOD_TEST_FLAG column. If the value of that column is a 'Y', then the function will return 'Yes'. If the value is 'N', the function will return 'No'. If the value is NULL, the function will return 'None'. If none of these value/pairs is selected, the column is presumed to have an invalid value, and the word 'Invalid' will be returned.

The DECODE function can often be put to some creative uses in a SQL query. One technique is to turn what would otherwise be rows into columns. Consider the query in the following example:

```
SQL> SELECT TO_CHAR(TRUNC(BIRTH_DATE,'YEAR'),'YYYY'),
  2         COUNT(*)
  3  FROM AQUATIC_ANIMAL
  4  WHERE TO_CHAR(TRUNC(BIRTH_DATE,'YEAR'),'YYYY')
  5         IN ('1995','1996','1997')
  6  GROUP BY TO_CHAR(TRUNC(BIRTH_DATE,'YEAR'),'YYYY');

TO_C  COUNT(*)
----  --------
1995         1
1996         3
1997         1
```

This query tells you how many animals were born in the years 1995, 1996, and 1997. Each row in the query displays the count for a different year. What if, however, you really want those values displayed as three columns? You can make that happen through the creative application of DECODE, as shown in Listing B-1.

Listing B-1: A query using DECODE

```
SQL> SELECT SUM(
  2         DECODE(TO_CHAR(TRUNC(BIRTH_DATE,'YEAR'),'YYYY'),
  3                '1995',1,0)) born_1995,
  4         SUM(
  5         DECODE(TO_CHAR(TRUNC(BIRTH_DATE,'YEAR'),'YYYY'),
  6                '1996',1,0)) born_1996,
  7         SUM(
  8         DECODE(TO_CHAR(TRUNC(BIRTH_DATE,'YEAR'),'YYYY'),
  9                '1997',1,0)) born_1997
 10  FROM AQUATIC_ANIMAL
 11  WHERE TO_CHAR(TRUNC(BIRTH_DATE,'YEAR'),'YYYY')
 12        IN ('1995','1996','1997');

BORN_1995 BORN_1996 BORN_1997
--------- --------- ---------
        1         3         1
```

In this example, the BIRTH_DATE column is referenced three times to create three columns in the result set. The DECODE function is applied to each column in such a way as to filter the dates returned for one specific year. In the first column, for example, DECODE changes any 1995 dates to a 1 and any non-1995 dates to a 0. The SUM function then totals up the values to arrive at the number of animals born in 1995. The expressions in the other two columns perform the same process for the years 1996 and 1997.

DUMP

The DUMP function returns the internal representation of the data stored within a column or the data returned by an expression. The return value of DUMP is VARCHAR2. Following is its syntax:

```
DUMP(expression[, return_format[, start[, length]]])
```

Its arguments are described as follows:

expression The value that you want dumped.

return_format	Specifies the manner in which you want the data to be formatted. The following values are valid here: 8, use octal notation; 10, use decimal notation; 16, use hexadecimal notation; and 17, use single characters.
	Add 1,000 to any format code to also have the character set name returned. The default is to use decimal notation.
start	Specifies the starting point for the data to be returned. This is an optional argument. It can be useful for large columns that can't be dumped into the single 4,000-byte chunk allowed by a VARCHAR2 result.
length	Specifies the number of bytes to dump. This is an optional argument. By default, all data is dumped.

The following examples show the DUMP function being used to display the internal representation of the current date. The first example shows the entire date and uses decimal notation. The second example begins with the fourth byte and uses hexadecimal notation (decimal 24 = hexadecimal 18).

```
SQL> SELECT DUMP(SYSDATE) FROM dual;

DUMP(SYSDATE)
------------------------------------------
Typ=13 Len=8: 207,7,11,24,22,17,52,0

SQL> SELECT DUMP(SYSDATE,16,4) FROM dual;

DUMP(SYSDATE,16,4)
------------------------------------------
Typ=13 Len=8: 18,16,12,12,0
```

EMPTY_BLOB

The EMPTY_BLOB function returns an empty BLOB locator that can be used in an INSERT or UPDATE statement to initialize a BLOB column. Following is its syntax:

```
EMPTY_BLOB()
```

This function has no parameters. The following example shows EMPTY_BLOB being used to initialize a LOB column for a new row being inserted into a table:

```
INSERT INTO some_table
   (blob_column)
   VALUES (EMPTY_BLOB());
```

EMPTY_CLOB

The `EMPTY_CLOB` function performs the same function for CLOBs that `EMPTY_BLOB` does for BLOBs. It returns an empty `CLOB` locator that can be used in an `INSERT` or `UPDATE` statement to initialize a `CLOB` column. Following is its syntax:

```
EMPTY_CLOB()
```

This function has no parameters. The following example shows `EMPTY_CLOB` being used to initialize a `CLOB` column for a new row being inserted into a table:

```
INSERT INTO some_table
    (clob_column)
    VALUES (EMPTY_CLOB());
```

EXP

The `EXP` function returns the value of *e* raised to a specific power. In mathematics, *e* is used to represent a specific transcendental number (infinite number of decimal places) that takes the value $2.718...$, and forms the basis of natural logarithms. Following is its syntax:

```
EXP(exponent)
```

Its argument is described as follows:

> *exponent*   The power to which you want to raise *e*

The following examples illustrate the use of the `EXP` function:

```
EXP(1) = 2.7182818
EXP(3) = 20.085537 (2.7182818 * 2.7182818 * 2.7182818)
```

FLOOR

The `FLOOR` function takes a number as input, which could be a decimal number, and returns the largest integer less than or equal to the input value. The `FLOOR` function works similarly to `CEIL`, but in the opposite manner. Following is its syntax:

```
FLOOR(number)
```

Its argument is described as follows:

> *number*   Any number, including decimal values

The following examples illustrate the use of the FLOOR function:

```
FLOOR(5.1) = 5
FLOOR(-5.1) = -6
```

To understand how FLOOR and CEIL function when used against negative values, compare the result of FLOOR(-5.1) with the results of CEIL(-5.1).

GREATEST

The GREATEST function takes a list of values and returns the highest value in that list. You can use the GREATEST function with either numeric or character-string values. Following is its syntax:

```
GREATEST(value, value, value,...)
```

Its argument is described as follows:

value   A numeric or text value. Typically, you want all values to be the same datatype. If you mix datatypes, the value returned will match the datatype of the first parameter. All other parameters will be implicitly converted to that datatype as well.

The following examples illustrate how the GREATEST function operates:

```
GREATEST(1, 3, 9, 45, 93, 2, -100) = 93
GREATEST('Jenny', 'Jeff', 'Ashley') = 'Jenny'
GREATEST('11',101) = '11'
```

The third example illustrates what happens when you mix datatypes. Since the first datatype is a string, Oracle converts the numeric 1 to the string '1' to make the datatypes match. While the number 101 is greater than the number 11, the reverse is true when you convert both to strings. In that case, '11' is greater than '101' and is what the function returns.

Note   When used with text values, the return type is always VARCHAR2. That's true even if the input values are CHAR.

HEXTORAW

The HEXTORAW function converts a string of hexadecimal digits into a raw value. Following is its syntax:

```
HEXTORAW(string)
```

Its argument is described as follows:

string   A string of hexadecimal values

The examples shown in Listing B-2 illustrate using the HEXTORAW function:

Listing B-2: **HEXTORAW function examples**

```
SQL> CREATE TABLE xx (y raw(10));

Table created.

SQL> INSERT INTO xx VALUES (HEXTORAW('414243'));

1 row created.

SQL> SELECT DUMP(y) FROM xx;

DUMP(Y)
-------------------------------------------------
Typ=23 Len=3: 65,66,67
```

Notice that the values in the raw column are exactly what was specified in the call to HEXTORAW (decimal 65 = hexadecimal 41).

INITCAP

The INITCAP function takes a string and changes all the words in that string so that they start with an initial capital letter. Following is its syntax:

    INITCAP(*string*)

Its argument is described as follows:

string   Any VARCHAR2 or CHAR value

The following example illustrates using the INITCAP function:

    INITCAP('THIS is a test') = 'This Is A Test'

INSTR

The INSTR function tells you whether one string is contained inside another, and if so, where. Following is its syntax:

    INSTR(*string*, *substring*[, *start*[, *occurrence*]])

Its arguments are described as follows:

string	The string to search.
substring	The string that you are searching.
start	Specifies the character position from which you want to begin searching. The default is 1, which means that the search starts from the first character of the string. You can use negative values to specify the starting position based on the right end of the string instead of the left.
occurrence	Specifies the occurrence of the substring that you want to find. The default value is 1, which means that you want the first occurrence.

The INSTR function returns the index at which the substring was found. The following examples illustrate using the INSTR function:

```
INSTR('AAABAABA','B') = 4
INSTR('AAABAABA','B',1,2) = 7
```

In the second example, the occurrence parameter is 2, so the location of the second occurrence of 'B' is returned by the function.

INSTRB

The INSTRB function tells you whether one string is contained inside another, and, if so, where. The INSTRB function is the same as INSTR, except that the value it returns represents a byte index, not a character index. This difference has meaning only when a multibyte character set is being used. Following is its syntax:

```
INSTRB(string, substring[, start[, occurrence]])
```

Its arguments are described as follows:

string	The string to search.
substring	The string that you are searching for.
start	Specifies the character position from which you want to begin searching. The default is 1, which means that the search starts from the first character of the string. You can use negative values to specify the starting position based on the right end of the string instead of the left.
occurrence	Specifies the occurrence of the substring that you want to find. The default value is 1, which means that you want the first occurrence.

The `INSTRB` function returns the index at which the substring was found. The following examples illustrate using the `INSTRB` function:

```
INSTRB('AAABAABA','B') = 4
INSTRB('AAABAABA','B',1,2) = 7
```

In the second example, the occurrence parameter is 2, so the location of the second occurrence of `'B'` is returned by the function.

LAST_DAY

The `LAST_DAY` function takes a date as input and returns the last date of the corresponding month. Following is its syntax:

```
LAST_DAY(date)
```

Its argument is described as follows:

> *date*   A date value

The following examples illustrate using the `LAST_DAY` function:

```
LAST_DAY(TO_DATE('29-Dec-1988','dd-mon-yyyy'))
    = '31-Dec-1988
LAST_DAY(TO_DATE('1-Feb-2000','dd-mon-yyyy'))
    = '29-Feb-2000
```

LEAST

The `LEAST` function takes a list of values and returns the lowest value in that list. You can use the `LEAST` function with either numeric or character-string values. Following is its syntax:

```
LEAST(value, value, value,...)
```

Its argument is described as follows:

> *value*   A numeric or text value. Typically, you want all values to be the same datatype. If you mix datatypes, the value returned will match the datatype of the first parameter. All other parameters will be implicitly converted to that datatype as well.

The following examples illustrate the use of the `LEAST` function:

```
LEAST(1, 3, 9, 45, 93, 2, -100) = -100
LEAST('Jenny', 'Jeff', 'Ashley') = 'Ashley'
LEAST('110',12) = '110'
```

The third example illustrates what happens when you mix datatypes. Since the first datatype is a string, Oracle converts the numeric 1 to the string '1' to make the datatypes match. While the number 12 is less than the number 110, the reverse is true when you convert both to strings. In that case, '110' is less than '12' (based on the sort order), and is what the function returns.

Note   When used with text values, the return type is always VARCHAR2. That's true even if the input values are CHAR.

LENGTH

The LENGTH function returns the length of a string in terms of the number of characters that it contains. Following is its syntax:

```
LENGTH(string)
```

Its argument is described as follows:

> *string*   Any character-string value

The following examples illustrate the use of the LENGTH function:

```
LENGTH('This is short') = 13
LENGTH('This is a bit longer') = 20
```

LENGTHB

The LENGTHB function returns the length of a string in terms of the number of bytes that it contains. Except for when a multibyte character set is being used, LENGTHB will return the same values as LENGTH. Following is its syntax:

```
LENGTHB(string)
```

Its argument is described as follows:

> *string*   Any character-string value

The following examples illustrate the use of the LENGTHB function:

```
LENGTHB('This is short') = 13
LENGTHB('This is a bit longer') = 20
```

LN

The LN function returns the natural logarithm of a number. The natural logarithm of a number is the power to which *e* must be raised to yield that number as a result. Following is its syntax:

```
LN(number)
```

Its argument is described as follows:

> *number*   A numeric value that is greater than 0

The following examples illustrate how LN functions, and also show its relationship to EXP:

```
LN(10) = 2.3025851
EXP(2.3025851) = 10
```

As you can see, feeding the result of LN through the EXP function should give you back your original value.

LOG

The LOG function returns the logarithm (not natural) of a number. Following is its syntax:

```
LOG(logbase, number)
```

Its arguments are described as follows:

> *logbase*   Any positive number other than 0 or 1
>
> *number*   Any positive number

The following examples illustrate the use of the LOG function:

```
LOG(10,100) = 2
LOG(EXP(1),10) = 2.3025851 = LN(10)
```

The value for log base 10 of 100 is 2 because 10^2 equals 100. Note that LOG(e, x) is the equivalent of LN(x). You can use EXP(1) to get the value of *e*, as shown in the second example.

LOWER

The LOWER function returns the lowercase version of a string. Following is its syntax:

```
LOWER(string)
```

Its argument is described as follows:

string   Any VARCHAR2 or CHAR value

The following example illustrates the use of the LOWER function:

```
LOWER('THIS IS a Test') = 'this is a test'
```

LPAD

The LPAD function pads a string on the left. Following is its syntax:

```
LPAD(string, numchars[, padding])
```

Its arguments are described as follows:

string   Any VARCHAR2 or CHAR value.

numchars   The number of characters that you want in the resulting string.

padding   The character sequence that you want to use for the padding. This is optional and defaults to a single space.

The following examples illustrate the use of the LPAD function:

```
LPAD('Jenny',10) = '     Jenny' (5 leading spaces)
LPAD('Jenny',10,'*') = '*****Jenny'
LPAD('Jenny',10,'*!') = '*!*!*Jenny'
```

LTRIM

The LTRIM function removes leading characters, usually leading spaces, from a string. Following is its syntax:

```
LTRIM(string[, trimchars])
```

Its arguments are described as follows:

string   Any VARCHAR2 or CHAR value

trimchars A string containing the characters to remove

The following examples illustrate the use of the LTRIM function:

```
LTRIM('     Jeff') = 'Jeff' (leading spaces removed)
LTRIM('*****Jeff','*') = 'Jeff'
LTRIM('*!*!*Jeff','*!') = 'Jeff'
```

Note in the last example that all '*' and all '!' characters are removed. That's because both of those characters are listed in the *trimchars* string.

MOD

The MOD function returns the remainder of one value divided by another. Following is its syntax:

```
MOD(number, divisor)
```

Its arguments are described as follows:

number　　Any numeric value.

divisor　　Any numeric value. The MOD function will compute the remainder of number/divisor.

The following examples illustrate the use of the MOD function:

```
MOD(14,12) = 2 (1400 hours = 2:00 O'Clock)
MOD(10,10) = 0
MOD(10,0) = 10
```

Note that if the divisor is 0, the original number is returned.

MONTHS_BETWEEN

The MONTHS_BETWEEN function returns the number of months between two dates. Following is its syntax:

```
MONTHS_BETWEEN(date_1, date_2)
```

Its arguments are described as follows:

date_1　　A date value

date_2　　Another date value

If both *date_1* and *date_2* represent the same day of the month, or if they both represent the last day of the month, then MONTHS_BETWEEN will return an integer. Otherwise, the function will return a fractional value. Also, if *date_1* is less than *date_2,* the value returned will be negative.

The following examples illustrate the use of the MONTHS_BETWEEN function:

```
MONTHS_BETWEEN(TO_DATE('29-Dec-1999','dd-mon-yyyy'),
               TO_DATE('29-Dec-1988','dd-mon-yyyy'))
  = 132
MONTHS_BETWEEN(TO_DATE('29-Dec-1999','dd-mon-yyyy'),
               TO_DATE('24-Nov-1988','dd-mon-yyyy'))
  = 133.16129
```

In the first example, both dates represent the 29th of the month, so the result is an integer. In the second example, because the dates represent different days of the month, a fractional value, based on 31 days in the month, is returned.

NEW_TIME

The NEW_TIME function converts a date/time value between time zones. Following is its syntax:

```
NEW_TIME(date, oldzone, newzone)
```

Its arguments are described as follows:

date	A date value. In Oracle, all dates have a time-of-day component in addition to the date itself.
oldzone	A character string representing a time zone. Valid time zones are shown in Table B-3. The date value is presumed to be in this time zone.
newzone	Also a character string representing a time zone. The value of date is converted from the old time zone to this new time zone.

Table B-3
Time Zone Identifiers

Identifier	Time Zone
AST	Atlantic Standard Time
ADT	Atlantic Daylight Time
BST	Bering Standard Time
BDT	Bering Daylight Time
CST	Central Standard Time
CDT	Central Daylight Time
EST	Eastern Standard Time
EDT	Eastern Daylight Time

Identifier	Time Zone
GMT	Greenwich Mean Time
HST	Alaska-Hawaii Standard Time
HDT	Alaska-Hawaii Daylight Time
MST	Mountain Standard Time
MDT	Mountain Daylight Time
NST	Newfoundland Standard Time
PST	Pacific Standard Time
PDT	Pacific Daylight Time
YST	Yukon Standard Time
YDT	Yukon Daylight Time

The following example illustrates the use of the NEW_DAY function:

```
NEW_TIME(TO_DATE('25-Dec-1999 8:00','dd-mon-yyyy HH:MI')
        ,'EST','PST') = '25-DEC-1999 05:00'
```

NEXT_DAY

The NEXT_DAY function takes a date, determines the next occurrence of a specified day of the week from that date, and returns the result. Following is its syntax:

```
NEXT_DAY(date, weekday)
```

Its arguments are described as follows:

date   A date value.

weekday   A character string specifying the name of a day (for example, 'Monday', 'Tuesday', 'Wed'). You can use either the full name or an abbreviation, but whatever you use must be valid based on the date language setting for your session.

The following examples illustrate the use of the NEXT_DAY function:

```
NEXT_DAY(TO_DATE('24-Nov-1999','dd-mon-yyyy'),'FRIDAY')
    = '26-Nov-1999'
NEXT_DAY(TO_DATE('24-Nov-1999','dd-mon-yyyy'),'WED')
    = '01-Dec-1999'
```

Note that in the second example, the date 24-Nov-1999 falls on a Wednesday. However, the NEXT_DAY function returns the date of the subsequent Wednesday, which is 1-Dec-1999.

NLS_CHARSET_DECL_LEN

The `NLS_CHARSET_DECL_LEN` function, given a size in bytes, returns the width in terms of characters for an `NCHAR` or `NVARCHAR2` column. Following is its syntax:

```
NLS_CHARSET_DECL_LEN(bytecnt, csid)
```

Its arguments are described as follows:

`bytecnt`   The size of the column in bytes

`csid`   The NLS character set ID

The following example illustrates the use of the `NLS_CHARSET_DECL_LEN` function:

```
NLS_CHARSET_DECL_LEN(200, 1) = 200
```

NLS_CHARSET_ID

The `NLS_CHARSET_ID` function returns the ID number corresponding to a specific NLS character set name. Following is its syntax:

```
NLS_CHARSET_ID(charset_name)
```

Its argument is described as follows:

`charset_name`   The name of an NLS character set

The following example illustrates the use of the `NLS_CHARSET_ID` function:

```
NLS_CHARSET_ID('US7ASCII') = 1
```

NLS_CHARSET_NAME

The `NLS_CHARSET_NAME` function does the reverse of `NLS_CHARSET_ID`. It returns the character set name corresponding to a specified ID number. Following is its syntax:

```
NLS_CHARSET_NAME(charset_id)
```

Its argument is described as follows:

`charset_id`   A character set ID number

The following example illustrates the use of the `NLS_CHARSET_ID` function:

```
NLS_CHARSET_NAME(1) = 'US7ASCII'
```

NLS_INITCAP

The NLS_INITCAP function works like INITCAP, but it is designed for use with national character set strings. Following is its syntax:

```
NLS_INITCAP(string[, 'NLS_SORT=sort_seq_name'])
```

Its arguments are described as follows:

string	Any VARCHAR2, CHAR, NVARCHAR2, or NCHAR value.
sort_seq_name	The name of a linguistic sort sequence. The sort sequence specifies the capitalization rules for the language being used. This is an optional argument. If omitted, the default sort sequence for your session is used. You may also specify the keyword BINARY.

The following example illustrates the use of the NLS_INITCAP function:

```
NLS_INITCAP('chocolate','NLS_SORT=XSPANISH) = 'Chocolate'
```

NLS_LOWER

The NLS_LOWER function works like LOWER, but it is designed for use with national character set strings. Following is its syntax:

```
NLS_LOWER(string[, 'NLS_SORT=sort_seq_name'])
```

Its arguments are described as follows:

string	Any VARCHAR2, CHAR, NVARCHAR2, or NCHAR value
sort_seq_name	The name of a linguistic sort sequence or the keyword BINARY

The following example illustrates the use of the NLS_LOWER function:

```
NLS_LOWER('CHOCOLATE','NLS_SORT=XSPANISH') = 'chocolate'
```

NLS_UPPER

The NLS_UPPER function works like UPPER, but it is designed for use with national character set strings. Following is its syntax:

```
NLS_UPPER(string[, 'NLS_SORT=sort_seq_name'])
```

Its arguments are described as follows:

string	Any VARCHAR2, CHAR, NVARCHAR2, or NCHAR value
sort_seq_name	The name of a linguistic sort sequence or the keyword BINARY

The following example illustrates the use of the NLS_UPPER function:

```
NLS_LOWER('chocolate','NLS_SORT=XSPANISH') = 'CHOCOLATE'
```

NLSSORT

The NLSSORT function returns the string of bytes used to represent a value when that value is being sorted using a linguistic sort sequence. Following is its syntax:

```
NLSSORT(string[, 'NLS_SORT=sort_seq_name'])
```

Its arguments are described as follows:

string	Any character-string value.
sort_seq_name	The name of a linguistic sort sequence or the keyword BINARY. If you specify BINARY, the function returns the byte values for string.

The following examples illustrate the use of the NLSSORT function:

```
NLSSORT ('chocolate','NLS_SORT=XSPANISH')
   = '205A1E5A4B146E280002020202020202020200'
NLSSORT ('chocolate','NLS_SORT=XSPANISH')
   = '43686F636F6C61746500'
```

NVL

The NVL function takes two values as an argument. The second value represents an alternative to the first and is returned if the first value is null. Following is its syntax:

```
NVL(value, alternative)
```

Its arguments are described as follows:

value	A value, which may be null. This value is returned by the function if it isn't null.
alternative	The value to be returned in the event that the value is null.

The following example shows how NVL may be used to supply an alternate value for a database column in the event that the column contains a null value:

```
SELECT emp_id, NVL(emp_name,'Name Missing!'
FROM emp_table;
```

In this example, if an employee has a name, then that name will be returned by the NVL function. However, if an employee's name is null, then the text 'Name Missing!' will be returned instead.

POWER

The POWER function returns the result of raising a number to a specified power. Following is its syntax:

```
POWER(number, power)
```

Its arguments are described as follows:

number	Any numeric value.
power	The power to which you want *number* to be raised. The result of the function is number^{power}. If *number* is negative, *power* must be an integer. Otherwise, *power* may be any value.

The following examples illustrate the use of the POWER function:

```
POWER(10,2) = 100 (10 * 10)
POWER(10,3) = 1000 (10 * 10 * 10)
POWER(-10,3) = -1000
```

RAWTOHEX

The RAWTOHEX function converts a raw value to a string of hexadecimal values. Following is its syntax:

```
RAWTOHEX(raw_value)
```

Its argument is described as follows:

raw_value	A value of type RAW

The examples shown in Listing B-3 illustrate the use of the RAWTOHEX function:

Listing B-3: RAWTOHEX function examples

```
SQL> CREATE TABLE xx (y raw(10));

Table created.

SQL> INSERT INTO xx VALUES (HEXTORAW('414243'));

1 row created.

SQL> SELECT RAWTOHEX(y) FROM xx;

RAWTOHEX(Y)
--------------------
414243
```

REPLACE

The REPLACE function searches a string for a specified substring and replaces that substring with another. Following is its syntax:

```
REPLACE(string, substring[,replace_string])
```

Its arguments are described as follows:

string	The string to search.
substring	The substring to search for. All occurrences of this will be replaced by the replacement string.
replace_string	The replacement string. This is an optional argument. If it's omitted, all occurrences of substring are deleted.

The following examples illustrate the use of the REPLACE function:

```
REPLACE('This is a test','is','was') = 'Thwas was a test'
REPLACE('This is a test','is') = 'Th  a test'
```

ROUND (for dates)

The ROUND function rounds a date value to a specified element. Following is its syntax:

```
ROUND(date[, fmt])
```

Its arguments are described as follows:

date	A date value.
fmt	One of the date format elements listed in Table B-2. The date will be rounded to the element specified by this format. If you omit this argument, the date will be rounded to the nearest day.

The following examples illustrate the use of the ROUND function for dates:

```
ROUND(TO_DATE('24-Nov-1999 08:00 pm','dd-mon-yyyy hh:mi am'))
   = '25-Nov-1999 12:00:00 am'
ROUND(TO_DATE('24-Nov-1999 08:37 am','dd-mon-yyyy hh:mi am')
      ,'hh')
   = ' 24-Nov-1999 09:00:00 am'
```

Note that the rounding may result in date changes. In the first example, because 8:00 PM is actually closer to the next day, the rounded result is the 25th, not the 24th.

ROUND (for numbers)

The ROUND function is used to round off a value to a specific number of decimal points. Following is its syntax:

```
ROUND(value, places)
```

Its arguments are described as follows:

value	The value that you want to round.
places	The number of decimal places that you want in the result. This must be an integer, but it can be a negative integer. If negative, the number is actually rounded to the left of the decimal point.

The following examples illustrate the use of the ROUND function for numbers:

```
ROUND(89.985,2) = 89.99 (Note that .005 is rounded up.)
ROUND(89.985,-1) = 90
ROUND(89.985,-2) = 100
```

ROWIDTOCHAR

The ROWIDTOCHAR function converts a ROWID value to a character string. Following is its syntax:

```
CHARTOROWID(rowid)
```

Its argument is described as follows:

> rowid   A value of type ROWID

The following example illustrates the use of the ROWIDTOCHAR function:

```
SQL> SELECT ROWIDTOCHAR(ROWID) FROM dual;

ROWIDTOCHAR(ROWID)
------------------
AAAADCAABAAAAVUAAA
```

RPAD

The RPAD function pads a string on the right. Following is its syntax:

```
RPAD(string, numchars[, padding])
```

Its arguments are described as follows:

> string   Any VARCHAR2 or CHAR value.
>
> numchars   The number of characters that you want in the resulting string.
>
> padding   The character sequence that you want to use for the padding. This is optional and defaults to a single space.

The following examples illustrate the use of the RPAD function:

```
RPAD('Jenny',10) = 'Jenny     ' (5 trailing spaces)
RPAD('Jenny',10,'*') = 'Jenny*****'
RPAD('Jenny',10,'*!') = 'Jenny*!*!*'
```

RTRIM

The RTRIM function removes trailing characters, usually leading spaces, from a string. Following is its syntax:

```
RTRIM(string[, trimchars])
```

Its arguments are described as follows:

> string   Any VARCHAR2 or CHAR value
>
> trimchars   A string containing the characters to remove

The following examples illustrate the use of the RTRIM function:

```
RTRIM('Jeff    ') = 'Jeff' (trailing spaces removed)
```

```
RTRIM('Jeff*****','*') = 'Jeff'
RTRIM('Jeff*!*!*','*!') = 'Jeff'
```

Note in the last example that all '*' and all '!' characters were removed because both of those characters are listed in the *trimchars* string.

SIGN

The SIGN function returns an integer representation of a number's sign. The following values are returned: –1, the number is negative; 0, the number is zero; or 1, the number is positive. Following is its syntax:

```
SIGN(value)
```

Its argument is described as follows:

> *value*   The input value, for which you want to know the sign

The following examples illustrate the use of the SIGN function:

```
SIGN(-100) = -1
SIGN(0) = 0
SIGN(100) = 1
```

You can use the SIGN function together with DECODE to specify different expressions to be evaluated depending on whether a value is positive, negative, or zero.

SIN

The SIN function returns the sine of an angle. Following is its syntax:

```
SIN(angle)
```

Its argument is described as follows:

> *angle*   The angle for which you want to know the sine. This must be expressed in radians. See the description of the COS function for information in converting from degrees to radians.

The following examples illustrate the use of the SIN function:

```
SIN(90*3.1415926/180) = 1
```

```
SIN(0) = 0
```

SOUNDEX

The SOUNDEX function returns a phonetic representation of a string according to the following rules, which are performed in the following order:

1. The first letter of the string is retained.

2. All of the following letters are removed: a, e, h, i, o, u, w, and y.

3. Any letters remaining after the first character are assigned one-digit values as follows:

```
b, f, p, v = 1
c, g, j, k, q, s, x, z = 2
d, t = 3
l = 4
m, n = 5
r = 6
```

4. The result is truncated to a four-digit number.

Following is its syntax:

```
SOUNDEX(string)
```

Its argument is described as follows:

    string   Any character-string value

The following examples illustrate the use of the RTRIM function:

```
SOUNDEX('Gennick') = 520
SOUNDEX('Genik') = 520
SOUNDEX('Genyk') = 520
```

SQRT

The SQRT function returns the square root of a number. A square root multiplied by itself yields the original number. Following is its syntax:

```
SQRT(number)
```

Its argument is described as follows:

    number   The number for which you want to know the square root. This cannot be a negative value.

The following examples illustrate the use of the SQRT function:

```
SQRT(100) = 10 (because 10 * 10 = 100)
SQRT(10) = 3.1622777
```

SUBSTR

The SUBSTR function returns a specified portion of a string. Following is its syntax:

```
SUBSTR(string, start[, length])
```

Its arguments are described as follows:

string   Any character string.

start   The index of the first character to extract from the string. Indexing begins with 1. The first character of any string is always counted as 1. This value can be negative. If it's negative, then it is treated as an offset from the right edge of the string.

length   The number of characters to extract. This is an optional argument. If you omit it, you get all the characters beginning from start until the end of the string is reached.

The following examples illustrate the use of the SUBSTR function:

```
SUBSTR('JennyJeffJonathan',6,4) = 'Jeff'
SUBSTR('JennyJeffJonathan',-12,4) = 'Jeff'
SUBSTR('JennyJeffJonathan',-8) = 'Jonathan'
```

SUBSTRB

The SUBSTRB function returns a portion of a string. The SUBSTRB function is almost identical to SUBSTR, but the start and length arguments refer to bytes, not characters. This difference is apparent only when a multibyte character set is being used. Following is its syntax:

```
SUBSTRB(string, start[, length])
```

Its arguments are described as follows:

string   Any character string.

start   The index of the first character to extract from the string. Indexing begins with 1. The first character of any string is always counted as 1. This value can be negative. If it's negative, then it is treated as an offset from the right edge of the string.

length   The number of characters to extract. This is an optional argument. If you omit it, you get all the characters beginning from start until the end of the string is reached.

The following examples illustrate the use of the SUBSTR function:

```
SUBSTRB('JennyJeffJonathan',6,4) = 'Jeff'
SUBSTRB('JennyJeffJonathan',-12,4) = 'Jeff'
```

```
SUBSTRB('JennyJeffJonathan',-8) = 'Jonathan'
```

SYS_CONTEXT

The SYS_CONTEXT function returns the value of an attribute in an application context namespace. Following is its syntax:

```
SYS_CONTEXT(namespace, attribute)
```

Its arguments are described as follows:

namespace	A character string containing the name of a namespace that has been created using the CREATE CONTEXT command. The default namespace of USERENV may also be specified.
attribute	A character string containing the name of an attribute in the namespace. The value of that attribute becomes the return value for this function. Table B-4 lists predefined attributes that are available in the USERENV namespace.

Table B-4
Predefined Attributes in the USERENV Namespace

Attribute Name	Description
NLS_TERRITORY	The current NLS territory name.
NLS_CURRENCY	The current NLS currency indicator.
NLS_CALENDAR	The current NLS calendar name.
NLS_DATE_FORMAT	The current NLS date format.
NLS_DATE_LANGUAGE	The language currently being used for days of the week.
NLS_SORT	The sort base.
SESSION_USER	The name that the current user logged on with.
CURRENT_USER	The current user name. This can change; if a user invokes a stored procedure written by another user, the current username changes to the stored code owner while that code is being executed.
CURRENT_SCHEMA	The current schema name, which usually matches the current username.
SESSION_USERID	The ID number of the session user.
CURRENT_USERID	The ID number of the current user.
CURRENT_SCHEMAID	The ID number of the current schema.

Attribute Name	Description
IP_ADDRESS	The user's IP address. This is valid only if the user is connecting via TCP/IP.

The examples shown in Listing B-4 illustrate the use of the SYS_CONTEXT function:

Listing B-4: **SYS_CONTEXT function examples**

```
SQL> SELECT SYS_CONTEXT('USERENV', 'SESSION_USER')
  2  FROM DUAL;

SYS_CONTEXT('USERENV','SESSION_USER')
--------------------------------------------------
SEAPARK

SQL> SELECT SYS_CONTEXT('USERENV', 'NLS_TERRITORY')
  2  FROM DUAL;

SYS_CONTEXT('USERENV','NLS_TERRITORY')
--------------------------------------------------
AMERICA
```

Your results, of course, will vary from these depending on the settings for your system and your logon username.

SYS_GUID

The SYS_GUID function returns a 16-byte globally unique identifier. The return type is RAW. On most platforms, the value consists of a host identifier, a process or thread identifier, and a sequence number. Following is its syntax:

```
SYS_GUID()
```

The SYS_GUID() function takes no parameters. However, the empty parentheses must be included when invoking the function. The following example illustrates the use of the SYS_GUID() function:

```
SQL> SELECT SYS_GUID() FROM DUAL;

SYS_GUID()
--------------------------------
A3B7D624A27111D38137005004AD2DB6
```

In this example, the value is converted to a string of hexadecimal numbers. Every two characters represent one hexadecimal value, so 16 bytes are displayed as 32 characters.

SYSDATE

The SYSDATE function returns the current date and time resolved down to the second. Following is its syntax:

```
SYSDATE
```

The SYSDATE function takes no parameters. The following example illustrates the use of the SYSDATE function:

```
SQL> SELECT SYSDATE FROM DUAL;

SYSDATE
--------------------
24-Nov-1999 06:45:00 pm
```

Your results, of course, will vary from these depending on when you invoke the function.

TAN

The TAN function returns the tangent of an angle. Following is its syntax:

```
TAN(angle)
```

Its argument is described as follows:

angle   An angle, expressed in radians. See the description of the COS function for information on converting from degrees to radians.

The following examples illustrate the use of the TAN function:

```
TAN(0) = 0
TAN(225*3.1415926535/180) = 1
```

TANH

The TANH function returns the hyperbolic tangent of an angle. Following is its syntax:

```
TANH(angle)
```

Its argument is described as follows:

angle   An angle, expressed in radians. See the description of the COS
         function for information on converting from degrees to radians.

The following examples illustrate the use of the TANH function:

```
TANH(0) = 0
TANH(225*3.1415926535/180) = .99922389
```

TO_CHAR (for dates)

The TO_CHAR function for dates converts a date value to a character string.
Following is its syntax:

```
TO_CHAR(date[, fmt[, 'NLS_DATE_LANGUAGE=language']])
```

Its arguments are described as follows:

date   A value of type DATE.

fmt   A date format string composed of elements found in Table B-2.
            This controls the character representation of the date.

language   The language to use. This can affect the spelling used for days
            of the week and months.

The examples shown in Listing B-5 illustrate the use of the TO_CHAR function for dates:

Listing B-5: **TO_CHAR function examples**

```
SQL> SELECT TO_CHAR(SYSDATE,'dd-Mon-yyyy')
  2  FROM dual;

TO_CHAR(SYS
-----------
24-Nov-1999

SQL> SELECT
  2     TO_CHAR(SYSDATE,'Month','NLS_DATE_LANGUAGE=Spanish')
  3  FROM dual;

TO_CHAR(SY
----------
Noviembre
```

TO_CHAR (for numbers)

The TO_CHAR function for numbers converts a number value to a character string. Following is its syntax:

```
TO_CHAR(number[, fmt[, 'nlsparams']])
```

Its arguments are described as follows:

number	A numeric value.
fmt	A number format string composed of elements found in Table B-1. This controls the character representation of the number.
nlsparams	The language characteristics of the number. This parameter is a character string consisting of one or more of the following: NLS_NUMERIC_CHARACTERS = ''dg'', NLS_CURRENCY = ''currchar'', and NLS_TERRITORY=territory.

The values d and g represent the decimal point character and the group separator (a comma in the U.S.), respectively. The currchar value (a dollar-sign ($) in the U.S.) is used to denote monetary values. Both of these values must be quoted strings within quoted strings, hence the doubled-up single quotes. |

The following examples illustrate the use of the TO_CHAR function for numbers:

```
TO_CHAR(123.45) = '123.45'
TO_CHAR(123456.78,'$999,999.99') = '$123,456.78'
TO_CHAR(123456.78,'L999G999D99',
        'NLS_NUMERIC_CHARACTERS='',.'' NLS_CURRENCY=''!''')
   = '!123.456,78'
```

Note that for the NLS parameters to have any effect, you must use L, G, and D for the currency symbol, group separator, and decimal, respectively.

TO_DATE

The TO_DATE function converts a character-string value to a date. Following is its syntax:

```
TO_DATE(string[, fmt[, 'NLS_DATE_LANGUAGE=language']])
```

Its arguments are described as follows:

string	The character string that you want to convert.
fmt	A date format string composed of elements found in Table B-2. This controls the way in which the character string is interpreted. This is an optional argument. If omitted, the default date format for your database will be used.

language   The language to use. This can affect the spelling used for days of the week and months. This is an optional argument.

The following examples illustrate the use of the TO_DATE function. The first TO_DATE function interprets the date as 8-Nov-1915:

```
TO_DATE('11/08/1915','MM/DD/YY')
```

This next example interprets the date as 11-Nov-1915:

```
TO_DATE('11/08/1915','DD/MM/YY')
```

This last example interprets the date as 11-Nov-1915:

```
TO_DATE('11-Nov-1915,'DD-MON-YYYY')
```

TO_LOB

The TO_LOB function converts a value of type LONG or LONG RAW to one of the following: CLOB, BLOB, or NCLOB. You can use this function only in the subquery of an INSERT statement when selecting LONG values to be inserted into LOB columns. Following is its syntax:

```
TO_LOB(long_value)
```

Its argument is described as follows:

long_value   A value of type LONG or LONG RAW. The LONG type values are converted to CLOB or NCLOB, depending on the type of the destination column. The LONG RAW type values are converted to BLOBs.

The following example illustrates the use of the TO_LOB function:

```
INSERT INTO new_table (clob_value)
   SELECT TO_LOB(long_value)
   FROM old_table;
```

TO_MULTI_BYTE

The TO_MULTI_BYTE function is useful only where multibyte character sets are being used, and it converts all the singlebyte characters in a string to their corresponding multibyte characters. Any singlebyte characters that have no corresponding multibyte characters are left as they are. Following is its syntax:

```
TO_MULTI_BYTE(string)
```

Its argument is described as follows:

string   The character string that you want to convert

The following example illustrates the use of the TO_MULTI_BYTE function:

```
multibyte_string := TO_SINGLE_BYTE(singlebyte_string);
```

TO_NUMBER

The TO_NUMBER function converts a character string to a number. Following is its syntax:

```
TO_NUMBER(string[, fmt[, 'nlsparams']])
```

Its arguments are described as follows:

string   The character string that you want to convert

fmt   A number format string composed of elements found in Table B-1. This controls the way in which the character string is interpreted.

nlsparams   The language characteristics of the number. This parameter is a character string consisting of one or more of the following: NLS_NUMERIC_CHARACTERS = ''dg'', NLS_CURRENCY = ''currchar'', or NLS_TERRITORY=territory.

The values d and g represent the decimal-point character and the group separator (a comma in the U.S.), respectively. The currchar value (a dollar sign ($) in the U.S.) is used to denote monetary values. Both of these values must be quoted strings within quoted strings, hence the doubled-up single quotes.

The following examples illustrate the use of the TO_NUMBER function. The first example interprets the number as 123.45:

```
TO_NUMBER('123.45')
```

This next example interprets the number as 123,456.78:

```
TO_NUMBER('$123,456.78', '$999,999.99')
```

TO_SINGLE_BYTE

The TO_SINGLE_BYTE function is useful only where multibyte character sets are being used, and it converts all the multibyte characters in a string to their corresponding singlebyte equivalents. Any multibyte characters that have no corresponding singlebyte characters are left as they are. Following is its syntax:

```
TO_SINGLE_BYTE(string)
```

Its argument is described as follows:

string   The character string that you want to convert

The following example illustrates the use of the TO_SINGLE_BYTE function:

```
singlebyte_string := TO_SINGLE_BYTE(multibyte_string);
```

TRANSLATE

The TRANSLATE function allows you to translate one set of characters into another. Following is its syntax:

```
TRANSLATE(string, charset1, charset2)
```

Its arguments are described as follows:

string   Any character string

charset1   A set of characters that you want to translate

charset2   A set of new characters that correspond positionally to the characters in charset1

The TRANSLATE function scans the input string, finds characters that occur in *charset1,* and replaces each of those with a corresponding character from *charset2.*

The following examples illustrate the use of the TRANSLATE function:

```
TRANSLATE('this is a code',
          'abcdefghijklmnopqrstuvwxyz',
          'zyxwvutsrqponmlkjihgfedcba') = 'gsrh rh z xlwv'
TRANSLATE('abcde','abc','xyz') = 'xyzde'
TRANSLATE('abcde','abc','xy') = 'xyde'
```

Notice from the third example that any characters in *charset1* that don't have corresponding values in *charset2* are deleted.

TRANSLATE USING

The TRANSLATE USING function translates strings between the database character set and the national character set. Following is its syntax:

```
TRANSLATE(string USING {CHAR_CS|NCHAR_CS})
```

Its arguments are described as follows:

string   The string to be translated.

USING CHAR_CS   Converts the string into the database character set. In this case, the function returns a VARCHAR2 value.

USING NCHAR_CS   Converts the string into the national character set. In this case, the function returns an NVARCHAR2 value.

The following examples illustrate the use of the TRANSLATE USING function:

```
TRANSLATE(nvarchar2_string USING CHAR_CS)
TRANSLATE(varchar2_string USING NCHAR_CS)
```

TRIM

The TRIM function removes leading and/or trailing characters from a string. Following is its syntax:

```
TRIM([LEADING|TRAILING|BOTH] [trimchar FROM] string)
```

Its arguments are described as follows:

LEADING   Specifies that only leading characters are trimmed.

TRAILING   Specifies that only trailing characters are trimmed.

BOTH   Specifies that both leading and trailing characters are trimmed. This is the default behavior.

string   Any character string.

trimchar   An optional argument that specifies the character that you want to trim. This defaults to a space.

The following examples illustrate using the TRIM function:

```
TRIM('  Ashley  ') = 'Ashley'
TRIM(LEADING '*' FROM '***Ashley***') = 'Ashley***'
```

TRUNC (for dates)

The TRUNC function truncates a date value to a specified element. Following is its syntax:

```
TRUNC(date[, fmt])
```

Its arguments are as follows:

date   A date value.

fmt   One of the date format elements listed in Table B-2. The date will be truncated to the element specified by this format. If you omit this argument, the date will be truncated to the nearest day.

The following examples illustrate the use of the TRUNC function for dates:

```
TRUNC(TO_DATE('24-Nov-1999 08:00 pm','dd-mon-yyyy hh:mi am'))
   = '24-Nov-1999 12:00:00 am'

TRUNC(TO_DATE('24-Nov-1999 08:37 am','dd-mon-yyyy hh:mi am')
   ,'hh')
   = ' 24-Nov-1999 08:00:00 am'
```

Note   Compare the results of the TRUNC function with those shown for the ROUND function.

TRUNC (for numbers)

The TRUNC function truncates a number to a specific number of decimal places. The TRUNC function works similarly to ROUND, but instead of rounding up or down, unwanted decimals are simply chopped off. Following is its syntax:

```
TRUNC(number[,decimals])
```

Its arguments are described as follows:

number   The number that you want to truncate.

decimals   The number of decimal places that you want in the final result. This is an optional argument. If omitted, all decimal places are removed from the number.

The following examples illustrate the use of the TRUNC function for numbers:

```
TRUNC(89.985, 2) = 89.98
TRUNC(89.985) = 89
TRUNC(89.985,-1) = 80
```

Notice that a negative value for the decimals argument results in digits to the left of the decimal point being replaced by zeros.

UID

The UID function returns an integer that is unique to the current database user. Following is its syntax:

```
UID
```

The UID function takes no parameters. The following example illustrates the use of the UID function:

```
SQL> SELECT UID FROM dual;

      UID
---------
        5
```

This value comes from the USER# column in the V$SESSION view.

UPPER

The UPPER function returns the uppercase version of a string. Following is its syntax:

```
UPPER(string)
```

Its argument is described as follows:

> *string*   Any VARCHAR2 or CHAR value

The following example illustrates the use of the UPPER function:

```
UPPER('THIS IS a Test') = 'THIS IS A TEST'
```

USER

The USER function returns the name of the current user. Following is its syntax:

```
USER
```

The USER function takes no parameters.

The following example illustrates the use of the USER function:

```
SQL> SELECT USER FROM dual;

USER
-----------------------------
SYSTEM
```

When invoked from within a stored function or procedure, this function will return the name of the function or the procedure's owner.

USERENV

The USERENV function returns a variety of information about the current user. Following is its syntax:

```
USERENV(option)
```

Its argument is described as follows:

option   A character string containing one of the option values listed in Table B-5. The function returns the value described for the specified option.

Table B-5 USERENV Options	
Option	**Description**
ISDBA	Returns 'TRUE' if the ISDBA role is enabled. Otherwise, 'FALSE' is returned.
LANGUAGE	Returns the current language and territory settings.
TERMINAL	Returns an identifier for the current session's terminal.
SESSIONID	Returns an auditing session identifier.
ENTRYID	Returns an auditing entry identifier.
LANG	Returns the ISO abbreviation for the current language.
INSTANCE	Returns the instance identifier.

The following example illustrates the use of the USERENV function:

```
SQL> SELECT USERENV('LANGUAGE') FROM DUAL;

USERENV('LANGUAGE')
---------------------------------------------
AMERICAN_AMERICA.WE8ISO8859P1

SQL> SELECT USERENV('INSTANCE') FROM DUAL;

USERENV('INSTANCE')
-------------------
                  1
```

VSIZE

The VSIZE function returns the size, in bytes, of the internal representation of a value. Following is its syntax:

    VSIZE(value)

Its argument is described as follows:

>   value   Any type of value

The following example illustrates the use of the VSIZE function:

```
SQL> SELECT VSIZE(SYSDATE) FROM DUAL;

VSIZE(SYSDATE)
--------------
             8

SQL> SELECT VSIZE(DUMMY) FROM DUAL;

VSIZE(DUMMY)
------------
           1
```

The first example tells you that the internal representation of a date value consumes 8 bytes. The second example tells you that the internal representation of the DUAL table's DUMMY column uses only 1 byte.

◆   ◆   ◆

SQL*Plus Reference

This appendix describes the many commands available from SQL*Plus. Before presenting the list of SQL*Plus commands, the appendix describes command argument strings and display formats, including character, date, and number formats. Then the commands are presented in alphabetical order.

String Parameters in SQL*Plus Commands

Many SQL*Plus commands accept character strings as parameters. The DEFINE command is a good example. It's used to define user variables. You can get a good idea of how it works from this example:

```
SQL> DEFINE x = Animals
SQL> DEFINE x = 'Animals'
SQL> DEFINE x = "Animals"
```

Notice the three different ways that the strings can be represented. In the first command, no quotes are used to delimit the string. SQL*Plus allows this for most SQL*Plus commands. However, not quoting your strings can lead to problems. In some cases, it could be ambiguous whether a given string of characters represents a value or a clause in a command. It's better to quote your strings, and you can do so using either single or double quotes.

Note   If your string consists of more than one word, enclose it within quotes.

If you need to embed quotes within a quoted string, you can either double them up or use different quotes inside and outside the string. For example:

```
SQL> DEFINE x="The Animal's Home"
SQL> DEFINE x='The Animal''s Home'
```

The first example uses double quotes to enclose the string, which allows single quotes to be used inside the string. The second example uses single quotes to enclose the string, which means that a double single quote (' ') is used inside the string to represent one single quote.

SQL*Plus Display Formats

Several SQL*Plus commands use format strings either to format output or to specify the format in which a user must enter a value. The COLUMN and ACCEPT commands provide good examples. Three types of format strings exist: those used for characters, those used for dates, and those used for numbers.

Character format strings

Your options are simple when it comes to formatting text columns. SQL*Plus recognizes only one character format, and that is the A format. You use it to specify the width of a displayed value. Here are some examples:

```
COLUMN animal_name FORMAT A10
ACCEPT x CHAR PROMPT 'Enter X:' FORMAT A5
```

The first command causes the animal_name column to be displayed in a ten-character-wide field. The COLUMN command affects the format of the animal_name column returned by a SELECT query. The second example here uses a format string of A5 with an ACCEPT command that requires the user to enter a character string that is five characters long or less.

Date format strings

You can't use date format strings with the COLUMN command, but you can use them with ACCEPT. Consider this example:

```
ACCEPT x DATE PROMPT 'Enter Date:' FORMAT "mm/dd/yyyy"
```

This command prompts you to enter a date in the month, day, and year format commonly used in the U.S. You can use a number of date format elements in a format specification. See Table B-2 in Appendix B, "SQL Built-in Function Reference," for a complete list.

Number format strings

SQL*Plus supports most, but not all, of the same numeric format elements that you can use with the built-in TO_CHAR and TO_NUMBER functions. Table C-1 shows the elements that SQL*Plus supports.

	Table C-1	
	SQL*Plus Numeric Format Elements	
Element	**Sample**	**Description**
,	999,999	Marks the location of the comma in a formatted number.
G	999G999	Returns the group separator (usually a comma in the U.S.) as specified by the NLS_NUMERIC_CHARACTER setting. This is a language-dependent value.
.	9.99	Marks the location of the decimal point in a formatted number.
D	9D99	Marks the location of the decimal point as specified by the NLS_NUMERIC_CHARACTER setting. This is a language-dependent value.
$	$999,999.99	Marks the location of a leading dollar sign in a formatted number.
C	C999,999.99	Marks the location of the currency symbol as specified by the NLS_ISO_CURRENCY parameter. This is a language-dependent value.
L	L999,999.99	Marks the location of the currency symbol, as specified by the NLS_CURRENCY parameter.
0	0999	Marks a location in the number at which you want to begin displaying leading zeros.
9	9.99	Marks the location of a digit. Note that if no sign is specified in a number format, positive numbers will be formatted with one leading space to allow for a negative sign.
EEEE	999.9EEEE	Causes a number to be formatted using scientific notation.
MI	999,999MI	Formats negative numbers with a trailing negative sign and positive numbers with a trailing blank.
PR	999pr	Formats negative numbers within < and > characters.
RN	RN	Formats a number in uppercase Roman numerals.
rn	rn	Formats a number in lowercase Roman numerals.

Continued

Table C-1 *(continued)*		
Element	**Sample**	**Description**
S	s999,999 999,999s	Formats both negative and positive values with a leading – or + sign. The *S* may also be placed at the end of the number, in which case, the sign becomes a trailing sign.
V	999v999	Multiplies a value by 10 raised to the power specified by the number of 9s trailing the V character.

You can use the elements listed in Table C-1 with the COLUMN command to format numeric output. Consider these examples:

```
COLUMN id_no FORMAT 99999
COLUMN tank_no FORMAT 09999
```

The first example formats the ID_NO column to display in a five-digit-wide field. The second example performs the same task for the TANK_NO column, but with the added requirement that leading zeros be used. In both cases, SQL*Plus will leave one space in front of the number for possible negative signs.

SQL*Plus Command Reference

The remainder of this appendix lists SQL's functions in alphabetical order. The following example uses the SQL SELECT statement to illustrate the notation used in the syntax diagrams:

```
SELECT [ALL|DISTINCT] {*|column}
FROM table_name[,table_name...];
```

SELECT	Words in capitals denote syntax — usually the function names.
column	Lowercase italics represent items that you must supply when you invoke the function.
[ALL|DISTINCT]	Square brackets denote an optional choice, with the choices delimited by a vertical line. In this example, you may choose ALL, DISTINCT, or nothing.

`{* | column }`	Curly brackets denote a mandatory choice, with the choices delimited by a vertical line. In this example, you have to choose between * or *column*.
`table_name[,table_name...]`	Repetitions are indicated by repeating the item between square brackets and adding an optional delimiter and three trailing dots at the end. In this example, specify one or more data sources, each delimited by a comma.

##

You use the @ command to execute a SQL*Plus script file. Following is its syntax:

```
@filename [arg arg arg...]
```

The syntax elements are as follows:

filename	The name of the file that you want to execute. The file name may optionally include a directory path and an extension. The default extension is .sql. If no path is specified, SQL*Plus will look in the current working directory for the file. If it's not found there, SQL*Plus will then search the directories listed in the `SQLPATH` environment variable.
arg	An argument that you want to pass to the script. You can have as many arguments as you like. They must be separated from each other by at least one space, and they may optionally be enclosed within quotes.

To execute a file named `create_user.sql` in the current directory, enter the following:

```
SQL> @create_user
```

To execute the same file and pass a username as an argument, enter the following:

```
SQL> @create_user "kim"
```

##

You can use the @@ command from within one SQL*Plus script to invoke another. SQL*Plus will begin searching for the second script in the directory containing the first. If you have two scripts in the same directory and one calls the other, you should use the @@ command. Otherwise, if you have another script in the `SQLPATH` with the same name, you could run into problems. Following is its syntax:

```
@@filename [arg arg arg...]
```

The syntax elements are as follows:

filename   The name of the file that you want to execute. The file name
may optionally include a directory path and an extension. The
default extension is .sql. If no path is specified, SQL*Plus will
look in the directory containing the current script. If you
execute @@ interactively, it functions just like @.

arg   An argument that you want to pass to the script. You can have
as many arguments as you like. They must be separated from
each other by at least one space, and they may optionally be
enclosed within quotes.

In the following example, you want the create_user script to execute a
create_user_2 script. Both scripts are stored in the same directory.

```
@@create_user_2
```

/

The / command executes the SQL statement currently in the buffer. The buffer
always contains the most recent SQL statement or PL/SQL block that you have
entered or executed.

Note   Use the L command to display the statement currently in the buffer.

Following is its syntax:

```
/
```

In the following example, the L command is used to list the contents of the buffer,
and the / command is then used to execute those contents.

```
SQL> L
  1* SELECT USER FROM DUAL
SQL> /

USER
----------------------------
SYSTEM
```

ACCEPT

The ACCEPT command interactively prompts the user for input and accepts a
response. Following is its syntax:

```
ACC[EPT] user_var [NUM[BER]|CHAR|DATE]
```

```
[FOR[MAT] format] [DEF[AULT] default]
[PROMPT prompt_text|NOPR[OMPT]] [HIDE]
```

The syntax elements are as follows:

user_var	Specifies the name of a SQL*Plus user variable. Note that you don't need to declare this variable before using it.
NUMBER	Requires the user to enter a number.
CHAR	Allows the user to enter any string of characters. This is the default behavior.
DATE	Requires the user to enter a date.
FORMAT *format*	Allows you to specify the format in which the data must be entered. See the earlier section "SQL*Plus Display Formats" for information on format specifications.

Note   Avoid complicated date and numeric formats. This feature is poorly implemented, and specifying a complex format can result in a catch-22 situation where nothing that you enter is accepted. Try accepting a number using a format of $999. You'll see that no matter how you attempt to enter a number, it won't be accepted.

DEFAULT *default*	Allows you to specify a default value, which is used if the user responds to the prompt by pressing Enter.
PROMPT *prompt_text*	Defines a prompt that is displayed to the user.
NOPROMPT	Inhibits the display of a prompt.
HIDE	Prevents the user's response from being displayed on the screen as it is typed.

In the following example, ACCEPT is used to prompt for a name:

```
SQL> ACCEPT name CHAR PROMPT 'Enter your name:'
Enter your name:Kim Beanie
```

In this next example, ACCEPT is used to prompt for a numeric value. The format string $999 is used. The result is that nothing passes validation.

```
SQL> ACCEPT test NUMBER FORMAT $999
23
SP2-0598: "23" does not match input format "$999"
$23
SP2-0425: "$23" is not a valid number
233
SP2-0598: "233" does not match input format "$999"
$233
SP2-0425: "$233" is not a valid number
```

If you use format strings with numbers, stick with simple formats made up of "9"s and "."s.

APPEND

The APPEND command appends text to the end of the current line of the SQL buffer. Following is its syntax:

```
A[PPEND] text
```

The syntax elements are as follows:

    text   The text that you want to append

The example in Listing C-1 shows a SQL statement being entered, listed, and modified using the APPEND command. Note that APPEND may be abbreviated to A.

Listing C-1: **A SQL statement using the APPEND command**

```
SQL> SELECT
  2   FROM DUAL
  3
SQL> L
  1   SELECT
  2*  FROM DUAL
SQL> 1
  1*  SELECT
SQL> A  USER
  1*  SELECT USER
SQL> L
  1   SELECT USER
  2*  FROM DUAL
```

It's difficult to see on paper, but two spaces are used following the A to get one space between the words SELECT and USER.

ARCHIVE LOG

The ARCHIVE LOG command allows you to start and stop archiving from SQL*Plus. This command also allows you to view current information about archiving and to initiate the manual archiving of log files.

Note   You must be logged on as SYSDBA, SYSOPER, or INTERNAL to use this command.

Following is its syntax:

```
ARCHIVE LOG {LIST|STOP}
            |{START|NEXT|ALL|log_seq_num} [TO destination]
```

The syntax elements are as follows:

LIST	Displays information about the current state of archiving.
STOP	Stops automatic archiving.
START	Starts automatic archiving.
NEXT	Archives the next unarchived log file in sequence.
log_seq_num	A log sequence number. The corresponding log file is archived.
TO destination	Overrides the archive log destination for this one operation.

The following example shows the current state of archiving being displayed and then shows automatic archiving being stopped:

```
SQL> ARCHIVE LOG LIST
Database log mode              Archive Mode
Automatic archival             Enabled
Archive destination            d:\oradata\coin
Oldest online log sequence     16033
Next log sequence to archive   16038
Current log sequence           16038
SQL> ARCHIVE LOG STOP
Statement processed.
```

ATTRIBUTE

The ATTRIBUTE command allows you to specify the display format for an attribute of an object column. Following is its syntax:

```
ATTRIBUTE [type_name.attribute_name [option...]
option := {ALI[AS] alias_name
          |CLE[AR]
          |FOR[MAT] format
          |LIKE {type_name.attribute_name|alias_name}
          |ON
          |OFF}
```

The syntax elements are as follows:

type_name	Specifies the name of an Oracle8i object type.
attribute_name	Specifies the name of an attribute of the object type.

ALIAS *alias_name*	Defines an alternate name for the attribute that SQL*Plus will recognize. You can use this name in future ATTRIBUTE commands.
CLEAR	Resets the display format for the attribute to the default.
FORMAT *format*	Specifies a display format for the attribute. See the earlier section "SQL*Plus Display Formats" for information on format specifications.
LIKE	Allows you to define this display of this attribute to be like another. You can name the other attribute by name or by alias.
ON	Enables the display format that you have defined.
OFF	Disables the display format that you have defined. The default will be used instead.

Listing C-2 shows how the ATTRIBUTE command is used to control the display width of the ID_NO and TANK_NO attributes.

Listing C-2: **Using the ATTRIBUTE command**

```
SQL> SELECT * FROM a_animals;

ANIMAL(ID_NO, TANK_NO, ANIMAL_NAME, MARKINGS_DESCRIPTION, BIRTH_DATE,
DEATH_DATE)
--------------------------------------------------------------------------------
--
A_ANIMAL(505, 1, 'Barney', 'No markings', '01-JAN-00', NULL)
A_ANIMAL(506, 1, 'Blurry', 'No markings', '01-JAN-00', NULL)

2 rows selected.

SQL> ATTRIBUTE a_animal.id_no FORMAT 09999
SQL> ATTRIBUTE a_animal.tank_no FORMAT 09999
SQL> SELECT * FROM A_ANIMALS;

ANIMAL(ID_NO, TANK_NO, ANIMAL_NAME, MARKINGS_DESCRIPTION, BIRTH_DATE,
DEATH_DATE)
--------------------------------------------------------------------------------
--
A_ANIMAL(00505, 00001, 'Barney', 'No markings', '01-JAN-00', NULL)
A_ANIMAL(00506, 00001, 'Blurry', 'No markings', '01-JAN-00', NULL)
```

Notice that in the second set of results, after the ATTRIBUTE commands were issued, both columns displayed five digits wide with leading zeros.

BREAK

The BREAK command allows you to define report breaks. Following is its syntax:

```
BRE[AK] [ON element [action [action...]]...]

element := {column_name|expression|ROW|REPORT}

action := {SKI[P] lines|SKI[P] PAGE
           |NODUP[LICATES]|DUP[LICATES]}
```

The syntax elements are as follows:

column_name	The name of a column in a SQL query. This defines a column break, and the corresponding actions will be executed each time the column's value changes.

Note If you define column aliases in your SQL query, then use those aliases as column names in the BREAK command.

expression	Specifies an expression used in a SQL query. The expression must match exactly the one used in the query. This defines the equivalent of a column break, but for an expression. Note that it's usually easier to alias the expression instead.
ROW	Defines a break that executes for each row returned by a query.
REPORT	Defines a break that executes at the end of a report.
SKIP lines	Skips the specified number of lines when the break occurs.
SKIP PAGE	Skips a page when the break occurs.
NODUPLICATES	Eliminates repeating values in a column. This is the default behavior.
DUPLICATES	Allows repeating values to be displayed.

The most common use of BREAK is to eliminate repeating values from a column. Consider the example shown in Listing C-3.

Listing C-3: **Using the BREAK command**

```
SQL> SELECT tank_no, animal_name FROM aquatic_animal
  2  ORDER BY tank_no;

  TANK_NO ANIMAL_NAME
--------- -----------------------------
        1 Flipper
        1 Skipper
        1 Bopper
        2 Batty
        2 Shorty
        2 Squacky
        2 Paintuin
        3 Nosey
        3 Rascal
        3 Snoops

10 rows selected.

SQL> BREAK ON tank_no
SQL> SELECT tank_no, animal_name FROM aquatic_animal
  2  ORDER BY tank_no;

  TANK_NO ANIMAL_NAME
--------- -----------------------------
        1 Flipper
          Skipper
          Bopper
        2 Batty
          Shorty
          Squacky
          Paintuin
        3 Nosey
          Rascal
          Snoops

10 rows selected.
```

The BREAK command can also be used to skip a line between each group of animals, as shown in Listing C-4.

Listing C-4: Using the BREAK command to skip lines

```
SQL> BREAK ON tank_no NODUPLICATES SKIP 1
SQL> SELECT tank_no, animal_name FROM aquatic_animal
  2  ORDER BY tank_no;

 TANK_NO ANIMAL_NAME
--------- ------------------------------
       1 Flipper
         Skipper
         Bopper

       2 Batty
         Shorty
         Squacky
         Paintuin

       3 Nosey
         Rascal
         Snoops


10 rows selected.
```

Notice that each time the tank number changes, a line is skipped. The BREAK command defining this behavior contains two break actions. Even though it is a default action, NODUPLICATES is included so that you can see how multiple actions are specified.

Note When you define a column break, always make sure that the query results are sorted by the break column.

BTITLE

The BTITLE command defines a footer (bottom title) that appears at the bottom of each page of a report. Following is its syntax:

```
BTI[TLE] [printspec [text|user_var]... [printspec...]]
         |[OFF|ON]

printspec := {COL col_num
             |S[KIP] lines
             |TAB col_num
             |LE[FT]
             |CE[NTER]
```

```
|R[IGHT]
|BOLD
|FORMAT format}
```

The syntax elements are as follows:

text	Specifies text that you want to appear as part of the title.
user_var	Specifies the name of a user variable, the contents of which will appear in the title. This may also be one of the following predefined user variables: SQL.LNO for the current line number, SQL.PNO for the current page number, SQL.RELEASE for the current Oracle release number, SQL.SQLCODE for the current error number, and SQL.USER for the current username.
COL col_num	Indents to the specified column.
SKIP lines	Skips the specified number of lines.
LEFT	Causes subsequent text to appear left-justified in the current line.
CENTER	Causes subsequent text to appear centered in the current line. Note that the definition of center is controlled by the SET LINESIZE command.
RIGHT	Causes subsequent text to appear flush right. Note that the SET LINESIZE command also defines the right edge of the line.
BOLD	Causes text to be printed three times in succession, on three different lines.
FORMAT format	Specifies a display format to use for subsequent text or numeric values. See the earlier section "SQL*Plus Display Formats" for details on specifying format strings.
OFF	Turns the page footer off.
ON	Turns the page footer on.

The following example setting defines a two-line page footer:

```
SQL> BTITLE LEFT 'Page' FORMAT 999 sql.pno -
>        RIGHT 'Confidential' -
>        SKIP 1 CENTER 'Payroll Department'
```

Note   The hyphen in SQL*Plus is a line continuation character. When used, it must be preceded by a space.

Assuming a 50-character-wide line, this footer will display as follows:

```
Page    1                                    Confidential
                     Payroll Department
```

You can use the BTITLE command with no arguments to see the current title setting, as shown in this example:

```
SQL> BTITLE
btitle ON and is the following 102 characters:
LEFT 'Page' FORMAT 999 sql.pno        RIGHT 'Confidential'        SKIP 1
CENTER 'Payroll Department'
```

CHANGE

The CHANGE command allows you to perform string substitution on the current line of the SQL buffer. Following is its syntax:

```
C[HANGE] /old_text/new_text/
```

The syntax elements are as follows:

old_text	The text that you want to replace.
new_text	The new text that you want to use.
/	The separator character. You can use any character as the separator character. SQL*Plus interprets the first nonspace character following the CHANGE command as the separator. The trailing separator character is optional, unless your new_text value contains trailing spaces.

In the following example, a query is entered with the wrong column name in the SELECT list. The L command is used to list the first line, and the column name is replaced.

```
SQL> SELECT animal_name
  2 FROM aquatic_animal
  3
SQL> L 1
  1* SELECT animal_name
SQL> C /animal_name/COUNT(*)/
  1* SELECT COUNT(*)
SQL> L
  1  SELECT COUNT(*)
  2* FROM aquatic_animal
```

CLEAR

The CLEAR command allows you to erase various types of SQL*Plus settings. Following is its syntax:

```
CL[EAR] {BRE[AKS]
        |BUFF[ER]
        |COL[UMNS]
        |COMP[UTES]
        |SCR[EEN]
        |SQL
        |TIMI[NG]
```

The syntax elements are as follows:

BREAKS	Erases all break settings
BUFFER	Erases the contents of the current buffer
COLUMNS	Erases all column format settings
COMPUTES	Erases all COMPUTE settings
SCREEN	Clears the screen
SQL	Erases the contents of the SQL buffer
TIMING	Deletes any timers that you have created using the TIMING command

The following commands clear any break and column settings:

```
SQL> CLEAR BREAKS
breaks cleared
SQL> CLEAR COLUMNS
columns cleared
SQL>
```

COLUMN

The COLUMN command formats columns for display on a report. Listing C-5 shows its syntax.

Listing C-5: **COLUMN command syntax**

```
COL[UMN] [column_name [option option...]]

option := {ALI[AS] alias|
          CLE[AR]|
```

```
FOLD_A[FTER]|
FOLD_B[EFORE]|
FOR[MAT] format|
HEA[DING] heading_text|
JUS[TIFY] {LEFT|CENTER|CENTRE|RIGHT}|
LIKE source_column_name|
NEWL[INE]|
NEW_V[ALUE] user_var|
NOPRI[NT]|
PRI[NT]|
NUL[L] null_text|
OLD_V[ALUE] user_var|
ON|
OFF|
WRA[PPED]|
WOR[D_WRAPPED]|
TRU[NCATED]}
```

The syntax elements are as follows:

column_name	Identifies the column that you are formatting. If you use column aliases in your SQL statement, then those aliases become the column names as far as SQL*Plus is concerned.
ALIAS *alias*	Allows you to specify an alternate name for this column that SQL*Plus will recognize.
CLEAR	Resets the display format of this column back to its default.
FOLD_AFTER	Specifies that SQL*Plus should advance to a new line after displaying the column's value.
FOLD_BEFORE	Specifies that SQL*Plus should advance to a new line before the column's value is displayed.
FORMAT *format*	Allows you to specify a display format for the column. See the earlier section "SQL*Plus Display Formats" for more information.
HEADING	Allows you to define a column heading that displays at the top of the column.
JUSTIFY	Controls the justification of the heading text. Use one of these keywords: LEFT, RIGHT, CENTER, or CENTRE.

LIKE *source_column_name*	Defines the column's display format to be like that of another column.
NEWLINE	Has the same effect as FOLD_BEFORE.
NEW_VALUE *user_var*	Tells SQL*Plus to update the named user variable with the current contents of the column as the query executes.
NOPRINT	Inhibits the display of the column.
PRINT	Allows the column to be displayed.
NULL *null_text*	Specifies text to be displayed whenever the column contains a null value.
OLD_VALUE *user_var*	Tells SQL*Plus to update the named user variable with the current contents of the column as the query executes.
ON	Enables the column format that you have defined.
OFF	Disables the display format that you have defined.
WRAPPED	Causes SQL*Plus to wrap long values to fit within the column. This is the default behavior.
WORD_WRAPPED	Causes SQL*Plus to wordwrap long values.
TRUNCATED	Causes SQL*Plus to truncate values longer than the column is wide.

The following example shows the COLUMN command being used to set the display format and headings for two columns:

```
SQL> COLUMN id_no FORMAT 999 HEADING 'Animal ID'
SQL> COLUMN animal_name FORMAT A10 HEADING 'Name'
SQL> SELECT id_no, animal_name
  2  FROM aquatic_animal;

Animal ID Name
--------- ----------
      100 Flipper
      105 Skipper
      112 Bopper
      151 Batty
```

COMPUTE

The COMPUTE command allows you to define summaries for SQL*Plus to compute and display. Following is its syntax:

```
COMP[UTE] [function [LAB[EL] label_text]...
          OF {expression|column|alias}...
          ON {expression|column|alias|REPORT|ROW}...]
```

The syntax elements are as follows:

function   One of the functions listed in Table C-2.

Table C-2
Functions You Can Use with COMPUTE

Function Name	Description
AVG	Computes the average of all non-null values in the column.
COU[NT]	Computes the number of non-null values in the column.
MAX[IMUM]	Computes the maximum value of a column.
MIN[IMUM]	Computes the minimum value of a column.
NUM[BER]	Computes the number of rows. This is similar to COUNT but includes null values.
STD	Computes the standard deviation of the values in a column.
SUM	Computes the sum of the values in a column.
VAR[IANCE]	Computes the variance of the non-null values in a column.

label_text   An optional label for the computation. SQL*Plus attempts to display this in the column preceding the one named in the COMPUTE statement.

expression   An expression that identifies a column returned by a SQL query. This expression must match an expression in the SELECT statement.

column   The name of a column returned by a SELECT statement.

alias   An alias previously defined using the COLUMN command.

OF   Introduces the list of columns being summarized. You may summarize multiple columns with one command.

ON	Introduces the list of break columns for which the summarized values are displayed.
REPORT	Defines a report-level summary.
ROW	Defines a row-level summary.

Note

The COMPUTE and BREAK commands work together. You can have only one COMPUTE setting for a database.

The example shown in Listing C-6 uses the COMPUTE command to print a count of the animals in each tank.

Listing C-6: **Using the COMPUTE command**

```
SQL> COMPUTE COUNT LABEL 'Count' OF animal_name ON tank_no
SQL> BREAK ON tank_no
SQL> SELECT tank_no, animal_name
  2  FROM aquatic_animal;

TANK_NO ANIMAL_NAME
--------- ----------------------------
        1 Flipper
          Skipper
          Bopper
********* ----------------------------
Count                                 3
        2 Batty
          Shorty
          Squacky
          Paintuin
********* ----------------------------
Count                                 4
        3 Nosey
          Rascal
          Snoops
********* ----------------------------
Count                                 3
```

For COMPUTE to work, you must BREAK on the column listed in the ON clause of the COMPUTE command. You should also sort the results of your query based on that same column. Note that the label 'Count' is displayed in the column preceding the one being counted. Oracle determines the preceding column based on the order in the select list. If the previous column is defined as NOPRINT, then you won't see the compute label.

CONNECT

You use the CONNECT command to connect to a database from SQL*Plus. Following is its syntax:

```
CONN[ECT] [[username[/password][@service]]
    [AS {SYSOPER|SYSDBA}] [INTERNAL]]
```

The syntax elements are as follows:

username	Specifies your Oracle username
password	Specifies your password
service	Specifies a Net8 service name
SYSOPER	Connects you in the SYSOPER role
SYSDBA	Connects you in the SYSDBA role
INTERNAL	Connects you as the INTERNAL role

The following example shows how to connect normally using the SYSDBA role:

```
SQL> CONNECT system/manager
Connected.
SQL> CONNECT system/manager AS SYSDBA
Connected.
```

If you omit your password, SQL*Plus will prompt you for it, as follows:

```
SQL> CONNECT system@seapark_db
Enter password: *******
Connected.
```

COPY

The COPY command allows you to copy data from one table to another table. The tables may be in different databases. Following is its syntax:

```
COPY {FROM login|TO login}
    {APPEND|CREATE|INSERT|REPLACE}
    destination_table [(column_list)]
    USING select_statement

login := username/password@service
```

The syntax elements are as follows:

username	Specifies your Oracle username.
password	Specifies your password.
service	Specifies a Net8 service name.
APPEND	Creates the destination table if it doesn't already exist.
CREATE	Creates the destination table.
INSERT	Causes SQL*Plus to return an error if the destination table doesn't exist.
REPLACE	Deletes the data in the destination table before doing the copy. The table will be created if it doesn't already exist.
destination_table	Identifies the table to which you are copying the data.
column_list	Identifies the list of columns in the destination table that are to receive the data being copied.
select_statement	Specifies the SELECT statement that retrieves the data that you want to copy.

The example in Listing C-7 shows the COPY command being used to copy the ID_NO and ANIMAL_NAME columns of the AQUATIC_ANIMAL table to a new table in a remote database.

Listing C-7: **Copy example**

```
SQL> COPY TO seapark/seapark@seapark_remote -
>    CREATE aquatic_animal_copy -
>    USING SELECT id_no, animal_name -
>         FROM aquatic_animal;

Array fetch/bind size is 15. (arraysize is 15)
Will commit when done. (copycommit is 0)
Maximum long size is 80. (long is 80)
Table AQUATIC_ANIMAL_COPY created.

   10 rows selected from DEFAULT HOST connection.
   10 rows inserted into AQUATIC_ANIMAL_COPY.
   10 rows committed into AQUATIC_ANIMAL_COPY at seapark@seapark_remote.
```

DEFINE

The DEFINE command allows you to create a SQL*Plus user variable and assign it a value. The DEFINE command also allows you to list the values of all currently defined user variables. Following is its syntax:

```
DEF[INE] [variable [= text]]
```

The syntax elements are as follows:

variable	The name that you want to give the user variable that you are defining
text	The text string that you want to assign to the variable

The following examples show how to use the DEFINE command to define some user variables and then to display their definitions:

```
SQL> DEFINE x = "Seapark"
SQL> DEFINE x
DEFINE X               = "Seapark" (CHAR)
SQL> DEFINE
DEFINE _SQLPLUS_RELEASE = "801050000" (CHAR)
DEFINE _EDITOR         = "Notepad" (CHAR)
DEFINE _O_RELEASE      = "801050000" (CHAR)
DEFINE X               = "Seapark" (CHAR)
```

Using DEFINE with just a variable name causes SQL*Plus to display the value of the named variable. Using DEFINE by itself causes SQL*Plus to display the value of all user variables.

DEL

The DEL command deletes one or more lines from the SQL buffer. Following is its syntax:

```
DEL [{beg|*|LAST}[ {end|*|LAST}]]
```

The syntax elements are as follows:

beg	The line number of the first line that you want to delete.
end	The line number of the last line that you want to delete.
*	The currently selected line. This may be used for either the beginning or end of the range.
LAST	The last line in the buffer.

The example in Listing C-8 shows various ways to use the DEL command.

Listing C-8: **Using the DEL command**

```
SQL> L
  1  SELECT id_no,
  2         animal_name,
  3         tank_no,
  4         birth_date
  5  FROM aquatic_animal
  6* ORDER BY id_no
SQL> DEL 2 4
SQL> L
  1  SELECT id_no,
  2  FROM aquatic_animal
  3* ORDER BY id_no
SQL> DEL *
SQL> L
  1  SELECT id_no,
  2* FROM aquatic_animal
```

The first delete gets rid of lines 2 through 4. The second delete gets rid of the current line, which happens to be the last line.

DESCRIBE

The DESCRIBE command displays information about the columns in a table. Following is its syntax:

```
DESC[RIBE] [schema.]object[@dblink]
```

The syntax elements are as follows:

schema	The schema in which the object is stored. This is optional.
object	The name of an object. You can describe tables, object types, and packages.
dbline	A database link.

The following example shows the DESCRIBE command being used to display the structure of a table:

```
SQL> DESCRIBE AQUATIC_ANIMAL

 Name                              Null?    Type
 --------------------------------- -------- -------------
```

```
ID_NO               NOT NULL  NUMBER(10)
TANK_NO                       NUMBER(10)
ANIMAL_NAME                   VARCHAR2(30)
MARKINGS_DESCRIPTION          VARCHAR2(30)
BIRTH_DATE                    DATE
DEATH_DATE                    DATE
```

DISCONNECT

The DISCONNECT command disconnects you from a database. Following is its syntax:

```
DISC[CONNECT]
```

There are no parameters for this command. The DISCONNECT command is used as follows:

```
SQL> DISCONNECT
Disconnected from Oracle8i Release 8.1.5.0.0 - Production
With the Partitioning and Java options
PL/SQL Release 8.1.5.0.0 - Production
```

EDIT

The EDIT command invokes an external text editor and allows you to use it to edit the contents of the SQL buffer. The EDIT command also allows you to edit the contents of a text file. Following is its syntax:

```
ED[IT] [filename]
```

The syntax element is as follows:

> *filename*   The name of an existing file. If you pass a file name as a parameter, the contents of that file will be loaded into the editor. Otherwise, the contents of the SQL buffer will be loaded into the editor.

The EDIT command is invoked as follows:

```
SQL> EDIT
```

In most environments, this results in the full screen editor being invoked that operates outside the bounds of the SQL*Plus session.

Note You can specify the editor to be invoked by defining a user variable named _EDITOR. SQL*Plus invokes the editor that the EDITOR user variable points to. For example, to have SQL*Plus invoke the vi editor, execute the command DEFINE _EDITOR=vi.

EXECUTE

The EXECUTE command allows you to execute a single PL/SQL statement. Following is its syntax:

```
EXEC[UTE] statement
```

The syntax element is as follows:

statement   The PL/SQL statement that you want to execute

The following example illustrates how you can use the EXECUTE command:

```
SQL> EXECUTE DBMS_OUTPUT.PUT_LINE('Hello World');
Hello World

PL/SQL procedure successfully completed.
```

EXIT

The EXIT command terminates your SQL*Plus session. Following is its syntax:

```
EXIT [SUCCESS|FAILURE|WARNING|number|user_var|:bind_var]
     [COMMIT|ROLLBACK]
```

The syntax elements are as follows:

SUCCESS	Exits with a status of success. This is the default.
FAILURE	Exits with a failure status.
WARNING	Exits with a warning status.
number	Exits with the specified error code.
user_var	Exits and returns the value of the specified user variable as the status code.
:bind_var	Exits and returns the value of the specified bind variable as the status code.

The following example illustrates how to use the EXIT command:

```
SQL> EXIT
```

GET

The GET command loads the contents of a text file into the SQL buffer. Following is its syntax:

```
GET filename [LIS[T]|NOL[IST]]
```

The syntax elements are as follows:

filename	Specifies the file that you want to load.
LIST	Displays the file on the screen after loading. This is the default.
NOLIST	Loads, but doesn't display, the file.

The following example illustrates how to use the GET command:

```
SQL> GET from_dual
  1* SELECT USER FROM dual
```

You can use the SAVE command to write the contents of the buffer to a file.

HELP

In some environments, the HELP command will get you help on SQL*Plus commands. For this to work, you must also install the SQL*Plus help tables in your database. Following is the HELP command's syntax:

```
HELP topic_name
```

The syntax element is as follows:

topic_name	The name of a help topic. Each of the SQL*Plus commands is a help topic.

The following example illustrates how to use the HELP command:

```
SQL> HELP COMPUTE
```

Note   The HELP command isn't available from the Windows NT version of SQL*Plus.

HOST

The HOST command allows you to execute an operating system command from within SQL*Plus. Following is its syntax:

```
HO[ST] [command]
```

The syntax element is as follows:

command	The command that you want to execute

Listing C-9 illustrates how to use the HOST command.

Listing C-9: **Using the HOST command**

```
SQL> host time
The current time is: 22:20:22.78
Enter the new time:

SQL> host
Microsoft(R) Windows NT(TM)
(C) Copyright 1985-1996 Microsoft Corp.

C:\> dir about.html
 Volume in drive C has no label.
 Volume Serial Number is 07CF-060A

 Directory of C:\

10/03/99  09:59p                      929 about.html
              1 File(s)               929 bytes
                          455,639,040 bytes free

C:\> exit
```

INPUT

The INPUT command allows you to add one or more new lines of text to the SQL buffer. The lines are added following the current line. Following is its syntax:

    I[NPUT] [*text*]

The syntax element is as follows:

> *text*   A line that you want to insert. If you supply this argument, then only this one line is inserted. Otherwise, you may insert as many lines as you like.

The following example illustrates how to use the INPUT command:

```
SQL> L
  1   SELECT animal_name
  2* ORDER BY animal_name
SQL> 1
  1* SELECT animal_name
SQL> I
```

```
 2i FROM aquatic_animal
 3i
SQL> L
 1  SELECT animal_name
 2  FROM aquatic_animal
 3* ORDER BY animal_name
```

LIST

The LIST command lists all or part of the SQL buffer. Following is its syntax:

```
L[IST] [{beg|*|LAST}[ {end|*|LAST}]]
```

The syntax elements are as follows:

beg	Represents the number of the first line that you want to list
end	Represents the number of the last line that you want to list
*	Represents the current line and may be used to denote either the first or last line to list
LAST	Represents the last line in the buffer

The following examples illustrate how to use the LIST command:

```
SQL> L 2 3
 2          animal_name
 3* FROM aquatic_animal
SQL> L
 1  SELECT id_no,
 2          animal_name
 3  FROM aquatic_animal
 4* ORDER BY animal_name
```

The LIST command with no arguments causes SQL*Plus to display all lines in the buffer.

PASSWORD

The PASSWORD command allows you to change your Oracle password. It also allows you to change the password of another user, but only if you have the ALTER USER system privilege. Following is its syntax:

```
PASSW[ORD] [username]
```

The syntax element is as follows:

username	The name of the user whose password you want to change

When you issue the PASSWORD command, SQL*Plus will prompt you for the new password. For example:

```
SQL> PASSWORD
Changing password for SEAPARK
Old password: *******
New password: ******
Retype new password: ******
Password changed
```

PAUSE

The PAUSE command displays a line of text and waits for you to press the Enter key. Following is its syntax:

```
PAU[SE] text
```

The syntax element is as follows:

> text   The text that you want to display

The following example shows you how to use the PAUSE command:

```
SQL> PAUSE Press ENTER to begin deleting old data.
Press ENTER to begin deleting old data.
```

You can use the PAUSE command in scripts as a way to let the user know what's going to happen next.

PRINT

The PRINT command displays the contents of a bind variable. The PRINT command with no arguments displays the contents of all bind variables. Following is its syntax:

```
PRI[NT] [variable [variable ...]]
```

The syntax element is as follows:

> variable   The name of a bind variable that you want to display

The following example shows a bind variable being declared, initialized with data, and then displayed using the PRINT command:

```
SQL> VARIABLE X number
SQL> EXECUTE :x := 11
```

```
PL/SQL procedure successfully completed.

SQL> PRINT x

        X
---------
       11
```

PROMPT

The PROMPT command displays a line of text on the screen. Following is its syntax:

```
PRO[MPT] text
```

The syntax element is as follows:

> text   The text that you want to display

The following example illustrates how to use the PROMPT command:

```
SQL> PROMPT Generating the animal report...
Generating the animal report...
```

QUIT

See the EXIT command. QUIT is synonymous with EXIT.

RECOVER

The RECOVER command is used to initiate database recovery. Its syntax is shown in Listing C-10.

Listing C-10: **The RECOVER command's syntax**

```
RECOVER [DATABASE [[UNTIL
                  {CANCEL
                  |CHANGE scn
                  |TIME date_time}
                  [USING BACKUP CONTROLFILE]
                  [PARALLEL([DEGREE {num_procs|DEFAULT}
                              |INSTANCES {num_inst|DEFAULT}]...)
                  |NOPARALLEL]
         |TABLESPACE tablespace_name [,tablespace_name...]
                  [PARALLEL([DEGREE {num_procs|DEFAULT}
                              |INSTANCES {num_inst|DEFAULT}]...)
```

Continued

Listing C-10: *(continued)*

```
                        |NOPARALLEL]
        |DATAFILE datafile_name [,datafile_name...]
              [PARALLEL([DEGREE {num_procs|DEFAULT}
                            |INSTANCES {num_inst|DEFAULT}]...)
              |NOPARALLEL]
```

The syntax elements are as follows:

RECOVER DATABASE	Initiates media recovery on the entire database
RECOVER TABLESPACE tablespace_**name**	Initiates media recovery on the specified tablespace or tablespaces. You can recover up to 16 tablespaces with one command.
RECOVER DATAFILE datafile_name	Initiates media recovery on the specified datafile or datafiles.
UNTIL CANCEL	Gives you the opportunity to cancel recovery after each log file is processed.
UNTIL CHANGE scn	Recovers changes up to, but not including, the specified system change number (SCN).
UNTIL TIME date_time	Recovers changes committed prior to the specified date and time.
USING BACKUP CONTROLFILE	Recovers using a backup control file.
PARALLEL	Causes the recovery to be done in parallel.
NOPARALLEL	Prevents recovery from being done in parallel.
DEGREE {num_procs|DEFAULT}	Controls the degree of parallelism if PARALLEL is being used.
INSTANCES {num_procs|DEFAULT}	Specifies the number of instances to use in the recovery process. Applicable only if PARALLEL is specified.

The following example illustrates how to use the RECOVER command:

```
SQL> RECOVER TABLESPACE seapark_tables;
```

REMARK

The REMARK command allows you to embed comments within a SQL*Plus script. Following is its syntax:

```
REM[ARK] [comment]
```

The syntax element is as follows:

    comment   Commentary on the script

The following example illustrates how to use the REMARK command:

```
SQL> REM This script generates an animal report.
SQL>
```

Note You can also add comments to scripts by using the double-hyphen (--) or by using /*...*/.

REPFOOTER

The REPFOOTER command allows you to define a report footer that prints on the last page of a report. Following is its syntax:

```
REPF[OOTER] [printspec [text|user_var]... [printspec...]]
            |[OFF|ON]

printspec := {COL col_num
             |S[KIP] lines
             |TAB col_num
             |LE[FT]
             |CE[NTER]
             |R[IGHT]
             |BOLD
             |FORMAT format}
```

The syntax elements are as follows:

text	Specifies text that you want to appear as part of the report footer.
user_var	Identifies a user variable, the contents of which will appear in the title. This may also be one of the following predefined user variables: SQL.LNO for the current line number, SQL.PNO for the current page number, SQL.RELEASE for the current Oracle release number, SQL.SQLCODE for the current error number, and SQL.USER for the current username.
COL col_num	Indents to the specified column.

SKIP *lines*	Skips the specified number of lines.
LEFT	Causes subsequent text to appear left-justified in the current line.
CENTER	Causes subsequent text to appear centered in the current line. Note that the definition of center is controlled by the SET LINESIZE command.
RIGHT	Causes subsequent text to appear flush right. Note that the SET LINESIZE command also defines the right edge of the line.
BOLD	Causes text to be printed three times in succession, on three different lines.
FORMAT *format*	Specifies a display format to use for subsequent text or numeric values. See the section early in this chapter titled "SQL*Plus Display Formats" for details on specifying format strings.
OFF	Turns the report footer off.
ON	Turns the report footer on.

The following example illustrates how to use the REPFOOTER command:

```
SQL> REPFOOTER CENTER "End of Report"
SQL> SELECT * FROM DUAL;

D
-
X

              End of Report
```

Note The report footer will actually print just prior to the final page footer (BTITLE) for the report.

REPHEADER

The REPHEADER command allows you to define a report header that prints on the first page of a report. Following is its syntax:

```
REPH[HEADER] [printspec [text|user_var]... [printspec...]]
         |[OFF|ON]

printspec := {COL col_num
             |S[KIP] lines
             |TAB col_num
             |LE[FT]
             |CE[NTER]
             |R[IGHT]
             |BOLD
```

```
|FORMAT format}
```

The syntax elements are as follows:

text	Specifies text that you want to appear as part of the report header.
user_var	Identifies a user variable, the contents of which will appear in the title. This may also be one of the following predefined user variables: SQL.LNO for the current line number, SQL.PNO for the current page number, SQL.RELEASE for the current Oracle release number, SQL.SQLCODE for the current error number, and SQL.USER for the current username.
COL col_num	Indents to the specified column.
SKIP lines	Skips the specified number of lines.
LEFT	Causes subsequent text to appear left-justified in the current line.
CENTER	Causes subsequent text to appear centered in the current line. Note that the definition of center is controlled by the SET LINESIZE command.
RIGHT	Causes subsequent text to appear flush right. Note that the SET LINESIZE command also defines the right edge of the line.
BOLD	Causes text to be printed three times in succession, on three different lines.
FORMAT format	Specifies a display format to use for subsequent text or numeric values. See the section early in this chapter titled "SQL*Plus Display Formats" for details on specifying format strings.
OFF	Turns the report header off.
ON	Turns the report header on.

The following example illustrates how to use the REPHEADER command:

```
SQL> REPHEADER CENTER "The Seapark Animal Report" SKIP 2
SQL> SELECT animal_name FROM aquatic_animal;

            The Seapark Animal Report

ANIMAL_NAME
-------------------------------
Flipper
Skipper
Bopper
            End of Report
```

Note The report header will print just after the first page header (TTITLE).

RUN

The RUN command lists and executes the SQL statement or PL/SQL block currently in the SQL buffer. Following is its syntax:

```
R[UN]
```

This command has no parameters. The following example illustrates the use of the RUN command:

```
SQL> L
  1   SELECT USER
  2*  FROM dual
SQL> R
  1   SELECT USER
  2*  FROM dual

USER
------------------------------
SEAPARK
```

SAVE

The SAVE command writes the contents of the SQL buffer to a file. Following is its syntax:

```
SAV[E] filename [CRE[ATE]|REP[LACE]|APP[END]
```

The syntax elements are as follows:

filename	Specifies the name of the file to which you want to write the contents of the SQL buffer. The default extension is .sql.
CREATE	Creates a new file and causes the command to fail if the file already exists.
REPLACE	Creates a new file or replaces the file if it already exists.
APPEND	Appends the buffer contents to the end of the file.

The following example illustrates how to use the SAVE command:

```
SQL> SELECT animal_name
  2    FROM aquatic_animal
  3
SQL> SAVE c:\a\list_animals CREATE
Created file c:\a\list_animals
```

You can find the SQL statement in the file named `list_animals.sql` in the `c:\a` directory.

SET

The SET command changes a setting that controls how SQL*Plus operates. A large number of settings have been added over the years that allow you to closely control certain aspects of SQL*Plus' behavior. Its syntax is shown in Listing C-11.

Listing C-11: **The SET command's syntax**

```
SET APPI[NFO] {OFF|ON|app_text}
    ARRAY[SIZE] array_size
    AUTO[COMMIT] {OFF|ON|IMMEDIATE|statement_count}
    AUTOP[RINT] {OFF|ON}
    AUTORECOVERY {OFF|ON}
    AUTOT[RACE] {OFF|ON|TRACE[ONLY]} [EXP[LAIN]] [STAT[ISTICS]]
    BLO[CKTERMINATOR] block_term
    BUF[FER] {buffer_name|SQL}
    CLOSECUR[SOR] {OFF|ON}
    CMDS[EP] {OFF|ON|separator
    COLSEP column_separator
    COM[PATIBILITY] {V7|V8|NATIVE}
    CON[CAT] {OFF|ON|concat}
    COPYC[OMMIT] batch_count
    COPYTYPECHECK {OFF|ON}
    DEF[INE] {OFF|ON|prefix}
    DOC[UMENT] {ON|OFF}
    ECHO {OFF|ON}
    EDITF[ILE] editfile
    EMB[EDDED] {ON|OFF}
    ESC[APE] {OFF|ON|escape}
    FEED[BACK] {OFF|ON|row_threshold}
    FLAGGER {OFF|ENTRY|INTERMED[IATE]|FULL}
    FLU[SH] {OFF|ON}
    HEA[DING] [ON|OFF]
    HEADS[EP] heading_separator
    INSTANCE [service_name|LOCAL]
    LIN[ESIZE] line_width
    LOBOF[FSET] offset
    LOGSOURCE logpath
    LONG long_length
    LONGC[HUNKSIZE] size
    MAXD[ATA] max_row_width
    NEWP[AGE] {lines_to_print|NONE}
    NULL null_text
    NUMF[ORMAT] format
    NUM[WIDTH] width
```

Continued

Listing C-11: (continued)

```
PAGES[IZE] lines_per_page
PAU[SE] {ON|OFF|pause_message}
RECSEP {WR[APPED]|EA[CH]|OFF}
RECSEPCHAR separator
SCAN {OFF|ON}
SERVEROUT[PUT] {OFF|ON}
              [SIZE buffer_size]
              [FOR[MAT]
              {WRA[PPED]|WOR[D_WRAPPED]|TRU[NCATED]}]
SHIFT[INOUT] {VIS[IBLE]|INV[ISIBLE]}}
SHOW[MODE] {ON|OFF|BOTH}
SPACE num_spaces
SQLBLANKLINES {OFF|ON}
SQLC[ASE] {MIXED|UPPER|LOWER}
SQLCO[NTINUE] continuation
SQLN[UMBER] {OFF|ON}
SQLPRE[FIX] prefix
SQLP[ROMPT] prompt
SQLT[ERMINATOR] {OFF|ON|term}
SUF[FIX] extension
TAB {OFF|ON}
TERM[OUT] {OFF|ON}
TI[ME] {OFF|ON}
TIMI[NG] {OFF|ON}
TRIM[OUT] {ON|OFF}
TRIMS[POOL] {ON|OFF}
TRU[NCATE] {OFF|ON}
UND[ERLINE] {underline | {ON|OFF}}
VER[IFY] {OFF|ON}
WRA[P] {ON|OFF}
```

The syntax elements for the SET command are shown in Table C-3.

Table C-3
Syntax Elements for the SET Command

Element	Description
APPI[NFO] {OFF|ON|app_text}	Enables and disables the automatic registration of command files. The app_text argument allows you to specify the registration text to use when no command file is being run.

Element	Description
ARRAY[SIZE] *array_size*	Specifies the number of rows in a batch. A batch represents the number of rows that SQL*Plus will retrieve with each fetch from the database.
AUTO[COMMIT] {OFF|ON|IMMEDIATE|	Controls whether statements are *statement_count*}automatically committed after they are executed. OFF is the default; ON and IMMEDIATE both cause SQL*Plus to automatically commit each of your SQL statements. By supplying a *statement_count* value, you can have SQL*Plus commit each time that a specified number of statements have been executed.
AUTOP[RINT] {OFF|ON}	Enables or disables the automatic printing of SQL*Plus bind variables after each SQL statement execution.
AUTORECOVERY {OFF|ON}	Enables or disables automatic recovery.
AUTOT[RACE] {OFF|ON|TRACE[ONLY]} [EXP[LAIN]] [STAT[ISTICS]]	Controls the SQL*Plus autotrace functionality. Turning autotrace on causes SQL*Plus to gather and display statistics about each SQL statement executed. The EXPLAIN option causes SQL*Plus to show the execution plan. The STATISTICS option causes SQL*Plus to show statistics. The TRACEONLY option causes SQL*Plus to show the statistics and the plan, but not the actual data returned by the statement.
BLO[CKTERMINATOR] *block_term*	Specifies the character used to terminate a PL/SQL block without executing it. The default value is a period.
BUF[FER] {buffer_name|SQL}	Allows you to switch between buffers.
CMDS[EP] {OFF|ON|separator	Controls whether you can enter multiple SQL*Plus commands on one line, and also specifies the separator character that goes between those commands. The default behavior is not to allow multiple commands on one line.
COLSEP *column_separator*	Specifies the separator character to use between columns of SQL*Plus output. The default value is a space.

Continued

Table C-3 *(continued)*

Element	Description
COM[PATIBILITY] {V7│V8│NATIVE}	Specifies the release of Oracle that SQL*Plus needs to be compatible with. The default value is NATIVE, which means that the database determines the setting.
CON[CAT] {OFF│ON│*concat*}	Specifies the character that you use to terminate a SQL*Plus user variable name. The default is a period.
COPYC[OMMIT] *batch_count*	Specifies the number of batches that SQL*Plus will write during the execution of a COPY command before executing a COMMIT. The default value is 0, meaning that one COMMIT is done when the COPY command finishes.
COPYTYPECHECK {OFF│ON}	Allows you to suppress type checking when the COPY command is being used. The default value is ON.
DEF[INE] {OFF│ON│*prefix*}	Specifies the prefix character used to identify user variables and also allows you to enable or disable the recognition of those variables. The default prefix character is the ampersand (&).
ECHO {OFF│ON}	Enables or disables the echoing of commands as they are executed from a script file. The default is OFF.
EDITF[ILE] *editfile*	Allows you to specify the name used for the temporary work file created when you issue the EDIT command. The default file name is afiedt.buf.
EMB[EDDED] {ON│OFF}	Allows you to embed two reports on one page. The default setting, OFF, forces each new report to start on a new page. The ON setting inhibits the page break between reports.
ESC[APE] {OFF│ON│*escape*}	Defines the SQL*Plus escape character and also allows you to enable or disable recognition of that character.

Element	Description
FEED[BACK] {OFF|ON|row_threshold}	Controls whether you see feedback after issuing a SQL statement. By default, feedback is on and occurs whenever a statement affects at least six rows.
FLAGGER {OFF|ENTRY| INTERMED[IATE]|FULL}	Specifies the level of FIPS flagging that you need. The default setting is OFF.
FLU[SH] {OFF|ON}	Controls whether output is displayed immediately. By default, FLUSH is ON, and output is displayed immediately. You can set FLUSH to OFF to have output buffered.
HEA[DING] [ON|OFF]	Controls whether column headings print. The default setting is ON.
HEADS[EP] heading_separator	Specifies the separator character used to divide a column heading into two or more lines. The default value is a vertical bar (|).
INSTANCE [service_name|LOCAL]	Specifies the default instance to use for your session.
LIN[ESIZE] line_width	Specifies the width of a report line in terms of a number of characters. This setting affects centering and right justifying of report text.
LOBOF[FSET] offset	Specifies a starting byte position for CLOB and BLOB columns.
LOGSOURCE logpath	Specifies the directory containing your archived redo logs.
LONG long_length	Specifies the number of characters that will be displayed when a LONG value is selected. The default is 80.
LONGC[HUNKSIZE] size	Specifies the chunk size that SQL*Plus uses when retrieving a LONG value.
NEWP[AGE] {lines_to_print|NONE}	Specifies the number of blank lines to print to advance to a new page. The default value is 1. A value of 0 results in a formfeed character being printed.
NULL null_text	Specifies the text to display in place of a null column value. The default is to display blanks.

Continued

Table C-3 *(continued)*

Element	Description
NUMF[ORMAT] *format*	Specifies a default number display format.
NUM[WIDTH] *width*	Specifies a default number display width. The default width is ten characters.
PAGES[IZE] *lines_per_page*	Specifies the number of lines on a page. The default setting is 24 lines.
PAU[SE] {ON|OFF|*pause_message*}	Enables or disables the pausing of output after each page of a report. Also allows you to define a message that is displayed when a pause occurs.
RECSEP {WR[APPED]|EA[CH]|OFF}	Specifies when record separators are displayed between two records in a report. The default setting is WRAPPED and results in a separator line only when one or more column values wraps to a second line. The EACH option causes a record separator to be displayed after each line. The OFF option turns off the record separator feature completely.
RECSEPCHAR *separator*	Specifies the character to use for the record separator. The default value is a hyphen (-).
SCAN {OFF|ON}	Enables or disables scanning for SQL*Plus user variables.
SERVEROUT[PUT] {OFF|ON} [SIZE *buffer_size*] [FOR[MAT] {WRA[PPED] |WOR[D_WRAPPED]|TRU[NCATED]}}	Enables or disables the display of output from a PL/SQL block. Allows you to specify the size of the buffer used to hold that output. Allows you to control whether the output is wrapped, word-wrapped, or truncated to match the line size.
SHIFT[INOUT] {VIS[IBLE]| INV[ISIBLE]}}	Controls whether shift characters are visible. This setting applies only when an IBM 3270 terminal is being used. The default setting is INVISIBLE.
SHOW[MODE] {ON|OFF|BOTH}	Controls whether SQL*Plus displays the old and new values of a setting when you change it. The default setting is OFF. The ON setting enables this behavior. BOTH performs the same task as ON.
SQLBLANKLINES {OFF|ON}	Controls whether blank lines are allowed within SQL statements. The default setting is OFF.

Element	Description
SQLC[ASE] {MIXED|UPPER|LOWER}	Controls whether the case of SQL statements is adjusted before being sent to the Oracle server. The default setting is MIXED, which means that SQL statements are left unchanged. The UPPER setting causes SQL*Plus to uppercase everything. The LOWER setting causes SQL*Plus to lowercase each statement.
SQLCO[NTINUE] *continuation*	Specifies the continuation character to use for long SQL*Plus commands. The default is a hyphen (-).
SQLN[UMBER] {OFF|ON}	Controls whether numeric prompts are used for the second and subsequent lines of a multiline SQL statement. The default setting is ON.
SQLPRE[FIX] *prefix*	Specifies the SQL*Plus prefix character, which allows you to execute SQL*Plus commands while entering a long SQL statement. Just place the command on a line by itself and prefix it with the prefix character. The default prefix character is the number sign (#).
SQLP[ROMPT] *prompt*	Specifies the prompt to use. The default value is SQL>.
SQLT[ERMINATOR] {OFF|ON|*term*}	Specifies the character used to terminate and execute SQL statements, and controls whether that character is recognized by SQL*Plus. The default terminator character is a semicolon (;).
SUF[FIX] *extension*	Specifies the default file extension used for the GET, SAVE, EDIT, @, and @@ commands. The default value is .sql.
TAB {OFF|ON}	Controls whether SQL*Plus uses tab characters to format white space when outputting to the display. The default setting is ON.
TERM[OUT] {OFF|ON}	Controls whether SQL*Plus displays output on the screen. The default setting is ON. The OFF setting is respected only when commands are being executed from a script file.

Continued

Table C-3 *(continued)*	
Element	**Description**
TI[ME] {OFF|ON}	Specifies whether the date and time are displayed as part of each prompt. The default setting is OFF.
TIMI[NG] {OFF|ON}	Controls whether timing statistics are displayed for each SQL statement that is executed. The default setting is OFF.
TRIM[OUT] {ON|OFF}	Controls whether trailing spaces are removed from the output. The default setting is ON.
TRIMS[POOL] {ON|OFF}	Controls whether trailing spaces are removed from the output before it is written to a spool file. The default setting is OFF.
UND[ERLINE] {*underline* | {ON|OFF}}	Specifies the character used to underline column headings, and controls whether that underlining occurs. The default underline character is a hyphen (-).
VER[IFY] {OFF|ON}	Controls whether before and after images are displayed for lines containing SQL*Plus user variables. The default setting is ON.
WRA[P] {ON|OFF}	Controls whether SQL*Plus wraps long lines of output. The default setting is ON.

The following example illustrates how to use the SET command:

```
SQL> SET LINESIZE 80
SQL> SET PAGESIZE 50
```

SHOW

The SHOW command displays the current value of a SQL*Plus setting. Following is its syntax:

```
SHO[W] [option/ALL]
```

The syntax elements are as follows:

option	Any setting that you can set using the SET command
ALL	A keyword causing SQL*Plus to list the values of all settings

The following example illustrates how to use the SHOW command:

```
SQL> SHOW LINESIZE
linesize 80
SQL> SHOW ALL
appinfo is ON and set to "SQL*Plus"
arraysize 15
autocommit OFF
autoprint OFF
autorecovery OFF
autotrace OFF
...
```

The first example shows the value of one setting, the LINESIZE setting. The second example shows the value of all settings. The resulting list is quite long.

SHUTDOWN

The SHUTDOWN command shuts down a database. You must be connected as INTERNAL, SYSDBA, or SYSOPER to use this command. Following is its syntax:

```
SHUTDOWN [NORMAL|IMMEDIATE|TRANSACTIONAL|ABORT]
```

The syntax elements are as follows:

NORMAL	Performs a normal shutdown, allowing users to disconnect when they are ready. This is the default behavior.
IMMEDIATE	Performs an immediate shutdown, forcibly disconnecting users as soon as they have completed their current statement.
TRANSACTIONAL	Performs a transactional shutdown, forcibly disconnecting users as soon as they have completed their current transaction.
ABORT	Aborts the instance. All processes are stopped immediately.

The following example illustrates how to use the SHUTDOWN command:

```
SQL> CONNECT system/manager AS SYSDBA
Connected.
SQL> SHUTDOWN IMMEDIATE
Database closed.
Database dismounted.
ORACLE instance shut down.
```

SPOOL

The SPOOL command allows you to send SQL*Plus output to a file. Following is its syntax:

```
SPO[OL] [filename|OFF|OUT]
```

The syntax elements are as follows:

filename	Specifies the name of the file to which you want to write the output. Spooling starts immediately after you issue a command specifying a spool file name. The default file extension is operating-system-specific, but it is usually .lis or .lst.
OFF	Stops the writing of output to the spool file and closes the file.
OUT	Does the same thing as OFF, but also prints the file. However, in Windows environments, this option functions exactly like OFF.

The following example illustrates how to use the SHUTDOWN command:

```
SQL> SPOOL
not spooling currently
SQL> SPOOL c:\a\animal_report
```

Issuing the SPOOL command with no arguments, as done in the first instance here, causes the current state of spooling to be displayed.

START

The START command executes a SQL*Plus script file. This command functions the same as the @ command. Following is its syntax:

```
STA[RT] filename [arg [arg...]]
```

The syntax elements are as follows:

filename	The name of the file that you want to execute. The default extension is .sql.
arg	A command-line argument that you want to pass to the file.

The following example illustrates the use of the START command:

```
SQL> START create_user
```

STARTUP

The STARTUP command allows you to start an instance and open a database. You must be connected as INTERNAL, SYSDBA, or SYSOPER to use this command. Following is its syntax:

```
STARTUP [FORCE] [RESTRICT]
        [PFILE=filename]
        [MOUNT [OPEN [RECOVER]] [database_name]]
        [[EXCLUSIVE|PARALLEL|SHARED] [RETRY]] | [NOMOUNT]
```

The syntax elements are as follows:

FORCE	Forces an instance to start. If the instance is running, a SHUTDOWN ABORT is done first, thus ensuring that a startup occurs.
RESTRICT	Opens the database in restricted session mode.
PFILE=filename	Tells SQL*Plus to use the specified parameter file when starting the instance. If you don't specify this parameter, Oracle will use the default parameter file name for your platform. See Chapter3, "Oracle8i Architecture," for information on parameter files.
MOUNT	Causes SQL*Plus to mount the database but not to open it.
OPEN	Opens the database for normal operation.
RECOVER	Causes Oracle to perform media recovery if necessary and then open the database.
database_name	Allows you to override the value of the DB_NAME parameter in the initialization file.
EXCLUSIVE	Opens the database for exclusive use by the instance being started.
PARALLEL	Opens the database such that multiple instances can access it.
SHARED	Causes the same behavior as PARALLEL.
RETRY	Causes SQL*Plus to keep retrying if it fails to open the database on the first try.
NOMOUNT	Starts an instance but doesn't mount or open a database.

The following example illustrates how to use the STARTUP command:

```
SQL> CONNECT SYSTEM/MANAGER AS SYSDBA
Connected to an idle instance.
SQL> STARTUP
ORACLE instance started.

Total System Global Area   38322124 bytes
Fixed Size                    65484 bytes
Variable Size              21405696 bytes
Database Buffers           16777216 bytes
Redo Buffers                  73728 bytes
Database mounted.
Database opened.
```

STORE

The STORE command generates a text file with SET commands reflecting the current SQL*Plus settings. Following is its syntax:

```
STORE SET filename [CRE[ATE]|REP[LACE]|APP[END]]
```

The syntax elements are as follows:

filename	Specifies the name of the file to which you want to write the SET commands
CREATE	Creates a new file and returns an error if the file already exists
REPLACE	Replaces an existing file and creates a new one if necessary
APPEND	Appends commands onto the end of an existing file

The following example illustrates how to use of the STORE command:

```
SQL> STORE SET c:\a\settings.sql
Created file c:\a\settings.sql
```

The file c:\a\settings.sql now contains all the SET commands necessary to reset the SQL*Plus environment to its current state. You can change those settings and revert back later by using the @ command to execute the file.

TIMING

Allows you to start and stop a SQL*Plus timer. Following is its syntax:

```
TIMI[NG] [START [timer_name ] | SHOW | STOP]
```

The syntax elements are as follows:

START [*timer_name*]	Starts a new timer. You may optionally provide a name for the timer so that you can reference it later.
SHOW	Displays the elapsed time from the most recently started timer.
STOP	Stops the most recently started timer, displays its current elapsed time value, and then deletes it.

Note Using the TIMING command with no parameters causes SQL*Plus to display the number of active timers.

The following example illustrates the use of the TIMING command:

```
SQL> TIMING START egg_timer
SQL> TIMING SHOW
timing for: egg_timer
 real: 3856
SQL> TIMING STOP
timing for: egg_timer
 real: 7421
SQL>
```

The format for the elapsed time is platform-specific. On Windows platforms, the elapsed time is displayed in milliseconds. On most UNIX platforms, it's displayed in minutes and seconds.

TTITLE

The TTITLE command defines a header (top title) that appears at the top of each page of a report. Following is its syntax:

```
TTI[TLE] [printspec [text|user_var]... [printspec...]]
         |[OFF|ON]

printspec := {COL col_num
             |S[KIP] lines
             |TAB col_num
             |LE[FT]
             |CE[NTER]
             |R[IGHT]
             |BOLD
             |FORMAT format}
```

The syntax elements are as follows:

text	Specifies text that you want to appear as part of the title.
user_var	Specifies a user variable, the contents of which will appear in the title. This may also be one of the following predefined user variables: SQL.LNO for the current line number, SQL.PNO for the current page number, SQL.RELEASE for the current Oracle release number, SQL.SQLCODE for the current error number, and SQL.USER for the current username.
COL *col_num*	Indents to the specified column.
SKIP *lines*	Skips the specified number of lines.
LEFT	Causes subsequent text to appear left-justified in the current line.
CENTER	Causes subsequent text to appear centered in the current line. Note that the definition of center is controlled by the SET LINESIZE command.
RIGHT	Causes subsequent text to appear flush right. Note that the SET LINESIZE command also defines the right edge of the line.
BOLD	Causes text to be printed three times in succession, on three different lines.
FORMAT *format*	Specifies a display format to use for subsequent text or numeric values. See the section early in this chapter titled "SQL*Plus Display Formats" for details on specifying format strings.
OFF	Turns the page header off.
ON	Turns the page header on.

The following setting defines a two-line page header:

```
SQL> TTITLE CENTER "Animal Listing" SKIP 1 -
>        FORMAT 999 CENTER "Page " sql.pno
```

Assuming a 50-character-wide line, this footer will display as follows:

```
              Animal Listing
              Page    1
```

You can use the TTITLE command with no arguments to see the current title setting, as shown in the following example:

```
SQL> TTITLE
ttitle ON and is the following 72 characters:
CENTER "Animal Listing" SKIP 1          FORMAT 999 CENTER "Page " sql.pno
```

UNDEFINE

The UNDEFINE command undefines a SQL*Plus user variable. Following is its syntax:

```
UNDEF[INE] variable
```

The syntax elements are as follows:

> variable   The name of the user variable that you want to undefine

The following example illustrates the use of the DEFINE command:

```
SQL> DEFINE X = "Y"
SQL> DEFINE X
DEFINE X              = "Y" (CHAR)
SQL> UNDEFINE X
SQL> DEFINE X
SP2-0135: symbol x is UNDEFINED
```

In this example, the variable X was defined, displayed, and then undefined. When another attempt was made to display the value of X, an error message was returned.

VARIABLE

The VARIABLE command defines a SQL*Plus bind variable. Following is its syntax:

```
VAR[IABLE] variable data_type
```

The syntax elements are as follows:

> variable   The name of the bind variable that you want to define.
>
> data_type   One of the following datatypes: NUMBER, CHAR, VARCHAR2, NCHAR, NVARCHAR2, CLOB, NCLOB, and BLOB. You may specify a length for the character string variables, but not for NUMBER and not for the LOB types.

The following example illustrates the use of the VARIABLE command:

```
SQL> VARIABLE x NUMBER
SQL> VARIABLE y VARCHAR2(30)
SQL> VARIABLE z CLOB
```

In this example, X is a number, Y is a variable-length character string, and Z is a character-large object. The maximum string length that Y can handle is 30 bytes.

WHENEVER OSERROR

The WHENEVER OSERROR command allows you to specify an action to take in the event that an operating system error occurs. Following is its syntax:

```
WHENEVER OSERROR
        {EXIT [SUCCESS|FAILURE|value|:bind_variable|]
             [COMMIT|ROLLBACK]
        |CONTINUE [COMMIT|ROLLBACK|NONE]}
```

The syntax elements are as follows:

EXIT SUCCESS	Exit with a success status.
EXIT FAILURE	Exit with a failure status.
EXIT value	Exit and return the value specified as the status.
EXIT :bind_variable	Exit and return the value of the specified bind variable as the status.
CONTINUE	Do not exit if an error occurs. This is the default behavior.
COMMIT	Causes SQL*Plus to automatically commit the current transaction when an error occurs. This is the default behavior.
ROLLBACK	Causes SQL*Plus to roll back the current transaction when an error occurs.
NONE	Causes SQL*Plus to neither commit nor roll back when an error occurs. You can use this only with CONTINUE.

The following example illustrates the use of the WHENEVER OSERROR command:

```
SQL> WHENEVER OSERROR EXIT FAILURE
```

In this example, SQL*Plus will exit when an operating system error occurs, and an exit status indicating a failure will be returned to the operating system.

WHENEVER SQLERROR

The WHENEVER SQLERROR command allows you to specify an action to take in the event that a SQL error occurs. Following is its syntax:

```
WHENEVER SQLERROR
        {EXIT [SUCCESS|FAILURE|value|:bind_variable|]
              [COMMIT|ROLLBACK]
        |CONTINUE [COMMIT|ROLLBACK|NONE]}
```

The syntax elements are as follows:

EXIT SUCCESS	Exit with a success status.
EXIT FAILURE	Exit with a failure status.
EXIT value	Exit and return the value specified as the status.
EXIT :bind_variable	Exit and return the value of the specified bind variable as the status.
CONTINUE	Do not exit if an error occurs. This is the default behavior.
COMMIT	Causes SQL*Plus to automatically commit the current transaction when an error occurs. This is the default behavior.
ROLLBACK	Causes SQL*Plus to roll back the current transaction when an error occurs.
NONE	Causes SQL*Plus to neither commit nor roll back when an error occurs. You can use this only with CONTINUE.

The following example illustrates the use of the WHENEVER SQLERROR command:

```
SQL> WHENEVER SQLERROR EXIT SUCCESS ROLLBACK
```

In this example, SQL*Plus will exit when a SQL error occurs. The exit status returned to the operating system will indicate success, but the transaction will be rolled back.

✦ ✦ ✦

What's On the CD-ROM?

In the back of this book is the accompanying CD-ROM. It contains the following items:

+ Scripts to create the sample schemas used in the book

+ Example scripts and files for Chapter 10, "Using SQL*Loader"

+ Example scripts and files for Chapter 12, "Using Fine-Grained Access Control"

+ Oraxcel Lite, a software product that is described in the last section in this appendix

Sample Tables and Objects

The CD-ROM contains scripts that create and populate the tables used for the examples in this book. You can install the sample tables into your own Oracle8i database. When you do that, three new users are created:

1. SEAPARK — Owns the sample relational tables.

2. HAROLD — Used occasionally for examples involving multiple users.

3. AMY — Owns the object types and object tables.

Follow these steps to install the sample tables:

1. Log on to SQLPlus Worksheet as SYSTEM. The default password is MANAGER.

2. Open the maketables.sql script on the CD-ROM. The script is found in the Make directory.

3. Press the Execute button. The script will then create the users and tables, and it will then populate the tables with data.

4. Repeat steps 2 and 3, but this time for the file named makeobjects.sql.

5. Close SQLPlus Worksheet.

Note If you don't have SQLPlus Worksheet installed, you can also run the scripts using SQL*Plus.

When the maketables.sql script creates the SEAPARK, AMY, and HAROLD users, it sets their default tablespace to USERS and their temporary tablespace to TEMP. If you don't have tablespaces with these names in your database, either create some to match, or modify the script to use tablespaces that do exist in your database.

Chapter 10 Scripts

The folder on the CD-ROM named sql_loader_examples contains all the files used in the examples for Chapter 10. See the readme.txt file in that directory for detailed information on the individual files.

Chapter 12 Scripts

The folder named fine_grained_security_examples contains the scripts used in the Chapter 12 examples. You can use these to follow along as you read through the chapter.

Oraxcel Lite

Oraxcel Lite is a utility that gives you easy access to Oracle data from Microsoft Excel. To install Oraxcel Lite, unzip the file named oraxcelLITE23.zip, and follow the instructions in the readme.txt file. Oraxcel Lite is developed and marketed by Gerrit-Jan Linker, who wrote Appendix A, "SQL Statement Reference," for this book.

✦   ✦   ✦

Glossary

actual parameters The values that you pass as parameters to a procedure or a function at the time that you call the function. See also *formal parameter*.

Advanced Queuing A messaging feature introduced with Oracle8. Advanced queuing allows you to develop message-based applications. The message infrastructure is provided by the Oracle database.

application context A scratchpad area in memory that may be used to record values that you might need to reference while a user is connected to the database. Application contexts are designed to be used to implement fine-grained security.

application server A server that is used in three-tier environments and that exists to serve up the application logic to the clients. An application server sits between clients and the database server.

archive log destination The directory to which Oracle copies the redo log files from a database so that they can be accessed if the database needs to be recovered.

archivelog mode A mode in which a database can't reuse redo log files until copies have been made and stored in another directory. The destination directory is known as the archive log destination. An Archiver process handles the business of copying filled redo log files to the archive destination so they can be reused when needed.

Archiver The background process that copies filled redo logs to the archive destination.

assistant The Oracle term for what Microsoft calls a wizard.

autonomous transaction A transaction that executes independently of the parent transaction. You can be in the middle of one transaction, suspend that transaction, execute and commit an autonomous transaction, resume the parent transaction, roll back the parent transaction, and the autonomous transaction will stay committed.

background process A process that runs in the background and that forms part of an Oracle instance.

bad file The file to which SQL*Loader writes records that couldn't be loaded because loading them caused an error.

block The smallest unit of storage managed by Oracle. Could also refer to the smallest unit of storage managed by an operating system. Note that Oracle blocks and operating system blocks are not the same. Oracle blocks are usually sized to be an even multiple of the operating system block size.

Boolean expression An expression that returns a value of TRUE or FALSE. Boolean expressions are used most often in IF statements.

Cartesian product The product of all possible combinations of all possible rows from two tables. Cartesian products come about when you join between two tables without specifying any conditions in the WHERE clause of the query that limit the join to related records.

check constraint An arbitrary condition that must be true or unknown (in other words, not false) for every row in a table.

checkpoint A value in a database file indicating the most recent database change that is fully reflected in that file.

cold backup A backup that is performed while the database is completely shut down and all the files are closed. Once the database is closed, you perform the backup by copying the files to tape or to some other backup medium. Sometimes called an *offline backup.*

complete recovery A type of recovery that is allowed to proceed through all archived and online redo log files, thus bringing the database up-to-date with no loss of data. See also *incomplete recovery.*

constraint A rule regarding the data that you can store in a table. Oracle allows you to define the following four types of constraints: primary key, foreign key, unique key, and check.

Context Cartridge An Oracle8i add-on that allows you to search and manipulate large amounts of text.

conventional-path export An export that retrieves data from the database using a SQL query. See also *direct-path export.*

crash recovery The type of recovery performed after an instance crash. The redo log files are read to find changes that were logged but which were never recorded in the datafiles. When found, these changes are applied to the datafiles so that no data is lost as a result of the crash. Crash recovery involves only the online redo log files, never the archived log files.

Database Writer (DBW0) The background process that continuously writes modified data blocks from the buffer cache back to disk.

datablock The smallest logical unit of storage in an Oracle database. Datablocks are made up of one or more operating system blocks.

data definition language (DDL) The set of SQL statements that allows you to create, modify, and delete database objects.

data dictionary cache An area in the shared pool where frequently accessed data dictionary information is held so that it doesn't need to reread from disk.

datafile A database file that contains table data, index data, or stored code.

data manipulation language (DML) The set of SQL statements that allows you to manipulate and change data. These include INSERT, UPDATE, and DELETE.

DBA Management Pack A set of applications that ships with Oracle Enterprise Manager and that allows you to perform basic database administration tasks.

DBW0 See *Database Writer.*

definer's rights The execution of stored PL/SQL code using the system and object privileges granted to the user who created the stored code. Prior to Oracle8i, stored PL/SQL always executed with definer's rights. See also *invoker's rights.*

delimiter A character or a string of characters used to separate two values from each other.

dictionary cache An area in the shared pool used to cache frequently accessed data dictionary information.

dictionary-managed tablespace The type of tablespace that you could create prior to Oracle8i. Oracle uses the data dictionary to manage the space within these tablespaces. Therefore, dictionary-managed tablespaces can't be copied from one database to another. See also *locally managed tablespace.*

direct-path export An export that bypasses normal SQL processing to retrieve data from a database. See also *conventional-path export.*

DLL See *dynamic link library.*

DML See *data manipulation language.*

dynamic link library A library that a program links to and uses at run-time.

embedded dynamic SQL A simple way to generate and execute dynamic SQL statements using PL/SQL.

Enterprise Manager The GUI environment for managing Oracle databases.

environment variable An operating system variable that can be used to convey information to an application. Oracle uses environment variables to point to the directory containing the Oracle software and to point to the instance you are using.

equipartitioning The act of partitioning two tables, or a table and its indexes, on the same set of columns.

exception handler In the context of PL/SQL, a set of PL/SQL statements that is invoked when a specific type of error occurs. An exception handler in PL/SQL always begins with the keyword WHEN.

explicit cursor In PL/SQL, a cursor that you declare in the declaration section of a PL/SQL block, as opposed to implicit cursors, which are those that PL/SQL automatically creates for you.

extent A contiguous set of blocks that have been allocated to an object such as a table or an index.

fine-grained access control The ability, new with Oracle8i, to write PL/SQL code to enforce row-level security at the database level.

fine-grained security The Oracle term for what is essentially row-level security. By using security policies together with application contexts, you can transparently limit a user's access to specific rows in a table.

flat file A file containing data that must be read sequentially from beginning to end. It contains no internal structure, such as an index, to speed navigation to any particular record.

foreign key constraint A constraint that requires the values in a specific set of columns to also occur in another table. Foreign key constraints usually define parent-child relationships.

formal parameter A parameter that you list in the declaration of a function or a procedure.

hot backup A backup that is performed while the database is open and being used. The process for performing one is complex, and you must issue special commands to tell Oracle which tablespace's files are being copied. Sometimes called an *online backup*.

implicit cursor A cursor that PL/SQL declares for you, behind the scenes, so that you can execute a SQL statement.

incarnation A new incarnation of the database is created through the process of resetting the logs. You can't use logs from one incarnation to recover another incarnation.

incomplete recovery A form of recovery that isn't allowed to proceed to its conclusion. You can stop recovery so that the database reflects a state at some point in the past. Remaining redo log entries are then discarded when you open the database with the RESETLOGS option.

index-organized table (IOT) A table that is physically stored as if it were an index. The result is a potential savings on I/O, because Oracle doesn't need to do an extra read following an index lookup to retrieve a row.

Intelligent Agent A component of Oracle Enterprise Manager that runs on the database server and that performs tasks scheduled by the DBA.

invoker's rights The process of executing PL/SQL code using the system and object privileges granted to the user who called the stored code. The ability to create stored procedures that execute with invoker's rights is new with Oracle8i. See also *definer's rights*.

IOT See *index-organized table*.

Java database connectivity (JDBC) An interface that allows Java code to access relational data.

Java pool An area in memory that Oracle uses to hold Java classes and variables.

Java Virtual Machine The software within an Oracle database that executes Java byte code.

JDBC See *Java database connectivity*.

JServer The Oracle term for a Java-enabled database.

large object (LOB) An object, either character-based or binary, that can be up to 4GB in size. Oracle8i's large object types are CLOB, BLOB, BFILE, and NCLOB.

large pool An area in memory used by the multithreaded server.

least recently used (LRU) list A list that Oracle uses to track the use of buffers in the database buffer cache.

LGWR See *Log Writer*.

library cache An area in the shared pool used to store PL/SQL blocks and SQL statements.

Listener, Net8 Listener A process that runs on a server and monitors the network for database connection requests. Without a listener process, network users won't be able to connect to a database.

Listener Control The program used to manage the Net8 Listener.

LOB See *large object.*

locally managed tablespace A new type of tablespace introduced in Oracle8i. Extent allocation for a locally managed tablespace is tracked within the tablespace itself, not within the data dictionary. This makes the tablespace a self-contained unit that can be copied from one database to another.

logical record A representation of a record from the user's point of view, without regard for how that record may be stored physically. This term is often encountered when working with SQL*Loader. See also *physical record.*

LogMiner A new Oracle8i feature that allows you to retrieve and report on the contents of redo log files.

Log Writer (LGWR) The background process that writes a record of database changes to the redo log files.

LRU See *least recently used list.*

materialized view A view where the underlying SELECT statement is executed at the time of view creation, and the results are stored for later access by queries referring to the view. The SELECT statements for normal views are executed not at creation time, but instead are executed when the view is used in a query. Materialized views can provide significant performance enhancements for queries that summarize large amounts of data.

media recovery The type of recovery done after a datafile has been restored from a backup. The media recovery process uses entries from the archived and online redo log files to reapply changes to the restored file, bringing it up-to-date with other files in the database. The end result is that no data is lost because of having to restore the file.

Net8 Assistant A wizard-like program that allows you to configure Net8.

Net8 Configuration Assistant A wizard-like program that walks you through some common Net8 configuration tasks that need to be performed after installing Oracle.

Net8 Easy Config A wizard-like program that allows you to add and remove service names from your listener.ora file.

network adapter A software module that sits between Net8 and the underlying physical transport. Network adaptors convert Net8 calls to TCP/IP calls, SPX calls, or whatever other underlying network protocol is being used.

OAS See *Oracle Application Server.*

object-relational database A database that combines features from the object-oriented world and the relational world. Oracle8i is considered to be an object-relational database.

OFA See *optimal flexible architecture.*

offline backup A backup that is performed while the database is completely shut down and all the files are closed. Once the database is closed, you perform the backup by copying the files to tape or to some other backup medium. Often called a *cold backup.*

OLTP See *online transaction processing.*

online backup A backup that is performed while the database is open and being used. The process for performing one is complex, and you must issue special commands to tell Oracle which tablespace's files are being copied. Often called a *hot backup.*

online transaction processing (OLTP) A system characterized by short, well-defined transactions that are repeatedly executed throughout the day. An airline reservation system is a classic example of an OLTP system.

optimal flexible architecture (OFA) The Oracle guidelines for directory naming, for the placement of database files, and for the placement of software files. The OFA guidelines are intended to maximize flexibility in the face of changes to the system.

Oracle Application Server (OAS) An Oracle product that allows you to develop three-tier Web-based applications.

Oracle Call Interface The API that Oracle client software uses to communicate with an Oracle database server.

Oracle home directory The top-level directory in the directory tree containing the Oracle server software.

Oracle Names server A Net8 component that provides a central repository for Net8 service name definitions.

Oracle Objects for OLE A component that you can use in the Windows environment to connect an application to an Oracle database.

Oracle Parallel Server An Oracle feature that allows multiple instances to open and service the same database.

Oracle Reports An Oracle product used for developing reports.

outer join A join between two tables where one of the tables is optional.

overpunch A relic of the card punch days, when characters were represented by a pattern of holes punched in a card. An overpunch resulted when two patters were superimposed on top of one another. Overpunching was often used to mark the sign in numeric fields, enabling the sign to be recorded without using an extra character position.

package Usually refers to a PL/SQL package, which is a collection of related PL/SQL procedures and functions that are managed as a unit.

partition A segment of a table or an index that contains data for a specific range of values.

PGA See *program global area.*

physical record A record, such as a line in a text file, that is physically stored on disk. Sometimes multiple physical records combine to form one logical record.

PL/SQL program unit A generic term meaning any or all of the following: a stand-alone PL/SQL block, a procedure, a function, or a trigger.

PMON See *Process Monitor.*

precompiler A precompiler reads a source code file and translates SQL statements into function calls that represent valid syntax for the programming language in question.

primary key constraint A constraint that requires a set of columns to have a unique value for each row in a table. Null values aren't allowed; thus, each row may be uniquely identified by the values in the primary key columns.

Process Monitor (PMON) An Oracle background process that monitors the server processes created when users connect to the database.

program global area (PGA) An area in memory used to store information that is specific to a user or a program accessing the database.

program unit A generic term for procedures, functions, packages, and triggers.

QMN0 See *Queue Monitor.*

Queue Monitor (QMN0) A background process that manages the Oracle job queue processes.

RECO See *Recoverer.*

Recoverer (RECO) A background process that is involved in the recovery of distributed transactions.

recovery The process of reading entries from the database redo log and using those entries to bring datafiles up-to-date.

resource management The practice of allocating CPU time between users or groups of users.

role A defined grouping of database privileges that are granted as a unit.

Row ID An internal identifier used to uniquely identify a row in the database.

row-level security See *fine-grained security.*

Schema Manager The Enterprise Manager application used to create and modify tables, views, sequences, stored procedures, and other schema objects.

SCN See *system change monitor.*

Security Manager The Enterprise Manager application used to create and manage database users and to manage the privileges and roles granted to those users.

security policy A policy used to restrict a user's access to a specific set of rows within a table. Security policies are implemented by writing PL/SQL functions that append conditions onto the WHERE clause of data manipulation statements.

segment A collection of extents that belong to an object. Oracle creates a segment for each object. In the case of a partitioned object, Oracle creates a segment for each partition.

SGA See *system global area.*

shared pool An area in memory that Oracle uses to hold SQL statements, execution plans, PL/SQL code, and data dictionary information. The two major components of the shared pool are the library cache and the dictionary cache.

shared SQL area The area within the library cache used to store SQL statements and their execution plans.

SMON See *System Monitor.*

SQL buffer A memory buffer in SQL*Plus used to hold the most recently entered or executed SQL statement or PL/SQL block.

SQL*Loader An application used for bulk-loading data into an Oracle database.

SQL*Net The old name for Net8. In Oracle7, SQL*Net was used. Beginning with Oracle8, the name was changed to Net8.

SQL*Plus The primary command-line interface to an Oracle database.

SQLPlus Worksheet The Enterprise Manager application that wraps SQL*Plus functionality in an Enterprise Manager GUI.

SQL Trace An Oracle feature allowing you to trace execution plans and capture statistics for SQL statements.

Storage Manager The Enterprise Manager application used to manage disk storage for an Oracle database.

system change number (SCN) An internal number that identifies each change to a database. This number is recorded in redo log file headers and also in datafile headers, and it allows the Oracle software to easily determine if datafiles are consistent with one another and which log files to apply if they aren't. The acronym SCN is often used.

system global area (SGA) An area of memory shared by the background processes for an Oracle instance.

System Monitor (SMON) The background process that monitors the operation of an Oracle instance.

tablescan The act of reading all the rows in a table to find those that satisfy the WHERE clause of a query.

tablespace A logical container that is analogous to a file. Oracle stores objects such as tables and indexes in tablespaces. Ultimately, a tablespace has one or more files associated with it, and those files are where the tablespace data is physically stored.

three-tier A type of client/server architecture where the clients don't access the database server directly, but rather, access an application server. One or more application servers may be present, depending on the number of clients that need to be supported. The application servers communicate with the database server.fs.

transportable tablespace A special type of tablespace designed so that the underlying datafiles may be copied from one Oracle database to another.

trigger A PL/SQL code block that is automatically executed in response to a specific event. Traditionally, triggers could be defined only on data manipulation events such as inserts, deletes, and updates. With the release of Oracle8i, triggers can be defined on database events such as startup, shutdown, and so forth.

two-tier A type of client/server architecture where one or more clients are all accessing the database server directly.

unique key constraint A constraint that requires each row to have a unique set of values in a given set of columns. Unique key constraints are similar to primary key constraints, except that unique key constraints allow the columns to be null.

view A stored SELECT statement that may be used in DML statements in place of a table name.

zoned decimal A method of using the character digits 0 through 9 to represent numeric values. Signed values are represented through the use of overpunches on either the leading or trailing digit. The result is that those overpunched digits may appear as letters.

Index

Continued

F

G

Continued

Continued

Continued

Continued

U

Continued

Continued

IDG Books Worldwide, Inc. End-User License Agreement

READ THIS. You should carefully read these terms and conditions before opening the software packet(s) included with this book ("Book"). This is a license agreement ("Agreement") between you and IDG Books Worldwide, Inc. ("IDGB"). By opening the accompanying software packet(s), you acknowledge that you have read and accept the following terms and conditions. If you do not agree and do not want to be bound by such terms and conditions, promptly return the Book and the unopened software packet(s) to the place you obtained them for a full refund.

1. **License Grant.** IDGB grants to you (either an individual or entity) a nonexclusive license to use one copy of the enclosed software program(s) (collectively, the "Software") solely for your own personal or business purposes on a single computer (whether a standard computer or a workstation component of a multiuser network). The Software is in use on a computer when it is loaded into temporary memory (RAM) or installed into permanent memory (hard disk, CD-ROM, or other storage device). IDGB reserves all rights not expressly granted herein.

2. **Ownership.** IDGB is the owner of all right, title, and interest, including copyright, in and to the compilation of the Software recorded on the disk(s) or CD-ROM ("Software Media"). Copyright to the individual programs recorded on the Software Media is owned by the author or other authorized copyright owner of each program. Ownership of the Software and all proprietary rights relating thereto remain with IDGB and its licensers.

3. **Restrictions On Use and Transfer.**

   (a) You may only (i) make one copy of the Software for backup or archival purposes, or (ii) transfer the Software to a single hard disk, provided that you keep the original for backup or archival purposes. You may not (i) rent or lease the Software, (ii) copy or reproduce the Software through a LAN or other network system or through any computer subscriber system or bulletin-board system, or (iii) modify, adapt, or create derivative works based on the Software.

   (b) You may not reverse engineer, decompile, or disassemble the Software. You may transfer the Software and user documentation on a permanent basis, provided that the transferee agrees to accept the terms and conditions of this Agreement and you retain no copies. If the Software is an update or has been updated, any transfer must include the most recent update and all prior versions.

4. **Restrictions on Use of Individual Programs.** You must follow the individual requirements and restrictions detailed for each individual program in Appendix D of this Book. These limitations are also contained in the individual license agreements recorded on the Software Media. These limitations may include a requirement that after using the program for a specified period of

time, the user must pay a registration fee or discontinue use. By opening the Software packet(s), you will be agreeing to abide by the licenses and restrictions for these individual programs that are detailed in Appendix D and on the Software Media. None of the material on this Software Media or listed in this Book may ever be redistributed, in original or modified form, for commercial purposes.

5. Limited Warranty.

(a) IDGB warrants that the Software and Software Media are free from defects in materials and workmanship under normal use for a period of sixty (60) days from the date of purchase of this Book. If IDGB receives notification within the warranty period of defects in materials or workmanship, IDGB will replace the defective Software Media.

(b) **IDGB AND THE AUTHORS OF THE BOOK DISCLAIM ALL OTHER WARRANTIES, EXPRESS OR IMPLIED, INCLUDING WITHOUT LIMITATION IMPLIED WARRANTIES OF MERCHANTABILITY AND FITNESS FOR A PARTICULAR PURPOSE, WITH RESPECT TO THE SOFTWARE, THE PROGRAMS, THE SOURCE CODE CONTAINED THEREIN, AND/OR THE TECHNIQUES DESCRIBED IN THIS BOOK. IDGB DOES NOT WARRANT THAT THE FUNCTIONS CONTAINED IN THE SOFTWARE WILL MEET YOUR REQUIREMENTS OR THAT THE OPERATION OF THE SOFTWARE WILL BE ERROR FREE.**

(c) This limited warranty gives you specific legal rights, and you may have other rights that vary from jurisdiction to jurisdiction.

6. Remedies.

(a) IDGB's entire liability and your exclusive remedy for defects in materials and workmanship shall be limited to replacement of the Software Media, which may be returned to IDGB with a copy of your receipt at the following address: Software Media Fulfillment Department, Attn.: Oracle8i(tm) DBA Bible, IDG Books Worldwide, Inc., 7260 Shadeland Station, Ste. 100, Indianapolis, IN 46256, or call 1-800-762-2974. Please allow three to four weeks for delivery. This Limited Warranty is void if failure of the Software Media has resulted from accident, abuse, or misapplication. Any replacement Software Media will be warranted for the remainder of the original warranty period or thirty (30) days, whichever is longer.

(b) In no event shall IDGB or the authors be liable for any damages whatsoever (including without limitation damages for loss of business profits, business interruption, loss of business information, or any other pecuniary loss) arising from the use of or inability to use the Book or the Software, even if IDGB has been advised of the possibility of such damages.

(c) Because some jurisdictions do not allow the exclusion or limitation of liability for consequential or incidental damages, the above limitation or exclusion may not apply to you.

7. **U.S. Government Restricted Rights.** Use, duplication, or disclosure of the Software by the U.S. Government is subject to restrictions stated in paragraph (c)(1)(ii) of the Rights in Technical Data and Computer Software clause of DFARS 252.227-7013, and in subparagraphs (a) through (d) of the Commercial Computer — Restricted Rights clause at FAR 52.227-19, and in similar clauses in the NASA FAR supplement, when applicable.

8. **General.** This Agreement constitutes the entire understanding of the parties and revokes and supersedes all prior agreements, oral or written, between them, and may not be modified or amended except in a writing signed by both parties hereto that specifically refers to this Agreement. This Agreement shall take precedence over any other documents that may be in conflict herewith. If any one or more provisions contained in this Agreement are held by any court or tribunal to be invalid, illegal, or otherwise unenforceable, each and every other provision shall remain in full force and effect.

my2cents.idgbooks.com

Register This Book — And Win!

Visit **http://my2cents.idgbooks.com** to register this book and we'll automatically enter you in our fantastic monthly prize giveaway. It's also your opportunity to give us feedback: let us know what you thought of this book and how you would like to see other topics covered.

Discover IDG Books Online!

The IDG Books Online Web site is your online resource for tackling technology — at home and at the office. Frequently updated, the IDG Books Online Web site features exclusive software, insider information, online books, and live events!

10 Productive & Career-Enhancing Things You Can Do at www.idgbooks.com

- Nab source code for your own programming projects.

- Download software.

- Read Web exclusives: special articles and book excerpts by IDG Books Worldwide authors.

- Take advantage of resources to help you advance your career as a Novell or Microsoft professional.

- Buy IDG Books Worldwide titles or find a convenient bookstore that carries them.

- Register your book and win a prize.

- Chat live online with authors.

- Sign up for regular e-mail updates about our latest books.

- Suggest a book you'd like to read or write.

- Give us your 2¢ about our books and about our Web site.

You say you're not on the Web yet? It's easy to get started with IDG Books' *Discover the Internet,* available at local retailers everywhere.

CD-ROM Installation Instructions

The CD-ROM with this book contains: scripts to create the sample schemas used in the book; example scripts and files for Chapter 10; example scripts and files for Chapter 12; and a copy of Oraxcel Lite (a software product that allows easy manipulation of Oracle data while using Microsoft Excel). Appendix D describes this material in more detail.

If you install the sample tables in your own Oracle8i database, three new users are created: SEAPARK, HAROLD, and AMYC. Follow these steps to install the sample tables:

1. Log into SQLPLus Worksheet as SYSTEM. The default password is MANAGER. (If you don't have SQLPlus Worksheet installed, you may also run the scripts using SQL*Plus.)

2. Open the `maketables.sql` script on the CD-ROM. The script is found in the Make directory.

3. Press the Execute button. The script will create the users and tables, and it will then populate the tables with data.

4. Repeat steps 2 and 3, but this time for the file named `makeobjects.sql`.

5. Close SQLPlus Worksheet.

The folder on the CD-ROM named sql_loader_examples contains all the files used in the examples for Chapter 10. (See the readme.txt file in that directory for detailed information on the individual files.) The folder named fine_grained_security_examples contains the scripts used in the Chapter 12 examples. To install Oraxcel Lite, unzip the file named oraxcellLITE23.zip and follow the instructions in the readme.txt file.